P9-DVK-520

DATE DUE

Better Training for Distance Runners

SECOND EDITION

David E. Martin, PhD
Department of Cardiopulmonary Care Sciences
Georgia State University

Peter N. Coe
Coach of Sebastian Coe and Wendy Sly

Human Kinetics

Riverside Community College
Library
4800 Magnolia Avenue
Riverside, California 92506

GV 1065.17 .T73 M37 1997

Martin, David E., 1939-

Better training for distance
  runners

Library of Congress Cataloging-in-Publication Data

Martin, David E., 1939-
    Better training for distance runners / David E. Martin, Peter N.
  Coe. -- 2nd ed.
      p.   cm.
    Rev. ed. of: Training distance runners. c1991.
    Includes bibliographical references and indexes.
    ISBN 0-88011-530-0
    1. Marathon running--Training. 2. Running races. I. Coe, Peter
  N., 1919-   . II. Martin, David E., 1939- Training distance
  runners. III. Title.
  GV1065.17.T73M37   1997
  796.42'5--dc20   96-43851
                                                                    CIP

ISBN: 0-88011-530-0

Copyright © 1997, 1991 by David E. Martin and Peter Coe

All rights reserved. Except for use in a review, the reproduction or utilization of this work in any form or by any electronic, mechanical, or other means, now known or hereafter invented, including xerography, photocopying, and recording, and in any information storage and retrieval system, is forbidden without the written permission of the publisher.

This book is a revised edition of Training Distance Runners, published in 1991 by Human Kinetics Publishers, Inc.

Developmental Editor: Julie Rhoda; **Assistant Editor:** Sandra Merz Bott; **Editorial Assistants:** Jennifer Jeanne Hemphill and Amy Carnes; **Copyeditor:** Karen Bojda; **Proofreader:** Jim Burns; **Indexer:** Craig Brown; **Graphic Designer:** Robert Reuther; **Graphic Artist:** Tara Welsch; **Photo Editor:** Boyd LaFoon; **Cover Designer:** Jack Davis; **Photographer (cover):** Anthony Neste; **Illustrators:** Mark Fetkewicz, Jerry Thompson, David Gregory, Sara Wolfsmith; **Printer:** Versa Press

Human Kinetics books are available at special discounts for bulk purchase. Special editions or book excerpts can also be created to specification. For details, contact the Special Sales Manager at Human Kinetics.

Printed in the United States of America   10 9 8 7 6 5 4 3 2 1

Human Kinetics
Web site: http://www.humankinetics.com/

United States: Human Kinetics, P.O. Box 5076, Champaign, IL 61825-5076
1-800-747-4457
e-mail: humank@hkusa.com

Canada: Human Kinetics, Box 24040, Windsor, ON N8Y 4Y9
1-800-465-7301 (in Canada only)
e-mail: humank@hkcanada.com

Europe: Human Kinetics, P.O. Box IW14, Leeds LS16 6TR, United Kingdom
(44) 1132 781708
e-mail: humank@hkeurope.com

Australia: Human Kinetics, 57A Price Avenue, Lower Mitcham, South Australia 5062
(08) 277 1555
e-mail: humank@hkaustralia.com

New Zealand: Human Kinetics, P.O. Box 105-231, Auckland 1
(09) 523 3462
e-mail: humank@hknewz.com

CONTENTS

FOREWORD

Sebastian Coe

W.C. Fields was supposed to have been asked whether poker is a game of chance. "Not the way I play it," he drawled.

Minimizing the element of chance by trying to leave no stone unturned in the quest for coaching excellence is the cornerstone of Peter Coe's thinking. This philosophy kept me at hte forefront of world athletics for more than a decade. Coauthor David Martin holds the same creed; an established physiologist, his dedication to research and its practical application is total.

Together they have combined their expertise to produce a book that has been long overdue. Watching them work together has been like experiencing first-hand the partnership of composer and librettist. The result is a book of complementary disciplines and harmony.

Although sport scientists have made theoretical contributions to training knowledge, they have been less ready to apply their work to coaching. Similarly, many coaches are slow to realize that by working within a theoretical framework and by applying scientific evaluations, they can make much greater progress. Science is a discipline; coaching should be one also. Both scientists and coaches have much to contribute to each other, and this will come only with dialogue. In practice, their paths have often been only parallel; they have not touched frequently enough.

I feel privileged to have been helped by Peter and David along the way from club athlete to Olympic golds winner in 1980 and 1984—a voyage of discovery during which obstacles and hazards became navigable challenges.

Successful coaching is both an art and a science. *Training Distance Runners* is a synthesis of the two. This book is the pooling of two people's special talents, and, more than that, it is a very significant contribution to the literature on the sport of athletics. I believe it to be the best reference yet in linking together the science and the art of developing distance runners.

I had the privilege of writing the foreword to the first edition of *Training Distance Runners* and now I have been asked to write another to this latest edition, titled *Better Training for Distance Runners*.

It is a little daunting to add comments about a book that is already a classic of its kind, but this new edition is even *better* than the original. Data, or, if you prefer the word, facts, must be absorbed and understood before they can become useful knowledge. Clearly, much effort has been contributed to help coaches and athletes by the authors' simplifying and clarifying the opening chapters on biomechanics and physiology. They have given the same meticulous attention to covering additional events and to including the road-running fraternity.

I endorse all that I wrote in the first foreword and I am more than pleased that the same experts who helped me to Olympic Golds and world records are still hard at work helping all runners to succeed.

FOREWORD

Anne Marie Lauck

It is truly amazing to see how far women's distance running has come in such a relatively short amount of time. Competition is now a genuinely global affair with the addition of Asian and African women who have finally gained athletic acceptance within their respective cultures. Currently there is more opportunity than ever for female distance runners

Along with all of the increased opportunities and new challenges, comes the need for proper research and development for the female athlete. In distance running especially, smart planning is crucial for ultimate success. David Martin's expertise as a world-renowned exercise physiologist along with his ability to practically apply his knowledge make him an invaluable source to any distance runner. Peter Coe is also a contributor to athletic excellence as evidenced by his numerous years of coaching world-class athletes.

This new edition is a valuable guide to optimum training for distance runners. Throughout the book, Martin and Coe keep women in mind. The book is valuable for both the way it does, and does not, treat women differently than men. The authors have plenty of experience working with elite female runners, and they know that an athlete is an athlete, and training has the same objectives for everyone. But these two also know that a woman has different blood chemistry, training paces, race experiences, and cultural pressures to deal with. They address these issues with the knowledge and understanding that have made them and their athletes so successful.

I have had the privilege of working with David Martin for almost four years now as an athlete member of his Elite Athlete Project, and I have never known anyone so selflessly dedicated to the successful development of the distance runner. As a female distance runner who is world-ranked on both the roads and on the track, I am very grateful to David for being such a positive force in my running career. Of course, I am fortunate to work with David in his Elite Athlete Project. However, others can gain the same insights in *Better Training for Distance Runners*. This book is not only a top-rated synthesis on distance running in general, but it is also an invaluable tool for helping elite female runners as well as elite male runners achieve their dreams of athletic success.

PREFACE TO THE FIRST EDITION

If two people share a common goal long enough, there is a fair chance that they will meet. Looking back, it seems that, although we didn't know each other, living on separate continents and pursuing different professions, for nearly a decade during the 1970s we were already on the road to collaboration. Specifically, we both had the goal of linking together the craftiness of coaching artistry with the rapidly evolving body of knowledge in sport science and sports medicine so that the athletes with whom we were working could have the best opportunity for competitive success. The people most likely to achieve such a goal are those who not only have experience in scientific methodology but who also are working in the trenches at the front lines of battle preparing runners for top-level racing proficiency. When they combine their skills of data acquisition and analysis (both scientifically in the laboratory and practically in the field) with close personal working relationships with their athletes, they are in the best position to discover what works, what does not, and the best explanations for both. Delightfully, the two of us have enjoyed this most priceless privilege for what now between us totals nearly 40 years of our lives.

One of us (Peter Coe), a professional engineer, assumed the task of training a single athlete from the beginning as a young lad through a career that lasted more than 20 years. Sebastian Coe is arguably the greatest middle-distance runner in athletic history. Perhaps the most detailed and continuous daily record in existence for any elite-level runner's development and performance has produced a very powerful game plan with many elements that can be used sensibly and practically by others. The systematic approach developed for Seb's training did not change conceptually throughout this entire period, attesting to its basic worth.

Eventual expansion of activities led to a working relationship with more runners as well. Restricting attention to a very small group of individual athletes at any one time instead of becoming a coaching administrator for an entire club program has always ensured a focus on the most important task at hand, namely, the constant monitoring and subtle modifying of assigned work loads that best help athletes achieve their planned development. Initially it was not easy to persuade runners who already had tasted some measure of success with one type of training regimen to alter quite significantly their training to fit Coe's system, a system albeit tried and tested with singular success on one male athlete. Their willingness to work, along with Coe's careful nurturing, brought successful results.

At the moment, half of Coe's athlete charges are female. Women distance runners are mentally and physically just as durable and delightful to work with as men. They are competitive and desirous of success, even to the point of needing a restraining hand to save them from the problems caused by the excesses of overenthusiasm. At the 1988 British Olympic Trials one of his female runners earned a bronze medal at 800 m, and the other (Wendy Sly) won a bronze at 3,000 m and a silver at 10,000 m on consecutive days. As a result, Wendy was selected to a 3,000-m spot on the British team for her second Olympic Games. Although she lost considerable time in the years following the Los Angeles Olympics due to overtraining and overuse problems that resolved slowly, her progressive improvement when exposed to the system of multi-tier and multipace training that is described in this book provided her with the developmental sparkle she needed to regain her performance excellence at the highest level.

The other author (David Martin), a physiologist by profession, established a human performance evaluation laboratory in 1975. One of its goals was the identification and implementation of methodology to quantify aerobic and anaerobic fitness changes occurring during an athlete's training season. Another was to interpret these changes from the perspective of the specific kinds of training utilized by that athlete. By evaluating elite-level distance runners three to four times each year, sufficient knowledge was acquired that could permit practical suggestions, specific to each runner, to guide the athletes in fine-tuning their training for steady forward progress. Enhancing these studies was a comprehensive health evaluation program including blood chemistry profiling, musculoskeletal evaluation, and nutritional assessment, a primary goal being the early identification of overuse injury or overtraining. Initially, participation was limited to those elite-level athletes passing through Atlanta to or from competitions, as travel funds specifically for health and fitness profiling were difficult to acquire from either research grant sources or sporting goods companies with which athletes had promotional contracts. The success of the project through word-of-mouth reports from participants soon created a waiting list of athletes desiring involvement. Several athletes have continued to return for periods now approaching 10 years, and they are still reaping the benefits.

Since 1981, funding from the United States Olympic Committee (USOC) to the Athletics Congress of the United States (TAC/USA) has provided a continuity for these studies and has also increased the number of athletes that can be accommodated. The athletes who have received benefits from this USOC/TAC Elite Athlete Special Project form a contemporary Who's Who of American distance running. Some of those with whom we have been privileged to develop close working relationships spanning several years include, in alphabetical order, Dick Beardsley, Bruce Bickford, Keith Brantly, Tom Byers, Jim Cooper, Ed Eyestone, John and Chris Gregorek, Janis Klecker, Mike Pinocci, Pat Porter, Anthony Sandoval, Linda Sheskey, Jon Sinclair, Steve Spence, Jim Spivey, John Tuttle, and Craig Virgin. With a few of these athletes, a personal coaching relationship has developed. With others, a tripartite exchange between athlete, coach, and scientist has been equally productive. For still others, who are self-coached, the technical input has also been valuable.

The catalyst in the fusion of our special interests was Sebastian Coe, in whom we both recognized and appreciated a very special talent. Although one of us, of course, has been both father and coach, the other first met Seb at the European Championships (Prague) in 1978 purely by accident, in helping to resolve a translation problem as some of the East German media, familiar with Seb's then archrival Olaf Beyer, sought details of Seb's training. An abiding friendship was born.

Our own conversations together date back to the early 1980s, when we would meet, usually unexpectedly, at various European cross-country and track gatherings. Our track- or turf-side postmortem observations as we watched our athletes compete, together with our late-night discussions in local pubs, made us realize that much of what we perceived as gaps in knowledge or inaccuracies in application of scientific information to the practical realities of working with athletes was common to both sides of the Atlantic. From these discussions developed a joint yearning to do our best to resolve a few of these gaps and inaccuracies, thus permitting our own runners, to whom we were so dedicated, ultimately to benefit.

By this time Seb was an outstanding athlete with an already long career, and it was for the improvement and extension of that career that we joined forces in a practical way, encouraged by Seb himself. There is a great need for planning and management skills in coaching, and these were brought to bear in this most productive environment. Being a British-based coach did not prevent Coe from recognizing and, most importantly, using powerful (and friendly!) resources in the United States. (Chauvinism and parochialism are formidable obstacles to progress, and we have both steadfastly fought to be free of their entanglement!) The opportunity for Seb and Wendy Sly to combine wintering in Florida with access to a physiology laboratory in Atlanta as well as a scientist-coach in whom they could confide and discuss developmental strategies was too good to pass up. Then again, as Martin realized that athletics seemed far better researched in Europe than in the U.S., particularly with regard to long-term and individualized athlete care, his American base as a physiologist did not prevent him from frequenting the European scene—studying it and learning from it.

Seb became an important force in permitting these interactions to continue. The fruits of our labor bear witness to the value of that collaboration—Seb's unique second gold medal in Los Angeles for his Olympic-record 1,500-m performance, and his first major victory two years later in the 800 m at the 1986 European Championships. Although he happily commenced training in preparation for a third Olympic Games in Seoul, Seb's participation in those Games was not to be, snuffed out by a decision of his nation's athletic body that he not participate.

Each of us has thus been motivated by the desire to bring together the two languages of coaching and sport science as they pertain to distance running. Each discipline can learn so much from the other, yet they seem so far apart when viewed alone. The two knowledge bases should be woven into a unified whole. We owe this to our athletes, who urge constantly that we be of practical benefit to them, because the bottom line in our practical collaboration is their best preparation for an excellent race.

We have enjoyed taking the teacher's approach of putting our ideas and experiences into writing under cover of a book. It should be emphasized most clearly that this is not intended as a treatise on exercise physiology, nor is it an encyclopedia of coaching suggestions. It is, however, a summary of some of the major information areas that we have found important not only for our own understanding but also in teaching our athletes, so that they might know more about themselves as they seek excellence in their event specialties. Our goal has been to achieve a balance between describing basic principles and exploring controversial ideas, thereby providing an appreciation for both problems solved and the many problems we still face.

We hope we have provided clarity without oversimplification. At the same time, some topics are difficult to understand without considerable thought and some background knowledge. Other topics are fraught with misunderstanding and controversy, caused mainly by disagreements in the definition of terms or problems with precise conceptual descriptions. If coaches and athletes become a little distressed as the pace of reading slows considerably while they grapple with the lactate/ventilatory threshold, the Krebs cycle, and muscle fiber types, they can take comfort in realizing that their scientific friends will have equal challenge a few chapters later in comprehending the nuances of reps and sets in training plan design or planning strategy in 800-m versus 5,000-m racing! All of these topics are simply different facets on the diamond that represents athletic performance competence.

We hope that this book will serve as a legacy for the athletes from whom we have learned so much, and as a basis from which our continuing interest can help us (and others) learn more. We fully anticipate that some (in some respects nontraditional) elements of our total approach to working with distance runners may stimulate vigorous debate and reaction. Indeed, by the time this is read, the present explosion of knowledge may very well have already answered some of the questions we pose and proved incorrect some suggestions offered from more recent literature. Such change can serve only as an exciting stimulus for advancing a more reasoned view. As with all aspects of education, we are climbing mountains to see more mountains to climb. If better performances in distance running result from the thought and application resulting from such analysis of our ideas, we will have achieved our purpose.

David E. Martin, Atlanta

Peter N. Coe, London

PREFACE TO THE SECOND EDITION

As coauthors, we could not have been more pleased with the popularity of the first edition of this book. It was with trepidation back in 1986 that we undertook the challenge of creating a "textbook" on distance running that could serve the needs of elite-level racers and their coaches. Before putting pen to paper, we thought we knew so much. Then reality set in, as we found that it required four years of writing (not our predicted two) to put our thoughts together logically and correctly. Often our thinking differed from others', and it required hours of both journal searching and soul-searching to identify what in fact was correct, or at least the best current consensus.

The book has indeed been well received by elite-level athletes and their coaches in many countries around the world (there are even German and Spanish editions). But the book also has been discovered by a larger population of dedicated runners not quite elite in terms of genetic gifts, but whose interest in learning the technical aspects of human athletic performance is still extremely keen. The many letters we have received from around the world have given us plenty of constructive suggestions for further improvement, as well as delightful questions that we could not answer and fascinating stories or examples that often were better than ours at illustrating key points.

So much has happened since the first edition that a second edition seems warranted, and the publishers have agreed. Most of the distance-running world records have been broken, providing the impetus for asking whether this has occurred because of better genes, better training, or better racing. Meanwhile, Seb Coe's 800-m and 1,000-m world records of 1981 still remain unsurpassed. At the world level, the women's 5,000-m run has now replaced the women's 3,000-m run as the intermediate championship event between the shorter-distance 1,500-m metric mile and the longer-distance 10,000-m event, and the powers that be in the politics of track are strongly urging women to take up the steeplechase. Also, many track athletes interested in doing some road racing during the off-season requested some input of ideas on winning strategies for this quite different aspect of distance running.

We have responded to all of these concerns and issues, and more. Scarcely a section of the book has emerged unchanged in this updated and revamped edition. Updating the content has been fairly easy. Not only do we keep current with what's happening through technical journals, but also, by continually communicating and collaborating in a very personal way with elite-level athletes, sport scientists, and other coaches, we continue to acquire new experience and knowledge. As might be expected, it is from the athletes that we learn the most.

Revamping the text to make it more readable has required considerably more time. We have responded to many reader comments, suggestions, and criticisms and have implemented some changes that should prove useful. One frequent comment, particularly from coaches, is that while the scientific material (biomechanics, muscle anatomy and physiology, and energy dynamics) is important, it was too concentrated. We have thus divided the old chapter 1 into chapters 1 through 3, separating these major topics into smaller, more palatable packages, with additional practical examples to explain the importance of the principles described. The other chapters have been similarly scrutinized to provide more examples that practically apply technical information for better coaching.

Coaches should remember, however, that it is not important to struggle through all the superscience before moving on to the topics in chapters 5 through 8 that are of immediate practical interest. These later chapters frequently refer back to appropriate sections in the science-oriented chapters that provide technical background material for that particular topic. This permits appropriate delving into specific topics as they become relevant.

Several entirely new sections give deserved attention to the changing dimensions of the sport. The majority of these new sections are directly related to coaching information and technical information for athletic performance enhancement. Examples include the new sections on road racing, use of heart rate monitors in training, the steeplechase, altitude training, use of glycerin-induced hyperhydration for hot-weather training and racing, and suggestions for rewriting the record book in the 800 m.

New developments in scientific and medical areas have been summarized as well. As just one example, although much has been learned about injury prevention and about optimal nutrition, the recently defined female athlete triad of osteoporosis, amenorrhea, and eating disorders as a result of a recurring notion that one must "be thin to win" has been the focus of much attention. Because this problem can be career-threatening for certain groups of very talented athletes and is widespread, we have included a section in chapter 6 to discuss the problem.

On the American front, the steady improvements of those athletes who faithfully come to Atlanta for periodic testing and acquiring data for planning their program give us the impression that as a team we are progressing in the right direction. The laboratory performance evaluation that these athletes undergo when they come to Atlanta becomes ever more sophisticated as we learn more about which kinds of laboratory data best help to prevent overtraining, improve fitness, optimize recovery from injury, and identify the cause of injury so as to minimize future recurrence. We have also developed a comprehensive package of dietary profiling, bone density measurement, and assessment of daily energy dynamics to provide useful counseling for optimizing energy intake, ensuring calcium balance, and maintaining bone mineralization.

Recent Elite Athlete Project additions since the first edition of this book—from whom we have learned so much and with whom it is a genuine privilege to work—include, alphabetically, Kellie Archuletta, Mark Coogan, Karen Hecox, Dan Held, Laurie Henes, Julianne Henner, Libbie Johnson, Bob Kempainen, Anne

Marie Lauck, Amy Legacki, Jennifer Martin, Colette Murphy, Cathy Palacios, Reuben Reina, Ceci St. Geme, Kristen Seabury, Joy Smith, and Sarah Thorsett. Specializing in events from the 800-m through the marathon, they continue to provide a wonderful challenge for us to learn together how to achieve excellence.

The British front has had plenty of continuing activity as well. The British Milers Club, frequent lecturing, working on manuscripts for other writings related to athletics, and regular attendance at European track meetings ensures that we remain in touch with new faces and new developments in the sport.

As before, our ideas about training, racing, and sport science may spark considerable debate. We welcome that debate, for the logical end result will be what we all desire—a better understanding of distance running and better performance from the athletes with whom we so much enjoy working.

David E. Martin, Atlanta

Peter N. Coe, London

ACKNOWLEDGMENTS

We cannot name all those who have influenced us during our time devoted to athletics; there simply are too many. But each of us must mention those few who, from our individual perspective, have had a special place in making it all possible. It is appropriate that we name them separately.

From Peter Coe:

In coaching, there is my old friend Frank Horwill, who founded the British Milers Club. His devotion to miling has been obscured by his prickly and contentious ways, but nevertheless he has put a lot of thought into the sport. In 1970 he made what for me was a very seminal observation: In Britain the fastest milers were the 5,000-m athletes who had come down in distance, and the best half-milers were 400-m runners who had stepped up an event. This gave me a new direction in coaching and in structuring training around the correct paces.

In journalism, writers should not overglamorize, nor should they pen needlessly cruel copy; it must be analytical and fair. For me there are two particular writers who temper their analytical eyes with a passionate love of the game and are sensitive to the individual behind the medals and the records. Both are respected friends from prestigious journals. The first is Robert Parienté, editor of the great French newspaper *L'Equipe*, and the other is Kenny Moore of *Sports Illustrated*, a fine Olympian and marathoner as well. Kenny's search for the inside story borders on the extreme, and the results of his rambles are chronicled with class. He was brave enough on one occasion to join a painfully difficult training session with Seb Coe on an even harsher English winter day, a session that I, protected from the icy wind and rain, directed from a following car.

And finally, I thank meet promoter Andreas Brugger of Zürich, whose long-time assistance and friendship has helped me to cope with the many hazards and vicissitudes of the international circuit.

From David E. Martin:

Top-quality "people-power" and financial resources are at the heart of most successful endeavors, and the present situation is no exception. The close working relationships I established early on with coaches, athletes, and sport scientists at the forefront of both the European track and cross-country circuits, as well as the Asian marathon circuit, have been the sources of much knowledge I've needed to confront the technical and practical challenge of athlete preparation for top-level competitions.

The Center for Exercise Physiology and Pulmonary Function in the Department of Cardiopulmonary Care Sciences at Georgia State University has been the site of our scientific studies with distance runners. The dedication and expertise over many years by a small but devoted and talented cadre of professional colleagues—notably Donald F. May, Susan P. Pilbeam, Meryl Sheard, and Richard Eib—ensured an unusually high standard of test-retest reliability so indispensable for the success of periodic physiological data acquisition when the study subjects serve as their own controls. Their talents have been essential in helping to mesh the nuances of changing equipment and technology with the challenging demands of monitoring the performance capabilities of some of the most gifted athletes the sport of distance running has ever seen. Collaboration with David H. Vroon, MD, Director of the Clinical Laboratory of Grady Memorial Hospital, has been instrumental in providing the kind of long-term comprehensive blood chemistry profiling program required to document from many viewpoints the various metabolic changes occurring in distance runners as they proceed through a training season.

In recent years, I have desired to expand the kinds of health-care resources available to our visiting athletes, to serve them better. For runners, most injury risks begin at the foot, and thus it was deemed desirable to bring a very competent sports podiatrist into the fold. We welcomed Perry Julien, DPM, himself a devoted multi-sport enthusiast and thus able to identify with the "running mentality," and his input has been wonderful.

Another perceived need was in the area of nutrition. Energy fuels runners, and that means optimum nutritional intake. A myriad of important aspects of the health of hard-training distance runners center around nutritional concerns. Iron intake must be sufficient to reduce the risk of anemia and ensure adequate stores for producing fuel-metabolizing enzymes. Calcium intake must be adequate to ensure bone mineralization and minimize the risk of skeletal injuries. Especially for our women athletes, interaction between blood estrogen, menstrual cyclicity, bone density, and calcium dynamics is an important concern for good health. A professionally fruitful relationship has developed through colleague Dan Benardot, PhD, RD. His competence in nutrition, coupled with his research interest in understanding the special nutritional dynamics of top-class athletes (particularly gymnasts and runners), has led to the merging of our two laboratories into a joint Laboratory for Elite Athlete Performance. The new knowledge we are gaining from our collaboration has been pioneering, and our participating athletes are the first to benefit from its practical worth.

From 1981 through the late 1980s, substantial funding to defray travel and laboratory testing costs for elite-level athletes was acquired through the highly competitive research and support services grant programs of the USOC, administered through its Elite Athlete Special Project. Since then, continued (and equally competitive) funding has come directly through the national governing body for track and field (now known as USA Track & Field), particularly through its Sports Medicine and Men's Development Committees. The funding has permitted athletes to reap the practical benefits of long-term profiling, with visits scheduled at important points in their development to monitor their fitness changes and outline appropriate strategies for further progress. Additional funding has been provided by such sources as the Urban Life Foundation of Georgia State University and the Atlanta Track Club, and gratefully accepted.

Lastly, I shall always cherish the friendships developed with the athletes who have visited our laboratory. Their confidence that we could be of substantial benefit to their developing athletic careers has motivated us to work with a devotion matched perhaps only by their own, so that we might be of service to them. It has been a rare privilege to study with them the details of their training plans, to help them identify their performance strengths and liabilities, and to help design strategies for continuing their quest for athletic success. Those who have taken the greatest advantage of the program, by faithful scheduling of periodic laboratory visits and applying the data obtained in a practical manner to help themselves learn more about how optimum training and nutrition, coupled with injury-prevention, can be powerful tools for success, have reaped the greatest rewards. We have always challenged them to learn as much from us as we do from them. With few exceptions, they have indeed accepted and met that challenge!

Both of us as authors also owe a great debt of gratitude to Rainer Martens of Human Kinetics Publishers, who agreed with our view that this book could be of benefit to the athletics community. For the Second Edition, we are indebted particularly to Ken Mange for providing us with new insights and perspectives that started us on our way toward a Second Edition that would be truly useful for our readers. Developmental Editor Julie Rhoda then helped us immeasurably with the challenging task of finalizing the details. As a distance runner herself in addition to being a grand master at editing, we thoroughly enjoyed having her as "one of us," seeing this project to completion.

INTRODUCTION

It is quite simple to lump into a single word the tasks for any distance runner aspiring to further excellence: *train*. However, that word embraces a multiplicity of assignments. We see the following requirements for distance runners as ideally giving them the best chance for achieving success:

- Find a competent *coach* or advisor with whom to work, and try to learn as much as possible about the dynamics of training: what work loads best improve fitness, what kinds of changes occur with training, why adequate *recovery* following tissue breakdown from training is so crucial, and how to realize in advance when more breakdown will be counterproductive to improved fitness development.
- Define and create a development plan based on *achievable goals*.
- Do the *physical* and *mental training* necessary to improve performance.
- Develop a *support system* for maintaining good health, preventing overtraining, and monitoring fitness/performance assets and liabilities composed of qualified people who can interact effectively with both athlete and coach.
- *Evaluate* the results of development by a combination of carefully planned periodic time trials, laboratory physiological evaluation, and races.
- *Document* the results of training, racing, and physiological/health evaluation over time using charts, graphs, or notes and thus obtain a record that permits objective assessment.
- Enter each major competitive period with *confidence*, and deliver good performances.

The purpose of this book is to help athletes achieve success in distance running and to help the coaches and scientists working with them. The first four chapters provide the scientific foundation, and the last four chapters apply this basic information in a practical way for optimal athletic performance. Chapter 1 discusses some of the essentials of physiology and biomechanics that relate to movement in general and running in particular. Chapter 2 then outlines the function of skeletal muscles, which permit the movement to occur. Chapter 3 explains relevant aspects of energy metabolism, since it is energy derived from the breakdown of foods that permits muscles to function. These chapters connect the information on *movement*, *muscles*, and *metabolism* that is the basis on which the science of training and competing relies.

Chapter 4 outlines the means by which the cardiopulmonary system ensures the distribution of fuels and oxygen (O_2)—so essential for high-level work—to the various organs that interact to permit athletic performance. Since performance fitness is essentially a measure of the operating capabilities of these organ systems, we introduce here the details of evaluating a runner's aerobic and anaerobic fitness using appropriate physiological testing protocols.

Some parts of these chapters will seem challenging to understand, especially for those not well versed in biology and chemistry. Do not devote excessive time to details. The best approach at first is to see the forest, not the trees. Then, as the basic concepts become clearer, re-read the examples to help develop a conversational knowledge that will permit exchange of ideas among friends. Carrying even a basic knowledge into the final four chapters will set the stage for understanding the logic of the practical concepts described and should provide a background of information that will clarify the more technical details.

Based on a fairly comprehensive scientific understanding of athlete performance, chapters 5 and 6 specifically discuss the design of training plans. Chapter 5 introduces the concept of periodization, or systematic design, of a training plan and emphasizes the running-related activities for that plan. Chapter 6 then integrates all the other aspects of total-body fitness needed to convert a trained runner into a complete athlete—flexibility, strength and power training, and monitoring body composition for best sport performance.

Once athletes understand their bodies and how to train for fitness, it is time to race. Chapter 7 is an event-by-event analysis of racing strategies for the primary Olympic distance events, along with a special section on road racing. We hope that the presentation of strategies and ideas will serve as a catalyst for athletes to develop their own additional strategies as they enter the "School of Hard Knocks" that is the essence of hard-fought competition.

Finally, chapter 8 examines the problem of managing the enormous physiological and psychological stress load of athletes whose goal is top-level training and competition. This chapter offers strategies to effectively read the signs of overload and to deal objectively with appropriate behaviors to reduce the stressors that are causing the decline in performance. Some athletes train so arduously that overuse and overtraining result in exhaustion and injury, which can ruin their careers. Athletes' willingness to overtrain must instead be refined into a more reasoned approach of identifying what is necessary and how to master it. Important in this process is interaction with a practical and knowledgeable coach or advisor, who can help athletes design a useful plan, and with a good sport scientist, who can help monitor progress using the consistent laboratory profiling technology. (It would be ideal, of course, for athletes to team up with a coach who is a sport scientist, or a sport scientist who also is a coach—but those are rare birds indeed!) Some perspective on the roles of assistive personnel is appropriate at this point.

Defining the Role of a Coach

Finding a good description for the complex relationship that develops between athletes and the people who work closely with them isn't easy. Current English language usage doesn't help very much, either. The word *coach* when used as a verb means "to give instruction or advice to" (Flexner and Hauck 1987). The word *train,* however, when used as a verb can refer both to what the athlete does (i.e., "to get oneself into condition for an athletic performance through exercise, diet, practice, etc.") and to what a coach does (i.e., "to give the discipline and instruction, drill, practice, etc., designed to impart proficiency or efficiency"). We might conclude from this that both athletes and coaches are trainers, that is, people who train (themselves or others). Indeed, the word *trainer,* used as a noun, can refer to either "a person who trains" or "a person who trains athletes." (Not all coaches are athletes, however, although some athletes make good coaches.) But a trainer can also be "a staff member of an athletic team who gives first aid and therapy to injured players," as well as "a person who trains racehorses or other animals for contests, shows, or performances." The French word *entraineur* means "trainer (of horses) or coach (of a team)," the latter referring to humans (Mansion 1968). Indeed, most coaches whose primary language is not English use the term *trainer* rather than *coach* in reference to athletes' development. Interestingly, the official entry list for the 1984 Los Angeles Olympic Games, written in both French and English, used *coach/entraineur* as one heading for team staff and *trainer/soigneur* as another. The French verb *soigner* means "to attend to, to look after, to take care of."

In striving to improve and to win, athletes require excellent coaching, management, and competition. Frank Dick (1983) very nicely defines a coach as "the director of an athlete's athletic ambition" (p. 6). If we substitute the word *career* for *ambition,* the concept becomes clearer still. If a coach and an athlete have agreed to a collaboration leading in the direction of the athlete's achieving all-around excellence in competitive sport, then the coach must undertake to provide input into the plan and to manage all aspects of it. The thinking should be done first, before training begins. If athletes develop both *long-term* and *short-term goals,* these form a defined framework for all meaningful subsequent decisions. Training plans then become relatively simple to create. A good coach thus must provide a good example and also be well rounded to make value judgments with conviction and credibility.

The one-word definition we are seeking to sum up the concept of being a coach may be simply *manager.* Only recently has this concept caught on in the rest of the coaching world (Prendergast 1994). A good manager blends all the ingredients of a successful undertaking into a functional whole. A successful coach knows what to blend, how much of each ingredient to mix and when, and has an appreciation of how the end result may reflect more than simply the sum of all the ingredients. A competent coach is an expert at creating a master development plan and is able and willing to utilize the expertise of qualified and trusted people to assist with the execution of this plan. All along the way, a steady eye is kept on the path of progress for optimal athlete development. It is hoped that the coach's input of knowledge can provide the direction an athlete needs to help inherent skills develop optimally into continuing success in later years.

Coaching a talented athlete thus would appear to be almost a full-time job, or at the very least a job that cannot be done effectively with a large group of athletes. A one-on-one athlete-coach relationship is probably most productive in the long run (pun intended), but it is difficult to achieve in practice. A coach in a club situation may be required to work actively with a dozen or more athletes, all with different talents and levels of fitness. College and university coaches, in addition to managing the administrative details of an entire program, may be hostage to the "payment by results" system, threatened by dismissal every year if their team doesn't win. For a coach to create useful training plans individualized for athletes' needs, a sizable time commitment is required. The greater the ancillary demands on a person aspiring to coach a group of talented athletes, the less likely it is that those athletes will obtain the individualized care that they need and deserve.

To use an academic analogy, a coach is like a teacher who prepares students (athletes) to perform well in their examinations. Make no mistake: An important championship race is indeed a searching test of mastery! Good coaches are also good students, learning what others have done and documenting carefully what they are doing with their own athletes. Discovering blind alleys before entering them can save time and keep athletes on the path of progress. This path is the overall plan, and thus we return to the implicit need for *goals*—they give direction to the plan.

In preparing athletes, however, a coach cannot know it all. Today there are more and more information subspecialties, all of which can and should contribute to multifaceted athletic development. Coaches need to establish a working awareness of all these sources of assistance and to interweave their potential benefits effectively into the master development plan. Podiatric care, biomechanical film analysis, blood chemistry profiling, strength and circuit training, psychological preparation, nutritional counseling, laboratory treadmill testing to quantify key aspects of cardiovascular conditioning, and more all have their value. When implemented judiciously they can be an important part of the overall process of improving the environment in which athletes can refine their talents with minimal risk of injury or burnout. Added to these subspecialties are all the various aspects of athletes' interaction with the world around them that need effective management—not only in the short term (such as the details of upcoming competitions and training plan design), but also in the long term (completing college education, managing financial affairs, utilizing promotional opportunities, planning a baby, etc.). Sport is indeed a microcosm of life itself; the greater an athlete's success, the more complex this world becomes.

The Successful Athlete-Coach Relationship

An athlete must be self-motivated. A coach may, and should, broaden an athlete's horizon and suggest higher standards or goals to seek, as long as goals are within the boundaries of reason and good sense. But a coach cannot supply the inner drive that a winner must possess. That would be rather like the morbid story of the doctor who is the donor in a slow but continuing blood transfusion wherein doctor and patient both die. The best athletes are *coach-oriented* but not *coach-dependent*.

The best relationship is a *partnership*. When an athlete chooses a coach, he or she also assumes the obligation to submit reasonably to that coach's discipline. A primary example is doing no greater quantity or intensity of training than assigned. If the coach is unaware of such additional training, he or she may erroneously interpret the effect of the assigned work load. The coach then has difficulty in subsequently devising meaningful training plans. But the coach must also be sensitive to athletes' unique needs and must consider those needs in devising the master plan. If an athlete-coach relationship is to be a journey of mutual discovery, both minds must be working together, not separately.

As the athlete progresses in excellence, it may become entirely appropriate for certain aspects of athletic life to be handled independently of the coach. Highly media-visible athletes can acquire sizable financial rewards, for example, making the addition of a good financial manager to the team advantageous. This decision should be made jointly by coach and athlete but is usually initiated by the athlete. Other decisions involving the athlete and other members of the support team may also be handled independently of the coach. For example, periodic health care and performance profiling through the sport scientist should be scheduled jointly by the scientist and the athlete at points in the training cycle that provide optimal information to all parties involved.

Success depends so much on mutual trust. Even in the closest of partnerships, athletes will be away from their coaches for periods of time and may not even live in the same city as their coaches. A coach with the slightest doubt about an athlete's dedication or whether the athlete is doing the work assigned is a frustrated coach for whom dispassionate judgment is difficult. The coach must have the confidence (instilled by the athlete) that, within reason, agreed-upon assignments will be completed. The real champions are self-disciplined and willing to make considerable personal sacrifice. Communication between athlete and coach must be effective, because both utilize the knowledge provided by each other's perspective on the training process and its effects. Indeed, knowledge is power, and the synergism of two experts (coach and athlete) bound by a desire to create a superlative performance is powerful indeed.

Athletes are essentially unique "experiments of one," and the more elite the athlete, the more unique the experiment. Although athletes are all unique individuals, their similarities far outweigh their differences. It is only because the human body functions physiologically in known, laboratory-testable ways that training methods have gotten anywhere beyond guesswork. This is why it is very useful for a good coach to be well versed in the scientific essentials explaining human performance and its enhancement by adaptation to specific work loads. A college degree in the subject may not be necessary, but the knowledge is. Access to a human performance testing center may not be routinely possible, but the data obtained by such a facility, when interpreted properly, can be invaluable. Careful observations and recording of training responses and results of time trials can be adequate by themselves to permit meaningful analysis of progress and preparation. The coach and athlete must work closely to ensure the kind of communication that permits such analysis.

Of course, an obvious truth is that no one is completely knowable. Therefore, the best coach-athlete relationships are those in which each can tune in to the other with the greatest success. In part such understanding stems from classic intuition—seeing the truth without reason or knowledge. But in part it comes from years of working together. It is the coach's responsibility to assign the work of training, raising or lowering its intensity to adjust its tolerability. Thus, the coach constantly must have all antennae tuned in to pick up clues that will identify small changes that will ensure steady progress or identify areas needing improvement. The more intense the training, or the closer a major competition, the more sensitive this fine-tuning should be. Good coaches can arrive at a sense of what needs to be done, sometimes without being able to articulate fully the reasoning or the actions prompting that decision. This is a far different kind of assessment than simple gut reactions of quasi-coaches acting on impulse. Very often, a coach well tuned to an athlete will be able to discuss overall progress in such a way that both together delineate a sensible plan of action.

Successful Athletes Are High Achievers

Competitively successful athletes, like successful people in other walks of life, possess behavioral characteristics consistent with their achievement. Knowledge of these characteristics permits athletes to better understand themselves and also permits coaches to interact more effectively with them. For example, successful athletes have a high degree of persistence at practicing the tasks required to improve. Thus, it is important that they know which tasks are important for improvement, for which good coaching is beneficial. It is often said that our best coaches ought to work with our youngest athletes, and there is good reason for this. Wasting time and energy at tasks that do not necessarily improve the ability to perform in a particular sport event merely contaminates an athlete's development plan. This is a critical issue, especially in a sport such as distance running, which has injury risks from overuse and chronic fatigue.

High achievers also have a high completion rate for the tasks that are related to their goal of performance improvement. Their focus is more task-centered than person-centered. They are self-directed. Once given instructions, they proceed competently on their own, guided by their task-oriented focus. They assume responsibility willingly and enjoy involvement in making decisions about the design of tasks that will improve performance. As they continue to work, they strive for a high completion rate in their assigned tasks. A crucial implication of this behavioral characteristic is that the training work load must closely approximate the athlete's ability. If the load is too easy, frustration occurs because of insufficient challenge. If the assignment is too difficult, injury may occur because the athlete will persist relentlessly toward what is perceived as an achievable goal. The final result in a properly directed program of development for a highly motivated athlete is improved performance quality. It is evident that proper planning is essential for this to occur.

Scientific Evaluation of Health and Fitness

There is no doubt that hard work over an extended period of time is the primary means for achieving athletic performance potential. A combination of training, competing, and sharing of experiences and emotions with other athletes forms the primary basis for development of expertise. Successful training and racing, however, can occur only in the context of excellent general health. Thus, it becomes essential to ensure that a continual improvement in fitness results from the assigned training. Continual improvement involves the prevention of habituation to training and identification of optimal training. Habituation is simply an absence of further adaptation. If one habituates to a training load, one is no longer responding to the training environment by performance improvement. Effective training preferably results in continued, steady adaptation to the assigned work load. Continual adaptation is an important reason for the considerable interest among coaches and athletes for teaming up with knowledgeable scientists or for a competent coach to be well versed in sport science. Application of sport science allows coaches to monitor general health and prevent injury; to quantify training effectiveness by measuring fitness improvements in an objective, repeatable laboratory environment; and to identify fairly precisely the best short- and long-term training and racing strategies that will enhance performance. Long-term periodic evaluation of fitness and health in which the athletes' data serve as a standard for comparison provides a powerful tool for assessing the success of development, in addition to race results and subjective expressions of overall fitness. It permits the integration of the art of coaching and the science of sport into a unified whole.

Changes in tolerance to training loads over time can be determined subjectively by athlete and coach and interpreted along with objective evidence from time trials or small competitions. Coupled with this, careful laboratory monitoring of performance capabilities—with minimal contamination by such factors as temperature, wind, humidity, terrain, and tactics—can provide an additional objective assessment of changes in fitness over time. The more often this objective performance profiling is carried out and compared with race data and training results, the more accurate can be the identification of appropriate strategies for fine-tuning health, fitness, and performance. If athletes are in a training mode, the combined wisdom from training logs and laboratory data can suggest the best plan for further fine-tuning. If athletes are about to enter a racing mode, this combined wisdom can go far to suggest the best racing strategies that take advantage of performance strengths and that rely least on less-developed abilities (which in turn can be given their due attention during subsequent training).

Unfortunately, athletes and coaches have not always found the world of sport science very useful in helping them refine their training strategies. Too often in the past athletes have very willingly agreed to be evaluated in scientific laboratories but were provided with little or no direct feedback or useful information for their training. There have been at least two reasons for this. Although scientists have been fascinated with the amazing performance capabilities of elite athletes and the extent to which these abilities exceed the norm, a large proportion of studies have been simply descriptive with practical relevance not immediately obvious. Scientists who are not coaches or athletes also may not be as appreciative of the need for practical application of the laboratory results to training methodology.

A second reason is that quite often the discovery of information about how physiological processes function simply reinforces what athletes already have experienced. As just one example, a champion marathoner who finds training sessions of fast running difficult to accomplish and who has never excelled at shorter-distance races will learn little from a biopsy evaluation of his skeletal muscle fibers that shows a biochemical specialization for endurance rather than speed performance. This information by itself does little to improve training effectiveness. It is our view that the emphasis of studies done with elite athletes whose careers are determined solely by the quality of their competitive results should be directed toward acquisition of specific practical knowledge that, when incorporated properly into their training styles, can preserve excellent health or improve their fitness. Results in this area are improving significantly.

Three kinds of information have been identified as useful for assisting athletes and coaches with performance enhancement. The first kind includes information related to basic health. Using data from blood chemistry profiling to evaluate general health and the likelihood of overtraining is one general example. Detecting a trend toward anemia by observing steadily decreasing hemoglobin levels is a specific example. Data from nutritional evaluation that quantify the balance between energy intake and loss and the adequate intake of essential nutrients is still another example. The second kind of useful information includes that which indicates risks for disease or musculoskeletal injury. Evaluation of pulmonary function in athletes with exercise-induced asthma, with a view toward identifying the effectiveness of approved medications to cope with and minimize its debilitating effects, is an example. The third kind of useful information includes measurement of specific performance-related variables that can be affected by training. An example is cardiopulmonary system evaluation using treadmill runs to identify optimal training paces for delaying the onset of accumulated metabolic acid or for increasing the maximal oxygen uptake during fast running.

Changes in any single performance-related variable by itself are unlikely to be a guaranteed cause-and-effect predictor of individual competitive excellence. The effects of all the measured performance- and health-related training variables over time, plus others unmeasured, interact. And, of course, on the day of competition there is the inner mental drive to perform well that may never be exactly quantifiable. But a healthy athlete whose training plan has brought development to a peak at the appropriate moment has the ideal opportunity to combine the will to win with superlative fitness into a personal best performance. This book is about how serious distance runners can acquire fitness, maintain health, and quantify the status of these contributors to performance so that they can steadily become better distance runners.

References

Dick, F. 1983. Value judgements and the coach. *Track & Field Quarterly Review* 83(3):6-9.

Flexner, S.B., and Hauck, L.C. 1987. *The Random House dictionary of the English language.* 2nd ed. New York: Random House.

Mansion, J.E. 1968. *Heath's standard French and English dictionary.* Boston: D.C. Heath.

Prendergast, K. 1994. Coaching as a management exercise. *New Studies in Athletics* 9(1):57-63.

THE BIOMECHANICS OF RUNNING

Where there is life, there is movement. Walking and running are intricate motor skills that develop over time, with repeated practice, and are our most familiar forms of movement. Running is often considered humanity's oldest form of sport—a simple test of the ability to move quickly from the starting line to the finish. The Olympic motto *Citius, Altius, Fortius* literally means *faster, higher, braver* (or *swifter, higher, stronger,* the more common translation). From ancient Greece to modern times, running fast and far has been popular.

The desire to know how to run faster or farther is as old as our willingness to try harder. Talented athletes very often are highly motivated, even to the extent that their enthusiasm may need toning down rather than gearing up. Running is a neuromuscular skill, performed in accordance with the principles of biomechanics and dependent on metabolic energy. Practice, it is often said, makes perfect. When inefficient movement patterns are refined out of a runner's natural style through months of practice, which we call training, movement economy improves, permitting potentially greater speed or endurance. But it isn't just practice that brings perfection. Knowing *how* to practice is essential; athletes must have an effective plan derived from the best information available about the kinds of work that will bring improvement. The results of that practice then can provide essential feedback for more refined activity.

As soon as runners begin to improve their abilities over time through training, they become desirous of any and all information that might enhance this development. Coaches also continually search for answers to questions that might provide them with additional knowledge to help their athletes acquire the winning edge over their competitors. How is running acquired as a skill? How do the nervous and musculoskeletal systems interact to permit running to occur? Can an individual's running style be improved, and would this likely improve competitive performance abilities? How can running injuries be prevented? What occurs during the training process that makes muscles more fatigue-resistant? Are these changes related solely to the neuromuscular system, or does the cardiovascular system contribute to these changes? Because energy is required for movement, how are the various available fuels converted into energy? How is this energy stored and made available for use by working muscles? How can this knowledge be applied practically by athletes and coaches to provide the best possible physiological environment for adaptation to the various training loads that will be assigned over a season of training and competing?

It's a tall order to answer all these questions, but in the first four chapters of this book we'll try. In this chapter we identify some of the basic concepts relating to movement and to development of the running skill. Then we review some of the biomechanical principles governing how we run. From there we can conveniently consider in chapter 2 the function of working skeletal muscles to permit both speed- and endurance-oriented movement. The realization that this requires metabolic energy leads us to chapter 3, which proceeds to outline the general concepts of fuel metabolism and nutrition. Chapter 4 discusses the role of the cardiopulmonary system in performance. This overall knowledge base should provide an adequate foundation for considering the development of physical fitness for sport performance and competitiveness over the broad range of distances that are of interest to the middle- and long-distance athlete.

Kinesiology: The Study of Movement

Kinesiology is the science of human motion. It utilizes relevant principles from such disciplines as anatomy, physiology, and physics and applies them appropriately to the understanding of bodily movement. Our particular interest is to better understand the movement patterns that permit running. Each structure contributing to such body movements acts in obedience to biomechanical and physiological principles. Understanding these principles puts us in a better position to identify the best plan for helping runners become more skilled in their sport. Because running is such a fundamental aspect of human movement, it is a skill learned quite early in life. Improved skill combined with the benefits of training contribute to performance enhancement. Thus, once runners are in their high school, college, and postcollegiate years, increases in performance ability are achieved primarily through greater fitness.

Terminology and Concepts

We define *movement* as a positional change by any segment of the body. A more complex *movement pattern* is thus a sequence of movements in a particular time-space relationship. Running is a specifically structured movement pattern. Sometimes the phrases *motor activity* or *motor pattern* are substituted for movement pattern. A *motor skill* is defined as a group of simple, natural movements oriented toward achieving a predetermined goal. Three primary demands on muscular performance are imposed in acquiring any motor skill: strength, endurance, and speed. Coordination links these three together to permit smoothly executed movement patterns (Henatsch and Langer 1985).

Fundamental motor skills set the stage for the development of more advanced and specialized motor activities. *Fundamental motor patterns* thus are the general sequence of movements required to perform a fundamental skill. A small child just beginning to run a few steps has acquired fundamental motor patterns for running. Over time and with practice, marked improvement will occur. This refinement has various features that constitute the developmental motor pattern. As this developing athlete becomes more accomplished over time, the steady improvement in competence beyond the fundamental running motor pattern will be obvious to all. Thus, motor skills are learned. Inborn, natural (unconditioned) responses are eventually modified to permit their triggering by other than natural (conditioned) stimuli in new combinations and sequences. This occurs because the plasticity of the nervous system permits reinterpretation (and, it is hoped, a refinement) of nervous input over time and with repetition.

When asked to run laps around a 400-m track at a specific pace, novice runners typically demonstrate considerable variation in lap times. If the runner is asked to maintain a 75-second (s) pace, for example, for six laps, with half a minute (min) rest between laps, variation of as much as 2 to 3 s and more for each lap can be common. Not so with the majority of experienced distance runners, who after years of good coaching can achieve a consistent sense of pace, despite weather or progressive fatigue, that over distances from 200 to 800 m may not vary by more than a few tenths of a second.

A *sport skill* is a fundamental skill that has been refined and specialized to permit participation in a particular sport. Thus, whereas the simple act of running may be a fundamental skill, the art of running competitively is a sport skill. The concept of *form* or *style* refers to the visual effect produced by motor patterns. If the visual effect is smooth and efficient, then good form (style) ought to relate at least to some extent with increased skill. Finally, *performance* describes an assigned motor activity. A *sport performance* is thus an assigned, specialized sport activity with the intent of producing the best possible display of motor patterns.

Ability Versus Capacity

In all activities—athletic, artistic, literary—individuals who have subjected themselves to the same levels of intensive training typically demonstrate different levels of ability. The inference is that they must have started with unequal capacities to learn. There is thus a distinction between ability and capacity. *Capacity* is synonymous with readiness for use, whereas *ability* presupposes training. Each individual is thus endowed with a general motor capacity analogous to his or her general intellectual capacity. Whereas capacity is a condition, ability can be observed and measured. An ability is invariably the result of training, and the degree of ability is related to the quantity of such training. The common phrase *inherent ability* really refers to capacity.

The capacity of the brain to develop new motor patterns seems almost unlimited. Incorporation of incoming new sensory information leads to further perceptive and cognitive integration, which in turn permits progressively more effective motor responses. Not only can we create movements in the images of our thinking, but we also can improve their execution. This mental assimilation comes from training. There is no substitute for proper training if movement patterns are to develop optimally. The extent of performance improvement is greatest among athletes whose development programs have been not only very intense but also most specific to the sport skills being developed. Thus, the primary key to success is doing the correct amount of the type of training that best promotes the desired outcome: in the case of distance running, more endurance and more speed.

In essence, we are suggesting that the acquisition of human skill presupposes not only physical abilities but also the realization of distinct aims. The latter in turn are conceived in the image of historical, social, cultural, and scientific precedents. Thus, developing athletes become aware of the excellence of past athletes (such as Olympian Jesse Owens), identify with a particular event (such as the short sprints), and develop a yearning for excellence (such as a desire also to compete in the Olympic Games someday). This provides a base for their motivation and goal-setting toward achieving excellence (through collaboration with coaches who have demonstrated competence).

Development of Skill in Movement

Both training and technique are essential in improving sport skill levels. The human body is a self-optimizing machine in that it gradually adapts to a given movement challenge by improving the efficiency with which that movement is performed. This presumably permits the imposition of an even greater challenge, with eventual adaptation to that as well. Peak physical performance occurs when limits to further adaptation are reached. Peak performance is essentially the result of a balance between natural abilities (both physical and mental) and proper training. The results of training are seen in the biochemical and physiological adaptations occurring within cells. Skill is seen in improved movement pattern efficiency; outwardly we see an improved running style.

At least five characteristics are observable as a skilled performer optimizes energy expenditure to permit the highest quality of performance:

- Balance and coordination improve, thereby reducing postural work.
- Unnecessary and exuberant movements are eliminated.
- Necessary movements are refined to ensure that these occur in the proper direction, with optimal quickness to minimize loss of kinetic energy.
- The most important muscles for movement (the prime movers) are used more effectively, including the most efficient coordination of *agonist muscles* (those active for generating movement), *antagonist muscles* (those which have opposing motion and either are relaxed or stabilize the involved joints when the agonists are active), and *synergistic muscles* (those assisting the prime movers). The result is minimal energy devoted to initiating the movement, minimal opposing resistance, and minimal force required to terminate or reverse the direction of movement.
- Continually controlled movements are gradually replaced by ballistic strokes.

This final characteristic needs further elaboration. For practical purposes, the limiting factor in the rapidity of a movement—be it tapping a finger or running down a street—is set by the natural movement frequency of the involved body part; this is its *resonance*. A reciprocal movement such as running is essentially a series of ballistic strokes. A *ballistic stroke* can be conceptualized here as a single oscillation of a moving pendulum formed by the arm or leg. Movement is initiated by sudden generation of tension in shortening muscles until acceleration has been completed, at which time the limb continues to move under its own momentum. As movement patterns are being learned, the stroke velocity is slow because of uncertainty, and tension application may occur throughout much of the range of motion. As skill is acquired, movement velocity increases. With it, there is a gradual shift from prolonged muscle activity through the range of motion to short ballistic bursts that initiate limb acceleration in the precise direction and extent required to complete the movement.

Like acceleration, a decelerating action caused by tension generation in the antagonistic muscles continues for sufficient time to reverse the movement and initiate a ballistic stroke in the opposite direction. If the optimal resonant frequency of a limb is exceeded, movement becomes less efficient because more energy is required. Resonance thus limits the rate of running through limitation of stride frequency. Once the optimal frequency is attained, greater velocity occurs by lengthening the stride. This is achieved by strengthening, which comes with proper training over time. This explains why, for any aspiring great runner, the two fundamental determinants of running fast are *stride length* and *stride frequency.*

These concepts can help us understand the developmental process as runners progress from novice to elite levels. For example, if we compare two runners, each running at the same percentage of their maximal performance capacity and having the same height and leg length, the stronger and more powerful elite-level runner typically takes a stride that is several centimeters (cm) longer. This brings the thigh of the lead leg forward at closer to the maximal velocity permitted by resonance. In turn, this increased velocity requires more intense tension generation in the agonist muscles, and an equally greater relaxation of the antagonists to accommodate the increased range of motion.

If the quadriceps muscles, for example, are the agonist muscles providing forward thrust in running, then the hamstrings are the antagonists. Inflexible hamstrings can thus limit efficient stride maintenance at higher running intensities or can be prone to injury if the much stronger quadriceps group stretches them inappropriately. Thus, optimal relationships among muscle strength, muscle length, and joint range of motion are important not only for promoting faster-paced running, but also for promoting injury-free improvement in performance. As an accompaniment to a training plan that includes various patterns of running to provide specific development (see chapter 5), we also recommend a plan to develop these other more general aspects of fitness commonly called *total-body conditioning* (see chapter 6).

Brain Initiation and Execution of Movement

Many regions of the brain and spinal cord interact as a team to set the stage for and permit initiation of functionally useful and efficient movement. The cerebral cortex, as the seat of our volitional thoughts, is only one of the regions in the brain involved in directing movement. Many other brain and spinal cord regions are also involved with movement, and they interact with the cerebral cortex. Gaining a complete understanding of this topic would require some college courses in neuroanatomy and neurophysiology, but for our purposes, such advanced knowledge is not needed. We can briefly discuss some of the more important concepts, and these will be perfectly adequate for our understanding of how running occurs as a form of organized movement.

It is useful to view movement as a phenomenon in direct conflict with posture. Movement causes variable changes in the position of the body parts over time. In contrast, posture is exactly the reverse of movement: The body position is fixed. To resolve this paradox, the renowned neurologist Derek Denny-Brown suggested that we think of movement as simply a series of postures. In figure 1.1, from left to right, three 800-m runners (Seb Coe [Great Britain], Steve Cram [Great Britain], and Ryszard Ostrowski [Poland]) demonstrate what we shall later describe as, respectively, the midsupport, follow-though, and foot descent periods of a running cycle. Of interest to us at the moment, however, is

Figure 1.1 Three of many postures assumed during a running sequence. Shown here, from left to right and identifiable by their side numbers, are Sebastian Coe (GBR–#1), Steve Cram (GBR–#3) and Ryszard Ostrowski (POL–#2). Coe's right leg is in the mid-support period, Cram's left leg is in the follow-through period, and Ostrowski's left leg is in the foot descent period of the running cycle.

understanding which structures of the central nervous system interact to initiate and permit these very rapid sequential postural changes that we call running. While some may suggest that such consideration is too detailed for a text intended for coaches and athletes, we disagree. Only by having such appreciation can a clearer understanding be gained regarding the cause and management of overtraining, and attempts to change an individual's running style.

The *reticular formation* in the brain stem (see figure 1.2) plays a fundamental role. This is the oldest part of the brain, responsible for the three primary requirements of postural maintenance:

- Support against gravity
- Orientation in space
- Balance

Cues from several sensory systems help to satisfy this responsibility. The *visual system* provides visual orientation in space. The *vestibular system* in the inner ear provides cues about the position of the center of mass as well as changes in acceleration or deceleration. *Neuromuscular spindles* distributed among all the skeletal muscle fibers detect static as well as dynamic muscle length. *Golgi tendon organs* detect changes in tension or force in skeletal muscles. These various receptors are often grouped together as *proprioceptors*. The Latin prefix *proprio* refers to "one's own." Thus, proprioceptors identify the position of one's body in space. Information from all of these systems is sent to the reticular formation via nerve pathways in either the brain or spinal cord.

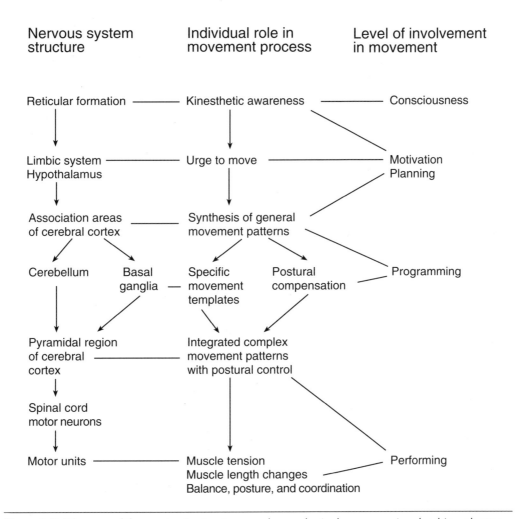

Nervous system structure | Individual role in movement process | Level of involvement in movement

Reticular formation ——— Kinesthetic awareness ——— Consciousness

Limbic system Hypothalamus ——— Urge to move ——— Motivation / Planning

Association areas of cerebral cortex ——— Synthesis of general movement patterns

Cerebellum   Basal ganglia — Specific movement templates   Postural compensation ——— Programming

Pyramidal region of cerebral cortex ——— Integrated complex movement patterns with postural control

Spinal cord motor neurons

Motor units ——— Muscle tension Muscle length changes Balance, posture, and coordination ——— Performing

Figure 1.2 Diagram of the anatomic structures and neurological processes involved in voluntary movement.

The *cerebellum* is another primitive brain region, acting like a computer to process incoming information from several levels of sophistication—volitional, automatic, and reflexive. It interacts with both the reticular formation and the cerebral cortex to ensure that volitional commands for movement sequences produce the most efficient and coordinated result possible while still maintaining appropriate posture.

The signals to initiate movement originate in regions just below the cerebral cortex, notably the *limbic system* and *hypothalamus.* Here is where motivation and the urge to move (the drive to act) are developed. Stimuli from these areas then activate regions of the cerebral cortex known as *association areas,* which generate signals to permit synthesis of movement patterns. Signals going to the cerebellum result in movement patterns involving ballistic strokes and great precision. Signals sent to the *basal ganglia* just below the cerebral cortex create movement templates that provide postural compensation when the movement begins. Both the basal ganglia and cerebellum send their integrated movement pattern signals back to the cerebral cortex, specifically to its motor or pyramidal region (so called because many of its large cell bodies resemble small pyramids).

Initiating signals are then sent from the cerebral cortex down through the spinal cord to the various muscles involved in both movement and postural maintenance. The beginning movement and postural alteration are monitored in exquisite detail via action of the proprioceptors. Such incoming information is used by the brain to help determine how much volitional output is required to permit efficient and effective movement. Figure 1.2 summarizes these various levels of organization and processes that permit voluntary movements.

Acquiring Skill Through Training

Achievement in sport is essentially the product of *testing capabilities* (how well one performs in either a competition, a time trial, or a practice session) and *skill level*. Motivation is required for both, but it is particularly influential in providing the persistence required for the training and practice necessary to improve skill levels. For achievement in any endeavor, one needs at least the following:

- Reasonable capabilities for that activity
- The capacity (motivation plus environment) to train diligently
- Effective use of learned skills in a test situation

Observing and thinking by themselves do not suffice for the acquisition of skills. In sports as well as the arts, a long period of conditioning and practice precedes mastery of a task. The personal history of every champion athlete reveals the determining role played by intensive and dedicated training. Sustained practice of precisely designed movement sequences establishes advanced levels of control, differentiation, and precision of motor patterns that are beyond the integrative control of the untrained individual. Along with basic neuromotor skill, the cognitive qualities of awareness and judgment are also required for performance excellence.

The eventual goal of motor learning is to develop the ability to perform with minimal conscious concern for exactly how the performance is being achieved. Frequent practice of a complex skill helps make it automatic rather than voluntary, and the increasing smoothness thereby reduces error frequency. The execution of all rapid movements depends greatly on timing—generating and relaxing tension in individual muscles in a closely planned sequence. People vary in their abilities to store such movement sequences within the brain. Considerable time is spent practicing to develop one's potential within the complex neurological framework that permits movement patterns in the context of postural balance. Once movement patterns have been learned, attention needs only to be shifted from the elements of the task to the initiating signal for skill competence. Thus, bowlers are taught to take their stance and then focus on the pins rather than on the ball or their body position behind the foul line. Tennis players are taught not to look at racquets or arms but rather at the oncoming ball being returned or served. Although running involves much more fitness than technique because it is not a complex, technique-oriented activity, there are useful skill-related hints that runners can focus on while running to perform more efficiently. These will be suggested shortly.

Runners in a race automatically select a stride length, stride frequency, and breathing rate that fit their level of exertion and running velocity. This permits other aspects to be dealt with more from a cognitive viewpoint, such as assessing their own level of perceived exertion and how it seems to compare with the level of the runners around them (listening to their breathing patterns, viewing their expressions, etc.) and determining the appropriateness of tactics for improving race position. Is this automatically selected combination of stride length and stride frequency in fact always the most energy efficient? To answer this question, we need to better understand some of the basic applications of biomechanics to running.

Running-Specific Movement

Successful distance runners improve steadily with training and experience minimum setbacks from structural injury in any parts of the connecting limbs (bones, tendons, muscles, joints). More training can bring better fitness and thus better performance capabilities, but only within limits. The challenge is to identify those limits *before* they are reached. This is primarily because the large volumes of training required to improve fitness result in an enormous net impact stress on the feet and legs, which predisposes an athlete to injury.

An example can illustrate the magnitude of the problem. Let us define a *running cycle* as beginning and ending with the same foot striking the ground (Mann 1982); it thus requires two strides, one with each foot. Some investigators substitute *stride* for cycle and *step* for stride (Cavanagh and Kram 1990). We prefer to equate stride with step, so that one cycle equals two strides, or two steps, or really, two landings. Assuming a stride (step) length of 60 inches (in), or 5 feet (ft), at a pace of 6:30/mile (mi), with each landing foot bearing the impact of twice the body weight, a 10-mi run for a 130-pound (lb) male runner would involve 5,280 landings per foot, with a total impact force per foot of 686 U.S. tons, as shown by the following calculations:

$$(1 \text{ stride}/5 \text{ ft} \times 5{,}280 \text{ ft}/\text{mi} \times 10 \text{ mi})/2 = 5{,}280 \text{ landings per foot} \qquad (1.1)$$

$$(130 \text{ lb} \times 2)/\text{landing} \times 5{,}280 \text{ landings per foot} \times 1 \text{ U.S. ton}/2{,}000 \text{ lb} = 686 \text{ U.S. tons per foot} \qquad (1.2)$$

As running velocity increases, stride length increases, reducing the number of landings per unit distance. But the ground impact force then increases to as much as four times body weight.

For readers more familiar with the metric system, let us recalculate the preceding example using metric equivalents:

$$(1 \text{ stride}/1.52 \text{ m} \times 16{,}100 \text{ m})/2 = 5{,}296 \text{ landings per foot} \qquad (1.3)$$

$$(59 \text{ kg} \times 2 \text{ times body weight})/\text{landing} \times 5{,}296 \text{ landings per foot} = 624{,}928 \text{ kg} \qquad (1.4)$$

A similar calculation for a female distance runner could be made by substituting 110 lb (50 kg) and a 55-in. (1.4 m) stride length at 6:30/mi (4:02/km). Using Imperial units, she would have 5,760 landings per foot, and a total impact force of 634 U.S. tons. With metric units, she would have 5,750 landings per foot, for a total of 575,000 kg of force.

Runners aspiring to excellence are in an almost no-win situation. Running is required as training to improve running skills. As records become more difficult to break, more training (quantity, quality, or both) is required to achieve the performance level necessary for such a feat. This is true for individual records (personal bests) as much as for world, Olympic, or school records. The greater the volume or intensity of distance run, the greater the stress and thus the risk of injury. As shown previously, even one run provides enormous stresses to the lower limbs. Not to train very extensively makes one ill-prepared to compete successfully with those who have done so but haven't (yet) been injured. At the top level, it is not unusual for an elite 10,000-m runner or marathoner to have several-week blocks of endurance-oriented training that can exceed 100 mi (161 km) each week (Kaggestad 1987). Using the arithmetic format illustrated in equation (1.1), a calculation of the number of footstrikes or amount of landing force for such a week gives results that are almost unimaginable. Try the calculations first, before you try the endurance training!

It should be clear that the conflict between the need for training for improvement and the limit imposed by load-related stress that results in injury has stimulated considerable interest in understanding what occurs during a running cycle, how biomechanics can be improved, and how the weakest links, which might predispose a runner to injury as repetitive stress accumulates, can be identified. If improved running mechanics in fact can decrease the energy costs associated with the muscular forces of running, the resulting improved efficiency should decrease the O_2 cost of running at any given submaximal pace. Presumably, this ought to increase the maximal maintainable pace, thereby improving performance. Athletes and coaches ought to understand these basic concepts, including the proper terminology related to running biomechanics. They then can communicate more effectively with the various experts—biomechanists, podiatrists, orthopedists, and other coaches—who have the skills to assist them in identifying optimal training conditions for performance enhancement with freedom from injury.

Applying Biomechanical Principles to Running

At least four important principles of biomechanics explain what occurs during a running cycle. Understanding these principles permits greater appreciation for the limb and postural adjustments that occur.

Force Must Be Applied to Change the Velocity of an Object in Motion

In humans, muscular tension generation serves as the producer of force. This force can start, accelerate, decelerate, stop, or change direction of movement. As an example, a runner experiences a slight loss of velocity during the airborne phase of each stride. Thus, to maintain continuity of motion, appropriate accelerative force must be applied by the support leg at takeoff.

Integration of Linear and Angular Motion Permits Optimal Performance of Movement Patterns

The lower limbs function by flexion and extension through the range of motion of their joints. The pelvis transmits the body weight to the alternating surface-striking limbs through the hip joints and the lumbothoracic spine. As the lower limbs alternate from support phase through swing phase, thigh extension and flexion are accompanied by rotary movements (to increase stride length), as well as abduction and adduction at the hips and lateral flexion and rotation of the spine. All these movements about various planes need to be complementary and not contradictory.

The Longer the Lever, the Greater the Potential Linear Velocity at Its End

In running, this principle is utilized in reverse. Thus, the knee of the recovery leg and the arms as well are bent in order to shorten these limb levers and bring them forward with a smaller energy requirement.

For Every Action There Is a Reaction Equal in Amount but Opposite in Direction

With every running footstrike, the landing surface pushes back with a force equal to the impact force, driving the runner upward and forward in a direction opposite that of impact.

There are, of course, additional biomechanical principles that describe the kinds of activities runners engage in during training. In chapter 6 we shall consider some of these, particularly those relating to development of leverage for the various aspects of strength training that constitute a total-body conditioning program.

Understanding Podiatric Principles

Podiatrists consider walking and running as an integrated series of anatomic rotations that propel the body through space. The so-called *kinetic chain* of bones that cope with the impact forces upon landing and the push-off forces upon takeoff extend from the spine to the foot. These bones include, in sequence, the lumbar spine, pelvis, proximal lower limb (femur), distal lower limb (tibia and fibula), rear foot (calcaneus and talus), midfoot (navicular and cuboid), and forefoot (cuneiforms, metatarsals, and phalanges). Figure 1.3 illustrates the bones from the distal lower limb to the foot. Joints connect each of these various bony links: the pelvis (hip to femur), the knee (femur to tibia), the ankle or talocrural joint (tibia and fibula to talus), the subtalar or talocalcaneal joint (talus to calcaneus), the two midtarsal joints—talonavicular and calcaneocuboid (talus to navicular and calcaneus to cuboid), and so on, through to the metatarsophalangeal joints (metatarsal bones to phalanges). These are also seen in figure 1.3. The

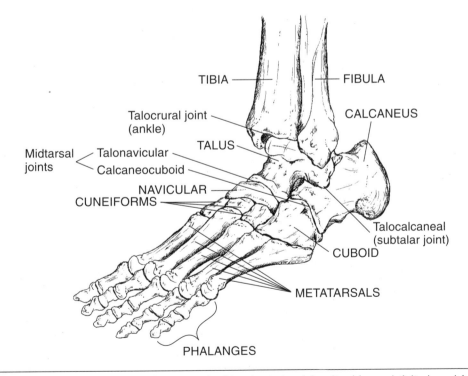

Figure 1.3 The major bones and joints in the kinetic chain of the distal lower left limb and foot (as viewed from the lateral, or outside, surface), which distribute running-related impact forces on landing and push-off forces on takeoff. Joints are indicated in lower-case letters, bones in all capital letters. (Line drawing courtesy of James E. Zelichowski, DPM.)

incredible complexity of foot structure and mechanics may now be better appreciated.

Muscles, tendons, ligaments, bones, and joint capsules work together to dissipate and manage the rotatory, angular, and compressive forces that occur during a gait cycle. Muscles are particularly important because they initiate movement, stabilize bones, and decelerate or dampen movement forces resulting from sudden weight bearing. Muscle fatigue reduces this protective function, increasing the risk of injury to the other tissues in the kinetic chain.

The body has three axes of rotation: *frontal, sagittal,* and *transverse.* Relative to the foot, frontal plane rotation represents *inversion* and *eversion,* sagittal plane rotation represents *dorsiflexion* and *plantar flexion,* and transverse plane rotation represents *abduction* (external rotation) and *adduction* (internal rotation). One confusing aspect of foot mechanics is that the ankle, subtalar, and midtarsal joints have axes of rotation that are oblique to these three body movement planes. Movements of these joints have components of all three motions. Thus, *pronation* consists of dorsiflexion, calcaneal eversion, and external rotation, whereas *supination* consists of plantar flexion, calcaneal inversion, and internal rotation. The talus bone lies just below the tibia and above the calcaneus and thus is a pivotal structure in linking the movements of the lower leg and foot. When it articulates with the tibia to form the ankle joint, it works as part of the foot to permit dorsiflexion and plantar flexion. When it articulates with the calcaneus at the subtalar joint, it works as part of the leg to permit pronation and supination.

The *support phase* of a running gait cycle consists of three distinct periods: *footstrike, midsupport,* and *takeoff* (sometimes called contact, midstance, and toe-off). During *forward recovery* there are also three periods: *follow-through, forward swing,* and *foot descent.* The follow-through and foot descent periods are sometimes also known as the periods of *float.*

Figure 1.4 illustrates pronation and supination during a normal gait cycle. Our subject (U.S. distance athlete Donna Garcia) is neither running nor walking, but rather posing to provide the best views of key moments in the gait cycle. She is demonstrating supination at heelstrike (figure 1.4a), pronation during midsupport (figure 1.4b), resupination as takeoff begins (figure 1.4c), and pronation near the transition from the takeoff aspect of the support period to actually leaving the ground (figure 1.4d). Slower-paced running (as well as walking) usually involves heelstrike, particularly among the serious fitness runners "back in the pack." As the pace quickens, runners gradually become midfoot strikers. In fact, at fast paces it is quite normal for only the forefoot of elite-level middle-distance runners to touch the ground.

The Sequence of Movement in a Running Cycle

We can briefly describe what occurs as a runner's limbs proceed through one running cycle. The relevant terminology and concepts are familiar to podiatrists, biomechanists, and orthopedists interested in gait, but this body of knowledge ought to be familiar to coaches and athletes as well. Several good reviews describe rather precisely what occurs during running (Adelaar 1986; James and Brubaker 1972; Mann, Moran, and Dougherty 1986; Slocum and Bowerman 1962; Slocum and James 1968). More than one set of descriptive terms exist for identifying the various aspects of gait cycle for running; we will use that of Slocum and James.

Running and walking are both fundamental skills, but they differ from many other such skills in that the movement pattern is designed to be continuous,

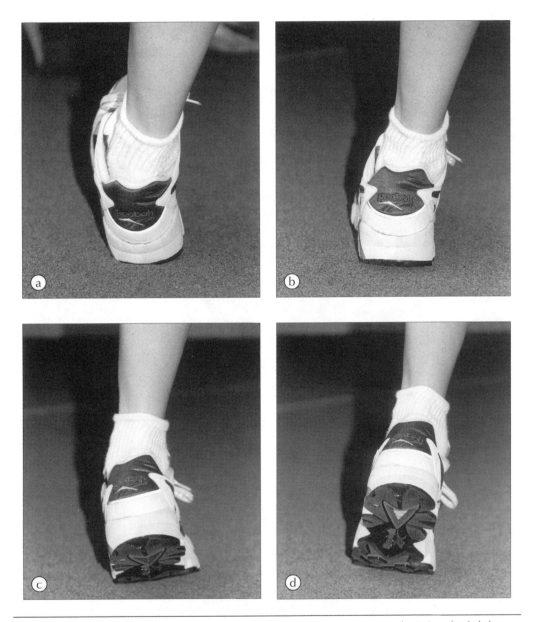

Figure 1.4 Rearview illustrations of foot dynamics during one running cycle, using the left foot. As footstrike is initiated, the foot is in supination (*a*). Then as contact progresses (*b*), pronation permits absorption of the forces of impact. As the transition from midsupport to takeoff begins (*c*), resupination occurs as the foot becomes a rigid lever. Just before toe-off (*d*) the foot is again in pronation. This is described further in the text. (Photos courtesy of Perry M. Julien, DPM.)

without interruption. We move one foot in front of the other, with the arms on each side moving synchronously but in the direction opposite that of the legs. Thus, as the left leg and right arm are moving forward, the right leg and left arm are moving backward. (This information makes it easy to tell when the runners are posed—that is, appearing as though they are running but really standing still to reduce problems with lens focusing—on the covers of running magazines.) In both walking and running the trunk should lean forward minimally to reduce the load on postural muscles, which will be stressed least if they keep the large percentage of body weight made up by the trunk and head (60%) directly over the point of ground support.

TECHNIQUE: THE RUNNING CYCLE

Forward swing

Forward swing

Float (follow through)

← Recovery →

Forward swing

Foward swing

Float (follow through)

← Recovery →

Figure 1.5 *a-l* Julianne Henner completes a running gait cycle starting with footstrike in the upper right corner (*a*). The photos were taken from a photographer standing on the infield of the track in order to ensure each photo was taken from the same distance.

Takeoff   Midsupport   Footstrike

← **Support** →

Takeoff   Midsupport   Footstrike

← **Support** →

Figure 1.5 *a-l* (continued)

The most important feature that distinguishes running from walking is that in running there is a period during which the runner is airborne, which does not occur during walking. This airborne period is very nicely illustrated in figures 1.5, *d* to *f* and *k* to *l*. The photo sequence in figure 1.5 shows 1995 University Games silver medalist and 1996 Olympian Julianne Henner running at a pace of approximately 68 s/400 m. We will describe this sequence in greater detail shortly. First, recall our earlier division of both walking and running into the sequential phases of support (or stance) and forward recovery (or swing). During walking the support phase accounts for perhaps 65% of the total cycle time, with both limbs on the ground simultaneously for part of its duration. During running the support phase is reduced in duration to as little as 30%, and the period of double-limb support disappears. If the support phase constitutes 40% of a running cycle, then the free-floating forward recovery phase occupies about 60%.

Although the period of free float is the most noticeable difference between walking and running, there are other differences as well. First, in walking the forward foot touches down heel first, before the toe of the other foot has pushed off. During running the push-off becomes so strong that the body is launched into the air; running is thus a kind of bounding. Second, in running the elbows flex more acutely. This shortens the arm lever and thereby allows more rapid arm swing as stride rate increases. In contrast, during walking the arms are nearly extended. Third, greater vertical displacement of the trunk (the bounding aspect) occurs with running than with walking. Last, there is more hip, knee, and ankle activity to accommodate the greater stresses with running than with walking. At landing a runner experiences a rapid knee and hip flexion and ankle dorsiflexion in response to the need for greater shock absorption. With walking there is ankle plantar flexion, not dorsiflexion.

We have already explained the difference between cycle and stride in running. *Running velocity* is the product of stride length and stride frequency. Stride length is best measured from the toe of the landing shoe rather than from the back of the heel. Although walking is almost universally a heel-to-toe action, some runners do not land on their heels. The majority of talented runners (60%) land on the forefoot, a sizable number land on the midfoot (30%), and the remaining 10% are rearfoot strikers (Cavanagh, Pollock, and Landa 1977). The forefoot is better able to absorb stress than the rearfoot, an advantage for forefoot strikers.

Now let's follow Julianne Henner through one of her running gait cycles. We will follow her right leg as it moves through its support and nonsupport phases. In figure 1.5a her foot is just touching the ground, initiating footstrike (see also figure 1.4a). Her foot still has a certain amount of supination as it contacts the surface. As she touches the ground, her foot is slightly ahead of her center of mass to minimize braking and to preserve linear forward momentum. Her subtalar joint plays the major role in converting the rotatory forces of her lower extremity into forward motion.

In the split second from foot contact to full support on the running surface (figure 1.5, *a* and *b*), the knee flexes, the tibia internally rotates, the ankle plantar flexes, and the subtalar joint pronates, causing heel eversion (seen from behind in figure 1.4b). This pronation permits absorption of compressive shock forces, torque conversion, adjustment to uneven ground contours, and maintenance of balance. The foot is a nonrigid, supple structure during this time, thus suited admirably for its role. Knee flexion occurs by eccentric tension in the vastus medialis, vastus lateralis, rectus femoris, and sartorius of the thigh (these muscles are shown clearly in figure 1.6, the anterior view of a runner landing). Eccentric tension in the posterior tibialis, soleus, and gastrocnemius muscles also causes a deceleration of subtalar joint pronation and lower extremity internal rotation. Pronation reaches its maximum during this time; sufficient resupination then occurs to permit the foot to pass through its neutral position (shown from behind in figure 1.4c) at midsupport. A certain amount of pronation is thus desirable to disseminate the energy of footstrike over the mid- and forefoot. Too little pronation transfers too much impact to the rearfoot, and excessive joint pronation causes too much calcaneal eversion, putting undue strain on the longitudinal arch.

The period of midsupport continues until the heel starts to rise upward into takeoff (figure 1.5c). During this time Julianne's foot must convert itself from a supple, mobile structure to a rigid lever to adequately support what at her pace can be two to three times her body weight. This change does not depend so much on muscle action as on change in position of the subtalar and midtarsal joints of the foot, the anatomic shape of the bones involved, and tension on the various ligaments. Supination of the subtalar joint establishes this rigid lever for forward propulsion. Thus, the knee joint extends, the lower extremity rotates externally, the calcaneus inverts, the midtarsal joint locks, and the foot becomes a rigid lever. The propulsive force is a thrust backward and downward, resulting from a combination of hip extension (gluteal and hamstring muscles), knee extension (quadriceps group), and ankle plantar flexion (soleus and gastrocnemius). The end result is a rise in the center of mass as the body becomes airborne. The wider forefoot than rearfoot helps provide balance and also increases the weight-bearing surface area.

As soon as Julianne's foot leaves the ground, she will be in the initial floating period of the forward recovery phase, called follow-through. Her left limb

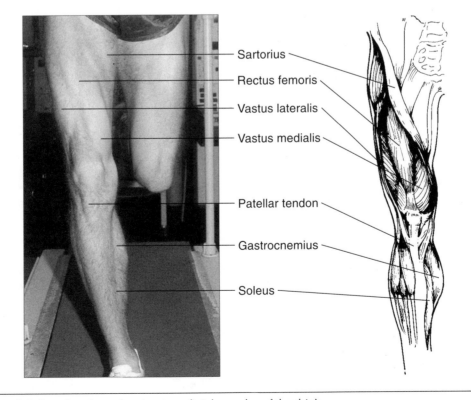

Figure 1.6 Anterior view of major superficial muscles of the thigh.

PLANTAR FASCIITIS

The *plantar fascia* limits the extent to which the longitudinal arch of the foot can depress and thus absorbs much of the landing force. Too little supination at takeoff also stresses this fascia. The fascia originates from a tubercle on the bottom of the calcaneus (figure 1.7) and divides into three bands as it continues forward along the plantar surface of the foot and attaches to the proximal parts of the toes. If microtears occur in this fascia from overuse, the resulting painful, localized inflammation—*plantar fasciitis*—can be quite debilitating. A very painful first step as one gets out of bed in the morning is a characteristic sign of plantar fasciitis.

Suggested causes of plantar fasciitis include excessive pronation, a tendency for a flat foot, a rigid foot, a tight Achilles tendon, training errors, and wearing inappropriate footwear (Warren 1990). Shoes should have adequate arch support, an optimally fitting toe box, a firm heel counter, and an optimally flexible sole. The shoe should match the foot type; that is, a high-arch foot should

not wear a shoe designed for low-arch feet. Training mistakes that predispose runners to plantar fasciitis include sudden and substantial changes in format without gradual adaptation: hard hill sessions, adding workouts, switching suddenly to hard or soft surfaces, and so on. Once plantar fasciitis occurs, it is extremely difficult to cure without substantial downtime and aggressive therapy. Thus, careful management of training dynamics and use of footwear to *prevent* its occurrence is very wise indeed.

The two most important therapeutic management techniques are icing and stretching, but evaluation of shoe-support dynamics is also useful. One suggestion for icing is to roll the bottom of the foot back and forth for 5-min periods on a frozen cylinder made by freezing a plastic cup filled with water. This will both massage and ice the fascia. Stretching the calf muscles is also essential. More aggressive therapy can include night splints, ultrasound, and deep-friction massage.

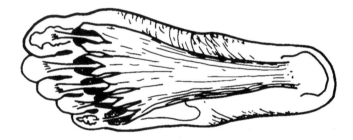

Figure 1.7 The plantar fascia of the foot. Sometimes called the *plantar aponeurosis*, this is a glistening white fibrous membrane that resembles a flattened tendon. Just as with tendons, circulation of blood is very poor. Its three collagen-containing bundles of fibers are tightly packed and arranged in parallel, giving great strength. It attaches to the medial process of the tuberosity of the heelbone and eventually becomes broader and more flattened. Near the metatarsal heads it expands to permit a band of tissue to extend to each of the toes.

movement will be counteracted (slowed) by the action of her hamstrings. The opposite knee is still flexed and high. The right trailing leg then decelerates, and the hip, knee, and ankle reach maximal extension (figure 1.5d). The left limb then begins to move forward, initiating forward swing (figure 1.5e).

This reversal of limb direction requires time and energy. Hip flexion and forward rotation of the pelvis start moving the left thigh forward (figures 1.5, *f-j*). Studies by Mann, Moran, and Dougherty (1986) suggest that *hip flexion*, achieved through action of the iliacus and psoas muscles (figure 1.8), is probably the single most important contributor to forward limb movement. Whereas the iliacus muscle has its origin at the base of the sacrum and the anterior surface of the ilium, the psoas muscle originates on the bodies and intervertebral cartilage of the last thoracic and all the lumbar vertebrae, as well as the transverse bony processes of the lumbar vertebrae. Both muscles then attach by the same tendon to that portion of the femur known as the lesser trochanter.

Knee flexion, which is mainly passive, assists this hip flexion by shortening the lever arm, thus permitting the thigh to move forward at a velocity considerably faster than the body's forward velocity. As soon as maximal hip flexion has been reached and the thigh is farthest off the ground, the final float period, called foot descent, begins (figure 1.5, *k* and *l*). Final preparations are made for the footstrike that will initiate the next cycle. Quadriceps muscle activity promotes knee extension for maximal forward movement of the lower limb. The hamstrings then slow the forward movement of the foot and leg by generating tension, antagonizing any additional knee extension. In slowing this limb movement, the hamstrings lengthen. Movement of the limb now slows to match that of the trunk. When the next footstrike occurs, the foot ideally will be moving backward with a velocity equal to the forward movement of the trunk.

Interesting Questions About Running Biomechanics

The technical details about running biomechanics just described often stimulate a wide variety of practical questions. We can address just a few of them here.

Does Running Pace Influence Stride Frequency and Stride Length?

Both stride frequency and stride length increase as we run faster, with stride length increasing more than stride frequency (figure 1.9). The exact combination

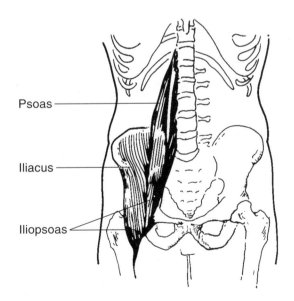

Figure 1.8 The iliacus and psoas muscles, important hip flexors for forward movement of the lower limbs. The psoas arises from the last thoracic vertebra and the five lumbar vertebrae, whereas the iliacus arises from the ilium. The two muscles join together and continue as the iliopsoas to insert on the lesser trochanter of the femur.

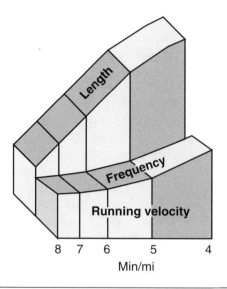

8 7 6   5   4

Min/mi

Figure 1.9 The relationship between stride frequency and stride length. As running velocity increases, stride frequency increases, but stride length increases even more, most likely from recruitment of additional skeletal muscle fibers. *Note.* From "Should You Change Your Stride Length?" by P. Cavanagh and K.R. Williams, 1979, *Runner's World*, 14(7), p. 64. Copyright 1979 by *Runner's World*. Adapted by permission.

of length and frequency at a given pace may differ slightly for each runner because of such variables as leg length, hip flexion, breathing rate, and state of fatigue. Considerable current knowledge about biomechanics of runners stems from the elegant studies done over a period of 12 years by Peter Cavanagh and Keith Williams with their associates (Cavanagh et al. 1985; Cavanagh and Kram 1990; Williams and Cavanagh 1987).

How Is Stride Length Related to Energy Cost?

A runner's most efficient stride length, that is, the stride length that is least energy costly in terms of O_2 consumption, typically occurs subconsciously. This self-selection develops with practice over time from cerebellar integration of incoming information from joint receptors that have been stimulated by hundreds of thousands of previous running cycles. Optimal joint mobility, coupled with increasing leg muscle strength from proper training, increases stride length naturally because of greater propulsive thrust. Intentionally lengthening or shortening the stride length predisposes a runner to premature exhaustion from excessive energy utilization. Figure 1.10 illustrates this, showing clearly how O_2 cost increases at stride lengths longer or shorter than the optimal value selected by that individual. Runners should not attempt to increase stride length beyond that which intuitively seems natural for them.

How Do the Back and Pelvis Interact With the Legs in Running?

It must be remembered that, although it is the foot that strikes the ground, the actual pivot point for the lever system that provides movement is really the lumbar spine and pelvis. During midsupport and takeoff the pelvis tilts forward through action of the lumbar muscles, and this helps provide greater backward thrust of the leg (figure 1.5, *b* and *c*). To minimize swaying from side to side, the entire trunk turns in a counterbalancing direction, that is, opposite to the direction of thrust. Major hip muscles such as the gluteus maximus and

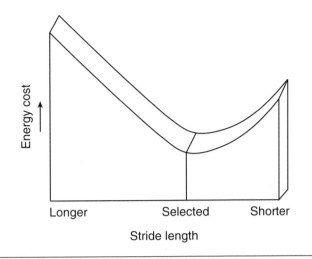

Figure 1.10 The relationship between O$_2$ cost and stride length, showing how a deviation from the selected stride length (typically minimal in energy cost) is less efficient. Depending on individual differences, it may be more energy costly to shorten or to lengthen stride. *Note.* From "Should You Change Your Stride Length?" by P. Cavanagh and K.R. Williams, 1979, *Runner's World*, 14(7), p. 64. Copyright 1979 by *Runner's World*. Adapted by permission.

gluteus medius are important in this regard. The lumbar spine reaches maximal extension during follow-through (figure 1.5*d*) and maximal flexion during forward swing (figure 1.5*g*).

How Can Stride Efficiency Be Increased?

The most efficient runners decelerate least at footstrike, have the least vertical oscillation, and get maximal forward movement with every stride. Footstrike deceleration tends to increase with overstriding, that is, landing well in front of the body's center of mass. Vertical oscillation relates to the combination of trunk length and leg length, determined by the extent of extension or flexion. Maximal forward movement relates in large measure to the torque-generating abilities of the primary muscles involved. In turn, torque generation is developed through increased motor unit recruitment and strengthening of lower-limb and hip muscles. Running efficiency changes as a result of subtle adjustments in these variables. Decreased vertical oscillation and reduced deceleration at footstrike both conserve energy. Increased lower-limb strength should lengthen the most energy-efficient stride length. We have already described the complex central nervous system activity and integration that produces a running cycle. Conscious attempts at changing individual aspects of this process must be well thought through to prevent other, unwanted, alterations in biomechanics that counteract the intended improvement in efficiency.

Do Taller and Shorter Runners Have Similar Biomechanics?

Although the answer is probably yes, taller and shorter runners have similar biomechanics, there are some disadvantages to being a tall runner. As people get taller, they get heavier. But the relationship is exponential; that is, people get heavier at a faster rate than they get taller. A survey of nearly 1,500 New York City marathoners (Stipe 1982) suggested that as height increases linearly, body weight increases exponentially (to the 2.5 power). Thus, if runner A is 66 in. (167.6 cm) tall, and runner B is 72.6 in. (184.4 cm)—a 1.1-fold difference—runner B's expected body weight (156 lb, or 70.8 kg) would be 1.3 times that of runner A

(120 lb, or 54.4 kg). This relationship suggests exponentially greater impact forces on landing. Do the feet increase in size appropriately, that is, by 1.3 times? No. Overall foot size, as well as the impact-absorbing surface area on the bottom of the foot, does not increase relative to the increase in body weight. Thus, taller runners have greater running loads to support, but they have a relatively smaller margin of safety for managing the impact stress of those loads. Cushioning or energy-absorption characteristics of shoes thus need to be increased appropriately as shoe sizes increase to accommodate these greater stresses.

Do Men and Women Have Similar Running Mechanics?

This question is in its infancy in terms of resolution. Only recently has a study of elite female runners been completed (Williams, Cavanagh, and Ziff 1987) as a companion to earlier work done with elite male runners (Cavanagh, Pollock, and Landa 1977). Although these studies do not represent a huge data base, nevertheless some gender differences seem identifiable. Elite male runners appear to have less hip flexion, shorter stride lengths in relation to leg length, and less vertical oscillation than elite female runners.

A problem with many reviews of clinical literature that suggest anatomic differences between men and women that could contribute to one or the other being more prone to injury is that there are variations both in requirements for individual sports as well as in body types of athletes most likely to perform well in each sport. Studies are needed to document clearly that those injuries found are in fact most prevalent among that specific sport and that those individuals of the specific gender involved do exhibit the greatest anatomic differences. Thus, it might be quite correct to state that women on average, when compared with men, have a wider pelvis with a resulting increased femoral anteversion (turning forward), genu valgum (a tendency toward knock-knees), and less development of the vastus medialis muscle in their upper legs (Hutchinson and Ireland 1995). The result of these differences is increased stress on the patellofemoral joint in a manner that increases the risk for various types of knee injury. But if elite female runners' measurements for the variables just mentioned, for example, tend more toward the mean for men, they may be protected from injuries that the average woman would likely acquire from such training. Thus, the elite female runners may be able to tolerate greater training loads, and thus attain greater fitness and performance capacity, than not-so-talented women whose structural dimensions make them more predisposed to injury. Much investigative work remains in this interesting area of sports injury epidemiology.

Do Running Injuries Have Biomechanical Origins?

Running injuries very likely have biomechanical origins. Let's consider one example. What happens when a runner pulls a hamstring? Recall from our discussion of the running cycle that there is a brief moment when both quadriceps and hamstrings groups are generating tension simultaneously. The quadriceps group permits hip joint flexion and knee joint extension for increased forward limb movement in preparation for foot descent and footstrike. The hamstrings attempt to restrain the extent of hip flexion and knee extension, true to their role as antagonistic muscles, and thus serve to decelerate the thigh and lower leg (Stanton and Purdam 1989). During early footstrike the hamstrings are maximally stretched across the hip and knee joints and generate tension together with the quadriceps and gluteals in a team effort to absorb the downward force of body weight as it impacts on the running surface. The net effect of the two antagonistic muscle groups acting simultaneously will be determined by their relative tension-generating abilities. The quadriceps group typically is stronger than the hamstrings group. If the hamstrings group has a limited range of motion due to inflexibility (e.g., from inadequate stretching) or has inadequate strength in the tendons that connect these muscles to the pelvis, tearing of tissue may occur during that brief period when both muscle groups are generating tension. The risk is greater with faster running velocities, as both the forces generated and the stretching required are increased. Although this kind of injury is thus more common in sprinters, it can still affect middle- and long-distance runners who include shorter intervals of running at near-maximal velocity during their peaking periods for important competitions.

THE IMPORTANCE OF HIP STABILITY IN RUNNING

The relationship between running injuries and biomechanics is only beginning to be investigated. Another example, in addition to the previous one, can serve as a provocative thought for athletes and coaches, as well as researchers. We are seeing increasing numbers of what are initially referred to as "hip problems" among those attempting to move to a higher level by increasing the volume of their training load, especially elite female runners. For some it is muscle pain in the iliopsoas, piriformis, or gluteals. For others it is lumbosacral or lower lumbar joint pain or nerve irritation, especially the sciatic nerve. Worse, symptoms could include several or all of these. Depending on whom they see for medical advice (orthopedist, podiatrist, chiropractor, physical therapist, massage therapist), runners get different opinions because of the various specialties' approach in diagnosis. As their discomfort over time may change (often because postural or stride compensation results in accompanying fatigue or irritation in other muscles or connective tissues), their description of symptoms, as well as suggested diagnoses from various experts, may also change.

According to biomechanical principles, probably no part of the body is more vulnerable to tissue stress than the lumbopelvic region, which also includes the fourth and fifth lumbar vertebrae. This region has a critical role in maintaining stability and balance when movements are performed with the legs and arms. It is truly the hub of weight bearing, the place where forces from above (torso, head, and arm movements) and forces from below (ground forces transmitted through the lower limbs) "interface." Running and jumping are particularly challenging in this regard. The faster the running, the taller the athlete, and the wider the

pelvis, the greater the rotational forces that must be managed.

The faster athletes run, the more powerful is their rotational arm and shoulder motion. This places increasing demands on their pelvic rotational stabilizer muscles and ligaments. The less developed their pelvic stability, the more their pelvis will rotate in one direction as it counteracts shoulder rotation in the other. Some hip rotation is appropriate in helping to increase stride length, but if hip rotation is excessive, an inefficient force application on accessory muscles instead of the prime movers not only decreases running efficiency, but also increases the risk of injury or irritation in either the involved muscles or their tendons. And if the cause is podiatric (wearing improper shoes for foot type, needing but not using appropriately corrective orthotics, etc.), no amount of attention devoted to rehabilitation of the lumbopelvic region will really correct the problem.

Runners tend to have weaker abdominal muscles than lower back muscles, because the latter are developed from running but the former are not developed enough by exercises such as sit-ups. This imbalance increases the tendency toward an anterior pelvic tilt. Excessive anterior tilt tends to limit hip range of motion, which decreases hip flexion and increases hip extension. For runners this tends to reduce stride length and increase ground contact time, both of which slow the maintainable pace. Attempting to force a faster cadence risks injury. It is no surprise that such problems as muscle spasms in the iliopsoas, piriformis, and gluteals occur among runners who have not emphasized a combination of strengthening and stretching of the muscles promoting forward motion as well as those providing pelvic rotational stability.

One practical training hint to emerge from this analysis is that, when doing abdominal exercises such as sit-ups, runners should include strengthening of the abdominal obliques by adding a rotational component to the sit-up. Another practical hint is that runners should be sure that their training shoes are correct for their foot type. A high-quality physical therapist and sport podiatrist are thus excellent members of a support group of professionals who ensure that runners stay healthy and train successfully.

Evaluating and Improving Running Biomechanics

Efficient running style is a blending of all the separate movements of the trunk and limbs so that, along with optimal mechanical efficiency, a runner also visually appears to use minimal effort for the task required. Thus, running style suggests a combination of biomechanics and visual appearance, or form. When judging running style with a view toward its improvement, we search for improvements in biomechanics that will help reduce the cost of movement. The end result is probably a smoother appearance as the individual runs. One element of efficient running style, for example, is an optimal combination of cadence and stride length. This will vary not only for each event but also for each runner's height and flexibility. As previously discussed, both overstriding and understriding are energy costly (figures 1.9 and 1.10). Running style for one event may be entirely inappropriate for another: The marathon cannot be run using a style that is appropriate for the 100-m dash or the 1,500-m run. To do so would require a pace that could not be sustained for 42,195 m.

An efficient running style does not automatically guarantee a great running performance, but poor running style can certainly be detrimental. Exceptions may exist, but there aren't many. Emil Zatopek's rather ungainly style has often been used as an example to illustrate that style is really not all that important, and doing what comes naturally, with little attempt at refinement, is best. After all, his record at the 1952 Helsinki Olympic Games speaks for itself—gold medals in the 5,000 m, the 10,000 m, and the marathon.

However, we could also argue that if Zatopek had been coached toward development of more efficient running mechanics, he might have raced even faster. Without the excessive counterrotation of his shoulders, his stiff and high arm action, and his strained facial and neck muscles that produced a characteristically agonized countenance as he rolled his head from side to side, Zatopek might have conserved considerable energy. The brutal fact is that Zatopek triumphed because he trained harder than the rest. He pioneered training with both a high volume of distance running and massive sets of short-distance repetitions. Compared with his contemporaries, his stamina was unmatched—as evidenced by his medals—but he never developed anything like the basic speed of today's long-distance runners. His best 1,500-m time was 3:52, which today can be matched by 16-year-old boys. Many of his 400-m repetitions were at paces no faster than the over-distance paces used by many of today's elite-level male runners.

To us, the school of thought that argues that one's so-called *natural* style is not only best but unchangeable represents a defeatist attitude. It ignores the reality that the nervous system has great adaptive capabilities to incorporate subtle changes in data input that create an improved movement pattern. In so many sports—golf, tennis, swimming, gymnastics, and more—the guidance of coaches expert in designing corrective exercises and instructional commands can bring observable changes in style that contribute to improved performance. The same can occur in running.

We see examples of this plasticity of nervous system development when we observe the changes that occur in running style over time as children mature. Marjorie Beck (1966) studied young American boys in elementary school grades 1 through 6, carefully noting the changes that occurred in their running as they matured. The changes represented improvements in running biomechanics and form. Effective coaching ought to assist more mature runners in defining their form in a similar manner. Beck observed five improvements as the boys matured:

- Longer running strides
- Footstrike coming closer to a point under the center of gravity
- More float time
- Decreased vertical oscillation
- Increased knee flexion at the end of forward swing

Seb Coe's style of running has been described by sportswriters and commentators as "poetry in motion," but it was not always so. He had a cramped, high arm action and excessive shoulder movement when he began training during his early teens. After a little more than three years of corrective effort through coaching, these faults were reduced, and the new version became his "natural" style. The true measure of success in correcting faults is when they fail to return when the athlete is under pressure. Obviously, the earlier in an athlete's career that attention is paid to correcting faults, the better, as movement patterns are less ingrained. But there is always time to attempt improvements in style if it is perceived that useful benefits in efficiency will accrue. Of course, a counterargument is equally apropos. In pursuit of perfection, seldom if ever is it reached, and coaching judgment should limit further attempts at correction if they will be counterproductive. Even today purists can see that one of Seb Coe's elbows is slightly wingy when he is moving quickly, but after 20 years of competitive running there wouldn't be much benefit in constantly picking away at him with corrective exercises to improve it.

An analysis of style involves assessing the principal parts of a running cycle with a view toward identifying aspects of excellence as well as areas for improvement. Let us begin with the feet.

Foot Placement

When an athlete runs in a straight line, successive foot placements should be parallel with each other (or very nearly so) and in the direction of running. This will help reduce rotational torque about the ankles and knees, as well as minimize stride shortening from turning out (splaying) of the feet. Because the hip, knee, and ankle joints are all subjected to severe loads during running, it is best to minimize rotatory torques in favor of torque that optimizes forward movement.

Figure 1.11 illustrates foot placements that vary in efficiency. The photo was taken very near the finish of the 800-m final at the 1986 European Championships in Stuttgart and shows the exciting British sweep of the medal positions. Seb Coe (326) and Tom McKean (351) took the gold and silver, respectively, and

Figure 1.11 Lower-limb running mechanics in three of Britain's best 1500-m runners. Note the optimal foot orientation parallel to the path of movement in Seb Coe (326) and Tom McKean (351), but excessive lower-limb rotation in Steve Cram (328).

their foot orientation parallel to the direction of forward movement is fairly obvious. The left foot of the bronze medalist (Steve Cram, 328), however, is markedly turned out (everted), as well as his left knee, giving that leg a reduced forward force vector as it generates propulsive thrust. An excessive amount of Cram's propulsive energy is being absorbed by the knee and ankle joints in resisting the torsional stresses generated by his everted foot plant. This style of foot plant not only increases the risk of lower-limb injuries, but also reduces his stride length by more than 1 cm. At his race pace and stride length in Stuttgart, Cram was losing a little more than 50 cm for every 100 m of distance covered. In today's races, this is an enormous disadvantage to overcome. Here is an excellent example in which an athlete's potential performance abilities might be enhanced considerably by a professional podiatric/orthopedic evaluation with a view toward developing an ongoing program of corrective exercises to either improve foot placement or strengthen the musculature that is being unduly stressed. It may also be of interest that over several of his competitive years Steve Cram was bothered by lower-limb running injuries, particularly to his calf muscles.

Ankle Flexibility

An important feature of the ankle joint to assess is its flexibility. Improved flexibility has a payoff in longer potential stride length. Ankle flexibility seems best displayed at major international track meets by African runners, particularly those who ran barefoot as children. Their style shows the knee of the supporting leg well in front of the ankle, giving the foot a greater range of motion throughout takeoff. It is a well-known physiological fact that a muscle can generate greater shortening if it has been prestretched before tension generation begins.

The longer the heel remains near to or in contact with the ground while the knee moves forward, the greater the prestretch on the calf muscles. This will increase both stride length and power. Figure 1.12 illustrates this effect of early and late takeoff caused by lesser or greater ankle flexibility.

High Knee Lift

Velocity determines style for the knee as well. High-velocity running requires a high knee lift, marathon running does not, and there is a pro rata accommodation in between. Runners with considerable spring in their style have such a rapid ballistic stroke during the forward-swing phase that the heel of the swing leg very nearly touches the buttock. In coaching jargon this increased knee flexion produces a greater *butt kick* or *heel flick*. Sprinters thus have both a high knee lift and a high heel flick as a natural result of the bounding aspect of their powerful push-off from rapid forward leg movement. Long-distance runners should not intentionally attempt to incorporate such motion in their running style. Their slower running velocity naturally produces a smaller bounding component, which decreases vertical oscillation.

Hip Flexibility

The pelvis is the next joint along the kinetic chain, and it too has a unique and crucial role in running. Its large size accommodates large muscles, which

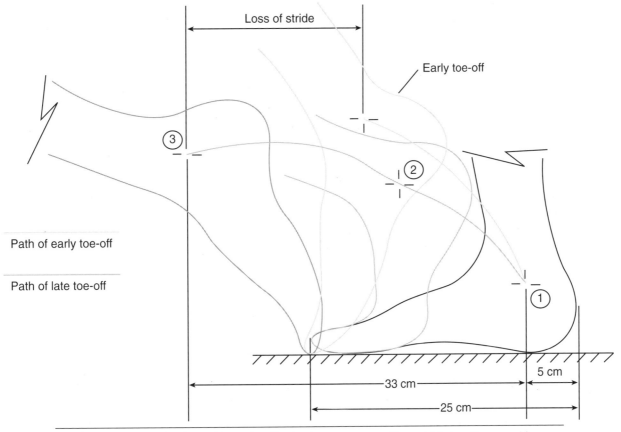

Figure 1.12 Effect of early and late takeoff (also known as toe-off) on stride length caused by, respectively, lesser and greater ankle flexibility. Early takeoff results in a shorter stride and more vertical displacement of the center of mass, creating a less efficient running style than later takeoff, which enhances stride length and lessens vertical displacement.

generate the powerful propulsive forward thrust of the plant foot, as well as the flexor thrust of the forward-swinging leg. Lack of hip joint mobility also limits stride length. The muscles that stabilize the hip against rotatory torque must be especially strong to prevent injury if they are strained excessively. Adductor muscle injuries are particularly slow to heal because of these muscles' small attachment areas. We have already mentioned the importance of the iliopsoas muscle group in hip flexion. Those muscles, together with the large gluteal muscles and adductor muscles, require specific strengthening and stretching to ensure an athlete's ability to complete long, powerful strides when fast running is required. The great Australian distance runner Ron Clarke often mentioned in conversations with athletes and coaches that a runner could never be too strong around the middle, and his idea is sensible. Forward trunk leaning often occurs as compensation for a lack of hip mobility. Thus, an increase in hip flexibility can often lead to a more vertical, energy-efficient running style.

Upper-Body Balance

The shoulders and upper arms are also important in running. Though they primarily provide balance at relatively slow speeds, they increase in importance in assisting the leg muscles as running velocity increases and as a runner climbs hills. Adequate arm and shoulder interaction reduces the need for counterrotation of the trunk musculature, which is more energy wasteful. Efficient running style suggests that the arms swing fairly loosely and be held quite naturally. Neither should the shoulders be hunched or pulled back, nor the chest thrust out in front. Unnecessarily tensed muscles suggest a needless waste of energy. The shoulders should be carried above the hips.

Arm action varies with running velocity; it is much more vigorous at faster than at slower velocities. Elbows kept close in toward the body minimize the tendency for the hands and lower arms to cross the midline of the chest. Hands and arms normally should only approach the midline. At a wide range of running velocities the elbow joint is flexed at about 90° and remains that way through the range of arm swing. However, at very fast racing velocities this elbow flexion angle unlocks and varies on either side of 90° to provide more fluidity. Arm swing and leg action are inextricably interwoven. If arm swing tends to be erratic, it detracts from optimal style and is energy costly.

The hands should be kept loose and relaxed at all times. Notice in figure 1.11 that this is true even in the final moments of the race as these 800-m runners are racing at top speed toward the finish line. Their thumbs are not sticking up like spikes, their wrists are fairly loose, and their fingers are slightly bent. Without flopping about like limp lettuce, their hands are still relaxed, again minimizing energy consumption.

Positioning the Head

Except for making a desperate dip at the finish of a race, the head should be poised well above the shoulders. It is a very heavy piece of anatomy, and if it is not positioned properly, it can cause either of two problems, both bad. If it is too far backward, it places an unnecessary strain on the neck muscles. If it is too far forward, it can restrict the airways and make breathing difficult.

Figure 1.13 illustrates three well-known runners, Seb Coe, Said Aouita, and Ingrid Kristiansen, at different race paces: 400 m, 5,000 m, and 10,000 m. Some comments are provided to assist readers in making their own style analyses. Runners are encouraged to have a friend take similar snapshots or videos of

Figure 1.13 Assessment of various features of running style in contemporary elite athletes running at various paces. In (*a*) Sebastian Coe (Great Britain) is running at a 50 s/400-m pace during training. In (*b*) Said Aouita (Morocco) is running a 64 s/400-m pace during a 5,000-m race. In (*c*) Ingrid Kristiansen (Norway) is running at a 75 s/400-m pace during a 10,000-m race. Both races were at the 1987 Rome World Championships. Each athlete has the hands relaxed with a 90° angle at the elbow joint. Stride length varies with pace; Coe requires a more powerful leg drive than the others, resulting in a more extended rear leg. The trunk is maintained in a vertical position; the head well poised. Kristiansen exhibits more tension in the muscles of her forehead than the others. Each is in the inside of the lane, conserving distance.

their running for analysis. Using the information provided here, athletes may be able to identify individual areas for improvement. Although such tasks as keeping elbows in or relaxing the hands must be practiced consciously at first, over time they can become automatic instead of voluntary movements and thus an inherent part of improved form. Appropriate flexibility, stretching, or strengthening exercises to improve mechanics can also be designed if required.

SUMMARY

Using Biomechanics Effectively

1. Running is one of our fundamental movement patterns, practiced from childhood and improved in biomechanical efficiency during our growing years.

2. The experience gained over many years of running tends to result in an optimally energy-efficient combination of stride frequency and stride length. Thus, runners get the greatest amount of forward movement for the least energy cost.

3. The details of events during a running cycle have been described. The cycle has a support phase and a nonsupport phase. Each phase has three periods. The shorter support phase has periods of footstrike, midsupport, and takeoff; the longer, free-floating, forward-recovery phase has periods of follow-through, forward swing, and foot descent. An effective training plan not only strengthens the muscle groups that allow this motion to occur, but also enhances joint mobility for achieving the required muscle lengthening.

4. As they run faster, runners impact on the ground with greater force, causing more stress on the entire musculoskeletal system. Thus, although faster-paced training is essential for improving the ability to race quickly, careful attention to proper musculoskeletal development and wearing proper footwear will help training occur with minimal injury risk.

5. Mature athletes interested in becoming competitively competent performers typically focus primarily on improving their fitness rather than on improving their biomechanics. Understanding some of the principles of the biomechanics of running, however, provides an additional avenue for performance enhancement.

References

Adelaar, R.S. 1986. The practical biomechanics of running. *American Journal of Sports Medicine* 14:497-500.

Beck, M. 1966. The path of the center of gravity during running in boys grade one to six. PhD diss., University of Wisconsin, Madison.

Cavanagh, P.R.; Andrew, G.C.; Kram, R.; Rodgers, M.M.; Sanderson, D.J.; and Hennig, E.M. 1985. An approach to biomechanical profiling of distance runners. *International Journal of Sports Biomechanics* 1:36-62.

Cavanagh, P.R., and Kram, R. 1990. Stride length in distance running: Velocity, body dimensions, and added mass effects. In *Biomechanics of distance running,* ed. P.R. Cavanagh, 35-60. Champaign, IL: Human Kinetics.

Cavanagh, P.R.; Pollock, M.L.; and Landa, J. 1977. A biomechanical comparison of elite and good distance runners. *Annals of the New York Academy of Sciences* 301:328-345.

Cavanagh, P., and Williams, K.R. 1979. Should you change your stride length? *Runner's World* 14(7):62-66.

Henatsch, H.-D., and Langer, H.H. 1985. Basic neurophysiology of motor skills in sport: A review. *International Journal of Sports Medicine* 6:2-14.

Hutchinson, M.R., and Ireland, M.L. 1995. Knee injuries in female athletes. *Sports Medicine* 19:288-302.

James, S.L., and Brubaker, C.E. 1972. Running mechanics. *Journal of the American Medical Association* 221:1014-1016.

Kaggestad, J. 1987. So trainiert Ingrid Kristiansen 1986. *Leichtathletik* 38:831-834.

Mann, R.A. 1982. Foot problems in adults. *Instructional Course Lectures* 31:167-180.

Mann, R.A.; Moran, G.T.; and Dougherty, S.E. 1986. Comparative electromyography of the lower extremity in jogging, running, and sprinting. *American Journal of Sports Medicine* 14:501-510.

Slocum, D.B., and Bowerman, W. 1962. The biomechanics of running. *Clinical Orthopedics* 23:39-45.

Slocum, D.B., and James, S.L. 1968. Biomechanics of running. *Journal of the American Medical Association* 205:721-728.

Stanton, P., and Purdam, C. 1989. Hamstring injuries in sprinting—The role of eccentric exercise. *Journal of Orthopaedic and Sports Physical Therapy* 10:343-349.

Stipe, P. 1982. Scaling of body size and cushioning in running shoes. *NIKE Research Newsletter* 1(2):3-4.

Warren, B.L. 1990. Plantar fasciitis in runners. *Sports Medicine* 10:338-345.

Williams, K.R., and Cavanagh, P.R. 1987. Relationship between distance running mechanics, running economy, and performance. *Journal of Applied Physiology* 63:1236-1245.

Williams, K.R.; Cavanagh, P.R.; and Ziff, J.L. 1987. Biomechanical studies of elite female distance runners. *International Journal of Sports Medicine* 8(suppl. 2):107-118.

MUSCLE PHYSIOLOGY FOR RUNNING

Every organ system in the body contributes in its own way to the coordination of movement that permits daily activities. Skeletal muscles could be a prime candidate for the one organ system that contributes most to athletic performance. They typically make up about 40% of the total body mass in a man of average stature and 35% in an average woman. This mass of tissue at rest may consume as much as 15% to 30% of the total O_2 intake. It is the largest tissue mass devoted to a single function, namely, movement of the skeleton. These muscles, however, cannot function alone. The nervous system is responsible for activating skeletal muscles. Thanks to a superb interaction between blood and the cardiovascular system, the working muscles are provided with adequate nutrition and O_2 to permit a high level of metabolism.

Training distance runners involves to a large extent training skeletal muscles to perform optimally when challenged. Coaches and athletes are inundated with literature from various manufacturers of training equipment, all of which suggests that one or another brand of equipment, along with its strategy of use, is best for developing optimal performance. Terms such as fast-twitch and slow-twitch muscle fibers, fiber interconversion, motor unit recruitment, hypertrophy, and many more frustrate those without technical backgrounds but with keen athletic interests. Much has been learned in the past few years, making muscle physiology a rather labile science. Today's hypotheses may be tomorrow's facts or fallacies. A brief synthesis of what seems correct at the moment should not only help enhance communication among athletes, coaches, and scientists, but also allow more intelligent assessment of training concepts for improving skeletal muscle function.

Anatomic Aspects of Neuromuscular Integration

Estimates of the number of skeletal muscles in the human body range from 435 (Gregor 1989) to around 650 (Thomas 1989), depending on the system of nomenclature. Most of these muscles occur in pairs, and a runner in intense competition will actively involve the majority of them. Muscles come in a wide variety of sizes. The stapedius muscle of the middle ear is but 2 to 3 millimeters (mm) in length, whereas the sartorius of the upper leg (figure 1.6) can be more than half a meter long in a tall individual. Skeletal muscles are typically surrounded by a thin layer of connective tissue called the *epimysium* (figure 2.1). Each skeletal muscle comprises from dozens to hundreds of muscle cells (also called muscle fibers). A typical muscle cell might be 50 micrometers (µm) in diameter and extend the length of the muscle. These muscle fibers attach to bones by tendons. The epimysium extends into the body of each muscle, encircling small groups of half a dozen muscle fibers. This surrounding connective tissue is now called the *perimysium*, and the bundles of muscle fibers are called *fascicles*. These fascicles are sometimes large enough to be seen without a microscope, being 250 µm or more in diameter.

Muscles are also often covered by glistening, white, dense fibrous connective tissue called *fascia*. We see this fibrous connective tissue in other places as well: Tendons connect bones to muscles, and ligaments connect bones to each other. The term *fascia* derives from the Latin word for band, and it might be useful to think of fascia around muscles as a kind of bandage that assists in postural stability. The fascia perhaps most well known to runners is the *iliotibial band*, located within the *fascia lata*, illustrated in figure 2.2. The fascia lata begins at the iliac crest as a broad, fibrous connective tissue sheath along the lateral aspect of the leg, continues past the knee, and attaches to the lateral tibial tubercle. Two muscles, the *tensor fasciae latae* (a thigh flexor) and *gluteus maximus* (a thigh extensor), insert into the iliotibial band, a thicker lateral tendon within this fascia. This band is a stabilizing ligament between the tibia and the lateral femoral condyle of the knee. Tension in this fascia helps stabilize the knee joint.

The arrangement of fascicles in skeletal muscles in part determines muscle power and the range of motion of the joint to which they connect. The arrangement of fibers in skeletal muscles varies considerably. Figures 1.6, 2.2, 2.3, and 2.4 illustrate some of these possibilities, using a combination of sketches and

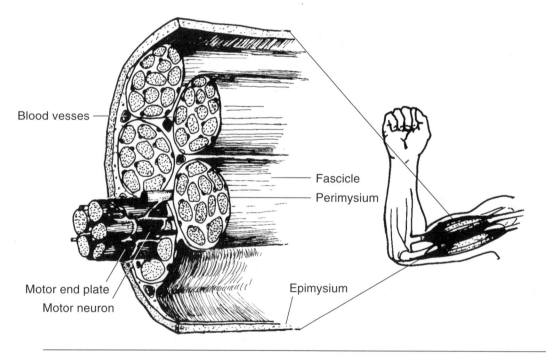

Blood vesses

Fascicle
Perimysium

Motor end plate
Motor neuron

Epimysium

Figure 2.1 General arrangement of skeletal muscle into small groups of muscle cells, called fascicles, with each fascicle surrounded by a connective tissue perimysium. Each muscle cell is innervated by a branch of a motor neuron.

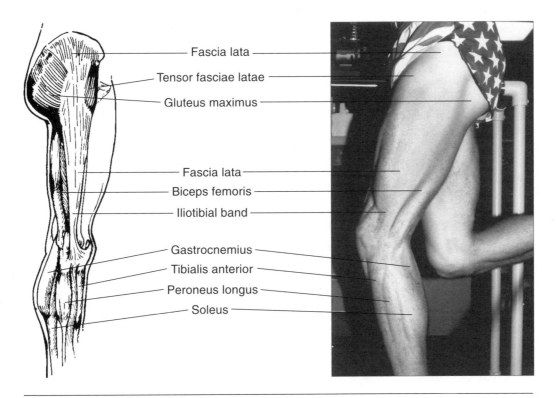

Figure 2.2 Lateral view of lower limb, showing the gluteus maximus and tensor fasciae latae muscles of the hip, the lateral fascia of the upper limb (fascia lata and iliotibial band), and some of the lower-limb muscles.

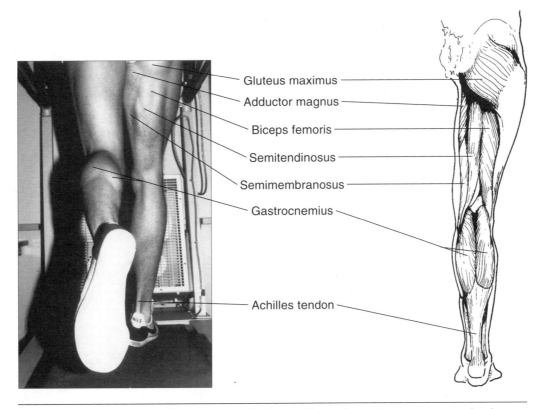

Figure 2.3 Posterior view of the muscles of the hip and lower limb, showing in particular the three muscles of the hamstrings group.

photographs of elite runners' muscles to provide the best practical view of these arrangements. One of the muscles of the *quadriceps* group (the rectus femoris) has its fascicles arranged much like a feather plume, with the tendon in the middle and fascicles converging toward it from two sides (figure 1.6). It is called a *bipenniform* muscle. A few muscles of the *hamstrings* group (such as the semimembranosus and semitendinosus) have a feather-plume arrangement as well, but with their tendon along one side (figure 2.3). These are *penniform* muscles. The longitudinal muscles, best exemplified by the sartorius (figure 1.6), are straplike and thin, with fibers arranged in parallel along the full length of the muscle.

In figure 2.4, middle-distance star Tom Byers illustrates the pectoralis major and deltoid muscles, which have several different actions. The *pectoralis* is known as a triangular muscle because of its fan-shaped appearance; muscle fibers radiate outward from the narrow attachment at the humerus toward the sternum and collarbone (clavicle). The middle portion of the deltoid muscle is *multipenniform*, with several tendons present and muscle fibers extending diagonally between them. Other parts of the deltoid are *fusiform*, or spindle-shaped. Another multipennate muscle is the gluteus maximus (figures 2.2 and 2.3). The gluteus medius and minimus are fan-shaped. The fiber arrangement of all these various muscles is optimally advantageous for their special functions. Thus, penniform muscles typically are more powerful in relation to their size due to the greater functional cross-sectional area of their muscle cells but have less range of motion than nonpenniform muscles (Wirhed 1984).

Skeletal muscles attach to the skeleton at two points. One of these attachments is called the *origin,* which is the less movable end closer to the axial skeleton. The other attachment is called the *insertion,* and this is the more

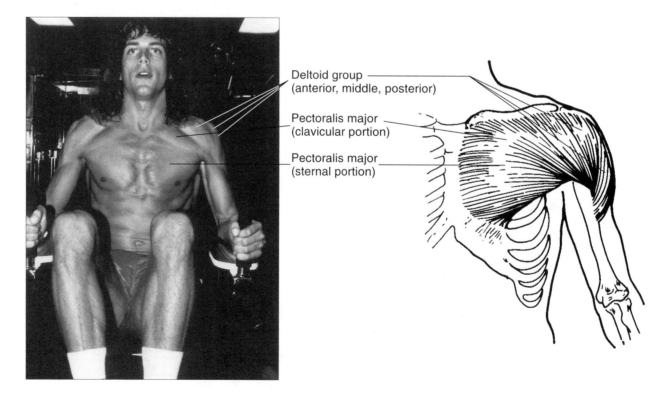

Deltoid group
(anterior, middle, posterior)

Pectoralis major
(clavicular portion)

Pectoralis major
(sternal portion)

Figure 2.4 Anterior view of superficial muscles of the shoulder joint, including the pectoralis major and deltoids.

movable end farther away from the axial skeleton. Virtually all muscles connected to joints have actions that are opposed by the actions of other muscles. In such pairs of muscles if one muscle of the pair initiates a particular movement, it is called the *agonist;* the other muscle, called the *antagonist,* provides a stabilizing action for the involved joint, remaining relaxed while the agonist is active or permitting the opposite motion to occur. One of the most familiar pairs is the biceps and triceps of the upper arm; the former flexes the elbow, and the latter extends it.

Motor innervation is the key to muscle function. A *motor nerve* contains many dozens of individual nerve cells (also called neurons), each of which branches and connects to variable numbers of muscle cells. The *motor point* is the site of entry of a nerve into a skeletal muscle. Such sites are well known to physical therapists, who are trained to evaluate muscle function by examining the dynamics of muscle tension generation using electrical stimulation. At the motor point a minimal amount of electrical current will excite the muscle.

One *motor unit* is defined as a single motor neuron plus all the skeletal muscle fibers innervated by it. These fibers are dispersed throughout the muscle rather than closely adjacent to each other, permitting a more uniform change in muscle shape when they are activated. This arrangement also prevents a large number of active muscle fibers from all competing for the same blood supply, except, of course, when the entire muscle is extremely active. Figure 2.5 illustrates several motor neuron branches, each connecting to a muscle fiber via a neuromuscular junction (see also figure 2.1). The number of muscle fibers per motor neuron varies widely, depending on the specificity of muscle activity. The medial head of the human gastrocnemius muscle, for example, has as many as 1,900 muscle fibers per motor unit and nearly 580 motor units (Gregor 1989). This muscle can

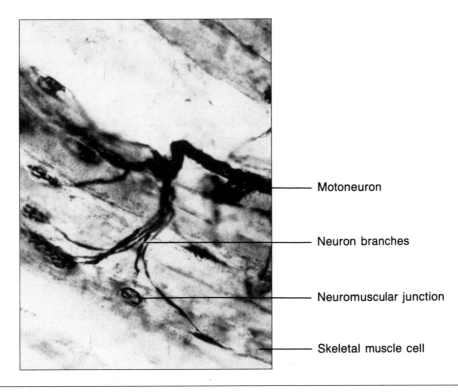

Figure 2.5 Components of a motor unit: a motor neuron, with its many branches, connecting to individual muscle fibers via neuromuscular junctions.

perform only gross, relatively nonspecific activity. By contrast, laryngeal muscles (used for speaking) have only two to three muscle fibers per neuron and are very precise in their action. There is very little overlap of muscle fibers in any given motor unit; that is, the fibers are well dispersed throughout the muscle.

Generation of Muscle Tension

Normally, neuron and muscle cell membranes are electrically polarized. When a motor nerve is stimulated sufficiently, a very brief wave of cell membrane depolarization (called an *action potential*) travels along its various neurons (and along their branches) until it reaches each neuromuscular junction. The depolarization wave crosses these junctions and is reinstated as a muscle cell action potential along the surface of the muscle cell. At certain points this wave will be carried deep within the muscle cell as well by means of *transverse tubules* (T tubules) that serve as inward extensions of the muscle cell membrane (figure 2.6).

Notice that each muscle cell has dozens of *myofibrils* arranged in parallel (figures 2.6 and 2.7) with several types of *cellular organelles* in between. The organelles perform many specialized functions required to keep cells alive and functional. The nucleus, for example, is responsible for cellular division. Each myofibril is composed of many parallel *myofilaments*, which include the two primary tension-generating proteins, *actin* and *myosin*. The thicker myosin filaments are arranged around the thinner actin filaments in such a manner that regularly repeating segments, called *sarcomeres*, result. Another organelle, called the *sarcoplasmic reticulum*, is a storehouse for calcium (Ca^{2+}) ions, which are required for the physicochemical interaction of actin and myosin.

Mitochondria are the organelles of greatest importance for energy and movement (figures 2.7 and 2.8). In these organelles are found the enzyme systems that permit complete breakdown of fuels by eventual interaction with O_2, with liberation of large amounts of energy available to provide movement. The en-

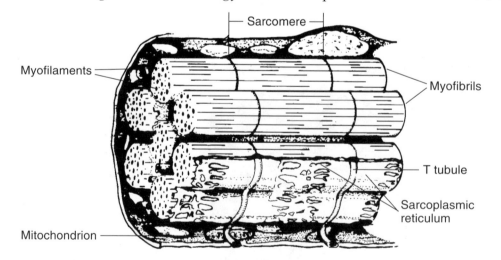

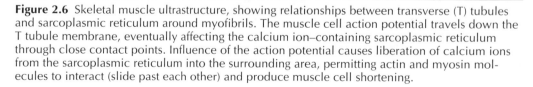

Figure 2.6 Skeletal muscle ultrastructure, showing relationships between transverse (T) tubules and sarcoplasmic reticulum around myofibrils. The muscle cell action potential travels down the T tubule membrane, eventually affecting the calcium ion–containing sarcoplasmic reticulum through close contact points. Influence of the action potential causes liberation of calcium ions from the sarcoplasmic reticulum into the surrounding area, permitting actin and myosin molecules to interact (slide past each other) and produce muscle cell shortening.

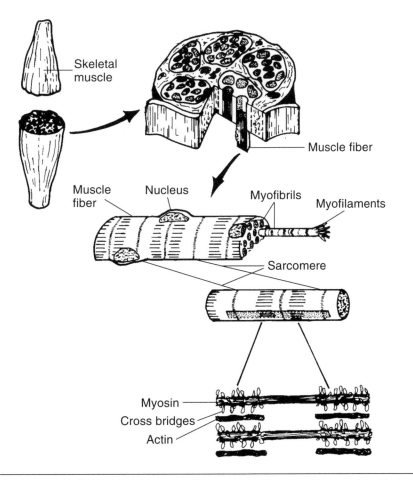

Figure 2.7 Microscopic details of skeletal muscle structure, illustrating sequential subdivision into myofibrils and myofilaments. The two major types of myofilaments are actin and myosin. Myosin molecules are thicker and heavier and have enzymatic activity at localized sites known as cross bridges. At rest, actin and myosin are prevented from interacting by the presence of other protein molecules, the troponin-tropomyosin complex, located between them but not shown here.

ergy released from such breakdown is stored in a molecule called *adenosine triphosphate* (ATP), which will be described in greater detail shortly. Because of their role, mitochondria are often thought of as the powerhouses of the cell. They are typically 1 to 2 μm long and 0.3 to 0.7 μm wide but can vary considerably in size and shape depending on their tissue location and its metabolic state. They have a peculiar double-membrane structure such that the inner membrane is folded into leaves called *cristae*; these greatly increase the membrane surface area. As much as 25% of the total protein content of this inner mitochondrial membrane is made up of all the various enzymes required for aerobic fuel breakdown. Part of the process of getting fit through training at the cellular level involves an increase in both the size and number of mitochondria, together with their fuel-metabolizing enzymes, so that the maximal energy-producing capacity of the trained muscle can increase.

Actin molecules have ATP bound to them. Myosin molecules have enzymatic activity so that they can break down ATP; that is, they are *ATPases*. Normally these two molecules are blocked from interacting and generating tension by the presence of several proteins, which for simplicity we can group together as the *troponin-tropomyosin complex*. When actin and myosin interaction is inhibited,

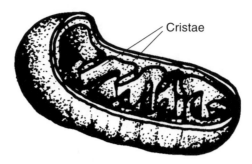

Cristae

Figure 2.8 Anatomical structure of a mitochondrion. These organelles are ovoid in shape, roughly 2 µm long and 0.7 µm wide, and have two very different membrane structures. The inner mitochondrial membrane is greatly folded, forming cristae. The enzymes, which are responsible for oxidative metabolism of fuels, are an integral part of the cristae.

the muscle is resting, that is, generating minimal tension. One function of the electrical stimulus wave that passes along the cell membrane is to release Ca^{2+} ions from their storage sites within the sarcoplasmic reticulum. Calcium ions temporarily remove the blockade by the troponin-tropomyosin complex, permitting actin and myosin interaction to occur, owing to the energy released through enzymatic breakdown of ATP. The interactions between actin and myosin molecules are referred to as *cross-bridge linkages* and form the basis for molecules to generate tension. A so-called *sliding filament theory* for muscle tension generation, postulating that the actin and myosin molecules simply slide past each other as their cross-bridge linkages are rapidly formed and broken, was proposed more than 40 years ago by two separate groups of investigators (Huxley and Hanson 1954; Huxley and Niedergerke 1954). This shortening or lengthening of sarcomeres causes corresponding changes in muscle length. This theory has been proved essentially correct.

Tension may be maintained with no change in muscle length (called isometric or *static tension*) or may result in the myofilaments sliding past each other. This sliding may cause lengthening (*eccentric tension*) or shortening (*concentric tension*), depending on the arrangement of the muscle and its load. Once tension generation has occurred, reaccumulation of Ca^{2+} ions back into their storage sites promotes relaxation. Increasing the frequency of stimulation as well as the magnitude of stimulation (increasing the number of motor units activated) increases the total muscle tension.

A specific relationship exists between the amount of tension (and thus force) that a muscle can develop and the velocity with which shortening or lengthening occurs. The faster the rate of cross-bridge linking between actin and myosin myofilaments, the faster they can slide past each other, and the faster the rate of tension generation in the muscle. However, the faster the rate of cross-bridge linking, the smaller the number of linkages in place at any given moment, and thus the smaller the net tension generated. The suggestion here is that one cannot be both strong and quick at the same time.

One can imagine that the application of this information provides a practical dilemma for sprinters, who indeed *must* be both strong and quick at the same time (i.e., very powerful). The only way they can achieve this is to recruit large numbers of muscle fibers and develop them through extensive prior training designed to increase the amount of protein in each cell. This explains in part why excellent sprinters typically have large upper-leg muscles. Figure 2.9 depicts the force-velocity relationship. Muscle force is plotted on the vertical axis

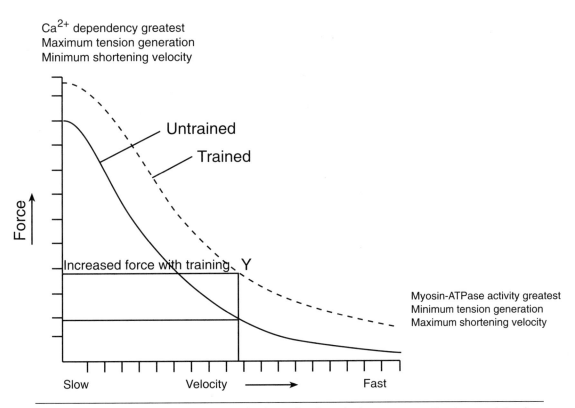

Ca^{2+} dependency greatest
Maximum tension generation
Minimum shortening velocity

Untrained

Trained

Force

Increased force with training Y

Myosin-ATPase activity greatest
Minimum tension generation
Maximum shortening velocity

Slow   Velocity ⟶   Fast

Figure 2.9 Relationship between muscular force developed (also conceptualized as work load, muscle tension, or torque) and velocity of muscle shortening. Training a muscle for greater work-load tolerance brings adaptations within the muscle cells to permit, at submaximal velocities, greater work output.

(ordinate), and velocity of muscle movement is plotted on the horizontal axis (abscissa). As velocity of muscle shortening or lengthening increases, the tolerable work load decreases. Training increases the tolerable work load at any given velocity (point Y on the graph) due to an increase in quantity of muscle protein and an increased ability to recruit more fibers into action. For whole muscle, extreme force production at very slow velocities is prevented by neurological inhibition; this is not seen when single muscle fiber preparations are stimulated experimentally.

Skeletal Muscle Fiber Types

As far back as the late 19th century, gross differences in coloration of skeletal muscles not only within animal species but also among different species were noted in the scientific literature (Ranvier 1873). We need only visit the meat department of a grocery store and compare the white and dark meat of chicken or the red cuts of beef and grayish cuts of pork to realize that considerable variation occurs. Such obvious individual differences in muscles prompted what has become an extremely detailed study of this tissue in an attempt to learn whether these color differences might help explain the physiological properties of individual tension-generating muscle cells. As a result, we probably know more about the functioning of skeletal muscle—even down to the molecular level— than about any other organ system. The explanation for the color difference has been reasonably easy to solve. In addition to the red-pigmented *hemoglobin* that transports O_2 in the bloodstream, within individual muscle cells two additional red-pigmented molecules play an important role in the complete metabolism of fuels. One is *myoglobin*, an O_2-binding pigment similar to hemoglobin in its function. The other is an entire group of molecules called *cytochrome enzymes*, which we shall find later to be associated with the metabolic interaction between complete fuel breakdown, energy release, and interaction with O_2.

Skeletal muscles that have a more whitish appearance are composed of cells with considerably less myoglobin and cytochrome enzymes than those that are brilliant red. Muscles of intermediate coloration are heterogeneous in their fiber composition, having a mixture of both cell types. The important question for those interested in work and exercise is whether those features of muscles that relate to their color also explain their performance.

Early physiological investigations of muscle function suggested some general relationships between structure and function. In general, more muscles with a major role in posture (the antigravity muscles) were of the red variety, whereas the gravity-assisted muscles often were lighter colored. This brought the term *tonic* (or fatigue-resistant) into use for describing the red fibers, and *phasic* (or fatigue-susceptible) for referring to the white fibers.

During the late 1960s and early 1970s, particularly with the advent of laboratory methods of enzyme histochemistry, continuing interest in understanding the details of muscle structure and function directed investigational focus not only toward the specific enzymes related to metabolism, but also toward different types of myofibrillar proteins. Muscle tissue was obtained in the form of needle biopsy specimens from willing volunteers. (In a needle biopsy a local anesthetic administered around the biopsy site minimizes pain, but it still is a painful procedure.) Once obtained the piece of muscle tissue is immediately deep-frozen and kept for later sectioning and study using a variety of laboratory procedures. The results of these refined analyses created several different fiber classification schemes. Unfortunately, not all of these schemes are exactly interchangeable for various technical reasons quite interesting to muscle biologists but of little interest in our discussion. Excellent reviews of progress made in these areas exist (Gollnick and Hodgson 1986; Rice et al. 1988; Saltin and Gollnick 1983). Our purpose is to provide only some of the most useful basic information—terms, concepts, and conclusions—for an appreciation of the significance of muscle fiber types from the viewpoint of exercise performance.

One set of terminology stems from the work of Brooke and Engel (1969). These workers studied the behavior of myosin ATPase in the myofibrils and divided muscle fibers into two groups, which they arbitrarily termed *Type I* and *Type II*. Their Type I fibers roughly corresponded to fatigue-resistant fibers, with Type II equating to the fatigue-susceptible fibers. Edstrom and Nystrom (1969) labeled the Type I fibers as red and the Type II fibers as white. The Type II fibers, however, were soon found to fit two subcategories, depending on whether they demonstrated high (*Type IIa*) or low (*Type IIb*) oxidative enzyme activity (Brooke and Kaiser 1970).

Subsequent physiological studies by Gollnick, Armstrong, Saubert, Piehl, and Saltin (1972) showed that the Type I muscle cells require a longer time to reach peak tension when stimulated than do the Type II cells (75 versus 35 milliseconds). This is illustrated in figure 2.10. The terms *slow-twitch* (ST) and *fast-twitch* (FT) thus came into vogue to describe, respectively, Type I and Type II fibers. Table 2.1 indicates some of the basic differences between these two primary fiber types, although we should emphasize that this breakdown is an oversimplification, as additional subdivisions using other criteria have developed since.

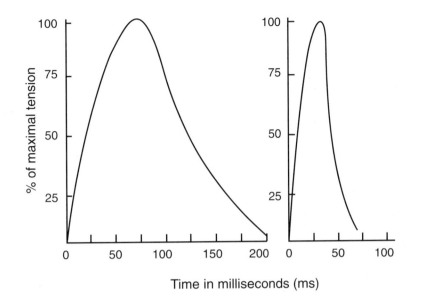

Figure 2.10 Difference between the twitch characteristics of fast-twitch and slow-twitch skeletal muscle fibers. Slow-twitch fibers, on the left, reach their maximal tension in about 75 ms after stimulation and have fully recovered after about 200 ms. Fast-twitch fibers, however, reach peak tension more quickly (30 to 35 ms) and recover very quickly (by about 70 ms). *Note.* From "Relationship of Strength and Endurance With Skeletal Muscle Structure and Metabolic Potential" by P.D. Gollnick, 1982, *International Journal of Sports Medicine*, **3** (Suppl. 1), p. 26. Copyright 1982 by Georg Thieme Verlag. Reprinted by permission.

TABLE 2.1

Characteristics of Slow Oxidative and Fast Glycolytic Fibers

Slow-twitch (ST) muscle fibers	Fast-twitch (FT) muscle fibers
Loosely referred to as red or tonic fibers	Loosely referred to as white or phasic fibers
Example of predominant ST muscle in human: soleus	Example of predominant FT muscle in human: triceps brachii
Longer muscle fibers, therefore a greater total length-change capability	Shorter fibers, therefore a smaller total length-change capability
Maintenance of posture	More rapid, voluntary movements
Quicker recruitability; lower threshold for stimulation (−70 mV) and smaller connecting neuron	Slower recruitability; higher threshold for stimulation (−85 mV) and larger connecting neuron
Longer time to reach peak tension (75 ms)	Shorter time to reach peak tension (35 ms)
Fewer muscle cells per motor unit; less strength capability	More muscle cells per motor unit; greater strength capability
Good endurance, slow fatigability	Poor endurance, rapid fatigability
Oxidative enzymes predominate	Glycolytic enzymes predominate
More mitochondria	Fewer mitochondria
Contain H form of lactic dehydrogenase	Contain M form of lactic dehydrogenase
Greater surrounding capillarization	Lesser surrounding capillarization
No change in glycogen content after repeated stimulation for 2 hr at 10/s	Stimulation at relatively low frequencies (5/s) reduces stored glycogen
Greater myoglobin content	Larger stored calcium pool for interaction with tension-generating proteins

At about the same time J.B. Peter and his group (1972) further studied the properties of the two categories of Type II fibers. They offered another set of terminology that combined tension-generating and metabolic properties to identify the various fiber types. Type I cells were termed *slow oxidative* (SO); the term *oxidative* (or aerobic) refers to the use of O_2 for complete fuel metabolism. Type II cells were classified as either *fast glycolytic* (FG), the term *glycolytic* referring to an emphasis on glycogen and glucose breakdown to pyruvic acid, which does not require O_2, or *fast oxidative-glycolytic* (FOG), suggesting both a capability for complete (oxidative, or aerobic) metabolism as well as incomplete (glycolytic) metabolism. FG fibers thus are similar to Type IIb fibers, and FOG fibers are similar to Type IIa fibers.

With these details in mind let us consider human skeletal muscles from the viewpoint of fiber type and performance.

Fiber Type Content in Human Muscles

Unlike those of certain other mammals, human skeletal muscles are never solely FT or ST. Most are considerably heterogeneous. Even within any muscle there is a variation in fiber arrangement in different regions. As an example, Bengt Saltin and his colleagues (1977) showed that muscles, such as the gastrocnemius in the lower leg, the vastus lateralis and rectus femoris in the upper leg, and the biceps brachii in the arm, in untrained subjects have essentially equal numbers of FT and ST muscle fibers. The soleus muscle in the lower leg (an antigravity muscle) is predominantly ST (75%-90%), however, and the triceps brachii in the upper arm is primarily FT (60%-80%).

What Determines Fiber Type Percentage in Skeletal Muscles?

Studies done by Komi et al. (1977) with identical twins suggests that genetic endowment determines fiber type in skeletal muscles. Additional elegant work by Buller, Eccles, and Eccles (1960) indicates that the nervous system determines whether a muscle cell is FT or ST. Subsequent studies by Close in 1969 and by Barany and Close in 1971 using laboratory animals and involving cross-reinnervation (i.e., the sectioning of nerves that innervate predominantly FT and ST muscles, followed by rejoining their opposite ends) demonstrated this even more strikingly. In the rat and the cat, FT muscles became ST after cross-reinnervation not only in their myosin characteristics, but also in other physiological features such as mitochondrial density, enzyme composition, and even the number of capillaries around individual muscle cells (ST fibers have more than FT).

Do Men and Women Differ in Muscle Fiber Types?

Men and women apparently do not differ in muscle fiber types, on the basis of the few data available. Two well-known studies of male (Fink, Costill, and Pollock 1977) and female (Costill et al. 1987) elite distance runners, carried out by some of the same investigators, revealed quite similar fiber ratios and fiber composition (mitochondrial size and enzyme activity profiles) for athletes specializing in similar events. Thus, marathoners tended to have a higher ST endowment than middle-distance runners.

However, one consistently observed gender difference occurring among both athletes and sedentary people is a larger muscle fiber cross-sectional area in men than in women (Miller et al. 1993). This is probably a result of the muscle protein-building action of testosterone, which exists in higher concentration among men than women and which acts to make each muscle cell a little larger. Otherwise, the number of muscle fibers, number of motor units, strength per unit of muscle cross-sectional area, and ability to recruit motor units are similar.

Fiber Type Differences in Endurance Versus Strength Athletes

Considerable evidence suggests that endurance-specialized athletes, such as marathon runners, do have greater numbers of ST fibers than quickness-oriented athletes, such as sprinters, who in contrast tend to have a greater proportion of FT fibers. However, in reported studies these athletes were not biopsied *before* they began their serious training. Thus, the contributing effect of training along with what seems to be a genetic predisposition is still not well understood. Did each group find their particular event an easy one in which to excel because, in addition to their hard training, they had a genetic predisposition toward success in that event as a result of the appropriate fiber-type preference? We just do not know the answer unequivocally. As an example, the lateral head of the gastrocnemius muscle of 14 elite male long-distance runners showed a range of 50% to 98% ST fibers (Fink, Costill, and Pollock 1977) compared with the range of 50% to 64% among the untrained population (Rice et al. 1988). However, because the ST fibers in the elite runners were 29% larger than the FT fibers, on the average 82% of the muscle cross-sectional area was composed of ST muscle. Thus, training can selectively increase the size of muscle fibers; we shall describe shortly some of the changes that can occur with training.

Within this group of elite runners, however, individual ST:FT ratios correlated poorly as a predictor of running success as judged by personal best performance time. This poor correlation has been reported elsewhere (Gollnick and Matoba 1984). The explanation is simply that many additional factors also contribute to successful athletic preparation, including the desire to endure long years of difficult training, a proper training plan to permit development without injury, and improved running efficiency. Many variables also set the stage for an excellent competitive performance, such as achievement of peak physical fitness when it counts most, a psychological profile and readiness that is optimal for success, and near-perfect competitive circumstances.

Finally, there is considerable overlap in the extent to which various fiber type combinations can explain sport performance. Consider, for example, the following set of six performances by Morocco's Said Aouita during three months of 1986:

Event	Time	Date	Rank of performance in the world in 1986
1 mi	3:50.33	August	Fourth fastest performer
2,000 m	4:51.98	September	Fastest performer
3,000 m	7:32.23	August	Fastest performer
2 mi	8:14.08	September	Fastest performer
5,000 m	13:00.86	August	Fastest performer
10,000 m	27:26.11	July	Second fastest performer

Uniform excellence over a wide range of distances within a very short competitive period is clearly evident in Aouita's incredible achievement, which hasn't been matched before or since. On the short-distance side, a generous FT endowment is essential, but the 10,000 m cannot be raced without a sizable ST endowment to provide the aerobic capabilities. In view of the variability found among published studies relating performance with fiber type, the suggestion could thus be plausibly offered that if Aouita had several of his major running muscles biopsied, percentage ratios of FT:ST fibers ranging anywhere from 60:40 through 50:50 to 40:60 might all be appropriate to explain his performance range. In the present-day running scene, Ethiopia's Haile Gebrselassie has demonstrated even greater athletic excellence over the 3,000 m through 10,000 m range, as shown by his excellent summer of 1995:

Event	Time	Date	Rank of performance in the world in 1995
3,000 m	7:35.90	September	Fastest performer
2 mi	8:07.46	May	World record
5,000 m	12:44.39	August	World record
10,000 m	26:43.53	June	World record

Arrangement and Recruitment of Skeletal Muscle Fibers

Motor units are either all FT or all ST; there is no fiber intermixing within motor units. There are two available mechanisms for increasing the tension generated by skeletal muscle. One is termed *rate coding*—the *intensity* of activity of stimulated neurons increases. The other is termed *recruitment*—additional numbers of motor neurons are brought into action. As reviewed recently by Deschenes (1989), the principle of recruitment (on the basis of neuron size) seems to be the predominant mechanism, although rate coding may come into play during higher-intensity work loads. At relatively low work rates the ST fibers are utilized predominantly. This is because their innervation is primarily by smaller neurons that are activated by low-intensity stimulation. Increasing loads require activation of more muscle protein, achieved by recruitment of additional motor units.

Figure 2.11 depicts this relationship more clearly. ST motor units will respond to meet the needs of all the easier submaximal work loads, with FT Type IIa and IIb motor units contributing as work loads become more challenging and approach maximal intensity. This is a beautifully designed system to provide optimal use of muscle fibers specialized for complete metabolism during lighter work loads, to minimize the anaerobic metabolite accumulation (such as lactic acid) that would result if FT Type IIa (and particularly FT Type IIb) fibers were mobilized, and to permit use of both types of fuels (carbohydrates and fatty acids). As work loads become more intense, instead of FT fibers substituting for ST fibers, FT fibers additionally contribute to the output of ST fibers already activated, in teamwork fashion. The practical significance of this for endurance runners is that, if months pass by without any training at higher work intensities, a sizable number of muscle fibers—the entire FT complement—will fail to receive even a minimal training stimulus to improve their performance potential. This is a physiological explanation for a training tenet that will be emphasized again later in this book: *Although the pace may vary throughout a training year, it is essential to include an ongoing program of faster-paced work to ensure maintenance of the performance capabilities of FT fibers.*

Fiber Type Conversion?

Can the stimulus of serious endurance or strength training convert FT fibers to ST, and vice versa? This question has been pursued carefully for many years in controlled longitudinal studies involving both humans and laboratory animals (Pette 1984). The evidence is still inconclusive that a complete fiber interconversion (FT to ST or ST to FT) with enzymatic changes, myofibrillar protein changes, and other physiological aspects can occur. A change in the rela-

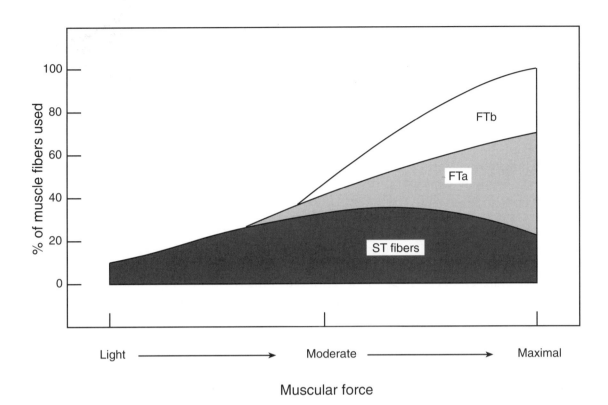

Figure 2.11 Relationship between exercise intensity and utilization of fast-twitch and slow-twitch muscle fibers. Assuming a hypothetical instance of an individual having roughly 45% slow-twitch fibers, 40% fast-twitch Type IIa fibers, and 15% fast-twitch Type IIb fibers, at maximal work loads more than half the total number of fibers in use will be of the fast-twitch variety. However, their relatively high threshold of stimulation makes the influence of slow-twitch fibers dominant during light and even moderate work intensities. *Note.* From "Weight Training for Swimmers—A Practical Approach" by R. Uebel, 1987, *National Strength and Conditioning Association Journal,* **9**(3), p. 39. Copyright 1987 by National Strength and Conditioning Association Journal. Reprinted by permission, National Strength and Conditioning Association, Lincoln, Nebraska.

tive numbers of FG and FOG fibers, however, has been rather clearly demonstrated (Henriksson and Reitman 1976; Ingjer 1979; Prince, Hikida, and Hagerman 1976). Thus, *FG (Type IIb) fibers can preferentially take on the characteristics of FOG (Type IIa) fibers* in response to the stimulus of the chronic, submaximal-pace training stimulus of distance running, providing a greater oxidative capacity for the working muscles. This response maintains the anaerobic aspects of cell function while enhancing the aerobic aspects, thereby improving competitive capabilities. The opposite change (FOG to FG conversion) can also occur with strength training.

Effects of Training on Skeletal Muscle Performance

Skeletal muscle tissue has an enormous capacity for adapting to increased exercise loads, both strength- and endurance-oriented. The changes involve structural, biochemical, nutritional, and cardiovascular improvements in working capacity. The resulting improved strength and tolerance to submaximal work increases performance capabilities, in turn permitting continued resistance (within reasonable limits) to injury. Two reviews of progress in this area have been published (Holloszy and Coyle 1984; Nadel 1985).

One beneficial adaptation to endurance training is as much as an 80% increase in myoglobin content in skeletal muscles (Pattengale and Holloszy 1967). This report confirmed what had been more or less assumed ever since G.H. Whipple showed back in 1926 that hunting dogs had more myoglobin in their working leg muscles than sedentary dogs. The increased myoglobin provides an O_2 reservoir within the working skeletal muscle cells for use when circulatory O_2 supplies are inadequate, as with near-maximal or maximal work loads, for example.

Along with a larger intracellular O_2 reservoir, training adaptation also improves O_2 delivery capability to the cytochrome enzymes within muscle cells. The studies of Brodal, Ingjer, and Hermansen (1977) have shown a more extensive capillarization in the working muscles of endurance-trained men compared to untrained men. Notice in table 2.1 that untrained skeletal muscles generally reveal fewer capillaries around the FT fibers than around the ST fibers—typically about four capillaries around ST and FT Type IIa fibers and three around FT Type IIb cells, according to the studies of Saltin et al. (1977). Endurance training significantly increases the number of capillaries around ST fibers. This decreases the diffusion distance for O_2 as it moves from capillary blood into the working muscle cells. As illustrated in figure 2.12, Karlsson (1986a) has shown a positive relationship between percentage of ST fibers in working muscles and the maximal volume of O_2 (abbreviated as $\dot{V}O_2$max) that can be taken up over time during exercise. Similarly, Saltin et al. (1977) demonstrated a relationship between skeletal muscle fiber capillarization and $\dot{V}O_2$max. The cardiopulmonary aspects of O_2 delivery and capillarization as they relate to endurance performance will be discussed in chapter 4.

Holloszy (1967) demonstrated that during endurance training many more fuel-metabolizing enzymes are found in the mitochondria, enlarged by training, of both FT Type IIa and ST cells. Thus, the rate of replenishment of ATP—the storage form of energy in cells—can increase. The number of mitochondria also increases (Hoppeler et al. 1973). The net effect of these adaptations is somewhat akin to putting a larger engine inside an automobile. In the context of the body, trained skeletal muscles become more similar to heart muscle in their ability to sustain prolonged submaximal work loads. Only those muscles affected by the training show these increased mitochondrial dynamics. The explanation for this lies partly in the important principle of *symmorphosis* (Taylor and Weibel 1981), which states that adaptation will be only as extensive as the requirement provided by the stimulus. That is, overadaptation probably never occurs; it is metabolically too costly. All this adaptation takes time, dictated by the limits of intracellular turnover and manufacture of materials. Taking a practical example from the everyday world, bricklayers already working at their fastest pace will not lay more bricks if they are paid more, simply because the increased recompense doesn't increase the dexterity with which they perform their skilled task. The more prolonged the intense period of system challenge, the greater the extent of adaptive response, which is reflected in muscle fiber performance characteristics.

Muscle glycogen supplies in the working muscles can also increase. In part this is caused by increased enzymatic activity in these cells, which promotes the synthesis of more glycogen for storage. But the majority of the increase occurs as a result of the stimulus of exercise, which through depletion of muscle carbohydrate supplies, stimulates enhanced storage during the recovery phase (Saltin and Gollnick 1983). In chapters 3 and 7 we discuss further the importance of carbohydrates in exercise and techniques that long-distance runners use to en-

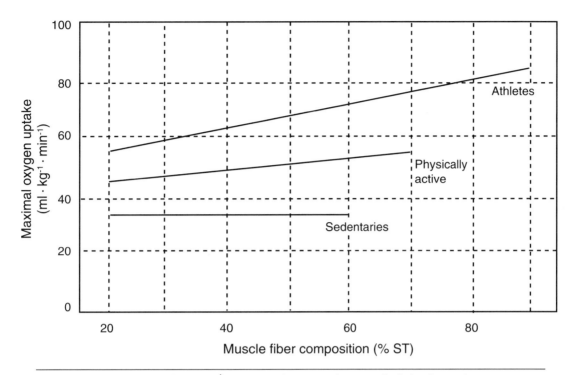

Figure 2.12 Relationship between $\dot{V}O_2$max and percent slow-twitch skeletal muscles in primary muscle movers. Endurance training improves the work capacities of these muscles. People with a greater percentage of slow-twitch fibers respond more than those with fewer slow-twitch fibers and increase their maximal oxygen uptake capacity to a greater extent. *Note.* From "Muscle Fiber Composition, Metabolic Potentials, Oxygen Transport and Exercise Performance in Man" by J. Karlsson. In *Biochemical Aspects of Physical Exercise* (p. 4) by G. Benzi, L. Packer, N. Siliprandi (Eds.), 1986, Amsterdam: Elsevier Science. Copyright 1986 by Elsevier Science. Reprinted by permission.

hance their carbohydrate stores before long endurance racing. Although lipid stores are adequate for even the longest of competitive events, increased carbohydrate storage is of great benefit in delaying the onset of fatigue. The reason for this relates to the interesting interrelationship between the use of these two major fuels during exercise, which will be discussed shortly.

Strength training can also improve muscle function along with endurance training. In particular, strength training offers an important nervous system stimulus that isn't as evident with endurance training. Motor units become better synchronized and recruitable (Sale et al. 1983). Thus, there is better teamwork among motor units, with more units contributing to the task at a given work load and with each functioning at a lower intensity.

Changes in cross-sectional area of skeletal muscle cells, resulting in skeletal muscle enlargement (hypertrophy), tend to occur with high-intensity resistance training, initiated by increased muscle strain itself (McDonagh and Davies 1984). The cross-sectional area of FT fibers seems to increase more than that of ST fibers, however, even though both types are stimulated. This may be caused by a variable responsiveness of the two types of myosin in these cells to quite different intracellular levels of acidity. This different response might explain why elite long-distance runners, with their increased numbers of ST fibers, do not experience the accompanying muscle cell hypertrophy of athletes endowed with a majority of FT cells, even though they may include serious strength training as part of their development (to increase joint strength and thereby reduce injury risk).

Thus, the body has the potential to adapt in many ways to the stimulus of serious training. Each organ system responds in its own particular way, with the ultimate goal of accommodating a sizable training stress and making it more easily tolerable. Then an even greater stress can be applied, permitting further adaptation and, it is hoped, better performance in training and competition. It is essential to realize that the adaptation takes time (one does not get fit overnight) and that the stimuli must be reasonable—that is, not excessive—as well as appropriate. Chapters 5 and 6 will consider the various training modalities, and chapter 8 will consider the challenge of keeping the stress of training within manageable limits.

SUMMARY

Using Muscle Physiology for Better Training

1. Skeletal muscles form the largest organ system in the body, capable of an enormous range of intensities and durations of movement—from the twitching of an eyelid to the completion of an ironman triathlon.

2. The variation among muscles' responses to exercise stimuli is caused by the interaction of genetics, innervation, intracellular organelles, and training. Understanding these principles provides an awareness of how best to improve on genetic potential by optimal training.

3. The simplest division of types of skeletal muscle cells (fibers) shows fast-twitch (FT) and slow-twitch (ST) varieties. Although we all have generous quantities of both types, elite athletes tend to show a preference for one type or the other. This explains why some athletes find speed training, or endurance training, so much easier than other types of training. Effective coaching provides for optimization of both characteristics.

4. Men and women differ more in their relative quantities of muscle protein (muscle mass) than in muscle performance properties; hence the two genders are similarly trainable.

5. Muscles interact with their related connective tissues (tendons) and bone to exert force through appropriate lever systems. Imbalance in the strength of various muscle groups can set the stage for performance decrements from injury or fatigue. Perfect balance can permit incredible feats of skill, as seen in current world records for the various running distances. Training consists as much in remaining injury-free as in improving muscle performance.

6. The skeletal muscle training process consists of a combined increase in muscle mass, muscle cell recruitability, and fuel storage and mobilization within the cells.

References

Barany, M., and Close, R.I. 1971. The transformation of myosin in cross-innervated rat muscle. *Journal of Physiology* 213:455-474.

Brodal, P.; Ingjer, F.; and Hermansen, L. 1977. Capillary supply of skeletal muscle fibers in untrained and endurance-trained men. *American Journal of Physiology* 232:H705-H712.

Brooke, M.H., and Engel, W.K. 1969. The histographic analysis of human muscle biopsies with regard to fiber types. I. Adult males and females. *Neurology* 19:221-233.

Brooke, M.H., and Kaiser, K.K. 1970. Muscle fiber types: How many and what kind? *Archives of Neurology* 23:369-379.

Buller, A.J.; Eccles, J.C.; and R.M. Eccles. 1960. Interaction between motoneurons and muscles in respect of the characteristic speeds of their response. *Journal of Physiology* (London) 150:417-439.

Close, R.I. 1969. Dynamic properties of fast and slow skeletal muscle after nerve cross-union. *Journal of Physiology* 204:331-346.

Costill, D.L.; Fink, W.J.; Flynn, M.; and Kirwan, J. 1987. Muscle fiber composition and enzyme activities in elite female distance runners. *International Journal of Sports Medicine* 8:103-106.

Deschenes, M. 1989. Short review: Rate coding and motor unit recruitment patterns. *Journal of Applied Sport Science Research* 3:34-39.

Edstrom, L., and B. Nystrom. 1969. Histochemical types and sizes of fibers in normal human muscles. *Acta Neurologica Scandinavica* 45:257-269.

Fink, W.J.; Costill, D.L.; and M.L. Pollock. 1977. Submaximum and maximum working capacity of elite distance runners. Part II. Muscle fiber composition and enzyme activities. *Proceedings of the New York Academy of Sciences* 301:323-327.

Gollnick, P.D. 1982. Relationship of strength and endurance with skeletal muscle structure and metabolic potential. *International Journal of Sports Medicine* 3(suppl. 1):26-32.

Gollnick, P.; Armstrong, R.; Saubert, C.; Piehl, K.; and B. Saltin. 1972. Enzyme activity and fiber composition in skeletal muscle of untrained and trained men. *Journal of Applied Physiology* 33:312-319.

Gollnick, P.D. and D.R. Hodgson. 1986. The identification of fiber types in skeletal muscle: A continual dilemma. *Exercise and Sports Sciences Reviews* 14:81-104.

Gollnick, P.D. and H. Matoba. 1984. The muscle fibre composition of muscle as a predictor of athletic success. *American Journal of Sports Medicine* 12:212-217.

Gregor, R.J. 1989. The structure and function of skeletal muscles. In *Kinesiology and Applied Anatomy*, 7th ed., ed. P.J. Rasch, pp. 32-47. Philadelphia: Lea & Febiger.

Henriksson, J., and J.S. Reitman. 1976. Quantitative measure of enzyme activities in type I and type II muscle fibers of man after training. *Acta Physiologica Scandinavica* 97:392-397.

Holloszy, J.O. 1967. Biochemical adaptation in muscle. Effects of exercise on mitochondrial oxygen uptake and respiratory enzyme activity in skeletal muscle. *Journal of Biological Chemistry* 242:2278-2282.

Holloszy, J.O., and E.F. Coyle. 1984. Adaptation of skeletal muscles to endurance exercise and their metabolic consequences. *Journal of Applied Physiology* 56:831-838.

Hoppeler, H.; Luthi, P.; Claassen, H.; Weibel, E.R.; and H. Howald. 1973. The ultrastructure of the normal human skeletal muscle. A morphometric analysis on untrained men, women, and well-trained orienteers. *Pflüger's Archiv für die gesamte Physiologie* 344:217-232.

Huxley, A.F., and R. Niedergerke. 1954. Structural changes in muscle during contraction. *Nature* 173:971-973.

Huxley, H.E., and J. Hanson. 1954. Changes in the cross-striations of muscle during contraction and stretch and their structural interpretation. *Nature* 173:973-976.

Ingjer, F. 1979. Effects of endurance training on muscle fibre ATPase activity, capillary supply and mitochondrial content in man. *Journal of Physiology* 294:419-432.

Karlsson, J. 1986a. Muscle exercise, energy metabolism and blood lactate. *Advances in Cardiology* 35:35-46.

———. 1986b. Muscle fiber composition, metabolic potentials, oxygen transport and exercise performance in man. In *Biochemical aspects of physical exercise*, eds. G. Benzi, L. Packer, and N. Siliprandi, 12. Amsterdam: Elsevier Science.

Komi, P.V.; Viitasalo, J.H.T.; Havu, M.; Thorstensson, A.; Sjödin, B.; and J. Karlsson. 1977. Skeletal muscle fibers and muscle enzyme activities in monozygous and dizygous twins of both sexes. *Acta Physiologica Scandinavica* 100:385-392.

McDonagh, M.J.N., and C.T.M. Davies. 1984. Adaptive response of mammalian muscle to exercise with high loads. *European Journal of Applied Physiology* 52:139-155.

Miller, A.E.J.; MacDougall, J.D.; Tarnopolsky, M.A.; and D.G. Sale. 1993. Gender differences in strength and muscle fiber characteristics. *European Journal of Applied Physiology* 66:254-262.

Nadel, E.R. 1985. Physiological adaptation to aerobic exercise. *American Scientist* 73:334-343.

Pattengale, P.K., and J.O. Holloszy. 1967. Augmentation of skeletal muscle myoglobin by a program of treadmill running. *American Journal of Physiology* 213:783-785.

Peter, J.B.; Barnard, R.J.; Edgerton, V.R.; Gillespie, C.A.; and K.E. Stempel. 1972. Metabolic profiles of three fiber types of skeletal muscles in guinea pigs and rabbits. *Biochemistry* 11:2627-2633.

Pette, D. 1984. Activity-induced fast to slow transitions in mammalian muscle. *Medicine and Science in Sports and Exercise* 16:517-528.

Prince, F.P.; Hikida, R.S.; and F.C. Hagerman. 1976. Human muscle fiber types in power lifters, distance runners, and untrained subjects. *Pflüger's Archiv für die gesamte Physiologie* 363:19-26.

Ranvier, L. 1873. Propriétés et structures différentes des muscles rouges et des muscles blancs chez les lapins et chez les raies. *Compte Rendu Hebdomadaire des Séances de l'Académie des Sciences (D) Paris* 77:1030-1034.

Rice, C.L.; Pettigrew, F.P.; Noble, E.G.; and A.W. Taylor, 1988. The fibre composition of skeletal muscle. *Medicine and Sport Science* 27:22-39.

Sale, D.G.; MacDougall, J.D.; Upton, A.R.M.; and A.J. McComas. 1983. Effect of strength training upon motoneuron excitability in man. *Medicine and Science in Sports and Exercise* 15:57-62.

Saltin, B., and P.D. Gollnick. 1983. Skeletal muscle adaptability: Significance for metabolism and performance. In *Handbook of physiology: Sec. 10. Skeletal muscle*, eds. L.D. Peachey, R.H. Adrian, and S.R. Geiger, 555-663. Washington, DC: American Physiological Society.

Saltin, B.; Henriksson, J.; Nygaard, E.; and P. Andersen. 1977. Fiber type and metabolic potentials of skeletal muscles in sedentary man and endurance runners. *Annals of the New York Academy of Sciences* 301:3-29.

Taylor, C.R., and E.R. Weibel. 1981. Design of the mammalian respiratory system. I. Problem and strategy. *Respiration Physiology* 44:1-10.

Thomas, C.L. 1989. *Tabor's Cyclopedic Medical Dictionary*. 16th ed. Philadelphia: Lea & Febiger.

Uebel, R. 1987. Weight training for swimmers—A practical approach. *National Strength and Conditioning Association Journal* 9(3):38-41.

Whipple, G.H. 1926. The hemoglobin of striated muscle. I. Variations due to age and exercise. *American Journal of Physiology* 76:693-707.

Wirhed, R. 1984. *Athletic ability & the anatomy of motion*. London: Wolfe Medical Publications, Ltd., pp. 15-20.

THE ENERGY DYNAMICS
OF RUNNING

Whatever the specific details of training plan design, a training plan must always remain within the limits of energy availability for the muscles being challenged. Thus, energy fuel dynamics within the working muscle cells must be appropriate. It is fitting to turn our attention to the metabolic aspects of running and to consider the biochemical processes that provide energy for movement.

Sizable quantities of chemical energy are involved in muscle tension generation. In contrast, most artificial devices for doing mechanical work typically use heat or electrical energy. Skeletal muscle's metabolic rate can undergo a greater increase from its resting level than any other body tissue, and enormous mechanical work can be done. Study of these performance dynamics at the cellular level becomes, in a real sense, a study of nutritional biochemistry. Understanding these chemical energy dynamics in the context of the tension-generating processes of muscle permits a more complete understanding of how the body can accomplish mechanical work—in our application, running.

It is not essential to understand the precise details of every chemical reaction involved in the conversion of foodstuffs into energy, but it is important to comprehend the concepts. Many practical questions are often presented to coaches and athletes that involve applying nutritional knowledge to running. Nutrition is very much the science of consumable chemistry. What is the best diet for an elite distance runner? How is the food we eat converted into energy? Are some foods better than others for highly fit athletes? Are vitamin supplements useful? Is a high-carbohydrate diet preferable to one containing substantial quantities of fat for endurance athletes? How does lactic acidosis relate to fuel metabolism? How can lactic acid production or its debilitating effects on performance be minimized?

Athletes and coaches do not need to become food biochemists. But the more they know of important basic concepts, the more intelligently they can pursue their professions. To use an analogy, it is more essential to know the rules of soccer than to know the names of the players if we truly desire to understand how the game is played. Once the game is understood, knowing some personal details about the players and the various teams then adds delightful subtleties that increase satisfaction in watching the game. Thus, a working knowledge of the general principles of metabolism—the fuels that are used, how much energy can be produced, and how energy production is regulated—permits a practical understanding of the limitations and capabilities of the body for providing energy. With these principles clearly in mind, coaches and athletes are in a better position to apply them to suit their purpose, which is performance enhancement in running.

Thermodynamics Made Easy

The discipline of thermodynamics governs metabolism. *Thermodynamics* is the study of the relationships between all the various forms of energy: chemical, heat, mechanical, and so on. Two of its laws are appropriate for our consideration. The *first law of thermodynamics* states simply that the total energy of the universe remains constant. We can define *energy* as all forms of work and heat. The *second law of thermodynamics* states, again very simply, that the entropy of the universe increases. We will define *entropy* as disorder or randomness.

How do these two laws relate to running? Running requires energy, which is obtained by the breakdown of energy-containing fuel. Of the total energy released in aerobic fuel breakdown, such as during an easy distance run, about 27% will be converted into movement (Jéquier and Flatt 1986). The other 73% is released in the form of heat, as runners soon discover when they start sweating during their training run—even when the day is cool. Our stored fuel reserves are assimilated from the foods we eat. Thus, an understanding of metabolism needs to include a knowledge of fuel intake, processing, and storage as well as fuel breakdown and utilization.

Solar energy is the source of all biological energy. Green plants utilize this energy. Green plants have a pigment, chlorophyll, that converts radiant light energy into chemical energy. This chemical energy, in turn, is used to produce glucose by chemical reduction of atmospheric carbon dioxide (CO_2). The process is termed *photosynthesis*. Molecular O_2 is formed during photosynthesis and given up to the atmosphere. Following is the overall equation for this photosynthetic reaction:

$$6\ CO_2 + 6\ H_2O + \text{Energy} \longrightarrow C_6H_{12}O_6 + 6\ O_2 \tag{3.1}$$

Because glucose ($C_6H_{12}O_6$) is a more complex molecule than the two simpler molecules involved in its formation, in thermodynamic jargon we say that the entropy (disorder) of the chemical system has decreased. This synthesis required a considerable amount of heat energy, which can be quantified using units of *calories* (cal) or *joules* (J). These can be interconverted as follows:

$$1\ \text{cal} = 4.186\ \text{J} \qquad 1\ \text{J} = 0.24\ \text{cal} \tag{3.2}$$

$$1{,}000\ \text{cal} = 1\ \text{kilocalorie (kcal)} \qquad 1{,}000\ \text{J} = 1\ \text{kilojoule (kJ)} \tag{3.3}$$

Our living cells require the complex, energy-rich products of photosynthesis as fuel and as a carbon source. This is because we are unable to use such simple molecules as CO_2 either as fuel or as building blocks for synthesizing the components of our cells. We rely on the plant world as the ultimate source of our food and energy, providing us with *fatty acids* (stored as triglycerides), *sugars* (stored as complex carbohydrates such as glycogen), and *amino acids* (bound together and stored as proteins). We eat these fuels, and in the stomach and small intestine they are then broken down by digestive enzymes to their smallest component parts: simple sugars, fatty acids, and amino acids. This process is called *catabolism*. After absorption into the blood circulation system and transport to the various tissues, these energy fuels are then reassimilated, by a process called *anabolism*, and stored in various quantities. Skeletal muscle cells, of course, can use the potential energy from further breakdown of such stored fuels to produce movement.

Assuming that complete fuel breakdown results from this so-called *cellular respiration*, the stable end products of CO_2 and H_2O result. The equation for cellular respiration in its simplest form is thus virtually the opposite of the equation for photosynthesis. Using glucose, a simple carbohydrate, as an example, we may write the following equation:

$$C_6H_{12}O_6 + 6\,O_2 \longrightarrow 6\,CO_2 + 6\,H_2O + \text{Energy} \qquad (3.4)$$

Again, considering this equation in thermodynamic perspective, a considerable amount of heat energy is released, along with energy used for movement. We say that the entropy is positive (has increased), indicating that glucose breakdown has brought more disorder (randomness) to the chemical system.

Several important observations should be made at this point. First, protein typically is not a primary fuel source, although protein breakdown and reassimilation may occur with hard work. Carbohydrates (represented by glucose) and fats (represented by fatty acids) are our primary fuel sources. Many of the details of both synthesis and breakdown of these two fuel sources are similar, as we shall see, although some important differences exist as well. Table 3.1 compares glucose (a typical carbohydrate) and palmitic acid (a fatty acid) as cellular fuels. It can be seen that the energy value of palmitic acid is nearly 2 1/2 times greater per gram than that of glucose.

Second, the very sizable heat-energy aspect of metabolism should be familiar to all who exercise. Our resting body temperature is about 37° C (98° F). We have evolved mechanisms for getting rid of this metabolic heat through sweating and dilation of skin blood vessels. During exercise, body temperature rises. This promotes an increased blood flow to the skin for heat loss through sweating and dilated skin blood vessels. In turn, this shunting diminishes the flow available for working muscles. This explains the typically slower training and competitive paces by endurance athletes in very warm weather.

Third, although the equation for breakdown of glucose as a typical fuel appears simple, this is deceptive, because there are a few dozen separate, sequential, enzymatically controlled steps required in the chemical breakdown of glucose to CO_2 and H_2O. These are outlined in figure 3.12, and we will describe only a few of the relevant details later. We will emphasize only the most important steps in these metabolic pathways, particularly those that are relevant for performance enhancement during training or competition. First, however, we

TABLE 3.1

Metabolic Aspects of Carbohydrates and Fatty Acids as Fuels

	Carbohydrate (glucose)		Fatty acid (palmitic acid)	
Structure	CH_2OH ... $CH_3(CH_2)_{14}COOH$			
Molecular weight, gm	180		256	
% carbon and hydrogen	47		88	
% oxygen	53		12	
Relative stored energy	3.81 kcal/gm	15.9 kJ/gm	9.1 kcal/gm	38.1 kJ/gm
Total stored energy	686 kcal	2,872 kJ	2,340 kcal	9,795 kJ
Energy generated as ATP	360 kcal	1,507 kJ	1,300 kcal	5,442 kJ
Energy value	19 kcal/ATP	79.5 kJ/ATP	18 kcal/ATP	75.4 kJ/ATP
O_2 needed for catabolism	130 L		515 L	
Energy production per liter of O_2	5.28 kcal	22.1 kJ	4.54 kcal	19.0 kJ
CO_2 produced in catabolism	130 L		358 L	
Energy production per liter of CO_2	5.28 kcal	22.1 kJ	6.54 kcal	27.4 kJ
CO_2 produced per O_2 used (respiratory exchange ratio)	1.00		0.71	

Note. From "Dynamics of pulmonary gas exchange" by B.J. Whipp, 1987, *Circulation,* **76** (Suppl. 6), 18-28. Reprinted by permission of the American Heart Association, Inc.

should describe briefly how the free energy produced from fuel breakdown is actually harvested and stored in chemical form for eventual use in permitting movement.

Energy Storage in Tissues: Adenosine Triphosphate and Creatine Phosphate

We have already mentioned that the energy released from complete cellular breakdown of fuels is stored in the form of adenosine triphosphate (ATP). Oxygen is required for this complete catabolism, and thus the phrase *oxidative metabolism* is commonly used to describe the reactions involved. Figure 3.1 shows the structure of the parent molecule called *adenosine monophosphate* (AMP), to which additional phosphate (PO_4^{3-}) groups can bind, forming first adenosine diphosphate (ADP) and then ATP itself. This chemical bonding, however, requires considerably more energy than that found in the other bonds linking the various atoms together. The wavy line denotes these so-called *high-energy bonds,* in contrast to the straight-line notation for lower-energy bonding. High-energy PO_4^{3-} bonds are a kind of gold standard of metabolic energy currency in the biological world.

The free energy available from oxidation of food is used to link together a PO_4^{3-} group to adenosine diphosphate (ADP), thereby forming a molecule of

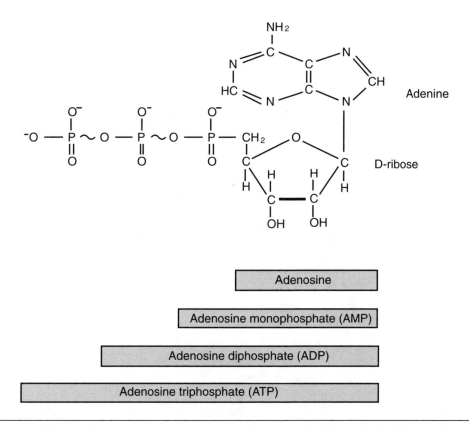

Figure 3.1 Chemical structure of adenosine monophosphate (AMP), to which additional high-energy phosphate groups can be chemically bonded, forming adenosine diphosphate (ADP) and adenosine triphosphate (ATP).

ATP. When cells require energy for biosynthesis of other substances for chemical interactions, such as those of actin and myosin in muscle for tension generation, ATP is used. By the coupling of oxidation (the use of O_2 to permit complete breakdown of fuels with release of energy) to phosphorylation (the storage of this energy as ATP), the free energy available from breakdown of fuels can be used for mechanical work.

Historically, the realization that phosphates were the storage form of the free energy from fuel oxidation dates back to 1925. Gustav Embden, a German biochemist, observed that much more PO_4^{3-} would diffuse into the solution bathing an isolated, twitching skeletal muscle preparation than into that around a resting muscle. Two years later, in 1927, two groups of investigators simultaneously discovered a substance called *creatine phosphate* (CP), a very unstable derivative of a nitrogen-containing substance called *creatine* (figure 3.2). Creatine exists in sizable concentrations in muscle and nerve cells, with skeletal muscles having the largest supplies. Then in 1929 ATP and ADP were discovered independently by Karl Lohmann in Germany and by two American scientists. The ensuing few years saw work proceed toward the unraveling of how these various PO_4^{3-}-containing substances interacted in energy storage and release (Lehninger 1982).

The classic study came in 1934 when Lohmann demonstrated that cell-free muscle extracts of CP would split PO_4^{3-} from creatine only in the presence of ADP, which resulted in the formation of ATP. His explanation of the situation was simple. CP is a reservoir of PO_4^{3-} (in effect a reservoir of energy), usable

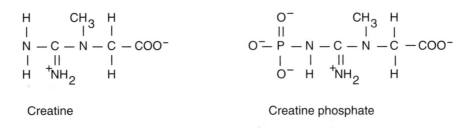

Figure 3.2 Structures of creatine and creatine phosphate.

only if there is first a need for ATP. Lohmann envisioned muscle tension generation as somehow involving ATP breakdown directly into ADP. As soon as ADP was formed, available CP would rephosphorylate it back into ATP. Subsequent research proved him correct, and the following equations (3.5) and (3.6) are often termed the *Lohmann equations* to recognize his brilliance in identifying what was occurring:

myosin ATPase

$$ATP + H_2O \longrightarrow ADP + H_3PO_4 \tag{3.5}$$

creatine kinase

$$\text{creatine phosphate} + ADP \rightleftharpoons \text{creatine} + ATP \tag{3.6}$$

Equation (3.6) is reversible, as shown. That is, it can proceed in either direction, but its equilibrium normally is shifted toward the right, keeping the ADP phosphorylated as ATP at all times by use of CP. Thus, the CP pool represents a small but labile reservoir of high-energy PO_4^{3-} groups. When ATP is plentiful, so also is CP. If a sudden, enormous ATP requirement occurs in muscle cells, such that metabolism of carbohydrates and fats cannot occur in time to provide the needed energy, CP can provide it. In sprinting, for example—whether in the 100-m dash or the final 50-m rush to victory in a 10,000-m run—CP will play an important role. Skeletal muscle is thus biochemically capable of generating tension for brief periods (perhaps 20 s) even without any energy derived from ongoing carbohydrate or fat breakdown. A CP shuttle exists between the cytoplasm and mitochondria, as shown in figure 3.3. In the myofibrillar region of the cytoplasm, PO_4^{3-} is taken from CP to allow ADP conversion to ATP. This provides a ready source of ATP for muscle tension generation. When CP arrives back to the mitochondrial membrane, creatine becomes rephosphorylated.

The *creatine kinase* (CK) enzyme shown in equation (3.6) occurs in three forms, known as *isoenzymes.* These are restricted to skeletal muscle (CK-MM), cardiac muscle (CK-MB), and brain tissue (CK-BB), although skeletal muscle also produces some CK-MB. When these tissues are challenged by trauma (such as in a boxing match), by circulatory shutdown (as with a clot in a coronary artery of the heart), or by fuel exhaustion (during and following a marathon race), clinically elevated levels of the appropriate CK isoenzymes will appear in the bloodstream for several days following these insults (Rogers, Stull, and Apple 1985). Thus, particularly for distance runners, measurement of serum CK levels can serve as a marker for excessive training or competitive stress, signaling a need for temporary training reduction and increased appropriate therapeutic modalities to enhance recovery.

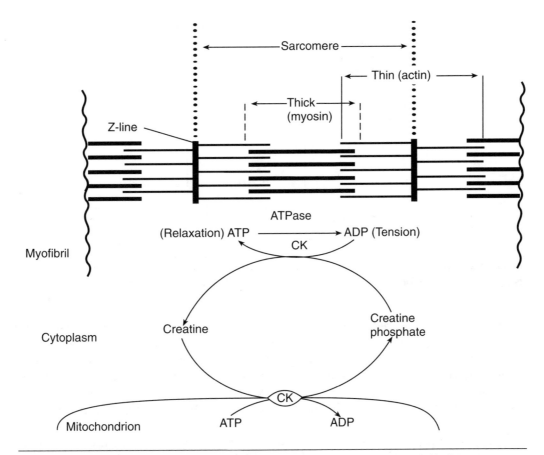

Figure 3.3 Creatine phosphate shuttle between mitochondria and muscle myofibrils. During muscle tension generation, ATP contributes energy, forming ADP, and this energy supply must be regenerated. Creatine kinase (CK) in the vicinity of the tension-generating proteins (myosin and actin) permits regeneration of ATP. Similarly, at the mitochondrial membrane CK provides for regeneration of creatine phosphate using energy provided from fuel metabolism. A healthy diet provides adequate creatine, and special supplementing is not necessary.

The Four Energy Systems

The essence of metabolism (figure 3.4) is in the conversion of fuels to end products, with appropriate storage of the energy as a usable form (ATP) for cellular function. It is interesting that ATP is present in only very small quantities in cells. A warm-blooded skeletal muscle may have typically about 6 micromoles (μmol) of ATP per gram, compared with between 20 and 30 μmol of CP per gram. According to Lehninger (1982), a sedentary 70-kg man has only about 50 gm of ATP in his entire body, yet he would probably require the equivalent of 190 kg of ATP to provide his daily energy requirements!

The ATP content of muscle and other cells is thus recycled between ATP and ADP many times per minute, with PO_4^{3-} groups alternating from CP to ADP to ATP. Extremely heavy work loads reduce the CP supply, but afterward CP is rapidly regenerated by continued metabolism. This *CP-ATP system* can provide energy needs without any breakdown of fuels such as glucose or fatty acids for perhaps 15 to 20 s of intense work. It is one of the four primary energy systems of the body—often referred to scientifically as the *phosphagen system* (Hawley and Hopkins 1995), but just as often known practically as the *sprinters' energy system* because of its major role in energy provision for short sprints.

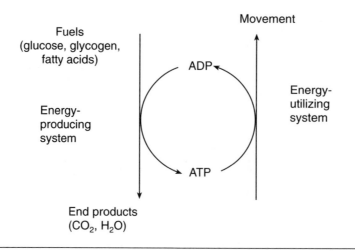

Figure 3.4 The essence of metabolism. Available fuels are broken down, and the resulting energy is stored as a usable form (ATP) for purposes such as skeletal muscle tension generation and thus the production of movement.

Another of the three systems does not require O_2 for fuel metabolism. The term *anaerobic glycolysis* is used to describe this system. It is an incomplete breakdown of carbohydrates that provides a high level of energy for a small period of time. The other two systems involve complete breakdown of fat and carbohydrate in mitochondria. Because of an interaction with O_2, these are referred to as *aerobic glycolysis* and *aerobic lipolysis*. The term *aerobic* signifies the presence of O_2.

Oxygen provision in the working skeletal muscles may be limited by any of several circumstances. There may be insufficient circulation of blood (caused in part by dehydration), or the rate of physical activity may be so great as to challenge the ability of even an optimally functioning circulatory system to provide adequate O_2. The inability to respond when the mind says "go" but the body says "no," as a runner tries to increase speed in a race or a training session when already fatigued from prior effort, attests to the very definite limits of aerobic and anaerobic metabolism. An important goal of training is to extend one's aerobic and anaerobic limits as far as possible.

Figure 3.5 graphically summarizes the relative contribution of these various energy systems for running. Energy contribution is plotted as a function of running distance. At the very short, so-called sprint distances, CP and ATP are the energy providers, with no requirements for O_2, carbohydrate, or fat. Over what are typically referred to as the middle distances, anaerobic metabolism provides the majority of the required energy, because the intensity level required is so great that adequate O_2 cannot be provided to permit complete carbohydrate metabolism. Over the longer distances, where exercise intensity is not as great, blood circulation of O_2 is adequate to permit both fat and carbohydrate metabolism to occur more completely (i.e., aerobically), releasing enormous quantities of energy and producing minimal accumulating acidosis. During this longer distance running, anaerobic metabolism will contribute energy as well, but to a decreasing extent as the distance lengthens.

For O_2 to be available in mitochondria, it must be brought from the outside environment into metabolizing cells. This movement requires an intricate pathway through the respiratory passageways, then through the bloodstream, into and through the extracellular fluid, and finally into the cytoplasm of individual cells. Along each step of the way, O_2 moves by diffusion down its concentration

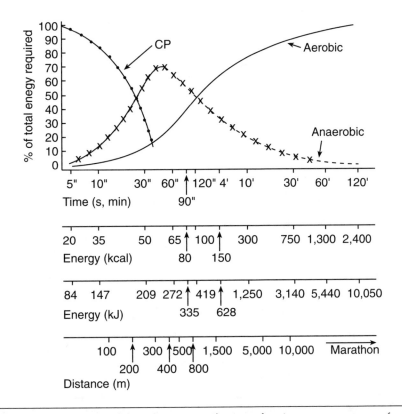

Figure 3.5 Graphic summary of the relative contribution of various energy sources for maximal effort over the spectrum of distances from the sprints through the marathon. For the short sprints creatine phosphate (CP) is the primary energy supplier, with an increasingly substantial contribution from anaerobic glycolysis up through events lasting about 1 min. For events longer than 1 min, CP supplies would have already been depleted, and aerobic (complete) breakdown of fuels (fatty acids and glucose) becomes increasingly important; for marathon racing aerobic metabolism is by far the predominant energy source.

gradient—that is, from a region of higher availability to successive regions of lower availability. The term O_2 *cascade* is often used to suggest this stepwise movement of O_2 toward cells awaiting its arrival. The *partial pressure* exerted by O_2 (PO_2), both in the atmosphere and in dissolved fluids such as blood and cell cytoplasm, is typically expressed in units of millimeters of mercury (mmHg). Figure 3.6 shows the various PO_2 values that are found from the external environment to mitochondria.

Comparing Aerobic and Anaerobic Metabolism

The generalized equation for aerobic breakdown of a carbohydrate such as glucose results in enormous amounts of energy for work, as shown below:

$$C_6H_{12}O_6 + 6\ O_2 \longrightarrow 6\ CO_2 + 6\ H_2O + 36\ ATP \tag{3.7}$$

For fatty acid breakdown the reaction is similar in principle and also releases plenty of energy. Fatty acid breakdown is summarized by the following equation, using palmitic acid as an example:

$$C_{16}H_{32}O_2 + 23\ O_2 \longrightarrow 16\ CO_2 + 16\ H_2O + 130\ ATP \tag{3.8}$$

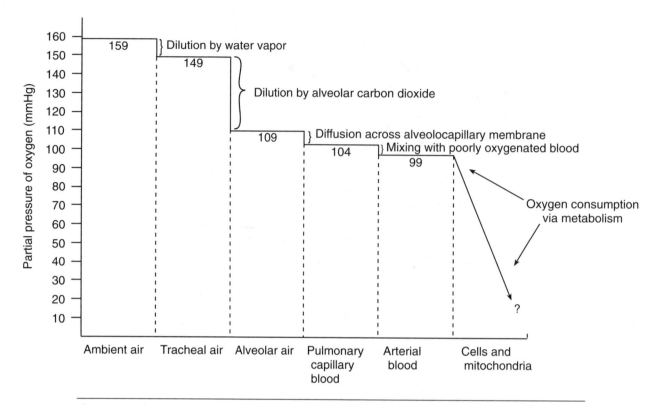

Figure 3.6 The oxygen cascade, showing how oxygen moves down its concentration gradient from environmental air to the mitochondria of living cells. Dilution steadily lowers its partial pressure, and then its utilization in metabolism decreases its concentration enormously within cells.

If insufficient O_2 is available for complete fuel breakdown, a small amount of energy can be released with glucose conversion to an intermediate substance, *pyruvic acid*. In turn, pyruvic acid can be converted into *lactic acid*. Both of these reactions occur in the cytoplasm, with no involvement of mitochondria. In contrast, no such anaerobic energy release is possible with fatty acids; their stored energy can be accessed only when they are completely broken down. Under physiological conditions the lactic acid produced from anaerobic carbohydrate metabolism dissociates almost immediately and completely (Gladden 1989) into *lactate ions* (Lac⁻) and *hydrogen ions* (H⁺). The same is true for a large number of other metabolic acids that we will encounter in fuel metabolism. It is accepted biochemical jargon to refer to these acids by the name of their negative ion, for example, lactate (Lac⁻) for lactic acid or oxalacetate for oxalacetic acid. We will use this convention here as well.

A summary equation for the anaerobic conversion of glucose to lactate is given in the following equation:

$$C_6H_{12}O_6 \longrightarrow 2 \text{ ATP} + 2 \text{ Lactic acid} \rightleftharpoons 2 H^+ + 2 \text{ Lac}^- \tag{3.9}$$

By comparing the ATP generated in equations (3.7) and (3.9), we can see that anaerobic metabolism provides only 1/18—about 5.5%—as much energy as aerobic metabolism (2 ATP as compared to 36). Thus, anaerobic fuel metabolism is extremely substrate costly, meaning that large amounts of glucose are consumed with minimal energy return. Also, the rapid accumulation of H⁺ ions (commonly called *protons*) as a result of lactic acid dissociation eventually inhibits the enzymatic breakdown sequence. The enzymes involved in fuel breakdown operate best within a specific narrow range of acidity. Acidity is determined by the number of available protons. Excessive tissue acidity (acidosis) inhibits the activity of many of the enzyme reactions for fuel metabolism. Thus, optimal cell function depends on adequate O_2 to maximize energy (ATP) production via aerobic metabolism. Improving performance fitness in skeletal muscles involves adaptation in any and all ways to provide a higher level of ATP-derived energy release with minimal tissue or blood acidification.

Carbon dioxide is also an acid. An *acid* is defined as a substance that donates H^+ ions to its surrounding solution. When CO_2 dissolves in body water, it becomes hydrated to form carbonic acid (H_2CO_3), which then dissociates into H^+ ions and bicarbonate (HCO_3^-) ions according to the following equation:

$$CO_2 + H_2O \rightleftharpoons H_2CO_3 \rightleftharpoons H^+ + HCO_3^- \qquad (3.10)$$

Carbon dioxide is called a volatile acid because it can be eliminated as a gas when the blood containing it is returned to the heart from the working tissues and then sent to the lungs. The lungs thus are important not only for their role in blood oxygenation, but also as the body's most powerful organ for acid excretion. Lactate, on the other hand, is a nonvolatile acid and is not eliminated via the lungs. Although the Lac^- portion of lactic acid can be used by many tissues as a fuel, the inhibitory effects of the H^+ ion on its metabolism must be minimized. One substance that minimizes the influence of H^+ ions in this regard is sodium bicarbonate ($NaHCO_3$). This substance circulates in the bloodstream and also is in the interstitial fluid that bathes cells. Equation (3.11) illustrates the so-called *buffer action* of $NaHCO_3$ in the blood perfusing working tissue. Many of the H^+ ions resulting from lactate production combine with the HCO_3^- ion of $NaHCO_3$ to form H_2CO_3. This decreases the rate of formation of acidosis, since only the H^+ ions themselves contribute to acidity. As blood H_2CO_3 passes through the lungs, it can dissociate to CO_2 and H_2O, with CO_2 being excreted. The NaLactate contributes Lac^- ions to working tissues as a source of fuel.

$$Na^+ + HCO_3^- + H^+ + Lac^- \rightleftharpoons NaLactate + H_2CO_3 \rightleftharpoons H_2O + CO_2 \qquad (3.11)$$

Excessive acidity in tissues has several undesirable effects. We have already mentioned its inhibitory effects on optimal enzyme functioning for efficient metabolism. Another is its destabilization of cell membranes, allowing some of their vital enzymes to leak out into either the bloodstream or the interstitial fluid. A third is its tendency to cause H_2O to enter cells in an attempt to maintain osmotic equilibrium between the cells and their surrounding fluid environment. An acidotic cell cytoplasm has excessive numbers of ions, or *electrolytes*, dissolved in its fluid portion (H^+, Lac^-, Na^+, HCO_3^-, etc.). As a result, there are relatively fewer H_2O molecules per unit volume than in surrounding solutions such as blood or extracellular fluid. An osmotic inflow of H_2O attempts to restore fluid-electrolyte balance. When this occurs in highly active muscle cells, which normally are elongated and thin, the increase in fluid content makes them shorter and thicker. Functionally, athletes sense this after a hard training session as a decreased joint range of motion. The next morning, this can be particularly noticeable as stiffness.

Maintenance of increased circulation following such training, typically in the form of easy running, will enhance recovery. This is often referred to simply as *cool-down*, because during this process the body temperature gradually decreases from its maximum during exercise back toward its resting level. It is an important intermediate step in the activity continuum from the highly active state on one end to the resting condition on the other. The enhanced circulation, maintained aerobically and at little energy expense, helps restore fluid and electrolyte balance in the working muscles. It also provides continued perfusion of O_2-rich blood into the working muscles, which facilitates complete breakdown of Lac$^-$ ions from anaerobic metabolism.

How can athletes increase their performance potential by minimizing blood and tissue acidosis during training and competing? From the preceding discussion, two suggestions can be offered:

- Ensure adequate fluid and energy-rich nutritional intake soon after the race or the hard training session to restore blood volume for adequate tissue perfusion, to permit rejuvenation of muscle energy stores, and to allow recovery of an aerobic metabolic state.

- Ensure adequate musculoskeletal recovery by a cool-down session (easy running, a relaxing swim, etc.), and restore flexibility through stretching exercises and massage.

Comparing Carbohydrates and Fatty Acids as Fuels

Table 3.2 provides a quantitative idea of the available energy substrates in the body. The principal storage form of carbohydrates is *glycogen*. Glycogen is essentially polymerized glucose—long chains, sometimes branching, as depicted in figure 3.7. These glycogen polymers are sometimes so large that histologic sections of tissue, when stained appropriately, will reveal them as cytoplasmic glycogen particles, larger in the liver than in skeletal muscle. When glycogen is broken down to glucose (a process called *glycogenolysis*), one ATP is produced per mole of glucose removed.

Adipose tissue and the liver provide the greatest reservoir of fat-related energy. The much greater reservoir of fat than of carbohydrate can be seen in table 3.2. Muscle cells have a large capacity to utilize fat, which can diffuse easily across the muscle cell membrane. Endurance training increases both carbohydrate and fat supplies in skeletal muscle. Cardiac muscle, with its never-ending activity in generating more than 100,000 heartbeats every day, is specially endowed with fat stores and mitochondria to satisfy its needs.

Fats are essentially water insoluble and exist in the body as *triglycerides*. These result from the linking together of glycerol with three fatty acid molecules—a process called *esterification* and illustrated in figure 3.8. Fat found in food (e.g., butter, bacon, margarine, oils) is chiefly in the form of triglycerides. Fats that are liquid at room temperature tend to be of plant origin, whereas the solid fats are principally animal-derived. The number of H$^+$ ions bound to fatty acids (known as its extent of hydrogenation or saturation) determines their melting point and thus whether they will be liquid or solid at room temperature. Cooking oils, such as safflower or corn oil, are polyunsaturated, that is, not very extensively hydrogenated. Animal fat, such as lard, is much more saturated. We shall see that hydrogenation affects the amount of energy released when these fats are broken down as fuels.

TABLE 3.2

Energy Substrates Available for Metabolism

	kg	kcal	kJ
Tissues			
Fat	15	141,000	590,000
Protein	6	24,000	100,500
Muscle glycogen	0.35	1,400	5,900
Liver glycogen	0.085	340	1,400
	21.435	166,740	697,800
Circulating fuels			
Extracellular fluid glucose	0.020	80	335
Fatty acids	0.0004	4	17
Triglycerides	0.003	30	126
	0.0234	114	478

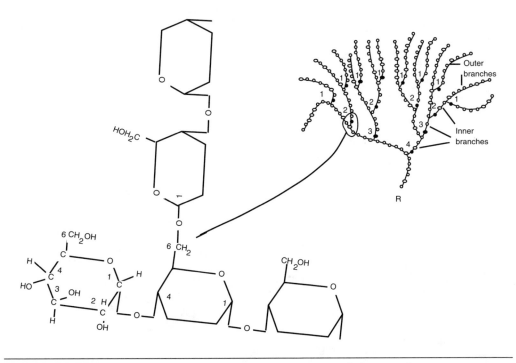

Figure 3.7 The glycogen molecule, showing branches made up of glucose subunits.

When fats are ingested, they are first broken down from triglycerides into *fatty acids* (sometimes called non-esterified fatty acids because they are not bound to glycerol). These are absorbed into the bloodstream and then bind to *albumin*, our most common plasma protein, for transport. Because the plasma fatty acid concentration is typically higher than that in such tissues as liver, adipose, and muscle cells, this gradient permits a steady fatty acid influx into these cells. No active transport mechanism for fatty acids is known, and as they enter the cells, the freed albumin then becomes available for assistance in transport of other fatty acids. As shown in figure 3.9, the fatty acids are eventually bound again as triglycerides and stored for later use by these metabolizing cells.

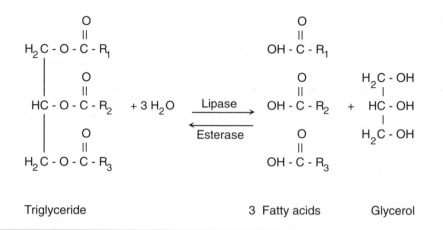

Figure 3.8 Breakdown of a triglyceride into three fatty acids. A lipase enzyme permits removal of fatty acids from the glycerol molecule to which they were bound. An esterase enzyme permits the storage of fatty acids, bound to glycerol as a triglyceride; this storage process is called esterification.

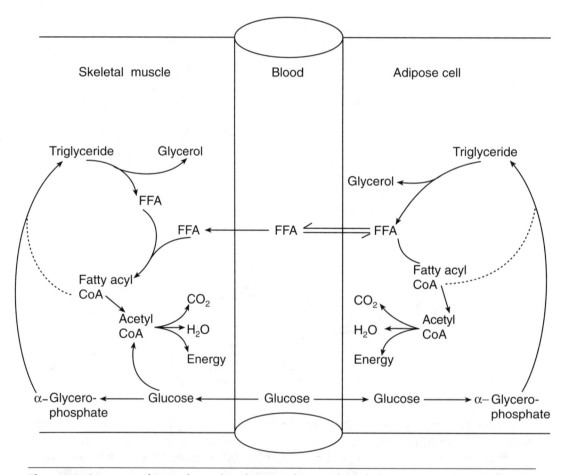

Figure 3.9 Summary of interrelationships between fatty acids and glucose in metabolism. Blood glucose can enter either skeletal muscle cells, for eventual breakdown, or adipose cells, for eventual conversion to triglyceride. Fatty acids can also enter either skeletal muscle cells or adipose cells. In the former, they are typically metabolized for energy; in the latter they can be stored for later release and transport to muscle tissue. FFA = free fatty acid; CoA = coenzyme A.

By studying equations (3.7) and (3.8) along with table 3.2, several interesting differences between carbohydrates and fats as fuels can be seen. First, note that carbohydrate is a less efficient form of stored energy than fat. Fats are 88% carbon and hydrogen with 12% O_2, compared with 47% carbon and hydrogen and 53% O_2 for carbohydrates. Oxygen atoms in a molecule of stored energy merely add more bulk, as they generally can be obtained from the environment as needed. However, as exercise intensity increases, this small amount of stored O_2 in fats can be a liability, making carbohydrates a preferred fuel over fats as O_2 requirements begin to approach O_2 supply capabilities. Also, carbohydrates require less O_2 for metabolism than fats. Thus, for glucose 36 ATP are produced per 6 O_2 utilized (36/6 = 6). For palmitic acid, a saturated fat, 130 ATP are produced per 23 O_2 utilized (130/23 = 5.7). Unsaturated fats (those more likely to be liquid at room temperature) produce somewhat less energy on catabolism (Hunt and Groff 1990).

Second, it can be seen that carbohydrates are more acidic than fats; that is, more CO_2 is produced *per quantity* of O_2 used in carbohydrate breakdown than in fat breakdown. This ratio of CO_2 produced by cells to O_2 consumed by cells is termed the *respiratory quotient* (RQ). More practically, we measure the volumes of O_2 and CO_2 exchanged by the lungs. Here, the ratio of CO_2 to O_2 is referred to as the *respiratory exchange ratio* (R). For glucose,

$$R = 6 \, CO_2 / 6 \, O_2 = 1.00 \tag{3.12}$$

For palmitic acid,

$$R = 16 \, CO_2 / 23 \, O_2 = 0.70 \tag{3.13}$$

Third, fat is less bulky than carbohydrate; that is, fats are higher in energy content per unit mass than carbohydrates. Oxidation of one gram of fat forms 508 mol of ATP as compared to 211 mol for an equal weight of carbohydrate.

An individual at rest consuming a normal diet will have a resting R value of about 0.80, indicating that the majority of ongoing energy requirements are met by fat oxidation, with perhaps one third by carbohydrate. If this person begins to exercise at a steadily increasing work rate, carbohydrate metabolism increasingly becomes the dominant energy source. We could follow the course of this change by monitoring the rise in R. Table 3.3 shows this nicely as part of a set of data obtained when one of our elite female runners underwent a performance evaluation using treadmill running to allow estimation of $\dot{V}O_2$max. The data point marked *Rest* indicates baseline values before her test began. The next four data points show the progressive rise in R values as well as other accompanying physiological responses to the steadily increasing work load. The final five data points were obtained during the few minutes just prior to the point of voluntary exhaustion, she "ran out of reasons for running" and stepped off the treadmill. Her R actually exceeded 1.00 due to her very high level of acidosis. Production of CO_2 was in excess of that explainable by pure carbohydrate metabolism and was exhaled due to her increased breathing.

Metabolism of Carbohydrates

It is well known that a progressive fall in working muscle glycogen occurs during vigorous exercise, and when fatigue is noticeable in those muscles glycogen

TABLE 3.3

Effect of Increasing Work Load During a Treadmill Stress Test on Oxygen Consumption, Carbon Dioxide Production, and Elevation of Respiratory Exchange Ratio (R)

Elapsed time (min)	Heart rate (beats/min)	Respiratory rate (breaths/min)	Oxygen consumption (ml/min)	Oxygen consumption (ml · kg^{-1} · min^{-1})	Carbon dioxide production (ml/min)	Respiratory exchange ratio (R)
Rest	60	14	320	6.8	260	0.79
1/2	136	32	1,522	29.4	1,293	0.84
1	136	33	1,612	31.2	1,364	0.85
1 1/2	140	33	1,904	36.8	1,625	0.86
2	145	35	1,914	37.0	1,634	0.86
14 1/2	167	46	3,220	62.3	3,053	0.95
15	170	46	3,353	64.9	3,206	0.96
15 1/2	176	47	3,414	66.0	3,329	0.97
16	180	47	3,474	67.2	3,503	1.02
16 1/2 End	188	48	3,691	71.4	3,862	1.04

depletion is a likely explanation (Costill et al. 1971). Higher exercise intensities reduce available glycogen supplies much more quickly than low-level exercise. How is glycogen mobilized to permit exercise? And how can glycogen be stored and replenished in working muscles?

The glycogen content of tissues varies considerably, depending on nutritional status, level of physical training, premeasurement exercise level, and the influence of several hormones. *Cortisone* (from the adrenal cortex) and *insulin* (from the pancreas) elevate the glycogen content in tissues by increasing its synthesis from glucose. *Adrenaline* (from the adrenal medulla) and *glucagon* (from the pancreas) reduce the glycogen content of tissues such as the liver and muscle by stimulating its breakdown to glucose.

The release of *noradrenaline* (from the sympathetic nervous system) along with adrenaline stimulates glycogen mobilization during exercise. Statements made by athletes referring to "a surge of adrenaline" and "getting the juices flowing" in a real sense have some truth to them and suggest the *fight, flight, or fright syndrome* that characterizes sympathetic nervous system activation. In addition to mobilizing glucose reserves through glycogen breakdown, these substances also raise the heart rate and blood pressure, thereby increasing blood flow to working tissues.

Glycogenolysis: Glycogen Breakdown to Glucose

Glycogen breakdown occurs through the action of an enzyme called *phosphorylase*, as shown in figure 3.10. Not all of the steps are shown, but the end result is the formation of glucose-1-PO$_4$. The phosphorylase enzyme typically exists in an inactive form. Its activation results from a rather complex series of chemical events. Any of three circulating blood substances—two hormones (adrenaline and glucagon) and noradrenaline from the sympathetic nervous system—have the ability to interact with a specific enzyme located in cell membranes called *adenyl cyclase*. This interaction permits breakdown of intracellular ATP to a substance called *cyclic 3',5'-AMP*. Magnesium ions are also required for this reac-

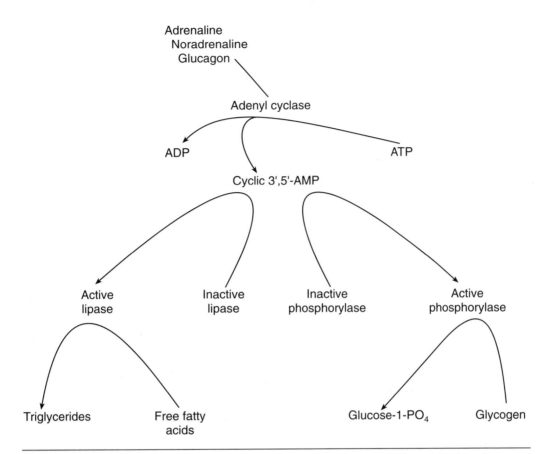

Figure 3.10 Mechanism by which circulating substances, such as adrenaline, noradrenaline, and glucagon, can promote mobilization of both free fatty acids and glucose when required for energy metabolism. In each instance an inactive fuel breakdown enzyme is activated by the presence of cyclic 3', 5'-AMP, which in turn is produced by the action of adenyl cyclase on ATP. The three involved substances, when bound to adenyl cyclase, permit this enzyme to function.

tion to proceed. Cyclic AMP in turn activates the phosphorylase enzyme, permitting cleavage of a glucose fragment from glycogen.

Continued circulation of adrenaline, glucagon, or noradrenaline will extend cyclic AMP production in both liver and muscle cells, providing both with supplies of glucose. However, there is an important basic difference between these two cell types in terms of how this glucose is utilized. In liver cells, glucose-1-PO_4 can either be metabolized completely to CO_2, H_2O, and ATP to satisfy the energy needs of the cell or be converted back to free glucose (i.e., glucose not bound to PO_4^{3-}). This free glucose can diffuse out of the cell, whereas the phosphorylated form cannot. Thus, as illustrated in figure 3.11, liver cells have two important enzymes, *hexokinase* and *glucose-6-phosphatase*. The former permits glucose to enter into cellular metabolic pathways, and the latter allows glucose the option of returning to the bloodstream. Once in the bloodstream, the glucose can be transported to muscle cells.

Muscle cells do not possess glucose-6-phosphatase and thus cannot release their glucose, when cleaved from glycogen, back into circulation. This situation creates an interesting dilemma. Glycogen reserves of nonworking muscles cannot be transferred to the working muscles, because once inside a muscle cell, glucose must remain there and be metabolized within that cell. Thus, a partial explanation for why competitors in a long endurance event such as marathon

Glucose dynamics in a muscle cell

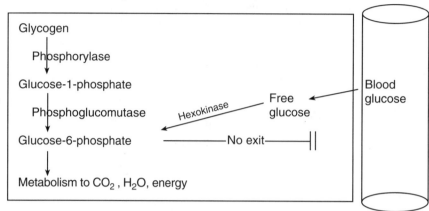

Glucose dynamics in a liver cell

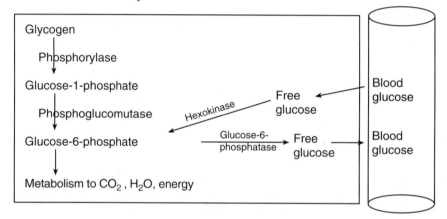

Figure 3.11 Glucose dynamics in muscle as compared to liver cells.

running often prefer race courses with periodic, slight elevation changes may be that the accompanying variation in muscle activation permits the sharing of glycogen reserves among a larger number of working muscles.

For every gram of glycogen stored, approximately 3.0 gm of H_2O are stored with it to maintain osmotic equilibrium (Costill and Miller 1980). This contributes in part to weight gain as marathon runners taper their training before a race and continue their carbohydrate intake. Such weight monitoring is done commonly by these longer-endurance-event athletes as they attempt to maximize their carbohydrate stores a few days before the race. As glycogen is metabolized during the race, this bound H_2O, together with the H_2O released from fuel breakdown, can serve as an important contribution to available body H_2O supplies. On a warm day, as H_2O is lost from perspiration, this can be an asset.

Anaerobic Glycolysis: Glucose Breakdown to Pyruvate

Both glycogen and glucose are metabolized in the fluid portion of cells—the *cytoplasm*, or in the jargon of muscle physiologists, the *sarcoplasm*. The entire process, from breakdown of glycogen to glucose and then to pyruvic acid, can proceed without O_2 involvement; hence it is termed anaerobic. The major chemical reactions involved in this conversion are summarized in figure 3.12.

Notice in figure 3.12 that we have divided glycolysis into two phases. The initial phase requires an input of ATP and eventually splits the glucose molecule (which has six carbon atoms) into two 3-carbon units. Each of these is then broken down to pyruvate, with generation of small quantities of ATP. We must subtract the energy input in this initial phase from the energy output obtained during the second phase to determine the net energy production. This is an interesting task, because there is a difference in the energy dynamics of glucose derived from muscle glycogen breakdown versus glucose derived from the liver and sent through the blood to that same muscle. Figure 3.13 illustrates this.

When glucose within a muscle cell is obtained from glycogen, one ATP is required to provide energy and initiate the breakdown process. Enough energy to create four ATPs will be generated. The net gain is three ATPs. Glucose entering a muscle cell from the liver via the blood requires two ATPs to initiate breakdown, with four ATPs again generated. This is a net gain of only two ATPs. The implication of this is that, for purposes of metabolic efficiency, muscle cells should rely on their own stored glycogen instead of on glucose mobilized from the liver. Indeed, for distance races through the half-marathon distance and for training runs under 30 km (18.6 mi) this is not a problem, because muscle glycogen stores are probably adequate. Marathoners, however, have some logistical problems regarding their energy dynamics, which will be discussed in chapter 7 in connection with their prerace training preparation.

In phase I of glycolysis shown in figure 3.12, notice the substance labeled *NAD*, permitting conversion of fructose-1,6(PO_4)2 to 1,3-diphosphoglycerate. This substance is called *nicotinamide adenine dinucleotide* (NAD), and its structure is indicated in figure 3.14. Biochemists call it a *coenzyme*, of which several can be identified. Notice that an integral part of its structure is nicotinic acid; this is *vitamin B_5*. We shall see that several water-soluble vitamins are essential to the success of glucose metabolism, which emphasizes the need for adequate dietary vitamin intake. The oxidized form of NAD is required to catalyze the reaction that produces 1,3-diphosphoglycerate. In the process, NAD is reduced (or hydrogenated) to $NADH_2$. Under aerobic conditions, O_2 eventually permits the removal of H^+ ions from this coenzyme, regenerating NAD and permitting more substrate (glucose) breakdown to occur. Thus, adequate O_2 implies adequate NAD, which permits continuing glycolysis.

However, we know that glycolysis can occur anaerobically. How do we produce NAD in the absence of adequate O_2? The answer is relatively simple. Pyruvate already available is converted to lactate, using $NADH_2$ and the enzyme lactic dehydrogenase (LDH). The equation for this reaction is as follows:

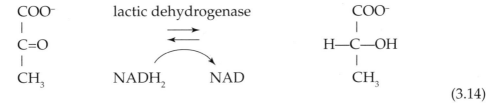

$$\text{(3.14)}$$

This therefore is the biochemical reasoning that can explain lactate production in muscles when O_2 supplies are inadequate. It provides a mechanism for NAD production, which in turn allows glycolysis to continue. The LDH enzyme occurs in two forms, depending on location. In the heart, as well as in ST skeletal muscles, the *H-LDH isoenzyme* (H for heart) exists, and its action shifts the

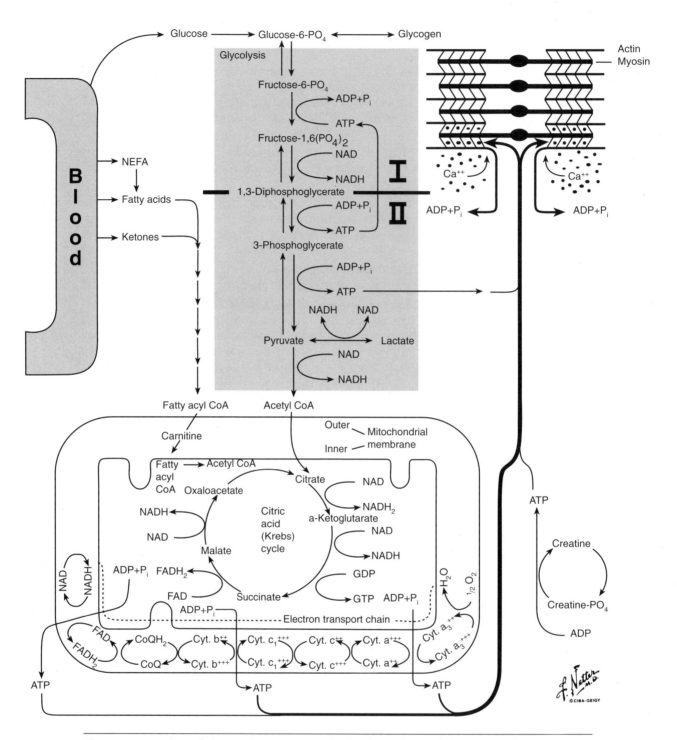

Figure 3.12 Outline of chemical reactions involved in breakdown of glucose and fatty acids for energy. For glucose, initial breakdown occurs in the cytoplasm (anaerobically), with eventual formation of small two-carbon (acetyl) fragments that combine with coenzyme A (CoA) for entry into the mitochondria as acetyl coenzyme A units. Each acetyl group can combine with oxalacetate to form citrate, which then is further degraded in a series of reactions collectively known as the citric acid (Krebs) cycle. Hydrogen atoms released by this breakdown sequence (or their corresponding electrons) are eventually transferred by way of the electron transport chain to oxygen. Energy released by this transfer is directed toward formation of ATP from ADP. In this manner, energy from fuel breakdown is available for crucial cellular functions such as tension generation in muscle cells, which utilizes energy stored as ATP. *Note.* From *Musculoskeletal System, Part I* (The Ciba Collection of Medical Illustrations, Vol. 8) (p. 162) by F.H. Netter, 1987, Summit, NJ: CIBA-GEIGY. Reproduced with permission from the CIBA collection of Medical Illustrations by Frank H. Netter, MD. All rights reserved.

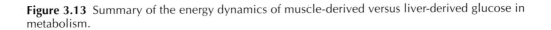

Muscle cell-derived

Glycogen ⟶ glucose-1-PO₄: no ATP needed

Glucose-1-PO₄ ⟶ pyruvate: one ATP needed

Glucose-1-PO₄ ⟶ pyruvate: four ATPs produced

Net gain: three ATPs

Liver cell-derived

Free glucose (from liver
via blood) ⟶ glucose-1-PO₄: one ATP needed

Glucose-1-PO₄ ⟶ pyruvate: one ATP needed

Glucose-1-PO₄ ⟶ pyruvate: four ATPs produced

Net gain: two ATPs

Figure 3.13 Summary of the energy dynamics of muscle-derived versus liver-derived glucose in metabolism.

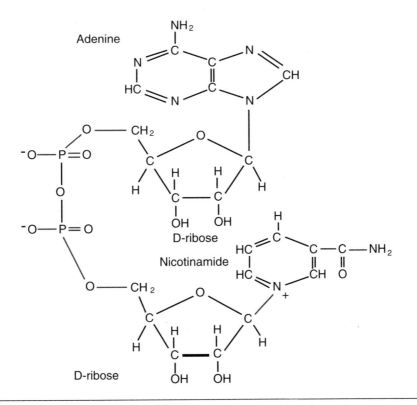

Figure 3.14 Chemical structure of nicotinamide adenine dinucleotide (NAD), a coenzyme that contains a sugar (ribose), adenine, and nicotinic acid (vitamin B_5).

direction of the reaction toward the left, thereby minimizing lactate formation. In FT skeletal muscles, the *M-LDH isoenzyme* (M for muscle) favors a right-shifted equilibrium, thereby permitting more lactate to form.

Runners attempting to race or train at near-maximal paces over distances between 200 m and 800 m cannot continue for very long at those intensities. Despite excellent adaptations with training for aerobic metabolism (increased myoglobin and hemoglobin for O_2 storage and transport, increased capillarization, increased CO_2 excretion and acid buffering, and increased reservoirs of high-energy PO_4^{3-}), O_2 demand still exceeds O_2 supply. Anaerobic metabolism adds to the total energy supply available, but the process is both inefficient and self-limiting. How is this process inefficient? Recall equations (3.7) and (3.9), which indicate that anaerobic metabolism of glucose requires 18 times more substrate than aerobic metabolism to produce the same amount of ATP.

How is it self-limiting? As the acidity within working muscle cells increases, the functional capability of certain key glycolytic enzymes decreases, thereby slowing the rate of fuel breakdown. This is a safety mechanism to prevent cell destruction. Should acidosis become excessive, it could be catastrophic for muscle cell activity due to the presence of intracellular organelles called *lysosomes*. These contain a variety of enzymes capable of causing digestion of the muscle cells themselves. Their outer membrane is unstable under acidic conditions. If rupture occurs, cell death will result. Thus, anaerobic metabolism must be a powerfully self-limiting process that shuts itself off when it produces such "environmental" pollution that its own existence is threatened.

The need for such an all-powerful inhibition is obvious when we observe runners in events such as the 400-m dash and the 800-m run, particularly the final stages. They struggle valiantly to maintain pace, more than willing to endure almost any amount of discomfort if it will produce victory. Gradual inhibition of metabolism in their prime movers brings an inevitable slowing of pace unless other accessory muscles can be implemented to provide additional energy output. This is often seen as they start to toe out, thereby utilizing additional leg muscles that still have aerobic capabilities. Biomechanically this may not appear very stylish, but it just may make the difference between winning and losing. If these runners didn't have metabolic inhibition to shut down their excessively acidotic cells, extensive cell death and dissolution of their leg muscles could occur. Indeed, this does occur in certain pathological situations and is termed *rhabdomyolysis*.

Can athletes take precautions prior to beginning their intensive training sessions or races to manage excessive muscle acidity? There certainly are, and one of them is the familiar prerun *warm-up*, defined as a period prior to more intense activity when mild exercise is performed. Along with cool-down following hard work, warm-up is another necessary step in the energy continuum. Enzymes work optimally at temperatures slightly above the normal core temperature of about 37° C (98° F). Initial easy jogging with transition into faster but still easy running raises metabolism and thus body temperature and improves circulation. Not only is enzyme-controlled fuel breakdown enhanced, but the muscles also improve their elasticity, permitting greater range of joint movement.

Aerobic Glycolysis: Metabolism of Pyruvate

If glucose metabolism is to continue beyond the formation of pyruvate and lactate with eventual release of large amounts of energy, then adequate O_2 must be available for the complete breakdown of these intermediate substances. Earlier we referred to this aerobic glycolysis as one of the four primary energy systems for living tissues (Hawley and Hopkins 1995). Whereas anaerobic glycolysis occurs in the cytoplasm, the chemical reactions for aerobic glycolysis occur in the mitochondria. Thus, pyruvate must be transported across the mitochondrial membrane. Figures 3.12 and 3.15 help to illustrate how this occurs.

Notice that pyruvate is first degraded further to a two-carbon fragment called an *acetyl group*, with a loss of CO_2 in the process. This acetyl group combines with a molecule called *coenzyme A*, forming *acetyl coenzyme A*. Figure 3.16 illustrates the structure of this coenzyme. Notice how it is similar to both NAD and ATP. All three molecules have adenine coupled to a sugar called ribose. NAD and coenzyme A have vitamins attached to the sugar. NAD has nicotinic acid and coenzyme A has pantothenic acid (*vitamin B_3*). In figure 3.15 the acetyl group of pyruvate is circled, allowing us to observe how coenzyme A participates in transferring this group across the mitochondrial membrane and to the four-carbon substance called oxalacetic acid (oxalacetate). The combination of the two-carbon acetyl group with the four-carbon oxalacetic acid molecule forms the six-carbon compound citric acid. Coenzyme A thus serves to transfer cytoplasmic glucose fragments into the mitochondria without itself being altered. The renowned British biochemist Sir Hans Krebs (1970) first delineated the complete set of reactions whereby citric acid is subsequently broken down to oxalacetic acid, permitting a repetitive cycle whereby additional acetyl groups from pyruvate can be utilized to form more citric acid. This series of reactions is commonly referred to as the *Krebs cycle* or *citric acid cycle.*

Through subsequent degradation involving several intermediate steps indicated in figure 3.12, the two-carbon acetyl group is degraded to CO_2 and H^+ ions. Each step is enzymatically controlled, and no O_2 is consumed directly in the process. For glucose, eight H^+ ions are generated (four for each two-carbon acetyl group). The steps in which H^+ ions are removed are called *dehydrogenation* steps. Notice that NAD serves as the hydrogen acceptor in three of them. In the fourth, FAD does this. FAD is *flavin adenine dinucleotide*, a relative of NAD except that still another vitamin, riboflavin (*vitamin B_2*), is substituted for nicotinamide. Figure 3.17 depicts the structure of FAD.

Four points concerning this Krebs cycle reaction sequence are important.

- First, O_2 plays only an indirect role, because its presence in the cell permits oxidation of $NADH_2$ to NAD (through removal of two H^+ ions to form H_2O). Without NAD, which permits conversion of dihydrolipoic acid to lipoic acid (lipoate), acetyl coenzyme A production could not occur (figure 3.15).

- Second, this series of reactions connects anaerobic and aerobic aspects of carbohydrate breakdown. Metabolism of glucose via the formation of acetyl coenzyme A occurs in the cell cytoplasm, but further degradation of the acetyl group can only occur in mitochondria.

- Third, note that this reaction sequence, from pyruvate to acetyl coenzyme A, marks the first instance where a glucose-derived carbon atom is lost (in the form of CO_2). Thus, this sequence is irreversible and for that reason alone exceedingly important. This is a key transition in glucose utilization from a biochemical viewpoint.

- Fourth, notice in figure 3.15 that an additional vitamin, thiamine (*vitamin B_1*), plays a vital role in this sequence by mediating the transfer of the acetyl group of pyruvate to lipoate.

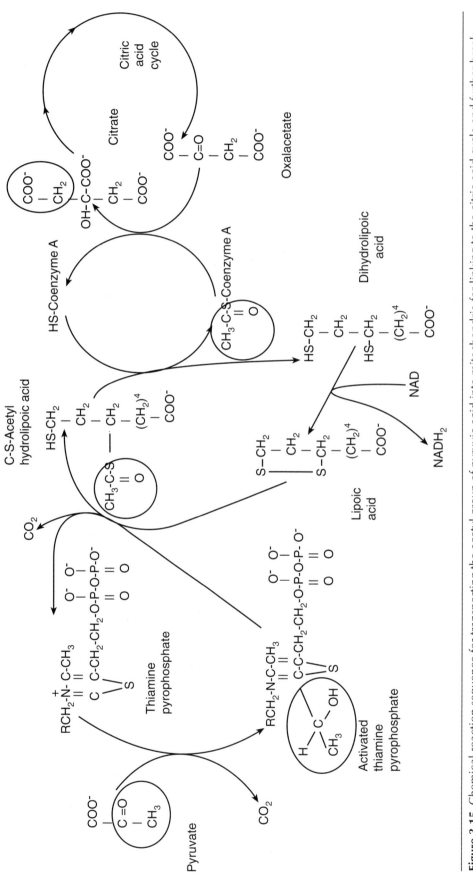

Figure 3.15 Chemical reaction sequence for transporting the acetyl group of pyruvic acid into mitochondria for linking to the citric acid cycle and further breakdown.

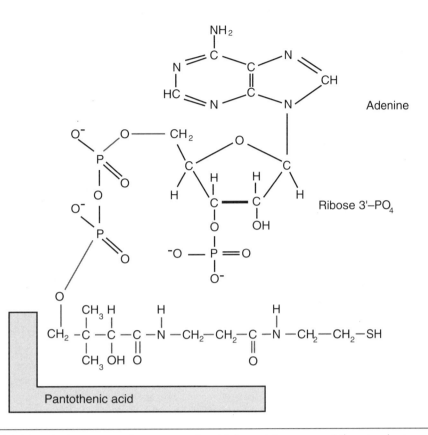

Figure 3.16 Chemical structure of coenzyme A, which contains a sugar (ribose), adenine, and pantothenic acid (vitamin B$_3$).

Electron Transport Chain

Although the Krebs cycle indeed describes the fate of the carbon skeleton of the acetyl portion of pyruvate, the cycle itself is not concerned directly with the mechanism of energy conservation. Energy conservation involves the H$^+$ ions (with their electrons) that have been gathered up and bound to NAD or FAD (figures 3.14 and 3.17). These reduced molecules, NADH$_2$ and FADH$_2$, will donate their electrons to another series of enzymes, collectively termed the *electron*

THE IMPORTANCE OF VITAMINS

Vitamins are organic substances that the body cannot synthesize but that are required for metabolic reactions. We have, through evolution, lost the genes required for their synthesis, and thus they must be ingested as part of our normal food intake. The *minimum daily requirement* (MDR) is the quantity of each of these essential nutrients required to permit normal physiological function without signs of deficiency. The *recommended dietary allowance* (RDA) in the United States is the level of daily intake considered in the judg-

ment of members of the U.S. Food and Nutrition Board as adequate to meet the known nutritional needs of practically all healthy people. RDA values are usually higher than MDR values.

A common interest among exercise-conscious people is to ensure that they have enough vitamins. Fair enough, as they're important in metabolism. But how much is enough? Glowing testimonials by over-the-counter health food product manufacturers in fitness magazines suggest improved capability to train or race following the use of specific brands of megavitamin supplements or individual vitamin preparations available only from mail-order outlets or specialty shops often referred to as health food stores (Jarvis 1983). Proprietors of such establishments argue for the people's right to freedom of choice and urge the correct choice (obviously, their specific product). The alternative, of course, is the more practical mode of consuming nutritious fresh foods that have plenty of vitamins in wide variety, along with necessary energy fuels, H_2O, and trace elements.

Because metabolism proceeds in a precise fashion, specific quantities of each vitamin are required. Water-soluble vitamins, such as the B series described previously, that are ingested through megadose supplementation but are not required in such excess will be excreted through the urine. This seems a waste of money. In terms of the B vitamins, excellent nonmanufactured sources include green leafy vegetables, nuts, and yeast. This explains why many so-called health food stores emphasize specialized mixtures of yeasts or nuts and seeds. The cost of these mixtures typically exceeds that of equally excellent and tasty sources of these vitamins such as a daily tossed salad of fresh vegetables obtained from a local grocery store or farmer's market (both of which, incidentally, also are "health food stores").

There is no sensible justification for megavitamin ingestion in terms of performance enhancement (Weight, Myburgh, and Noakes 1988). Even athletes devoting several hours each day to their training do not require as much nutrition or energy as is often suspected. A marathon run by a 132-lb (60-kg) runner requires approximately 2,600 kcal (10,880 kJ), roughly equivalent to that individual's daily energy requirement without training. In other words, that runner has gained a day's requirement in meals. True, this is a sizably increased energy requirement, but it is perhaps twice the normal required vitamin intake, not the many-times-greater-than-RDA often provided in megavitamin preparations. And seldom do runners engage in the equivalent of a marathon's energy requirement in a day's training.

It is often suggested that large supplemental vitamin ingestion may be required if an athlete is so busy that he or she skips meals. The practice of skipping meals itself should be reevaluated. Adequate nutritional intake is essential to maintain supplies of energy fuels, minerals, and vitamins.

Athletes would be well-advised to stay away from the nutritional supplement industry and to resist the many seemingly wonderful offers of "new products" "tested in the Orient" and "used by other top-class athletes" that "yield greater fitness gains." The well-established standards in the food industry and the drug industry that prevent industry fraud do not extend to the supplement industry. While the active ingredient may in fact be present in the concoction, there is no guarantee that it will be absorbed and no guarantee that the filler will not cause diarrhea or constipation. While testimonials by high-visibility athletes may add "star power" to the potential worth of the supplement in question, these typically are paid for, which creates a questionable bias. Also, elite athletes' credibility is with their athletic performances rather than with the requisite technical knowledge of the product's legitimacy. Remember the old adage that "if it seems too good to be true, it probably is." The supplement industry is all about market share: Acquiring a small percentage of the share of what people consume—a huge market—in turn brings a sizable profit. Grandma was correct: Nutritious and tasty meals are both essential and enjoyable and ensure proper food balance with all the required vitamins in their correct proportions. Plenty of quality nutrition through healthy foods should be a top priority for any athlete; this is an important (and delightful) part of the training process!

transport chain, illustrated at the bottom of figure 3.12. This is the final common pathway by which energy derived from the various cellular fuels—fatty acids, carbohydrates, and even proteins—is harvested, ultimately through interaction with O_2, the final oxidant or electron acceptor in aerobic cells. This phase of fuel breakdown is thus the "financial end" of the business of cellular metabolism, for this is where the metabolic "currency," ATP, is produced.

The complex sequence of reactions in the electron transport system involves several molecules of quite diverse structure, of which only a few are illustrated

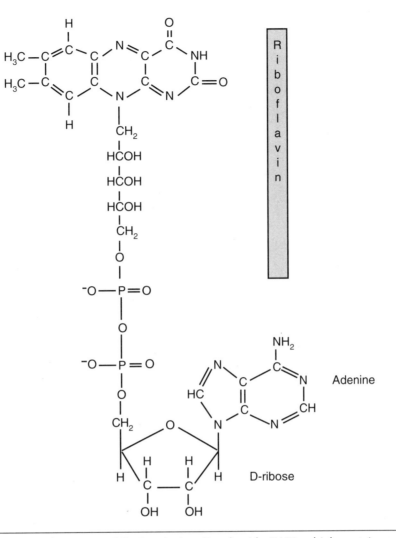

Figure 3.17 Chemical structure of flavin adenine dinucleotide (FAD), which contains a sugar (ribose), adenine, and riboflavin (vitamin B_2).

in figure 3.12. A group of proteins, known collectively as *cytochromes* (abbreviated *cyt*), have a molecular similarity to hemoglobin; one important difference is in the oxidative state of iron within their molecular structure. In hemoglobin, iron exists in the ferrous (Fe^{2+}) state, but in cytochromes it is in the ferric (Fe^{3+}) state. Each cytochrome in its oxidized form (i.e., with Fe^{3+}) can accept an electron from a hydrogen atom and become reduced (Fe^{3+} becomes Fe^{2+}). The hydrogen atom becomes a H^+ ion and thus contributes to the acidity of the medium. In turn, this cytochrome can then donate its electron to the next carrier in its oxidized form, and so on, almost like the children's game of tossing a hot potato. Notice, for example, how cytochrome b^{3+} transfers an electron to cytochrome c_1^{2+}, forming cytochrome c_1^{3+} and cytochrome b^{2+}. The final cytochrome, called cytochrome a_3^{3+} or cytochrome oxidase, gives up its electron to molecular O_2 directly. As two electrons attach to an oxygen atom, two H^+ ions also bind, and H_2O forms as a result. Each electron transfer releases considerable free energy, which is harvested as ATP. Figure 3.12 represents only a simplified version of a much more complex system. In addition to the cytochrome pigments, other substances are involved, including coenzyme Q (CoQ) and FAD and NAD as well.

We may now write an energy balance sheet for glucose oxidation, as shown in figure 3.18, and summarize how much energy is produced and from where in the overall metabolic pathway outlined in figure 3.12. We need two ATPs to initiate glycolysis, and four ATPs are recovered. Four hydrogen atoms are released in the anaerobic phase of glycolysis bound as $NADH_2$. For every two hydrogen atoms carried, three ATPs are produced if delivery into the electron transport system is via NAD. Thus, these four hydrogen atoms yield six ATPs of energy. Four hydrogen atoms are released in the transfer of pyruvate to coenzyme A; this yields six ATPs because NAD is again the carrier. In the Krebs cycle, six sets of two hydrogen atoms are released to NAD, yielding 18 ATPs. Two sets of two hydrogen atoms are released to FAD, and here only four ATPs are generated (two ATPs per hydrogen atom pair). Thus, the Krebs cycle production of ATP is 11 ATPs per acetyl group, or 22 ATPs per mole of glucose. The processes preceding the Krebs cycle produce 16 ATPs, with 2 ATPs lost in sequence initiation. The net ATP production, therefore, is 22 + 16 − 2 = 36.

Metabolism of Fats: Aerobic Lipolysis

We have thus far emphasized carbohydrate metabolism, but we must realize that this is only part of the story of providing energy for metabolism. Far more stored energy is available in fats than in carbohydrates. Thus, it is fats that provide the main energy supply for the entire exercise continuum that ranges from rest through marathon racing and beyond. This so-called *aerobic lipolysis* is the fourth primary energy system in living tissues (Hawley and Hopkins 1995). The higher the potential for fatty acid oxidation in muscle, the better the endurance performance capacity of that muscle. In the heart this capacity is enormous.

Glycogen and triglycerides have a similar initial pattern of catabolism. An activated phosphorylase and lipase, respectively, interact with cyclic 3',5'-AMP to initiate the fuel breakdown sequence (figure 3.10). Fatty acids released by this process must then enter the mitochondria for subsequent catabolism. Movement across the double mitochondrial membrane requires coupling to a substance called *carnitine*. This occurs in a three-step process. First, coupling of acetyl coenzyme A to the fatty acid molecule produces a fatty acyl coenzyme A, which crosses the outer mitochondrial membrane, as shown in figure 3.12. Then, the enzyme *carnitine acyltransferase I* exchanges carnitine for coenzyme A, forming fatty acylcarnitine. This crosses the inner mitochondrial membrane. Finally, *carnitine acyltransferase II* exchanges carnitine for intramitochondrial coenzyme A, reforming fatty acyl coenzyme A. The coupling of carnitine to fatty acyl coenzyme A is thus the rate-limiting step for the speed of fatty acid oxidation. This may also explain why endurance-trained runners have more carnitine in their skeletal muscles—it provides a greater capability for utilizing fatty acids as fuel (de Palo et al. 1986).

Now a systematic, enzyme-directed cleavage of two-carbon units begins from the multicarbon fatty acid skeleton. This reaction sequence is called *beta oxidation*, because cleavage occurs at the second (beta) carbon instead of the first (alpha). With the 16-carbon palmitic acid, for example, seven cleavages of acetyl groups would achieve complete breakdown. Each two-carbon acetyl fragment combines with coenzyme A inside the mitochondrion to form acetyl coenzyme

2 ATP required to initiate glycolysis

4 H$^+$ released in anaerobic glycolysis and bound as NADH$_2$		+ 6 ATP
4 ATP produced in anaerobic glycolysis		+ 4 ATP
4 H$^+$ released in pyruvate conversion to acetyl CoA and bound as NADH$_2$		+ 6 ATP
6 sets of 2 H$^+$ released in Krebs cycle and bound as NADH$_2$		+18 ATP
2 sets of 2 H$^+$ released in Krebs cycle and bound as FADH$_2$		+ 4 ATP
(2 ATP required to initiate glycolysis)	Total ATP less 2 lost	38 - 2
	Net ATP	36

Figure 3.18 Energy balance sheet for glucose oxidation.

A (figure 3.12). Interaction with oxalacetate and formation of citrate, as with carbohydrate breakdown, permits eventual energy release in accordance with principles that we have already discussed regarding the Krebs cycle and electron transport chain.

Interaction of Carbohydrate and Fat Metabolism During Exercise

During rest, fats available as plasma fatty acids (from adipose tissue stores) and muscle triglycerides are our dominant source of energy. Carbohydrates also contribute energy, available as muscle glycogen and plasma glucose. Think of fats as the main burner of a gas stove, and carbohydrates as the pilot light. Now let's compare the relative contributions of these energy stores at three increasing work levels: when walking (25% of $\dot{V}O_2$max), when running at marathon race pace (65%-85% of $\dot{V}O_2$max), and when racing over the 10-km distance (85%-92% $\dot{V}O_2$max) (Coyle 1995). Although there is a steady increase in the *total* energy expenditure from *both* fats and carbohydrates, a dramatic change occurs in the *relative* contributions of each fuel source for providing the energy.

At 65% of $\dot{V}O_2$max there is a greater relative energy contribution from plasma glucose and muscle triglycerides and a decrease in relative contribution from plasma fatty acids. The contribution from muscle glycogen is negligible. From 65% $\dot{V}O_2$max to 85% $\dot{V}O_2$max, the increasing contribution from plasma glucose continues, and the energy contribution from both muscle triglycerides and plasma fatty acids declines. A very large contribution from muscle glycogen provides a majority of the additional required energy. Training increases the amount of intramuscular triglyceride available for this purpose. However, beyond 85% $\dot{V}O_2$max the increased O$_2$ demands for such exercise rapidly exceed

O_2 intake capability for complete metabolism. Only carbohydrate can be utilized for this anaerobic metabolism, and thus carbohydrate plays an increasingly important role.

Training increases both the numbers and the size of mitochondria in the skeletal muscles. It is here that the enzymes are located for complete metabolism of fats and carbohydrates—these are the familiar Krebs cycle enzymes, and they are the same for either fuel. Having more of these enzymes increases the potential fuel metabolic rate in those tissues; if these are working muscles, their movement capability is increased. In particular, endurance training increases intramuscular triglyceride and glycogen stores. The mandatory requirement for carbohydrate at faster paces, as well as the requirement for carbohydrate intake to replace the always fairly low supplies of it in comparison to fats, means that there is little justification for the recent trend among purveyors of energy bars to promote a higher dietary fat intake (Coyle 1995; Sherman and Leenders 1995).

Running pace and the length of time that this pace can be maintained are thus related inversely. Running too fast for too long starts to limit continued performance at that pace because of accumulation of tissue and blood lactic acid. The H^+ ions from excessive lactate accumulation inhibit the action of phosphofructokinase, thereby decreasing glycolysis. These H^+ ions also compete with Ca^{2+} ions for the binding sites that regulate actin-myosin interaction (Katz 1970). Thus, although H^+ ions seem to be "metabolic monsters" in causing such inhibition of fuel breakdown, their presence is beneficial from two points of view. By slowing the rate of metabolism, they keep acidity levels from reaching a critical point where lysosome-mediated cell destruction could occur. Also, they directly inhibit smooth muscle tone in adjacent arterioles delivering blood to the region, thereby enhancing perfusion and with it the distribution of fuel, O_2, and buffers.

SUMMARY

Better Training Through Chemistry

1. The primary purpose of training is to increase our biochemical potential: to increase the rate at which we can metabolize fuel and the duration that this rate can be maintained. Energy resulting from this metabolism permits movement. Effective racing is all about sustained, high-level energy production. Four energy-producing systems have been described: the phosphagen system, anaerobic glycolysis, aerobic glycolysis, and aerobic lipolysis. Each has its place in metabolism for sport.

2. The energy currency for muscular work is ATP (1 mol represents about 46 kJ or 11 kcal of energy). ATP is provided through release of energy from high-energy phosphate bonding to creatine (as creatine phosphate, or CP) and adenosine diphosphate (ADP). Depending on the intensity with which training or competitive work is carried out, CP or ADP will be the primary energy source.

3. Short bursts of high-speed sprinting of about 20 s can be managed entirely by available stores of CP in the muscles. These CP stores will be replenished during this brief space of time by ATP without the need for other types of metabolism. Such explosiveness, however, is seen more in sprinting than in middle- and long-distance running.

4. Work at high intensity carried out over a longer time period—that is, between 20 s and about 4 min—demands far more energy than can be provided by the intake of O_2 to provide complete (or aerobic) fuel breakdown. The O_2 consumption for racing distances such as 200 m to 400 m, for example, is in excess of 100 ml $\cdot$ kg^{-1} $\cdot$ min^{-1}, which has never been achieved in humans. The highest $\dot{V}O_2$max ever recorded is around 92 ml $\cdot$ kg^{-1} $\cdot$ min^{-1}. Thus, we must produce the extra energy anaerobically.

5. The fuel used for this anaerobic metabolism is carbohydrate, such as glucose. The process is very inefficient: For every unit of glucose broken down, only about 1/18 as much energy is released as when it is metabolized completely using O_2. The process is also self-limiting, because a rapid buildup of lactic acid shuts off the metabolic system to prevent its destruction.

6. As racing times lengthen from about 4 min through 90 min, it becomes increasingly possible for metabolic O_2 demands to be better met by ongoing O_2 intake. Muscle cell stores of glycogen and triglyceride are available as fuels for aerobic metabolism (aerobic glycolysis and lipolysis), as well as bloodborne glucose and fatty acids. The continuing requirement for variable amounts of anaerobic metabolism will be provided by anaerobic glycolysis. The maintainable pace for any selected race distance depends on the tolerable discomfort caused by H$^+$ ion accumulation.

7. At marathon distances and beyond, metabolism essentially must remain below the threshold at which anaerobic metabolites such as lactic acid accumulate in the bloodstream, otherwise the discomfort cannot be tolerated for this extended period. The slower rate of fat metabolism than carbohydrate, as well as its requirement for adequate O_2 for its complete metabolism, makes it a steadily more important fuel source for very long distances, especially those well beyond the marathon distance.

8. The goal of training is to improve the ability of muscle cells to increase O_2 utilization so that at any particular pace the anaerobic contribution is smaller than before. Then, when anaerobic contributions become sizable, the goal is to have increased the ability of muscle cells to manage (buffer) the effects of acidosis. Long-term training increases the number and size of mitochondria, where the enzymes for aerobic glycolysis and lipolysis are located, and so the size of the "metabolic engines" increases. The amounts of stored energy sources (muscle creatine phosphate) and fuels (muscle glycogen and triglyceride), as well as an increased plasma volume, increase the metabolic potential and the capability for diluting metabolic acids.

9. The working tissues will be best able to manage the rigors of hard training when they are metabolically ready. A process of warm-up before exercise increases muscle blood flow gradually and adequately, thereby ensuring that the tissues have increased their metabolism aerobically and that blood flow to the entire region is increased. After this generalized warm-up, still more intense effort, the nature of which depends on the proposed race event or training assignment, will provide sufficient vasodilation through lactic acid formation that blood flow is enhanced even further. In turn, the increased O_2 availability sets the stage for optimal muscle performance when the activity begins.

10. Similarly, when training is completed, a period of cool-down—easy running—begins the process of restoring resting metabolism by continued perfusion of stressed muscles with nutrition for energy replenishment and with O_2 for complete metabolism of anaerobic metabolites such as lactate.

11. A healthy diet will permit the intake of all the necessary fuels, vitamins, minerals, and electrolytes that are required for this high level of metabolism. There is no need for specialized nutrient supplementation from the incredible variety of individualized potions and mixtures offered in pill, tablet, and other forms, despite the hype. This is merely an attempt to take away market share from purveyors of wholesome, nutritious, well-balanced foods. A wide variety of tasty fresh fruits and vegetables; pasta and breads; meat, poultry, and fish; and dairy products ought to form the mainstay of any runner's diet. Eating is a very important part of the training process, and it should be enjoyable. A rule of thumb is to "shop around the walls" of grocery stores, as the fresh items are typically arranged there. Healthy athletes should aim for a diet that is roughly 60% carbohydrate, 25% fat, and 15% protein.

References

Costill, D.L.; Bowers, R.; Branam, G.; and Sparks, K. 1971. Muscle glycogen utilization during prolonged exercise on consecutive days. *Journal of Applied Physiology* 31:834-838.

Costill, D.L., and Miller, J.M. 1980. Nutrition for endurance sport: Carbohydrate and fluid balance. *International Journal of Sports Medicine* 1:2-14.

Coyle, E.F. 1995. Fat metabolism during exercise. *Sport Science Exchange* 8(6):1-6.

de Palo, E.; de Palo, C.; Macor, C.; Gatti, R.; Federspil, G.; and Scandellari, C. 1986. Plasma free fatty acid, carnitine and acetylcarnitine levels as useful biochemical parameters in muscular exercise. In *Biochemical aspects of physical exercise*, eds. G. Benzi, L. Packer, and N. Siliprandi, 461-467. Amsterdam: Elsevier Science.

Embden, G. 1925. Chemismus der Muskelkontraktion und Chemie der Muskulatur. In *Bethes' Handbuch der normalen und pathologischen Physiologie,* vol. VIII/1, 369. Berlin.

Gladden, L.B. 1989. Lactate uptake by skeletal muscle. *Exercise and Sports Sciences Reviews* 17:115-155.

Hawley, J.A., and Hopkins, W.G. 1995. Aerobic glycolytic and aerobic lipolytic power systems. *Sports Medicine* 19:240-250.

Hunt, S.M., and Groff, J.L. 1990. *Advanced nutrition and human metabolism.* St. Paul, MN: West.

Jarvis, W.T. 1983. Food: Faddism, cultism, and quackery. *Annual Review of Nutrition* 52:3-35.

Jéquier, E., and Flatt, J.-P. 1986. Recent advances in human energetics. *News in Physiological Sciences* 1:112-114.

Katz, A.M. 1970. Contractile proteins of the heart. *Physiological Reviews* 50:63-158.

Krebs, H. 1970. The history of the tricarboxylic acid cycle. *Perspectives in Biology and Medicine* 14:154-170.

Lehninger, A.L. 1982. *Principles of biochemistry.* New York: Worth.

Lohmann, K. 1934. Über die enzymatische Aufspaltung der Kreatinphosphorsäure; zugleich ein Beitrag zum Chemismus der Muskelkontraktion. *Biochemische Zeitschrift* 271:264.

Netter, F.H. 1987. *Musculoskeletal system, Part 1.* Vol. 8 of *The Ciba collection of medical illustrations.* Summit, NJ: Ciba-Geigy.

Rogers, M.A.; Stull, G.A.; and Apple, F.S. 1985. Creatine kinase isoenzyme activities in men and women following a marathon race. *Medicine and Science in Sports and Exercise* 17:679-682.

Sherman, W.M., and Leenders, N. 1995. Fat loading: The next magic bullet? *International Journal of Sports Nutrition* 5:S1-12.

Weight, L.M.; Myburgh, K.H.; and Noakes, T.D. 1988. Vitamin and mineral supplementation: Effect on the running performance of trained athletes. *American Journal of Clinical Nutrition* 47:192-195.

Whipp, B.J. 1987. Dynamics of pulmonary gas exchange. *Circulation* 76(suppl. 6):18-28.

HEART, LUNG, AND BLOOD ADAPTATIONS TO RUNNING

Observing a group of elite distance runners warming up before an important race is much like seeing a diesel locomotive idling in a railroad yard, its 100 or so freight cars being connected in preparation for its next trip. There is no way that we can really appreciate the enormous work capabilities of these two "engines" until we see them in action—runners competing at a near-world-record pace and the locomotive ascending a mountain grade with relative ease.

Once nerves and skeletal muscles have been stimulated to create movement, it is the combined activity of the heart and blood vessels, the lungs, and the blood flowing through the highly active tissues that determine how intensely, and for how long, a runner can perform. Thus, a working knowledge of how these systems interact is important for coaches and athletes to develop effective strategies for improving functional abilities. The overall view of the cardiopulmonary system involves a pump that can vary its output (the *heart*) and a given volume of fluid (the *blood*) that is contained within a space that can vary in its volume (the *vascular capacity* of the blood vessels). This blood interfaces with a gas exchanger (the *lungs*) each time it circulates through the body. The pressure on the blood vessel walls is determined by the existing blood volume and the variable muscle tone in those vessel walls, which tends to make the vascular capacity larger or smaller. Lung blood flow increases along with lung ventilation, and the venous blood returning to the lungs from the rest of the body exits the lungs almost fully oxygenated and free of excess CO_2. Thus, blood flow, blood volume, blood gas (O_2 and CO_2) concentration, blood pressure, and blood distribution all exist within a framework of *variability* to meet ongoing needs and cope with changing demands.

We can begin to comprehend the magnitude of the performance increase from the idling to the competing state of an elite distance runner by comparing values for a few physiological variables at rest and during all-out exercise. One of the most impressive increases is in the amount of O_2 used by the tissues. Resting O_2 consumption averages 3.5 ml per kilogram of body weight per minute (in the jargon of exercise physiology this is written as $3.5 \text{ ml} \cdot \text{kg}^{-1} \cdot \text{min}^{-1}$); for a 60-kg athlete this is 210 ml/min. But this O_2 uptake can increase to as much as $85 \text{ ml} \cdot \text{kg}^{-1} \cdot \text{min}^{-1}$ and more in highly trained male runners—more than 5 L/min. This so-called $\dot{V}O_2max$ for trained endurance athletes is more than twice that typically found among untrained people. Clearly, an enormously successful teamwork occurs among the various tissues of the body to move O_2 from the mouth to the mitochondria of highly active muscle cells. There is a functional *coupling* of *external respiration* (breathing O_2 into the body) with *internal respiration* (cellular O_2 utilization) in meeting the challenge of exercise (Wasserman 1984). Breathing rate can increase to 45 or 50 breaths/min, compared with roughly 12 at rest. Total expired airflow can increase 30 times, from 6 to 180 L/min. Blood pumped out of the heart (the *cardiac output*) may increase eightfold, from 5 L/min at rest to more than 40 L/min in highly trained endurance athletes during maximal exercise (Ekblom and Hermansen 1968). The working skeletal muscles may increase their blood flow requirements from 20% of the output of the heart at rest to more than 85% during maximal exercise. Skeletal muscle blood flow may increase from 1.2 L/min to more than 22 L/min (figure 4.1). This means that many other tissues, notably the viscera, will have blood shunted away from them; there just isn't enough to go around. But they still will receive sufficient flow so that their function will not be compromised.

Along with O_2 delivery to working muscles at rates that are as much as 20 times higher than at rest, the body must manage the dynamics of transporting the various products of metabolism. We identified in chapter 3 the two major types of metabolic acids: *volatile acids* such as CO_2 (which is excreted as a gas via the lungs) and *nonvolatile acids* (the best example of which is *lactic acid*). Fuels need mobilization from storage sites in the liver and fat tissue and transport through the bloodstream to supplement fuel reserves in the highly active working muscles. Finally, heat production will increase by as much as 100-fold, to 5,000 kJ/hr (1,194 kcal/hr) and higher. This heat must be eliminated, and the primary process involved is evaporation of sweat, production of which can exceed 2 L/hr in some who sweat profusely during hot weather when they are working hard. The other major source of heat loss is through convection from dilated skin surface blood vessels (heat and fluid loss can also occur through the expired air, but this loss is small by comparison). Fluid losses through perspiration will be derived from body water everywhere, but primarily from blood plasma. If sweat losses are excessive, the eventual decrease in blood volume can compromise effective tissue perfusion.

The ultimate goal of training is to increase the functional capacity of the organ systems most concerned with generating movement. Primarily these are cardiac and skeletal muscle tissues. We have already seen in chapter 3 how this functional capacity from a biochemical viewpoint involves the use of O_2 to permit complete fuel breakdown, with subsequent removal of the CO_2 produced and harnessing of energy as ATP. It becomes the integrated role of the lungs, blood, and blood vessels to satisfy the goal of getting the necessary O_2 and fuels to the skeletal muscles and heart for their use in generating movement and maintaining blood flow. The purpose of this chapter is to (1) permit a better understanding of how these systems interact, (2) explain how genetic endowment as well as proper training contribute to maximal performance abilities for improv-

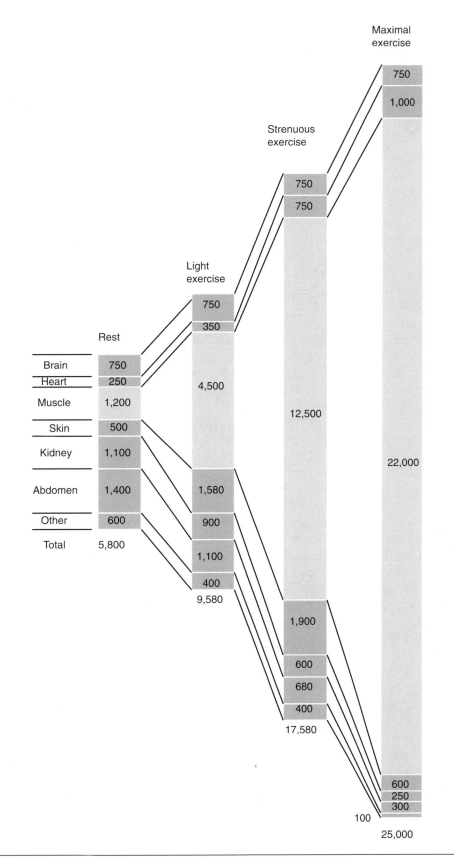

Figure 4.1 Redistribution of blood flow to working skeletal muscles with increasing exercise. Blood flow in ml/min is shown for the various organs. *Note.* From "The Physiology of Exercise" by C.B. Chapman and J.H. Mitchell, 1965, *Scientific American,* **212**(5), p. 91. Copyright 1965 by Scientific American, Inc. Adapted by permission.

ing athletic performance, and (3) identify how these abilities can be measured and monitored using laboratory evaluation.

Aerobic and Anaerobic Contributions to Performance

In chapter 3 we mentioned in general terms that, as a runner makes the transition from rest to hard exercise, O_2 demands for complete metabolism in the working muscles are not always met with available O_2 supply. Let us now consider this topic in greater detail and identify the major metabolic and cardiopulmonary interactions that occur as an athlete proceeds through a continuum of activity starting from the resting level, increasing stepwise in intensity by running faster and faster, and ending about 20 min later with voluntary cessation due to exhaustion and work load intolerance. This progression is often done using treadmill stress testing protocols. Testers collect the expired air from the trained athlete for analysis of O_2 uptake and CO_2 production and also insert an indwelling catheter in an arm blood vessel from which they can collect small samples of blood for measurement of lactic acid as exercise proceeds. Fingertip blood sampling instead of blood vessel catheterization and a mixture of level and uphill running are frequent variations of the test format previously suggested, depending on laboratory and athlete preferences. Still other laboratories prefer to keep blood collections for lactic acid measurement until the very end of the test session, relying on careful study of ventilatory patterns during the test to indicate noticeable increases in blood lactic acid values (Billat 1996).

In figure 4.2 running paces typical of the ability level of a talented, trained male runner prepared for hard competition are plotted on the horizontal axis. After a pretest warm-up run our athlete starts from a standing, resting situation (point P) and begins to run at what for him is an easy initial pace of 7:30/mi (4:40/km). This is a velocity of 215 m/min (12.9 km/hr). Note that coaches and athletes typically think of movement in terms of *pace* (the time elapsed in covering a specific distance), whereas scientists usually think in terms of *velocity* (distance traversed during a specific time period). The runner's O_2 consumption at this pace (or velocity), plotted along the vertical axis, is about 35 ml · kg^{-1} · min^{-1}, already 10 times greater than at rest. Runners not quite so talented or fit would start their runs at a slower pace, but this sudden increase in energy requirement occurs for them as well, so the same physiological response will occur. As the work load of the exercise protocol gradually increases, we can observe this runner's changing responses to progressive exercise and note the paces at which these changes occur.

One response known to all athletes is that breathing, heart rate, and blood flow do not immediately speed up to exactly match the blood flow requirements for the working muscles to keep their metabolism completely aerobic. There is a time lag, represented by the distance between points P and Q, during which O_2 demands are greater than O_2 supply. Anaerobic glycolysis in the skeletal muscles provides the additional required ATP-derived energy for this initially elevated activity. According to the essentials of anaerobic fuel metabolism discussed in chapter 3, as glucose is catabolized to pyruvate, some of the accumulating H$^+$ ions are available to convert pyruvate to lactate through interaction with lactic dehydrogenase (LDH) and NADH$_2$. At this relatively easy initial pace, pri-

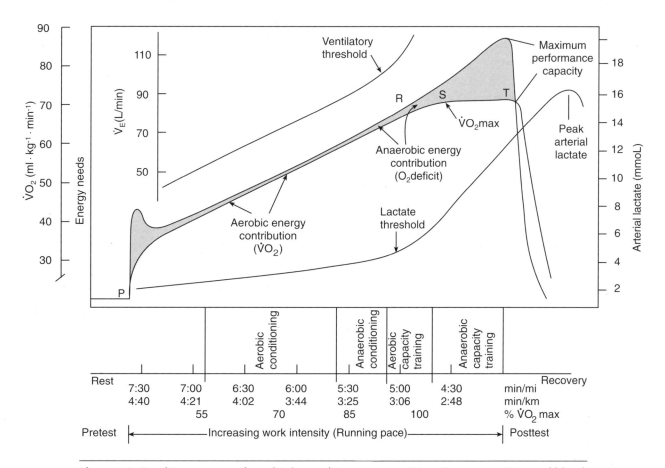

Figure 4.2 Graphic summary of aerobic/anaerobic energy provision, O_2 consumption, and blood lactic acid during a treadmill test of an elite male runner's performance abilities. The exercise intensity steadily increased until voluntary exhaustion at about 20 min. Starting pace was 7:30/mi (*P*). Initially, O_2 demand exceeded uptake, with anaerobic mechanisms providing needed energy. By *Q* aerobic metabolism was providing almost all required additional energy, and this continued until *R*. Aerobic metabolism could no longer match energy needs, and effects of increasing anaerobic metabolism were seen as more rapid blood lactate accumulation. VO_2max was reached at 4:35/mi pace (*S*), but additional work could be performed using more anaerobic reserves. When maximum work tolerance was reached (*T*), the test was stopped, with cool-down accompanied by continued elevated breathing and heart rates until recovery was complete. Blood lactate level peaked at about 5 min posttest.

marily ST skeletal muscle fibers are utilized. LDH exists in two different isoenzyme forms. In ST muscle fibers the H-LDH isoenzyme form (H for heart) maintains the equilibrium preferentially shifted toward pyruvate shown here, which minimizes lactate formation and permits H⁺ ions to accumulate:

$$\text{Pyruvate} + NADH_2 \overset{\text{H-LDH}}{\underset{\text{M-LDH}}{\rightleftarrows}} \text{Lactate} + NAD \tag{4.1}$$

It is interesting that the very presence of accumulating H⁺ ions helps to initiate a marked increase in local blood flow to the working muscles and to enhance their O_2 supply. Both H⁺ ions (from anaerobic glycolysis) and CO_2 (from mitochondrial oxidation) are potent inhibitors of smooth muscle tension generation in blood vessels. This action dilates the small, local blood vessels in the working skeletal muscles, which increases local blood flow. Greater O_2 availability from increased circulation and breathing permits more aerobic metabolism. Removal of CO_2, lactate, and H^+ ions helps to slow the development of acidosis in these active tissues. Eventually, increases in circulation and respiration permit O_2 delivery to catch up with demand almost completely (point Q). It has been thought by some that the so-called *second-wind phenomenon*—which we may define as a sudden improvement in general comfort and ability to tolerate pace following several minutes of running—may correlate with initial achievement of this aerobic metabolic dominance (point Q), when external respiration catches up with internal respiration. No one really knows for sure.

Once our athlete has achieved a predominantly aerobic metabolic state in his working muscles, although he is still gradually quickening his pace, the testers try to keep the rise in work load slow enough to permit a steady increase in O_2 uptake, circulation, and utilization sufficient for meeting metabolic demands. A near-balance situation is achieved between acidic metabolite production and removal. CO_2 is excreted through the lungs and does not accumulate. Nearly all lactate is metabolized or converted back to glucose by other tissues, and during the range of pace increase from point Q to point R, blood lactate concentration will rise only a small amount. Although both fatty acids and glucose are major fuel sources, the latter is becoming increasingly important.

Eventually, the continuing increase in pace results in a work load (point R) where again aerobic metabolism by itself can no longer meet the additional energy requirements. This is caused in part by the increased recruitment of FT skeletal muscle fibers. These fibers are specialized more for anaerobic than for aerobic metabolism and convert glucose rapidly to pyruvate. In these fibers the M-LDH isoenzyme (M for skeletal muscle) directs equation (4.1) preferentially toward the right, permitting formation of additional lactate. At this exercise intensity (point R) blood lactate starts to accumulate at a faster rate because increased lactate production by working muscles, and its release into the blood, is greater than its utilization (as a fuel) by other tissues. This can be termed the *lactate threshold*. Ongoing measurements of the increasing ventilation during exercise usually also show a change in ventilatory pattern here as well. In figure 4.2 point R indicates this *ventilatory threshold* as well as the lactate threshold. The change in breathing intensity at this work load is often sensed by runners—to use runners' jargon, "this is where the conversation stops!"

Despite these various metabolic changes with increasing pace, our athlete manages the situation well and continues to run faster and faster, eventually reaching his maximal O_2 power, or $\dot{V}O_2$max (point S). Although this work load is quite stressful, being similar to 5,000-m race pace, if he continues to be encouraged and possesses good racing fitness and a desire to do his very best, he will be able to run even faster for as long as a few minutes. Anaerobic glycolysis now provides the additional energy requirements for whatever work load he can manage beyond point S, and the blood lactate level rises exponentially. Voluntary exhaustion occurs at point T, and our athlete has completely "run out of reasons for running," achieving his maximal performance capacity.

Upon termination of this test run to voluntary exhaustion, our athlete quickly slows his pace to an easy jog for a cool-down, and recovery begins. Breathing and heart rate quickly slow toward their resting levels but remain elevated for a variable period as metabolic recovery proceeds. This maintenance of increased circulation and ventilation provide O_2 to the working tissues that fell behind in their ability to completely metabolize their available fuels, and it also permits removal of CO_2. Blood lactate will continue to rise, peak at about 5 min posttest, and then start to fall (Gollnick, Bayly, and Hodgson 1986). In chapter 3 we identified the purpose of such a cool-down following hard exercise: to maintain an enhanced circulation and thus speed the recovery process.

Physiological Indicators of Performance

In figure 4.2 there are three particular exercise intensities that have physiological significance. One of these, which we have termed the *maximal performance capacity,* is very easy to sense because it is the exercise termination point, but it is much less easy to quantify. It is the sum of the effects of maximal anaerobic metabolism superimposed on maximal aerobic metabolism. Increasing anaerobic glycolysis occurs after $\dot{V}O_2$max is achieved; because $\dot{V}O_2$max has plateaued, the additional increase in energy provision is solely from anaerobic sources, with the end product, lactate, diffusing out of the working muscle cells into the blood. This increased energy production by anaerobic glycolysis is as enormous as it is inefficient—18 times more fuel breakdown is required than for aerobic glycolysis to produce the same amount of ATP. The rapid buildup of H^+ ions in muscle tissue, even though much of it can diffuse into the bloodstream, limits further effort.

Margaria, Cerretelli, and Mangili (1964) reported that such exercise beyond the achievement of $\dot{V}O_2$max could occur for no more than 30 to 40 s, depending on fitness. When we evaluate the fitness of the extraordinarily talented runners with whom we have been privileged to work close to their period of competition, our experience suggests that this post-$\dot{V}O_2$max effort tolerance can reach 2 min. They thus have enormous tolerance to the stress of intense anaerobic work. When we consider techniques for fitness profiling, we shall identify some measurable quantities that can help to describe the magnitude of this maximal performance capacity.

The other two exercise indicators of performance identified in figure 4.2 are $\dot{V}O_2$max and the *lactate/ventilatory threshold.* These can be quantified rather easily in the laboratory. The dynamics of fuel metabolism and O_2 availability determine how large $\dot{V}O_2$max can become and at what work intensity the lactate/ventilatory threshold will occur. At the cellular level the essence of the process of getting fit is in increasing the number of mitochondrial enzymes in the working skeletal muscles along with the number of surrounding capillaries, so that the combination of increased O_2 delivery and increased enzyme activity permits an increased work rate. Before we discuss just how the various organ systems adapt with training to increase $\dot{V}O_2$max and lactate/ventilatory threshold, it is appropriate to further describe these two important variables at least in general terms. When quantified, they can serve as the basis for defining appropriate training paces to further improve aerobic and anaerobic fitness.

Maximal Aerobic Power ($\dot{V}O_2$max)

$\dot{V}O_2$max functionally represents the maximal amount of oxygen that can be removed from circulating blood and used by the working tissues during a specified period (Mitchell and Blomqvist 1971; Mitchell, Sproule, and Chapman 1958). Whether the relationship between increasing O_2 consumption and running speed is linear or curvilinear has been a subject of great interest and varying opinion ever since the early experiments of Hill and Lupton (1923). The studies of Rodolfo Margaria and his colleagues (Margaria et al. 1963), showing that the submaximal aerobic energy demand for running was approximately 1 kcal per kilogram of body weight per kilometer of distance covered, provided a basis for estimating energy utilization for a variety of other activities. This was also the basis for the aerobic exercise programs popularized by Kenneth Cooper (1968) for maintaining fitness and optimal body weight. Although figure 4.2 illustrates a linearity in O_2 consumption with increasing submaximal work until $\dot{V}O_2$max is reached, this by no means represents the final word. In 1986 the American College of Sports Medicine (ACSM) presented an equation for estimating the $\dot{V}O_2$ used at any given velocity while running over level ground, assuming that a linear relationship exists:

$$\dot{V}O_2 = (\text{velocity} \times 0.2) + 3.5 \tag{4.2}$$

where $\dot{V}O_2$ is in ml $\cdot$ kg^{-1} $\cdot$ min^{-1}, velocity is in m/min, and 0.2 ml O_2 $\cdot$ kg^{-1} $\cdot$ min^{-1} are consumed for every m/min increase in velocity. The value of 3.5 ml $\cdot$kg^{-1} $\cdot$ min^{-1} represents the typical resting metabolic energy level without exercise (often referred to as 1 *MET*). There is no difference in O_2 consumption between level treadmill and over-ground running. When running up a grade, however, treadmill running is less energy demanding than over-ground running. The equations for the additional O_2 consumption that must be added to the horizontal component to calculate the vertical component are as follows, with grade expressed as a decimal (for example, 2% = 0.02):

$$\dot{V}O_2 = \text{velocity} \times \text{grade} \times (0.9 \text{ or } 1.8) \tag{4.3}$$

where 0.9 and 1.8 ml O_2 $\cdot$ kg^{-1} $\cdot$ min^{-1} are consumed, respectively, for treadmill and for over-ground running for every m/min velocity increase.

Influence of Training, Genetics, and Aging

A young, sedentary female (20-29 yr) of average fitness has a $\dot{V}O_2$max of 35 to 43 ml $\cdot$ kg^{-1} $\cdot$ min^{-1} (Nagle 1973), whereas an elite-level female distance runner similar in age would have a $\dot{V}O_2$max ranging from 61 to 73 ml $\cdot$ kg^{-1} $\cdot$ min^{-1} (Pate et al. 1987). Similarly, although a man of average fitness has a $\dot{V}O_2$max range from 44 to 51 ml $\cdot$ kg^{-1} $\cdot$ min^{-1} (Nagle 1973), an elite male distance runner has a $\dot{V}O_2$max ranging from 71 to 84 ml $\cdot$ kg^{-1} $\cdot$ min^{-1} (Pollock 1977). Our own experience suggests that the range of values for elite-level (i.e., genetically gifted as well as physically fit) runners is closer to 60 to 75 ml $\cdot$ kg^{-1} $\cdot$ min^{-1} for women and 71 to 90 ml $\cdot$ kg^{-1} $\cdot$ min^{-1} for men.

A large portion of this difference between sedentary and athletic values—anywhere from 30% to 50%—can be attributable to training (Klissouras 1972; Shephard 1984). As either active or sedentary people undertake serious aerobic training, their $\dot{V}O_2$max typically increases. Thus, the capacity to adapt to increased endurance work loads is a *trainable* attribute of healthy people, and $\dot{V}O_2$max is an appropriate indicator of the improved aerobic fitness.

The extent to which quantities such as $\dot{V}O_2$max can improve with training is not the same in everyone, however. As Claude Bouchard et al. (1988) put it, there are *high and low responders* to training, and this is hereditary. There is also genetic variability in the determinants of endurance performance (Bouchard and

Lortie 1984), probably the most notable being the differing FT and ST fiber composition of skeletal muscles. In addition, not everyone begins to respond to training at the same age; some are more responsive at an early age, others later. Olympic gold medal prospects thus are most likely to be those who have

- an interest in training,
- an inherited endowment of physiological attributes related to high-level aerobic and anaerobic performance,
- a high sensitivity of response to training,
- resistance to injury due to excellent musculoskeletal symmetry, and
- a well-designed training program.

Thus, in the words of Per-Olof Åstrand (1982, 193), "Top athletes in endurance events are only partly products of a tough training program." Another important factor that changes $\dot{V}O_2$max is the aging process. As we get older, performance gradually deteriorates; aging is the price we pay for living! Åstrand and Rodahl (1977) suggest that $\dot{V}O_2$max declines about 1% per year from around age 25 onward among individuals who lead relatively sedentary lifestyles. Many changes occurring as part of the aging process contribute to the gradual decline in $\dot{V}O_2$max during later years. The maximum attainable heart rate in beats per minute declines at a rate of about six beats per decade, and this is an important component of $\dot{V}O_2$max. Unless stroke volume increases appropriately, maximum cardiac output declines. After age 60 among sedentary people, muscle cells seem to deteriorate more rapidly than previously, which contributes to a gradual decrease in skeletal muscle strength. Campbell, McComas, and Petito (1973) have suggested that these changes may be induced by accelerated nervous system degeneration during the later years, especially in sedentary people.

The addition of serious fitness training as an integral part of lifestyle can substantially slow these processes. Endurance-trained athletes during their second and third decades of life probably will experience very little reduction in $\dot{V}O_2$max, provided they continue in serious training. The coupling of genetic trainability with continued effective aerobic training can provide a rather extended period of comparable-quality performances, provided that interruption does not occur from injury. The marathon is the most aerobically dependent Olympic running event and has contributed several well-known athletic examples of such interaction. Many will recall the men's 1984 Los Angeles Olympic gold medal marathon performance (2:09:21) by 37-year-old Carlos Lopes of Portugal. (His 2:07:12 at Rotterdam the following April was a new world best.) The 1990 Boston Marathon world best master's (or veteran's) performance of 2:11:04 by New Zealander John Campbell at the age of 41 is equally outstanding. Among the women, two of the more brilliant marathoners include Priscilla Welch, with her British record of 2:26:51 at age 42 in 1987, and Sweden's Evy Palm, who at age 47 set a new national record of 2:31:04 in 1989. Both of these records were established over the fast London Marathon course.

It is difficult to quantify exactly how $\dot{V}O_2$max and other performance criteria of such athletes change over time. This is because as athletes grow older, their lifestyles also change, often decreasing the amount of time they can devote to training. Moreover, a greater requirement for recovery following hard training decreases their manageable weekly training volume, which slows the rate of adaptation possible.

Male-Female Differences

Women as a group have smaller absolute $\dot{V}O_2$max values (ml/min) than men. Typically, men are taller (and thus heavier) than women, but if $\dot{V}O_2$max values are expressed in ml · kg⁻¹ · min⁻¹, the difference still remains. It is assumed, of course, that in studies reporting such differences both groups are comparably trained, but ensuring this has been difficult. Inclusion as study subjects of male and female athletes specializing in similar events and performing at a similar competitive level has often provided the basis for that assumption, but whether they have been doing comparable training can still be debated. Because men have been competing at distance running events longer than women, the top standard for women may not be quite as refined as that for men.

Some scientists have suggested that it might be more informative to express $\dot{V}O_2$max values as ml · kg⁻¹ · min⁻¹ of fat-free body mass (or lean body mass) when comparing men's $\dot{V}O_2$max to women's (Åstrand 1984). Women have a larger percentage of body fat than men as a result of their higher concentration of fat-storing estrogen hormones. Also, men have a larger amount of skeletal muscle mass than women as a result of their higher circulating testosterone levels. Fat tissue consumes O_2 but does not contribute to the ability to increase work rate. If anything, it impedes maximal work output, because it must be transported during running. When comparisons of $\dot{V}O_2$max are made using fat-free body mass measurements, the difference between men's and women's $\dot{V}O_2$max diminishes somewhat but still remains.

Another factor contributing to the gender difference relates to a larger quantity of hemoglobin circulating in men than in women of similar fitness and absolute body weight. This is also in part caused by the anabolic (protein-building) effects of testosterone. In men this hormone not only stimulates production of higher levels of erythropoietin, the glycoprotein hormone that stimulates the bone marrow to release more red blood cells, but it also promotes the production of more hemoglobin, also a protein. Because 98.5% of the bloodborne O_2 is transported by hemoglobin, more hemoglobin means a greater O_2-carrying capability. For men a hemoglobin level of 15 gm per deciliter (dl) of blood multiplied by 77 ml blood volume per kilogram of body weight results in 11.6 gm hemoglobin/kg. For women 14 gm hemoglobin/dl × 66 ml blood volume/kg = 9.2 gm hemoglobin/kg. Thus, women have roughly 21% less hemoglobin per kilogram than men. In the bloodstream similar calculations that will be illustrated later reveal that women have about 11% less circulating O_2 per deciliter than men.

Influence of Running Economy

Almost all of the highly trained elite-level distance runners that we have tested have lower O_2 consumption values at submaximal running paces than those predicted by the ACSM formulas [equations (4.2) and (4.3)]. This is illustrated in table 4.1, which summarizes mean values from our athletes over time, but it has been reported by others as well (Bransford and Howley 1977; Conley and Krahenbuhl 1980). Thus, either genetic factors or the enormous volumes of training that these runners indulge in during their athletic years provide them with sufficient thriftiness in O_2 consumption that they have become more efficient, or economical. To help quantify this concept Daniels (1974) defined *running economy* as the O_2 required for an individual to maintain any particular submaximal running pace.

Notice also in table 4.1 that there seems to be no difference in running economy between the men and women although there is no uniform agreement on this

TABLE 4.1

Comparison of Submaximal O_2 Consumption of Elite Men and Women Runners With ACSM-Predicted Estimates

Velocity		Pace		O_2 consumption, ml $\cdot$ kg^{-1} $\cdot$ min^{-1}		
mi/hr	m/min	min/mi	min/km	Men	Women	ACSM-predicted
8.0	215	7:30	4:40	37.3	36.9	46.5
8.6	230	7:00	4:21		39.4	49.5
9.0	241	6:40	4:09	41.4		51.7
9.2	248	6:30	4:02		41.7	53.1
10.0	268	6:00	3:44	46.8	47.4	57.1
10.6	284	5:40	3:31		51.5	60.3
11.0	295	5:30	3:25	52.1		62.5
12.0	322	5:00	3:06	58.5		67.9

topic (Anderson 1996; Davies and Thompson 1979). One must ensure that both groups are comparably trained in order to make such comparisons. In our situation both groups represent the best of U.S. distance runners, who are essentially "at the top of their game" and in hard (yet manageable) training.

To an extent, we become more economical at running simply through running. For example, we tend naturally to develop an optimal combination of stride length and frequency that requires minimal O_2 cost. Fatigue, however, affects economy in a negative way, increasing aerobic demand through the use of increasingly tired prime movers plus others brought into action to help maintain pace. Well-coached runners, when it is time to race, ensure that they are fresh and completely recovered from the performance-slowing effects of prior hard training. In this manner they keep aerobic demand as low as possible at their race pace. As they approach exhaustion toward the end of the race, their running will likely become less economical.

Just as we can see variations in running economy within populations, we can determine whether a runner has improved economy from training over a period of time by comparing the aerobic demand at the beginning and end of this period. As an example, if we determined a runner's O_2 consumption in November as 47 ml $\cdot$ kg^{-1} $\cdot$ min^{-1} at a 6 min/mi pace (268 m/min; 3:44/km), and then five months later, with no change in the runner's percentage body fat or body weight, remeasured and found the O_2 consumption at the same pace to be 41 ml $\cdot$ kg^{-1} $\cdot$ min^{-1}, we might (correctly) conclude that this runner was now performing more economically in April than in November.

Ideally, runners are most concerned with being optimally economical at race pace. The longer the race and thus the smaller the anaerobic racing component, the greater will be the influence of running economy on performance quality. Thus, marathoners can probably benefit most either from above-average running economy through genetic factors or from specific training to improve it. This has been offered as an explanation for the rather low $\dot{V}O_2$max values recorded among some top-level marathon runners.

One such example is the Australian Derek Clayton, whose 2:08:34 once was a world best. He was studied by Costill, Thomason, and Roberts (1973) and found to have a $\dot{V}O_2$max of 69.7 ml $\cdot$ kg^{-1} $\cdot$ min^{-1}. Another is the Swedish marathoner

Kjell-Erik Stahl (personal best of 2:10:38), with 65 marathon performances under 2:20:00 (at last count) between 1979 and 1995. He was studied by Sjödin and Svedenhag (1985) and found to have a $\dot{V}O_2$max of 66.8 ml $\cdot$ kg^{-1} $\cdot$ min^{-1}. Both athletes were slightly more economical at submaximal work loads than even our elite-level runners. Published data for Clayton and Stahl indicate an O_2 consumption of 59.5 and 59.7 ml $\cdot$ kg^{-1} $\cdot$ min^{-1}, respectively, at 20 km/hr (3:00/km; 333 m/min; 4:50/mi). But we (as well as others) have studied marathon runners with personal best credentials just as excellent and who possess considerably higher O_2 consumption rates at both submaximal and maximal loads than those described here. Would they be world-record breakers if they were more economical? Or is there more to performance than economy? We are reminded of the words of Mark Twain: "Few things are harder to put up with than the annoyance of a good example!"

Clearly, there is considerable diversity among athletes, and the influence of running economy interacts with other performance characteristics in the total analysis of athletic excellence. In this chapter we will explain what is physiologically required to optimize both running economy and $\dot{V}O_2$max, and then in chapter 5 we can provide practical details of how to develop these attributes through training.

Blood Lactate and Ventilatory Thresholds

It was probably Hill and Lupton (1923) who first suggested that when skeletal muscles are subjected to gradually increasing work loads, eventually their metabolic demands exceed those that can be served solely by complete (aerobic) metabolism. To meet these increased needs, anaerobic metabolism occurs, with glucose being converted to pyruvate and lactate. In 1930 W. Harding Owles provided the first catchphrase that seemed to encapsulate this concept. He referred to a *critical metabolic level* of exercise intensity (using walking, not running) beyond which the blood lactate level increased above that found in the resting state. Also in 1930 Harrison and Pilcher found that patients with heart disease produced more CO_2 during exercise than normal, healthy subjects doing the same exercise. These scientists hypothesized that the excess CO_2 was released from plasma HCO_3^- as a result of chemical buffering of increased lactate that was produced from a failing heart.

For many years it was technologically difficult to analyze, simultaneously and on-line during exercise, both O_2 and CO_2 to measure changes in exercise responsiveness. Such pioneers as Issekutz, Birkhead, and Rodahl (1962) made great strides in this technology, as did a team headed by Karlman Wasserman in California. It was Wasserman and McIlroy (1964) who first used the term *anaerobic threshold* to define a particular work load at which blood lactate levels first begin to rise above their resting levels during a test to measure exercise tolerance. An increase in the rate of rise in *expired ventilation* ($\dot{V}_E$) in milliliters per minute that was greater than the rate of ongoing increase in O_2 uptake also began to occur. The term *anaerobic threshold* seemed logical to suggest the notion that anaerobic metabolic processes had begun to increase their role in supplementing aerobic processes to provide energy for movement. The term *anaerobic* literally means without O_2 but refers here to anaerobic metabolism. The term *threshold* refers to a region of change. As we shall describe shortly, this is not the same lactate/ventilatory threshold that we identified in figure 4.2. That depicted threshold is one of rapid blood lactate accumulation rather than one of moderate rise. The anaerobic threshold of Wasserman occurred in our athlete in figure 4.2 somewhere between points P and Q.

An enormous controversy began shortly following the appearance of Wasserman's paper and shows little sign of abating after more than 30 years. It wasn't the quality of Wasserman's research that was in doubt; that has always been superb. But as scientists around the world attempted to confirm his work using diverse groups of subjects (patients, sedentary controls, and athletes) and diverse methodologies (varying test durations and intensities, use of treadmill vs. bicycle ergometers for evaluation, blood lactate vs. measurements of ventilatory changes), great confusion arose. One reason for the controversy is the existence of two thresholds where anaerobic influences can be observed. The first is observed with mild work (accompanied by breathing changes and a small rise in blood lactate), whereas the other is observed with more intense exercise (accompanied by additional breathing changes and a steadily accumulating blood lactate). The details of what causes the ventilatory and blood lactate changes and whether these are exactly coupled have still not been completely explained. Most of the general concepts, however, have been identified, and we can describe them in the context of practical application for development of distance runners.

Dynamics of Blood Lactate

Lactate has a varied role in metabolism that is appropriate to review here, as part of the anaerobic threshold controversy has revolved around the notion by some that *no* anaerobic metabolism (and thus *no* lactate production) occurs at rest. This is incorrect, because lactic acid is being produced even during the quietest of resting states, as well as in increasing amounts as exercise intensity increases. Red blood cells are one well-known source, as they are capable of glycolysis but have no mitochondria. Thus, pyruvate and lactate, instead of accumulating, diffuse out of the red blood cells into the plasma. Lactate can be also produced and released into the bloodstream by the intestines and skeletal muscles. Along with this production of lactate is its use as a fuel. Nonexercising skeletal muscle will metabolize lactate (Essen et al. 1975). So will the liver (Wahren, Hagenfeld, and Felig 1975), the kidneys (Yudkin and Cohen 1975), and also the heart (Welch 1973). Even exercising skeletal muscle can metabolize lactate. We know it is an important energy source, released from both FT and ST skeletal muscle cells and usable as a fuel especially by ST muscle cells. Thus, lactate is not some kind of gremlin molecule to be maligned as an internal poison. Rather, it is produced in a well-understood manner and usable as an important energy source.

The blood lactate level measured at rest or at any particular level of exercise represents a balance between its rate of production and release into the blood and its removal; in biochemical terms this balance is called *lactate turnover rate*. This turnover rate determines the baseline lactate concentration in the blood. An untrained individual in an overnight fasted state who has a sample of blood collected in the morning from an arm vein before any exercise has a lactate level ranging from about 4 to 15 mg/dl. (Many clinical laboratories express lactate levels in millimoles per liter [mmol/L, or mM/L]. Because 1 mg/dl = 0.1112 mmol/L, this resting blood lactate level can also be expressed as 0.44 to 1.7 mmol/L.) We find that our trained elite distance runners typically have a lactate level near the low end of this range (around 3 to 5 mg/dl, or 0.3 to 0.6 mmol/L) if they are not overtrained. (However, one residual effect of either a very hard single training session or a period of overtraining is a morning postabsorptive lactate level that is either very high normal or clinically elevated.)

The First Threshold

As runners begin a training session, gradually increasing their pace to a comfortable aerobic level (e.g., transitioning from points P to Q in figure 4.2), their arterial blood lactate level typically increases into the range of 15 to 22 mg/dl (1.7 to 2.4 mmol/L), and then remains relatively unchanged despite subsequent reasonable submaximal pace increases. The particular threshold of work intensity that initiates such a small elevation of blood lactate beyond resting baseline levels was termed the anaerobic threshold (Wasserman and McIlroy 1964), as described previously. Others have given it a different name: the *aerobic threshold* (Skinner and McLellan 1980), the *lactate threshold* (Ivy et al. 1980), the *onset of plasma lactate accumulation* (Farrell et al. 1979), the *first threshold* (Heck et al. 1985); and the *aerobic threshold (2 mmol)* (Kindermann, Simon, and Keul 1979).

Both ventilatory and blood lactate increases can be observed at this first threshold. The ventilatory rise is explainable on the basis of blood HCO_3^- buffering mechanisms. The H^+ ion resulting from lactate dissociation combines with available HCO_3^- to form H_2CO_3. By action of the enzyme carbonic anhydrase, H_2CO_3 is converted into H_2O and CO_2. As hypothesized by Harrison and Pilcher (1930), these changes are stoichiometrically equivalent; that is, one H^+ ion from lactic acid combines with one HCO_3^- from the $NaHCO_3$ buffer supply to form CO_2 via carbonic acid. Recall equation (3.11) in chapter 3 where this relationship was introduced.

This additional CO_2 beyond that normally produced by aerobic metabolism— 22 ml of CO_2 for every millimole of lactate buffered—provides an additional ventilatory stimulus. Thus, there is a disproportionate rise in expired ventilation ($\dot{V}_E$) in comparison to the ongoing rise in $\dot{V}O_2$. Therefore the $\dot{V}_E/\dot{V}O_2$max ratio (called the *ventilatory equivalent for O_2*) increases without an accompanying increase in $\dot{V}_E/\dot{V}CO_2$ (known as the *ventilatory equivalent for CO_2*). Or, in other words, the number of liters of inspired air required to deliver one liter of O_2 increases without an increase in the number of liters of expired air required to remove one liter of CO_2. $\dot{V}CO_2$ continues to rise at a rate similar to $\dot{V}_E$, however. The term *isocapnic buffering* is often used to describe this phenomenon; *isocapnic* refers to the relatively equal rate of rise of CO_2 with $\dot{V}_E$, and *buffering* refers to the relatively stable acidity during this period. More than 90% of the buffering of lactate is carried out by the action of $NaHCO_3$. This threshold usually occurs at 35% to 60% of $\dot{V}O_2$max, when R is between 0.85 and 0.90.

Once this threshold is reached, the work load can increase rather sizably (e.g., from points Q to R in figure 4.2) with only gradual and relatively small increases in circulating lactate. Trained male marathon runners, as an example, can maintain reasonably stable arterial lactate levels (ranging from around 26 mg/dl [2.9 mmol/L] to 44 mg/dl [4.9 mmol/L]) during running work loads reaching paces exceeding 5:00/mi (19.3 km/hr; 3:06/km; 322 m/min). Women marathoners can retain this blood lactate stability at faster than 5:50/mi (16.6 km/hr; 3:37/km; 276 m/min). For less fit or less talented runners, this pace range for stable blood lactate is considerably slower.

The Second Threshold

At work loads greater than those described or at comparable paces for other runners (75% to 90% of $\dot{V}O_2$max when R is around 1.0), the blood lactate level then begins a more rapid rise (occurring at point R in figure 4.2). The threshold at which this sudden rise occurs can also be termed an *anaerobic threshold* (Skinner and McLellan 1980), but it has also been termed the *respiratory compensation for metabolic acidosis* (Wasserman 1984), the *lactate turnpoint* (Davis et al. 1983), the *onset of blood lactate accumulation to 4 mmol* (Sjödin and Jacobs 1981), the *individual anaerobic threshold* (Stegmann, Kindermann, and Schnabel 1981), the *second threshold* (Heck et al. 1985), and the *anaerobic threshold (4mmol)* (Kindermann, Simon, and Keul 1979).

Both ventilatory and blood lactate changes occur at the second threshold as well. At the work intensity where the blood lactate concentration begins to accumulate rapidly, elevated ventilatory removal of CO_2 can no longer maintain blood acidity (measured as pH) within reasonable limits. As blood lactate levels rise rapidly, blood pH begins to fall, and this rising H^+ ion concentration (remember that a decrease in pH implies an increase in H^+ ions) provides an additional powerful ventilatory stimulus.

Perhaps the saddest part of this controversy is that no universal satisfaction among scientists exists with any of these terms to this day, showing perhaps that their competitiveness in defending various terminologies as "the best" is matched only by the aggressive assault on first place by athletes in a race. Not even *anaerobic threshold* is considered an acceptable term anymore (Walsh and Banister 1988).

We will be referring primarily to the *second threshold*, as this is the region of metabolic change that is of greatest interest in training elite-level distance runners. When we are referring to this second threshold as identified by blood lactate measurements, we shall use *lactate threshold*. We shall use *ventilatory threshold* to refer to this second threshold when specifically identified by respiratory changes. Otherwise, we shall use the combined term *lactate/ventilatory threshold*. Doll and Keul (1968) reported that, during an incremental exercise test similar in principle to that described earlier, untrained healthy people demonstrated this sudden rapid increase in blood lactate concentration beginning at about 50% of their $\dot{V}O_2$max. However, our experience with measuring the ventilatory threshold of trained distance runners indicates that it occurs at typically between 80% and 90% of $\dot{V}O_2$max (Martin, Vroon, May, and Pilbeam 1986).

Two of the previously mentioned synonyms for the lactate threshold refer to a 4 mmol/L value. The significance of this dates back to the work of Mader et al. (1976), who reported on a group of subjects in whom the threshold for rapid lactate accumulation typically began at a level of 4 mmol/L (36 mg/dl). Because of this report, it became popular to assume that this was true for all endurance athletes, and therefore that those athletes interested in identifying a training intensity to further raise this threshold should train at the 4 mmol/L running pace. Stegmann, Kindermann, and Schnabel in 1981 reported that this simply was not universally true, either logically or in fact. They found that the threshold at which blood lactate begins to rise had considerable individual variation, varying from around 2 to 7 mmol/L (18 to 63 mg/dl). It can only be imagined how many elite-level distance runners have suffered training misfortunes over the years as a result of following advice for training paces that were assigned arbitrarily using a 4 mmol/L work intensity as unequivocally representing their lactate threshold. Some doubtless were overtrained, incurring needless fatigue and staleness, whereas others were undertrained and did not achieve their intended goals in quickening the pace at which their lactate threshold occurred.

USING PHYSIOLOGICAL PRINCIPLES TO ASSESS ATHLETIC POTENTIAL

Four components contribute to an individual's maximal sustainable pace in distance running:

- The genetic composition of skeletal muscle cells (i.e., a large percentage of ST cells)
- A gradual lowering (with proper training) of the aerobic demand to run at any submaximal pace (i.e., greater economy of movement)
- An improvement in the O_2 consumption capabilities of the working muscles (more intracellular mitochondria, better blood perfusion, etc.)
- A gradual improvement in ability to buffer the effects of increasing acidosis as increased numbers of FT fibers are recruited to manage the work load at higher intensities.

If we can quantify these components—either in the laboratory or on the track—we shall find that the athlete who has the highest $\dot{V}O_2max$ plus the quickest lactate/ventilatory threshold pace plus the greatest running economy plus the greatest ability to tolerate metabolic acidosis has the greatest potential for winning a race. The combined effects of hereditary endowment, training emphasis, and training responsiveness determine which of these variables will be higher or lower in any given athlete at any moment in time.

There is no doubt that a high $\dot{V}O_2max$ constitutes a kind of membership card for entrance into the world of top-level middle- and long-distance running excellence. But anaerobic aspects of performance also contribute to the difference between finishing first and second in a race, because they interact with $\dot{V}O_2max$. Thus, two important physiological variables are important in evaluating distance-running abilities. One is the velocity at anaerobic threshold (vAT)—the pace at which blood lactate just starts to rise substantially. Marathon race pace is slightly slower than this. The other is the velocity at $\dot{V}O_2max$ (v $\dot{V}O_2max$), which typically is close to 3,000 race pace (Billat and Koralsztein 1996).

This concept is perhaps discussed most frequently among those interested in marathon racing. The great length of this event precludes accumulation of blood lactate except at the end. In-

deed, it has been shown clearly that the performance potential for a marathoner among a homogeneous population (i.e., all very talented marathon specialists) correlates better with the pace at their lactate/ventilatory threshold (expressed either by itself or as a percentage of $\dot{V}O_2max$ pace) than to $\dot{V}O_2max$ (Farrell et al. 1979; Sjödin and Svedenhag 1985). Costill, Thomason, and Roberts (1973) have referred to this relationship between lactate/ventilatory threshold and $\dot{V}O_2max$ as the *fractional use of the aerobic capacity.*

Let's take a practical example and apply the principles that we have identified. Jim and John both have $\dot{V}O_2max$ values of 75 ml · kg^{-1} · min^{-1}. They also have identical running economies, and they are running side by side over a level surface at a fairly fast pace—85% of $\dot{V}O_2max$ pace. Jim's anaerobic threshold pace is at 85% of $\dot{V}O_2max$ pace, whereas John's is limited to 81%. Other aspects being equal, Jim will be able to manage this pace for a longer time period than John, because John will begin to experience accumulating blood lactate before Jim.

This principle holds true over the entire spectrum of distance racing—from the marathon, where athletes attempt to compete at the fastest sustainable aerobic pace, through the 800 m, where they must cope with additional large anaerobic accumulations over a few minutes' time. The larger their $\dot{V}O_2max$, the smaller their total anaerobic contribution will be at any given pace, or the faster they can run before anaerobic effects start to impair performance. But once $\dot{V}O_2max$ has been elevated about as high as possible without inordinate additional training volumes, anaerobic development will make the additional difference between being optimally fit (i.e., able to use all trainable performance characteristics) and marginally fit (i.e., not fully trained).

Athletes and coaches are always interested in applying physiological data in a meaningful way to improve training or racing effectiveness. Figure 4.3 graphically summarizes how the fitness variables that we have just identified can increase performance when trained. In a fashion similar to figure 4.2, we have plotted O_2 uptake and blood lactate concentration on the vertical axes and increasing exercise load (represented by running

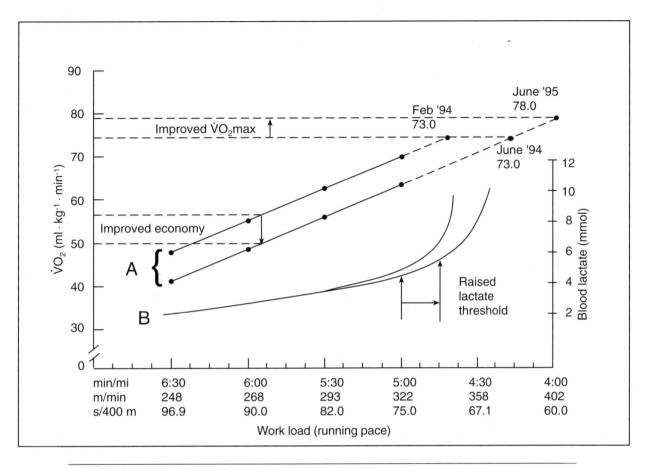

Figure 4.3 Graphic plot of O_2 consumption and blood lactate as a function of running velocity to show that a higher $\dot{V}O_2$max, an improved running economy, and a higher lactate/ventilatory threshold can increase performance potential in racing.

pace) on the horizontal axis. Consider runner A, who has attempted to improve his performance by appropriate training to increase $\dot{V}O_2$max and running economy, and runner B, who has attempted to raise lactate threshold. Runner A trained effectively between February 1994 and June 1994 and experienced a measurable improvement in running economy but no change in $\dot{V}O_2$max, which remained stable at 73 ml · kg^{-1} · min^{-1}. If this athlete competed at 92% of $\dot{V}O_2$max for a 10,000-m race, his race finish time would clearly be faster in June 1994 than in February 1994.

Between June 1994 and June 1995, runner A's $\dot{V}O_2$max improved from 73 to 78 ml · kg^{-1} · min^{-1}, with no changes in body weight. However, in this training year from 1994 to 1995, runner A experienced no improvement in running economy. As shown, if this athlete races at 92% of $\dot{V}O_2$max pace, as in a 10,000-m race, his June 1995 finish time would also be considerably faster than that

of June 1994 as a result of the improvement in $\dot{V}O_2$max.

Runner B engaged in a training program that provided greater tolerance to anaerobic work. Initially the pace at which blood lactate levels began to markedly rise (his lactate threshold) was at 5:00/mi (3:06/km); upon retesting several months later this pace has quickened to about 4:45/mi (2:57/km). If this athlete's $\dot{V}O_2$max and running efficiency were unchanged, he would be able to race at a faster pace simply because he is more fit from the standpoint of managing a greater work load before lactate starts to accumulate.

Wouldn't it be nice if coaches and athletes could identify specific kinds of workouts that could produce such improvements in $\dot{V}O_2$max, running economy, and lactate/ventilatory threshold? And wouldn't it also be nice if athletes could be tested periodically to learn whether the training they are doing is actually bringing about such changes? If these changes are occurring, fine—the athlete will be race fit in due course. But if the changes are not occurring, a sound basis is established for making some training modifications and then re-testing later on.

Can such evaluations be done? Sure, no problem—read on. Notice in figure 4.2 that we have used the lactate/ventilatory threshold and $\dot{V}O_2$max points to delineate four zones, or pace ranges, named for the predominant physiological benefit resulting from training in each. In chapter 5 we will describe in detail both the kinds of training appropriate to each zone and the resulting physiological adaptations. Before considering these practical training details, however, let us return to the basics and identify the major concepts of cardiopulmonary and blood physiology that explain how the various possible adaptations can occur with training. And let us also describe how such adaptations can be measured using laboratory performance profiling or field tests such as time trials.

Exercise as a Challenge to the Heart, Lungs, and Blood

Of all the vital signs that anyone considers in evaluation of health, surely to a runner the pulse or heartbeat must be the one most symbolic of working capacity. The pounding heartbeat felt as the apex of the heart thumps the inside of the chest wall just following all-out exercise is familiar to all. An elevated pulse rate during the few days following difficult training sessions is a sure sign of the need for some additional recovery time. Heart rate as an indicator of exercise intensity or adequacy of recovery before beginning another interval of higher-speed running is commonly measured in training. Gradual reduction in resting heart rate following a successful endurance training program—a decrease from between 60 to 80 beats/min down to as low as 30 to 40 beats/min—is common among endurance athletes. How does a runner's heart adapt to the stress of exercise? Surely it must become a more functional pump, but how is this accomplished? How are its needs met for providing more and more blood through its own circulation (the coronary vessels) to ensure that its cells are properly supplied with O_2 and fuel? Familiarity with the essentials of cardiopulmonary physiology can help us appreciate how the heart, lungs, and blood adapt remarkably well to the needs of exercise and how their own capacities in turn set limits on maximal exercise capacity.

The Heart and Its Circulation

Functionally, we have two hearts: The *right heart* delivers blood to the lungs, and the *left heart* delivers blood everywhere else. Each heart has two primary operating variables: its beat (or cardiac) frequency (f_c), or *heart rate*, and the volume pumped out per beat, or *stroke volume* (Q_s). The product of the two equals the *cardiac output* (CO), typically measured in milliliters or liters of blood. Thus,

$$f_c \times Q_s = CO \tag{4.4}$$

As an example using untrained resting values, a heart rate of 70 beats/min and a stroke volume of 70 ml/beat provides a cardiac output of 4,900 ml/min. Using maximum values for an elite-level trained runner, a heart rate of 190 beats/min and a stroke volume of 190 ml/beat yields 36,100 ml/min.

The heart can deliver to the arterial side of the body only that blood which returns to it from the venous side. Thus, cardiac output must equal venous return. In a resting individual, four principal factors control venous return:

- The tone or caliber of the venous vessels
- The position of the body in space
- The total body blood volume
- The depth of breathing

As exercise begins, a fifth factor becomes important: the milking action of skeletal muscles that helps push blood through the veins back toward the heart.

The interaction of these factors should be easily understandable and can be illustrated using three examples. First, if the blood volume is large or if an individual has high blood pressure, which would tend to force the incompressible blood into a smaller volume, venous return will be easily maintained or even increased. Second, as breathing produces alternately increased and decreased intrathoracic subatmospheric pressures, venous return will alternately rise and fall. The increased breathing volume with each breath during exercise makes such fluctuations greater.

Third, if venous tone is reduced, blood will pool in the periphery and decrease venous return. This can occur during heavy exercise as blood flow increases to the working muscles. Suddenly stopping exercise reduces venous return because of diminished muscular activity, and fainting could occur from inadequate perfusion to the brain. Runners' practice of bending over at the end of a hard, fast race (figure 4.4) is understandable with this information in mind.

Figure 4.4 Competitive middle-distance runners immediately following an 800-m race. By bending forward, bringing the head closer to the level of the heart, less blood pressure is required to ensure adequate cerebral perfusion. Extreme vasodilation in the skeletal muscles, as well as an absence of milking action of skeletal muscles to enhance venous return, contributes to a temporary reduction in blood pressure.

These runners would probably faint if they remained standing upright, because the large quantity of blood pooling in the periphery cannot be returned to the heart quickly enough to guarantee delivery of adequate blood flow to the brain. Bending at the waist lowers the head to the level of the heart, thereby reducing the pressure needed to maintain adequate cerebral blood flow.

The heart muscle itself receives a substantial blood flow even at rest—about 80 ml · 100 gm^{-1} tissue · min^{-1}, which is about 5% of the resting cardiac output. During exercise, this flow may increase as much as fivefold. If we examine the anatomy of the *coronary arteries*, as diagrammed in figure 4.5, we see that these vessels are embedded for a sizable portion of their length along the outer surface of the heart. The *left coronary artery* is very short and divides almost immediately into two branches. The large *circumflex artery* extends to the left in a groove between the left atrium and ventricle and continues as a large vessel that descends on the rear surface of the left ventricle. It supplies the left atrium as well as the upper front and whole rear portion of the left ventricle. The other branch is the *anterior descending artery*, circling to the left of the pulmonary artery and then running downward in a furrow to the apex of the heart. It supplies the front wall of the left ventricle and a small part of the rear of the right ventricle. The *right coronary artery*, embedded in fat, runs to the right in a groove between the right atrium and ventricle and carries blood to both structures. It also has two branches, the *posterior descending artery* and the *marginal artery*. Four specific characteristics of cardiac muscle and its perfusion via the coronary circulation contribute to the heart's ability to adapt to exercise stress: O_2 extraction, vessel size, protection from an O_2 debt, and blood flow.

O_2 Extraction From Coronary Arterial Blood is High

When blood is sampled from the coronary arteries and from the coronary venous sinus and analyzed for its O_2 content, it is found that an exceedingly large amount

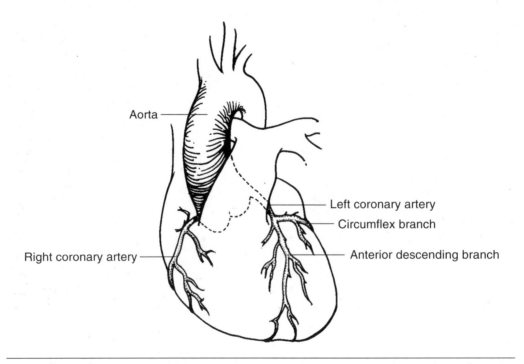

Figure 4.5 Position of right and left coronary arteries and their main branches on the surface of the heart.

of O_2 has been removed—much more than when we compare arterial blood with mixed venous blood from the entire body. In the language of cardiovascular physiology, we use the term *arteriovenous O_2 difference* (a-$\bar{v}O_2$ difference) to refer to this arterial O_2 content minus venous O_2 content. Typically, the usual arterial blood O_2 concentration averages about 20 ml/dl, and the mixed venous blood O_2 returning to the heart from its circuit through the body (representing the average O_2 used by all of the tissues) is about 15 ml/dl. This gives an overall a-$\bar{v}O_2$ difference of 5 ml/dl. The heart, even while the body is at rest, extracts much more O_2 than the other body tissues because it is metabolically so active. Thus, the venous blood O_2 concentration returning from the heart, measured in the coronary sinus, may be only 1 or 2 ml/dl. We can then calculate the coronary a-$\bar{v}O_2$ difference as 20 – (1 or 2) = 19 or 18 ml/dl. This O_2 utilization is much higher than that found in highly active skeletal muscles, whose venous blood O_2 concentration is around 4 to 5 ml/dl. That would give these working skeletal muscles an a-$\bar{v}O_2$ difference of 20 – (4 or 5) = 16 or 15 ml/dl. This normally very high O_2 extraction from coronary blood does not permit additional removal during increased exercise. Thus, any additional O_2 uptake by cardiac muscle can result only from an increased blood flow through its perfusing vessels.

Endurance Training Increases Coronary Vessel Size

As the heart enlarges with training, the coronary vessels also enlarge. Coronary flow increases as a logical consequence of these larger vessels. However, the powerful vasodilator effect of CO_2 is effective here just as in other actively metabolizing tissue beds. Thus, as metabolism in the heart increases during exercise, compensatory vasodilation from this important metabolite also enhances coronary blood flow.

Postmortem examination of the hearts of accomplished long-distance runners has seldom been done, but in those instances where this has been possible, the findings have often been very interesting. Probably the most famous case involves Clarence DeMar, veteran of more than 100 marathons, three-time Olympian, seven-time winner of the Boston Marathon, and a lifelong runner who between the ages of 21 and 69 participated in more than 1,000 long-distance races.

DeMar was a willing subject in some of the earliest treadmill studies conducted at the Harvard Fatigue Laboratory during the mid-1920s. His willingness to be tested for performance abilities allowed significant insights into the cardiovascular adaptations of highly talented runners. He died in 1958 of metastatic rectal carcinoma. An autopsy was conducted and reported in the scientific literature by the famed cardiologist Paul Dudley White (Currens and White 1961). DeMar's heart weighed a normal 340 gm, but his left ventricular wall was 18 mm thick, compared with the average adult thickness of 10 to 12 mm. His right ventricle was 8 mm thick, twice the average adult value. His heart valves were normal-sized, but his coronary arteries were estimated as two to three times the average adult size. He had visible signs of developing arteriosclerosis in his coronary vessels, as do most people at his age. His very large coronary arteries, however, gave him a large margin of safety to protect against loss of functional coronary flow and also allowed his heart an enormous blood flow during the many years of his racing career.

The Heart Is Protected From Developing an O_2 Debt

An increased coronary artery flow and increased O_2 extraction from the blood are both desirable features for an exercising heart. A primary reason for the elevated O_2 extraction involves a maintained high gradient for O_2 movement into the cardiac muscle cells from the coronary vessel blood. Within the heart cells themselves are adaptations to utilize large quantities of O_2. The heart simply cannot, under any circumstances, incur an O_2 debt. It is constantly very active, and there would never be a time when such a debt could be repaid effectively. Thus, cardiac muscle is the supreme example of a "twitch now, pay now" muscle. By contrast, the FT skeletal muscles can work very intensively for short periods, but then need periods of recovery; they are therefore often referred to as "twitch now, pay later" muscles.

Because the heart is constantly active, any adaptation developed by the ST skeletal muscle cells through endurance training is present to a greater extent in cardiac muscle cells. Cardiac muscle cells contain more myoglobin (the intracellular O_2-storing pigment) than other ST muscle cells. Huge numbers of mitochondria are also present, and cardiac muscle cells can metabolize lactate very effectively in addition to fatty acids and glucose. During exercise, this lactate uptake is so great that it becomes the preferred fuel, even above fatty acids. This ability has obvious value in delaying the onset of metabolic acidosis during intense physical activity.

Endurance Training Increases Heart Blood Flow

An interesting challenge to providing adequate blood flow to the cardiac muscle is discovered when we consider the circulation of blood through this muscle during its normal cycle of activity. Each *cardiac cycle* has a tension generation phase, called *systole* (when blood is ejected from the heart), and a relaxation phase, called *diastole* (when the heart again fills with blood). During systole, muscle tension generation by the spirally arranged cardiac muscle essentially reduces the size of the chambers that it surrounds, thereby emptying the heart of blood. In doing so, however, this wringing action applies considerable force on the blood vessels contained within the heart muscle. This action of the cardiac muscle on its blood vessels is termed *extravascular compression,* and its effect is different in the left and right heart. A higher left ventricular systolic pressure causes enough extravascular compression to almost stop the left coronary artery flow at the point where this vessel penetrates into the heart muscle tissue. Flow through the tissues perfused by the right coronary artery is less affected and continues, although reduced, all through systole.

The longer each diastolic interval, the more thorough the perfusion can be. Thus, it is better to have fewer but longer perfusion periods than more but shorter perfusion periods. This is exactly what occurs in the trained heart. As a result of cardiac chamber enlargement, the stroke volume at any given work load is larger and the heart rate lower, increasing the available perfusion time. Even with the extended diastolic perfusion time in a trained heart, however, the left ventricle can develop signs of hypoxia (inadequate oxygenation) during exhaustive exercise. This is seen especially among individuals with worsening coronary artery disease. In contrast, the right ventricular systolic pressure shows much less increase during exercise, and hence perfusion of the right heart muscle via that coronary artery generally proceeds effectively.

Cardiovascular Contributions to $\dot{V}O_2max$

We have already discussed the measurement and importance of $\dot{V}O_2max$ as a determinant of performance excellence. $\dot{V}O_2max$ can be expressed mathematically in terms of the cardiovascular dynamics of O_2 transport. $\dot{V}O_2$ is equal to the product of cardiac output times O_2 extracted from the blood. O_2 extraction is measured by subtracting the mixed venous blood O_2 concentration from the arterial blood O_2 concentration. This is the a-vO_2 difference discussed earlier. Therefore, we can write the following equation:

$$\dot{V}O_2max = (f_{cmax} \times Q_{smax}) \times max\ a\text{-}\bar{v}O_2\ difference \tag{4.5}$$

Cardiac output is graphed as a function of a-$\bar{v}O_2$ difference in figure 4.6. The typical resting $\dot{V}O_2$ as well as $\dot{V}O_2max$ values in a trained runner are depicted. Changes in any of these variables, as might occur with training or during exercise, can alter $\dot{V}O_2$. Changes in heart rate and stroke volume constitute the so-called *central adjustments* in circulation; in contrast, a change in blood O_2 extraction by the tissues is a *peripheral adjustment*. It is of great interest, therefore, to understand how training can improve the capacity of these variables in their response to exercise and to appreciate the magnitude of possible changes in these variables with exercise at varying intensities. We shall see that maximal heart rate is either unchanged or slightly reduced by endurance training, and that maximal a-$\bar{v}O_2$ difference peaks at about 16 ml/dl. Thus, the heart's capacity to increase the body's aerobic power is improved primarily by increases in maximal stroke volume.

Determining and Regulating Heart Rate

All of the various cell types in the heart are functionally, anatomically connected by microscopic structures called *intercalated disks*. Thus, activity in one cell can be transmitted quickly to all other cells. Certain regions of the heart have nodes of tissue that are not specialized for tension generation but that are composed of

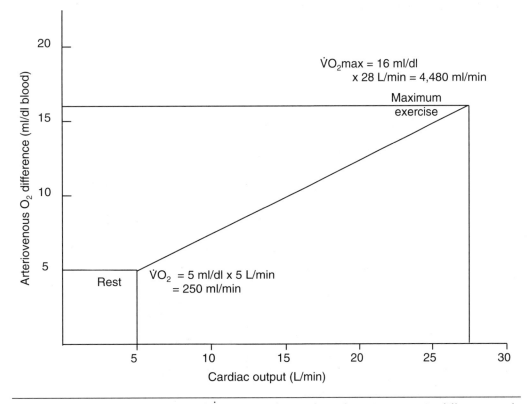

Figure 4.6 Graphic representation of $\dot{V}O_2max$ as the product of arteriovenous O_2 difference and cardiac output. In turn, cardiac output is the product of heart rate × stroke volume.

cells that are neither muscle nor nerve. Their cell membranes are rather unstable, particularly regarding the maintenance of a stable ionic equilibrium between the surrounding fluid and their cytoplasm. A slow, ongoing inward Ca^{2+} ion leakage across the cell membrane brings a gradual depolarization until a sudden, almost explosive cell membrane ionic disruption occurs. This *action potential* is transmitted through the heart and results in depolarization, with momentary sudden tension generation (systole), in all of the muscular cells in the heart. Very rapid recovery occurs, and it is this ongoing repeated process of cellular depolarization and repolarization, causing tension generation and relaxation, that forms the basis for the ongoing heart rhythm. The *sinoatrial node* is the primary tissue responsible for this periodic cardiac depolarization and as such is often termed the *pacemaker* of the heart. It has an intrinsic, basal rhythm of about 105 depolarizations each minute.

Transmitter chemicals from the two divisions of the autonomic nervous system (parasympathetic and sympathetic) each affect this intrinsic rate of depolarization of sinoatrial node tissue, thus changing the heart rate. Figure 4.7 depicts these two innervations to the heart. *Acetylcholine*, released from the *vagus nerves* (parasympathetic system), increases the stability of the nodal cell membranes. In turn, this decreases the rate of depolarization and *lowers* the heart rate. When we are at rest, and particularly during sleep, the parasympathetic nervous system dominates. Its stimulation of the heart via the vagus nerve keeps the heart rate at its lowest value. Apprehension or arousal as the time for exercise approaches—whether a training session or competition—brings an increase in sympathetic nervous system activity, with its *noradrenaline* release from the *cardiac accelerator nerves*, as well as *adrenaline* release from the adrenal medulla. The action of these two chemicals will increase the rate of depolarization and thus *increase* the heart rate.

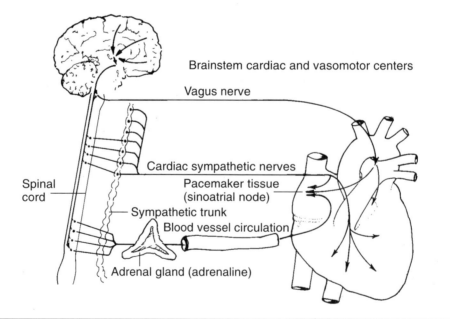

Figure 4.7 Autonomic nervous system connections to the heart. Vagus nerve fibers, from the parasympathetic nervous system, connect primarily to the pacemaker tissue. Their stimulation decreases the heart rate. Cardiac accelerator nerve fibers, from the sympathetic nervous system, extend from the spinal cord through the adjacent sympathetic trunk and then to the heart. Stimulation of these accelerates heart rate. Sympathetic nervous system activation can also increase adrenaline release from the adrenal medulla, which also increases heart rate.

Thus, the heart rate determined at any moment reflects a balance between the relative activity of these three physiological influences on the basal intrinsic rhythm. At rest, parasympathetic tone dominates over sympathetic, giving a net resting heart rate of about 60 to 70 beats/min in sedentary people. As exercise begins, this vagal tone is gradually released, up to about 100 beats/min; sympathetic tone then increases significantly.

Breathing also influences heart rate by mechanisms involving blood pressure receptors located in the carotid arteries. These pressure receptors (called *carotid sinus baroreceptors*) are optimally positioned to monitor blood pressure generated by the heart as it pumps blood toward the brain. The slightest decrease in perfusion pressure to these receptors will be sensed with an appropriate increase in nervous impulse traffic to the brain centers for regulating blood pressure and heart rate. As we inhale, the increased volume occupied by the lungs in the thoracic cavity temporarily impedes venous return, thereby lowering cardiac output, illustrated in figure 4.8. This slight reduction in aortic blood flow is sensed by the baroreceptors, and a brief reflexive increase in heart rate occurs by increased nervous activity to the cardiac centers in the brain. In turn, this reduces parasympathetic nervous activity (via the vagus nerve); the heart rate rises, and blood pressure is maintained. By that time, however, expiration has occurred, with venous return and cardiac output increasing as a result of a decreased lung volume in the thoracic cavity. This too is sensed by the baroreceptors as an increased blood flow and pressure in the carotid arteries. The resulting rhythmic increase and decrease in heart rate caused by breathing is often termed the *respiratory* or *rhythmic arrhythmia*. The term is essentially a misnomer, because *arrhythmia* suggests disease when there in fact is none. It simply represents a breathing-induced heart rate fluctuation.

It can thus be seen that a delicate interplay between the activity of the nervous and respiratory systems keeps the resting pulse changing in a rhythmic fashion. In the electrocardiographic tracing from a trained marathon runner in figure 4.8, the varying time intervals between each heartbeat are clearly evident. This athlete has a lower resting heart rate (in the range of 45 to 55 beats/min) than the norm of 70 beats/min seen in the sedentary population. The breathing-induced heart rate fluctuation is more pronounced in athletes and is truly striking among those highly trained runners who have resting heart rates as low as 30 beats/min. The electrocardiographic tracing illustrated shows the difficulty in attempting to determine an individual's resting heart rate solely on the basis of time difference between two sequential beats. Typically, a series of beats is recorded over a time frame of 10 or 20 s (and then multiplied by, respectively, 6 or 3) to give the heart rate in beats per minute.

What causes the decrease in resting heart rate observable in trained endurance runners? The possible mechanisms are twofold: an increase in parasympathetic nervous system activity or a decrease in sympathetic nervous system activity (Frick, Elovainio, and Somer 1967). Increased vagus nerve stimulation decreases the rate of spontaneous depolarization of the specialized cells in the sinoatrial node, which when activated sufficiently triggers a myocardial depolarization that initiates a heartbeat. Decrease in the activity of these cells thus decreases the frequency of heartbeat generation. The reverse occurs with cardiac accelerator nerve activation. Available evidence suggests that both sympathetic decreases and parasympathetic increases occur in cardiac function as a result of training. But exactly what triggers these adaptive changes in distance runners isn't clear. The end result is the often-seen decreased resting heart rate, known as *bradycardia*, and a decreased maximal heart rate as well.

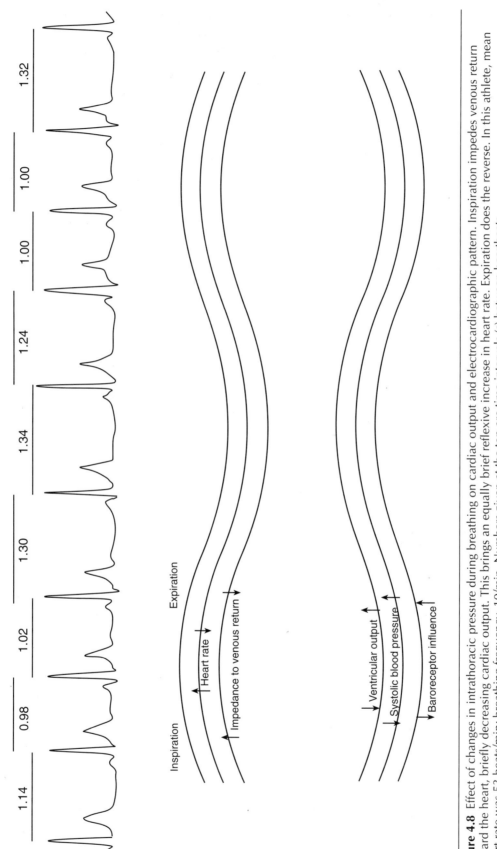

Figure 4.8 Effect of changes in intrathoracic pressure during breathing on cardiac output and electrocardiographic pattern. Inspiration impedes venous return toward the heart, briefly decreasing cardiac output. This brings an equally brief reflexive increase in heart rate. Expiration does the reverse. In this athlete, mean heart rate was 53 beats/min; breathing frequency, 10/min. Numbers given at the top are time intervals (s) between heartbeats.

Increase in Stroke Volume

Trained distance runners have an increased stroke volume both at rest and during exercise in comparison to sedentary people. What causes this increase in stroke volume? There are several possible contributing factors. One is the end-diastolic volume, sometimes called *ventricular preload*. This is the amount of blood in the ventricles just prior to the next heartbeat. One study (Rerych et al. 1980) involving 18 college endurance athletes who trained for six months did show such a increase in the end-diastolic volume. Most likely this is explained by the decreased resting heart rate as a result of developing aerobic fitness.

Another possibility is simply an *increased circulating blood volume* as an adaptation to endurance training. This has indeed been demonstrated as an increase in both plasma volume and red blood cell mass (Brotherhood, Brozovic, and Pugh 1975). These workers found a 16% increase in blood volume, which involved a 13% increase in red cell mass and an 18% increase in plasma volume. This lowered *hematocrit*—the percentage of blood that is red cells—decreases blood viscosity, helping it flow more easily through the vessels. Because the total red cell mass in trained runners is actually increased, the term *dilutional pseudoanemia* has been used to describe this altered blood volume relationship (Eichner 1986).

A third factor in increased stroke volume involves increased *cardiac dimensions*. A larger ventricular chamber should provide a greater stroke volume upon emptying. In 1927 an English translation of a book published in German in 1924 by Felix Deutsch and Emil Kauf provided the most detailed study ever attempted to document heart size among athletes. No study has matched it, and the authors' conclusions are still significant today. In comparing athletes to sedentary subjects, they showed that competitive athletes engaged in such sports as rowing, cycling, skiing, swimming, and running have a statistically large incidence of enlarged hearts (although this was not found in Clarence DeMar's heart—he had thicker ventricular walls and larger coronary arteries). The cardiac enlargement involves an increase in size of the heart chambers (dilation) as well as an increase in the mass of heart muscle. Chambers of both the right and left heart are affected.

The increase in heart muscle mass is the result of an increase in size of existing myocardial cells, called *hypertrophy*, and not an increase in the number of cells, known as *hyperplasia*. An increase in the number of mitochondria and myofilaments increases the diameter of each cell. There is also an increase in the number of sarcomeres, which increases the length of these muscle cells. Unfortunately, very little data exist on heart sizes in these people *before* they began to engage in the training that gave them their status as trained athletes. Do certain athletes born with larger-than-usual hearts find endurance athletics easier than those athletes less endowed and hence participate in those activities, enlarging their hearts even more? Or is it solely the great devotion of these individuals to endurance athletics, together with the adaptive abilities of the heart to enlarge with stress, that produces the observed result? We just do not know at present.

The response of the heart to exercise is specific to the type of loading to which it is subjected. Echocardiographic studies comparing the hearts of endurance-trained athletes (swimmers and runners) with strength-trained athletes (wrestlers and shot-putters) have been especially informative (Morganroth et al. 1975). Table 4.2 compares the net effects of these two training emphases on four aspects of cardiac adaptation. Endurance athletes devote most of their training to submaximal work and thus present their hearts with long periods of increased venous return. We call this *volume loading* of the heart. The cardiac response to such an exercise challenge is lengthened ventricular muscle fibers and thus an increased ventricular chamber volume, with no appreciable change in ventricular wall thickness. This produces a larger stroke volume both at rest and during exercise. In turn, a slower heart rate at any given work load can still maintain cardiac output, thereby enhancing perfusion of the cardiac muscle during the diastolic (rest) period. Because the maximal achievable heart rate changes very little, endurance training increases the maximal cardiac output, which contributes to an increased $\dot{V}O_2$max.

In contrast, athletes engaged in strength-oriented training (such as weight lifters and shot-putters) have a left ventricular response that is an adaptation to short-term, high-pressure loading. During periods of maximal or near-maximal activity the working skeletal muscles provide such a large compressive force against the blood vessels within them that flow is essentially stopped. In turn, the heart generates enormous muscular tension in an attempt to overcome this high resistance to blood flow. As summarized in table 4.2, the heart's adaptation to permit this is an increased left ventricular wall thickness in an attempt to provide the additional tension-generating protein. With this so-called *pressure loading,* there is thus minimal change in maximal stroke volume and cardiac output, and minimal improvement in $\dot{V}O_2$max. This does not affect these athletes' performance, because their specialty is not endurance-oriented competition.

A fourth factor in increased stroke volume involves *myocardial contractility.* Both healthy, sedentary people and endurance athletes have a high level of *myocardial vigor,* which is defined as the combined features of optimal speed and force of cardiac muscle tension generation. However, there is little evidence that training itself makes the heart more vigorous in its ability to function, as its functioning is already honed virtually to perfection. Each beat essentially empties the heart chambers, leaving only a very small *residual volume.* However, during exercise this residual volume gets even smaller, contributing to an increase in stroke volume.

A fifth possible factor is *arterial blood pressure,* sometimes referred to as *ventricular afterload.* Again, as with myocardial vigor, no evidence exists that endurance training itself brings changes in arterial blood pressure that would contribute to an increased stroke volume. If anything, mean arterial blood pressure may be slightly reduced at $\dot{V}O_2$max among athletes. We know, of course, that skeletal muscle blood flow increases with training, but if there is no real increase in blood pressure, the only explanation is that more small skeletal muscle blood vessels (capillaries) are open to permit more flow. This is often referred to as an increased skeletal muscle vascular conductance.

TABLE 4.2

Comparison of the Effects of Isotonic (Endurance-Oriented) Versus Isometric (Strength-Oriented) Training on Cardiac Adaptation to Exercise

Variable	Isotonic	Isometric
Heart wall thickness	Unchanged	Increased
End-diastolic ventricular volume	Increased	Unchanged
Cardiac mass	Increased	Increased
Cardiac output	Increased	Unchanged

Development of this combined increase in stroke volume and decrease in heart rate at any given work load provides some of the most crucial adaptations to the higher-speed training that is an integral part of the advanced preparation of all middle- and long-distance runners. Anaerobic conditioning sustainable for between 15 and 20 min and done at lactate/ventilatory threshold pace provides the kind of volume-overload stimulus that eventually increases ventricular chamber size. At the same time, the intrinsic pacemaker rhythm decreases by a small increment, in turn lowering the maximal attainable heart rate. Table 4.3 summarizes these changes in cardiac dynamics—decreased heart rate and increased stroke volume—that can occur both at rest and at maximal exercise among elite distance runners as compared to sedentary people. Figure 4.9 summarizes the means by which the primary adaptations seen with endurance training all contribute to improved performance potential: a decrease in heart rate and increases in ventricular chamber size, blood volume, skeletal muscle capillarization, and muscle cell enzyme content.

Increase in Arteriovenous O_2 Difference

Figure 4.10 shows the changes in arterial and venous O_2 content of blood observable as athletes increase their exercise intensity. Arterial O_2 content may rise slightly because of the movement of fluid into the active muscle cells and fluid space outside the capillaries, whereas mean venous O_2 content decreases dramatically. Saltin and Gollnick (1983) explained that a major reason for this increased O_2 extraction comes from an increase in skeletal muscle capillary density with training. More capillaries around each skeletal muscle fiber reduce the diffusion distance for O_2 as it moves from the circulatory system to muscle tissues. Also, there is an increased mean transit time for blood moving through working muscle.

It is interesting that the total blood volume in the skeletal muscles does not increase as a result of the observed increase in capillary blood volume. Physiologically, this would be unwise, because more blood would be in the periphery, decreasing stroke volume and ventricular filling pressure. It appears that skeletal muscle blood volume is maintained by a combination of increased capillary volume and reduced venous volume.

Other factors contribute to the a-$\bar{v}O_2$ difference as well. Skeletal muscle myoglobin levels increase with endurance training. This O_2-binding pigment provides an effective O_2 reservoir when the partial pressure of O_2 in intensely active muscle begins to fall to low levels. There is also an increase in the total

---

TABLE 4.3

Changes in Heart Rate and Stroke Volume at Rest and Maximal Exercise in Sedentary People and Endurance-Trained Runners[a]

Variable	Resting conditions		Maximal exercise	
	Nonathlete	Elite runner	Nonathlete	Elite runner
Cardiac output (ml/min)	4,900	4,515	22,800	36,100
Stroke volume (ml)	70	105	120	190
Heart rate (beats/min)	70	43	190	190
$\dot{V}O_2$ (ml · kg^{-1} · min^{-1})	3.5	3.5	46	85

[a]Data are from two 60-kg male subjects.

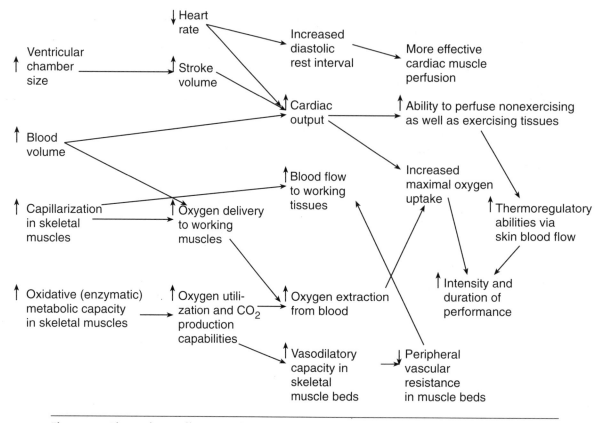

Figure 4.9 Flow scheme illustrating how major adaptations occurring with endurance training (increases in ventricular chamber size, blood volume, skeletal muscle capillarization, and intracellular enzyme content and a decrease in heart rate) all contribute to the potential for improved performance.

mitochondrial enzyme content in trained skeletal muscles, permitting greater O_2 usage.

An additional possible contributory factor could involve greater shunting of blood away from the nonexercising tissues in the visceral region and into the working muscles. Endurance exercise training, however, does not appear to improve this, because near-maximal vasoconstriction can occur in these tissues even among untrained individuals asked to exercise at their maximal capacity. The maximal overall a-$\bar{v}O_2$ difference found in healthy people is about 16 ml/dl, which represents extraction of about 85% of available O_2 from blood into tissues.

Pulmonary System Responses to Exercise

The pulmonary system plays a critical role in permitting exercise because it is the primary site for both O_2 acquisition into the blood perfusing the working tissues and CO_2 removal from those tissues. Thus, not only do the lungs permit aerobic metabolism in working tissues because of their O_2 delivery capabilities, but they also serve as the body's primary organ for acid (CO_2) excretion. In contrast to organ systems such as the heart and skeletal muscles, extensive morphological adaptations by the pulmonary system to the rigors of long-term endurance exercise do not develop. Instead, there are accommodative changes in response to the demands of exercise. This means that the pulmonary system is essentially already equipped as a result of its existing structure to deal reason-

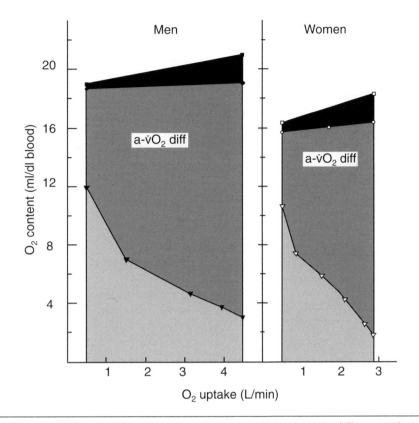

Figure 4.10 Changes in arterial and venous O_2 content of blood (a-$\bar{v}O_2$ difference) during increasing exercise intensity. For both men (left), the response is similar. The darkest shaded area at the top represents the difference between calculated O_2-binding capacity and actual O_2 content in arterial blood. The bottom shaded area represents calculated mixed venous blood O_2 content, which decreases as work load (measured in L/min of O_2 uptake) increases. The shaded middle area indicates the increasing arteriovenous O_2 difference. *Note.* From *Textbook of Work Physiology* (2nd ed., p.183) by P.-O. Åstrand and K. Rodahl, 1977, New York: McGraw-Hill. Copyright 1977 by McGraw-Hill, Inc. Adapted by permission.

ably well with demands placed on it to maintain unchanging O_2 (*iso-oxic*) and unchanging CO_2 (*isocapnic*) concentrations in the arterial blood perfusing the working tissues.

Getting O_2 From Lungs to Blood

Our normal breathing rate of about 12 breaths/min, with each breath about 500 ml, produces a resting *respiratory minute volume* (RMV), or *expired ventilation* ($\dot{V}_E$), of about 6 L/min. This air swirls through a complex series of breathing tubes, beginning with the mouth and nose and continuing through the pharynx, larynx, trachea, bronchi, and bronchioles, to eventually circulate in about 300 million tiny air sacs called alveoli. In any single resting breath, about 67% of the air becomes the *alveolar volume*, which can exchange with gases in the blood. The remaining 33% remains in airways above the alveoli, and is called *dead space volume* (V_D). Pulmonary capillaries are immediately adjacent to alveoli. The wall thickness of this so-called *alveolocapillary membrane* ranges from 0.5 to 1.5 μm. Across it, the respiratory gases (O_2 and CO_2) flow in opposite directions (fig. 4.11). Assuming a resting cardiac output of 4,900 ml/min and a pulmonary capillary blood volume of about 70 ml, these capillaries are emptied and refilled 70 times per minute! During maximal exercise, the $\dot{V}_E$ can exceed 170 L/min, and cardiac output can exceed 40 L/min—an enormous increase beyond resting conditions. How is gas exchange managed under such circumstances?

The primary task of the pulmonary system in accommodating the needs of an endurance athlete for either hard training or competition is to provide adequate gas exchange between alveoli and arterial blood with minimal work required by the lungs and chest. Otherwise, the added O_2 cost would not justify the O_2 gain. Two challenging problems are presented to the lungs as exercise becomes more intense. One involves the need to increase the amount of blood flowing through the pulmonary capillaries without increasing pulmonary system blood pressure. Such an increase would cause fluid to leak into and accumulate within the alveoli or the interstitial space between alveoli and capillaries, producing *edema.* This problem is managed nicely in two ways. First, exercise increases the filling of capillaries that were essentially nonperfused at rest, thereby providing a passive expansion of the pulmonary blood volume without increasing the pulmonary blood vessel resistance. Second, if any tendency toward extravascular fluid accumulation does occur, the lungs are equipped with a very extensive lymphatic drainage system (Staub, Nagano, and Pearce 1967), ensuring prompt fluid removal and maintenance of effective lung function.

A second problem involves the movement of ever-increasing quantities of O_2 from ambient air into the blood. A greatly increased O_2 extraction from tissue capillary blood during exercise makes the returning venous blood considerably less oxygenated than during the resting state. This so-called *mixed venous blood* flows from the right heart into the lungs via the pulmonary artery and then into the smaller arterioles that eventually empty into lung capillaries. Oxygen flows down its concentration gradient from the air-filled alveoli across the alveolocapillary membranes and into the pulmonary capillaries during the brief period that the blood in the lungs flows through those capillaries (figure 4.11). It is only across these alveolocapillary membranes that gas exchange with the blood can occur.

Oxygen movement from the atmosphere into blood is determined by

- its concentration difference between alveolus and pulmonary capillary,
- its solubility in blood, and
- the amount of hemoglobin to which it can bind once in the bloodstream.

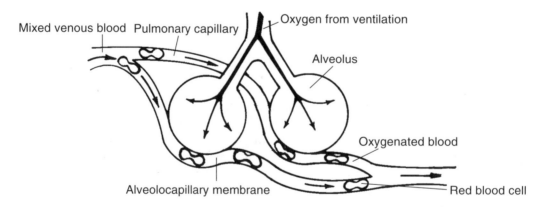

Figure 4.11 Gas exchange across the alveolocapillary membrane. Normally, the fusion of capillary endothelium with alveolar epithelium provides a membrane of 0.5 to 1.0μm in thickness, ideal for rapid exchange of gases (O_2 and CO_2) between pulmonary capillary blood and alveolar gas. Red blood cells, being about the same or greater diameter as the capillaries through which they move, may twist and bend as they proceed.

Our environmental air is a mixture of gases, with O_2 making up about 20.9% of the total. Physical laws explaining gas movement tell us that each gas in the atmosphere behaves independently, without chemical interaction with the others. Thus, each gas contributes independently to the total pressure exerted by the gas mixture as it moves down its concentration gradient from one place to another (recall figure 3.6). If sea-level barometric pressure, for example, is 760 mmHg, with O_2 making up 20.9% of the atmosphere, then the inspired partial pressure exerted by O_2 (written as P_IO_2) can be calculated as follows:

$$P_IO_2 = 760 \times 0.209 = 158.8 \text{ mmHg} \tag{4.6}$$

Whether the air we inhale is dry or moist, it will get completely humidified well before it moves into the alveoli. This dilution with water vapor helps to lower the alveolar O_2 partial pressure (P_AO_2) down to about 100 mmHg. As pulmonary arteriolar blood enters the capillaries, a very rapid O_2 transfer into the blood begins, along with CO_2 transfer from blood into the alveoli. Normally, a complete equilibrium is nearly reached, and the arterial blood O_2 partial pressure (P_aO_2) is about 97 mmHg. Thus, at rest the *alveolo-arterial O_2 gradient*—written as (A-a)PO$_2$ gradient—is about 3 mmHg (table 4.4). This is the same for men and women.

This slight imperfection in the equilibrium of O_2 between alveolar and arterial blood, even at rest, is relatively unimportant. This is because in addition to the total quantity of O_2 *dissolved* in the blood (measured as PO$_2$), a very much larger quantity of O_2 is *chemically bound* to hemoglobin. This is why it is so important for healthy runners to ensure that they have adequate quantities of hemoglobin, and why many runners travel to altitude so that the low O_2 levels there will stimulate more hemoglobin production. Oxygen has a very strong affinity for hemoglobin. When O_2 enters the bloodstream it diffuses through the

TABLE 4.4

Values for Selected Cardiopulmonary Variables at Rest and During Hard Exercise in Trained Male Runners

Variable	Rest	Hard exercise
Alveolar ventilation ($\dot{V}_A$) (L/min)	4.2	140
Tidal volume (V_T) (L)	0.5	3
Breathing rate (f_R) (per min)	12	55
Expired ventilation ($\dot{V}_E$) (L/min)	6	180
O_2 consumption ($\dot{V}O_2$) (ml/min)	270	5,500
O_2 consumption ($\dot{V}O_2$) (ml · kg^{-1} · min^{-1})	3.5	85
Alveolar PO$_2$ (P_AO_2) (mmHg)	100	120
Arterial PO$_2$ (P_aO_2) (mmHg)	97	90
(A-a)PO$_2$ difference (mmHg)	2-10	30
Mixed venous PO$_2$ ($P_{\bar{v}}O_2$) (mmHg)	46	20
Arterial PCO$_2$ (P_aCO_2) (mmHg)	40	25-32
Arterial pH	7.4	7.2-7.3
Pulmonary blood flow (L/min)	5	30
Lung capillary blood volume (ml)	70	250
Mean red blood cell transit time (s)	0.75	0.5

plasma, crosses each red blood cell membrane, and then attaches to hemoglobin molecules contained within the red blood cells.

We can calculate the *total O_2 content* of arterial blood as the sum of the dissolved plus bound oxygen. As an example, using some "typical" or average healthy values, let us consider a male runner with a hemoglobin concentration of 15 gm/dl and a P_aO_2 of 98 mmHg. We will assume that he has the typical binding affinity of O_2 for hemoglobin, namely 1.31 ml O_2 per gram of hemoglobin, and we'll assume that O_2 is attached to 96% of the available sites (this is referred to as 96% hemoglobin saturation). At a P_aO_2 of 98 mmHg, the dissolved O_2 is 0.29 ml/dl. The bound O_2 is determined by the product of hemoglobin concentration times O_2 binding affinity times percent O_2 saturation ($15 \times 1.31 \times 0.96$). Thus, the O_2 content would be calculated as

$$O_2 \text{ content} = 0.29 + (15 \times 1.31 \times 0.96) = 19.15 \text{ ml/dl} \tag{4.7}$$

For a female runner, again using typical healthy values, taking a hemoglobin concentration of 13.5 gm/dl, and assuming a dissolved O_2 level of 0.29 ml/dl and 98% hemoglobin saturation with O_2, the O_2 content would be calculated as follows:

$$O_2 \text{ content} = 0.29 + (13.5 \times 1.31 \times 0.98) = 17.62 \text{ ml/dl} \tag{4.8}$$

Thus, using these two specific hemoglobin values as examples, which are normal mean values for men and women, women have about 8% less O_2 per deciliter of blood than men. There is, of course, a range of healthy values for hemoglobin for males and females. As an example, a male with a hemoglobin value of 14 gm/dl would still be considered normal (toward the low end of the range), as would also a hemoglobin value of 14 gm/dl for a female be considered normal (toward the high end of the range). These two individuals, thus, would have the same blood O_2 content.

Figure 4.12 illustrates the relationship between blood PO_2 and the percentage of potential O_2 binding sites on hemoglobin that are saturated with O_2. The S-shaped curve of the binding relationship, as well as the fact that arterial blood hemoglobin is very nearly saturated with O_2 under normally existing PO_2 conditions, means that a considerable reduction in P_vO_2 can occur without much reduction in total arterial O_2 content.

When blood reaches the systemic capillaries, dissolved O_2 diffuses rapidly across the capillary membrane and into the adjacent tissues. This reduces the capillary PO_2, which in turn promotes the release of a portion of the O_2 reservoir of hemoglobin out into the surrounding plasma to help raise the capillary PO_2. As blood leaves the systemic capillaries, a sizable part of the O_2 reservoir of hemoglobin typically has been depleted, and the PO_2 is somewhat reduced. Notice in figure 4.12 that the PO_2 of mixed venous blood (P_vO_2, the mixture of blood returning to the lungs from all the various tissue beds) has fallen from just under 100 mmHg to about 40 mmHg. At this P_vO_2, there still remains about 76% of the total blood O_2 reservoir bound to hemoglobin. During intense exercise, the P_vO_2 can fall to as low as 20 mmHg.

During high-intensity exercise, does the (A-a)PO_2 gradient of 2 to 10 mmHg remain? No, and this points out one limitation of the pulmonary system to exercise that has been found to occur in some highly trained, elite-level distance runners. Dempsey, Hanson, and Henderson (1984) have reported a steady reduction in dissolved arterial O_2—called *arterial hypoxemia*—as highly trained

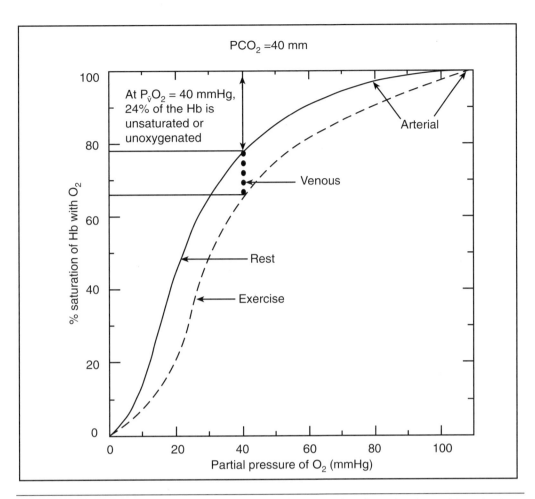

Figure 4.12 The oxyhemoglobin dissociation curve. A sigmoid (S-shaped) relationship exists in relation to the binding of oxygen to hemoglobin (Hb) when hemoglobin is exposed to increasing quantities of oxygen dissolved in red blood cell water. Arterial saturation (P_aO_2 = 100 mmHg) is nearly 100%; mixed venous saturation (P_vO_2 = 40 mmHg) is about 75%. Increasing blood PCO_2 decreases binding affinity of hemoglobin for O_2, as seen by the right shift of the curve (dashed line). This occurs with exercise. As shown, at any given $PaCO_2$ this decreased affinity permits release of sizable quantities of additional O_2 into the fluid portion of blood (as dissolved O_2), thereby ensuring a gradient of O_2 movement from blood into working tissues. *Note.* From *Respiratory Anatomy and Physiology* (p.190) by D.E. Martin and J.W. Youtsey, 1988, St. Louis: C.V. Mosby. Copyright 1988 by C.V. Mosby. Reprinted by permission.

runners approach their maximal performance capacities. This (A-a)PO_2 gradient can be 20 to 30 mmHg at O_2 consumption values of 4,000 ml/min and as high as 40 mmHg at O_2 consumption values of 5,000 ml/min (table 4.4). Although this so-called *diffusion disequilibrium* is developing at these high work rates, adequate O_2 is still available for the working tissues. It has not yet been accurately determined whether this disequilibrium actually limits performance for these athletes.

What is the explanation for the decrease in P_aO_2 (and decreased hemoglobin saturation with O_2) seen with near-maximal exercise in trained runners? It is caused by a combination of two factors: the need to add much more than the usual quantity of O_2 to blood perfusing the lung capillaries and the reduced amount of time that blood remains in contact with the alveolar surface. Figure 4.13 shows that at rest a red blood cell will be in a pulmonary capillary for about 0.75 s, well within the time required for nearly complete oxygenation to occur.

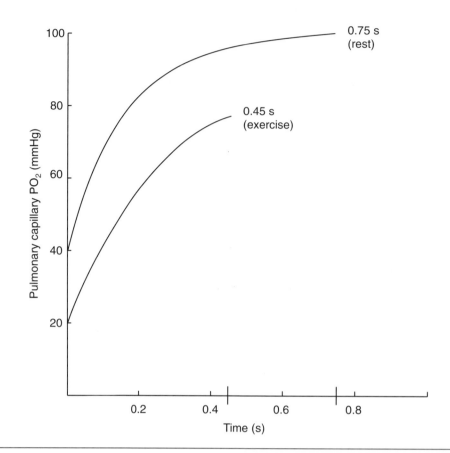

Figure 4.13 The time course of O_2 and CO_2 movement across the alveolocapillary membrane at rest and during exercise. At rest, with 0.75 s available, only abut 0.6 s is required to achieve an acceptable arterial PO_2 of 95 mmHg. However, during maximal exercise in very highly trained distance runners, only 0.45 s may be available due to increased blood transit time through pulmonary capillaries. Thus, PO_2 values of not much more than 85 mmHg may be reached in blood destined for the systemic arterial circulation

Only about 0.6 s is required. As exercise increases in intensity, this so-called *pulmonary capillary transit time* increases, and eventually is so rapid that only about 0.45 s is available for alveolar gas exchange. Though this may be adequate for CO_2 removal, it probably isn't enough for optimal O_2 uptake.

Breathing Dynamics With Increasing Exercise

The ventilatory system's efficiency for providing airflow is self-optimizing. As for blood flow, where $CO = f_c \times Q_s$, for breathing the *expired ventilation* ($\dot{V}_E$) is the product of *breathing rate* (f_R) and *tidal volume* (V_T), the volume expired per breath. Thus,

$$\dot{V}_E = f_R \times V_T \tag{4.9}$$

Excessively deep breaths, few in number, would be too energy costly. Very many breaths, each small in volume (as observed when dogs pant to cool themselves evaporatively) would not provide effective alveolar gas exchange. And so we optimize our breathing, with V_T never more than about 60% to 65% of the *vital capacity*, defined as the maximum amount of air that can be exhaled after a maximal inspiration. Thus, among our highly trained athletes undergoing a maximal exercise evaluation, we commonly record maximal f_R values no greater than about 55 per minute. If each breath (V_T) is about 3,000 ml, this gives a $\dot{V}_E$ of about 165 L/min. Quite often, runners synchronize their f_R to their stride frequency. Thus, if two footstrikes occur during the time required for each inhalation and exhalation, a common cadence of 196 footstrikes/min is also accompanied by a f_R of 49 breaths/min. One practical implication of this information relates to the usefulness of shortening stride and quickening cadence when climbing hills. The resulting increased f_R with increased stride frequency helps increase O_2 intake.

The *diaphragm* is the primary respiratory muscle used during resting breathing, but exercise recruits a large number of *accessory muscles* to assist with ventilation. Some, such as the abdominal muscles, are primarily *expiratory* in their contribution. Their powerful expiratory force helps optimize the available inspiratory time as breathing depth increases. This also helps to lengthen the diaphragm, increasing the tension it can exert when it is stimulated. Other muscles, notably the intercostals, scalenes, and sternocleidomastoids, provide marked *inspiratory* assistance. Subtle but important activity in still other muscles also makes breathing easier. Stimulation of laryngeal abductor muscles, for example, increases the diameter of this narrowest portion of the respiratory tract, thereby decreasing resistance to flow through it (Dempsey, Aaron, and Martin 1988).

At the beginning of exercise V_T increases with each breath, and the portion of air in the alveoli (alveolar volume) increases more than the portion in the airways above (dead space volume, V_D). Pulmonary physiologists thus say that the V_D/V_T ratio decreases as exercise increases, at least initially. A steadily increasing elevated breathing depth (V_T) and rate (f_R) will match increased metabolic needs. This increased breathing to meet metabolic requirements is termed *exercise hyperpnea*, and will continue until V_T reaches a plateau that corresponds to the first (ventilatory) threshold. As exercise intensity increases beyond this threshold, the most efficient means for continuing to steadily increase the alveolar ventilation is to increase f_R.

Indeed, during long-duration exercise at relatively low work intensities, such as between 50% and 60% of $\dot{V}O_2$max for about 2 hr, a gradual but measurable rise in breathing rate (15% to 40%) does occur. This is accompanied by a reduction in V_T of about 10% to 15%. The term used to describe this change is *tachypneic ventilatory drift*. The decrease in V_T does not exactly compensate for the increased frequency, because $\dot{V}_E$ increases as well. This drift is not observed during the short-duration runs (1 hr or less) that characterize most training sessions.

We could suspect that this slight increase in breathing rate is more energy wasteful than that seen during resting breathing. There is now a slight increase in the V_D/V_T ratio because of greater net air movement in relation to actual alveolar ventilation. With ventilatory drift the small net decrease in alveolar ventilation causes a slight accumulation of CO_2 in arterial blood. We know that CO_2 is a powerful ventilatory stimulant, and this small rise in P_aCO_2 probably increases the $\dot{V}_E$ by 10% to 30%. The level of $\dot{V}_E$, with its removal of CO_2, thereby serves as the major determinant of arterial H^+ ion concentration during this submaximal long-term work (i.e., at work loads ranging from a long training run to marathon or ultradistance racing). These subtle changes in volume and rate dynamics are controlled automatically to optimize mechanical efficiency while maintaining normal blood O_2 and CO_2 concentrations. Thus, it is unwise for coaches or athletes to attempt voluntary regulation of breathing patterns.

Body temperature modifies the hyperventilatory response. As body temperature increases—for example, with running on a warm and humid day—ventilation increases (MacDougall et al. 1974). Cooling, as permitted by running in conditions of low humidity that permit evaporative heat loss, in turn reduces the magnitude of hyperventilation.

Physically fit individuals typically can maintain a steady-state ventilation and blood acid-base equilibrium over long time periods. We see this among athletes racing over distances from the marathon to the longest ultradistance event. This steady state is just below the *lactate/ventilatory threshold pace*—ranging from around 50% of $\dot{V}O_2$max in serious fitness athletes to more than 80% of $\dot{V}O_2$max in the elite level group. Because $\dot{V}O_2$max will also likely rise among these athletes as they train at this pace, this prolonged performance level represents a remarkable accommodation capability of the pulmonary system. When exercise intensity exceeds this threshold—for example, more than 50% of $\dot{V}O_2$max in serious fitness runners and more than 80% of $\dot{V}O_2$max in well-trained elite runners—then the steady state is no longer maintainable. The tachypneic ventilatory drift is observable, and prolonged exercise at such intensities has a definite time limitation.

These limitations in part explain the intensity at which various competitive distance events can be managed. As an example, the 10,000-m event is raced by a trained athlete typically at roughly 90% to 92% of $\dot{V}O_2$max, and the marathon at about 85% of lactate/ventilatory threshold pace. Accumulating metabolic acidosis from the faster pace limits the time that 10,000-m runners can race effectively at that intensity. Developing fatigue (from acidosis in 10,000-m runners and from fuel depletion and dehydration in marathoners) decreases running efficiency, thereby increasing the metabolic rate required to maintain pace. In turn, heat production increases, raising core temperature. Increasing dehydration from fluid loss provides a smaller reservoir for perspiration, decreasing evaporative potential and also increasing body temperature. Both of these factors (dehydration and fatigue) contribute to the tachypneic ventilatory drift. Increased diversion of blood to maintain ventilatory muscle function occurs. Dempsey, Aaron, and Martin (1988) refer to this as "stealing" by the ventilatory muscles of blood flow from the pool available for the limb muscles. The extent of energy drain for maintaining effective ventilatory muscle activity during vigorous exercise has not been accurately quantified because of measurement difficulties, but it could be as high as 25% during hard work (Pardy, Hussain, and Macklem 1984).

Trained endurance runners tend to exhibit a reduced ventilatory response to very intense exercise. One could suggest that, because *dyspnea* (defined as a sensation of breathlessness) is a limiting symptom for exercise tolerance, removing it might permit greater exercise tolerance. Particularly in view of the reservoir of O_2 bound to hemoglobin, it might be possible for trained runners to optimize for a slightly reduced ventilation at the expense of greater arterial hemoglobin desaturation, thereby permitting increased high-level work tolerance. Indeed, such *arterial hemoglobin desaturation* does occur, as described in the literature (Dempsey, Hanson, and Henderson 1984) and seen in our own experience with trained runners.

One advantage of decreased ventilation during heavy work loads could be a decreased ventilatory stealing of blood from the highly active limb muscles, or it could prolong these limiting effects from being influential until an even greater work load has been reached. Thus, athletes undergoing arduous endurance training have been invaluable in identifying some of the limitations of the pulmonary system to high-level performance. There is (1) a limitation in gas exchange between alveoli and blood, (2) an increase in ventilatory cost, and (3) an inability to sustain breathing at high rates. This same training has also provided a means for us to observe some of the temporary overrides for permitting such extremely intense exercise, which might never be observed by studying the responses of less-trained people.

Evaluating Pulmonary Function Among Trained Athletes

Do trained distance runners have improved pulmonary function? When they are compared cross-sectionally with age-, height-, and sex-matched untrained controls, they show improvements in some aspects. But because these same athletes were not evaluated before they began training, it is not known to what extent hereditary components may also affect pulmonary function. Are these subjects excellent runners because they possess pulmonary function capabilities greater than generally observed, or has training actually brought specific beneficial changes? We do not know.

Clinically, a *pulmonary function test* (PFT) assesses three different aspects of system performance: the size of the lungs (*lung volumes*), the dynamics of flow through the pulmonary system (*flow rates*), and the ability of O_2 to diffuse from the environment through the lungs into the bloodstream (*diffusing capacity*). Standard guidelines were published by the American Thoracic Society in 1979 for quantification of various lung volume, flow rate, and diffusing capacity values. Using such guidelines, we have done PFT evaluations on a sizable population of trained distance runners, both men (Martin, May, and Pilbeam 1986) and women (Martin and May 1987), in an attempt to identify possible differences from an age-, height-, and sex-matched untrained control group. There is little statistical difference between the two population means due to considerable individual variation within each group, but quite large differences do exist among individual athletes. Another reason for conducting PFT evaluations is to screen for disease or to quantify the extent of disease processes that do occur. Some of our athletes have various degrees of exercise-induced asthma. PFT evaluation (illustrated in figure 4.14) allows better identification of the extent of this breathing disorder as well as evaluation of the effectiveness of approved medications for treatment.

Among the various flow rate variables, one that we frequently find elevated among both trained male and female runners is *maximum voluntary ventilation* (MVV). This is determined by a 12- to 15-s test of maximal airflow generation. Such increased performance is predictable, as distance running requires the muscles of breathing to be moderately active during long runs and highly active during fast-paced sessions. Although MVV may be an indicator of short-term endurance, however, it may not be a good indicator of *maximum sustainable ventilation* (MSV). MSV can be measured during the final moments of treadmill testing as athletes approach their performance limits. MSV is also elevated among trained runners when compared with matched, untrained controls. MVV is typically larger than MSV by about 35%.

One complicating factor in appreciating pulmonary system performance is that runners nearing their MSV in treadmill tests to determine maximal performance are operating at a lower remaining lung volume at the end of each breath than when they perform the MVV clinical test. The former condition is more efficient than the latter because the diaphragm is longer and able to generate tension more efficiently. We are only beginning to explain the mechanism whereby these athletes respond to their clinical evaluation in a physiologically

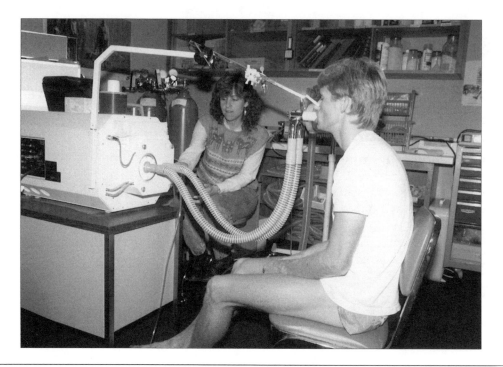

Figure 4.14 Pulmonary function evaluation of a trained distance runner (1995 U.S. men's marathon champion, Keith Brantly). Typically, such studies include assessment of lung volume, flow rate, and diffusing capacity.

different manner than their natural breathing style during running. It may relate to how they perceive and perform their assigned task. During the MVV test athletes are seated, at rest, and encouraged to blow into and out of the collecting tube as rapidly and deeply as possible. The forced time urgency of the clinical test is likely greater than that of maintaining breathing during a treadmill exercise stress test, and this may stimulate a slightly earlier inspiratory effort. And, of course, when MSV values are obtained, the athletes are running, not sitting.

One of the variables related to lung flow that seems consistently increased in trained runners is the *forced expiratory flow* (FEF). FEF is measured during the middle portion of a maximum forced expiration, thus explained the clinical term ($FEF_{25\%-75\%}$) used to refer to it. Powerful expiratory muscles are required to achieve this high expiratory flow, which then permits the next inspiration to occur more quickly. The abdominal muscles are especially effective in this regard, emphasizing the importance of sit-ups in training.

Lung diffusing capacity represents the largest amount of O_2 that can transfer across the alveolocapillary membrane and bind to hemoglobin molecules in the pulmonary capillary blood adjacent to that membrane. There is thus a *membrane component* (related to the thickness, surface area, and physicochemical properties of the alveolocapillary membrane) as well as a *perfusion component* (determined by pulmonary capillary blood volume and hematocrit). We find rather consistent increases in resting diffusing capacity among highly trained runners as compared with their matched sedentary controls, and the reason for this has not yet been clearly identified. The actual size of the lungs doesn't seem to increase with endurance training. But resting cardiac output (Henderson, Haggard, and Dolley 1927) and total blood volume (Brotherhood, Brozovic, and Pugh 1975) tend to be increased. This should bring more extensive lung perfusion, with a possibly greater pulmonary blood volume, and thus an increased diffusing capacity. Active investigation of this interesting topic is underway in several laboratories around the world.

Blood O_2 Transport

Metabolizing tissues require O_2 in quantities far in excess of solely those dissolved in the bloodstream. Thus, an additional reservoir of O_2 is mandatory. Hemoglobin binds to O_2 and thus serves this need admirably. In fact, it carries 98.5% of all the O_2 in the bloodstream; only 1.5% is dissolved. Although hemoglobin has additional important roles in the transport of CO_2 and H^+ ions, which make it a major buffer against acidosis, its role as an O_2 reservoir is primary.

On every pass through the circulatory system during resting conditions, each 100 ml (1 dl) of blood typically gives between 5 and 6 ml O_2 to the body tissues for their metabolic needs (this is the a-$\bar{v}O_2$ difference). If hemoglobin did not exist, insufficient O_2 would be available in the dissolved form to provide this requirement. Under resting conditions of blood flow (about 5 L/min flowing out of the right and left heart each), the dissolved arterial O_2 partial pressure (P_aO_2) would need to be 2,000 mmHg. But our resting, sea-level P_aO_2 approaches only 100 mmHg, limited by existing atmospheric conditions. Apart from breathing high concentrations of pure O_2 from a tank, the only other possibility to meet O_2 demands by dissolved O_2 alone would be to increase blood flow, but then we would need 80 L/min to provide enough O_2 to meet just resting needs. This is impossible, because even during maximal exercise the human heart isn't capable of permitting more than about 40 L/min of blood flow. Clearly, hemoglobin is a crucial molecule in solving the body's needs for a large quantity of available bound O_2.

The structure of hemoglobin gives many clues about how it acts in carrying respiratory gases. It is a roughly spherical molecule consisting of four units, each of which has a long protein chain called *globin*, composed of about 150 amino acids, linked to a complex organic chemical ring structure called a *porphyrin*. CO_2 and H^+ ions bind to the globin portion of the molecule, whereas O_2 binds to *heme*, which is the term given to the porphyrin ring plus an iron atom bound to its center.

Many molecules resembling hemoglobin exist in the living world. Chlorophyll, for example, closely resembles heme. The substitution of iron for the magnesium found in chlorophyll allowed heme to form, thus paving the way for the organic evolution of animals. Recall that the cytochrome enzymes of the electron transport chain have a heme structure as well, but with iron in the ferric (Fe^{3+}) oxidation state instead of the ferrous (Fe^{2+}) state found in hemoglobin.

Myoglobin is an O_2-carrying pigment related to hemoglobin but different in several ways. It has only one heme unit and one globin chain and thus is only one fourth as large as hemoglobin. Myoglobin binds only one O_2 molecule (hemoglobin binds four), but its affinity for O_2 is much greater than that of hemoglobin. Hemoglobin is fully saturated with O_2 at a PO_2 of about 100 mmHg (typically approached in arterial blood), whereas myoglobin is saturated at a PO_2 of only 27 mmHg. Myoglobin is found in muscle tissue, not blood, and serves as a muscle O_2 reservoir. The two pigments interact very nicely: Hemoglobin serves to transport O_2 from the lungs through blood to the working tissues, and myoglobin maintains an O_2 supply in the muscle tissue to meet metabolic needs during high demand, as with intense exercise. Myoglobin is thus an integral part of the so-called O_2 *cascade* as O_2 moves down its concentration gradient, from lungs to blood to tissues and finally to mitochondria.

The precise nature of the interrelationships between hemoglobin, O_2, and CO_2 were discovered at the start of the 20th century. In 1904 Christian Bohr, one of Denmark's leading physiologists, and two of his students, August Krogh and Karl Hasselbalch, described the nature of the O_2-binding relationship to hemoglobin illustrated in figure 4.12. Inadvertently, they also discovered a strong influence of CO_2 on the binding of O_2 to hemoglobin. If the PCO_2 was increased, the entire curve shifted to the right. If blood pH was lowered, the curve also shifted to the right. These phenomena are often referred to as the *Bohr effect*. The increased acidity can occur from fever or exercise; both are situations of increased metabolism. During exercise, the body temperature rises up to as high as 40° C (104° F) in active muscles. Thus, in the tissues CO_2 entering capillary blood assists hemoglobin with its unloading of O_2, maintaining the gradient of O_2 flow from blood toward skeletal muscle mitochondria.

In the lungs the reverse occurs. There the blood PO_2 rapidly increases as O_2 moves from alveolus into capillary blood. Does this increased PO_2 decrease the amount of CO_2 that the blood can carry (the opposite of the Bohr effect existing in metabolizing tissues)? Yes, it does, because the increased oxygenation of hemoglobin decreases the amount of CO_2 that can be bound to it. Of course, in the pulmonary capillary CO_2 can quickly diffuse into adjacent alveoli. The influx of O_2 thus actually helps CO_2 leave the blood by favoring the movement of hemoglobin-bound CO_2 into solution. These relationships in the lung were reported in 1914 by Joanne Christiansen, Charles Douglas, and John Scott Haldane at Oxford.

Iron's Role in O_2 Transport and Utilization

Of all the substances in metabolism that contribute to the beneficial adaptations seen with endurance training, a powerful case could be made for *iron* as the most critical for at least four reasons. One relates to hemoglobin. We have already described the increased circulating blood plasma volume and red cell mass that occur as an adaptation to endurance training (Brotherhood, Brozovic, and Pugh 1975). Hemoglobin fills about one third of the volume of each red blood cell, so an increase in red cell mass results in an increased total hemoglobin. Without iron, hemoglobin cannot be manufactured.

An increased red cell mass means that the rate of production of red blood cells must be stepped up in endurance-trained athletes. In untrained people, typical dynamics of the red blood cell synthesis-breakdown continuum are such that about 233 million cells are released from the bone marrow into the bloodstream each second, with an equal number destroyed (Cronkite 1973). This number is even larger among trained runners because of an increase in cell production to meet the increased rate of destruction.

A red blood cell has no nucleus and thus divides no further, but because all its precursor cells do, this cellular division requires enormous DNA turnover. The rate-limiting enzyme for DNA synthesis, *ribonucleotide reductase*, contains iron (Hoffbrand et al. 1976), and without adequate iron this enzyme cannot be produced in the quantities required.

Endurance training is characterized among other things by an increased myoglobin content in skeletal muscle (Pattengale and Holloszy 1967). Myoglobin contains iron; limitations in iron supply should reduce its availability as an O_2 storage reservoir in skeletal muscle.

We mentioned in chapter 3 that the volume and quantity of mitochondria increase in the skeletal muscles of trained endurance runners. The enzymes for oxidative phosphorylation are located in these organelles. Among these are the

Krebs cycle enzymes, more than half of which contain iron (Dallman, Beutler, and Finch 1978), and the cytochrome proteins, which allow eventual interaction of O_2 with H^+ ions to form H_2O, completing the large-scale energy release from fuel breakdown.

Thus, although even at rest there is a varied and essential *iron requirement* to ensure (1) *blood O_2 transport,* (2) *intracellular muscle O_2 storage,* and (3) *complete enzymatic fuel breakdown,* for athletes undergoing high-volume endurance training this requirement is increased. Given this iron requirement, the hypothesis could be advanced that endurance training challenges the body's ability to acquire and store adequate iron reserves and that this limit may compromise the magnitude of adaptations to the training response.

To examine this hypothesis, it is appropriate to ask the following seemingly simple question: Do elite-level endurance runners exhibit discernible indications of reduced iron stores? The best answer is that they apparently can, and rather commonly (Haymes and Lamanca 1989). Given this, several other questions follow. First, what are the characteristics of this reduction? Second, could iron inadequacy compromise training effectiveness and, if so, how? Third, is the inadequacy caused by iron intake problems? Fourth, can strenuous training contribute to an increased loss of iron stores? Fifth, could dietary iron supplementation be useful in maintaining optimal iron stores in runners with diminished supplies? Sixth, what are the mechanisms by which reduced iron availability might impair training effectiveness? This latter question has been particularly significant (Newhouse and Clement 1988) because of its very practical relevance to athletes striving toward successful long-term adaptation to training.

Iron Depletion in Endurance Athletes

When we first began to evaluate the performance characteristics of highly trained distance runners, we were intrigued by literature reports of what seemed to be an increased incidence of anemia among Olympic team endurance athletes. The Dutch team was surveyed in 1968 (DeWijn et al. 1971), the Australian team in 1972 (G.A. Stewart et al. 1972), and the Canadian team in 1976 (Clement, Asmundson, and Medhurst 1977). Hemoglobin levels were frequently lower than among the general population, particularly in distance runners. We know now, of course, that this decrease may occur because of a correspondingly slightly greater increase in plasma volume caused by endurance training. It is now well known that such training increases the body's release of such hormones as aldosterone, vasopressin, and renin, causing a net retention of Na^+ and H_2O and thus a volume expansion of the blood and a dilutional pseudoanemia. Of interest, over the many years that we have been collecting blood from elite-level distance runners, we have seen on only few occasions a decrease in blood hemoglobin in the athletes we profiled, and these were definitely anemic athletes. This difference in findings among published work and our own athletes has continued to keep us keenly interested in better understanding the importance of iron in the dynamics of oxygen transport and fuel metabolism.

Table 4.5 summarizes blood chemistry data collected from 15 of our male athletes whose specialty at the time was marathon training and racing. Their range of personal best race performances certainly attests to their status as talented athletes, but it by no means suggests that they had consistently good health or race performances over time. On the contrary, they were more often fraught with downtime from injury or periods of profound fatigue, and they wanted to learn how to turn this situation around. We gained some helpful clues about their tendency for breakdown and how to prevent it as we carefully studied their training logs and coupled this study with the results of treadmill stress testing and comprehensive blood chemistry profiling.

Hemoglobin levels among these athletes were, as mentioned, entirely within the normal reference range, and all but two were within the normal mean range of 15 to 16 gm/dl. Hemoglobin is contained within the red blood cells, and these athletes' red cell count was also within the normal reference range, as was their hematocrit. Assuming that our runners had the plasma volume increase characteristic of this population, they must have been using additional iron from their available stores to produce the extra hemoglobin required to keep its concentration unchanged.

Ferritin is the body's primary iron-storage molecule in all cells. The individual ferritin values for the athletes in table 4.5 were almost all outside the accepted range for healthy, untrained people. Only two athletes were as high as the low-normal range; the rest were lower. In adults most red blood cells are produced in the bone marrow. The level of circulating blood ferritin correlates quite well with bone marrow iron stores. Four of the 15 ferritin values were below 20 ng/ml. In our assay a ferritin level of 20 ng/ml or lower in the blood indicates zero bone marrow iron stores. Interestingly, those athletes with the lowest ferritin levels also had the lowest blood hemoglobin and red blood cell concentrations.

We continue to find this trend among both middle- and long-distance runners engaged in hard training. Instead of a dilutional pseudoanemia with lower-than-normal hemoglobin values, in endurance runners we routinely find normal hemoglobin levels accompanied by low ferritin levels. In these highly fit athletes, the body's top priority for iron utilization seems to be directed toward producing hemoglobin, thereby ensuring the capability for adequate oxygen transport. This may leave inadequate iron available for the increased requirements for producing iron-containing enzymes as skeletal muscles attempt to adapt to training.

Four of these runners demonstrated an increased bone marrow response to the stress of training, as shown by greater bone marrow activity to produce more red blood cells (their ferritin levels were > 25 ng/ml). This response was seen as an elevation in the blood level of *reticulocytes* and the presence of *shift cells*. Reticulocytes are immature red blood cells, and shift cells (also called stress reticulocytes) are slightly more immature cells normally restricted to the bone marrow. The increased presence of these cells in blood is a clinical indication that the marrow is responding to the need for additional O_2 carrying capacity. The high

---

TABLE 4.5

Selected Erythrocytic and Hematological Variables in Elite Male Marathoners[a]

Variable	Reference range	Athlete mean[b]
Erythrocytes (billion/ml)	4.5-6.2	5.08 ± 0.27
Hematocrit (%)	38-45	44.9 ± 2.1
Hemoglobin (gm/dl)	14-17	15.7 ± 0.74
Serum iron (mgm/dl)	50-165	97 ± 39.2
Ferritin (ng/ml)	50-150	30.1 ± 12.7
Haptoglobin (mg/dl)	27-139	27.6 ± 21.4
Reticulocytes (thousand/ml)	10-50	55.3 ± 36.8

[a]n = 15; mean age = 27 yr (range 24-30); mean best marathon time 2:13:41 ± 2:13.
[b]All values ± 1 standard deviation.

end of the reference range for reticulocytes is 50,000/µl, and in our laboratory more than 75,000/µl indicates a vigorous response. However, four athletes were in the low-normal range (< 20,000/µl), and their ferritin levels were less than 20 ng/ml. The remaining seven athletes fell between these extremes but had ferritin levels greater than 20 ng/ml. These data suggest that only when iron stores are adequate can bone marrow activity responsively meet increased O_2 delivery requirements by producing more hemoglobin-containing red blood cells.

The clinical picture, then, for many of these runners is *iron depletion* (low body stores of iron) rather than *iron deficiency* (low hemoglobin levels, or *anemia*, in addition to iron depletion). Similar findings have been published by others studying both male and female distance runners (Clement and Asmundson 1982; Dufaux et al. 1981).

Haptoglobin is a normally circulating plasma protein whose function is to bind to free hemoglobin that gets released into the plasma when red blood cells break down (called *hemolysis*), either after their normal life span of about 120 days or for other reasons. Serum haptoglobin levels in our 15 runners also averaged below the normal limit of 50 mg/dl in untrained people. Our reference range is 27 to 139 mg/dl, and 7 of the 15 runners were below this limit. This haptoglobin-hemoglobin complex is captured either by the liver (Magnusson et al. 1984) or by specialized cells located along the linings of blood vessels (called the reticuloendothelial system), where iron is reclaimed and redistributed. Serum ferritin reflects metabolism of iron stores from either of these routes (Letsky et al. 1974).

A decrease in available haptoglobin suggests that red blood cell breakdown is elevated, because only unbound haptoglobin is quantified by the assay procedure. When enough hemoglobin is liberated by intravascular hemolysis, the haptoglobin concentration falls quickly and can reach zero within 8 to 12 hr. Return toward normal then begins because of the continued release of haptoglobin into the circulation from the liver. Should the haptoglobin level fall to zero, remaining unbound hemoglobin may be filtered by the kidneys, resulting in a loss of iron from the bloodstream (Allison 1957).

A recent study has confirmed that the major cause of hemolysis during running is mechanical trauma to red blood cells from increased foot impact forces (Miller, Pate, and Burgess 1988), as illustrated in figure 4.15. Running shoe technology has brought marvelous improvements in impact shock absorption, but athletes training 15 mi/day (24 km/day) still subject themselves to over 15,000 footstrikes with more than twice their body weight impacting on plantar surfaces. Hemolysis is thus inevitable in the plantar capillaries of the feet. This is an extension of the so-called *march hemoglobinuria* first observed in soldiers more than a century ago (Fleischer 1881) and later observed in apparently healthy athletes after they ran long distances (Attlee 1937).

Another cause of hemolysis is an increased red blood cell membrane instability caused by acidosis (Yoshimura et al. 1980), which results from faster-paced anaerobic training. Red blood cells on the slightly more acidic venous side are more fragile and susceptible to hemolysis.

A third cause of hemolysis is mechanical trauma from an increased velocity of movement through the bloodstream. As the cardiac output rises during intense training or racing, movement velocity of blood increases. Red blood cells are barely small enough to pass through capillaries, and often they must bend and twist to do so. Flow through larger vessels may become turbulent instead of laminar, which also increases their susceptibility to damage. Extravascular compression by skeletal muscles generating tension also makes blood vessels smaller and can even force them completely shut, causing additional trauma to the cells within.

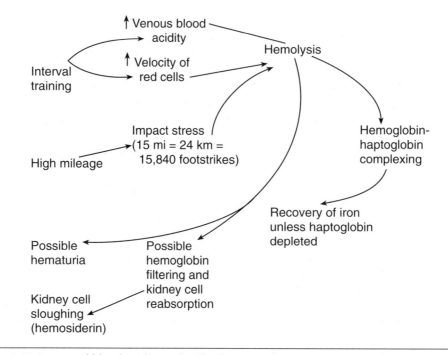

Figure 4.15 Increased blood acidity, red cell velocity, and impact stress can all increase the red blood cell destruction rate, with a risk for increased urinary iron loss unless hemoglobin can be recovered.

Because of the time course of haptoglobin decline and return following training hemolysis, the timing of blood evaluation to observe such changes is important to assess maximal-effect responses of specific training sessions. Our blood collections from athletes are in the early morning, fully 15 or more hours after their previous training. Thus, although we often see values below 10 mg/dl among those athletes as a residual effect of very hard training, we have never seen levels that are so low as to be immeasurable. We do suspect that this occurs, however, because of information we have gained through urine analysis. The kidney tubules have a maximum absorption rate for iron, after which any excess filtered hemoglobin is excreted in the urine (this is called *hematuria*). Iron stored in these tubule cells is bound to an insoluble protein called *hemosiderin*. As part of kidney cell homeostasis and normal sloughing of cells, hemosiderin appears in the urine and can be visualized using appropriate staining techniques. Among athletes with very low blood haptoglobin, a urine hemosiderin test is commonly positive.

Clearly, the greater an individual's level of endurance fitness, the greater the O_2 demand and the more extensive the body's system of iron storage and utilization must be to ensure that these demands are met, but there are other demands as well. It is tempting to suggest that the body manages iron supplies so as to give top priority to providing adequate O_2-carrying abilities via hemoglobin and second priority to distributing iron to the many iron-containing enzymes essential for aerobic metabolism. Clinically normal or moderately low hemoglobin values may not constitute functional anemia in sedentary populations, but they may indeed do so in physically active populations (Pate 1983). As more iron-containing enzymes are required in the working skeletal muscles as part of getting fit, this synthesis draws even more heavily upon existing iron reserves. If adequate iron is not available, this synthesis likely will not occur, and the athlete essentially does not progress in cellular adaptation to training. The resulting scenario is easy to predict: As the athlete increases the intensity or volume of training load as part of the normal progression through a training block, the requisite increase in production of iron-containing enzymes in the working muscles must occur, otherwise the increased metabolic capacity (increased $\dot{V}O_2$max, quickening anaerobic threshold pace, etc.) is not achieved. Continual progressive increase in training load will predictably result in fatigue, illness, or injury.

The increased loss of iron from hemolysis and inadequate iron recapture raise other questions concerning iron availability, some of which were mentioned earlier. It turns out that decreased dietary iron intake and increased iron loss are important considerations in understanding the dynamics of iron availability in such athletes. Each of these aspects is discussed briefly.

There are two primary dietary sources of iron. One is consumption of red meat, with its accompanying hemoglobin and myoglobin; this is called *heme iron* because of the iron's attachment to the heme portion of these molecules. Of all the available dietary forms of iron, heme iron is the most easily absorbed (Conrad et al. 1967). The human species evolved as omnivorous hunter-gatherers and thus has maintained a hereditary preference for heme iron.

The other source of iron is a variety of foods that do not contain heme iron. Iron is plentiful in raisins, leafy vegetables, lima beans, dates, baked or boiled potatoes, dried fruits, baked beans with molasses, broccoli, brussels sprouts, and soybeans. Cooking with iron pots and skillets also provides a source of elemental iron. Absorption of nonheme iron depends on the presence of accompanying ligands in food that will either enhance or inhibit conversion of iron from the Fe^{3+} to the Fe^{2+} oxidation state. A phosphoprotein in egg yolk, polyphenols such as tannin prevalent in coffee and tea, and bran fiber in wheat and cereals all inhibit absorption. Also, calcium and zinc compete with iron for the same receptor site and decrease iron absorption if also present in sizable quantities. Enhancement of iron absorption occurs in the presence of ascorbic acid and citric acid in fruits and in the presence of amino acids derived from the digestion of red meat and fish. This underscores the importance of at least a modest portion of lean red meat in the diet as both a source of heme iron and an enhancer of nonheme iron absorption (Snyder, Dvorak, and Roepke 1989). The prevalence of nutritional iron deficiency rises as the amount of dietary animal protein diminishes.

Current dietary practices for elite runners in many parts of the world, as well as for much of American society, emphasize low saturated fats and cholesterol, which imply a minimum of red meat intake, and a greater emphasis on vegetable protein and complex carbohydrates. For athletes scheduling two training sessions per day and who require a high energy intake that can be assimilated easily and quickly, such emphasis is useful. However, this diet is likely to have a lowered iron content.

As athletes increase their training intensity, particularly in anaerobic interval sessions, the accompanying gastrointestinal tract ischemia (localized tissue anemia), with blood flow being reduced by as much as 80% (Clausen 1977), commonly decreases appetite. Stored fat reserves are then used for required energy needs, typically observed over time as a decreased percentage of body fat. Though this decrease may enhance performance, as there is less body mass to transport, an extended period of decreased iron intake may reduce the total amount of iron assimilation into the enzymes of aerobic metabolism. The decrease in energy intake as well as intake of other nutritional elements may also compromise performance if prolonged. A side effect of the gastrointestinal ischemia from intense training may be an increased rate of cell sloughing in the gastrointestinal tract, causing loss of already absorbed iron that has not yet entered the bloodstream (Green et al. 1968). It is suspected that hypoxia is the ultimate cause of the increased cell sloughing. These aspects of physiology all need closer investigative scrutiny in distance runners before the full practical extent of this problem of dietary iron intake and loss is realized.

Runners also appear to have elevated iron losses in comparison to the sedentary population. At least three possible routes exist for iron loss from the body: perspiration, the gastrointestinal tract, and the urinary tract. The final story has certainly not been discovered on this subject either, and more research should provide a better basis for deciding which routes may be most important in iron loss. Early studies of iron losses via perspiration (Paulev, Jordal, and Pedersen 1983; Vellar 1968) suggested that this route was of considerable importance, but a more recent study (Brune et al. 1986) concluded that iron losses in sweat (obtained from people in a sauna) are minor. The differences in composition of sweat from exercising athletes and that from people in a sauna need to be quantified.

Although it has been suggested that runners may lose iron from the gastrointestinal tract during hard races (J.G. Stewart et al. 1984), a more routine loss can occur from the use of aspirin. It is common for elite runners to ingest therapeutic doses of aspirin as both an analgesic and an anti-inflammatory agent during periods of particularly intense training. One gram of aspirin per day causes about 1 ml of blood loss, which represents anywhere from 0.5 mg (Wintrobe et al. 1981) to 1.5 mg (J.G. Stewart et al. 1984) of iron loss.

SUGGESTIONS FOR MAINTAINING OPTIMAL IRON STORES

To apply the concepts about iron stores described previously, one can envision a likely (but unfortunate) scenario involving an athlete aspiring to a successful college championship or other track season peak, which typically occurs during early or late summer. The athlete has successfully endured many months of hard work in preparation for a superlative competitive result. However, training and lifestyle patterns favor a net iron loss rather than a balance between iron intake and output, and the stage is set for an eventual inadequacy in iron availability. Let us take the example of late spring and early summer training. The days get warmer, and losses of iron through sweat increase. Training gets more intensive, and thus hemolysis from both impact stress and blood acidosis increases. Gastrointestinal ischemia from such higher-intensity training and an accompanying decrease in appetite result in lowered iron intake.

It is almost an occupational hazard of such a lifestyle for progressive depletion of available iron supplies to occur when they are most needed. The athlete progresses very well through the middle of the season, with several weeks remaining before championship time, but then takes a turn for the worse. For no apparent reason, the athlete develops a state best characterized as burnout, with sleepless nights, more fatigue than usual, and decreased ability to manage even less-intense training than was easily tolerated a few weeks before. Training continues, because the championships are impending, but the athlete never recovers and instead experiences progressively poorer-quality training, a developing bad attitude, and a dismal showing at the championships. This scenario happens all too often, and when we are contacted (typically too late) by an athlete in such a state, a blood chemistry evaluation shows acceptable hemoglobin but very low ferritin, haptoglobin, and reticulocyte levels and a positive hemosiderin test. This athlete's iron stores may not have been adequate to meet the various metabolic adaptations required beyond adequate O_2 transport.

We have had many opportunities to evaluate blood chemistry profiles from runners in the middle of such late-spring, warm-weather build-ups to important championships, and we have found the same pattern of values. If it is inappropriate to increase iron intake through more iron-containing foods in the diet, the athlete may find it appropriate to improve iron stores by taking an oral iron supplement (0.5 to 1.0 mg/kg body weight) in the form of ferrous sulfate, gluconate, or fumarate. For a 60-kg (132-lb) athlete, this would be 30 to 60 mg, compared with the recommended dietary iron allowance of 15 mg per day for adult women and 10 mg per day for adult men (Food and Nutrition Board 1989). Our common experience with blood profiling of athletes after such iron supplementation is that reticulocyte count increases, a small increase in hemoglobin occurs, ferritin rises, and both haptoglobin and hemosiderin data remain unchanged unless training changes.

Because even a small amount of iron supplementation can cause side effects ranging from constipation to gut aches to dark stools, evening intake is optimal because training does not occur again for many hours. Also, substances that inhibit iron absorption are typically absent from the evening meal. For most athletes, a turnaround in tolerance to training occurs within two weeks—they can manage previous work loads, they lose the sensation of profound fatigue, and they regain a positive attitude to training. The explanation might simply be a placebo effect, but this is not likely the case, because taking a pill becomes such a simple daily habit that the mental association of why it is being taken disappears. (This has been difficult to specifically assess, because the side effects of iron supplementation are difficult to duplicate in a placebo pill to be used in a double-blind, randomized trial study design.)

We certainly are not stating that iron supplementation is the instant and permanent cure for illness and fatigue in seriously training endurance runners. Inappropriately excessive training will eventually prove disastrous to any athlete. We do suggest, however, that athletes enduring high-volume and high-intensity training for several weeks have considerably increased skeletal muscle cell needs for iron above the requirement for hemoglobin production, and unless these are satisfied, symptoms of performance reduction similar to those found with iron deficiency are likely even though only iron depletion exists.

This point is emphasized because recent articles (Eichner 1988; Peota 1989) suggest that the notion of performance impairment in athletes as a result of iron store depletion may be more fallacy than fact. Unfortunately, this is a generalization; conclusions from study subjects who fit the category of "active people" or athletic individuals with moderate training schedules cannot be applied to elite-level endurance runners whose distance running training schedules require 80 or more miles (130 or more kilometers) per week on a continual basis. Such extension of conclusions from one subject group to another is inappropriate here. Highly trained distance runners are athletes with performance requirements quite different from people engaged in serious fitness programs. Especially for sea-level athletes who are contemplating a training sojourn to altitude, increasing iron intake is also essential to compensate for the increased iron requirements associated with producing additional numbers of red blood cells (Martin 1994).

Iron supplementation should not continue indefinitely and should not be done without blood chemistry monitoring three to four times a year. A small percentage (about 5% to 10%) of the population is subject to iron overload, or *hemochromatosis*, which causes symptoms of fatigue and malaise (Herbert 1987) similar to those of iron inadequacy. In these subjects, serum ferritin may rise above 300 ng/ml and can be easily detected using blood chemistry profiling.

Perhaps even more important than the consideration of iron supplementation are suggestions for improving the training environment in a manner that helps to reduce iron loss and enhance iron acquisition:

- Train as often as possible on packed dirt trails or low-cut, smooth grass surfaces.
- Eliminate unnecessary volumes of low-intensity running that simply burn fuel without improving aerobic fitness, add impact stress, and give the logbook a high number for weekly completed distance.
- Train during the cool parts of the day.
- Eat a modest amount of lean red meat.
- Stay away from beverages such as coffee and tea, which reduce iron absorption and contribute to dehydration due to their diuretic effect.
- Plan occasional days with no running to per-

mit dietary replenishment, mental refreshment, and physical recovery.

• Women with excessive menstrual flow are likely to be at higher risk for inadequate iron stores and thus should be more cognizant of the need to monitor blood chemistry values (hemoglobin, ferritin, and haptoglobin) and urine hemosiderin to ensure optimal health.

Measuring Cardiopulmonary Fitness in the Laboratory

We have now identified the major kinds of cardiopulmonary and blood responses and adaptations that occur with training, and we have also indicated that it is useful to identify specific training pace ranges that will best permit these kinds of adaptations. Scientists for many years have been devising various test protocols to evaluate individual responsiveness to exercise tolerance. Coaches and athletes have also been doing this in a less specific manner, using time trials over a measured distance or race simulations.

It is quite possible, and indeed in vogue, to devise laboratory test protocols that satisfy everyone: Scientists obtain interesting data concerning the physiological response of the tested individual to exercise, and athletes and coaches can directly apply the results to training. Sets of data from a large athlete population of comparable fitness can be contrasted with similar results from an age-matched, untrained population; scientists call this a *cross-sectional study*. Athletes and coaches tend instead to prefer *longitudinal studies*—sets of data obtained several times during the course of a training season and then from year to year, with the athlete serving as his or her own control—to identify changes in such variables as $\dot{V}O_2max$, lactate/ventilatory threshold, and running economy and also to develop suggested training paces based on these data.

Coaches unaware of the benefits of laboratory monitoring sometimes question the worth of such testing: "It doesn't mimic a race," they say. "My athlete does not race or train on a treadmill, and in addition, in a race situation many other extraneous variables contribute to the outcome." Though all this is true, these coaches are missing the underlying rationale for laboratory profiling. Scientists in the laboratory specifically attempt to *remove* as many extraneous variables as possible, such as weather, terrain, and tactics, because then the responses observed are more likely to indicate strengths and weaknesses in existing fitness. Isn't this what all coaches are seeking—informative, objective data? Increased fitness since the previous test suggests successful training adaptation: The training plan is working. No change suggests that the training plan is not bringing improvements. Decreased fitness suggests developing fatigue from either overtraining or excessive lifestyle stresses (often called lifestyle overload). Increases in $\dot{V}O_2max$ but not lactate/ventilatory threshold, or the reverse, point to specific aspects of fitness that need additional work. Such testing shortly before a race can provide information about the best racing strategy to take advantage of existing fitness. When done at the start of a training block, such testing indicates areas requiring greatest emphasis. All this testing assists the athlete's development and fine-tuning.

Treadmill training can also help athletes develop a working knowledge of the effort sense or stress level required for running at specific paces, particularly the optimal sub–lactate/ventilatory threshold race pace for marathon runners. As athletes then train in varying weather and terrain, their over-ground pace can vary as they instinctively maintain effort sense. Prevention of overtraining in such circumstances is an important legacy of the intelligent use of such information. Particularly as athletes achieve greater excellence and require a stronger training stimulus for improvement, such specific training takes on added value.

Scientists first began to study the physiological capabilities of trained athletes during the early part of this century. Some of the best scientists of the day—Lindhard (1915) in Denmark, Liljestrand and Stenstrom (1920) in Stockholm, and Hill and Lupton (1923) in London—designed equipment and protocols that, although pioneering, were so sound that the principles underlying their use are still applied today. Equipment presently available for this purpose is sophisticated, and computerization has relieved much of the tedium of data collection and analysis. Because of the importance of O_2 in metabolism and because the amount of O_2 that can be taken up and used is an endpoint that can be identified easily, $\dot{V}O_2$max has long been the most widely used criterion for assessing maximal endurance performance. This value quantifies the net ability of the cardiorespiratory system to transport O_2 to all the active tissues and the ability of these tissues to use it (Åstrand 1976).

Many methods have been developed for quantifying $\dot{V}O_2$max, but *treadmill running* and *bicycle ergometry* are used most frequently (Hermansen and Saltin 1969). Evaluation of untrained people who have had very little experience with either running or bicycling usually shows them to have a higher $\dot{V}O_2$max value when using a treadmill than when using a bicycle ergometer. Treadmill testing can lead to higher values by as much as 4% to 23% (Åstrand 1976; Hermansen and Saltin 1969; Kamon and Pandolf 1972). Because a larger total muscle mass is active (the upper as well as the lower limbs), venous blood return to the heart is greater. Venous return typically equals cardiac output, which is an important variable affecting $\dot{V}O_2$max (Shephard et al. 1968).

Improvements in $\dot{V}O_2$max occur with training and are best identifiable using a test protocol that challenges the body in the manner most similar to the mode of training (Clausen et al. 1973; McArdle et al. 1978). Trained cyclists thus are at a disadvantage using a treadmill test when compared to a bicycle ergometer (Hagberg, Giese, and Schneider 1978). Analogously, runners are at a disadvantage when tested using a bicycle (Pannier, Vrijens, and Van Cauter 1980). Thus, as demonstrated in figure 4.16*a* by U.S. road-racing star Jon Sinclair, we use a treadmill for our maximal performance tests of runners. However, for certain specialized tests—such as cold-air challenge tests to evaluate exercise-induced asthma—a bicycle, as illustrated in figure 4.16*b* by Britain's two-time Olympic 3,000-m finalist Wendy Sly, is perfectly acceptable because the purpose is to produce a mild exercise response rather than to determine $\dot{V}O_2$max.

How high can one raise $\dot{V}O_2$max by training? In part, the answer relates to inherent genetic endowment, but the level of fitness at which one begins the training program also plays a role. Recent studies (Makrides et al. 1986) have shown that untrained people over a broad age range who embark on a serious aerobic fitness development program can raise their sedentary-lifestyle $\dot{V}O_2$max values as much as 40% or more (for example, from 35 to 50 ml · kg^{-1} · min^{-1}). Among already-established top-level runners this percentage increase is considerably less. Although some researchers claim that $\dot{V}O_2$max among elite-level runners changes little over the course of a year, we find substantial differences as either training load or training emphasis shifts. As an example, the $\dot{V}O_2$max of one of our elite male middle-distance runners increased 18%, from 4,695 to 5,525 ml/min, over a seven-month period (his weight remained unchanged).

We mentioned earlier in this chapter that the interaction of aerobic with anaerobic capabilities determines an individual's performance ability in an all-out competitive effort. Does aerobic power by itself relate to successful performance in

Figure 4.16 The two most popular modes of evaluating endurance exercise capabilities in the laboratory: (*a*) a treadmill run and (*b*) bicycle ergometry.

competitive distance running? For any given competitive distance being considered, this relationship depends on the nature of the population. Unfortunately, the wide variation among research study populations has also resulted in a wide range of correlation coefficients (from $r = .08$ to $r = .91$) relating $\dot{V}O_2$max to race performance (McConnell 1988). In statistical analysis, a correlation coefficient (r) of .91 suggests a rather strong linear relationship between the two compared variables.

If the subject population is heterogeneous, that is, comprising a broad spectrum of aerobic fitness (for example, a range of $\dot{V}O_2$max values from 35 to 85 ml $\cdot$ kg^{-1} $\cdot$ min^{-1}), then there is a high statistical correlation between aerobic power and competitive performance. If the group of people under consideration is homogeneous, however—for example, the fastest 20 male marathon runners in the world—then the correlation between performance and $\dot{V}O_2$max is poorer. If the subjects were all highly fit and competed together in a single race, and if we could have determined their $\dot{V}O_2$max from laboratory treadmill testing under controlled conditions, the order of finish would very likely not correlate well to the rank order of $\dot{V}O_2$max values.

The explanation for this poor correlation is that within such a homogeneous population other variables influence race performance along with $\dot{V}O_2$max. A group of runners judged homogeneous simply by their competition results is probably rather heterogeneous in their *combination* of aerobic and anaerobic performance capabilities. The contribution to this homogeneous group's finish-time performances comes from $\dot{V}O_2$max, lactate/ventilatory threshold (both in absolute terms and as a percentage of $\dot{V}O_2max$), blood volume, iron-containing enzymes, hemoglobin concentration, and training emphasis (aerobic versus anaerobic). $\dot{V}O_2max$ is merely one of those several variables. Some of these variables are health related, for example, anemia (decreased hemoglobin) or dehydration (decreased blood volume). Others are training related.

A problem exists in attempting to steadily increase aerobic and anaerobic capabilities through training. The greater the increase in such performance indicators as $\dot{V}O_2max$, lactate/ventilatory threshold pace, and whatever maximal anaerobic work indicators are used, the greater the subsequent intensity and volume of training required for any further increases. Thus, higher volumes of aerobic running bring so little performance benefit that the increasing risks of overuse injury or development of symptoms of overtraining outweigh the potential performance gains. In other words, the *risk-benefit ratio* becomes excessively high. Sjödin and Svedenhag (1985) have thus quite sensibly questioned the benefits of more than 115 to 120 km/wk (71 to 75 mi/wk) at lower-intensity aerobic conditioning paces for distance runners seeking to improve their $\dot{V}O_2max$ values. Marathon runners are a special case in requiring very high training volumes in order to stimulate greater fuel storage abilities in their working muscles. They also realize that they must build greater connective tissue tolerance to prolonged impact stress, but they well know that this is done at the increased risk of overuse injury. As suggested earlier in this chapter, once aerobic conditioning has provided the initial stimulus, it should then be followed by lower total weekly volume with higher-intensity (quicker pace, shorter distance) aerobic capacity training sessions to bring $\dot{V}O_2max$ to its peak for that particular training period.

The age-old question thus remains: How much and what kind of training is ideal and sufficient? *Optimal training* can be defined as doing the least amount of the most specific work that will continually bring improvement in fitness. Any additional training will simply increase the risk for injury or burnout. Information gained from the use of laboratory performance testing, training logs that record what has been done for training, and subjective indications of how the body and soul are managing this load all should be studied together to help answer this question. If laboratory testing can identify strengths and weaknesses in a fairly objective manner, and if it is known which kinds of training can best improve these aspects of fitness, then the stage is set for the creation of a meaningful development plan. Chapter 5 attempts to integrate all of this information.

Treadmill Stress Tests

The term *graded exercise test,* or GXT, refers to a cardiopulmonary fitness evaluation in which the test subject is assigned a protocol involving a graded increase in work load that produces either voluntary exhaustion at a maximal working capacity or achievement of some predetermined submaximal exercise criterion. Very often such a test involves walking or running uphill, and this has caused some semantic confusion. Note that the term *graded* refers to a *gradual* increase in work load, rather than to a specific percentage grade of inclination up a hill. Thus, even a bicycle GXT is a graded test, because it involves pedaling against a gradually increasing resistance.

Test protocols tend to vary widely, having been developed to suit available equipment, subjects studied, and investigator preferences. Our elite-level, highly fit athletes prefer a single treadmill test that essentially mimics a competition: a continuous test that will measure all necessary fitness-related variables with no stopping along the way for such things as intermittent blood sampling. The most important variables to be measured are

- O_2 consumption at several submaximal training paces (running economy),
- the threshold at which steady-state work can no longer be maintained (lactate/ventilatory threshold), and
- the absolute limits of aerobic performance ($\dot{V}O_2$max) and anaerobic performance (several will be discussed).

These variables can essentially all be assessed by monitoring heart rate and expired air to determine ventilation, CO_2 production, and O_2 uptake. Collecting a blood specimen before and after the test allows comparison of resting and maximal blood lactate concentrations. Some laboratories prefer two separate tests, one for $\dot{V}O_2$max and the other for running economy and some of the other variables, including intermittent blood sampling for identification of lactate threshold. If correct technique is combined with sensible methodology, the actual values obtained for the measured variables should be similar with each protocol.

Some general constraints in designing treadmill test protocols can be outlined here to help athletes and coaches better understand the logistics of test implementation. First, test length should be optimum for accurate data collection. Taylor and colleagues (1963) concluded that all major physiological adaptations to permit such high-level exercise are functioning within about 10 min. For measurement a relatively short test is also advantageous, because testers desire physiological changes large enough to be identifiable. Variations in sequential measurements caused by analytical noise must be substantially less than the various threshold changes being studied. Thus, our athletes are on the treadmill for 18 to 22 min, and only the final 11 to 13 min of their test are noticeably stressful. Our protocol is an initially stepwise series of steady-state pace increases every few minutes, changing to a rampwise format with steadily increasing work rates. Metabolic measuring systems use either mixing chambers (from which expired air collected over prescribed periods is collected and sampled periodically, for example, every 20 s) or breath-by-breath analyses of gas composition.

A second constraint of treadmill testing is that, because a higher $\dot{V}O_2$max value is obtained by having subjects climb a grade rather than run on a solely level surface, uphill running should form the final portion of the test protocol. Saltin and Åstrand (1967) recommended a 2.6% grade rise every 3 min. Shephard et al. (1968) suggested 2.5% grade increments every 2 min. In our specific protocols for elite runners, after 14 min of level-grade running at several increasing paces to assess running economy, we use 2% grade rises every 2 min during the final portion of the test.

A third constraint during the GXT is that the various running paces should fit comfortably within the training habits of the tested athletes (McConnell 1988). The intensity of each work load should increase by an increment in energy cost similar to the preceding one. Pollock (1977), in his studies with elite male runners, suggested a range of 10.5 to 12 km/hr (9:12 to 8 min/mi) for sedentary controls and 16.1 to 19.4 km/hr (6 to 5 min/mi) for trained runners. For men our GXT protocol range is from 12.9 to 19.4 km/hr (7:30 to 5 min/mi); the women have a smaller range, from 12.9 to 17.0 km/hr (7:30 to 5:40/mi).

The fourth testing constraint is that environmental data collection conditions should be kept as constant as possible to optimize detection of changes in athletes' fitness from one test session to the next. We keep relative humidity at 35%

to ensure effective evaporative cooling. We also maintain our laboratory room temperature at a relatively cool 17° C (63° F) during testing as suggested by Rowell, Taylor, and Wang (1964). It is also appropriate to keep the treadmill running conditions as similar to over-ground running as possible. At least through velocities as fast as 6 min/mi (268 m/min), submaximal O_2 uptake as measured with treadmill running is insignificantly different from that measured with track running (McMiken and Daniels 1976). Biomechanical differences in running stride between the moving treadmill belt and over-ground running are minimal.

Although over-ground running creates air resistance, such resistance brings an added aerobic demand only at velocities considerably faster than those routinely used in our evaluations. According to the studies of Pugh (1970), the effect of air resistance starts to increase O_2 consumption measurably only at faster paces. As an example, at a pace of 4:35 min/mi (13 mi/hr; 350 m/min), the additional aerobic demand is 5.7 ml · kg^{-1} · min^{-1}. Indeed, this added energy demand to a front-runner in a fast-paced race is used to advantage as a tactical maneuver by runners who remain in that athlete's wind shadow. We position a variable-speed fan in front of our runners to provide evaporative cooling and to simulate as much as possible the conditions of a breeze created by over-ground running.

Preparing Athletes to Deliver a Good GXT Effort

Athletes always want to deliver their best possible efforts when they train and compete, and this is equally true for time trials and GXT evaluations. We find it useful to explain clearly the essentials of what will be done and how it will be done so that the athletes can best perform these activities for providing meaningful data.

Athletes should already have made some preparations for their maximal performance GXT a few days before the day of the test. Neither very long distance runs nor intense anaerobic interval sessions should be done in training during the two days preceding a test. These will decrease skeletal muscle glycogen stores and alter normal energy substrate balance, in turn decreasing both submaximal and maximal blood lactate concentrations during and following the performance test (Busse, Maassen, and Boning 1987; Foster et al. 1988; Fric et al. 1988; Jacobs et al. 1981). Similarly, dramatic changes in dietary habits, such as carbohydrate loading or increased lipid intake, respectively, will elevate or lower the blood lactate response to hard work (Ivy et al. 1981). Thus, their typical diet is recommended. Because we want the athletes to work to their absolute voluntary performance limits, we suggest that they treat the test as a time trial or race effort and schedule a defined, repeatable, relatively easy training regimen during the two days preceding the test.

We schedule each athlete's GXT at a similar biological-clock time to minimize the effects of circadian fluctuations in physiological variables, such as heart rate (Reilly, Robinson, and Minors 1984), basal metabolism (Aschoff and Pohl 1970), and body temperature (Roe et al. 1966) that may alter performance. Thus, the actual time during the day that we test athletes varies depending on the number of time zones they crossed in coming for evaluation; we attempt to test everyone at a time that would be late morning for them. This precludes testing several athletes as a group.

Before our athletes undergo a GXT for data collection purposes, we ensure that they have all gained prior experience of at least 30 min of treadmill running and of running hard with the appropriate laboratory headgear or gas collection mouthpiece affixed. This allows them to develop the confidence and experience essential for a successful test, ensures practice in maintaining a natural running style, provides a review of test protocols, and allows them experience at getting on and off the moving belt at various speeds. Thorough familiarization with the test protocol minimizes the unexpected.

We typically assess the resting metabolic status of each athlete before beginning the GXT. This is easily accomplished; the athlete sits comfortably in a chair and breathes normally through the gas collection equipment for about 10 min. Analyses typically show a resting O_2 consumption of between 250 and 300 ml · kg^{-1} · min^{-1}. During this same period, resting heart rate and blood pressure can be determined. We typically do not use the complete 12-lead electrocardiographic (ECG) monitoring system that would be considered essential for evaluating patients with known cardiac risk or unknown physical fitness. Instead, a simpler ECG system is employed to provide accurate measurement of heart rate as well as detection of the primary arrhythmias observed occasionally in trained athletes (Huston, Puffer, and Rodney 1985). As illustrated in figure 4.17a by U.S. marathoner Don Janicki, common practice in many laboratories is to affix ECG electrodes on parts of the chest to minimize background interference from skeletal muscle activity. We prefer, as do our athletes, to affix ECG electrodes to the back (figure 4.17b), which interferes less with arm motion during running.

A thorough warm-up period, similar to that done in preparation for a competition, should be provided before the test. This is important because in functional terms an evaluation of maximal performance is a serious competitive effort with the best possible result desired. Considerable motivation and mental

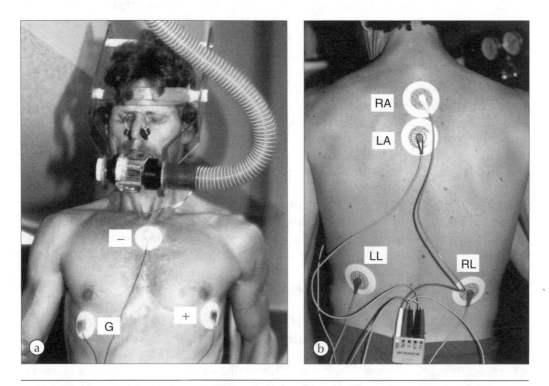

Figure 4.17 Suggested positioning of electrocardiographic electrodes for treadmill testing of distance runners. Some testers use the limb lead II arrangement (figure 4.17a) with positive (+), negative (-), and ground (G) electrodes positioned as indicated. We use the arrangement shown in figure 4.17b, permitting the monitoring of four standard limb leads. Here, RA and LA = right and left arm; RL and LL = right and left leg. In addition, placement of one chest electrode (the cable can be seen at the left) also permits monitoring of lead V5.

preparedness is required for athletes to deliver a best-effort result. Such a warm-up may include 15 to 30 min of running, before or after stretching exercises. We affix ECG electrodes (and perform our resting metabolic studies) before this warm-up period so that the GXT can begin very shortly after warm-up has been completed.

We find that it is also useful to explain some of the technical details of gas collection and analysis to the athletes. This helps them become more comfortable with items that can be sources of distraction unless their need is appreciated. In many laboratories rather bulky headgear is affixed to the head of the athlete, as shown in figure 4.18a. Notice the large plastic *breathing valve*, which permits sampling of the athlete's expired air during the test. On inhalation, air enters the mouth through one side of the valve (via the nearest hose), and exhaled air enters a tube connected to the other side of the valve. This exhaled air enters the mixing chamber of the metabolic measurement system. Analysis of this air quantifies the magnitude of increasing O_2 consumption and CO_2 production with increasing work loads. This is known as an *open-circuit spirometry system*.

Often such headgear either fits so snugly as to cause discomfort or fits so loosely that it comes loose during the test. This dilemma was an early source of frustration to testers and subjects alike. The ingenuity of one of our laboratory colleagues, Meryl Sheard, permitted the design and use of a *floating gas collection valve* positioned at an appropriate spot above the treadmill surface directly in front of the athlete's face and suspended by an ingenious pulley arrangement. This is illustrated in figure 4.18b. Notice that the athlete now has freedom of movement without problems from poorly fitted headgear. We are now replacing even this user-friendly technology by the smaller gas collection unit illustrated in figure 4.18c. This new technology permits *breath-by-breath gas analysis* as well as estimates of additional physiological information such as cardiac output and lactic acid accumulation that were not possible previously. Notice finally that all three of these athletes are wearing a white plastic *nose clip*; this ensures that O_2 intake into the body occurs only through the mouth.

Some athletes desire verbal encouragement during the test; others do not. Such requests are respected and consistently followed to minimize variability. Some laboratories attempt to obtain a subjective estimation of effort sense from athletes being tested as an accompaniment to the physiological data acquisition. One means for assessing effort sense is *rated perceived exertion* (RPE). Gunnar Borg (1973) was instrumental in developing scales that can be used for quantifying effort sense during performance evaluation of athletes. Particularly when the lactate/ventilatory threshold is reached, there is a noticeable effort-sense breakpoint. Beyond this work intensity, effort sense is too great to permit the kind of almost indefinite performance that characterizes marathon racing. Below this level athletes feel quite confident that the work load can be maintained. The Borg scale in its various formats consists of a dozen or more verbal labels describing effort. Terms such as "hard," "very hard," and "very, very hard" are used. Numerical codes beside each label permit exercising subjects to indicate the number corresponding to their perception of effort. A printed copy of the scale can be placed periodically alongside the athlete during the test, and they can simply point to the appropriate value. (Because athletes have a mouthpiece and headgear affixed to collect expired air samples, they cannot provide this information verbally.)

One study involving a combination of active people and trained athletes suggested an RPE value of "somewhat hard" as equivalent to the stress at the onset

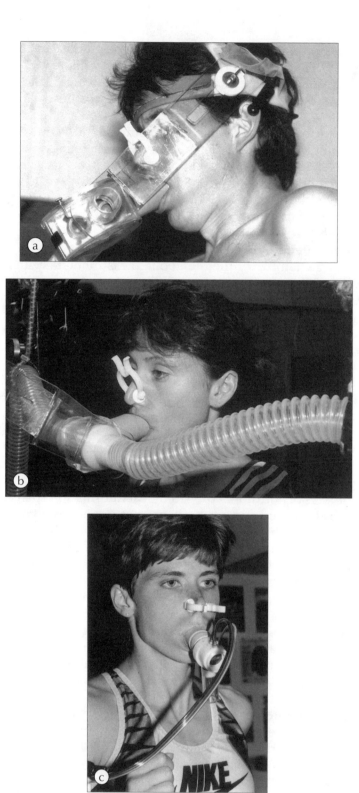

Figure 4.18 Headgear worn during treadmill stress testing of elite distance runners. (*a*) Anthony Sandoval, 1980 U.S. Olympic marathoner, wears early equipment, still used in some laboratories, fitted to the athlete's head. If too tight or loose, it can be distracting. Note the ear oximeter affixed to measure changing hemoglobin saturation. (*b*) Road racer Colette Murphy demonstrates a free-floating headgear designed and presently used in our laboratory. (*c*) 1996 U.S. marathon Olympian Anne Marie Lauck illustrates a newly developed gas collection system that provides breath-by-breath gas analysis.

of blood lactate accumulation (Purvis and Cureton 1981). The effectiveness of such a rating system, however, relies on the premise that everyone perceives "very hard" work equivalently, and this is most likely not universally true. In part there are semantic variations, and there are also differences in work effort tolerance among individuals. Accuracy of such reporting is based on the presumption that during a performance test the athlete not only is willing to interrupt concentration to categorize feelings, but also can objectively compare present effort sense with effort sense yet to be experienced because the test is still in progress. At present we are still uncertain that with highly trained athletes including such documentation during treadmill tests provides training-related information of sufficient value for athlete and coach to justify the intrusion on the athlete's concentrated competitive effort, which jeopardizes the attainment of maximal performance capacity.

Our athletes themselves terminate their tests on voluntary exhaustion, step off to the side of the treadmill, and then begin their recovery according to prearranged plans. Various protocols exist among laboratories for the transition back to the resting state after test completion. Continued easy jogging or walking, or complete rest either by sitting or lying down are all used. We routinely measure peak blood lactate levels after this maximal exercise test and observe how quickly such variables as heart rate, respiratory exchange ratio, and $\dot{V}_E$ return to baseline levels. Such monitoring demands a standardized pattern of posttest activity (Fujitsuka et al. 1982; Ohkuwa et al. 1984). Our experience and that of the Japanese investigators suggest that as soon as the treadmill can be slowed and leveled, an immediate slowdown to an easy walk maintained for 3 min to permit continued collection of metabolic recovery data provides a safe, acceptable, and repeatable posttest protocol. Such data that documents recovery dynamics is also of considerable value and should be collected in a consistent and repeatable manner. Blood for maximal lactate determination is then collected immediately after this cool-down, which is 5 min after test termination (Gollnick, Bayly, and Hodgson 1986).

Computer-interfaced instrumentation permits rapid analysis, calculation, and display of results while the test is in progress. This is not always used or available, however. For example, if data are to be collected from athletes running around a 400-m track, as shown in figure 4.19, it becomes more appropriate to collect the expired air in large balloons for temporary storage and transport to gas analyzers located in a nearby laboratory setting. Regardless of the mode of collection, because the inspired concentrations of O_2 and CO_2 are known (O_2 typically is 20.93%, CO_2 almost negligible at 0.04%), measurement of expired volumes of O_2 and CO_2 permits calculation of O_2 utilized and CO_2 produced with relative ease. From these values, the respiratory exchange ratio (R) can be calculated as $\dot{V}CO_2 / \dot{V}O_2$

Interpreting the GXT Data

Table 4.6 summarizes the kinds of data that can be obtained during an incremental treadmill test. These data were obtained from an elite male distance runner (a specialist in the steeplechase), peaked for an excellent performance in the 1988 U.S. Olympic trials. At the top of each column appear abbreviations for the various data that were collected and reported at 20-s sampling intervals. Some values are probably familiar: O_2 consumption ($\dot{V}O_2$ in ml/min and in ml $\cdot$ kg^{-1} $\cdot$ min^{-1}), CO_2 production ($\dot{V}CO_2$, also in ml/min), and heart rate (in beats/min). Breathing frequency (f_R in breaths/min) and total expired ventilation ($\dot{V}_E$, in L/min) are also measured. From these data, other variables have been calculated.

Figure 4.19 Field-test collection of expired gases using meteorological balloons. Elite-level U.S. marathoner Ken Martin is shown here at the U.S. Olympic Training Center. Note the gas collection equipment monitoring from the golf cart.

One is the respiratory exchange ratio (R) calculated as $\dot{V}CO_2/\dot{V}O_2$ (no units). Tidal volume (V_T), the size of each breath, is equal to $\dot{V}_E/f_R$.

Oxygen pulse is calculated as the volume of O_2 extracted per heartbeat ($\dot{V}O_2/f_c$), and can be used to estimate maximal stroke volume (Q_s) at peak exercise. This was one of the earliest indicators considered as a measure of maximum cardiovascular function (Henderson and Prince 1914). It was suggested that optimal training of the aerobic system should not be so high as to cause a decrease in O_2 pulse because any additional energy production would be derived purely through anaerobic sources. We can rearrange equation (4.5) as follows:

$$O_2 \text{ pulse} = \dot{V}O_2\text{max}/f_c = Q_s \times \text{max a-}\bar{v}O_2 \text{ difference} \qquad (4.10)$$

Remember that max a-$\bar{v}O_2$ difference is about 16 ml/100 ml. Q_s can then be estimated. The data in table 4.6 show that for several minutes O_2 pulse was between 29 and 30 ml/beat, with maximal Q_s approaching 190 ml. Using equation 4.10, $30 = Q_s \times 16/100$, and $Q_s = 188.7$ ml. The beginnings of cardiac limitation in the final 40 s of exercise (seen by the decrease in O_2 pulse to an average of 28.5 ml/beat), suggest reduction of SV to about 178 ml.

Oxygen Consumption

We can express O_2 consumption data both in absolute terms (ml/min) and relative to body weight (ml · kg^{-1} · min^{-1}). Expression in absolute terms is least ambiguous (Åstrand 1984), because it prevents changes in body weight from being

TABLE 4.6

Treadmill Evaluation of a Male Distance Runner—Physiological Data

Elapsed time (min)	Heart rate (beats/min)	O_2 pulse (ml/beat)	$\dot{V}_E$ (L/min)	$\dot{V}O_2$ (ml/min)	$\dot{V}O_2$ (ml · kg⁻¹ · min⁻¹)	$\dot{V}CO_2$ (ml/min)	R	$\dfrac{\dot{V}_E}{\dot{V}O_2}$	$\dfrac{\dot{V}_E}{\dot{V}CO_2}$	f_R (br/min)	V_T (ml)	Hb (sat. %)
:20	125	21.9	70	2,739	40.3	2,418	0.88	26	29	37	1,890	95
:40	125	21.0	68	2,624	38.6	2,288	0.88	26	30	42	1,610	94
1:00	125	20.1	63	2,518	37.0	2,171	0.85	25	29	42	1,500	94
1:20	125	18.4	55	2,302	33.9	1,953	0.85	24	28	33	1,660	95
1:40	125	22.3	70	2,793	41.1	2,423	0.86	25	29	42	1,670	93
2:00	125	19.6	57	2,444	35.9	2,070	0.84	23	27	33	1,730	94
2:20	125	21.4	63	2,673	39.3	2,247	0.84	24	28	44	1,440	95
2:40	125	21.6	64	2,695	39.6	2,289	0.84	24	28	37	1,710	94
3:00	125	23.0	70	2,869	42.2	2,525	0.88	25	28	38	1,850	93
3:20	125	22.5	67	2,815	41.4	2,433	0.87	24	28	40	1,680	94
3:40	130	23.1	71	3,005	44.2	2,607	0.87	24	27	40	1,770	94
4:00	135	22.0	72	2,967	43.6	2,580	0.88	24	28	41	1,780	93
4:20	135	22.2	73	3,000	44.1	2,630	0.88	24	28	44	1,860	93
4:40	136	22.3	74	3,034	44.6	2,649	0.87	25	28	42	1,770	93
5:00	136	22.5	74	3,061	45.0	2,691	0.88	24	28	36	2,060	93
5:20	136	23.2	77	3,157	46.4	2,795	0.88	24	28	45	1,740	94
5:40	136	21.7	75	2,952	43.4	2,652	0.90	25	28	43	1,760	94
6:00	140	22.6	81	3,159	46.5	2,835	0.90	26	29	45	1,810	94
6:20	140	22.0	74	3,085	45.4	2,707	0.87	24	27	40	1,870	93
6:40	145	23.6	88	3,427	50.4	3,093	0.91	26	29	44	1,990	93
7:00	145	22.3	80	3,235	47.6	2,931	0.91	25	27	36	2,230	93
7:20	145	24.3	89	3,526	51.9	3,161	0.90	25	28	42	2,130	94
7:40	145	22.9	85	3,314	48.7	2,984	0.89	26	28	42	2,020	92
8:00	145	23.9	88	3,464	50.9	3,130	0.90	25	28	40	2,190	92
8:20	145	22.6	85	3,277	48.2	2,946	0.90	26	29	44	1,940	92
8:40	145	23.3	86	3,372	49.6	3,037	0.90	26	28	41	2,080	92
9:00	148	23.3	91	3,445	50.7	3,154	0.91	27	29	43	2,140	94
9:20	148	24.0	93	3,545	52.1	3,221	0.92	26	29	42	2,210	92
9:40	150	24.8	97	3,717	54.7	3,447	0.92	26	28	42	2,300	93
10:00	150	25.4	103	3,803	55.9	3,547	0.93	27	29	45	2,280	91
10:20	155	23.0	92	3,568	52.5	3,311	0.93	26	28	39	2,350	93
10:40	155	25.5	102	3,951	58.1	3,657	0.93	26	28	39	2,620	92
11:00	160	24.7	107	3,947	58.0	3,701	0.93	27	29	45	2,400	92

Pace groupings (left margin): 7:30 pace (:20–2:00), 6:40 pace (2:20–5:00), 6:00 pace (5:20–8:00), 5:30 pace (8:20–11:00)

(continued)

TABLE 4.6 (continued)

	Elapsed time (min)	Heart rate (beats/min)	O_2 pulse (ml/beat)	$\dot{V}_E$ (L/min)	$\dot{V}O_2$ (ml/min)	$\dot{V}O_2$ (ml · kg^{-1} · min^{-1})	$\dot{V}CO_2$ (ml/min)	R	$\dot{V}_E/\dot{V}O_2$	$\dot{V}_E/\dot{V}CO_2$	f_R (br/min)	V_T (ml)	Hb (sat. %)
5:00 pace	11:20	160	22.5	99	3,602	53.0	3,414	0.95	28	29	42	2,350	91
	11:40	160	23.9	103	3,828	56.3	3,540	0.93	27	29	48	2,130	90
	12:00	167	23.0	106	3,848	56.6	3,595	0.94	27	29	45	2,370	90
	12:20	167	23.0	106	3,849	56.6	3,628	0.95	27	29	45	2,350	90
	12:40	167	24.9	113	4,159	61.2	3,956	0.94	27	29	45	2,520	89
	13:00	167	25.0	119	4,177	61.4	4,093	0.99	29	29	45	2,650	89
	13:20	167	23.6	108	3,941	58.0	3,800	0.97	28	29	41	2,650	88
	13:40	167	24.5	120	4,084	60.1	3,989	0.98	29	30	46	2,590	89
	14:00	167	25.2	113	4,206	61.9	4,005	0.96	27	28	42	2,680	89
6:00 4%	14:20	167	25.8	122	4,313	63.4	4,143	0.96	28	29	45	2,700	88
	14:40	167	23.9	114	3,989	58.7	3,853	0.96	28	29	42	2,720	87
	15:00	167	24.7	117	4,130	60.7	3,978	0.96	28	29	42	2,770	88
	15:20	167	25.2	112	4,207	61.9	3,938	0.93	27	29	42	2,680	88
	15:40	167	25.1	114	4,192	61.7	3,942	0.93	27	29	41	2,750	87
	16:00	167	23.9	111	3,987	58.6	3,789	0.95	28	29	41	2,700	87
6:00 6%	16:20	167	25.7	121	4,299	63.2	4,130	0.96	28	29	46	2,650	86
	16:40	167	26.2	120	4,377	64.4	4,210	0.97	27	28	46	2,620	87
	17:00	167	28.1	129	4,694	69.0	4,501	0.96	27	29	45	2,860	88
	17:20	170	26.7	128	4,534	66.7	4,458	0.99	28	29	43	2,990	87
	17:40	170	27.6	131	4,700	69.1	4,622	0.99	28	28	45	2,920	86
	18:00	170	28.4	138	4,826	71.0	4,785	1.00	29	29	47	2,930	85
6:00 8%	18:20	170	26.8	122	4,549	66.9	4,464	0.99	27	27	45	2,690	85
	18:40	170	29.5	145	5,010	73.7	5,025	1.00	29	29	48	3,020	86
	19:00	170	28.9	142	4,921	72.4	5,006	1.02	29	28	47	3,050	87
	19:20	180	28.2	151	5,083	74.8	5,249	1.02	30	29	50	3,060	87
	19:40	180	29.0	154	5,216	76.7	5,431	1.04	30	28	51	3,040	84
	20:00	180	28.0	149	5,044	74.2	5,238	1.03	30	29	48	3,100	84

Time												
20:20	180	29.0	159	5,219	76.8	5,489	1.04	31	29	53	3,040	85
20:40	180	29.3	162	5,266	77.4	5,589	1.07	31	29	53	3,080	84
21:00	180	29.1	165	5,299	76.9	5,672	1.09	31	29	54	3,050	84
21:20	180	29.2	164	5,251	77.2	5,659	1.07	31	29	54	3,030	83
21:40	180	30.7	175	5,532	81.4	6,054	1.10	32	29	57	3,070	85
22:00	180	29.7	172	5,354	78.7	5,935	1.10	32	29	57	3,000	84
6:00 10%												
22:20	180	29.5	170	5,307	78.0	5,918	1.10	32	29	57	2,990	82
22:40	188	28.6	177	5,377	79.1	6,119	1.15	33	29	60	2,960	80
23:00	188	28.4	176	5,332	78.4	6,070	1.15	33	29	62	2,850	76
6:00 11%												
23:20	188	26.6	172	5,006	73.6	5,744	1.14	34	30	61	2,820	78
23:40	188	17.0	130	3,192	46.9	3,747	1.18	41	35	50	2,600	86
24:00	150	18.0	114	2,707	39.8	3,218	1.19	42	35	51	2,250	88
24:20	150	18.2	123	2,735	40.2	3,618	1.33	45	34	50	2,460	88
24:40	125	18.8	93	2,344	34.5	3,330	1.42	40	28	32	2,900	89
25:00	125	16.6	97	2,071	30.5	2,987	1.45	47	32	39	2,470	93
25:20	115	17.8	97	2,045	30.1	2,991	1.45	47	32	39	2,500	92
25:40	115	15.7	87	1,802	26.5	2,544	1.43	48	34	39	2,200	91
26:00	115	14.5	82	1,670	24.6	2,343	1.39	49	35	41	2,020	93
Recovery												

TABLE 4.7

Expressing $\dot{V}O_2$max Data in Absolute and Relative Terms

Date of $\dot{V}O_2$max measurement	October	February	June
Body weight (kg)	60	60	57
Absolute $\dot{V}O_2$max (ml/min)	4,700	4,900	4,950
% change in absolute $\dot{V}O_2$max	⊢———— +4.3 ——→⊢	⊢———— +1.0 ————→	
Relative $\dot{V}O_2$max (ml · kg⁻¹ · min⁻¹)	78	82	87
% change in relative $\dot{V}O_2$max	⊢———— +5.1 ——→⊢	⊢———— +6.0 ————→	

confused as changes in O_2 consumption. Table 4.7 shows some of the difficulties that can occur in interpreting data expressed in the two formats. We use the example of a trained male runner who had a physiological performance evaluation in October, February, and June as a training plan progressed to bring him toward a fitness peak during June. Notice that between October and February his weight was constant at 60 kg. Thus, his *relative $\dot{V}O_2$max* improved from 78 to 82 ml · kg⁻¹ · min⁻¹, an increase of 5.1%. But his *absolute $\dot{V}O_2$max* increased by 4.3%, from 4,700 to 4,900 ml/min. Between March and June, his training gradually shifted toward maintaining $\dot{V}O_2$max and increasing anaerobic capabilities. This was reflected in the form of an essentially unchanged $\dot{V}O_2$max in absolute terms—from 4,900 ml/min to 4,950 ml/min (an insignificant 1% increase). However, his weight decreased from 60 to 57 kg, a reduction of 5%. Relative $\dot{V}O_2$max, calculated as 4,950/57 = 87 ml · kg⁻¹ · min⁻¹, increased by 6%. The improvement in $\dot{V}O_2$max during the entire training period from October to June expressed in relative terms was 11.5%, whereas the absolute increase was 5.3%.

We could consider the $\dot{V}O_2$max of the runner of table 4.6 as the largest observed $\dot{V}O_2$ value, which is 81.4 ml · kg⁻¹ · min⁻¹. Instead, by averaging that value with the four subsequent values (78.7, 78.0, 79.1, and 78.4), we obtain what we term a mean *sustainable $\dot{V}O_2$max* of 79.1 ml · kg⁻¹ · min⁻¹. The duration of this plateau becomes an important indicator of anaerobic work tolerance, because once $\dot{V}O_2$max is achieved, anaerobic metabolism provides the additional energy for continued work.

What is the error associated with such $\dot{V}O_2$ measurements? In other words, how much change in a given $\dot{V}O_2$ value actually represents an increase or a decrease in fitness rather than technological or biological variability? In today's era of excellent technology most laboratories take great care to perform proper calibrations, maintain constant room temperature and humidity for repeat test procedures, and ensure consistency in technician competence. Even so, $\dot{V}O_2$max values obtained on different days from the same athlete will not be identical. No more than 10% of the variation should be caused by technological variability. The remaining 90% of the variability will be biological; that is inherent within the individual being tested—subtle differences in psychological determination, hydration status, and so on. Gibson, Harrison, and Wellcome (1979) suggested that the coefficient of variation of $\dot{V}O_2$max can be held within ± 3%. Our laboratory experience is similar. Thus, using the $\dot{V}O_2$max value of 81.4 ml · kg⁻¹ · min⁻¹ as an example, values within 3% (that is, between 79.0 and 83.8 ml · kg⁻¹ · min⁻¹) cannot be guaranteed as training related because they fall within the expected error range of the measurement system.

Running Economy

The first part of our GXT evaluation is concerned largely with assessing O_2 consumption at a series of submaximal paces, which identifies running economy as defined by Daniels (1974). Notice in the data summary of table 4.6 that there is an initial warm-up period at a pace of 7:30 min/mi (4:40 min/km). Following this warm-up, economy is assessed by collecting 3 min of $\dot{V}O_2$ data at the four level-grade running paces of 6:40, 6:00, 5:30, and 5:00 min/mi (4:09, 3:44, 3:25, and 3:06 min/km). Using scientific (velocity) jargon rather than coaching (pace) jargon, these four level running velocities are 241, 268, 293, and 322 m/min (14.5, 16.1, 17.6, and 19.4 km/hr). This pace/velocity range encompasses the aerobic range of this athlete during all but higher speed track-oriented training sessions. For our female runners, we use running paces of 7:00, 6:30, 6:00, and 5:40 min/mi (230, 248, 268, and 284 m/min; 13.8, 14.8, 16.1, and 17.0 km/hr) to measure running economy. Those desiring to develop their own test protocols that best match their athletes' fitness can do so using convenient guidelines developed by the American College of Sports Medicine (1986), based on equations (4.2) and (4.3).

Note in table 4.6 that adaptation to each work load is not instantaneous, and a measurable upward creep in results of expired gas analyses occurs. Our experience with these work loads for highly trained runners has been that, for the paces indicated, adaptation is sufficient by the end of 3 min so that continued running at each pace for a fourth minute or longer does not reveal $\dot{V}O_2$ or $\dot{V}CO_2$ values significantly different from those obtained during the third minute. Having our athletes run at these submaximal test paces for only as long as necessary thus minimizes boredom during the test and also decreases total sweat loss. We estimate the submaximal O_2 demand (economy) at each pace as the average of the three 20-s expired gas samples collected during the final minute of running at that pace. Using the statistical technique of *regression analysis*, an equation can be written using these four pairs of pace and $\dot{V}O_2$ data that best describes each runner's O_2 consumption with increasing work load. For example, using linear regression, an equation of the type

$$y = mx + b \tag{4.11}$$

would be generated, where $y = O_2$ demand, b = the y ordinate intercept, x = velocity, and m = slope of the line of best fit of the data. This regression equation determined from data obtained during level running permits extrapolation to the level-ground pace at which the athlete would be running at $\dot{V}O_2$max intensity. One need only insert the $\dot{V}O_2$max value into the equation, rearrange, and solve for velocity. This is called the *velocity at $\dot{V}O_2$max, or v-$\dot{V}O_2$max*. The term was first coined by Daniels et al. in 1986, and the concept has been useful because combining $\dot{V}O_2$max and running economy into a single factor can explain differences in running performance not distinguishable by measures of $\dot{V}O_2$max or running economy alone. This value has been quite useful from a coaching viewpoint (Billat and Koralsztein 1996) because, as described earlier, when coupled with other values such as the pace for the lactate/ventilatory threshold, pace ranges can be identified for the four training zones identified in figure 4.2 (these will be described more fully in chapter 5).

Such extrapolation is valid, however, only if the rate of change in O_2 consumption outside the range of measured data points follows the same mathemical relationship as it did within the range. As an example, let us hypothesize that the relationship between O_2 consumption and velocity is not linear, but curvilinear instead. If the pace range used for producing the regression equation involves relatively slow running velocities and is not wide enough to fully characterize the curvilinearity at the other end, where $\dot{V}O_2max$ occurs, then the extrapolated v-$\dot{V}O_2max$ pace will be overestimated. If, however, the relationship between running velocity and O_2 consumption is linear throughout, then the extrapolated v-$\dot{V}O_2max$ pace will be accurate.

Is the relationship between running velocity and O_2 consumption linear or curvilinear? Daniels (1985, 333) hedges the answer by stating that "work done since 1950 *generally* supports the concept of a linear or *very nearly* linear relationship . . . during *submaximal* running, where energy demands are met aerobically and where the range of running speeds is *rather limited*" (emphasis added). Thus, although one study generated performance tables using a curvilinear relationship between $\dot{V}O_2$ and velocity (Daniels and Gilbert 1979), subsequent reports, typified by a study of female middle- and long-distance runners (Daniels et al. 1986), used linear regression to describe the same relationship. This inconsistency in data analysis, even among individual investigators, suggests that the final conclusion is still unknown about whether this relationship between $\dot{V}O_2$ and running velocity is linear or curvilinear across its entire range in humans. The present evidence seems almost in favor of curvilinearity. If the relationship was linear throughout, the slope of the regression lines obtained by most workers who evaluate the economy of distance runners should be essentially parallel, differing only in that the more efficient runners are positioned lower than the less efficient runners because of their decreased O_2 cost at submaximal paces. Such appears not to be true; both Daniels (1985) and Kearney and Van Handel (1989) state or summarize information from other published studies suggesting that a range of faster running velocities results in a steeper slope than a range of lower running velocities.

One plausible explanation is that the several sets of data have been obtained from different parts of a relationship between $\dot{V}O_2$ and work load, which varies according to the influence of other factors (such as the effects of anaerobic energy demands and running mechanics). The frequently reported suggestions of a linear relationship between O_2 consumption and work load may thus be based on data collected from a rather narrow submaximal range of work intensities. Thus, although the studies of Cavagna and Margaria are quoted frequently regarding the relationship whereby 1 kcal of energy is required per kilogram of body weight per kilometer of distance covered submaximally (Cavagna, Saibene, and Margaria 1964; Margaria et al. 1963), this linearity may not necessarily be true for energy demands beyond the lactate/ventilatory threshold and approaching $\dot{V}O_2max$.

Clearly, additional work is needed in this area to elucidate more fully the details of this relationship between O_2 consumption and work load. For best accuracy in preparing useful regression equations to extrapolate v-$\dot{V}O_2max$ pace when linear regression is to be used, the fast end of the level-ground submaximal pace range should not be too far away from $\dot{V}O_2max$. If curvilinear regression is to be used, then a sufficiently wide pace range is needed (including higher-intensity work loads) to ensure identification of the extent of curvilinearity. As a practical suggestion for coaches, athletes should perform a track time trial a few days following their treadmill test, lasting somewhere between 10 and 12 min (this is about the longest period of time that $\dot{V}O_2max$ can be sustained). Knowing the distance covered and the elapsed time will permit a field-test estimation of v-$\dot{V}O_2$max. This can serve as a check on the accuracy of treadmill test data interpretation.

What factors can alter running economy, and can training improve running economy? It has been suggested that anaerobic capacity training (repeated intervals of shorter faster running) improves running economy (Daniels 1985), but the same author states elsewhere (Daniels et al. 1986) that "training seems to play a minimal, if any, role in narrowing the between-individual variations that exist" (66). Thus, the specific kinds of training that may improve running economy have yet to be clearly identified. Intuition suggests that the larger volumes of aerobic conditioning, which begin to produce in a runner the ability to manage elevated training loads as a development season begins, would provide an improvement in fitness, strength, and coordination that is reflected in an improved economy of O_2 consumption. But it hasn't been easy to document this.

Some of our elite-level athletes experience increases in running economy over the course of a training macrocycle, and some do not. Those who do typically are the middle-distance experts, who have sizable differences in their ratios of aerobic-to-anaerobic training loads over the course of a year. The longer-distance stars are not influenced as much by such changes. Our suspicion is that it is the higher-intensity training that adds components of increased neurological recruitment and increased muscle power output to aerobic fitness and that these components make it relatively easier for athletes to manage particular submaximal paces.

It is possible that increased volumes of aerobic training alone can improve fitness and provide a similar economy of motion. The studies of Scrimgeour and colleagues (1986), which report that athletes training less than 60 km/wk have as much as 19% less running economy than athletes training more than 100 km/wk, might support this suggestion. But those athletes running less than 60 km/wk were not asked to average more than 100 km/wk for a prolonged period to determine whether aerobic running in that particular group of individuals actually *caused* an improvement in economy. Those athletes doing the high-volume training might simply have found the training easier to manage than the lower-volume athletes because their economy was greater before they began training.

Many factors extraneous to training can also affect economy. Rainy weather, for example, increases the weight of socks and shoes, thereby increasing O_2 cost and decreasing economy. Wearing lighter racing flats instead of heavier training shoes decreases O_2 consumption at submaximal paces and thus improves economy. For our GXT evaluation of athletes, we recommend that they run in racing flats, primarily for consistency but also because they wear them in competitive racing situations.

Lactate/Ventilatory Threshold

A complete explanation of the possible interrelationships between the exercise-induced ventilatory changes and lactate production by working muscle has still not been developed. The threshold increases in blood lactate and ventilation (which we have termed the lactate/ventilatory threshold) occur together with high correlation among metabolically normal people (Caiozzo et al. 1982; Clode and Campbell 1969; Davis et al. 1976). If one of the factors limiting exercise from the athlete's perspective is an increasing subjective ventilatory discomfort, this heightened respiratory stress may be a more important variable to measure than a blood chemistry variable such as lactate, although it is presumably the acidosis that initiates the increased ventilatory drive.

Laboratories specializing in studies of human performance often can measure both lactate and ventilatory thresholds. The problems inherent in quantifying blood lactate, which will be described shortly, may make its measurement less informative than that of ventilatory changes. Individual subject variability sometimes makes one or the other threshold less easy to discern. This is another reason that both variables are sometimes determined during a GXT. The preferred measurement seems to depend on the fundamental research bent of the investigators as well as the nature of the exercise test protocol (i.e., bicycle versus treadmill and laboratory versus field study).

The ventilatory threshold is best estimated by using graphic plots of $\dot{V}_E$ versus increasing work load, to identify the change in linear rate of rise in $\dot{V}_E$. Often, at about this same time, $\dot{V}CO_2$ produced exceeds $\dot{V}O_2$ utilized, and this crossover can also be graphed. Using such plots, we estimated that our athlete's ventilatory threshold in table 4.6 occurred at about 72 ml $\cdot$ kg^{-1} $\cdot$ min^{-1}. This is about 88.5% of his absolute $\dot{V}O_2$max and 91% of his mean sustainable $\dot{V}O_2$max.

The ventilatory equivalents have also been used to suggest that, certainly at sea level, ventilation in athletes with healthy lungs is probably not a limiting factor in running performance. Let us compare healthy resting values of $\dot{V}_E$ and $\dot{V}O_2$ of our trained male runner in table 4.6 at maximal effort (177 L/min and 5.5 L/min, respectively). We can compute $\dot{V}_E/\dot{V}O_2$ as increasing from 5/0.25 = 20 to 177/5.5 = 32. Notice the greater rise in ventilation than in O_2 consumption. The limitations to maximal exercise are thus more likely those of cardiovascular O_2 transport or tissue utilization than they are of ventilatory effectiveness.

Measuring Blood Lactate

Analysis of blood lactate was simplified in the 1980s with the advent of reasonably accurate and rapid enzymatic microassay techniques, requiring only a lancet puncture of a fingertip or earlobe to obtain a small sample of peripheral blood. For sequential collection of blood at various work loads during a treadmill test or after field-test runs around a track, such collection is preferred by athletes to blood collection via syringe or indwelling catheter in a blood vessel. It is this simplicity that has most likely stimulated the enormous wealth of scientific literature concerning the quantitation of onset of blood lactate accumulation during exercise.

We see a number of difficulties with such analyses. First, we find that athletes prefer a racelike, uninterrupted treadmill protocol, which obviously cannot be maintained if athletes must stop periodically for fingertip or earlobe blood collection. Second, there are technical quality-control problems in analyzing capillary as opposed to venous blood. Capillary blood collected following lancet puncture will certainly be contaminated with interstitial fluid and possibly with sweat as well. Only if the lancet puncture is firm enough to provide plenty of free-flowing blood will it be essentially arterialized (meaning that arterioles have been severed) rather than predominantly capillary blood. If the first drop is wiped away, as it will be contaminated with interstitial fluid, collection of the next drop must be rapid to prevent clotting at the puncture site. Third, along with the lactate sample, either a second drop must be collected and analyzed for hemoglobin and hematocrit, or another lancet puncture must be performed. The site must not be massaged to enhance flow, because this will alter the blood composition.

Why is it necessary to measure hemoglobin if the blood lactate changes are of interest? The answer is simply that there are sizable fluid movements out of the bloodstream during exercise, and we need to measure hemoglobin to quantify the extent of this hemoconcentration. During a treadmill test, which lasts 20 min or more, a sizable body weight loss occurs (as much as 3 lb) from sweat (Martin, Vroon, and Sheard 1989), which comes primarily from blood plasma. During more prolonged exercise, particularly in warm weather, both sweat loss and osmolar movement of water out of the bloodstream because of increased electrolyte accumulation in the plasma and because of plasma protein movement into the interstitial fluid can amount to as much as 15% of plasma volume (Nadel 1988). Because of this hemoconcentration from several sources, even if there were no increases in lactate derived from anaerobic metabolism during exercise, the blood lactate concentration in a postexercise sample would appear larger than in a sample obtained near the beginning of exercise. The posttest lactate value is being expressed in millimoles (per liter) or milligrams (per deciliter) of a now-decreased blood volume. This hemoconcentration varies among runners from 5% or less to as high as 13% (Martin, Vroon, and Sheard 1989). It does not appear to relate to fitness level or sex, and it can vary considerably even among individuals whose treadmill test endurance times are similar.

Dill and Costill (1974) have described how correction for hemoconcentration can be made using hemoglobin data from the collected blood samples (preexercise and during or after exercise). To ensure consistent analysis and adequate sample volume, we find venipuncture preferable to capillary sampling using lancet puncture. Percentage hemoconcentration of a posttest blood sample as a result of volume loss is given by the following equation:

$$\% \text{ hemoconcentration} = 100 - (\text{pretest Hb}/\text{posttest Hb} \times 100) \qquad (4.12)$$

To correct the posttest lactate value for hemoconcentration, the following equation is appropriate:

$$\text{corrected lactate} = \text{pretest Hb}/\text{posttest Hb} \times \text{posttest lactate} \qquad (4.13)$$

An example from our own unpublished data can help illustrate this concept. One of our elite female marathoners ran for slightly longer than 20 min during a treadmill test. Her $\dot{V}O_2$max was 72 ml $\cdot$ kg^{-1} $\cdot$ min^{-1}. Her pretest and posttest hemoglobin values were 13.3 and 15.0 mg/dl, respectively. Her posttest maximal blood lactate was 88 mg/dl (9.8 mmol/L). Her percentage hemoconcentration was calculated as

$$\% \text{ hemoconcentration} = 100 - (13.3/15.0 \times 100) = 11.3\% \qquad (4.14)$$

If we correct for this hemoconcentration, her posttest maximal lactate is given by

$$\text{corrected lactate} = 13.3/15.0 \times 88 = 78.0 \text{ mg/dl } (8.7 \text{ mmol/L}) \qquad (4.15)$$

Typically, in published reports describing blood lactate concentrations during or after exercise in runners, such volume corrections for hemoconcentration appear not to have been made (e.g., Fay et al. 1989; Sjödin and Jacobs 1981; Sjödin and Svedenhag 1985). This prevents an accurate appreciation for the actual magnitude of blood lactate rise as a result of varying intensities of exercise.

It also adds to the error involved in estimating training paces based on preset blood lactate concentrations such as 4 mmol/L.

Maximal Performance Capacity

Although O_2 consumption eventually peaks and plateaus, in trained distance runners anaerobic contributions from additional recruited FT fibers at high work rates both extend and increase total work output. This anaerobic capability is a crucial part of an athlete's physiological competitiveness and is thus deserving of careful assessment. This is why we encourage our athletes to endure absolutely as long as possible during their treadmill tests. Recall from chapter 3 that it is the H^+ ion–induced inhibition of Ca^{2+} binding to the tropomyosin complex in the muscle filaments, as well as a reduced production of ATP due to the H^+ ion–induced blockade of the phosphofructokinase enzyme in the glycolytic pathway, that shuts down not only tension generation but also the means to produce it. Studies have indicated that intracellular muscle pH may fall to as low as 6.2 during heavy exercise, with plasma pH as low as 6.8 (Hermansen and Osnes 1972). Athletes working very hard sense this acidosis subjectively. Thus, the increasing metabolic acidosis becomes an intolerable stress. Exactly what limits exercise is therefore probably more easily answered subjectively as a symptom-limiting situation involving an intolerable effort sense in either the limb muscles or the breathing muscles (Jones 1988). We can evaluate anaerobic responsiveness from test to test in several ways. Perhaps the most quantitative way is to measure the accumulated O_2 deficit using a protocol described by Medbø et al. (1988). But there are other observations that can be made from data such as that in table 4.6. One is to note the length of time the $\dot{V}O_2max$ plateau is maintained. Another is to compare the length of time the athlete is working with a respiratory exchange ratio (R) greater than 1.0, which indicates a respiratory compensation to increasing metabolic acidosis, and to identify the maximum R value achieved during the test. A third is to compare the $\dot{V}CO_2max$. A fourth is to compare the 5-min posttest maximal blood lactate level. Although effective endurance training ought to lower blood lactate concentrations observed at any given submaximal work load, a higher maximal lactate suggests greater tolerance to anaerobic work (Holloszy and Coyle 1984). Finally, a fifth observation is to evaluate subjectively the athlete's stability during the final few moments before test termination: Is running form maintainable throughout the test or beginning to deteriorate?

For the athlete whose data are summarized in table 4.6, it can be seen that

- his sustainable $\dot{V}O_2max$ plateau lasted 80 s;
- his maximum R during the test was 1.15, and R was above 1.0 for 4:40;
- his $\dot{V}CO_2max$ was 6,119 ml/min, or 96 ml $\cdot$ kg^{-1} $\cdot$ min^{-1}; and
- his maximal blood lactate was 119 mg/dl (13.2 mmol/L) after correction for a 9.1% hemoconcentration during the test.

For this athlete, we were hard-pressed to offer him any suggestions for further improvement of his fitness. His $\dot{V}O_2max$ was his highest, and his anaerobic threshold (88.5% of $\dot{V}O_2max$) was also his highest over the three-year period of working with him. We had tested this athlete on two other occasions in the year leading up to those Olympic trials and had given him training suggestions based on previous data. In each instance the training assignments did improve his fitness in the direction we desired, and he peaked at the appropriate moment.

He arrived at the starting line of the trials healthy, injury free, and fit. And he performed very well.

SUMMARY

Training and Monitoring the Heart and Lungs for Better Running

1. Two important tasks of the cardiovascular system, pulmonary system, and blood are to transport fuels to the working muscles, including O_2 for complete fuel metabolism, and to remove the resulting products of metabolism. These products include volatile acids such as CO_2 and nonvolatile acids such as lactate.

2. Such factors as maximal oxygen consumption ($\dot{V}O_2$max), the ability to work for long periods at near-$\dot{V}O_2$max intensity with minimal lactate accumulation, and the capacity to work for short periods at intensities far in excess of $\dot{V}O_2$max are all trainable to a varying extent (depending on fitness level) by means of specific stimuli to the cardiopulmonary and musculoskeletal systems, although there is a hereditary component as well. Their net effects couple with psychological readiness and knowledge of tactics to produce a good competitor.

3. The interaction of all of these factors explains why, in a homogeneous population of gifted and trained endurance runners, all with excellent competitive credentials, no one of these physiological aspects of performance by itself explains very well the superiority of one athlete over another.

4. Training brings specific adaptations in the cardiovascular system, the pulmonary system, and the blood. These adaptations can improve the maximal oxygen uptake ability ($\dot{V}O_2$max), raise the lactate/ventilatory threshold, and improve running economy and maximal anaerobic capacity. Such improvements directly increase aerobic and anaerobic performance capabilities.

5. Specific cardiovascular adaptations to training have been identified. There is an increased blood volume, which permits better perfusion of tissues, and a larger fluid reservoir for sweat production and dilution of metabolic acids. The ventricular chambers of the heart expand to permit greater stroke volume per beat. This in turn permits an adequate cardiac output with minimal increase in heart rate, thereby ensuring optimal time between beats for perfusion of the heart tissue with blood through the coronary vessels. Greater perfusion permits increased O_2 extraction from blood, seen as an increased arteriovenous (a-$\bar{v}O_2$) difference.

6. $\dot{V}O_2$max is determined by heart rate, stroke volume, and rate of extraction of O_2 from blood. It is lower in women than in men, because women have less O_2-carrying capacity. It decreases with age. Elite-level and trained distance runners can have $\dot{V}O_2$max values more than twice those of untrained controls. Both training and heredity factors contribute to the observed difference.

7. Lactate/ventilatory threshold can refer to either of two work intensities where changes in the influences of anaerobic metabolism in supplementing aerobic metabolism are observed. For distance runners the work intensity marked by the onset of blood lactate accumulation, typically accompanied by an increase in ventilation, is commonly used as part of the training regimen intended to improve competitiveness at longer distances. This threshold does not always

occur at a blood lactate level of 4 mmol/L as often suggested, but varies among individuals and also within individuals as a result of training. As a runner becomes better trained, not only does the $\dot{V}O_2$max rise, but so does the lactate/ventilatory threshold, both in absolute terms and as a percentage of $\dot{V}O_2$max.

8. The multifaceted importance of iron in aerobic metabolism makes adequate iron supply crucial to successful long-term endurance performance. Iron is a part of hemoglobin and myoglobin molecules, a part of the enzymes that metabolize fuels aerobically, and a part of the enzyme that controls cell division among the several precursors of red blood cells. Hard training and dietary preferences while in training can decrease iron intake. Hemolysis from footstrike impact and the acidosis of intense training predisposes an athlete to iron loss via the urine, and iron losses through sweat may also be important in some instances. Monitoring of blood variables such as ferritin (to assess iron stores), haptoglobin (to evaluate hemolysis), reticulocytes (to assess red blood cell production), and urinary hemosiderin (to identify urinary loss) as well as hemoglobin levels can be useful for assessing the extent to which an athlete is managing the stress of training in terms of O_2 transport and fuel metabolism. Dietary iron supplementation (coupled with measurement of iron-related blood chemistry variables) may be appropriate to restore adequate iron stores if they become depleted.

9. Repeated GXT evaluation at various points over a training year provides knowledge of which aspects of performance—$\dot{V}O_2$max, lactate/ventilatory threshold, running economy, and maximal performance capacity—have changed as a result of training. This provides a fine-tuning mechanism for assignment of subsequent training or a best estimate of strengths for best race strategies. Running economy, or the aerobic demand of running at submaximal paces, can be determined for a series of such paces. By using a regression equation constructed from these data, we can calculate training paces at $\dot{V}O_2$max and lactate/ventilatory threshold as well as pace ranges for each of four identified training zones: aerobic and anaerobic conditioning, and aerobic and anaerobic capacity training.

10. Athletes who want to obtain the best results from a GXT should (a) mentally consider the test as a competitive event; (b) taper their training a few days prior to the test to ensure freshness and minimal metabolic effects of very long or very intense runs; (c) become familiar with both treadmill running and the test protocol; (d) include a thorough warm-up similar to that done before a competition; and (e) strive to work as hard as possible until voluntary exhaustion to ensure not only $\dot{V}O_2$max determination but also maximal anaerobic performance aspects.

11. Acceptable test-retest reliability is obtained by (a) keeping laboratory conditions (temperature, humidity, test equipment, and test decorum) as constant as possible; (b) minimizing circadian fluctuations by testing at the same time of day; and (c) using a protocol that is of appropriate length to provide exhaustion without more than about 10 min of intense effort.

12. Blood sampling is often used in GXT evaluation, either after the test to measure maximal lactate or at intermittent points during the test to identify the work load at which lactate accumulation begins. Hemoconcentration occurs primarily from sweat losses. Lactate measurements thus should be accompanied by measurements of hemoglobin and hematocrit to correct lactate values for

this hemoconcentration. Values obtained by venipuncture must not be confused with values obtained by fingertip or earlobe puncture.

References

Allison, A.C. 1957. The binding of haemoglobin by plasma proteins (haptoglobins): Its bearing on the "renal threshold" for haemoglobin and aetiology of haemoglobinuria. *British Medical Journal* 2:1137.

American College of Sports Medicine. 1986. *Guidelines for exercise testing and prescription.* 3rd ed. Philadelphia: Lea and Febiger.

American Thoracic Society. 1979. ATS statement—Snowbird workshop on standardization of spirometry. *American Review of Respiratory Diseases* 119:831-838.

Anderson, T. 1996. Biomechanics and running economy. *Sports Medicine* 22:76-89.

Aschoff, J., and Pohl, H. 1970. Rhythm variation in energy metabolism. *Federation Proceedings* 154:29-35.

Åstrand, P.-O. 1976. Quantification of exercise capability and evaluation of physical capacity in man. *Progress in Cardiovascular Disease* 19:51-67.

———. 1982. Muscle oxygen supply in exercise. In *Oxygen transport to human tissues,* eds. J.A. Loeppky and M.L. Riedesel, 187-94. New York: Elsevier/North Holland.

———. 1984. Principles in ergometry and their implication in sports practice. *International Journal of Sports Medicine* 5:S102-S105.

Åstrand, P.-O., and Rodahl, K. 1977. *Textbook of work physiology.* 2nd ed. New York: McGraw-Hill.

Attlee, W.H.W. 1937. Hemoglobinuria following exertion. *Lancet* 1:1400.

Billat, L.V. 1996. Use of blood lactate measurements for prediction of exercise performance and for control of training. *Sports Medicine* 22:157-175.

Billat, L.V., and Koralsztein, J.P. 1996. Significance of the velocity at v-$\dot{V}O_2$max and time to exhaustion at this velocity. *Sports Medicine* 22:90-108.

Bohr, C.; Hasselbalch, K.A.; and Krogh, A. 1904. Über einen in biologisches Beziehung wichtigen Einfluss den die Kohlensäurespannung des Blutes auf dessen Sauerstoffbindung übt (Concerning an important influence in the biological relationship which the CO_2 tension of blood has on its O_2 binding). *Skandinavisches Archiv für Physiologie* 16:402-412.

Borg, G. 1973. Perceived exertion: A note on history and methods. *Medicine and Science in Sports* 5:90-93.

Bouchard, C.; Boulay, M.R.; Simoneau, J.-A.; Lortie, G.; and Perusse, L. 1988. Heredity and trainability of aerobic and anaerobic performances. *Sports Medicine* 5:69-73.

Bouchard, C., and Lortie, G. 1984. Heredity and endurance performance. *Sports Medicine* 1:38-64.

Bransford, D.R., and Howley, E.T. 1977. Oxygen cost of running in trained and untrained men and women. *Medicine and Science in Sports* 9:41-44.

Brotherhood, J.; Brozovic, B.; and Pugh, L.G.C. 1975. Haematological status of middle and long distance runners. *Clinical Science and Molecular Medicine* 48:139-145.

Brune, M.; Magnusson, B.; Persson, H.; and Hallberg, L. 1986. Iron losses in sweat. *American Journal of Clinical Nutrition* 43:438-443.

Busse, M.W.; Maassen, N.; and Boning, D. 1987. The work load-lactate curve: Measure of endurance capacity or criterion of muscle glycogen storage? I. Glycogen depletion. *International Journal of Sports Medicine* 8:140.

Caiozzo, V.J.; Davis, J.A.; Ellis, J.F.; Azus, J.L.; Vandagriff, R.; Prietto, C.A.; and McMaster, W.L. 1982. A comparison of gas exchange indices used to detect the anaerobic threshold. *Journal of Applied Physiology* 53:1184-1189.

Campbell, M.J.; McComas, A.J.; and Petito, F. 1973. Physiological changes in aging muscles. *Journal of Neurology, Neurosurgery, and Neuropsychiatry* 36:174-182.

Cavagna, G.A.; Saibene, F.B.; and Margaria, R. 1964. Mechanical work in running. *Journal of Applied Physiology* 19:249-256.

Chapman, C.B., and Mitchell, J.H. 1965. The physiology of exercise. *Scientific American* 212(5):88-96.

Christiansen, J.; Douglas, C.C.; and Haldane, J.S. 1914. The absorption and disassociation of carbon dioxide by human blood. *Journal of Physiology* 48:244.

Clausen, J.P. 1977. Effect of physical training on cardiovascular adjustments to exercise in man. *Physiological Reviews* 57:779-815.

Clausen, J.P.; Klausen, K.; Rasmussen, B.; and Trap-Jensen, J. 1973. Central and peripheral circulatory changes after training of the arms or legs. *American Journal of Physiology* 225:675-682.

Clement, D.B., and Asmundson, R.C. 1982. Nutritional intake and hematological parameters in endurance runners. *Physician and Sportsmedicine* 10(3):37-43.

Clement, D.B.; Asmundson, R.C.; and Medhurst, C.W. 1977. Hemoglobin values: Comparative survey of the 1976 Canadian Olympic Team. *Canadian Medical Association Journal* 117:614-616.

Clode, M., and Campbell, E.J.M. 1969. The relationship between gas exchange and changes in blood lactate concentrations during exercise. *Clinical Science* 37:263-272.

Conley, D.L., and Krahenbuhl, G.S. 1980. Running economy and distance running performance of highly trained athletes. *Medicine and Science in Sports* 12:357-360.

Conrad, M.E.; Benjamin, B.I.; Williams, H.L.; and Fox, A.L. 1967. Human absorption of hemoglobin-iron. *Gastroenterology* 53:5-10.

Cooper, K. 1968. *Aerobics.* New York: Bantam.

Costill, D.L.; Thomason, H.; and Roberts, E. 1973. Fractional utilization of the aerobic capacity during distance running. *Medicine and Science in Sports* 5:248-252.

Cronkite, E.P. 1973. The erythrocyte. In *Best and Taylor's physiological basis of medical practice.* 9th ed., ed. J.R. Brobeck, 4-24. Baltimore: Williams and Wilkins.

Currens, J.H., and White, P.D. 1961. Half a century of running. *New England Journal of Medicine* 265:988-993.

Dallman, P.R.; Beutler, E.; and Finch, B.A. 1978. Effects of iron deficiency exclusive of anemia. *British Journal of Haematology* 40:179-184.

Daniels, J. 1974. Physiological characteristics of champion male athletes. *Research Quarterly* 45:342-348.

———. 1985. A physiologist's view of running economy. *Medicine and Science in Sports and Exercise* 17:332-338.

Daniels, J.T., and Gilbert, J. 1979. *Oxygen power: Performance tables for distance runners.* Tempe, AZ: Oxygen Power.

Daniels, J.T.; Scardina, N.; Hayes, J.; and Foley, P. 1986. Elite and subelite female middle- and long-distance runners. In *The 1984 Olympic Scientific Congress proceedings.* Vol. 3, *Sport and elite performers,* ed. D.M. Landers, 57-72. Champaign, IL: Human Kinetics.

Davies, C.T.M., and Thompson, M.W. 1979. Aerobic performance of female marathon and male ultramarathon athletes. *European Journal of Applied Physiology* 41:233-245.

Davis, J.A.; Caiozzo, V.J.; Lamarra, N.; Ellis, J.F.; Vandagriff, R.; Prietto, C.A.; and McMaster, W.C. 1983. Does the gas exchange threshold occur at a fixed blood lactate concentration of 2 or 4 mM? *International Journal of Sports Medicine* 4:89-93.

Davis, J.A.; Vodak, P.; Wilmore, J.H.; and Kurtz, P. 1976. Anaerobic threshold and maximal aerobic power for three modes of exercise. *Journal of Applied Physiology* 41:544-550.

Dempsey, J. A.; Aaron, E.; and Martin, B.J. 1988. Pulmonary function and prolonged exercise. In *Perspectives in exercise science and sports medicine, 1,* eds. D.R. Lamb and R.R. Murray, 75-124. Indianapolis: Benchmark Press.

Dempsey, J.A.; Hanson, P.; and Henderson, K. 1984. Exercise-induced arterial hypoxemia in healthy human subjects at sea level. *Journal of Physiology* (London) 355:161-175.

Deutsch, F., and Kauf, E. [1924] 1927. *Heart and athletics.* Trans. L.M. Warfield. St. Louis: Mosby.

DeWijn, J.F.; deJongste, J.L.; Mosterd, W.; and Willebrand, D. 1971. Hemoglobin, packed cell volume, serum iron, and iron-binding capacity of selected athletes during training. *Nutrition and Metabolism* 13:129-139.

Dill, D.B., and Costill, D.L. 1974. Calculation of percentage changes in volumes of blood, plasma, and red cells in dehydration. *Journal of Applied Physiology* 37:247-248.

Doll, E., and Keul, J. 1968. Zum Stoffwechsel des Skelettmuskels. II. *Pflüger's Archiv für die gesamte Physiologie* 301:214-229.

Dufaux, B.; Hoederath, A.; Streitberger, I.; Hollmann, W.; and Assman, G. 1981. Serum ferritin, transferrin, haptoglobin, and iron in middle- and long-distance runners, elite rowers, and professional racing cyclists. *International Journal of Sports Medicine* 2:43-46.

Eichner, E. 1986. The anemias of athletes. *Physician and Sportsmedicine* 14(9):122-130.

———. 1988. Other medical considerations in prolonged exercise. *Perspectives in Exercise Science and Sports Medicine* 1:415-442.

Ekblom, B., and Hermansen, L. 1968. Cardiac output in athletes. *Journal of Applied Physiology* 25:619-625.

Essen, B.; Pernow, B.; Gollnick, P.D.; and Saltin, B. 1975. Muscle glycogen content and lactate uptake in exercising muscles. In *Metabolic adaptations to prolonged physical exercise,* eds. H. Howald and J.R. Poortmans, 130-134. Basel: Dirkhauser.

Farrell, P.A.; Wilmore, J.H.; Coyle, E.F.; Billing, J.E.; and Costill, D.L. 1979. Plasma lactate accumulation and distance running performance. *Medicine and Science in Sports and Exercise* 11:338-344.

Fay, L.; Londeree, B.R.; LaFontaine, T.P.; and Volek, M.R. 1989. Physiological parameters related to distance running performance in female athletes. *Medicine and Science in Sports and Exercise* 21:319-324.

Fleischer, R. 1881. Über eine neue form von Haemoglobinurie beim Menschen (Concerning a new form of hemoglobinuria in people). *Berliner Klinische Wochenschrift* 18:691-694.

Food and Nutrition Board. 1989. *Recommended dietary allowances.* 10th ed. Washington, DC: National Academy of Sciences.

Foster, C.; Snyder, A.C.; Thompson, N.N.; and Kuettel, K. 1988. Normalization of the blood lactate profile in athletes. *International Journal of Sports Medicine* 9:198-200.

Fric, J., Jr.; Fric, J.; Boldt, F.; Stoboy, H.; Meller, W.; Feldt, F.; and Drygas, W. 1988. Reproducibility of post-exercise lactate and anaerobic threshold. *International Journal of Sports Medicine* 9:310-312.

Frick, M.R.; Elovainio, R.O.; and Somer, T. 1967. The mechanism of bradycardia evolved by physical training. *Cardiologia* 51:46-54.

Fujitsuka, N.; Yamamoto, T.; Ohkuwa, T.; Saito, M.; and Miyamura, M. 1982. Peak blood lactate after short periods of maximum treadmill running. *European Journal of Applied Physiology* 48:289-296.

Gibson, T.M.; Harrison, M.H.; and Wellcome, R.M. 1979. An evaluation of a treadmill work test. *British Journal of Sports Medicine* 13:6-11.

Gollnick, P.D.; Bayly, W.M.; and Hodgson, D.R. 1986. Exercise intensity, training, diet, and lactate concentration in muscle and blood. *Medicine and Science in Sports and Exercise* 18:334-340.

Green, R.; Charlton, R.W.; Seftel, H.; Bothwell, T.; Mayet, F.; Adams, B.; Finch, C.; and Layrisse, M. 1968. Body iron excretion in man. A collaborative study. *American Journal of Medicine* 45:336-353.

Hagberg, J.M.; Giese, M.D.; and Schneider, R.B. 1978. Comparison of the three procedures for measuring $\dot{V}O_2$max in competitive cyclists. *European Journal of Applied Physiology* 39:47-52.

Harrison, T.R., and Pilcher, C. 1930. Studies in congestive heart failure. II. The respiratory exchange during and after exercise. *Journal of Clinical Investigation* 8:291.

Haymes, E.M., and Lamanca, J.J. 1989. Iron loss in runners during exercise: Implications and recommendations. *Sports Medicine* 7:277-285.

Heck, H.; Mader, A.; Hess, G.; Mücke, S.; Müller, R.; and Hollmann, W. 1985. Justification of the 4-mmol/L lactate threshold. *International Journal of Sports Medicine* 6:117-130.

Henderson, Y., and Prince, A.L. 1914. The amount of O_2 consumed by the body from the blood of one systolic discharge of the heart. *American Journal of Physiology* 35:106-115.

Henderson, Y.; Haggard, H.W.; and Dolley, F.S. 1927. The efficiency of the heart and the significance of rapid and slow pulse rates. *American Journal of Physiology* 82:512-524.

Herbert, V. 1987. Recommended dietary intakes (RDI) of iron in humans. *American Journal of Clinical Nutrition* 45:679-686.

Hermansen, L., and Osnes, J.B. 1972. Blood and muscle pH after maximal exercise in man. *Journal of Applied Physiology* 32:304-308.

Hermansen, L., and Saltin, B. 1969. Oxygen uptake during maximal treadmill and bicycle exercise. *Journal of Applied Physiology* 26:31-37.

Hill, A.V., and Lupton, H. 1923. Muscular exercise, lactic acid, and the supply and utilization of oxygen. *Quarterly Medical Journal* 16:135-171.

Hoffbrand, A.V.; Ganeshaguru, K.; Hooton, J.W.L.; and Tattersall, M.H.N. 1976. Effects of iron deficiency and desferrioxamine on DNA synthesis in human cells. *British Journal of Haematology* 33:517-520.

Holloszy, J.O., and Coyle, E.F. 1984. Adaptations of skeletal muscle to endurance exercise and their metabolic consequences. *Journal of Applied Physiology* 56:831-838.

Huston, T.P.; Puffer, J.C.; and Rodney, W.M. 1985. The athletic heart syndrome. *New England Journal of Medicine* 313:24-32.

Issekutz, B., Jr.; Birkhead, N.C.; and Rodahl, K. 1962. Use of respiratory quotients in assessment of aerobic work capacity. *Journal of Applied Physiology* 17:47-50.

Ivy, J.L.; Costill, D.L.; Van Handel, P.J.; Essig, D.A.; and Lower, R.W. 1981. Alterations in the lactate threshold with changes in substrate availability. *International Journal of Sports Medicine* 2:139-142.

Ivy, J.L.; Withers, R.T.; Van Handel, P.J.; Elger, D.H.; and Costill, D.L. 1980. Muscle respiratory capacity and fiber type as determinants of the lactate threshold. *Journal of Applied Physiology* 48:523-527.

Jacobs, I.; Sjödin, B.; Kaiser, P.; and Karlsson, J. 1981. Onset of blood lactate accumulation after prolonged exercise. *Acta Physiologica Scandinavica* 112:215-217.

Jones, N.L. 1988. *Clinical exercise testing*. Philadelphia: Saunders.

Kamon, E., and Pandolf, K.B. 1972. Maximal aerobic power during laddermill climbing, uphill running, and cycling. *Journal of Applied Physiology* 2:467-473.

Kearney, J.T., and Van Handel, P.J. 1989. Economy: A physiologic perspective. *Advances in Sports Medicine and Fitness* 2:57-89.

Kindermann, W.; Simon, G.; and Keul, J. 1979. The significance of the aerobic-anaerobic transition for the determination of work load intensities during endurance training. *European Journal of Applied Physiology* 42:25-34.

Klissouras, V. 1972. Genetic limit of functional adaptability. *Internationale Zeitschrift für angewandte Physiologie* 30:85-94.

Letsky, E.A.; Miller, F.; Worwood, M.; and Flynn, D.M. 1974. Serum ferritin in children with thalassaemia regularly transfused. *Journal of Clinical Pathology* 27:652-655.

Liljestrand, G., and Stenstrom, N. 1920. Respirationsversuche beim gehen, laufen, ski- und schlittschuhlaufen (Gas exchange experimentation with walking, running, skiing, and skating). *Skandinavisches Archiv für Physiologie* 39:167-206.

Lindhard, J. 1915. Über das minutenvolum des herzens bei ruhe und bei muskelarbeit (Concerning the cardiac output at rest and with exercise). *Pflüger's Archiv für die gesamte Physiologie* 161:233-283.

MacDougall, J.D.; Reddan, W.G.; Layton, C.R.; and Dempsey, J.A. 1974. Effects of metabolic hyperthermia on performance during heavy prolonged exercise. *Journal of Applied Physiology* 36:538-544.

Mader, A.; Liesen, H.; Heck, H.; Philippi, H.; Rost, R.; Schuerch, P.; and Hollmann, W. 1976. Zur Beurteilung der sportartspecifischen Ausdauer-leistungsfähigkeit im Labor (Estimation of sport event–specific endurance work capacity during exercise). *Sportarzt und Sportmedizin* 4:80-88.

Magnusson, B.; Hallberg, L.; Rossander, L.; and Swolin, B. 1984. Iron metabolism and "sports anemia." *Acta Medica Scandinavica* 216:149-164.

Makrides, L.; Heigenhauser, G.J.F.; McCartney, N.; and Jones, N.L. 1986. Physical training in young and older healthy subjects. In *Sports medicine for the mature athlete*, eds. J.R. Sutton and R.M. Brock, 363-372. Indianapolis: Benchmark Press.

Margaria, R.; Cerretelli, P.; Aghemo, P.; and Sassi, J. 1963. Energy cost of running. *Journal of Applied Physiology* 8:367-370.

Margaria, R.; Cerretelli, P.; and Mangili, F. 1964. Balance and kinetics of anaerobic energy release during strenuous exercise in man. *Journal of Applied Physiology* 19:623-628.

Martin, D.E. 1994. The challenge of using altitude to improve performance. *New Studies in Athletics* 9(2):51-57.

Martin, D.E., and May, D.F. 1987. Pulmonary function in elite women distance runners. *International Journal of Sports Medicine* 8:S84-S90.

Martin, D.E.; May, D.F.; and Pilbeam, S.P. 1986. Ventilation limitations to performance among elite male distance runners. In *The 1984 Olympic Scientific Congress proceedings*. Vol. 3, *Sport and elite performers,* ed. D.M. Landers, 121-131. Champaign, IL: Human Kinetics.

Martin, D.E.; Vroon, D.H.; May, D.F.; and Pilbeam, S.P. 1986. Physiological changes in elite male distance runners training for Olympic competition. *Physician and Sportsmedicine* 14(1):152-171.

Martin, D.E.; Vroon, D.H.; and Sheard, M.M. 1989. Effects of hemoconcentration during maximum-effort treadmill tests on blood lactate levels in trained distance runners. In *First IOC World Congress on Sport Sciences proceedings*, 37-38. Colorado Springs: United States Olympic Committee.

Martin, D.E., and Youtsey, J.W. 1988. *Respiratory anatomy and physiology.* St. Louis: Mosby.

McArdle, W.D.; Magel, J.R.; Delio, D.J.; Toner, M.; and Chase, J.M. 1978. Specificity of run training on $\dot{V}O_2$max and heart rate changes during running and swimming. *Medicine and Science in Sports* 10:16-20.

McConnell, T.R. 1988. Practical considerations in the testing of $\dot{V}O_2$max in runners. *Sports Medicine* 5:57-68.

McMiken, D.F., and Daniels, J.T. 1976. Aerobic requirements and maximum aerobic power in treadmill and track running. *Medicine and Science in Sports* 8:14-17.

Medbø, J.I.; Mohn, A.C.; Tabala, I.; Bahr, R.; Vaage, O.; and Sejersted, O.M. 1988. Anaerobic capacity determined by maximal accumulated O_2 deficit. *Journal of Applied Physiology* 64:50-60.

Miller, B.J.; Pate, R.R.; and Burgess, W. 1988. Foot impact force and intravascular hemolysis during distance running. *International Journal of Sports Medicine* 9:56-60.

Mitchell, J.H., and Blomqvist, C.G. 1971. Maximal oxygen uptake. *New England Journal of Medicine* 284:1018-1022.

Mitchell, J.H.; Sproule, B.J.; and Chapman, C.B. 1958. The physiological meaning of the maximal oxygen uptake test. *Journal of Clinical Investigation* 37:538-547.

Morganroth, J.; Maron, B.J.; Henry, W.L.; and Epstein, S.E. 1975. Comparative left ventricular dimensions in trained athletes. *Annals of Internal Medicine* 82:521-524.

Nadel, E.R. 1988. Temperature regulation and prolonged exercise. *Perspectives in Exercise Science and Sports Medicine* 1:125-151.

Nagle, F.J. 1973. Physiological assessment of maximal performance. *Exercise and Sports Science Reviews* 1:313-338.

Newhouse, I.J., and Clement, D.B. 1988. Iron status in athletes. *Sports Medicine* 5:337-352.

Ohkuwa, T.; Kato, Y.; Katsumata, K.; Nakao, T.; and Miyanura, M. 1984. Blood lactate and glycerol after 400 m and 3,000 m runs in sprinters and long distance runners. *European Journal of Applied Physiology* 53:213-218.

Owles, W.H. 1930. Alterations in the lactic acid content of the blood as a result of light exercise, and associated changes in the CO_2-combining power of the blood and in the alveolar CO_2 pressure. *Journal of Physiology* 69:214-237.

Pannier, J.L.; Vrijens, J.; and Van Cauter, C. 1980. Cardiorespiratory response to treadmill and bicycle exercise in runners. *European Journal of Applied Physiology* 43:243-251.

Pardy, R.L.; Hussain, S.N.; and Macklem, P.T. 1984. The ventilatory pump in exercise. *Clinics in Chest Medicine* 5:35-49.

Pate, R.R. 1983. Sports anemia: A review of the current research literature. *Physician and Sportsmedicine* 11(2):115-131.

Pate, R.R.; Sparling, P.B.; Wilson, G.E.; Cureton, K.J.; and Miller, B.J. 1987. Cardiorespiratory and metabolic responses to submaximal and maximal exercise in elite women distance runners. *International Journal of Sports Medicine* 8(suppl. 2):91-95.

Pattengale, P.K., and Holloszy, J.O. 1967. Augmentation of skeletal muscle myoglobin by a program of treadmill running. *American Journal of Physiology* 213:783-785.

Paulev, P.E.; Jordal, R.; and Pedersen, N.S. 1983. Dermal excretion of iron in intensely training athletes. *Clinica Chimica Acta* 127:19-27.

Peota, C. 1989. Studies counter myths about iron in athletes. *Physician and Sportsmedicine* 17(11):26-27.

Pollock, M.L. 1977. Submaximal and maximal working capacity of elite distance runners. Part I: Cardiorespiratory aspects. *Annals of the New York Academy of Sciences* 301:310-321.

Pugh, L.G.C.E. 1970. Oxygen intake in track and treadmill running with observations on the effect of air resistance. *Journal of Physiology* (London) 207:823-835.

Purvis, J.W., and Cureton, K.J. 1981. Ratings of perceived exertion at the anaerobic threshold. *Ergonomics* 24:295-300.

Reilly, T.; Robinson, G.; and Minors, D.S. 1984. Some circulatory responses to exercise at different times of day. *Medicine and Science in Sports and Exercise* 16:477-482.

Rerych, S.K.; Scholz, P.M.; Sabiston, D.C.; and Jones, R.H. 1980. Effects of exercise training on left ventricular function in normal subjects: A longitudinal study by radionuclide angiography. *American Journal of Cardiology* 45:244-252.

Roe, C.F.; Goldberg, M.J.; Blaw, C.S.; and Kinney, J.M. 1966. The influence of body temperature on early postoperative oxygen consumption. *Surgery* 60:85-92.

Rowell, L.B.; Taylor, H.L.; and Wang, Y. 1964. Limitations to the prediction of maximum oxygen uptake. *Journal of Applied Physiology* 19:919-927.

Saltin, B., and Åstrand, P.-O. 1967. Maximal oxygen uptake in athletes. *Journal of Applied Physiology* 23:353-358.

Saltin, B., and Gollnick, P.D. 1983. Skeletal muscle adaptability: Significance for metabolism and performance. In *Handbook of physiology.* Sect. 10. *Skeletal muscle,* eds. L.D. Peachy, R.H. Adrian, and S.R. Geiger, 555-631. Washington, DC: American Physiological Society.

Scrimgeour, A.G.; Noakes, T.D.; Adams, B.; and Myburgh, K. 1986. The influence of weekly training distance on fractional utilization of maximum aerobic capacity in marathon and ultramarathon runners. *European Journal of Applied Physiology* 55:202-209.

Shephard, R.J. 1984. Test of maximum oxygen uptake: A critical review. *Sports Medicine* 1:99-124.

Shephard, R.J.; Allen, C.; Benade, A.J.S.; Davies, C.T.M.; di Prampero, P.E.; Hedman, R.; Merriman, J.E.; Myhre, K.; and Simmons, R. 1968. The maximal oxygen uptake. *Bulletin of the World Health Organization* 38:757-764.

Sjödin, B., and Jacobs, I. 1981. Onset of blood lactate accumulation and marathon running performance. *International Journal of Sports Medicine* 2:23-26.

Sjödin, B., and Svedenhag, J. 1985. Applied physiology of marathon running. *Sports Medicine* 2:83-99.

Skinner, J.S., and McLellan, T.M. 1980. The transition from aerobic to anaerobic metabolism. *Research Quarterly for Exercise and Sport* 51:234-248.

Snyder, A.C.; Dvorak, L.L.; and Roepke, J.B. 1989. Influence of dietary iron source on measures of iron status among female runners. *Medicine and Science in Sports and Exercise* 21:7-10.

Staub, N.C.; Nagano, H.; and Pearce, M.L. 1967. Pulmonary edema in dogs, especially the sequence of fluid accumulation in lungs. *Journal of Applied Physiology* 22:227-240.

Stegmann, H.; Kindermann, W.; and Schnabel, A. 1981. Lactate kinetics and individual anaerobic threshold. *International Journal of Sports Medicine* 2:160-165.

Stewart, G.A.; Steel, J.E.; Tayne, M.B.; and Stewart, M.H. 1972. Observations on the hematology and the iron and protein intake of Australian Olympic athletes. *Medical Journal of Australia* 2:1339-1342.

Stewart, J.G.; Ahlquist, D.A.; McGill, D.B.; Ilstrup, D.M.; Schwartz, S.; and Owen, R.A. 1984. Gastrointestinal blood loss and anemia in runners. *Annals of Internal Medicine* 100:843-845.

Taylor, H.L.; Wang, Y.; Rowell, L.; and Blomqvist, G. 1963. The standardization and interpretation of submaximal and maximal tests of working capacity. *Pediatrics* 32:703-715.

Vellar, O.D. 1968. Studies on sweat losses of nutrients. *Scandinavian Journal of Clinical and Laboratory Investigation* 21:157-167.

Wahren, J.; Hagenfeld, L.; and Felig, P. 1975. Glucose and free fatty acid utilization in exercise: Studies in normal and diabetic man. *Israeli Journal of Medical Science* 11:551-559.

Walsh, M.L., and Banister, E.W. 1988. Possible mechanisms of the anaerobic threshold. *Sports Medicine* 5:269-301.

Wasserman, K. 1984. Coupling of external to internal respiration. *American Review of Respiratory Diseases* 129:S21-S24.

Wasserman, K., and McIlroy, M.B. 1964. Detecting the threshold of anaerobic metabolism in cardiac patients during exercise. *American Journal of Cardiology* 14:844-852.

Welch, H.G. 1973. Substrate utilization in muscle—adaptations to physical effort. In *Exercise testing and exercise training in coronary heart disease,* eds. J.P. Naughton and H.K. Hellerstein, 193-197. New York: Academic Press.

Wintrobe, M.W.; Lee, G.R.; Boggs, D.R.; Bithell, T.C.; Foerster, J.; Athens, J.W.; and Lukens, J.N. 1981. Iron deficiency and iron-deficiency anemia. In *Clinical hematology,* 8th ed., 617-645. Philadelphia: Lea and Febiger.

Yoshimura, H.; Inoue, T.; Yamada, T.; and Shiraki, K. 1980. Anemia during hard physical training (sports anemia) and its causal mechanism, with special reference to protein nutrition. *World Review of Nutrition and Dietetics* 35:1-86.

Yudkin, J., and Cohen, R.D. 1975. The contribution of the kidney to the removal of a lactic acid load under normal and acidotic conditions in the conscious rat. *Clinical Science and Molecular Biology* 48:21-131.

DEVELOPING RUNNING WITH PERIODIZATION OF TRAINING

I keep six honest serving men,
They taught me all I knew;
Their names are What and Why and When
And How and Where and Who.

This old rhyme of Rudyard Kipling echoes down through the years and is the foundation on which any logical system of achievement is based. In athletic development, just as in the design and building of a piece of precision equipment, these "six serving men" allow completion of the job with relative ease and certainty. They represent the six most searching questions that must be answered in the construction of an effective training plan:

- What should be done?
- Why is it being done?
- When should it be done?
- How is it done best?
- Where should it be done?
- Who should do it?

The answers to these questions may not be perfectly obvious at first glance as athlete and coach try to design a specific training plan. *What* defines the details of each session—for example, running a certain number of times up a hill that is of a certain distance and grade, with a specific recovery time in between each effort. It also defines the overall goals of the entire training plan. *Why* identifies the reason for the specific physiological training zone, or muscle groups, being challenged in a training session. *When* addresses the time of day or the point during a particular training cycle when development of the system being challenged is most sensible or safest. *Where* demands a decision as to the best site to get the job done—a track versus a grassy hill, or a gymnasium versus a weight room. It also can refer to scheduling training camp situations in specific locations to take advantage of weather, altitude, or special facilities. *How* demands a decision as to the best method for developing the system in question—level or uphill sprinting versus free-weight exercises (or both) for building strength (or power, or endurance) in the leg extensor muscles, for example. *Who* refers to event specialty or level of development—is the athlete an 800-m runner or a marathon runner, a runner at the beginning or near the end of a development year or a career?

By continually seeking answers to these questions, the training plan will become ever more reasoned and finely tuned. And so will the quality of the finished product, namely, an athlete honed into a very fit and able competitor. Always ask these questions—they will "concentrate the mind wonderfully" (in the words of the venerable lexicographer Samuel Johnson), and ensure that no stone has been left unturned in a quest to produce an athlete who is both injury free and in the best condition at the appropriate moment.

Goal Setting

Athletes who strive to compete at the highest levels must realize that it takes time to build the excellence required. This in turn requires effective joint planning by the coach and athlete that is directed at steady improvement. Good planning mandates achievable intermediate goals along the way to a larger, ultimate goal, such as a personal best, a championship victory, or an Olympic medal. Goal setting is crucial at the outset because it demands an answer to a very important question asked of each athlete: "What do you want from running?" Once this answer is identified, it becomes the ultimate goal; working backward from that goal to the present is then much easier.

The Importance of Long-Term Planning

Anyone desiring instant gratification—and probably we all do to some extent—will by now have sensed that the goals we are identifying are not achieved quickly. We are discussing goals for a training year, for an Olympiad, or for a career. A cycle of training, recovery, focusing, and competing is not a cycle of activity that repeats frequently. When we discuss training concepts themselves, we shall see that short-term goals—those extending only a few weeks into the future—will also be an important part of the plan. Short-term goals delineate desired outcomes of day-to-day training and are thus the building blocks of the overall plan to reach long-term goals. For most athletes it is difficult to put an entire year's training into a functional perspective unless these day-to-day building blocks are laid out to show the path toward progress. An old adage has great meaning here: "The hunting dog must see the rabbit for an effective chase." The long-term goals allow short-term goals to be outlined more easily.

Not only must goals be seen on the horizon, but there also must be some success along the way. Staying enthusiastic for 6 to 10 months of a developmental season or 6 to 10 years in a career is not easy when so many sacrifices are required in the life of a dedicated athlete. Fortunately, in most countries many variably competitive opportunities, if scheduled optimally, can serve as stepping stones toward a major championship.

In the United States, for example, each state typically has county and regional championships in the high school–age divisions prior to the state championship. In colleges and universities the same concept exists: dual or triangular meets (with neighboring schools), conference meets, and finally the national collegiate division championships. For athletes not attending educational institutions, track meets as well as road race opportunities exist throughout the nation, conducted most often under the aegis of the national governing body for athletics, USA Track and Field (USATF), or of the Road Runner's Club of America (RRCA). Because no clear hierarchy exists for these postcollegiate activities, athletes and coaches must decide for themselves which event has the greatest significance—another example of goal setting. The USATF outdoor championship, for example, is often the selection meet for major international traveling teams, making it an important goal for track-oriented distance runners.

In Britain, Oceania, and most European countries the athletic scene is rooted firmly in the club system, with relatively little school competition. Thus, in contrast to the United States, where high schools and colleges schedule frequent and important competitions far in advance as part of the academic program, in Britain the number of scheduled competitions that demand good performance is far smaller. These few competitions can be given greater focus and scheduled comfortably as intermediate goals between blocks of time that allow for adequate training on the way to major competitive efforts.

Table 5.1 summarizes Seb Coe's major event titles as a good example of how longevity in an athlete's career can result from careful attention to prevention of overtraining and overracing. The table represents a span of 19 years as he progressed from a junior to a senior athlete. To add more insight to Seb's record progression, figure 5.1 depicts the administrative areas of England's Amateur Athletic Association (AAA). Throughout his career, but especially in the early days, Seb placed strong emphasis on a training plan to ensure his readiness for the various administrative championships. The reason for this was simple: These were the logical stepping stones for progression into steadily more and more challenging competitions. Thus, early on, each year Seb competed initially in the city (Sheffield) school championships, then progressed through the county (Yorkshire) championships and into the national championships. Good performances along the way as a junior athlete could (and did) lead to Seb's selection for the European Junior Championships and then eventually into higher-level European track and field meetings. Not always could perfect preparation be guaranteed, even with these relatively few periodic meetings; the exigencies of life didn't permit it. But long-term and short-term goals set on paper well in advance allowed construction of a development plan to synchronize the timing of excellent fitness with the time of the competition.

Goals to Optimize Racing Effectiveness

The essential specialization required for success at the top level mandates that runners not spread their energies too thin. Otherwise, they may be decent competitors all year long but never achieve real excellence at any specific point. Long-term goal setting permits an athlete to assign relative importance to the various aspects of a training year. This in turn provides the variation in focus that can yield winning results at some periods and good performances during other periods.

TABLE 5.1

Sebastian Coe's Major Championship Performances

Age	Meeting	Rank	Event	Class
14	Yorkshire County Championship	1	1,500 m	Boy
16	Northern Counties Championship	1	1,500 m	Youth
	UK Championship	1	1,500 m	Youth
	English Schools Championship	1	3,000 m	Youth
18	UK Championship	1	1,500 m	Junior
	European Outdoor Championship	3	1,500 m	Junior
20	UK Indoor Championship	1	800 m (CBP)	Senior
	European Indoor Championship	1	800 m (UKR, CWR)	Senior
21	Memorial Ivo Van Damme	1	800 m (UKR)	Senior
	European Outdoor Championship	3	800 m	Senior
	Coca-Cola	1	800 m (UKR)	Senior
22	UK Indoor Championship	1	3,000 m	Senior
	UK Outdoor Championship	2	400 m	Senior
	Europa Cup	1	800 m	Senior
	Bislett Games	1	800 m (WOR)	Senior
	Weltklasse	1	1,500 m (WOR)	Senior
	IAAF Golden Mile	1	1 mile (WOR)	Senior
23	Bislett Games	1	1,000 m (WOR)	Senior
	Olympic Games	2	800 m	Senior
	Olympic Games	1	1,500 m	Senior
24	UK vs. GDR Indoor	1	800 m (WIR)	Senior
	Florence International	1	800 m (WOR)	Senior
	Oslo Games	1	1,000 m (WOR)	Senior
	Weltklasse	1	1 mile (WOR)	Senior
	IAAF Golden Mile	1	1 mile (WOR)	Senior
	World Cup	1	800 m	Senior
25	European Outdoor Championship	2	800 m	Senior
	European Outdoor Championship	Fastest leg	4 × 800-m relay (WOR)	Senior
26	UK vs. USA Indoor	1	800 m (WIR)	Senior
	Oslo Indoor	1	1,000 m (WIR)	Senior
27	Olympic Games	2	800 m	Senior
	Olympic Games	1	1,500 m (OR)	Senior
28	European Outdoor Championship	1	800 m	Senior
	European Outdoor Championship	2	1,500 m	Senior
	Rieti	1	1,500 m (PR)	Senior
32	AAA UK Championships	1	1,500 m	Senior
	World Cup	2	1,500 m	Senior

CBP, championship best performance; UKR, United Kingdom record; WIR, world indoor record; PR, personal record; CWR, commonwealth record; OR, Olympic Games record; WOR, world outdoor record.

As an example, running cross-country or road races during the fall and winter may be perfectly acceptable for a track racer who desires the summertime months as an ultimate peak. However, unless the athlete is unusually gifted, winning performances in these cross-country and road racing events may come very seldom. If they do come often, either the competition is not very stiff, or the athlete will have focused so completely on these events that burnout occurs before the summer season arrives. Typically, top-level road races and cross-country races are highly contested by many talented athletes for whom this season is, in fact, their focal point.

We believe that it is unwise for athletes to be urged to "train through" a higher-level competition—that is, schedule a competition without making a serious

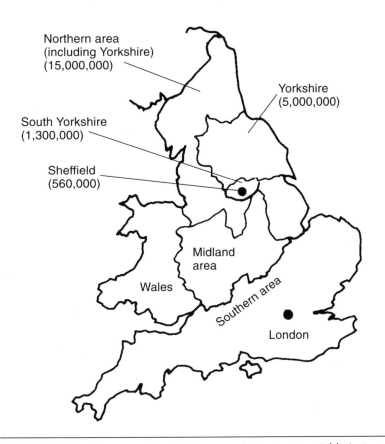

Figure 5.1 Division of England's administrative areas in its Amateur Athletic Association. Within the United Kingdom, the normal progression for an athlete is from city (schools) to county (analogous to a state in the U.S.) to area (analogous to a region in the U.S.) and finally to the national championships. Such progress will always elevate the level of competition since the catchment population for athlete selection increases. With Sebastian Coe, starting upward from Sheffield (population 560,000), moving through the South Yorkshire (1,300,000), Yorkshire (5,000,000), and eventually the Northern Counties championships (15,000,000), this was a 30-fold increase in population base for athlete selection. Moving toward the national championships represented another threefold increase beyond that (the population of England is 46,500,000).

attempt to perform well. The need to simply score points for the team or to be seen in a sponsoring firm's new line of sportswear without being prepared to do one's best is a very difficult pill to swallow for an athlete who desires excellence. The really good athletes are neither accustomed to nor interested in making excuses about not performing as well as might have been expected. Racing and training are very different entities and demand different mental attitudes. It is unwise to develop a habit of coming to the starting line of a race with only a haphazard interest in attempting to run well; this attitude may occur again when least desired! It might be better to arrange a time trial on a track or over a known road course, either alone or with some friends to help push the pace. This provides the opportunity for a more challenging effort, yet not quite as serious as a real race. It is also quite easily changeable if the athlete doesn't feel up to par at the last moment or if the weather changes drastically for the worse.

An important point here relates to using excessive racing in the school setting as intermediate goals. The coach-athlete relationship ought to exist with the aim of long-term benefit to the athlete (i.e., post–high school, postcollegiate) rather than solely immediate benefit (gratification of school or college via the coach's win-loss record). Demanding pressures placed on young athletes to perform at their maximum too often can be more debilitating to the spirit than beneficial to improvement. And they can produce injury.

Long-term goals permit a focus on the overall design of a year-long season; each phase of the program can benefit the other phases sensibly. The United States' Craig Virgin is a good example of a track-oriented athlete who for many years was also excellent at cross-country competition internationally. His yearly philosophy was to use the fall and winter to build strength and endurance, with the world Cross-Country Championships during March providing his ultimate test of progress. As a result, he earned berths on 10 USA World Cross-Country teams in 11 years, winning the world title on two occasions. Following cross-country, Craig either continued in a racing mode for a few more weeks followed by a break or took his break immediately. Building on this well-developed base of endurance fitness, he then began the kind of faster endurance and speed training needed for the fluidity and finesse required of a potential track champion at his June national championships. Again, either he followed those championships with a brief racing period on the early summer European circuit and then took a break, or he immediately took a break in preparation for a later summer peak during August or September. By identifying the goals for each of these racing seasons well in advance, Craig arranged the details of training, racing, and recovery in their proper context for meaningful development.

Nowadays, extreme pressures are placed on top-level athletes to disrupt their development and overall goals by traveling to far-flung destinations and racing for huge sums of money to satisfy the whims of meet directors trying to establish or maintain the integrity of their particular competitive events. Similar financial pressures (so great that athletes can become rich almost beyond their imaginations) are exerted by meet directors to entice athletes to change events—the 10,000-m runner being driven by dollars to debut in the marathon is one of the saddest examples.

One could well argue whether such infusion of money into the sport is for the athlete's (or the sport's) ultimate good when the athlete is relegated to the role of a short-lived tool in corporate machinations. Still, when faced with these challenges, the athlete and coach with well-defined goals are far better off in terms of at least considering workable ways to accommodate some of these opportunities than those whose planning is limited to day-by-day guesswork with little organized basis for logical forward progress.

How to Set Appropriate Goals

Let us consider two examples in this game of goal setting, one conceptual and the other real, to learn more about how it can be effective in organizing an athlete's career. The thought of running 5,000 m in 13 min may sound a bit too audacious even to consider for any aspiring male distance runner just turning 20 years old. Similarly, for a talented, enthusiastic young female runner, breaking 14:50 for 5,000 m may seem an impossible task. But if these talented athletes have indeed demonstrated some potential by delivering some quality performances at a young age, that talent should be nurtured, methodically and sensibly. Why not aim for the best, if that's really a desired goal? Are these athletes dreaming? Yes, of course. But if they do not dream, then there is no hope of that dream ever becoming reality. Such is the essence of breaking records. So how does one logically identify goals to help these athletes achieve their dreams?

The answer is to attempt to design a long-range plan with achievable goals. The focus of such a career plan is to identify the competitive event for which excellence can most likely be achieved and the age at which athletes typically will be at their best for that distance. With this knowledge, annual best-time performance goals can be calculated. Let us take an example of a 20-year-old male athlete specializing in the 5,000-m event, who wants to achieve his career-best performances at around 27 years of age. We can then outline yearly goals for our 20-year-old athlete, as illustrated in table 5.2. We'll assume his birthday is January 1 and that he presently has a personal best 5,000-m time of 14 min. Essentially, he needs to lower his time by 1 min in seven years, starting with the day he reaches 21 and ending with his 28th birthday. His peak performances will be during the northern hemisphere summer track circuit. Assuming that improvements in his performance will become more difficult as he reaches his peak, a weighted per-year time reduction is more realistic than an unweighted 10 s per year. The weighting is determined as follows: With each passing year a diminishing age difference will occur as the athlete approaches the target year $(27 - 20 = 7; 27 - 21 = 6$, etc., the last being $27 - 26 = 1)$. The sum of all these differences (28) is then divided into the total time to be removed from the initial performance best (here, 60 s): $60/28 = 2.14$. Multiplying this value by each yearly age difference gives the weighted reduction in number of seconds as a goal for that year. Thus, for the 21st year, $2.14 \times 7 = 15$ s as the goal for improvement over 14 min, or 13:45 as the performance goal.

Table 5.2 illustrates the expected annual progression of his yearly best times, if progress goes according to plan. We can see that 13 min may now seem a little more achievable. Each year the desired improvement is sensible—for example, a 15-s improvement over the space of the first year is not really so huge, and neither athlete nor coach need even consider performances such as 13:12 for four years! A crucial requirement over this seven-year development scheme, however, will be protecting the athlete from overuse injuries, thus creating an optimal environment for steady improvement.

Is it appropriate for a young distance runner to dream of achieving his career-best performances at about 27 years of age? We thought so when we wrote the first edition of this book, and came to this conclusion by determining the mean age of the top ten athletes, as of the end of 1989, for the commonly contested track distances. Except for the 800 m, whose athletes averaged 24.3 years (for men) and 25.6 years (for women), all of the other event means ranged from 26.1 to 29.2 years, and the overall mean was 27.2 years. Since then, mean age of the

TABLE 5.2

Setting Goals Toward a Predicted Improvement
From 14:00 to 13:00 for 5,000 m

Present personal best	14:00	Present age	20
Desired personal best	13:00	Target age	27

Age difference	Improvement (s)	Annual target
$27 - 20 = 7$	$7/28 \times 60 = 15$	14:00
$27 - 21 = 6$	$6/28 \times 60 = 13$	13:45
$27 - 22 = 5$	$5/28 \times 60 = 11$	13:32
$27 - 23 = 4$	$4/28 \times 60 = 9$	13:21
$27 - 24 = 3$	$3/28 \times 60 = 6$	13:12
$27 - 25 = 2$	$2/28 \times 60 = 4$	13:06
$27 - 26 = 1$	$1/28 \times 60 = 2$	13:02
Goal = 27	60	13:00

fastest ten competitors in the 800 m and in the men's marathon have not changed, but a consistent trend toward younger athletes at the top level has lowered the mean age of the top ten athletes in the other events. Table 5.3 summarizes these new data as of the end of the summer of 1996, 6 1/2 years later. The explanation is not immediately apparent, but one factor may involve a greatly increased possibility for younger athletes to compete at the highest levels, thanks to the IAAF's outdoor World Junior Championships.

Returning to our athlete's plan to peak by age 27, what should be done if, during the second year of his plan, a breakthrough allows him to reach the third year's target? Our opinion is quite clear. Additional progress should not necessarily be sought that year, or even the next. The athlete is on schedule. However, if several races during the year are each consistently ahead of the planned program, this is grounds for careful reconsideration. As we shall detail in the specifics of training, goals are best achieved by doing the least amount of work necessary, not the most, because the goal is freedom from injury as well as continued improvement over the next several years. The greedier athletes become, the sooner they are spent.

Now let us consider a real example of long-term goal setting. Seb Coe started running at age 12. By the time Seb was 13, his coach had constructed a plan shaped around relevant age-related minor championships initially but culminating with the 1980 Olympic Games. The plan was specific enough to set achievable goals, yet flexible enough to accommodate all the nuances of academic life from early schooling through postgraduate university work. By shifting emphases to fit examination periods, minor illnesses, and the like, the plan was kept intact.

The concept of the plan was relatively simple. In 1972 Seb's coach estimated on paper what he believed the world records in the 800 m, 1,500 m, and mile would be when Seb was ready to attack them, roughly by 1980 or 1981. The prediction was 1:43 for the 800 m; Seb's first 800-m world record (in 1979) was 1:42.33 at age 22. The prediction was 3:48 for the mile: Seb's first mile world record (also in 1979) was 3:48.95. Thus, the accuracy of estimation was good, but an element of surprise came in their arrival a year or so ahead of schedule. The forecasted 1,500-m time, however, was delayed by seven years—the estimate of 3:30 was achieved (3:29.77) only in 1986. Thus, no system is perfect, but this one was close. What made Seb's coach think that this was an athlete with world-record potential and thus an athlete who could likely achieve this level of performance? No evidence, really, beyond the facts that Seb enjoyed running, running seemed to come easily to him, and at his early age he was running nearly

---

TABLE 5.3

Average Age of Career-Best Outdoor Performance for the Fastest 10 Athletes in Common Distance Running Events

Event	Men	Women
800 m	24.2 ± 1.8	25.1 ± 3.4
1,500 m	26.3 ± 2.6	26.2 ± 3.8
3,000 m	24.9 ± 2.8	24.7 ± 4.5
5,000 m	25.0 ± 2.5	24.9 ± 4.5
10,000 m	24.5 ± 3.6	25.0 ± 3.4
Marathon	29.3 ± 4.9	26.8 ± 3.9

Note. Performance marks as of 01 September 1996; all values in years ± 1 standard deviation.

as well as anyone had at that age previously. A crucial issue here is that Seb and his coach dared to plan ahead: They dared to identify a logical approach from which they could sensibly deviate if appropriate later on. It turned out that they didn't have to change their plan.

Principles of Periodization

In athletic circles worldwide, one word is mentioned more frequently than any other when athletes and coaches discuss goals and plans: *periodization*. This impressive-sounding term refers simply to the specific time scale and format for all the various parts of a training plan. Such a format takes into consideration the four primary aspects of adaptation to training:

- Initial tissue catabolism that occurs from the load applied (running, weight lifting, etc.) and causes an initial reduction in performance capabilities
- Adaptation to the stress of training as a result of tissue recovery and improved mental outlook from having successfully completed the work
- Retention and likely improvement in such performance characteristics following a tapering of training
- Reduction in performance if training volume is decreased for too long a period

Thus, the training life of an athlete is a constant cycle of hard work (with fatigue), recovery (with regeneration), improvement in performance (for a brief period), and brief layoff (for mental and physical rest) to permit another cycle to repeat.

Preparing a training outline involves the delineation of several kinds of information. First, all the units required to achieve the various goals must be identified. By *units* we mean *general training assignments*. Some examples include longer-distance runs at moderate speed, upper-body strength training, and shorter-distance, faster runs. Second, training schedules need to identify the sessions appropriate to each unit. A *session* is a specific training assignment that identifies the volume, intensity, and density of effort that should provide a beneficial training effect. (These three parameters will also be defined shortly.) One session might include 6×800-m runs at 80% maximal effort up a 4% hill with a 2-min rest between runs. Another might include $8 \times 1,500$-m runs at 90% of $\dot{V}O_2$max pace, with a 3-min recovery between runs. Still another might include 3×15 split squats with a 20-kg weight on the shoulders. Finally, specific intermediate test situations (small races, time trials, a treadmill stress test, etc.) need to be scheduled as training proceeds to evaluate progress in achieving the ultimate goal of being ready for the major competitive period at the proper time.

In short, the value of periodization is that it permits a documented, methodical, incremental, and logical growth and development outline for the individual athlete and coach. Both must consider carefully what will be done. Their ideas are thrust into the spotlight of reason. *The objective of training is to bring an athlete to a peak fitness level at the proper time,* with all the requirements for good performance brought along in balance. Periodization permits this balanced progression by ensuring that the appropriate mix is put together into a unified plan. Much has been written about periodization because it is essential for organizing athletic development (Bompa 1988, 1993; Charniga et al. 1986-87; Dick 1975; Freeman 1989).

Now that we've identified the need for a comprehensive, periodized, master plan, it may seem contradictory to state that the essence of a good master plan is its malleability—its ability to be changed as required to ensure its optimal effectiveness. In a periodization scheme it is unnecessary and impractical to write initially the exact details of each day's training on a day-to-day basis for a year in advance. Some coaches do, and their athletes become locked into (and victims of) a plan that becomes less appropriate over time. Continual adjustment of a training scheme is required to recognize (and take advantage of)

- variable rates of adaptation to specific training,
- small setbacks such as a minor injury, and
- personal life vicissitudes that temporarily demand increased attention.

Thus, a generalized but well-thought-out master plan, with all its parts laid out in perspective, provides a reference point from which an intelligent beginning and reasoned continuity can occur. Without such a plan, athlete and coach are perpetually adrift, not knowing what to do or why and thus selecting training by whim.

Training and Periodization Terminology

Good communication is easiest when clear understanding exists between communicator and listener. Hence the origin of the familiar phrase "Say what you mean and mean what you say." Reasonably specific terminology is used for describing the periodization of training and the kinds of adaptation that occur. To familiarize readers with these terms, we will summarize their definitions.

Training is a sequence of activities done for the purpose of increasing efficiency and effectiveness in sport performance. In this instance, *performance* refers to quality of training and racing. Training improves several performance variables, identified many years ago by Nett (1965), including *strength*, defined as the quantity of muscular force exerted against resistance, and *speed*, which is the ability to perform body movements quickly, successively, and successfully. A good sprinter has excellent speed.

Endurance is also required for good running and racing; this is simply the ability to sustain submaximal activity for a prolonged period. A good marathoner has enormous endurance. There are two types of endurance. *Aerobic endurance*, or *stamina*, is the ability to cope with fatigue while working primarily aerobically at a high effort load over a long (but not indefinite) period. Stamina is sometimes thought of as the ability to handle speed over time. A male 10,000-m runner doing a session of 2 × 3,000 m at 85% of his 5,000-m race pace is developing stamina. So is a female 5,000-m runner coping with a track session of 3 × 2,000-m runs at 80% of her 5,000-m race pace. *Anaerobic endurance*, or *speed endurance*, is the ability to tolerate fatigue and maintain both pace and form while running at near-maximal intensities for relatively short distances. Repeat 400-m training is one example of work that will develop speed endurance. *Fatigue* is a sensation of increasing difficulty in performing at a given work load while still maintaining previous efficiency. (These definitions receive closer scrutiny in chapter 8 where we discuss overtraining.)

Three terms—macrocycle, mesocycle, and microcycle—describe various phases of a training period. A *macrocycle* is a developmental period of considerable length directed toward achievement of a peak of maximal performance fitness. For many athletes, particularly track-oriented middle-distance runners, this may require nearly a year. As an example, an athlete may begin training during the fall and aim ultimately for best performance at the national championships the following late spring or early summer (or even later). For others, such a long period may not be required. For example, top-level marathon runners who remain injury free with excellent general fitness can work well with a cycle that repeats every four to five months. There are 10 to 12 weeks of intense preparation, a few weeks of tapering, then the race, and a month of mental and physical recovery (Lenzi 1987). This is why the world's healthiest and most consistent marathoners typically compete no more than two to three times a year.

Training macrocycles are compartmentalized into several smaller developmental periods. A *mesocycle* is a period of anywhere from a few weeks to a few months, typically with a specific developmental objective different from the mesocycle preceding and following it. One mesocycle may emphasize development of an endurance base; another may represent a period of fine-tuning. Each mesocycle consists of at least one *microcycle*—a period of no more than two weeks during which a meaningful and focused block of training can be completed. Figure 5.2 illustrates the use of these cycles during a hypothetical training period. Intermediate-level competitive events or time trials may be scheduled along the way, typically at the end of a microcycle or mesocycle, to permit the assessment of developing fitness.

After goal identification has permitted the outline of an overall training macrocycle, the next task is to delineate the objectives and goals for each mesocycle and microcycle. A wide variety of activities should be planned. Running and comprehensive conditioning obviously form the backbone of the training plan, with other aspects included as well, such as a stretching program, recuperative modalities (e.g., massage), and periodic health and fitness evaluation. But how do we describe the details of each training session of each microcycle that constitute the work load outlined to achieve the developmental goals of optimal preparation when it counts?

Several terms permit specific description of each day's training sessions. They relate closely to the classic questions that athletes ask their coaches when they meet for a training period. We'll use the running portion of training as an example.

"How far must I run?" That's *volume*. (The answer to the athlete might be "Ten runs of 200 m on the track.")

"When are we going to do these again?" That's *frequency*. ("Once more this microcycle, six days from now.")

"How fast must I run them?" That's *intensity*, or duration. ("Start at 33 s/200 m, eventually quickening to 30 s/200 m.")

"How much recovery (rest) can I have between each run?" That's *density*. ("One-and-a-half minutes in jogging back to the 200-m mark on the track.")

Jogging for most runners is defined as very slow running—7 to 8 min/mi for talented young-adult men (4:21 to 4:58 min/km) and 8 to 9 min/mi for talented young-adult women (4:58 to 5:36 min/km). For runners not so talented, as well as for older runners, these paces would be slower. Jogging is more energy costly than walking.

Now let's define more formally these descriptors of training load. Training *volume* is simply the quantity of training done during a given time period— work done per microcycle, total push-ups done on a given day, total weight lifted in one session, total distance run on a day of repeated 200-m runs, and so on. It is a specific quantity that can be expressed in any of several time frames. Training *frequency* refers to the number of sessions completed during

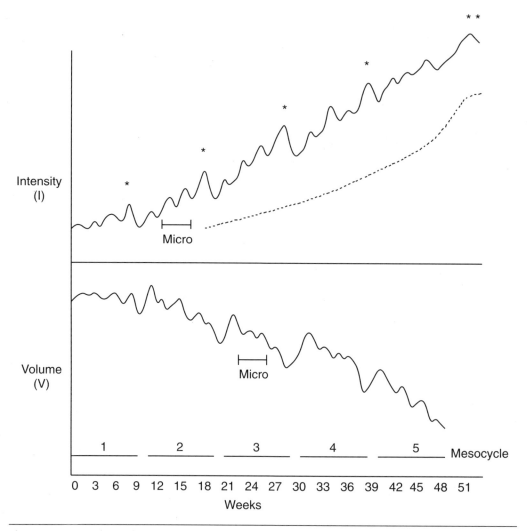

Figure 5.2 Hypothetical representation of a training period (here, 52 weeks), termed a macrocycle, divided into five smaller phases called mesocycles. During each successive mesocycle, the volume (V) of work done may either gradually lessen (as shown here) or be stable for a few mesocycles and eventually decrease. The intensity (I) of effort gradually increases as easier aerobic work is supplemented or replaced by more difficult anaerobic loads. The * symbols suggest periodic test points to determine progress at the end of mesocycles. The ** symbol indicates the major peak of that macrocycle. The dotted line (···) suggests competitive performance abilities, which should increase steadily as development proceeds but rapidly improve near the final week or two of tapering and rest. Each mesocycle is divided into a few training blocks, or microcycles, that permit appropriate cycling of training work loads.

a particular time period, or to the recurrence of a given training session during such a period, be it macrocycle, mesocycle, or microcycle. Some microcycles, for example, will have a training frequency of two sessions each day. On the other hand, repeated 1,000-m runs may be assigned a frequency of once every two weeks. Some exercises may be done nearly every day, such as sit-ups, push-ups, or aerobic conditioning runs. Other exercises, such as upper-body strengthening in the weight room, may be done once or perhaps twice each week.

Training *intensity* identifies the quality of completed effort and is related inversely to volume. Thus, as training intensity rises, the volume assigned decreases. A medium-intensity, high-volume run might be 10 mi at a 6:15 min/mi pace (3:53 min/km) for a good female 10,000-m runner. However, five repeated mile runs at a 5:00 min/mi pace (3:06 min/km) for that athlete would represent a far more intense training stimulus, but with reduced volume. The analog in strength training (weight lifting) would be the relationship of the load lifted with each repetition to that athlete's one repetition maximum.

Figure 5.2 illustrates the relationship between volume and intensity as conceptualized by Matveyev (1981) and Bondarchuk (1988) in their descriptions of the periodization process. As a macrocycle progresses, although the net weekly training load may remain the same, total volume decreases because intensity increases. Also, more event-specific special exercises are emphasized as the eventual final peak is approached. For each event specialty, these exercises may be quite different, but they typically also involve shorter, more intense training sessions.

Training *density* defines the rest pause between work bouts. The shorter the rest pause, the greater the stimulus density. Two 300-m runs on a track, each done in 44 s with a 2-min rest between, are a stimulus of greater density than two 300-m runs at the same speed but with a 3-min rest between each run. The rest pause can vary from a few seconds to several minutes, depending on the purpose of the session. Confusing jargon has developed among coaches in categorizing or identifying daily training sessions. It would be far preferable to be specific and informative, but such seems not to be in vogue, the result being worldwide difficulty in communications. Thus, one reads or hears about "cutdowns," but there is no knife or scissors involved. There are "breakdowns," but no one wants to really break down an athlete. There are "go's," meaning that after a specific recovery time (e.g., 2 min) the athlete begins the next run (a 2-min "go"). There are "ladders" (but no one is climbing), "clocks," "pyramids," and many more. All are simply variations on the theme of runs and rests, but they cause needless confusion since acceptable terminology is already established. Then there are phrases such as "tempo running," "interval running," and "repetition running" (Daniels and Scardina 1984; Wilt 1968), whose meanings vary quite a bit not only around the English-speaking world, but also between middle-distance and long-distance coaches. For example, some correctly use the term "interval" for the *distance* run, but others consider it the recovery time *between* runs. If a single factor has prevented effective coaching interchange in the sporting world, it is this all-too-frequent use of jargon that has different meanings to different people and event specialties.

Such complexity and confusion is unnecessary. Any running assignment should include specific directions, using terms that have clear meanings in common usage. Assignments given by one coach to a group of athletes should be unambiguous to another group of athletes being tutored by a different coach. The terminology is as follows. Athletes run a specific distance for a specific period of time; this is the *interval* of running. Chances are that they'll do this more than once. Several intervals of the same distance are referred to as *repetitions* (reps). Following each running interval, a specified *recovery* time permits a varying amount of rest, complete or incomplete. Groups of intervals are called *sets*, and the recovery time between sets is typically longer than the recovery time between runs within a set. Finally, each run is done at an assigned velocity, or *pace* or *tempo*. If the athlete is running as fast as possible, that's *maximal pace*. If it is slower than maximum, it's *submaximal pace*. It's as simple as that.

Using the preceding terminology, one example of a training session is 10 intervals of 200 m at 28-s pace (i.e., 10 runs of 200 m are each done in 28 s) with a 55-s jog between repetitions. In coaches' shorthand, this might be written as 10 × 200 m @ 28 s (55-s jog). This session would be quite difficult: The athlete is running quickly and has very little recovery rest. Another example is a series of fast interval runs at 85% of maximal pace, the first lasting 5 min, the second 4 min, the third 3 min, the fourth 2 min, and finishing with four 1-min runs. The first two recovery times are 4 min, the next two are, respectively, 3 and 2 min, and there is 1 min of recovery between each of the 1-min efforts. Again, using coaching shorthand, this session could be written as 5 min (4 min rec) + 4 min (4 rec) + 3 min (3 rec) + 2 min (2 rec) + (4 × 1 min) (1 min rec each).

The examples of training assignments given here represent only two of myriad combinations of higher-intensity, good-quality repetitions of an interval of distance run at a given tempo. Typically, such runs fit into the physiological performance zones of anaerobic conditioning or aerobic and anaerobic capacity training. Later in this chapter we will provide guidelines for more exact categorization of training assignments into these various zones. In turn this will provide a basis for intelligent structuring and manipulation of such assignments to best fit developmental needs.

Ensuring Training Balance and Specificity

One sensible method for injury-free performance progress over the course of a macrocycle involves harmonious interdevelopment of strength, speed, stamina, and endurance all during the year, never eliminating any of these entirely from the overall training plan. We define *multipace training* as the inclusion of training assignments at a variety of different paces over the entire training year. We tend to disagree with coaches who prescribe large volumes of solely longer-distance running over an initial period of weeks, followed by a similarly concentrated bolus of solely higher-intensity speed sessions over succeeding weeks. Instead, we view such training as an invitation for injuries from overuse and maladaptation. If for no other reason, such an emphasis on slow-paced training for too long causes decreased fitness among the FT muscle fibers, which we learned in chapter 2 are only stimulated by higher-paced work (see figure 2.11).

We also prefer to provide a smooth transition from a lower level of fitness to big-meet readiness by using a variety of training modalities (running, strength training, mobility exercises, etc.), the combination of which is changed periodically to meet the changing developmental focus. We define *multi-tier training* as the organization of training around several levels, or tiers, each of which builds on the preceding one. This is illustrated in figure 5.3. Each tier has a specific and different focus of development, and the combination contributes to well-rounded performance improvement.

The most valuable ingredients in the pursuit of any objective include the correct assessment of what is required and the proper pursuit of those requirements. The fundamental rationale for our belief in the effectiveness of multi-tier training is scientifically based. It is the experience of orthopedic and podiatric experts in sports medicine that lower-limb musculoskeletal injuries from overuse are more likely to occur when athletes suddenly change their ongoing load emphasis with inadequate transition—for example, from level surfaces to hills, from grass or dirt surfaces to hard asphalt, from solely slower-paced training to inclusion of fast-paced track intervals, from training flats to track spikes, or from slower over-distance sessions to quick, short sessions (Renström and Johnson 1985). The explanation is simply that the musculoskeletal system needs time to adapt gradually to changing stimuli. If adequate time is not provided, a high-volume or high-intensity training stress will likely be excessive and provoke injury. We are uninterested in developing injury-prone athletes. Multi-tier train-

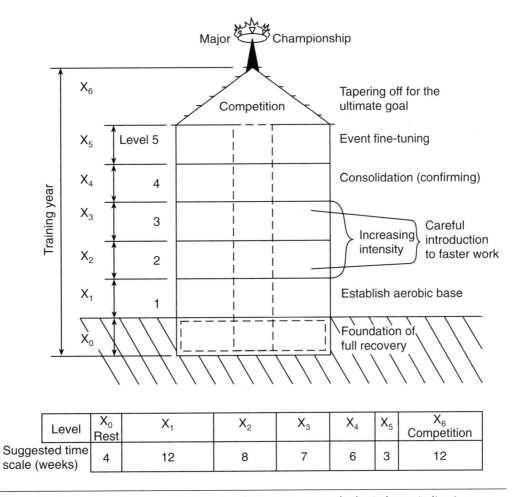

Level	X_0 Rest	X_1	X_2	X_3	X_4	X_5	X_6 Competition
Suggested time scale (weeks)	4	12	8	7	6	3	12

Figure 5.3 Diagrammatic representation of multi-tier training as the basis for periodization.

ing continually exposes athletes to a wide range of training stimuli with varying emphasis, thereby decreasing risk for injury or excessive fatigue.

There is yet another practical rationale for our approach, for which reference back to figure 2.11 again may be helpful. It makes little sense, in our view, for athletes to permit their FT type IIb skeletal muscle fibers to detrain from insufficient use during a long initial portion of a macrocycle devoted solely to development of an aerobic endurance base. Such detraining would occur if only low-intensity over-distance training was done for that period, because the FT type IIb motor units are stimulated only at higher work rates. This would decrease mobilizable speed that, when challenged suddenly, can bring injury from such motor units' reduction in readiness for use. When we refer to speed, we mean the repeatable, sustained speed of a 400-m runner, not the explosive, short-lived speed of a sprinter. Both aerobic and anaerobic components are involved. Middle- and long-distance racing is about *endurance and speed together*. Endurance will get a runner to the finish line, but endurance with speed will get a runner there first. One of our maxims, first and foremost, has been that *if speed is important, then never venture very far away from it*. Practically, this means that because speed must be practiced to be done well (to improve neural recruitment and permit cardiac and skeletal muscle strength adaptations), speed practice should continue, to varying degrees, all through a macrocycle.

Recent research studies involving comprehensive physiological evaluation of male Kenyan distance runners have been quite illuminating in helping to explain whether it is genetics (such as FT/ST muscle fiber ratios) or lifestyle (altitude residence, a hard lifestyle in younger years), or both, that combine with national pride in distance running excellence to explain the success of so many runners from a relatively small nation without a financially well-endowed developmental substructure for sport. As seen by the recent studies of Saltin et al. (1995), from a physiological perspective, probably the most important characteristic of these runners that sets them apart from their European and American counterparts is their slightly higher running economy, higher anaerobic threshold, and higher $\dot{V}O_2$max. These physiological advantages most likely are developed from the utilization of running as a part of their childhood lifestyle (shepherding farm animals, going to and from school and other villages, etc.), before they begin more structured training intended to improve fitness for competitive racing. Their greater musculoskeletal strength and endurance (helping to provide greater injury resistance) in comparison to their European and American counterparts, as well as their slightly greater cardiopulmonary fitness, provides a slight performance edge that continues over time as they age and continue to train as professional runners. Thus, it may be simply the situation of successful accommodation to stress loading in the formative years, rather than genetic factors, that sets the stage for their success.

Notice that we emphasize speed *with* endurance for the kind of training preparation that wins races. This is true from the 800 m through to the marathon. An 800-m or 1,500-m runner may need to endure back-to-back racing for three to four days in a major championship; the final race will be the most difficult. Doing an 800 m–1,500 m double—as Seb Coe managed with good success in two Olympic Games—may require seven races in nine days. Is preparation for speed with endurance really necessary for the marathon as well? Japanese national television thrilled millions of Sunday viewers on 30 January 1994 as three of their top female marathoners raced into Osaka's Nagai stadium side by side with a lap on the track after their trek through the city streets. Tens of thousands had waited in the cold for more than two hours to watch the outcome: It was a gut-wrenching sprint down the finishing straight. Tomoe Abe won, and Nobuko Fujimura came in second; both timed in at 2:26:09! Third place went to Junko Asari, 1 s behind. All three were faster than their national record. Yes, racing is indeed about endurance *and* speed together.

Periodization Using Multi-Tier Training

Training is much like constructing a multistory building. We need various kinds of building materials (aerobic and anaerobic running, comprehensive conditioning, flexibility, etc.). Several kinds of materials (training intensities and modalities) should be utilized in an ongoing fashion to complete the goal of a finished building—or a competitively fit athlete. Depending on progress in the construction plan, the relative mix of all these materials will vary. As a training season develops, for example, comprehensive conditioning work for strength and endurance will gradually change to an emphasis on power, with the substitution of intensity for volume in determining the total training load. Similar transitions occur with the pattern of running. An expert in periodization of training thus has a job similar to that of a good building contractor. Both are responsible for arranging the availability, quantity, and pattern of use of all the various components for completing the task at hand.

A Brief Analysis of Strategies for Training Runners

Many training systems for developing distance runners have evolved during this century. Various athletes have immortalized themselves by their superb middle- and long-distance running achievements, setting world records and earning Olympic and other major championship medals. In chronicling these marvelous achievements, the media have traditionally posed two major questions to the athlete and his or her coach: to the athlete, "What was the secret to your successful performances?" and to the coach, "Tell us about your athlete's training." This plan immortalized the coach. Who knows whether another plan could have produced better results with that gifted athlete?

It is useful to examine a few of the better-known athlete-coach relationships and their unique characteristics. In the 1920s and early 1930s the legendary Paavo Nurmi (22 world records between 1,500 m and 10,000 m; 12 Olympic medals) and his Finnish distance coach, Lauri Pikkala, placed a significant emphasis on a sizable number of weekly training periods of shorter duration, with adequate rest, rather than a focus on longer, slower distance running. Understanding of the details of skeletal muscle physiology and cellular biochemistry was in its infancy during that period, so no one realized that specifically Nurmi's greater emphasis on faster training was providing a good training stimulus for his FT skeletal muscle fibers, which required a more intense stimulus to respond (see figure 2.11). Many subsequent training systems have been little more than modifications of the principle that *those who race fast train fast*—provided that the companion requirement of recovery is also incorporated appropriately.

During the early 1940s, Woldemar Gerschler (coach of Rudolf Harbig) proposed that rest periods between short running intervals (100 m to 200 m) be determined by monitoring the heart rate (waiting until the pulse returns to about 120 beats/min). Mihaly Igloi (coach of Sandor Iharos during the 1950s) developed the concept of sets of short distances run quickly (in any set the recovery time between runs is minimal, with a longer rest between sets) to permit (unknowingly) a greater total FT type IIb and IIa muscle fiber stimulus. Arthur Lydiard (coach of the 1960 Rome Olympic gold medalists Peter Snell [800 m] and Murray Halberg [5,000 m]) preached the initial development of a profound aerobic (endurance) base on which to build faster running, as well as emphasis on total-body development. This included hill running to improve arm and shoulder action. A subsequent brief period of short-distance, fast-speed training permitted development of anaerobic stamina. Over the years the pendulum has swung between the extremes of speed emphasis and endurance emphasis. But there is often little logic to fashion, and such extremes lack a sensible rationale. As with most arguments, once both sides have been presented, the best solution is often an incorporation of an appropriate mix of each.

Our view is that two elements have been missing from these various training systems. One needed element is the inclusion of training over a rather wide range of running paces all through the year, with continual and careful assessment of the extent to which adaptation to paces slower and faster than the race pace occurs. This ensures rapid identification of the liabilities in performance—those aspects (aerobic or anaerobic) for which the athlete is less genetically gifted and to which a more careful developmental emphasis must be given. The other needed element is consideration of the running portion of an athlete's training as only one aspect of a program of total-body conditioning. Ensuring health maintenance and the prevention of injury or staleness requires that all facets contributing to performance adaptation—positive mental attitude, strength, speed, endurance, stamina, flexibility, and recovery—must be developed optimally. Our multi-tier training concept attempts to incorporate these facets. We do not consider our system revolutionary or new because we have been using it for years. Recently published articles and books describing the views of well-established coaches of distance runners (Bondarchuk 1988; Daniels 1989; Vigil 1987, 1995) and experts on periodization (Bompa 1988; Freeman 1989; McInnis 1981) describe concepts that have similar features but different terminology.

Our system for training athletes is holistic in that we realize that all parts of the system must be fully operational to ensure long-term success. Using an analogy to biological ecosystems, disruption of even a small facet of the ongoing order can bring profound negative consequences to every organism because a harmonious interdependence of all systems provides the balance for survival. A similar imbalance often occurs when athletes de-emphasize one aspect of development in favor of an excess of another. It is possible for athletes to be quite fit but not healthy—nonfunctional from a competitive point of view. They may be injured as a result of overtraining and left to languish in an athletic purgatory while they recover. Being in excellent health sets the stage for becoming totally fit. Extraordinary fitness sets the stage for competitive excellence and is achieved only after complete adaptation to rigorous training.

Training over a broad range of paces—those appropriate for distances both longer and shorter as well as equal to the athlete's primary event—provides optimal preparation for that primary event. Thus, the concept of multipace training is interwoven into the fabric of multi-tier training. Longer-distance runs of moderate intensity build aerobic endurance. Fast-paced, longer-distance running improves stamina, whereas very fast, shorter-distance running improves strength and quickness. A 1,500-m specialist needs 5,000-m distance training as well as 800-m speed training. A 10,000-m specialist can benefit from a periodic very long run (although probably not as long as those done by marathon specialists) but needs some of the speed training of a 5,000-m runner as well. Training at the primary-event race pace teaches awareness of the event itself.

Table 5.4 shows that the best event specialty around which to focus training for year-round development of mature runners is the 5,000 m (3,000 m for younger athletes). Both are raced at very close to 100% of $\dot{V}O_2$max pace. Thus, stamina is the central developmental focus for such a runner, enhanced on one hand by a strong speed component and on the other by sustainable endurance running. Upon a sizable (but not overdone) endurance base is superimposed the ability to run quickly and to sustain that quick pace. As specialization becomes more appropriate, the focus can be switched to shorter or longer events with minimal injury risk and minimal learning of new skills. Moving up to the 10,000-m event simply requires a subtle shift regarding more emphasis on endurance work. Moving down to the 1,500-m event requires an appropriate shift of emphasis toward more anaerobic work. When both speed and endurance are developed simultaneously, as occurs with multipace training even early into a year-long macrocycle, it is easy for the coach to learn where an athlete's natural capabilities reside, because genetic predisposition will soon reveal that one or the other is developing more easily. The task of deciding on a likely best event for the final focus then is simplified for both athlete and coach.

Running assignments, however, are only one facet of the overall development of distance runners. Because runners are specialists at running, of course the running portion of training will occupy the bulk of a training plan and provide the specific stimulus for greatest improvement in competitive excellence. However, flexibility exercises and comprehensive conditioning through circuit and specific strength training are also crucial for the consistency and longevity

TABLE 5.4

The Difference in Energy Sources That Contribute to Racing Performances in Common Distance Events

Event	World record Men	World record Women	Approx. % $\dot{V}O_2$max	Race characteristic	% energy contribution Phosphate	Lactate	Aerobic
100 m	9.85	10.49	NA	All-out; short speed	70	22	8
200 m	19.73	21.34	NA	All-out; short speed	40	46	14
400 m	43.29	47.60	NA	99% all-out; long speed	10	60	30
800 m	1:41.73	1:53.28	135	98% all-out; endurance speed	5	38	57
1,500 m	3:27.37	3:50.46	112	95% all-out; speed endurance	2	22	76
3,000 m	7:20.67	8:06.11	102	90% all-out; endurance with speed	<1	12	88
5,000 m	12:44.39	14:36.45	97	85% all-out; long endurance with speed	<1	7	93
10,000 m	26:43.53	29:31.78	92	Long endurance with some speed	<1	3	97
Marathon	2:06:50	2:21:06	82	Paced aerobic; long endurance; possibly speed	<1	<1	99

Note. NA = not applicable. Data adapted from Matthews (1996, pp. 247-258); Péronnet and Thibault (1989, pp. 453-465); and Léger, Mercier, and Gauvin (1986, pp. 113-120).

of an athletic career. In addition, the use of recuperative and restorative modalities, proper nutrition, and adequate rest are all part of this building process. The coach should be a key facilitator in helping athletes develop effective working relationships with experts who can provide assistance in these various developmental areas.

The Mesocycles of Multi-Tier Training

Figure 5.3 illustrates our concept of training using a multi-tier framework. We can continue our earlier analogy to constructing a building. During one macrocycle (or complete training period, typically approximating one year) the building will be constructed (i.e., the training will be completed). Each level of the building represents a mesocycle (or tier), indicated by X. Thus, multi-tier training is a training plan with several mesocycles, or levels, each of which has a different assigned goal for athletic development. The length of each mesocycle may vary depending on event requirements, athlete fitness, and the time available.

The *recovery mesocycle* (X_0) has already been identified as a restorative period of general activity that produces an athlete who has recovered from the previous training macrocycle and is committed to beginning the new one. The first or *aerobic-dominant mesocycle* (X_1) establishes a substantial aerobic conditioning base. In our suggested time scale for a hypothetical distance runner, this may require 12 weeks.

An example from Keith Brantly's training log of the mid-1980s (when his primary specialty was the 5,000 m and 10,000 m) can serve as an illustration of the starting-up of a training macrocycle. His University Games gold medal performance at 10,000 m in Kobe in late August 1985 ended his 1984-85 training macrocycle. He began his 1985-86 training macrocycle with a six-week mesocycle (X_0), the first four weeks of which were active nonrunning rest. He was entirely uninjured from the previous macrocycle and still quite fit from the summertime competition mesocycle (X_6). Thus, instead of the traditional easy aerobic endurance running characteristic of X_0, his two-week period of swimming, sailing, biking, and other sport activities quite removed from running kept him aerobically fit but permitted the rejuvenation of hunger to "train like a runner." The final two weeks of his six-week mesocycle X_0 included a reorientation to daily running.

Then, mesocycle X_1 began with an average of about 80 mi/wk for two weeks—primarily aerobic conditioning with a single session each week of quick, short intervals. During the third week he reduced his training to 49 mi, and included a 10-km road race in which he placed second. Following three additional weeks averaging 80 mi/wk, his next week was only 46 mi, but with another 10-km road race. Following this was a transition into five weeks of slightly less aerobic conditioning but with the substitution of a weekly session of long intervals (2,000 to 3,000 m) run at 5-km to 10-km race pace. Three more road races varying in their competitive intensity were included during this period, each preceded by a few days of ample rest. The combination of long but easy aerobic sessions, a few aerobic capacity training sessions, plenty of recovery, and road racing when fresh to ensure positive and challenging experiences gave him four victories, enough income to pay his bills, and a completed 11-week aerobic endurance mesocycle. He was healthy, happy, fit, secure, and had developed an adequate base to begin mesocycle X_2.

It should be clear from the description of mesocycle X_1, and this is true for all mesocycles as well, that occasional recovery days must be included for both physiological and psychological reasons. Although arduous training has its ultimate positive benefits, it is very difficult. It isn't wise or necessary for athletes to feel that they are on a kind of never-ending training treadmill, committed to weeks and weeks of daily hard work with no letup. The recovery days or phases are essential, because the regeneration of normal metabolic function in the working tissues (hydration, energy supplies, connective tissue recovery) makes continued training possible.

Through the next two *increasing-intensity mesocycles* (X_2, X_3) emphasis on higher-quality training increases—faster aerobic work as well as anaerobic training. This training load must be regulated carefully, and as adaptation occurs it must be varied in volume, intensity, and density to ensure progress without fatigue. Typically, the volume of aerobic work gradually begins to be reduced somewhat in order to keep the total load slowly increasing but always manageable.

During the *consolidation mesocycle* (X_4) the quality of progress in each of the many kinds of training modalities during the previous three mesocycles is carefully assessed. It is expected that not every phase of the athlete's development will have progressed precisely at the rate expected. One or two consolidating microcycles during this mesocycle should provide the optimal balance of additional training to improve speed, stamina, or endurance. Time is provided here for this "rounding out" to occur, whether it be an additional improvement in $\dot{V}O_2max$ or greater anaerobic work tolerance. A remarkably small amount of such higher-intensity training is required to provide substantial additional gains in fitness (Knuttgen et al. 1973). Each athlete's own genetic endowment and training success will have permitted better adaptation to faster or slower running over the shorter or longer distances.

Benchmarks of progress are required at reasonable points during each mesocycle for coach and athlete to verify that they are still on target for completing their goals. These benchmarks can include races, time trials, and laboratory physiological evaluations (such as a treadmill graded exercise test [GXT] and blood chemistry profiling). Target times for a variety of track distances (from 400 m through 3,000 m) should already have been defined as goals at various points during the year, based on experience during previous macrocycles. For long-distance runners, road or track races appropriate in quality to match the skills of the athlete can also serve as indicators, provided the weather is comparable from year to year.

The athlete should not make elaborate attempts to actually peak for these impending tests. Coaches and athletes should be uninterested in eliciting the athlete's absolute best *rested performance*. It is expected that the performance should indeed be slower than if complete recovery and the emotion of a top-level competition were included. These tests are simply timely indicators occurring in an environment of hard training, and nothing more. However, some tapering is important for two reasons. One is that a reasonable indication of developing fitness is desired through testing, otherwise the test is meaningless. Second, doing a fairly stressful test in a profoundly fatigued state is risking injury and may not be accompanied by adequate mental freshness to ensure a good effort. Some subtle shifting in a few days of the training plan within the microcycle should handle this dilemma nicely. With these benchmarks of progress, whether in the laboratory or in the field, the athlete is serving as his or her own control over time. As progress is made through the macrocycle, the compared results of these with other indicators along the way characterize the extent and nature of the athlete's progress (for example, faster performance times at a given distance raced earlier, or a similar track session pace now manageable over a longer distance).

Now the athlete enters the *fine-tuning mesocycle* (X_5), where the finishing touches are added. The construction of our house (the development of our athlete) is virtually complete. If there is ever to be a departure from an emphasis on balanced development, this is the period. We have scheduled three weeks for our hypothetical athlete. Emphasis now involves developing any specialized performance abilities germane to the event or honing particular skills that are a special asset of this athlete, such as a few additional longer runs, interval sessions, or acceleration practice during shorter intervals. Following completion of this mesocycle is a tapering period for the ultimate goal of a major championship performance or racing series.

During the final portions of the mesocycle X_5 and on into the *competition mesocycle* (X_6, shown in figure 5.3 as extending for 12 weeks), training by no means ceases completely. As in levels X_1 through X_4, work continues on each aspect of training. However, the volume of work is greatly decreased, leaving a freshness of both body and mind. A true peak, with best performances accompanied by very little maintenance effort, can be held for only about three weeks. During the remainder of this competition period, however, low-volume, moderate- to high-intensity training is arranged to fit around competition. (In contrast, during the previous mesocycles any small race or test situation would have been arranged around training, which was higher in volume and variable in intensity.) Such continued low-level, "quality maintenance" training prolongs the time during which the athlete can be successful competitively. For athletes who schedule four to six competitions during their peak competitive level, the integration of tapering training fits nicely into this portion of the mesocycle.

If tapering and regeneration are timed properly, the results of competitive performance will likely be exceptional. Yakovlev (1967) termed this phenomenon *supercompensation*, that is, results better than predicted on the basis of previous ongoing evaluations (figure 5.4). Explaining supercompensation is simple; timing racing performance to coincide with it is more difficult. The phenomenon has three components. There are physiological adaptations to the training

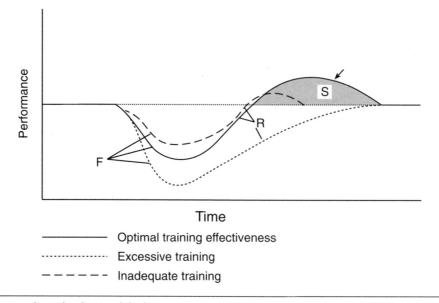

Figure 5.4 The Yakovlev model of supercompensation (S). Training places a physiological load on the body, resulting in fatigue (F) and a decrease in maximal performance abilities. Following a training load, improvement in performance can occur only with adequate recovery (R). Inadequate training may bring only small, short-lived improvements. Overtraining requires excessive recovery time and may not bring any improvements to overall performance. An appropriate recovery period can bring temporarily improved performance abilities due to increased metabolic potential (more fuel reserves, cardiovascular adaptation, etc.). If coupled with a tapering phase, the additional reduction in neural fatigue and increased psychological readiness for competition can bring a more extended period of excellent performance—a supercompensation (S). This model is viable for both short- and long-term blocks of training.

just completed (more and bigger mitochondria, more blood volume, greater skeletal muscle protein, more stored muscle fuels, etc.). There is a neurological recruitment effect, caused by a reduction in neural fatigue from the continued high-level training stimulus. Finally, an increased psychological readiness comes from a combination of rest from training, the motivation to perform well, the confidence that preparation has been optimal, a focus on competition, and a full stadium or crowds along the way ready to enjoy the drama. This supercompensation response has been likened to the adaptive recovery response of bone following a stress fracture. Repair is so good at the fracture site that the recovered part of the bone is actually stronger than the part surrounding it. Just as with bone repair, it is crucial in tapering that adequate time be permitted for attainment of this additional performance capacity.

The Yakovlev model can also be applied to a single training session within a microcycle, or to the training within a mesocycle. For example, a given day of hard training will produce fatigue and a temporary decline in performance, and regeneration occurs during the ensuing hours or days, depending on the training volume. Success in daily training resides in the optimal timing of each training stimulus so as to prevent excessive fatigue and to permit the most difficult sessions to occur when regeneration is optimal.

In keeping with the philosophy that athletes cannot generally be successful at simultaneously training hard and competing well, during the competitive period athletes must acquire the confidence that they indeed have done the work required during their previous mesocycles and that it is absolutely appropriate to turn off the focal emphasis on training and tune in to competing. Such a switch is crucial in order to bring on as dominant emotions the excitement to race, the yearning to win, and the striving to plow new turf by attempting personal best performances. These kinds of attitudes provide the proper beginning for athletes to start on a roll toward success. A few races that are longer or shorter than the athlete's event specialty against athletes of various (but probably known) abilities will create a mental framework conducive to competing again. Racing well and winning both create such an emotional high that the athlete desires overwhelmingly to experience it again. The trick is to start this process at the proper moment. Peaking at the appropriate race is one of the most elusive quests in the art and science of physical training. Training, recovery, and mental preparation all combine with environmental distractions and synergists. Thus, there are no guarantees, because not all contributing factors are positive and controllable. The athlete works hard within a sensible plan and hopes everything else comes together properly.

When the ultimate goal has been contested, then it may be appropriate to enter into the recovery phase and "shut down the engines." This may not always be done immediately. Often, other sport meetings will be scheduled just following the major competition; they provide the athlete with less total stress but still offer the athlete the opportunity of a quality performance, because the field of talent will all be at nearly their best performance levels. The athlete's emotional relief from the hype of a major competition combined with excellent fitness has often provided an environment for personal best performances and world records. Witness the two world records at the Zürich Weltklasse meeting of 1995 (in the men's 5,000 m and steeplechase) one week after the 1995 Göteborg World Championships. It isn't wise, however, to overdo such a competitive streak because the effects of reduced training will result eventually in performance decrements. This increases the risk of injury, and the sudden falloff in performance can be mentally discouraging.

If the results of the major championship or competitive season have been satisfying, then it is quite easy for athlete and coach to relax and enjoy a rest. If disappointment occurred, the sense of nonachievement or failure can be heartbreaking at best, disastrous at worst. But failure must always be handled with positive thinking; this provides a meaningful opportunity to determine what might have gone wrong. When instances of performance disaster are studied carefully, it can frequently be seen that the athlete pursued a development plan that was directed poorly toward improvement. The athlete trained and enjoyed training, but either training was overdone, or else improvement in all areas was simply not adequate, and these areas were either overlooked or not identified soon enough. There is no substitute for knowledge and organization in increasing the odds for an excellent end result.

The Seven Domains of Multi-Tier Training

We mentioned earlier that multi-tier training includes multipace running as well as a variety of other activities that contribute to total-body fitness during each level of development (from mesocycles X_1 through X_5). Table 5.5 illustrates this in greater detail. On each floor (tier) of our building (i.e., during each mesocycle), the same number of rooms (or training domains) exist (i.e., the same basic kinds of training and development modalities are utilized). Two domains (circuits and weights, and general mobility) include comprehensive conditioning, which will be described in chapter 6. Another domain, analogous to a maintenance service shaft in our building, will always be accessible from any level. This represents ongoing health care delivery, recuperative modalities such as massage and various forms of therapy, and laboratory performance evaluation to assess progress.

TABLE 5.5

The Seven Domains of Multi-Tier Training

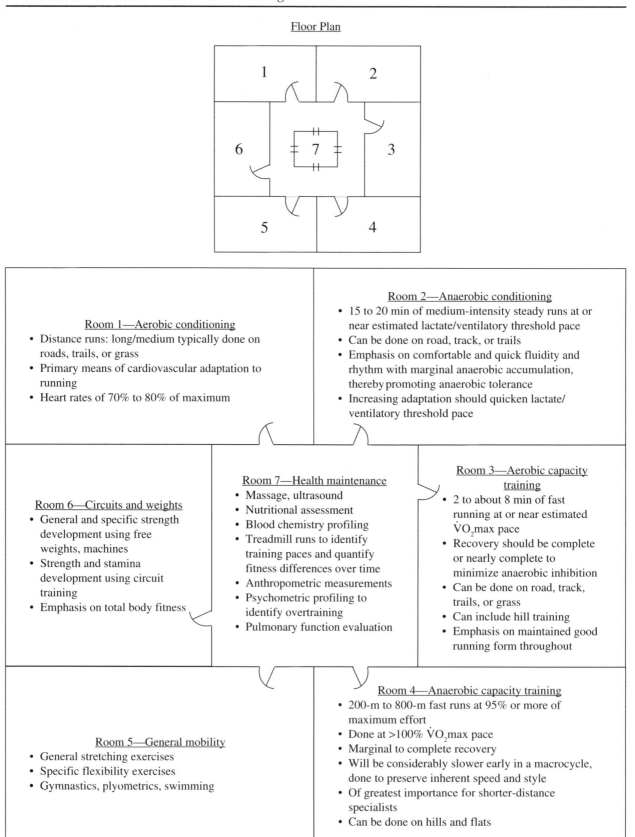

Floor Plan

Room 1—Aerobic conditioning
- Distance runs: long/medium typically done on roads, trails, or grass
- Primary means of cardiovascular adaptation to running
- Heart rates of 70% to 80% of maximum

Room 2—Anaerobic conditioning
- 15 to 20 min of medium-intensity steady runs at or near estimated lactate/ventilatory threshold pace
- Can be done on road, track, or trails
- Emphasis on comfortable and quick fluidity and rhythm with marginal anaerobic accumulation, thereby promoting anaerobic tolerance
- Increasing adaptation should quicken lactate/ ventilatory threshold pace

Room 6—Circuits and weights
- General and specific strength development using free weights, machines
- Strength and stamina development using circuit training
- Emphasis on total body fitness

Room 7—Health maintenance
- Massage, ultrasound
- Nutritional assessment
- Blood chemistry profiling
- Treadmill runs to identify training paces and quantify fitness differences over time
- Anthropometric measurements
- Psychometric profiling to identify overtraining
- Pulmonary function evaluation

Room 3—Aerobic capacity training
- 2 to about 8 min of fast running at or near estimated $\dot{V}O_2$max pace
- Recovery should be complete or nearly complete to minimize anaerobic inhibition
- Can be done on road, track, trails, or grass
- Can include hill training
- Emphasis on maintained good running form throughout

Room 5—General mobility
- General stretching exercises
- Specific flexibility exercises
- Gymnastics, plyometrics, swimming

Room 4—Anaerobic capacity training
- 200-m to 800-m fast runs at 95% or more of maximum effort
- Done at >100% $\dot{V}O_2$max pace
- Marginal to complete recovery
- Will be considerably slower early in a macrocycle, done to preserve inherent speed and style
- Of greatest importance for shorter-distance specialists
- Can be done on hills and flats

The other four domains involve various intensities and volumes of running that stimulate development in the four training zones identified in figure 4.2, which we shall describe in greater detail shortly.

As the athlete progresses from mesocycle X_1 toward X_5, the training load (intensity or volume) will increase gradually. Careful integration of daily sessions will provide optimal stimulation of the various energy systems to ensure progress without excessive fatigue or injury. To complete our construction analogy, any particular room (domain) on any tier (mesocycle) may be larger or smaller and may be entered more than once.

As mentioned earlier, multi-tier training suggests that a development plan for all distance runners should have similar components over the entire training year. This seems not in keeping with the concept of event specificity; an 800-m runner is indeed not a marathon expert. Thus, we have an apparent paradox. A paradox has no solution, only a resolution. Here, it is simple: depending on the athlete, the event, and the time frame within the macrocycle, *we vary the emphasis* on any of the types of training identified. Varying the emphasis refers not only to how many units from each training domain might be assigned during a given microcycle, but also to their intensity. In this manner, none of the components of training is ignored or eliminated. All are included because all are important. In fact, the risk of injury increases if such balance is not maintained or if specific modalities are inserted suddenly following neglect. Varying the mix of activities selected from the groups identified as training domains according to event specialty and according to the mesocycle of development optimizes training specificity.

The individuality of each athlete—genetic talent, existing fitness level, risk for injury, and superimposed challenges such as asthma or a full-time job—requires that the best training plans be individualized. This requires time, thought, and dedication. Ensuring the proper mix of work to be accomplished is the task of a competent coach. Athletes often are too close to their training to complete this task objectively. Because considerable work is involved, it is possible for a coach to work effectively with only relatively few athletes, or else he or she gambles that a few will always run well in spite of inadequate supervision (which isn't fair to the athletes being coached). Athletes desiring long-term success ought to seek out coaches who are dedicated to working well with a few athletes rather than those who have an unmanageable number.

Each specific assigned running distance (interval)—easy long run, short fast run, or something in between—provides a different physiological stimulus. If the stimulus is sizable and adequate recovery occurs, the physiological adaptation will also be sizable. The athlete and coach want the best adaptation appropriate for the athlete's event specialty. They do not want the athlete to train excessively (which increases the risk of injury) or inadequately (because optimal adaptation will not occur). By understanding the kinds of physiological adaptation that occur in each of the four training zones identified in figure 4.2, each of which has its own domain in table 5.5, and then determining for each zone what is required for performance excellence in each competitive running event, coaches and athletes are in the best possible position to develop meaningful training assignments that make good physiological as well as athletic sense.

Table 5.5 and figure 5.5 both summarize some of the physiological characteristics of performance within each of the four zones. In figure 5.5 we have constructed a pyramid with several levels. The width of each level represents both the distance run (interval) and the running pace (tempo). Thus, the greater the width, the longer the interval and the slower the pace. Recovery times will vary.

Physiological adaptations	Blood lactate	% max heart rate	% $\dot{V}O_2$max	Training interval run time	Systems challenged	Common jargon describing sessions	Training interval distance	Race pace for
Speed and strength ST and FT fiber development Increased neurological recruitment Improved blood buffering ability Tolerance to stress of acidosis	> 9 mmol 8 mmol	100 95	130 (Sprint) 100	30 s → 2 min	Anaerobic capacity	Short interval Repetitions Short speed	200 m → 1,000 m	800 m 1,500 m
Speed ST and FT fiber development Some increase in neurological recruitment Some increase in blood buffering ability Increased glycolytic enzymes	8 mmol 7 mmol 5 mmol	95 90	100 ($\dot{V}O_2$max) 98 90	2 min → 8 min	Aerobic capacity	Long interval Long speed	800 m → 3,000 m	3,000 m 5,000 m 10,000 m
Stamina ST and some FT Type IIa development Increased heart chamber size Increased stroke volume Increased oxidative/glycolytic enzymes Increased blood volume	5 mmol 4 mmol 3.5 mmol	90 80	90 75 (Lactate/ventilatory threshold)	8 min → 20 min	Anaerobic conditioning	Tempo training Pace training Marathon training Steady-state training	Marathon race pace 15-20 min	Marathon
Endurance ST fiber development Increased blood volume Increased connective tissue development Increased muscle fuel storage Increased oxidative/glycolytic enzymes Increased capillarization	3.5 mmol 2 mmol	80 70	75 60 55	20 min → 2 hr	Aerobic conditioning	Over-distance running Base work	All longer distances	

Figure 5.5 The primary training zones of performance during running.

Longer-distance intervals at slower tempos require less recovery time than shorter-distance intervals at a fast tempo. As fitness improves, recovery times following all intervals will likely decrease.

The uppermost portion of the pyramid in figure 5.5 represents the pure sprint speed of the 100-m through 400-m specialists (speed strength). This facet of performance isn't emphasized particularly for middle- and long-distance training, although some fast running over very short distances is indeed important. The remaining four tiers of the pyramid represent the four primary training zones in which middle- and long-distance runners do their daily work. Figure 5.5 can serve as a companion diagram to figure 4.2, the former providing more of a coaching (practical) perspective, the latter more of a physiological (scientific) perspective. Let us now describe each of these four training zones in greater detail.

Aerobic Conditioning

Aerobic conditioning represents the largest percentage of a distance runner's training, varying with event emphasis and over the training year. The lowermost level of the training pyramid for running illustrated in figure 5.5 is the foundation upon which other running is based. The mainstay of such a program is sizable volumes of continuous, longer-distance running at below race pace for any of the middle- and long-distance running events. It is often referred to as *base work*, and sometimes called *conversational running*, because it is slow enough to permit conversation during the run. The relatively easy nature of such training makes it appropriate for athletes of comparable ability to train together, providing camaraderie and adding enjoyment to sessions that for marathoners may last two hours or more.

It is convenient to express the intensity of running pace appropriate for each of these four training zones as a percentage of $\dot{V}O_2$max pace. Thus, aerobic conditioning runs typically are done at 55% to 75% of $\dot{V}O_2$max pace, depending on distance covered and level of fitness. In figure 4.2 the appropriate pace range for the male runner whose treadmill test data are graphed is between 5:50 and 6:50 min/mi. How can one determine $\dot{V}O_2$max pace? It can be easily identified using treadmill testing, but this is not always available. It can also be estimated from a track time trial, recognizing that 100% $\dot{V}O_2$max pace can be maintained for no more than 10 min. As an example, let's use the same athlete whose data were graphed in figure 4.2. If he covers 3,500 m in 10 min (600 s), the following equation can be written using simple arithmetic:

$$3,500 \text{ m}/600 \text{ s} = 1,609 \text{ m}/x \text{ s} \tag{5.1}$$

Solving equation 5.1 for x, we obtain

$$3,500x = 965,400 \quad \text{and} \quad x = 275.8 \text{ s} = 4{:}35.8 \text{ min/mi} \tag{5.2}$$

for $\dot{V}O_2$max pace. Or, for a result using the metric system,

$$3,500 \text{ m}/600 \text{ s} = 1,000 \text{ m}/x \text{ s} \tag{5.3}$$

Solving equation 5.3 for x, we obtain

$$3,500x = 600,000 \quad \text{and} \quad x = 171.4 \text{ s/km} = 2{:}51.4 \text{ min/km} \tag{5.4}$$

Running slower than 55% of $\dot{V}O_2$max pace brings little measurable aerobic improvement and merely adds to impact stress. Running faster than 75% $\dot{V}O_2$max pace causes the beginnings of anaerobic glycolytic activity, which may mark the beginning of lactic acid accumulation that is not appropriate for training emphasis in this zone.

Shorter-distance aerobic conditioning runs might range from 8 to 15 km (5 to 9 mi), depending on event specialty and years of experience, and longer runs might range from 10 to 35 km (6 to 22 mi). A talented 16-year-old high school boy averaging 30 mi/wk (48 km/wk), with an interest in racing 1,500 m or 1,600 m, may find a 6-mi (10-km) run at a 7:30-min/mi (4:40-min/km) pace an appropriate aerobic conditioning stimulus. A top-quality collegiate male 10,000-m runner averaging 75 mi/wk (121 km/wk) may find it more appropriate to cover 10 mi (16 km) at a 6:30-min/mi (4:02-min/km) pace to achieve a comparable conditioning stimulus. The explanation for this difference is that the young athlete's $\dot{V}O_2$max is not quite so well developed as it will be after he has attained the overall maturation and tolerance to chronic elevated training loads that characterize the collegiate athlete.

Heart rate values between 70% and 80% of maximum (Karvonen, Kentala, and Mustala 1957) are optimal for aerobic conditioning. Maximal heart rate varies considerably among individuals, depending on heredity and prior training. Thus, specific heart rate values are best calculated by athletes after they determine their own maximum values. For example, if a runner's maximal heart rate is 188 beats/min, 70% to 80% of this as an aerobic conditioning heart rate range would be 132 to 150 beats/min. This range is typical for men, but women's are generally a little higher (women's hearts are smaller in relation to body size than men's).

Aerobic conditioning serves to improve oxidative metabolic capabilities in cardiac muscle and in those skeletal muscle cells that are activated. It also provides a stimulus for improving joint and tendon strength without the excessive impact stress that would result at faster paces. Increases occur in the quantity of stored fuels (carbohydrates and fatty acids) as well as in the number and size of mitochondria in the stimulated muscle cells. Increasing blood volume and capillary density in trained muscles improves O_2 delivery and CO_2 removal by increasing the net transit time of blood through these working tissues and decreasing the diffusion distance between the interior of capillaries and the mitochondria in adjacent muscle cells.

Because aerobic conditioning is not a very intense training stimulus, it should form the mainstay of the initial return to training (mesocycle X_0) among those athletes who periodically take complete breaks from formal conditioning. It provides a gentle, yet sizable and important, adaptation to the work load provided, with both cardiovascular and musculoskeletal improvements. However, even from mesocycles X_1 through X_3 within a training year, aerobic conditioning still constitutes a sizable portion of the total work load, because it can serve as a maintenance stimulus for cardiovascular conditioning and as a continuing developmental stimulus for connective tissue adaptation. The sustained increased venous return to the heart, particularly during longer runs, provides an initial stimulus toward enlarging ventricular chambers, eventually increasing stroke volume and permitting a given volume of blood to be pumped at a lower heart rate than if this training effect were not present. This cardiac adaptation is first noticed as a lower resting (morning) heart rate.

Aerobic conditioning stimulates primarily the ST skeletal muscle motor units because their motor neurons are more responsive to lower-intensity activity than those of FT motor units. This was discussed in chapter 2. The adaptations in muscle cell and cardiovascular working capabilities occurring with training permit each ST motor unit to work at any given submaximal intensity with less fatigability. Thus, fewer motor units are required for maintaining a given pace, or those activated do not need to work as hard as before (in relation to their maximal output). Improved conditioning among specific muscle groups that serve as the prime movers reduces the need for contributions by accessory muscles for producing movement. This helps to improve running economy because less muscle activity is involved (and less O_2 consumption is required) in producing movement. Runners perceive this, often remarking that they "feel smoother and stronger." In actuality, this change isn't as much a strength increase (meaning more force production) as it is greater endurance (better fatigue resistance caused by better perfusion and less anaerobic metabolic influences at typical training paces).

The primary liability of such over-distance training is the relatively slower and less complete adaptation of connective tissue. Tendons and ligaments do not improve their circulation or increase their size as extensively as muscles do to permit appropriately increasing tolerance to their chronic work load. This probably accounts for the greater incidence of debilitation from inflammation and injury in connective tissue than in the muscles. Runners should avoid training on crowned road surfaces because the left and right footstrike surfaces are at slightly (but importantly) different elevations, giving asymmetric impact stress. Sidewalks, trails, or grassy surfaces such as firm, flat pastures or golf courses are preferable training surfaces to cambered or rough, uneven surfaces.

Anaerobic Conditioning

A proper balance of greater volume-oriented, slower-paced work with greater intensity-oriented, faster-paced work all through the training year permits a large base of endurance fitness, on top of which is an essential element of raw sustainable speed. Higher-intensity training falls into three categories, as diagrammed in figures 4.2 and 5.5, one of which is anaerobic conditioning. Training at a higher intensity than aerobic conditioning brings appropriate adaptations in those muscle cells that are only stimulated by such higher-intensity stimuli and also increases the adaptational response of the heart and cardiovascular system. Thus, judicious inclusion of higher-intensity training (below the limits that produce injury from excessive connective tissue overloading) are both beneficial and essential for the competitive athlete interested in training to race rather than simply training to train.

We can provide some examples of effective anaerobic conditioning, or anaerobic threshold pace. As introduced in chapter 4, the lactate/ventilatory or anaerobic threshold pace is the work intensity beyond which blood lactic acid begins to accumulate at an increasing rate. Longer-distance athletes might be able to identify the anaerobic threshold pace as fairly similar to that used in racing over the 15-km and half-marathon distances. (By contrast, their 10,000-m race pace would be roughly 3% to 4% faster than their anaerobic threshold pace and their 5,000-m race pace would be roughly 5% to 7% faster.) This pace is marginally too fast for maintaining conversation and is best described as "comfortably hard" (although some runners who call aerobic conditioning "moderate" often use the term "steady-state" for anaerobic threshold running).

Because acidosis has a stimulatory effect on ventilation, this increased ventilation typically can be both measured in the laboratory and sensed by runners. This increased rate and depth as well as eventual rise in working tissue acidity contribute to the subjective sensation of an increased work load that cannot be maintained indefinitely. Hence, selecting an appropriate length of run as well as running pace is important in planning manageable training sessions. Working at a pace slightly faster than lactate/ventilatory threshold pace optimally stimulates the kinds of adaptive physiological changes that eventually quicken the pace at which this threshold occurs. Although aerobic aspects of performance also improve with training in this pace range, the anaerobic conditioning response is the predominant training benefit.

If treadmill testing is unavailable to specifically identify anaerobic threshold, we suggest that athletes make an initial arbitrary assumption that the threshold occurs at 80% of $\dot{V}O_2$max pace. (Typically, this will be a slight underestimation, but it's better to be too low than too high.) Thus, $\dot{V}O_2$max pace should be reduced by 20% and then two 20-min runs tried at that pace with a 5-min recovery at an aerobic conditioning pace in between. The training session should be "comfortably hard," not so easily manageable that it really is aerobic conditioning, but also not so difficult that it is inordinately stressful. Depending on outcome, the training pace can be slightly increased or decreased to better match fitness.

Depending on heredity and fitness level, the threshold pace may vary from about 75% to as high as 90% of $\dot{V}O_2$max pace. This may represent a heart rate from about 80% to as high as 90% of its maximum value in men, often higher in women because of their smaller hearts. For the runner in figure 4.2 this pace occurred at 86% of $\dot{V}O_2$max pace, or 5:12 min/mi (3:14 min/km), and $\dot{V}O_2$max pace was 4:36 min/mi (2:51 min/km). The faster-paced training in this region can be maintained with minimal accumulating discomfort for anywhere from 15 to 20 min before it is appropriate to slow the pace, permit recovery, and start no more than one additional repetition. For the athlete described in figure 4.2 an appropriate anaerobic conditioning session might include a few kilometers of warm-up, then a 20-min run at lactate/ventilatory threshold pace (5:12 min/mi or 3:14 min/km), one recovery mile at 6 min/mi (3:44 min/km), and a 15-min run at 5 min/mi (3:06 min/km).

Although ST fiber stimulation is emphasized with such training because this pace of training has an even more sizable aerobic stimulus than with aerobic conditioning, there is also an increased activity among FT Type IIa (and perhaps even some FT Type IIb) motor units in the working muscles. Increased glycolytic as well as oxidative enzyme utilization promotes an increased number of such enzymes as part of the adaptation process, along with additional increases in capillarization and plasma volume. The increased metabolic rate in all these fibers does stimulate glycolysis, but there is minimal blood lactate accumulation, making the training load reasonably well tolerated. The ST fibers utilize their specialized form of lactic dehydrogenase to minimize lactate formation, and the small amount of lactate formed by the FT fibers can be used as fuel by nearby oxidative muscle fibers or by other tissues. The relatively high submaximal work load, sustained for a somewhat prolonged period, promotes adaptive changes in cardiac function most noticeable as an increase in ventricular chamber size, thereby increasing stroke volume. The end result of all these adaptations is that submaximal prolonged training becomes more easily manageable.

The most effective marathon race pace is ever so slightly slower than lactate/ventilatory threshold pace. This permits the fastest long-term sustainable running pace without requiring increasing anaerobic energy contributions until near the end of the race, when anaerobic reserves can help initiate a quick finish (Lenzi 1987). Race pace at shorter distances (10,000 m and less), however, is typically faster than the pace at which this threshold occurs. Athletes with a quicker lactate/ventilatory threshold pace have the advantage in that they can race at a faster pace. The best method for introducing an initial training stimulus to raise this lactate/ventilatory threshold pace is faster-paced training sustained for a period long enough to initiate physiological adaptation, yet not so long that needless training discomfort occurs. The reward is a faster sustainable marathon race pace.

One method for determining lactate/ventilatory threshold heart rate is based on the hypothesis that the rate of heart rate rise during exercise of increasing intensity slows at the lactate/ventilatory threshold. This has been termed the *Conconi test*, after Francesco Conconi, who initially described it (Conconi et al. 1982). Figure 5.6 illustrates the use of this test with a set of data obtained from an elite male marathon runner. The athlete wears a portable heart rate monitor and runs around a 400-m track, beginning with a very easily manageable aerobic pace (e.g., a heart rate of about 130-135 beats/min). At each 200-m interval, the pace is increased perceptibly but not greatly (ideally no more than 1 s/200 m). Heart rate values can be either called out at the end of each 200 m by the athlete or stored by the monitor (depending on its sophistication). The coach or an assistant carefully times each 200-m interval and provides feedback to the athlete regarding whether the pace increases are appropriate. Ideally, by about 12 to 16 pace increases the running pace will have increased sufficiently so that the linear rate of heart rate rise will change to a slower but still linear rate. When graphed, this change in slope can be seen easily. The pace at which the rate changed can be determined from the 200-m time just previous to its occurrence. Training sessions can then be designed specifically for this athlete.

Although other investigators have also found Conconi's concept attractive (Bunc et al. 1995), for several reasons the idea has met with considerable skepticism. First, other investigators attempting to duplicate Conconi's observations have not been very successful (Lacour, Padilla, and Denis 1987; Tokmakidis and Léger 1988, 1992). We also find that the kind of clearly seen relationship graphed in figure 5.6 is more a rarity than a common result. Typically the heart rate response does not exhibit a regular and linear change in rate of rise. Second, we find quite frequently that the heart rate of elite-level female distance runners at lactate/ventilatory threshold pace is the same as or very nearly their maximal heart rate; thus, no deflection in rate of rise could occur. Third, there doesn't yet appear to be any good physiological rationale to explain the mechanism by which either an increase in the rate of rise of ventilation or the onset of blood lactate accumulation, each of which characterize the lactate/ventilatory threshold, should be functionally linked to an increase in heart rate. Thus, the best practical method for runners to sense when they have exceeded anaerobic threshold pace is to be sensitive to increased breathing (stopping of conversation, focus shifts from simply passing time while running to the actual work of running).

Aerobic Capacity Training

Once there is a sizable foundation of musculoskeletal and cardiopulmonary development, it is appropriate to insert periodic training sessions intense enough to provide a stimulus to both ST and FT skeletal muscle cells and thus to provide a vigorous but not maximal challenge to both aerobic and anaerobic systems. Aerobic capacity training challenges the maximal aerobic capabilities (although a sizable anaerobic component occurs at the same time) and is carried out at paces similar to those found in racing events from 3,000 m through 10,000 m. The intensity is about 90% to 100% of $\dot{V}O_2$max pace, or about 90% to 95% of maximal heart rate in men (95% to 98% in women). Because this is fast running, each interval of distance run cannot be too long, or the accompanying anaerobic

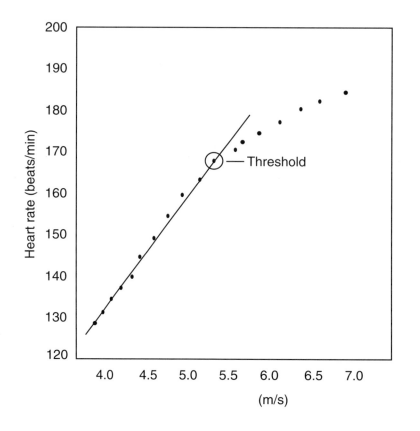

200-m increment	200-m time (s)	Cumulative distance (m)	Pace (m/s)	Heart rate (beat/min)
1	50.5	200	3.96	128
2	49.2	400	4.06	132
3	48.0	600	4.12	135
4	47.0	800	4.26	137
5	45.8	1,000	4.36	141
6	44.7	1,200	4.47	145
7	43.5	1,400	4.60	149
8	41.9	1,600	4.77	154
9	40.1	1,800	4.98	159
10	38.8	2,000	5.15	163
11	37.5	2,200	5.33	168
12	36.0	2,400	5.56	171
13	35.1	2,600	5.70	173
14	33.7	2,800	5.93	175
15	32.1	3,000	6.23	178
16	30.9	3,200	6.47	180
17	29.7	3,400	6.73	182
18	28.4	3,600	7.04	184

Figure 5.6 Use of the Conconi test to determine lactate/ventilatory threshold heart rate.

energy contribution brings excessive fatigue. The first few minutes of each run will be largely anaerobic before circulation and breathing increase to result in aerobic dominance. Then, about 5 or 6 min of aerobically dominant training can occur before the session begins to feel too stressful.

Adequate recovery and rest between running intervals is essential to permit reduction of blood acidity toward resting levels. Otherwise, premature performance debilitation will affect the subsequent running interval. Early exhaustion will require recruitment of additional (accessory) muscles. This not only costs more in fuel usage, because these muscles are not those optimally intended for the movement pattern, but also increases the risk of overuse injury. The tendons of the accessory muscles may not be conditioned sufficiently to accommodate such stress. As fitness improves during a training session, experienced runners find that their required rest between running intervals decreases even though pace is maintained. This is a sure sign of positive accommodation to the training.

Depending on event orientation (middle distance vs. long distance), the acceptable running interval time should not exceed 6 to 9 min, with the pace being quicker or slower depending on the time run. Subsequent recovery (with jogging or slower-paced running) will occur typically within 4 to 5 min, because blood acid accumulation has not been excessive, and the continued increased breathing will provide adequate tissue oxygenation to metabolize the majority of blood acid before the next running interval begins. The typical distances run during aerobic capacity training include repetitions of anywhere from 1,000 m to 3,000 m, depending in part on the athlete's event specialty. The entire training session load can range from about 6,000 m to 8,000 m. In our coaching of longer-distance runners we find it quite effective to cycle such aerobic capacity sessions around a five-week mesocycle, with one such session each week. For example, we might use a week-by-week sequence of $2 \times 3,000$ m, $3 \times 2,000$ m, $4 \times 1,600$ m, and $6 \times 1,000$ m, returning to $2 \times 3,000$ m the fifth week. The longer runs will be more similar to 10,000-m race pace, and the shorter runs more similar to 5,000-m or 3,000-m pace. If physiological adaptation to such training has occurred, the fifth-week session should be more tolerable than the same session done four weeks previously. As improvement occurs, it is not appropriate to quicken the pace beyond 100% $\dot{V}O_2$max intensity. This merely increases the anaerobic component, and that is not the purpose of aerobic capacity training. Instead, the running interval should be lengthened.

The physiological adaptations resulting from this kind of training include:

- an increase in oxidative and glycolytic enzymes in working muscles,
- activation of additional FT muscle fibers that were not stimulated by less-intense training, and
- a small increase in blood buffering capacity.

This is in keeping with the results of research by Fox and colleagues (1973), who suggested that intensity rather than volume of training provides the most complete stimulus for raising $\dot{V}O_2$max to its limits. Near-maximal aerobic metabolism is emphasized in both ST and FT fibers, with anaerobic metabolism providing the additional energy requirements for pace maintenance. The nature of the training stimulus (moderate running time, adequate recovery) keeps blood acidity at a tolerable level. The increased blood acidity does, however, bring a noticeable increase of ventilation, adding to the subjective training stress.

In addition to track-oriented level running, where pace, distance, and time can be controlled precisely, hill running sessions can also be done for aerobic capacity training. However, with longer-distance hill runs, the deviation from level-ground running cannot be very large. Also, the pace needs to be reduced from that maintained over level ground to compensate for the ascent. As an example, a 5:00 min/mi pace (3:06/km) over level ground is roughly equal to a 6:00 min/mi pace (3:44 min/km) at a 4% elevation (2.3°). The exaggerated arm and shoulder action and hip flexor and high–knee lift actions not seen during level-ground running both require added energy. This further increases energy requirements, causing excessive anaerobic accumulation unless pace is appropriately reduced.

Anaerobic Capacity Training

This is very intense training, at anywhere from 100% to 130% of $\dot{V}O_2$max pace and at 95% or more of maximal (all-out) pace—at or close to maximal heart rate. The primary goal of anaerobic capacity training is to improve short-distance racing speed and strength. Anaerobic capacity and high tolerance to acidity must be well developed, particularly for athletes specializing in events in which it is essential to change pace quickly and effectively; to sustain long, fast, end-of-race maximal-intensity running; or to run an entire race faster than $\dot{V}O_2$max pace. Neural capacity to recruit more skeletal muscle fibers is also mandatory. The middle-distance events (800 m, 1,500 m, 3,000 m, and 3,000-m steeplechase) are all contested at paces faster than 100% $\dot{V}O_2$max pace, requiring tolerance of steadily accumulating lactate levels in blood and working muscle tissue. The longer-distance events, particularly 5,000 m and 10,000 m, will also be raced best by those who can maintain the fastest possible pace with the least lactate accumulation until near the end and who then add a large sustained anaerobic component during the final stretch to the finish. Such racing demands that all skeletal muscle fibers (ST and FT) be trained as well as possible. When we study the physiological characteristics of middle-distance runners, we thus find that they have not only relatively high $\dot{V}O_2$max values but also tolerance to quite high maximal blood lactate values. Together, this suggests a generous FT and ST endowment, well-developed neural recruitability, and a high tolerance to tissue acidosis.

Training sessions that increase anaerobic capacity are done at a very fast pace, and thus the distances covered must be fairly short—typically 200 m through 800 m, with a total training session covering between 2,400 m and 4,000 m. Using our runner whose $\dot{V}O_2$max pace is 4:36 min/mi (2:51 min/km) as an example, 120% faster than this pace for a high-end anaerobic capacity training session is 1:50 for 800 m, 55 s for 400 m, and 27 s for 200 m. Because this athlete's best 800-m time is 1:49, it is inappropriate to ask him to attempt repeated 800-m intervals at essentially his personal best pace. However, the 400-m and 200-m intervals ought to be within his grasp. They are run at a pace that he must learn to tolerate longer and longer if he desires to improve his 800-m personal best. A session of two or three sets of (1 × 200 m in 27 s) + (1 × 400 m in 55 s) + (2 × 200 m in 27 s) with, respectively, 90 s, 180 s, and 90 s of recovery and a 10-min period for complete recovery between sets might be a useful anaerobic capacity training stimulus for this runner during the mid- to later stages of his seasonal development. Special emphasis should be given to maintaining excellent running mechanics throughout each run, despite coping with the effects of increasing fatigue.

A characteristic feature of a properly controlled aerobic and anaerobic capacity training session is that the final repetition is manageable at a considerably faster pace than the previous repetitions. For example, a world-class male 1,500-m or mile runner with a good aerobic base needs to develop the ability to manage 20 × 200 m in 28 to 29 s with a 60-s recovery before a racing season begins. Each year Seb Coe regained the ability to run 30 × 200 m in 27 or 28 s with a 45-s recovery. Toward the end of that session, however, he could also manage to run one or two intervals in the 23- to 24-s range. If he was not able to do so, then he was doing the first part of the session too intensely. This fast-paced repetition is the test of excessive anaerobic buildup during such an interval session.

Blood lactate levels continue to rise during the recovery period, and they remain high as the next interval begins, despite the relatively long recovery period. This prolonged high blood lactate level is helpful for improving the body's buffering capacity. A strong developmental stimulus is provided to FT Type IIa fibers, and these fibers seem to have the greatest capability to increase their total tension-generating protein as a training adaptation. This provides a strength-building stimulus, and runners often perceive after several such sessions that submaximal paces now seem considerably easier to maintain. This ease is probably due in part to additional strength, along with improved blood buffering ability, even greater blood volume, and an improvement in neuromuscular recruitment characteristics.

Glycogen and phosphate energy supplies will be utilized extensively in the stimulated skeletal muscle fibers during such high-speed training. ATP reserves will be regenerated within minutes, whereas carbohydrate reserves will require anywhere from 24 to 72 hr to be replaced, depending on intensity and volume of the session. Along with energy supply replacement, restitution of muscle cell electrolyte and osmotic balance and excretion of connective tissue breakdown products must occur for both aerobic and anaerobic capacity training. A wide variety of therapeutic modalities all have their proper place in the hours and days following such sessions. Gentle as well as deep muscle massage, ice water baths, anti-inflammatory medications such as aspirin or ibuprofen, and stretching sessions all are useful to enhance an athlete's timely recovery.

Monitoring Training Intensity Levels Using Heart Rate

If there is one single physiological variable that identifies the total stress load under which an athlete is performing, it is the heart rate. Normally, the heart rate is lowest when sleeping, and at its maximum when doing an all-out dash to the finish line in a race or quickness-oriented track session. A morning heart rate elevated above normal can indicate that full recovery from the prior day's training load hasn't yet occurred. Clearly, monitoring heart rate is of considerable value in evaluating the body's health status and readiness to perform work.

Earlier in this chapter we identified heart rate ranges for the four physiological zones of training. Figure 5.5 indicates heart rate ranges for each zone, expressed as a percentage of maximum. (This departure from the first edition of this book, in which we presented specific heart rate values in this figure, acknowledges the very considerable individual variation in maximum heart rate that makes specific values confusing.) One can determine maximal heart rate simply by setting up an 800-m time trial. After an initial warm-up period, as if preparing for a race, that includes some prerace strides to get the entire body revved up for an all-out effort, the heart rate during the final half minute of the 800 m will most likely be maximal.

How is maximal heart rate measured? Fortunately, today's technology has provided a wide range of heart rate monitors that can be worn on the wrist in a manner similar to a timepiece. In fact, some running wristwatches have a heart rate function built in. This permits instantaneous data while the athlete is still running. Without such a monitor the athlete must periodically stop to palpate either the radial or carotid artery and then count heartbeats for 10 s, a process that can be inaccurate because a fit person's heart rate starts to return to its resting value exponentially. The monitor has built-in sensing equipment to do this. Some heart rate monitors can even store data regarding maximal and minimal heart rates for interval sessions, which can then be uploaded to appropriate computer software for retrieval in the form of a paper record of the cardiac dynamics of that training session.

Many of our elite athletes find heart rate monitoring useful for quite various reasons. Some like to compare their heart rate data from specific training ses-

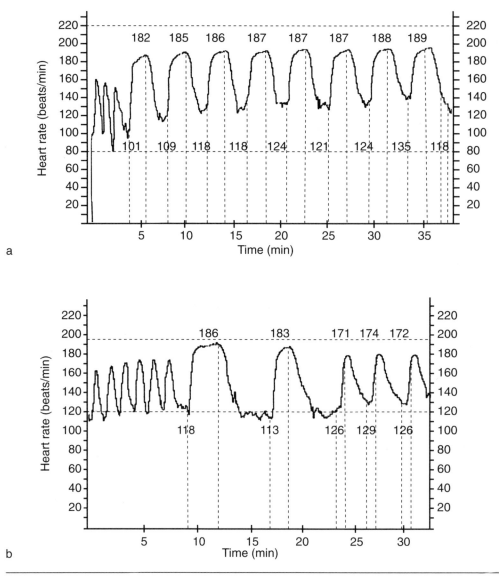

Figure 5.7 Heart rate profiles for an elite-level, female long-distance runner obtained during two track sessions, as described in the text. Maximal and recovery heart rates give useful information about the stress of the session on that particular day.

sions that are repeated periodically during a training mesocycle. If they are getting more fit, they should be able to more easily maintain the assigned running pace over time. This will be reflected in a decreased heart rate while they are running or in a quicker return of heart rate to a temporary resting value. Other athletes like to use heart rate monitoring on their easy days to ensure that they aren't unknowingly getting too carried away with what is intended to be an easy distance run. Still other athletes enjoy using their monitors during track interval sessions to monitor the return of their heart rate to the desired value before starting the next running interval. Athletes who train at altitude can compare the heart rate for a given pace at that altitude to that at sea level, which provides an idea of the added training stress. Over time this can also provide an indication of adaptation. Books have been written about the use of heart rate monitors for fitness evaluation (Edwards 1992), and articles appear yearly in the running magazines (Guralnick 1996).

Figure 5.7 includes actual data generated from a heart rate monitor used by one of our female long-distance runners during two interval track sessions. Heart rate is plotted against time. Figure 5.7a presents the heart rate response as she did the following session:

- 8 × 600 m @ 1:52 (74.6-s/400 m pace) with heart rate around 187 beats/min, with
- 2:00 recovery in the form of a 200-m walk back to the start line on the track.

Note the gradually increasing stress of the workout as seen by the steadily increasing heart rate, successively further from its initial resting value after each 2-min recovery period. Both coach and athlete can find such information quite useful. In this instance, reminding the athlete verbally to "run relaxed" during the interval can help to focus the athlete on a quality performance despite the increasing stress from fatigue.

Figure 5.7b indicates the heart rate dynamics of a more complex training session. We can outline the training session as follows:

- 6 × 100 m, beginning at 15-s/100-m pace and ending at 14-s/100-m pace (heart rate increasing to not more than 170 beats/min)
- 1 × 1,000 m @ 2:45 (66-s/400-m pace; max heart rate of 186)
- 400-m recovery walk (return to a heart rate of 113)
- 1 × 600 m @ 1:36 (64-s/400-m pace; max heart rate of 183)
- 400-m recovery walk (return to a heart rate of 126)
- 3 × 200 m @ 28-s/200-m pace with a 200-m walk as recovery (max heart rate in the low 170s)

These illustrations should indicate that heart rate monitoring can be both informative and fun, provided that athlete and coach do not become too obsessed with it. Care should be taken to purchase good-quality instrumentation. There is little worse for a highly charged athlete, warmed up and ready to perform, than the need to tinker with malfunctioning equipment before the session can begin. Athletes should be sure to shop around before purchasing such equipment, by asking shopkeepers to fully demonstrate each device and by asking fellow athletes about their experience.

Recovery

Five different facets of recovery are important in training: four physical, one mental. They can be identified as follows:

- The recovery between intervals
- The recovery between sets of intervals
- The recovery between hard training days
- The recovery required following injury or overtraining
- The pause needed for mental refreshment

Any good system of training must be flexible in its provision for recovery for two reasons. First, the optimal amount of recovery time can never be exactly determined in advance. Second, inadequate recovery carries with it a sizable injury risk, which should be minimized. Just as challenging sessions have a crucial purpose in providing an overload stimulus (putting the working muscles awash in lactates and initiating adaptive responses), so also the recovery period allows the adaptive regeneration to occur.

Recovery between intervals is related to the level of adaptation already achieved and should be only as long as required to permit performance of the next interval at the target pace. Thus, determining recovery time between intervals is important, because a quality effort from each interval is desired. As a particular mesocycle or microcycle progresses, the combination of running time and recovery time changes in such a way that training intensity is increased. Interval times and recovery times must both be estimated carefully to bring steady adaptation without undue stress. Again using Seb Coe's earlier diaries as an example, sessions of 300 m changed from an early macrocycle work load of 9 to 10 @ 41 to 42 s with a 3-min recovery to a subsequent stimulus of 6 @ 38 s with a 90-s recovery, and finally to 8 @ 38 s with a 45-s recovery. The last 300 m is always done at maximal velocity.

Determining the exact recovery between sets is not quite as critical. Recovery must be long enough to ensure that target paces are achieved during the next set, yet not so long that excessive physiological cool-down occurs or mental commitment is lost. In the early part of a macrocycle, it may not be possible to handle the pace required for intervals without a periodic longer recovery between sets. Dividing intervals into sets (for example, one set of 12 × 400 m into three sets of 4 × 400 m) allows enough intervals at a brisk pace to provide a training stimulus for muscular strength and speed. Both recovery periods (between sets and between intervals) should be active, such as easy jogging, to maintain circulation through the milking action of skeletal muscles on the blood vessels within them.

Recovery between days of hard sessions is sometimes difficult to quantify, but the concepts for assessment are simple enough. Any athlete who feels the aching tiredness in muscles and joints that follows a hard session, even during inactivity, knows without a doubt that recovery time is needed to rebuild muscle energy supplies and connective tissue integrity. This requirement applies to circuit and weight-room sessions as well as to all major running interval sessions at higher intensities. Individuality among athletes regarding tolerance to training intensity makes it appropriate to set a hard-easy-hard day pattern, or hard-hard-easy, or hard-easy-easy, and so forth. Recovery days programmed into each microcycle thus permit the rearrangement of trainings within that microcycle so that no sessions are missed.

SUGGESTIONS FOR SELECTING THE BEST RECOVERY TIMES

Once athletes and coaches have decided on a given number of and pace for intervals of running, the next question asked is, What should the interval of rest between each be? The simplest answer, of course, is enough to ensure that the athlete can complete each interval in the training session at the assigned pace while maintaining quality running mechanics. In turn, this will be determined by the combined effect of the length of the assigned running interval, the weather (temperature and humidity), and the athlete's level of fitness. It makes little sense to permit so little rest that exhaustion sets in before the assigned session has been completed. Mental composure will probably disappear as well. Thus, recovery needs to be adequate to permit the maintenance of good form for the succeeding interval. For longer runs at a slower pace, this recovery will be considerably shorter than the length of time run. For very short intervals, a far longer time than that required to run the interval distance may be appropriate. Table 5.6 provides a basis for estimating recovery times between running intervals expressed as fractions or multiples of the time spent running.

As can be seen from this table, required recovery time increases as running intensity increases. Physiologically, this makes sense. Recall the three major aspects of response and potential adaptation that occur with running. There is neuromuscular recruitment: Increasing intensity of effort stimulates more and more motor units, bringing FT as well as ST motor units into action. Second,

there is myocardial efficiency: Increasing ventricular chamber size produces an increased stroke volume and decreased heart rate at submaximal work loads. The increased volume of blood returning to the heart distends the ventricular chambers with each beat, eventually initiating their enlargement. Finally, there is a management of lactate dynamics: The anaerobic stimulus increases lactate production in skeletal muscles, which diffuses out into the blood. Its effects must be dealt with: Some tissues can use lactate as a fuel, but the accompanying H^+ ions also provide a direct stimulus to increase breathing. Tolerance to the discomfort of acidosis can be developed only through experience with it. As the intensity of running increases, regardless of how much adaptation has occurred, the more all of these performance systems are stimulated, and the longer is the recovery time required before they can be again challenged.

Determining the recovery time is only half the challenge, however. We need to identify the optimal run time, which serves as the basis for determining the recovery time. This is determined by distance; shorter distances can be run more quickly. We recommend a simple and fairly practical method to construct a plan for a fast-paced ($\dot{V}O_2$max or aerobic capacity training) session. We'll assume that the coach and athlete have made a rational decision about the interval distance to be run and the number of repetitions. We need to know the pace and the recovery. Take the athlete's

TABLE 5.6

Estimation of Recovery Times Between Running Intervals

Loading	Running time (RT)	Recovery time	Recovery activity
Short speed (all-out) (anaerobic capacity training)	10 s 20 s 30 s	3 × RT 3 × RT	Walking and/or stretching Jogging
Long speed (95%-100% of maximal effort) (anaerobic capacity training)	30 s 60 s 80 s	3 × RT 2 × RT	Jogging Jogging
Speed + endurance (90%-95% of maximal effort) ($\dot{V}O_2$max to aerobic capacity training)	80 s 2 min 40 s 3 min	2 × RT 1 × RT	Jogging Rest
Endurance (80%-90% of maximal effort) (anaerobic conditioning)	3 min 4 min 20 min	1 × RT 1 × RT	Rest Rest

best time for the interval of distance to be run and decrease it by 25%—that's the running interval time. Then use table 5.6 to determine recovery time.

For example, a female runner whose expertise is at the 5,000 m has a treadmill $\dot{V}O_2$max of 62 ml $\cdot$ kg^{-1} $\cdot$ min^{-1}, and her personal record (PR) for the 5,000 m is 16:34, which is a race pace of 5:20 min/mi (80 s/400 m). Her personal best for 400 m is 62 s, and she wants to do a session of 10 × 400 m at 100% of her $\dot{V}O_2$max. She should complete each run in 62 + (62 × 0.25) = 62 + 15.5 ≅ 78 s, with a recovery time of 78 × 2 = 156 sec = 2:36. As adaptation to this work load occurs and, one hopes, the athlete's $\dot{V}O_2$max increases, the pace can be quickened. After perhaps six weeks the athlete's best 400-m time need be slowed by only 20%: 62 + (62 × 0.20) ≅ 75 s, with a recovery time of 75 × 2 = 150 s = 2:30. When a session like this is done for the first time, plenty of feedback between coach and athlete is essential to determine just how well the athlete's assignment fits the formula. No formula fits all individuals with 100% satisfaction. If slightly more or less rest is appropriate, this information goes into the logbook and serves as the basis for implementation of the next session.

Whether we are working with high school–level athletes or world champions, the emphasis should be on quality work that at the same time is manageable. As performance quality improves, the pace required to maintain that quality will quicken or the length of time at which that pace can be maintained can increase. For 5,000-m and 10,000-m specialists the emphasis is initially on increasing the length of repetitions as development occurs and on decreasing the recovery time, rather than on increasing the tempo. For 800-m and 1,500-m specialists the emphasis is typically on decreasing the recovery time and increasing the tempo. Also remember when planning a session that it is a mistake to consider only the total distance run. At any given pace the intensity of effort is not directly proportional to the distance run. Thus, 30 × 200 m @ 32 s is easier than 15 × 400 m @ 64 s, although the total distance is the same. All these many variables must be considered carefully and, ideally, recorded as notes to permit an optimal rate of athlete development.

Coping with a mild injury or overtraining will be discussed more thoroughly in chapter 8. Should such an event occur, the healing processes of the body require considerable time, and the results of recovery are typically excellent, but one cannot increase the rate at which recovery processes occur. Premature resumption of training in a manner that has the slightest chance of causing a relapse into an injured or overtrained state is unwise. When an athlete is faced with the need for downtime, the important question should not be, "How quickly can I get back to training seriously again?" but rather, "How long should I remain away from serious training?" The difference may appear subtle, but the emphasis is important. The recovery, not the training, is of greatest importance at this point.

A pause for mental refreshment can either be programmed into the training process, or it can be inserted if it appears necessary. It can be very temporary, such as a day off from training, or it can be incorporated into an entire mesocycle in other ways. Athletic success comes only with great dedication and considerable sacrifice of many social pleasures. Thus, when possible, it is desirable to try to ensure an optimal mental attitude whenever possible in addition to a positive physical environment. Depending on resources, several possibilities exist. Particularly for athletes living in a winter climate, moving to a warmer climate for an entire mesocycle can permit quality work in a mentally satisfying situation. Many European distance runners combine a mesocycle of wintertime training (for them) in the summer weather of Australia and New Zealand with a judicious selection of outdoor track or outdoor road races as periodic performance tests along the way. In the United States, where northern winters are even more severe than in some parts of Europe, athletes tend to migrate southward during the winter to Arizona, California, or Florida. Care must be taken, however, to schedule the athlete's return to the home climate at a period when weather is tolerable. Coming back to winter weather can be dismal, particularly if it slows continued development or brings illness.

Objective Evaluation of Multipace Training

Is there any objective evidence that a mixture of both aerobic and anaerobic (distance and speed) training is more effective at building an athlete for better racing performance than simply a steady diet of long-distance running? Such evidence is available, particularly in two noteworthy studies presented at the Twelfth European Coaches Association annual meeting at Acoteias, Portugal, in 1983. Both were the work of Danish investigators.

One study was conducted by Henrik Larsen and Henning Bentzen (1983) from the August Krogh Institute at the University of Copenhagen. These scientists worked with a group of nine male athletes, each of whom had several years of experience in middle- and long-distance running. The first part of the study required that all nine athletes run an average of 100 km/wk (62.1 mi) at a pace of between 60% and 80% of $\dot{V}O_2$max (i.e., aerobically) for 26 weeks. After this period, a GXT was performed and a gastrocnemius muscle biopsy was obtained to assess physiological fitness prior to the next phase of the study. The GXT involved running against a steadily increasing work load to voluntary exhaustion to determine $\dot{V}O_2$max. These athletes were then divided into two groups. Five athletes reduced their total weekly running distance to 50 km (31.1 mi), but half of their training was made up of anaerobic efforts over a distance range of 60 to 1,000 m. This program was maintained for 14 weeks. The other four athletes continued their routine of 100 km/wk for the 14-week period.

Following the training regimen, the same evaluative tests were repeated to assess possible changes in fitness characteristics. The anaerobically trained athletes averaged a 7% increase in $\dot{V}O_2$max with a significant increase in maximal heart rate, whereas those with only aerobic training showed no change. Another evaluation involved two track races over distances of 1,000 m and 10,000 m. Those athletes with the anaerobic component added to their training improved an average of 4 s in the 1,000-m race, but the aerobically trained athletes showed no change. Neither group changed their 10,000-m race performance times significantly, although the trend was for the 10,000-m race times among the anaerobically trained athletes to improve.

Skeletal muscle biopsies were evaluated for biochemical changes that might better describe cellular adaptive specialization after training. None of the athletes had very many FT Type IIb fibers (specialized primarily for glycolytic [anaerobic] activity); most of the FT fibers were Type IIa (specialized for both glycolytic [anaerobic] and oxidative [aerobic] activity). The volume of FT Type IIa fibers of the anaerobically trained runners increased, however, suggesting an adaptive increase in anaerobic responsiveness.

In summary, this study by Larsen and Bentzen suggests that $\dot{V}O_2$max can be improved better by a combination of aerobic and anaerobic training than by aerobic training alone. The greater the aerobic reserve, the more intense can be the levels of performance when anaerobic performance begins to supplement (lactate/ventilatory threshold) and when the aerobic limit ($\dot{V}O_2$max) is reached. Because there is an anaerobic as well as an aerobic limit of work performance, it is optimal to train both, which ensures that aerobic capability is the highest possible at the time when performance requirements are greatest.

The second study was conducted by Thomas Okkels (1983), also at the August Krogh Institute. Its purpose was to study the effectiveness of two intensities of anaerobic training on performance. A group of 16 experienced runners was subjected to an initial, manageable, extended aerobic training period averaging 90 to 120 km/wk (56 to 75 mi/wk) for between 16 and 20 weeks. Accompanying this was a mix of circuit training, hill running, and fartlek running to provide a well-rounded developmental stimulus. Then baseline physiological performance evaluations (GXT and muscle biopsy) were carried out before the group was divided into two subgroups for specialized aerobic training.

The total weekly aerobic training for all 16 runners was then reduced from 90 to 120 km/wk down to 60 to 90 km/wk (37 to 56 mi/wk) for a seven-week period. Seven runners scheduled 3 days/wk of anaerobic capacity training (Okkels termed it "interval training," without further elaboration). These runners ran short-distance sessions (200 m to 600 m) at maximal or near-maximal intensity, with recovery limited to what would allow the runner to complete the session while still maintaining proper running form. The anaerobic capacity training aspects of such sessions were evidenced by capillary blood lactate concentrations of between 15 and 23 mmol/L (135 and 207 mg/dl) after the final repetition. (These lactate values were not corrected for hemoconcentration and thus lose considerable value in helping to explain adaptive changes.) The other nine runners scheduled 3 days/wk of what we would term aerobic capacity training—800 m to 1,500 m intervals done at a fast pace with recovery adequate to permit completion of the session with good running form. Blood lactate levels (uncorrected) following the final repetition were in the range of 10 to 11 mmol/L (90 to 99 mg/dl).

Results of the treadmill GXT to voluntary exhaustion revealed a 4% increase in $\dot{V}O_2$max among those athletes completing the anaerobic capacity training period, but no change in $\dot{V}O_2$max for those runners doing aerobic capacity training. An additional treadmill test was conducted to examine aerobic performance; it was a short-duration run at each athlete's maximal 800-m pace, again to voluntary exhaustion. Both groups of runners improved their anaerobic performance abilities, as measured by this test, by increasing their treadmill run time about 15%. Following this anaerobic treadmill test, blood lactate values measured at 1 min and 4 min posttest were increased by an average of 14% among the runners trained with aerobic capacity training, but were not changed significantly among the runners trained using anaerobic overload. This suggests that the sustained nature of the aerobic capacity training seems better for improving anaerobic output capabilities than are short-term, high-intensity work bouts at an even higher (but shorter) anaerobic work load.

Muscle biopsy studies (again from the gastrocnemius muscle) included evaluation of enzyme profiles. Glycolytic enzyme activity increased between 11% and 22% in the runners who included aerobic capacity training, whereas it either did not change or actually decreased in those doing anaerobic capacity training. Okkels did not discuss the implications of these findings, but several practical suggestions seem appropriate. First, the value of anaerobic capacity training for its ability to stimulate maximal neuromuscular recruitment should not be forgotten, as this is likely a beneficial effect. It probably contributed to the increase in $\dot{V}O_2$max seen in these subjects. However, the results described here suggest that anaerobic capacity training should not be overdone. If it is, the likely consequence is a diminution of glycolytic (anaerobic) performance potential. The cellular explanation for this may involve a combination of decreased available muscle carbohydrates as well as the inhibitory effects of extremely high acid levels on glycolysis itself.

These studies seem to confirm the scientific conclusions summarized in chapter 2 regarding the mobilization of skeletal muscle fibers. Higher-intensity (faster-paced) training will maintain a high level of adaptation in those fibers that are recruited only at higher work loads and may also stimulate synthesis of more skeletal muscle protein in the trained muscles. Both of these increase an athlete's strength capabilities, thereby providing the potential for increased speed and a decrease in perceived (and real) effort sense at given submaximal paces. Not including such higher-intensity training thus deprives athletes of developing their full potential by promoting detraining in muscle fibers that are not activated.

Constructing Your Own Effective Training Plan

The precise details of training plan construction soon come to haunt any coach or athlete; these details are the keys to achieving meaningful long-term development. How do longer-distance running, all the various faster running sessions, and comprehensive conditioning fit into a given time frame that ensures complete development and adequate recovery without undue fatigue? The most important part of any training plan is designing its details to match the needs and abilities of each athlete. Changing abilities to tolerate training stress may cause microcycles to vary in length anywhere between one and two weeks.

All too frequently coaches and athletes yearn to mimic specific day-to-day training plans of other athletes who have been successful. They may be inspired by the notion of quality by association; if the training brought success for that other athlete, then it must be good for them as well. They may also believe that if another athlete and coach have thought of some element of development that is so different from typical training routines, this in itself accounts for the excellence in the athlete's performance.

We suggest that copying such training strategies is not in the best interests of either coaches or athletes. First, their own creativity is stifled, and they are no longer masters of their own destiny. Second, virtually never do two training athletes have similar training environments, competitive racing goals, basic fitness, genetic gifts, and practiced ability to handle each other's training sessions. Third, even for an individual athlete, every training year will be different because of different patterns in scheduling of major races that have been identified as important goals.

Running magazines frequently publish excerpts of "a week in the training diary of . . . ," as if to suggest that "you too can run well—just do this!" Using such brief training plans out of context is seldom meaningful unless they describe a general weekly or fortnightly format that repeats in cyclic fashion for many weeks. Also, without a substantial summary of the previous training loads that have been endured to reach the level of fitness that this athlete has developed over time, readers will not be able to decide if the training load reported matches what they can manage. Athletes who are less fit have a sizable potential injury risk if they attempt such training unprepared.

Studying what others have done can certainly be useful, but such study should focus on development of a general picture of training strategy over weeks or months. The net effect of months of training is more important than the temporary effects of a week-long summary in bringing measurable fitness at the end of a training period. It is always tempting to consider some modifications of training to include new sessions, but it will be difficult to assess whether these alterations were the *specific* cause of any notable performance or fitness changes.

Starting a Training Macrocycle: Be Fully Recovered

Although one year by itself as an expanse of time may not appear very long, a year of hard physical training is. Athletes therefore have a genuine need for full recovery from the previous training period to permit a fresh attack on another year of similar dedicated effort. Complete physical rest and mental refreshment can do wonders, particularly if a break is allowed to last as long as a month or two. Considerable persuasion is needed to convince athletes to "hang up the shoes" for that long, but those who do are better for it, particularly as such a rest permits complete musculoskeletal repair from the accumulated stresses of the macrocycle just completed. Experienced runners most likely will suffer withdrawal symptoms from removal of the once- or twice-daily "fix" of running. Alternative exercises (swimming, biking, hiking, sailing, etc.) will never satisfy this mental training hunger, although they can maintain cardiorespiratory fitness and joint mobility reasonably well. But then, they shouldn't be a total replacement; no habit that is so important a part of one's lifestyle can be extinguished over a period of a month and casually replaced by something else. And oh, how the mind will gain in its enormous desire to begin serious development again!

Resuming training too early is much like pulling an onion out of the garden and discovering that it is not yet fully grown. One cannot thrust it back in and expect more growth! Physiological and psychological fatigue must be fully resolved if the total approach to beginning another training cycle is to be one of excitement, anticipation, and willingness to rededicate one's life to training. Time does heal everything, it is said, but that requires time off!

When various types of mild active rest (unstructured running, nonrunning activities such as hiking, sailing, tennis, swimming, biking) are continued, performance fitness does not deteriorate drastically. An interesting study by Cullinane and colleagues (1986) reported that 10 days of rest reduced plasma volume by 5% and raised resting heart rate by 9 beats/min, but $\dot{V}O_2$max was unchanged in 15 distance runners averaging 80 km/wk regularly prior to voluntary cessation from training. Probably the decrease in $\dot{V}O_2$max that should accompany decreased perfusion to the working muscles was offset by optimal recruitment of motor neurons and replenishment of muscle energy supplies as a result of the complete recovery. Mitochondrial size, enzyme concentrations, and energy storage capabilities in skeletal muscles were not evaluated, but the unchanged $\dot{V}O_2$max also suggests minor changes, if any, in these variables.

Because this recovery period is the first phase in a periodization scheme, coach and athlete need to discuss carefully the goals and objectives for the coming year, the strengths and weaknesses identified during the year just passed, and the possible inclusion of specific strategies during the coming year to remove or reduce weaknesses (increased flexibility exercises, for example, or increased focus on upper-body strengthening). A useful analogy is seen in annual, one-month, full-factory shutdowns that often occur in European industry. A factory overhaul, review of procedures, and incorporation of improvements set the stage for improved productivity during the next year.

Following a several-week layoff, easy and gradual aerobic running is important initially to readapt to impact stress. But not all is lost. When training is resumed, remarkably little time is required—as little as two to three weeks—for distance runners to again be able to handle 8- to 10-mi runs at 90% to 95% of earlier training paces. This is caused primarily by an increase in blood volume, because skeletal muscle mitochondrial content and capillarization are relatively unchanged, unless the layoff has been many months of complete rest due to injury (Coyle 1990). Attention to adequate rest, nutrition, fluid replacement, and

TABLE 5.7

Distribution of Training Load for a Middle- and Long-Distance Runner During a Training Macrocycle

A. Middle distance (800 m - 3,000 m)

Room / Period	Weeks	1 Aerobic conditioning	2 Lactate/ventilatory threshold	3 Aerobic capacity training	4 Anaerobic capacity training	Total running units	Total distance mi	km	5 Mobility	6 Circs & wts	Total units
X_1 (12 weeks) Establish aerobic base	4	5-6	0-1	0	0	5-7	30-40	48-64	4	0-1	9-12
	4	4-5	1-2	1-2	1	7-10	45-60	72-96	4	1-2	12-16
	4	4-5	2-3	2	2	10-12	65-75	104-120	4	2-3	16-19
X_2 (8 weeks) Increasing intensity	4	3	3	2	3	11	70-75	112-120	4	3	18
	4	3-4	4	2	3	12-13	75-80	120-128	4	3	19-20
X_3 (7 weeks) Harder tempo	4	3	5	2	3	13	70	112	5	2	20
	3	3	5	3	3	14	65	104	5	2	21
X_4 (6 weeks) Consolidate	3	3-2	4	3	4	14-13	60	96	4	1	18-19
	3	3-2	4	3	4	14-13	55	88	4	1	18-19

B. Long distance (5,000 m - marathon)

Room / Period	Weeks	1 Aerobic conditioning	2 Lactate/ventilatory threshold	3 Aerobic capacity training	4 Anaerobic capacity training	Total running units	Total distance mi	km	5 Mobility	6 Circs & wts	Total units
X_1 (12 weeks) Establish aerobic base	4	4-5	0-1	0	0	4-6	30-50	48-81	3	0-1	7-10
	4	4-5	1-2	1-2	1	7-10	55-70	89-112	3	1-2	11-15
	4	5-6	3-4	1	1	10-12	75-90	120-145	3	2-3	15-18
X_2 (8 weeks) Increasing intensity	4	4-5	3-4	2	1	10-12	80-95	128-153	3	3	16-18
	4	4-5	4-5	2	1	11-13	80-95	128-153	3	3	17-19
X_3 (7 weeks) Harder tempo	4	4-5	4-5	2	2	12-14	80	128	4	2	18-20
	3	4-5	4-5	3	2	13-15	75	120	4	2	19-21
X_4 (6 weeks) Consolidate	3	4-5	4-5	4	2	14-16	70	112	3	1	18-20
	3	4	4	3-4	2-3	13-15	70	112	3	1	17-19

flexibility maintenance will optimize the adaptive process. More formal training can then begin. The major question is how to structure this training.

Distributing Work Load Through a Training Cycle

Table 5.7 provides our view of one suggested format for the distribution of work load, expressed in units/wk, that might be appropriate for a middle-distance (1,500-m) and long-distance (10,000-m) runner, progressing through the first four training macrocycles (X_1 through X_4). Some caveats are appropriate to give this table proper perspective. First, recall our definition of training unit as a specific assigned modality of work. Second, realize that any given training period may contain more than one unit. A 40-min run of alternating fast and slow miles performed on grass, for example, will involve work in both the aerobic and anaerobic conditioning zones. This constitutes two units of training. Such a session might be followed by a gradual cool-down, and then a session of upper-body strength training in the weight room, adding a third unit to that day's training load.

Second, the schedules outlined in table 5.7 assume that a macrocycle lasts about one year. Starting with 4 weeks of recovery (X_0), then progressing through the 33 weeks of work outlined in mesocycles X_1 through X_4, and finishing with 3 weeks of fine-tuning (X_5) and 12 weeks of competition (X_6) covers 52 weeks. Is it possible to shorten this macrocycle and have two major peaks per year? Perhaps, but another rhetorical question could be asked: Could either peak match one single peak in excellence? To perform superbly at the level of today's major world competitions, multiple peaks of equal excellence may not always be possible. To achieve them, we would have to shorten the length of each microcycle, thus providing less total training and probably inadequate fitness to compete successfully at the highest level.

We mentioned earlier the example of the elite-level, already well-conditioned, uninjured marathon runner who may be able to begin a new macrocycle every four to five months. The slightest deviation in this runner's lifestyle balance—a small injury, a bout with the flu, the need for additional mental rest from the unending strain of focusing on training and competing—can disrupt this rhythm, adding weeks or months of additional preparation time until the next expected peak. Proper development simply cannot be hurried.

Athletes must decide their preference. Would they like to provide the sporting world with a few command performances of enormous quality when the time is ripe as a finale to a profoundly effective building period requiring most of a year? Or would they prefer to be somewhat successful year-round as a result of minor emphases here and there on a generalized plan of training that provides fitness without much substantial improvement? Increasingly, at the highest levels of sport the demands of television, corporate sponsors, and team selection races create the need for more competitive appearances with more performance peaks to permit eventual qualification into major championships. Producing a few truly great performances instead of simply competing at a high level requires both a physical and an emotional peak, which in turn can only be achieved by uncluttered nurturing of talent.

The third point to note in table 5.7 is the attention given to development of strength, power, joint mobility, and kinesthetic awareness by inclusion of several units each week that are labeled simply as *mobility* and *circuits and weights*. These units relate to the development of comprehensive conditioning, which is the subject of chapter 6—training for total-body fitness through activities different from actual running. It is assumed that runners will include appropriate joint-mobility and muscle-stretching exercises each day, particularly after running and before units of weight-room or circuit training, to ensure adequate joint range of motion and muscle length.

Fourth, marathon runners have a somewhat unique necessity for specific emphasis on high-volume aerobic conditioning each week. Thus, their total training distance will often be higher than outlined in table 5.7. The details of strategies for marathon race preparation are discussed further in chapter 7. A sizable increase in susceptibility to overuse injuries, however, occurs in this attempt to build additional aerobic capabilities. Plenty of rest, adequate nutrition to offset the energy losses, training on flat, soft surfaces with shoes that provide good support and impact absorption, and routine use of recuperative modalities such as massage all assume increased importance.

Fifth, training sessions that fit within a particular training zone for one athlete may be so much more difficult (or easy) to tolerate for another athlete that they really belong in a different zone. This may also be true of sessions for particular athletes as they increase their fitness. As one example, consider a session of 5 × 800 m @ 2:20, 2:16, 2:12, 2:08, 2:04 (2 min rec), or a session of 5 × 800 m @ 2:16 with recovery times of 2:00, 1:50, 1:40, 1:30, and 1:20. Such an intensity may be anaerobic conditioning or aerobic capacity training for an 800-m runner, but in the zone of aerobic capacity training or even anaerobic capacity training for a marathon runner. Alternatively, these work loads may be anaerobic capacity training (i.e., faster than $\dot{V}O_2$max pace) for a 1,500-m runner early in a macrocycle but aerobic capacity training (i.e., around $\dot{V}O_2$max pace) for that same athlete after several months of fitness improvement. By reviewing previous training diaries, using time trials or treadmill testing, and carefully monitoring sessions repeated throughout a development sequence, these changing fitness levels can be best identified. If there is ever doubt about optimal training intensity, recovery times should be overestimated and running speeds underestimated; this minimizes the risks of injury and overtraining.

Getting the Best Aerobic/Anaerobic Mix

Except for the majority of a marathon race, virtually all Olympic event distance racing is done at a pace that mandates a steady accumulation of anaerobic metabolites. The shorter the distance of course, the faster is the race pace, and the greater is the relative percentage of anaerobic effort required. Table 5.4 and figure 5.5 illustrates this transition from aerobic to anaerobic emphasis as the race distance shortens. Each race must be run at the proper pace for the particular distance and the particular athlete's ability. Too much anaerobic accumulation and the race will be lost due to fatigue. An excessive premature anaerobic accumulation can occur from three possible causes:

- Beginning too quickly due to a poor sense of pace
- Utilizing tactics that were metabolically too costly
- Being insufficiently fit to race at the required pace

Records in running continue to be broken. Records are broken because runners race ever faster. Over the past 60 to 70 years this rate of improvement has been enormous, yet it is a mere split second in the evolutionary span of our development as a species. In that short split second, we have not suddenly become biomechanically and physiologically more anaerobic or aerobic. Rather, greater participation and larger adaptive training loads produce a larger gene pool of athletes with greater aerobic and anaerobic abilities. As an example, Don Lash, an outstanding American distance runner of the 1930s (world-record holder for the 2-mi in 8:58.4; personal best of 31:06.9 for the 10,000 m, both in 1936), had a $\dot{V}O_2$max of 81.5 ml · kg^{-1} · min^{-1} (Robinson, Edwards, and Dill 1937). Our elite-level male 10,000-m athletes with personal bests faster than 28:00 all have $\dot{V}O_2$max values in excess of 81 ml · kg^{-1} · min^{-1}.

What has caused this quickening of pace for both men and women over time? One factor surely is the replacement of cinder tracks with artificial surfaces. Another likely factor is technical advances in shoe construction. A third is an unprecedented period of relative freedom from global strife, so that young men and women are able to turn their thoughts toward sport rather than war. A fourth is a great increase in the number of competitive opportunities, both financial and athletic, that permit a larger gene pool of athletic talent to remain competitively active for a longer time. A fifth is an improvement in health care provision—nutrition, rehabilitative and restorative modalities, and injury prevention—that permits athletes to train more effectively at a higher level. This in turn permits the addition of an increased anaerobic work tolerance on top of an already highly developed aerobic tolerance: those who buffer acidosis the best will beat the rest!

How can a judicious inclusion of marginally to distinctly anaerobic work be added each week to an already generous diet of aerobic long-distance running? Quite simply, use caution to avoid making the diet of distance volume too excessive. Depending on the extent of ST muscle fiber type dominance in the prime movers, no measurable cardiorespiratory improvement (measured as $\dot{V}O_2$max) will occur beyond more than 60 to 90 mi/wk (96 to 145 km/wk) of aerobic conditioning in elite-level long-distance runners (Costill 1986). Especially for young developing runners, the quantity of aerobic conditioning should be kept considerably below this volume until their working muscles and connective tissues develop the tolerance to such work. Including a well-designed program of comprehensive conditioning (see chapter 6) and some faster-paced running in addition to the endurance base produces a more balanced athlete with many well-developed talents: strength, speed, good range of joint mobility, and anaerobic work tolerance. Our concept of multi-tier training promotes this kind of development.

Tables 5.8 and 5.9 show an aerobic/anaerobic breakdown of Seb Coe's training early in his running career, when he was 16 and 18 years old, respectively. It can be seen that Seb's aerobic/anaerobic ratio in terms of training was roughly 65%:35%. Seb's coach felt that his performance expertise resided on the distance side of the 800-m to 1,500-m events rather than on the sprint side, and thus Seb's training focus was directed accordingly. These two very successful years for Seb, which resulted in national titles and a bronze medal in the European Junior Championships, suggest that his relative training emphasis was suited precisely to his racing needs. Total weekly aerobic distance running was kept to a minimum, and quality speed work was included to provide a complete training stimulus. This event-specific anaerobic training was required to compensate for the aerobic dominance that characterized Seb's (and most distance runners') fitness prior to competitive training.

Practical knowledge about FT and ST muscle fibers and their various properties relating to performance had not reached the lay press in the early- to mid-1970s. Even knowledge about the differing relative amounts of energy (aerobic vs. anaerobic) for the various events was not generally available in the coaching literature. We know now, of course, that long, slow distance running provides

TABLE 5.8

Training Summary and Analysis: Seb Coe, 1973, Age 16

Week	No. of training days	Miles	Km	% effort (aerobic)	% effort (anaerobic)	Races
5	5	11	18	100	0	
6	7	15	24	50	50	XC
7	6	24	29	75	25	
8	6	35	56	82	18	
9	7	47	75	87	13	
10	6	21	34	55	45	
11	5	27	43	49	51	Indoors 800 m
12	3	25	40	80	20	
13	6	34	55	57	43	XC
14	6	30	48	66	34	
15	6	14	22	33	67	
16	5	26	42	23	77	
17 (Apr.)	7	36	58	54	46	100 m; 800 m
18 (May)	6	20	32	75	25	800 m; 1,500 m
19	7	23	37	38	62	800 m in 1:56.0
20	6	21	34	28	72	
21	6	24	38	50	50	3,000-m city ch.
22	6	24	39	77	23	
23	7	39	63	36	64	3,000-m county ch.
24	6	9	14	0	100	1,500-m NCAA
25	6	29	46	73	27	
26	6	23	37	82	18	
27	5	28	45	59	41	3,000-m English schools ch.
28	7	28	45	64	36	
29	7	21	34	50	50	
30	7	29	41	46	54	
31	4	17	27	35	65	1,500-m youth
32	7	24	39	79	21	
33	3	7	11	0	100	3,000-m senior
34	5	26	46	100	0	
35	5	11	17	91	9	
36 (Sept.)	7	20	32	50	50	
37	4	8	13	0	100	1,500 m
38	4	15	24	75	25	
39	5	13	21	88	12	XC
40	5	20	32	100	0	
41	6	21	35	100	0	XC
42	5	23	37	100	0	XC
43	6	13	21	77	23	
44	5	7	11	55	45	
45	5	17	27	17	83	XC
46	4	16	26	100	0	XC
47	6	14	22	50	50	
48	6	26	42	81	19	XC
49	4	14	22	62	38	
50	1	2	3	0	100	
51	5	27	43	100	0	Road race
52	5	21	35	81	19	XC
48 weeks	264/336 days	1,025	1,635	61%	39%	23 races, not including heats
	Average =	21.4 mi/wk,	34.1 km/wk,	5.5 days/wk		

(Weeks 18–37 are bracketed as "Track season.")

Note. XC = cross-country; NCAA = Northern Counties Athletic Association.

TABLE 5.9

Training Summary and Analysis: Seb Coe, 1975, Age 18

Week	No. of training days		Miles	km	% Effort (aerobic)	%Effort (anaerobic)	Races
1 (Jan.)	7		41	66	50	50	
2	6		16	26	70	30	
3	7		47	76	82	18	7-km XC
4	6		34	55	50	50	
5	7		33	53	55	45	7-km XC
6	4		26	42	55	45	
7 (injured)	5		23	37	100	0	
8 (injured)	6		41	66	51	49	
9	7		39	63	45	55	
10	6		28	45	64	36	
11	7		42	68	50	50	
12	6		31	50	61	39	3,000-m indoor
13 (Mar.)	7		47	76	53	47	
14 (Apr.)	6		36	58	91	9	
15	7		31	50	58	42	1,500 m
16	6		28	45	78	22	
17	7		29	47	50	50	
18	6	T	38	61	100	0	1,500 m
19	6	r	19	30	75	25	
20 (injured)	0	a	0	0	—	—	
21 (injured)	0	c	0	0	—	—	
22	5	k	16	26	60	40	1,500 m
23	7	s	33	53	55	45	800 m
24	7	e	39	63	54	46	
25	6	a	25	40	56	44	1,500-m NCAA
26	7	s	31	50	50	50	3,000-m NCAA
27	7	o	37	59	40	60	
28	7	n	39	63	69	31	
29	6		36	58	61	39	
30	7		25	40	60	40	1,500-m AAA
31	6		29	47	60	40	
32	7		33	53	55	45	1,500 m
33	6		37	59	57	43	
34	7		22	35	89	11	1,500 m 3:45.2
35 (Aug.)	5		22	35	78	22	
36 (Sept.)	5		37	59	100	0	
37	6		29	47	89	11	
38	7		38	61	81	19	
39	2		10	16	90	10	
39 weeks 229/273 days 1,167			1,878		66%	34%	12 races, not including heats
Average =	29.9 mi/wk, 48.2 km/wk, 5.9 days/wk						

Note. XC = cross-country; NCAA = Northern Counties Athletic Association; AAA = Amateur Athletic Association. *Higher goals require a sharper focus on fewer targets. Note the reduction in number of races here compared with the number in table 5.8. This change reflects the maturing athlete's realization that bigger events require greater concentration and focus.*

little training stimulus to the FT muscle fibers, leaving any distance runner trained on such a diet unprepared for high-speed racing. But middle-distance runners need to develop endurance through such longer runs if they are to manage multiple high-speed races in a top-level championship. The longer runs help to provide the overall fitness base on which speed training can be placed for specialization. It thus seemed logical in Seb's development to train him specifically for both speed and endurance, keeping the total training load as small as possible to get the job done and having all systems in a progressively greater state of responsiveness. Only later was the beneficial connection between intuition and scientific logic discovered. Even for the longer distances, such as the 5,000 m and 10,000 m, an appropriate combination of speed and endurance is mandated if races are to be won at any competitive level.

We have already presented several examples of individual training sessions and how their intensity will be determined by the combination of natural and developed skills as well as position within a training macrocycle. Thus, no two coaches or athletes will be able to use identical training plans with similar effectiveness. In addition, varying terrain, weather, and availability of facilities all require additional individualization for the athlete to achieve the desired training stimulus. A variety of recently published books have suggested specific weekly and monthly training schedules for athletes of varying abilities and event ambitions. Some of these are quite good and can serve as a source of variations for daily training plan design (Dellinger and Freeman 1984; Galloway 1984; Humphreys and Holman 1985; Wilt 1968). The *optimal development plan* will

- use available training facilities,
- strike a balance between intensity and volume of training,
- be sensitive to individual abilities,
- use valid scientific concepts to progressively increase training volume and intensity, and
- ingeniously provide a continually stimulating and challenging training stimulus.

Table 5.10 provides a specific outline of a 12-day training block for a middle-distance (1,500-m) athlete and a 14-day block for a long-distance (10,000-m) athlete. Though specific in nature, these schedules permit identification of several key general principles. One principle involves the inclusion of rest. Note that there are one or two potential rest days, which can be positioned as needed. An essential part of training is regeneration, both mental and physical, from prior training. If this is best achieved by an entire day off, so be it. Training ought not to consume every single day of any runner's sport career. This puts the runner into a very deep rut indeed, and there is little difference between a rut and a grave, save for the depth. If easy training (mentally low key as well as physically manageable) is appropriate, that is fine as well. Typically, the day off (or off-day) serves to invigorate body and soul for good-quality training in the few days following.

A second principle involves use of the multipace concept—training at both faster and slower than race pace for the athlete's primary event. Notice how the middle-distance runner's 12-day block is constructed around a framework in which the faster sessions steadily get shorter in total distance and quicker in pace as the block progresses. Thus, as seen in table 5.10*a*, the total distance covered on day 10 (1,580 m) is much less (but more intense) than the 3,400 to 5,100 m done on day 8. Multipace training is implemented for the long-distance athlete as well, but with a different overall pattern.

Tables 5.11 and 5.12 provide some specific examples of how training plans can be constructed using the aforementioned guidelines. They have been extracted from Seb Coe's early training diaries and were selected particularly for the benefit of younger athletes and their coaches. Seb was 16 years old in 1973 (table 5.11), 18 in 1975 (table 5.12). Realize, of course, that many months of prior training had preceded these few-week blocks leading up to his important competitions, and he was in a tapering phase. Nevertheless, even then the multipace

TABLE 5.10

Generalized 12- and 14-Day Training Blocks

(a) Middle distance

Day	Session	Pace
1	3 × 2,000 m or [(3 × 1,200 m) + (2 × 800 m) + (2 × 400 m)][a]	5,000 m
2	Over-distance fartlek	
3	6 to 8 × 800 m[a]	3,000 m
4	Distance running on roads	
5	16 to 30 × 200 m alternating with 10 × 400 m[a]	1,500 m
6	Potential rest day (if race); if not, fartlek	
7	Race or time trial	
8	4 to 6 × 400 m alternating with 6 to 9 × 300 m	800 m
9	Distance running on roads	
10	(1 × 300 m) + (2 × 200 m) + (4 × 100 m) + (8 × 60 m)	400 m
11	Over-distance fartlek	
12	Rest if racing next day; if not, choose pace for next race	

[a]Will be run at a faster pace when in peaking stages for major races.

(b) Long distance

Day	Session	Pace
1	A.M. long run of 12-20 mi, easy	
2	A.M. no run; P.M. 7 mi easy	
3	A.M. 7 mi steady; P.M. (4 × 200 m with 200-m jog) + (4 × 2,000 m with 3-min jog) + (4 × 200 m with 200-m jog)	1,500/5,000 m
4	A.M. 7 mi easy; P.M. 10 mi easy with occasional accelerations to 10-km race pace, sustained for 2 min	
5	A.M. 15 mi easy; P.M. no run	
6	A.M. no run; P.M. (4 × 300 m with 300-m jog) + (6 × 800 m with 3-min jog) + (4 × 200 m with 200-m jog)	1,500/5,000 m
7	A.M. 9 mi easy; P.M. no run	
8	A.M. long run of 12-17 mi easy	
9	A.M. 5 mi steady; P.M. no run	
10	A.M. 9 mi easy; P.M. (4 × 200 m with 200-m jog) + (5 × 1,000 m with 2-min jog) + (4 × 200 m with 200-m jog)	1,500/5,000 m
11	A.M. no run; P.M. 7 mi easy	
12	A.M. 5 mi steady with several accelerations to 10-km race pace, sustained for 2 min	10,000 m
13	Single easy run if race the next day; if not, 2 distance runs, 5-7 mi and 7-10 mi, the latter with fartlek	
14	Race; if not, 2 × 15-20 min at lactate/ventilatory threshold pace	Marathon

development scheme permitted continuity in all aspects of competitive excellence, thereby preparing a well-rounded athlete for competition.

Identifying Strengths and Weaknesses

For any given athlete, it will be much easier to complete training at some paces than at others. There are a few reasons for this. One is different genetic predispositions. Athletes with a genetic emphasis on ST motor units may likely find short-distance, fast-speed training relatively more difficult than their friends with

TABLE 5.11

Prechampionship Buildup to Illustrate Multi-Tier Training: Seb Coe, Age 16

Day	English Schools Championships 3,000 m, July 1973	AAA Youth Championships 1,500 m, Aug. 1973
1	3-km steady warm-up (10 × 100 m) + (6 × 200 m) + (2 × 300 m) + (1 × 400 m)	School races, 800 m and 1,500 m
2	10-km cross-country running	15 km on road; first 7.5 km fast, second 7.5 km steady
3	7 × 800 m on road (2:15 per 800 m)	(4 × 400 m) + (4 × 150 m)
4	(1 × 300 m) + (2 × 200 m) + (4 × 100 m)	3 × (10 × 200 m) with 5-min recovery between sets
5	(4 × 400 m) in 56, 55, 57, 60 s	7 × 800 m (avg. 2:15 per 800 m)
6	Rest day	(2 × 150 m) + (6 × 100 m) + (2 × 200 m) + (8 × 80 m)
7	A.M. 10-km cross-country P.M. 5 × 200 m	(2 × 200 m) + (4 × 400 m) + (4 × 200 m)
	Week total = 25 mi (40 km)	Week total = 30 mi (48 km)
8	(20 × 200 m) with 45-s recovery	14-km cross-country running
9	A.M. 4 km fast; (4 × 800 m) + (1 × 400 m) P.M. (6 × 800 m)	Rest day
10	A.M. (30 × 100 m) up 10° hill P.M. 1,000 m + 400 m + 300 m + (4 × 200 m)	(7 × 800 m)
11	A.M. 10 km on roads P.M. (2 × 400 m) + (2 × 200 m)	(10 × 400 m)
12	A.M. 8 km P.M. 15 × 200 m	A.M. 8 km P.M. (5 × 200 m) + (2 × 300 m) + (3 × 100 m)
13	Rest day	(30 × 100 m) up 10° hill with jog-back recovery
14	Race 3,000 m (first place)	1,500-m heats
15		1,500-m final (first, in 3:55 with last 300 m in 42 s)
	Week total = 28 miles (45 km)	Week total = 17 mi (27 km)

a higher endowment of FT motor units. As the adaptive effects of training bring greater fitness, the running paces will quicken, and recovery times can decrease. The athlete will gradually increase fitness over the entire range of running paces. This subtle manipulation of intensity, volume, and recovery is the running world's version of the progressive resistance/overload concept that weight lifters have used in strength training since the 1940s. This concept will be more fully discussed in chapter 6.

Another reason is the varying rates of adaptation in different tissues. Acquisition of endurance typically takes longer than acquisition of speed, primarily because cardiovascular adaptations are slower to develop than neuromuscular adaptations. But speed training is more difficult because of its greater intensity. For this reason speed training sessions during the earlier mesocycles will of necessity be at slower paces, although the *relative intensity* of such training may be comparable to faster sessions later on. It is important for athletes and coaches to know whether the need for improvement is greater on the quickness end or the endurance end of the chosen distance specialty. Once this is known, some specialization in that direction can bring proper consolidation of overall skill. But how does one determine these so-called *equivalent multiple-event paces?* Table 5.13 provides one mechanism for answering this question.

We have constructed three sets of formulas for determining equivalent race performances over several distances when the performance for one distance is

TABLE 5.12

Prechampionship Buildup to Illustrate Multi-Tier Training: Seb Coe, Age 18

Day	NCAA 1,500-m/3,000-m Championships[a]	European Junior Championships
1	11-km distance running	A.M. weights P.M. 14-km distance running
2	Raced 800 m	A.M. 6.5-km distance running P.M. 20 × 200 m (28 s)
3	A.M. 8-km distance running P.M. 30 × 100 m (10° hill)	A.M. 6.5-km distance running P.M. (4 × 400 m) + (1 × 1,600 m)
4	7-mi distance running	4 × 150 m @ 18 s/150 m, 3 × 300 m @ 41 s, 1 × 400 m @ 60 s
5	7 × 800 m	A.M. 6.5 km distance running P.M. 10 × 400 m @ 60 s
6	11-mi distance running	Light weight training
7	A.M. 1 × (400 m + 300 m + 200 m + 150 m) P.M. 5-km recovery run	7 × 800 m (avg. 2:10 per 800 m)
8	4 × 1,200 m	1 × (200 m + 400 m + 200 m + 300 m) + 4 × 100 m
9	10 × 150 m	10-km distance running
10	A.M. 30 × 100 m (10° hill) P.M. 6.5-km distance running	6.5-km distance running
11	7 × 400 m	A.M. 6.5-km distance running P.M. strides and accelerations
12	11-km distance running	Raced 1,500-m heats
13	A.M. 6.5-km distance running P.M. 10 × 100 m	Raced 1,500-m final (3:45)
14	5-km distance running 14-day total: distance running = 83 km interval running = 22.75 km warm up and cool down before and after intervals = 63 km	11-day total: distance running = 56.5 km interval running = 20.2 km warm up and cool down before and after intervals = 32 km
15	Raced 1,500-m heat and final (3:50)	
16	Rest	
17	A.M. 6.5-km distance running P.M. 1 × (200 m + 400 m + 300 m + 200 m)	
18	A.M. 7-km distance running P.M. 20 × 200 m	
19	1 × (100 m + 300 m) + (2 × 400 m)	
20	A.M./P.M. 8-km distance running	
21	8-km easy pace running	
22	Raced 3,000-m final (8:14.2)	

[a]NCAA = Northern Counties Athletic Association.

known. Three tables are better than one because of each individual runner's specific event and ability to manage speed and endurance. To utilize a single table for all athletes would counter our concepts of individual and event specificity. Table 5.13*a* is primarily for the longer-distance specialists—those with competence at 8 km, 10 km, and 15 km who may also run marathons (or have an interest in doing so) but who also actively compete at 5,000 m for speed development. Table 5.13*b* is primarily for the 3,000-m and 5,000-m specialists who also enjoy racing either the next longer (10,000 m) or next shorter distance (1,500 m) on occasion, but who rarely compete in the 800 m. Table 5.13*c* serves the

TABLE 5.13

Suggested Formulas for Estimating Equivalent Times
Over Five Race Distances

Marathon	=	4.76 Y						
10,000 m	=	Y	10,000 m	=	2.1 Y			
5,000 m	=	0.48 Y	5,000 m	=	Y	5,000 m	=	3.63 Y
3,000 m	=	0.28 Y	3,000 m	=	0.58 Y	3,000 m	=	2.15 Y
1,500 m	=	0.13 Y	1,500 m	=	0.27 Y	1,500 m	=	Y
	A		800 m	=	0.13 Y	800 m	=	0.48 Y
			400 m	=	0.06 Y	400 m	=	0.22 Y
				B			C	

needs of the 800-m and 1,500-m runners who typically stay away from distances over 5,000 m. The shaded areas represent distances contested less frequently by each group.

In table 5.13 *a, b,* and *c,* respectively, Y = the athlete's 10,000-m, 5,000-m, and 1,500-m best performance. To calculate this athlete's comparable time for events longer and shorter than these distances, simply multiply Y by the indicated appropriate value. An example showing the use of this table can be given using data from one of our own athletes. Keith Brantly's best 10,000-m time (28:02) is a road mark set in February 1989 over a flat, certified loop course in a highly competitive race run under cool conditions. His best performance in the 1,500 m (3:45.49) occurred in late May in very warm and humid weather (in Florida) as a tune-up for a personal best 5,000-m effort of 13:40.20 at his national championships three weeks later in similarly difficult conditions (in Houston). Using table 5.13*a,* on the basis of his 10,000-m effort, Keith's 1,500 m and 5,000 m personal bests should be 3:39 and 13:27 if the races were run under conditions similar to those of the 10,000 m. These are faster than Keith has achieved, but they are reasonable expectations and show that the effect of weather slowed these performances by 2% to 3%. Keith at that time considered himself a 5,000-m to 10,000-m specialist and thus could utilize either table 5.13 *a* or *b* for estimating comparable performances. In this present instance, table 5.13*b* would not provide a meaningful estimate, as his 5,000-m personal best was slowed by weather. (Those calculations, for example, suggest a personal best at 10,000 m as 28:42, which is far too slow.)

Assessing Performance Improvements Over Time

Achieving personal best times is always enjoyable and an unequivocal indicator of improvement. As runners develop expertise over a range of distances, it becomes useful to learn whether developing excellence at one distance is comparable to doing so at another distance. As an athlete's, particularly a younger runner's, strength and endurance increase from growth as well as from training, such monitoring is important. For younger runners the equations presented in table 5.13 may not be quite as accurate. One method that has gained popularity in

TABLE 5.14

Esso Five-Star Award Scheme for Evaluating Athletic Performance Over Several Distances

Points	Sprints			Distance			Age
	100 m	200 m	400 m	800 m	1,500 m	3,000 m	18 years
Amount per extra point	0.05	0.1	0.2	1 s	2 s	4 s	16 years
100		22.6	50.3	1.57	4.02	8.48	
99	11.0	22.7	50.6	1.58	4.04	8.52	15 years
98		22.8	50.9	1.59	4.06	8.56	
97	11.1	22.9	51.2	2.00	4.08	9.00	
96		23.0	51.5	2.01	4.10	9.04	
95	11.2	23.1	51.8	2.02	4.12	9.08	
94		23.2	52.2	2.03	4.14	9.12	
93	11.3	23.3	52.6	2.04	4.16	9.16	
92		23.4	53.0	2.05	4.18	9.20	
91	11.4	23.5	53.4	2.06	4.20	9.24	
90		23.6	53.8	2.07	4.22	9.28	14 years
89	11.5	23.7	54.2	2.08	4.24	9.32	
88		23.8	54.6	2.09	4.26	9.36	
87	11.6	23.9	55.0	2.10	4.28	9.40	
86		24.1	55.5	2.11	4.30	9.44	
85	11.7	24.3	56.0	2.12	4.32	9.48	
84		24.5	56.5	2.13	4.34	9.52	13 years
83	11.8	24.7	57.0	2.14	4.36	9.56	
82	11.9	24.9	57.5	2.15	4.38	10.00	
81	12.0	25.1	58.0	2.16	4.40	10.05	
80	12.1	25.3	58.5	2.17	4.42	10.10	
79	12.2	25.5	59.0	2.18	4.45	10.15	
78	12.3	25.7	59.5	2.19	4.48	10.20	
77	12.4	25.9	60.0	2.20	4.51	10.25	
76	12.5	26.2	60.5	2.21	4.54	10.30	
75	12.6	26.5	61.0	2.22	4.57	10.35	
74	12.7	26.8	61.5	2.23	5.00	10.40	
73	12.8	27.1	62.0	2.24	5.03	10.45	
72	12.9	27.4	62.5	2.25	5.06	10.50	
71	13.0	27.7	63.0	2.26	5.09	10.55	
70	13.1	28.0	63.5	2.27	5.12	11.00	
69	13.2	28.3	64.0	2.28	5.15	11.05	
68	13.3	28.6	64.5	2.29	5.18	11.10	
67	13.4	28.9	65.0	2.30	5.21	11.15	
66	13.5	29.2	65.5	2.32	5.24	11.20	
65	13.6	29.5	66.0	2.34	5.27	11.25	12 years
64	13.7	29.8	66.5	2.36	5.30	11.30	
63	13.8	30.1	67.0	2.37	5.33	11.35	
62	13.9	30.4	67.5	2.39	5.36	11.40	
61	14.0	30.7	68.0	2.40	5.39	11.45	
60	14.1	31.0	68.5	2.42	5.42	11.50	
59	14.2	31.3	69.0	2.43	5.45	11.55	
58	14.3	31.6	69.5	2.45	5.48	12.00	
57	14.4	31.9	70.0	2.46	5.51	12.10	
56	14.5	32.2	70.5	2.48	5.54	12.20	

Data for Seb Coe are plotted from ages 12 through 18 to illustrate how progression in performance can be plotted over time. Some performances for ages 16 and 18 years are off the chart but are still plotted. The ideal situation would be to have these performance lines horizontal, indicating uniform development of speed as well as endurance over time. Deviations from horizontal thus indicate strengths or weaknesses which can be improved through appropriate specific training.

Britain for profiling such youthful performance improvement is the Esso-sponsored Amateur Athletic Association Five-Star Award Scheme. Youngsters convert results from track and field (athletics) performances into a point score modified by inclusion of bonus points. In table 5.14 we reprint a portion of one of these award schemes and superimpose data for Seb Coe over various distances as he developed from age 12 through age 18. Such tables permit comparison of relative quality of performances over various running distances and also permit analysis of improvement over time. Improvements over time have a greater point value and when graphed show a rise toward the top of the table.

A practical example of intelligent use of information from such performance ranking systems explains some fundamental decisions made early in Seb Coe's athletic development. When he was 12 years old, Seb joined an athletics club, and along with his school sports he had the opportunity to run occasional short sprint races. Although he was quite nimble because of his slim physique, his running showed a significant lack of endurance. To remedy this, some distance training and participation in boys' cross-country were included. The combined beneficial effect was marked indeed, as seen in table 5.14. Seb's performance results at age 13 soared in the longer track events, yet remained relatively static in the shorter events. An incorrect interpretation of these data, we believe, would be that Seb should have stopped his short-distance sprint training or that he was a "born marathoner" and should have begun to so specialize. The proper interpretation is that the improvement in endurance was caused by a shift in training specificity, the adaptation being appropriate to the stimulus applied.

As Seb progressed through his 14th year, a positive effort was made to improve the balance between speed work and endurance work—but neither one at the expense of the other. As can be seen in table 5.14, improvements occurred over the entire spectrum of tested distances, from 100 m through 3,000 m. Where the plotted points permitted the construction of a horizontal line through various test distances, this indicated the event range where Seb's development was of comparable quality. For Seb, it was easier to adapt to the training required for the 800 m and the 1,500 m than for the 400 m, indicating that he most likely had a generous endowment of *both* FT and ST skeletal muscle fibers rather than a predisposition toward FT as is more typical among sprinters. An attempt to maintain the performance line in table 5.14 as horizontal as possible ensured that neither the speed nor the endurance components of his training were unduly overemphasized.

Another way of profiling athletic performances across several events is to use the International Amateur Athletic Federation (IAAF) scoring tables. These can be useful in suggesting possible performance shortfalls as an athlete moves up the performance success ladder. In our earlier years of working with athletes we used the so-called Belgrade edition of these tables (International Amateur Athletic Federation 1977). More recently, the so-called Hungarian scoring tables (Spiriev, Spiriev, and Kovacs 1992) have been revised and updated to include tables for both men and women. As an example to illustrate the usefulness of such tables, depicted in figure 5.8*a* are the performances (with their appropriate Belgrade point values) that Seb Coe delivered for the 800 m, the 1,000 m, and the mile during his exciting summer of 1981—all world records. Though the world marveled at how he could manage to run so well in race after race, the fact was, as seen here, that the 1,000-m and mile efforts corresponded well in terms of fitness quality to his earlier 800-m performance.

A simple interpolation, however, also indicates that Seb should have been capable of running 3:29 for 1,500 m, but optimal racing conditions just never materialized. These finally occurred five years later, three weeks short of his

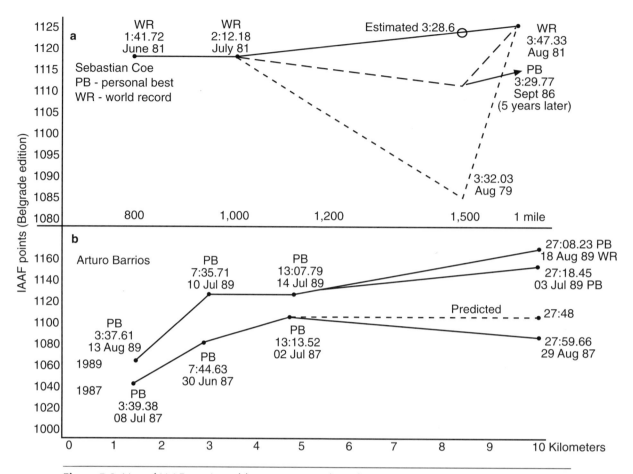

Figure 5.8 Use of IAAF scoring tables to assess quality of competitive race performances for Sebastian Coe (*a*) and Arturo Barrios (*b*). Details of racing strategies are found in the text, but as shown here, the higher the point value for a given performance, as indicated on the vertical axis, the greater is its degree of excellence. Graphing the relative positions of an athlete's best performances for several race distances during a single season permits identification of strong and weak events. A line connecting each performance for the year permits both delineation of one year from another, and assessment of relative success each year in the events being compared. The more horizontal the line that connects a series of compared performances, the more similar they are in quality.

30th birthday, in Rieti after the European Championships of 1986. The time was ripe; his fitness was appropriate as judged by his 800-m and 1,500-m Championships double at Stuttgart. Following that double, it was a simple decision to attempt to bring home the long-deserved mark in the 1,500 m rather than experiment with other events. Again, the world marveled, but to us the race and the result simply made logical sense (Miller 1992, 151-52).

A similar kind of assessment is effective for evaluating the performance of long-distance runners. During the summer of 1987, for example, Mexico's Arturo Barrios set as a goal to lower his personal best performances in shorter distance events in preparation for the Rome World Championships. His major competitive asset was his highly developed endurance capability, but his liability was less well developed raw speed. Improving his speed, combined with his endurance fitness, could give him optimal preparation for Rome. True to his desires, on the European track circuit during July he achieved personal bests in the 5,000 m (13:13.52), the 3,000 m (7:44.63), and the 1,500 m (3:39.38). Were these results comparable in quality? And what might he have expected as a possible goal for the Rome 10,000-m race under good conditions? Use of the IAAF scoring tables provides insight into these questions, and figure 5.8*b* graphs Arturo's performances in relation to their equivalent point values.

His longer distance performances were of the greatest quality, the 5,000 m and 3,000 m being similar in point value (1,106 and 1,083, respectively). His 1,500-m performance was slightly slower by comparison (1,040 points) but was still an improvement for him in the middle-distance range. A 10,000-m performance comparable to the 5,000-m and 3,000-m results would be, respectively, 27:48 and 28:05. He placed fourth at Rome with 27:59.66 despite stopping temporarily at the end of 24 laps due to reigning confusion among participants regarding elapsed laps.

During the summer of 1989 Arturo returned to Europe with the similar goal of improving his best track performances. Five of his major races in 1989 are graphed in figure 5.8*b*. His first race upon arrival was over 5,000 m (13:32.63), slowed somewhat by time zone acclimatization and less-than-ideal racing circumstances (not depicted). Eight days later he was ready to challenge his best 10,000-m time. In Stockholm, his 27:18.45 victory (as shown, worth 1,145 points) was outstanding indeed—nearly a 7-s personal best improvement. He followed this seven days later in Nice with a 7:35.71 for the 3,000 m (1,129 points), again a personal best improvement (by nearly 9 s). The Stockholm race was slightly better in quality using the IAAF point system, but the two were comparable. Four days later (on 14 July 1989), in London, he lowered his 1987 5,000-m personal best by nearly 5 s to 13:07.79 (1,123 points). Such consistency at the highest level led Arturo to believe that a brief period of rest followed by a modest additional dose of very high quality training to provide fine-tuning could give him the mental and physical preparedness for an assault on the world 10,000-m record.

His preparation proceeded optimally—recovery, training, travel back to Europe, a few tune-up races (one of which gave him a personal best of 3:37.61 for 1,500 m and proved that his speed was well honed), and he was ready. On the evening of August 18, five days after his 1,500-m best, with favorable racing conditions (good-quality athletes to set the initial pace and a supportive audience at Berlin's Olympic stadium), Arturo thrilled the world with a wonderful run of 27:08.23. This was a clear testament to the value of an athlete carefully planning a peak, racing seldom but under meaningful circumstances, and realizing that a foreign environment and challenging races both require time for physical and mental regeneration as well as preparation. We would thus urge those who read this book to become familiar enough with the formulas presented in table 5.13 and the 1992 (Hungarian version) IAAF scoring tables for performance comparisons. The time is well spent in carefully assessing an athlete's progress and differential rates of improvement, which suggest strengths and weaknesses, in the various events.

The advent of computer graphics has offered other possibilities for evaluating the progression of competitive performance quality over time. Figure 5.9 illustrates a graphic plot of one of our elite female middle distance runners' performances from 1993 through 1996. First we used computer-generated tables of what we call performance equivalents for each of her races, ranging from 800 m through 3,000 m (Daniels and Gilbert 1979), to obtain a comparable indicator of performance quality. The equivalents suggest the $\dot{V}O_2max$ that might be expected for an athlete capable of delivering the performances achieved, realizing that additional elements such as anaerobic threshold and running economy contribute to performance as well. Using Microsoft Excel, we simply listed her performance by date and performance equivalent and used the ChartWizard graphic

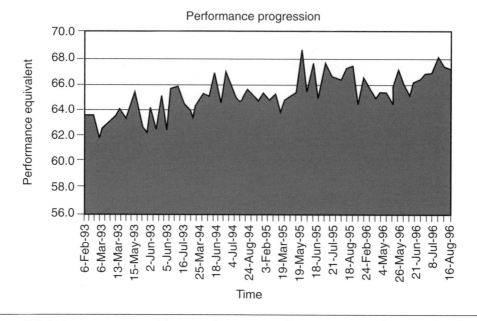

Figure 5.9 Using computer graphics to evaluate race performance is a good way to identify improvement, stagnation, or deterioration over time. Performances for races of different distances must first be converted into comparable units of quality. Shown here for a female distance runner are the performance equivalents for her race results from 1993 through 1996. Plotting point values using the Hungarian scoring tables could be equally informative.

capabilities to produce the illustration shown in figure 5.9. It is clear that this athlete has been steadily improving her performance ability. Her performance highs and lows are influenced by weather, fitness, quality of competition, and level of fatigue going into the competition, but the overall trend toward improvement is clearly visible. A similar plot would have resulted if we would have obtained the equivalent point value for each race using the Hungarian scoring tables.

A few other performance assessment systems exist for estimating performance potential in individual running events. One example is the Kosmin test for projecting performance in the 800 m. The athlete must run all-out for 1 min, followed by a 3-min recovery. The distance covered is measured accurately in meters. Then, another 1-min, all-out run is done; again, the distance covered is measured, and now the two distances are summed. By using the formula

$$T(800 \text{ m}) = 217.4 - (0.119 \times D) \tag{5.5}$$

where D = the distance run, the expected 800-m race time T can be estimated. Table 5.15 gives projected 800-m times based on 2×60-s test-run distances between 805 m and 950 m. This formula should be effective for athletes of all abilities. Obviously, those with little 800-m running experience will not cover nearly as much distance in their 1-min, all-out runs, indicating poorly developed anaerobic skills, and so their projected 800-m time will be considerably slower.

Suggestions for Better Use of Multi-Tier Training

A variety of different types of activities have been developed over the years to take advantage of training terrain and to simulate various aspects of racing.

TABLE 5.15

Use of the Kosmin Test to Project 800-M Race Times

Distance run in 2 x 60 s (m)	Projected 800-m time
805	2:01.6
810	2:01.0
815	2:00.4
820	1:59.8
825	1:59.2
830	1:58.6
835	1:58.0
840	1:57.4
845	1:56.9
850	1:56.2
855	1:55.7
860	1:55.1
865	1:54.5
870	1:53.9
875	1:53.3
880	1:52.7
885	1:52.1
890	1:51.5
895	1:50.9
900	1:50.3
905	1:49.7
910	1:49.1
915	1:48.5
920	1:47.9
925	1:47.3
930	1:46.7
935	1:46.1
940	1:45.5
945	1:45.0
950	1:44.4

Note. Recovery time between runs = 3 min; 800-m time (s) = 217.4 − (0.119 × distance run).

These activities add variety and spice to training sessions, and at the same time improve specific aspects of fitness. We list here those that we have found most useful and enjoyable.

Fartlek

Fartlek is a Scandinavian term roughly translating as speed-play. It consists of runs over mixed terrain at varied paces. In the past, it was part of Sweden's military training. The Swedish coach Gosta Holmer applied this concept of "go-as-you-please" training to the development of distance runners. On first consideration it sounds delightful. Training out in the forest, on wooded trails, and on back roads, runners who combine inventiveness, motivation, and self-discipline can run together or alone, changing pace at various points determined by arrival at some selected object (such as a telephone pole or large rock or tree). The constant pace changing, varied terrain, and soft footing provide quality fitness development in the natural beauty of the wilderness.

Although this may be a good training system for experienced athletes, younger and less experienced runners may require more structured assistance to achieve proper value from this style of training. Also, there is a risk of some problems if fartlek is carried out with a group of runners of mixed abilities. Some will tire less quickly than others and push the pace, leaving those less fit hanging on for dear life. For the tiring runners, this is not training; it is hell and a risk for injury, overtraining, and negative mental attitudes. Unless the coach of such a group is out on the course, he or she will most likely not learn who has profited well by the training and who has suffered until it is too late. We wonder whether the benefits of such an unstructured session outweigh the potential hazards.

A controlled version of fartlek training can be done on a golf course or in a park that has loops within earshot of a centrally placed coach. A grassy terrain with some hilly slopes and a quality running surface is really best. After an adequate 15- to 20-min warm-up, the athlete starts out on a prescribed route visible to the coach. When the coach blows the whistle, the athlete immediately quickens pace to between 75% and 90% of maximum for between 30 s and 2 min, until the next whistle blast signals a slowing to ongoing running pace. The emphasis is on maintaining excellent running mechanics and successfully negotiating hills or obstacles, despite these widely different running paces.

There are both assets and liabilities to this kind of session. What are the assets? The athlete must respond to an outside signal and surge hard, not necessarily when ready but rather when required; in the context of racing, this is when a competitor makes a move. Also, the athlete will not know in advance when it will be okay to back off and recover; this will not be known in a race either. So the simulation of a racing environment is excellent.

Now, what are the liabilities? This kind of session is advisable only for coaches who are masters of restraint, who understand their athletes very well, and who are in complete control of their own egos. The athlete is strongly controlled by the coach in this situation. The training load must be adjusted closely to the athlete's fitness level. If long sprints with short recoveries are demanded, then the session cannot last very long. Whether short or long, fast runs are stressful and must be appropriate to the total training load of that microcycle. In other words, the coach must plan in advance what is intended for development rather than thoughtlessly blasting inappropriate training demands through capricious use of a commanding whistle. Such a session is also inappropriate for a group of runners of mixed abilities, because as the group strings out, the signal to increase pace may be intended for those running uphill, but inappropriate for those not keeping up who may be running downhill too quickly for safety.

Better Hill Training

Three kinds of hill running are useful for distance runners. One is a series of gentle uphills and downhills as part of a road or cross-country distance run. Another is a series of runs up a long but manageable hill. The third is a speed session consisting of multiple repetitions up a short, steep hill. Not only does hill running increase the stress at any given pace because of the increased work necessary to counter the elevation change, but it also requires the use of arms, legs, and trunk musculature in ways that are different from level running. This different style is beneficial for improved racing abilities. For hilly, long-distance courses it is most beneficial to run steadily on the flat portion and vigorously up the hill. This optimizes the benefits of including the hills in that particular training session. The vigorous arm, shoulder, and trunk muscle activation from hill running just cannot be duplicated on flat surfaces. It closely mimics the muscular activity that occurs when a runner changes pace suddenly; thus, hill running is akin to an exaggerated pace-change session.

The downhills can serve as a respite for the cardiopulmonary system from the more vigorous flat and uphill portions of the run. The downhill portions should be treated with respect, however, for two reasons. First, the eccentric loading of muscles that occurs with such training activates fewer motor units at any given pace, placing more stress on those that are activated. Second, there is a greater impact force on the hip and knee joints from increased gravitational loading. Few runners have the luxury of a chauffeur accompanying them out on a long run, but it would actually be ideal if the runner could have a ride to the bottom of long, steep downhill portions of road training courses. Seb Coe did get such attention during his first five years of running. Training in the mountainous, sparsely populated Yorkshire countryside likely contributed to his longevity in the sport. His father followed behind him in the family car, letting him jump in at the crest of high plateaus for a quick lift to the bottom where he would resume his run.

Attacking hills during a long run provides a constantly recurring challenge. Each hill is a fresh obstacle to be overcome, testing an athlete's resolve and building mental toughness. Distance racing requires a similar resolve to counter other runners' attempts to break away from the field. In road and cross-country races some competitors will make a strong surge forward specifically at a hill to initiate the break. Hill training thus conditions the mind and the body in a specific and practical manner. Of course, not all distance runs should be on hilly courses run in the manner described. A session emphasizing hill running is just that: a specific kind of training stimulus to be used judiciously.

Intervals run on 800-m to 1000-m long uphills at a level-ground anaerobic conditioning pace may be equivalent physiologically to running at a level-ground intensity of aerobic capacity pace because of the added stress of the incline. The gradient of such hills should not be too steep, in the neighborhood of 1 in 14 (7%, or 4°). This is an excellent means for improving both aerobic and anaerobic power. However, unlike a track run, where it is relatively easy to jog back to the start and keep the rest as small as appropriate, a long run up an incline may require a jog back that provides too much recovery. The ideal, of course, would be a rising but mildly curving path that then continues back to the start. With a little searching, such courses can often be located.

Longer hill runs can become even more useful when there are slight changes of gradient along the way—one or two short level sections or a slight dip. Neither the dip nor the level stretches should be used to snatch a brief respite. Instead, the athlete should maintain running effort, using these stretches for acceleration. When the athlete reaches the final crest of the hill, he or she should continue over it at the same intensity as the uphill climb. The sudden increase in pace and lengthening of stride that occurs is exhilarating, and ought to be practiced, for it can provide a racing advantage over hilly cross-country and road races during competition. The change of pace and the lack of regular rhythm are both excellent race simulations performed under difficult conditions. If this is done well, the specific adaptations, both mental and physical, will be useful.

For many years of his training Seb Coe ran on a traffic-free cycle path that included a challenging 800-m section. After a steady 400-m climb, it leveled off for another 100 m only to climb still more steeply for another 250 m, finishing with 50 m slightly downhill. When preceded by a 3-mi warm-up and followed by a 2-mi cool-down, six to eight laps on this course completed a major workout for the day. It was finished relatively quickly and it challenged many aspects of competitive running in a very specific manner. Figure 5.10 shows another of Seb's favorite hills, very steep and only 180 m long, but with a varying gradient. Every serious distance runner should have one of these courses available for use when a hill session comes due on the schedule.

Short hill sessions run very quickly require only about 100 m of hill; a gradient of about 1 in 6 (17%, or 9.6°) is ideal. The short, jog-back recoveries make these runs predominantly anaerobic. An exaggerated running style is required to maximize speed, as these uphill runs spread the energy requirement to large muscle groups other than the legs. Once again, vigorous arm action, a quick and powerful knee lift by the hip flexors, and the powerful toe-off from each driving leg are all important elements for sudden dramatic pace changing and for continued dash-to-the-finish track racing. Figure 5.11 depicts a steep slope together with a suggested program to gradually build the ability to do many repetitions. It isn't wise to run up such hills aiming for specific transit times. Although these times may be kept for reference, the real reason for this kind of training is to build powerful and controllable (and therefore wondrous to behold!) hill-running ability. Excellent form should always be the watchword; achievement of specific paces is secondary.

Improving Acceleration

How can an athlete develop the ability to tolerate a steadily increasing running pace—gradual acceleration? All athletes realize that the finale of races is run faster than the earlier portions; this is achieved through an additional increase in anaerobic energy output added to that already being provided by aerobic

Figure 5.10 Illustration of a smooth-surface, traffic-free, aesthetically pleasing, somewhat steep 180-m-long hill suitable for running lactate/ventilatory threshold and VO_2max sessions. The river Thames is in the background.

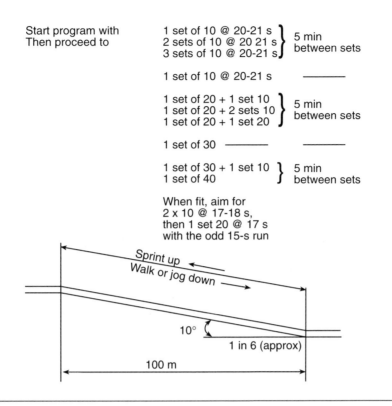

Start program with   1 set of 10 @ 20-21 s ⎫ 5 min
Then proceed to   2 sets of 10 @ 20 21 s ⎬ between sets
                      3 sets of 10 @ 20-21 s ⎭

                      1 set of 10 @ 20-21 s   ———

                      1 set of 20 + 1 set 10 ⎫ 5 min
                      1 set of 20 + 2 sets 10 ⎬ between sets
                      1 set of 20 + 1 set 20 ⎭

                      1 set of 30 ———   ———

                      1 set of 30 + 1 set 10 ⎫ 5 min
                      1 set of 40 ⎬ between sets

When fit, aim for
2 x 10 @ 17-18 s,
then 1 set 20 @ 17 s
with the odd 15-s run

Sprint up

Walk or jog down

10°

1 in 6 (approx)

100 m

Figure 5.11 Suggested model for developing a hill running program.

and some anaerobic energy sources. Those runners who have such a large aerobic potential that they have incurred minimal anaerobic accumulation up to the moment of this pace increase will have an edge over their opponents who aren't so well endowed. But those who can mentally tolerate the stress of anaerobic accumulation will have an edge as well over those who are not as well prepared. Once again, the interaction of speed and endurance sets the stage for racing to win.

Two types of shorter-distance interval sessions will help build the ability to accelerate during races. Figures 5.12 and 5.13 present the pace systems for permitting this. We have drawn lines through both figures to provide a specific illustration. The example shown is for a male runner who wants to run 1,500 m in 3:45 (approximately a 4:01 mile). We will also characterize him as more a 400-m and 800-m specialist with a fast 400-m time but somewhat short on stamina. It is stamina that we desire to improve. The first session involves running a series of steadily lengthening distances, each at a slightly faster pace. Recovery time increases because it involves a return to the start over the distance run. As illustrated in figure 5.12, we begin with a 100-m interval and increase each repetition by 10 m, the final interval being 200 m. Each interval is followed by a jogged recovery at the distance just run.

The time for his first (100-m) interval is 15 s, which is at the race pace (60 s/400 m) of his target 1,500-m race time. The pace for his final (200-m) interval is that of his best 400-m time (47 s), thus giving him 23.5 s for his 200-m distance. The next task is to determine the increase in time required for each successive intermediate interval. There will be 11 intervals of running but only 10 increases in distance. Thus, we need to determine the difference between the 100-m and 200-m interval times and divide this by 10. This will give the time increment by which each interval should be lengthened. Thus, 23.5 s – 15 s = 8.5 s/10 = 0.85 s.

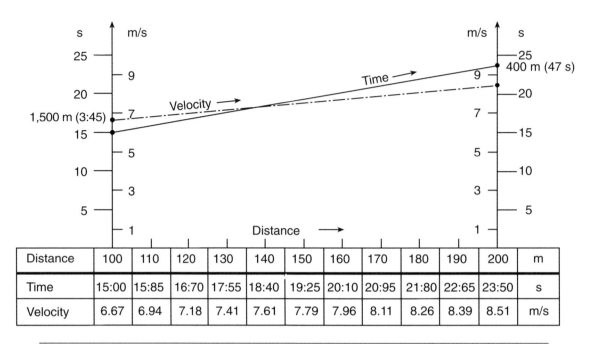

Distance	100	110	120	130	140	150	160	170	180	190	200	m
Time	15:00	15:85	16:70	17:55	18:40	19:25	20:10	20:95	21:80	22:65	23:50	s
Velocity	6.67	6.94	7.18	7.41	7.61	7.79	7.96	8.11	8.26	8.39	8.51	m/s

Figure 5.12 Plan for systematic increase of velocity and distance for a session of 11 repetitions run from 100 m to 200 m. Total distance run is 1,650 m (recovery period is a walk straight back to the start).

Using this increment, the 110-m interval will be covered in 15.00 + 0.85 = 15.85, the 120-m interval in 15.85 + 0.85 = 16.70 s, and so forth.

The pace session illustrated in figure 5.13 is more difficult and should be started only when the session in figure 5.12 has been practiced and mastered. Here the first interval is 200 m, increasing to 300 m in increments of 20 m. We use the same starting and finishing paces as before because this is the same runner doing the training. Thus, his 200-m interval will be at his 1,500-m pace (30 s), and his 300-m interval will be at a 47 s/400 m pace (35.25 s). There are five pace increases and six intervals. We can calculate the required time increase for each increment as the following: 35.25 s – 30 s = 5.25 s/5 = 1.05 s. Thus, the 220-m interval will be covered in 31.05 s, the 240-m interval in 32.10 s, and so forth.

The second type of repetition running also involves an increase in pace with an increase in distance, but now the recovery time is reduced. Again, mastery of the sessions described previously is essential before the athlete moves on to this session. Here, we use the data calculated from figure 5.13. Our runner will start at the 200-m mark and finish at the 400-m track finish line. He then will jog or walk around the track to the 200-m mark, which will remain the starting point for each successive interval. The second interval, however, will finish 20 m beyond the track finish line, giving him 20 m less recovery distance (and an appropriately reduced recovery rest) until the starting point for running is again reached. By the end of this session, athletes will have completed a fast 280 m and will have a recovery distance of only 120 m before beginning again.

To prevent this session from becoming too frustrating to complete initially, athletes may prefer to lengthen the recovery by slowing down the jog or walk. Athletes should make notes in their logbooks about what they found difficult and when they first noticed improvement. The object is to improve speed and speed endurance and not to bring undue duress in the athlete's development. Again, always err initially on the side of doing such sessions too slowly so as to

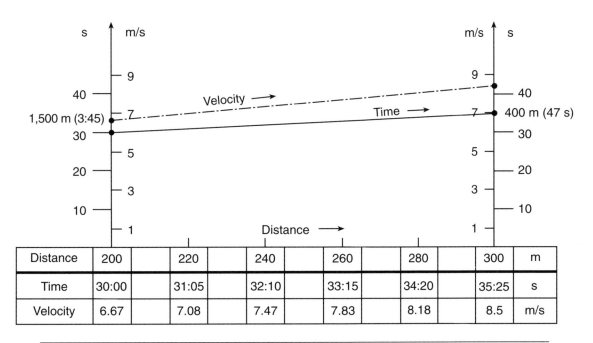

Distance	200		220		240		260		280		300	m
Time	30:00		31:05		32:10		33:15		34:20		35:25	s
Velocity	6.67		7.08		7.47		7.83		8.18		8.5	m/s

Figure 5.13 Plan for systematic increase of velocity and distance for a session of six repetitions run from 200 m to 300 m. Total distance run is 1,500 m, with recovery starting at a 3-min walk and reducing with development.

identify what can be managed, rather than beginning with a session so difficult that the athlete is floundering.

Speed Drills

Fast running is vastly different from easy aerobic distance running. Running stride is lengthened. Arm and shoulder action contribute more to the act of producing forward movement instead of primarily maintaining balance. All the various skeletal muscle motor units are now active—FT as well as ST. An athlete must develop tolerance to the discomfort of such stress, and this discomfort cannot be allowed to hinder the athlete's desire to perform.

There is a paradox in learning how to cope with speed. Consolidation of all the various facets that permit fast running—biomechanical, biochemical, and physiological—is required, and this can be achieved only through a large number of running repetitions. But this brings fatigue, a state in which the ability to tolerate the repetitions—and thus to learn—deteriorates rapidly. In such a state an athlete tends to replace correct technique with poorer technique, including the use of assisting muscle groups. Resolving this paradox requires the development of sufficient general conditioning and total-body fitness (see chapter 6) during the earlier mesocycles so that the anaerobic and neurological challenges provided by the speed stimulus can be managed effectively.

Once the techniques of speed running have been mastered, there is all the more reason for runners to include such work throughout their training macrocycle, with appropriate pace management.

Several drills to enhance speed development can be incorporated judiciously into the training plan, particularly during the later mesocycles (X_4 and X_5). A few of these drills that we have found enjoyable and practical are described below. They are not to be done all in one day, nor should they form a separate training session by themselves. Some of them can be substituted for a series of strides at the end of a distance run, or done after a warm-up as a transition into a track session involving faster-paced running.

Heel Flicks

This drill emphasizes rapid knee flexions and can be done during the warm-up period. We mentioned in chapter 1 the *heel flick*, where the heel nearly touches the buttock during the rapid forward-swing phase of the running stride. In a series of rapid, short steps during the warm-up period, initially every third or fifth step can become a smoothly executed, high heel flick. Gradual reduction of steps between high heel flicks ending with a brief sequence of continuous running with a high flick of each heel permits an easy and gradual transition to a sense of lower-limb quickness, even though the forward speed is quite slow.

High Knee Lifts

A second speed drill emphasizes hip flexions using a sequence of 10 to 20 high knee lifts. Well-developed iliopsoas muscle strength and endurance is important for these exercises. Forward movement again is quite slow, and arms must be moved vigorously through a wide range of motion. Elbows should be unlocked from their typical 90° position. A coaching suggestion is to "lift the knees as high as if they were en route to touching the chest." This is essentially an exaggeration of sprinting style, but the slow forward movement adds considerably more vertical oscillation (bounce). Plenty of recovery time should occur between each set to minimize mental and physical fatigue; these exercises are energy costly and demand concentration if they are to be done well. Two sets are plenty.

Short Accelerations

Short accelerations are another effective speed drill. Figure 5.14 shows a series of seven markers placed at 30-m intervals in a zigzag pattern. Beginning at point A, six sprint accelerations are made, with five 90° turns around the outside of each marker. Being forced to slow down to negotiate these turns without stopping requires the athlete to develop a combination of agility and acceleration-deceleration skills.

Straight Accelerations

Another acceleration drill consists of 30- to 50-m straight intervals beginning with a standing start three paces back from the sprint start line on a standard track. Crouch starts should not be used, as they represent an unnecessary risk for middle- and long-distance runners. These are anaerobic sessions, and thus the interval distance is purposely short. Middle-distance runners tend toward the shorter sprint accelerations (30 m), emphasizing quickness. Long-distance runners can opt for the longer distance (50 m), running not quite so quickly but still at high intensity to acquire an equivalent training stimulus. The tendency for most athletes is to take inadequate recovery, which brings premature fatigue. Unhurried walking recoveries ensure the fastest possible runs.

These straight acceleration drills are best done in sets of three or four runs, each set at increasing pace. An example, written in coaches' shorthand, which by now should be familiar, follows:

1. 4 × 30 m (85% max intensity); 2-min rec between intervals
   5-min rec before the next set
2. 4 × 30 m (90% max intensity); 2-min rec between intervals
   5-min rec before the next set

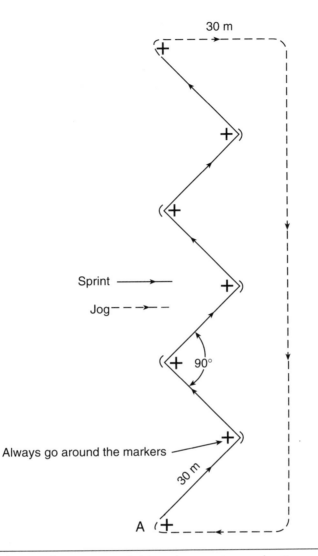

Figure 5.14 Suggested course layout to permit 30-m zigzag sprint accelerations as a speed drill. **A** is the starting point.

3. 4 × 30 m (95% max intensity); 2-min rec between intervals
   5-min rec before the next set
4. 4 × 30 m (100% max intensity); 2-min rec between intervals

When an athlete is training for maximal speed development, the demands of each running interval require that the recovery time between them be lengthened if pace and intensity are to be maintained. A better method is to reduce the length of each interval, keeping the intensity and recovery time the same. Two examples using a series of four fixed-distance intervals at 95% maximal intensity are the following:

1. 150 m, 120 m, 90 m, 60 m, with 3-min walked recovery
2. 120 m, 100 m, 80 m, 60 m, with 2 1/2-min walked recovery

Some perspective is appropriate here for longer-distance runners and their coaches who are contemplating such short-distance work. First, athletes specializing in the 5,000 m and longer will discover that such nearly all-out sprinting is very fatiguing when practiced hard for the first time. As always with specific training, the maxim is to run easy at first, become familiar with and adapted to the stress, and then raise the tempo as appropriate. The faster an individual's maximal sustainable pace for even relatively short distances, the higher will be his or her sustainable submaximal longer paces. This is primarily because of improved neurological recruitment abilities.

Second, preceding such speed drills with plenty of warm-up and flexibility exercises and following them with a cool-down period, stretching session, and massage are all essential parts of this high-level training process. Third, these sessions are not intended as a one- or two-time event done the week before an importance race. These sessions can begin to be inserted near the end of mesocycle X_4 and on into mesocycle X_5, initially at the lower intensities and with fewer total repetitions and progressing through the remainder of the macrocycle to provide a firmly developed speed stimulus. The end result will be the athlete's unusually fine ability to suddenly surge forward for several strides during a race at a point when such tactics are essential for positioning. Examples of when this is appropriate will be provided in chapter 7.

Better Pace Judgment

Very simply, there are two kinds of pace. One is the maximum, all-out, as fast as one can run. A runner requires no judgment to realize that he or she cannot run any more quickly. The second is submaximal, which encompasses all the other possible paces. The runner's judgment of submaximal pace can be altered by everything from fatigue or level of freshness to environmental temperature and humidity. Even a breeze—not a strong wind—can confuse judgment because it changes the effort required to maintain a given pace. Daylight versus nighttime illumination also affects pace judgment. A car being driven at night seems to be moving more quickly than in daylight even though the two velocities may be the same. This is because a person's limit of vision is closer at night from poorer illumination. In running at nighttime track meets held under artificial light, pace sense is similarly altered so that runners seem to be running more quickly than they actually are.

Pace sense to an extent is a gift; that is, even with practice, some 5,000-m or 10,000-m runners find it difficult to maintain pace consistency when fresh or tired, in warm weather or cool. Others do it with seeming ease. When the pace is increased in a race, however, a runner needs a well-developed ability to realize functionally the extent of the change. For example, a runner who increases the pace and takes the lead with the intention of breaking the field may estimate that it will take four laps at the current pace to do so. If this estimate turns out to be wrong (with several athletes still alongside), the confidence of knowing that sustaining this pace for a little longer should be adequate to achieve the purpose will prevent him or her from increasing the pace again, out of panic, to a level that may be unsustainable. Thus, pace sense and pace change are two valuable elements in a runner's racing armamentarium. Both need to be honed through practice.

How can pace practice be included in training? Pace sensing should not need incessant attention, because it isn't useful to have each training session serve as an intense cross-examination of pace detection abilities. However, if training routes have one or more sections accurately measured as one kilometer or one mile, pace can be checked easily against a watch worn during the run. Also, if the course involves the same route up to that particular measured segment, cumulative time can be estimated and compared to previous runs. Keith Brantly included a 400-m track as part of his running routes when he lived in Gainesville, Florida. Easy access to the track and the ability to maintain his training pace permitted a hassle-free means of accurate pace assessment and allowed him to mentally divide his longer distance runs into shorter segments.

Maintaining a sense of constant pace under changing track conditions can be developed by mixed-distance $\dot{V}O_2$max-pace runs done with different accompanying runners who are entering the workout in various degrees of freshness. One of Seb Coe's favorite summertime track challenges included careful lap-time recording during a $(2 \times 1{,}200 \text{ m}) + (1 \times 800 \text{ m}) + (2 \times 400 \text{ m})$ session, with various other club runners coming in alongside to accompany him. As an example, if his $\dot{V}O_2$max pace was 4:12 min/mi, his goal paces would be 3:08 for 1,200 m, 2:05 for 800 m, and 62.6 s for 400 m. As each lap was run, deviations from the prescribed intended pace could be determined. Maintaining pace when tired and not speeding up when fresh runners begin is an essential part of learning, ensuring, and refining pace judgment.

Can race-pace practice be included in training? The answer is a very definite *yes*. One example of the use of race-pace training includes what we call *incremental race-distance running*. In our experience, as just one example, we believe that many more elite-level female middle-distance runners striving to break the very desirable 2-min barrier could do it if they used this kind of training. For women hovering in the 2:20 to 2:04 range especially, weekly training sessions over a six-week period might include the following phases:

- **Phase 1.** Run 8×100 m in 14.8 s, with a 30-s recovery between each interval, and remain at this level until each 100-m interval can be run consistently at this pace.
- **Phase 2.** Repeat with slightly reduced recovery times, staying again at each training intensity level until the pace is perfectly identified.
- **Phase 3.** Repeat phase 2, using 4×200 m runs, with ever-shortening recovery times until a nonstop 800 m is recorded.

Training at actual race pace and also over the race distance can best be done by athletes specializing in the shorter events. During most of his youth and even afterward, Seb Coe used an undulating valley road as a test course. On this road, observed by his coach from a following car, Seb would run 6 to 8×800 m with short recoveries (as short as 1 1/2 min), all at his 800-m race pace. Apart from doing a very tough anaerobic work, Seb was learning to judge race pace when he was both fresh and very tired, not over limited distances but over his full race distance. Pace judgment at all levels of fatigue is an important sense to be developed.

Changing Pace

In any race longer than 400 m the ability to initiate a change of pace is very important. It must be done properly to be effective. Changing pace is different from sprinting and puts different demands on a runner. It is not initiated from a stationary start but occurs as a sequel to an already rather fast pace. Because it is a tactical maneuver, it may be called upon more than once, but not always for the same reason. Pace changing can and should be learned and practiced during training.

Three kinds of pace changes are used in racing. One is termed a *gradual,* or *economical,* change of pace. It is frequently used in races from the 3,000 m through the marathon and occurs during the bulk of the race; that is, not during the final few laps (when other kinds of pace changing occur). This is simply a firm and steady, but not necessarily rapid, quickening of the pace, which typically will split the field or open up a gap from the entire field. It can usually be achieved simply by a slight increase in stride length with no change in running cadence. For this reason, competitors in the race initially have no visual cues that it is occurring. Emphasis is on maintaining form and relaxation. The smoother and more steadily this is achieved, the more economical it is on energy reserves. It can be practiced in training during longer interval runs, such as 1,000 m to 3,000 m. Split times are recorded every 200 m or 300 m to determine the rate of the pace increase. The athlete is typically instructed to begin a steady increase in pace approximately midway through the interval until a subsequent signal, at which time running remains at that assigned pace. Too rapid a change will bring exhaustion because there is considerable distance yet to be covered. The purpose of this kind of training is to teach sensible pace increase as well as the ability to maintain good form despite steadily higher blood lactic acid levels and thus difficulty in maintaining quality running mechanics.

Another kind of pace changing is called *intermittent*. Varying amounts of acceleration will be required, but the effort is submaximal and quite brief. It may be repeated during a race, and it should not affect the athlete's ability to maintain the ongoing race pace, because there isn't sufficient anaerobic buildup to impair performance. One practical example of the need for such pace changing occurs in the 800-m and 1,500-m races when it becomes appropriate for the runner to remedy a poor race position. The runner may find it useful to accelerate quickly and pass three or four runners to reach a desired location. In this instance, it is most efficient for the runner to increase cadence fairly quickly but maintain stride length.

One method for developing this ability is for a group of four or five runners of similar abilities to run at 5,000-m or 10,000-m race pace for a long-interval track run of 2,000 m to 3,000 m. As the runners stay in single file, at each 200-m mark the rearmost runner quickly accelerates to take the lead and then slows to the group pace. Thus, if five runners are doing this session, every 1,000 m would see an acceleration by each of the runners moving into the lead.

Another example involves the use of fartlek runs to work on pace changing and the ability to surge forward in racing conditions. Recall the earlier example of the easy to steady fartlek pace, during which several rapid pace increases of 30 s to 2 min provide sudden challenges to be managed. A more advanced form of this session is to quicken the ongoing pace to anaerobic threshold pace, with a 20-min period during which several 45-s to 3-min surges to as fast as race pace are added.

The third change of pace is used only once, near the end of a race, and is termed a *sprint acceleration*. When making a final assault on the finish line, the athlete's effort must be total and the effect instantaneous. This is an important strategy in the sport of cycling and can win running races as well. For runners the key to success in sprint accelerations is to quicken the cadence. Arm swing depends on cadence, and as cadence quickens, the arms will naturally come up into their full sprinting style of carriage to provide the increased upper-body accompaniment to the higher knee lift and pronounced toe-off. As soon as maximal cadence is achieved, stride is again lengthened for maximal velocity. All of this is done smoothly and quickly. In a race the runner typically begins this final effort from one of two places. One is from the end of the back straight, so the runner can acquire the lead and fight off anyone attacking around the bend.

This will ensure unobstructed running toward the finish. The second is the final kick at the start of the finishing straight as the runner is leaving the bend, for a late, short drive to the tape. In chapter 7 we will use these principles to suggest strategies for specific event racing.

In these two sprint acceleration attacks, the runner is either entering or leaving a curve. To provide practice for this in training, bend running is essential, but it is important that athletes include this practice only when they are relatively fresh. Thus it is best for them to run individual laps beginning at the start/finish line, using the first bend and the back straight to build to a pace about 90% of maximal 400-m speed. For into-the-bend practice, at about 250 m out from the finish an acceleration signaled by a hand clap, shout, or whistle brings the runner into the back turn at full effort, which is sustained until he or she is at least halfway around the bend. In an actual racing situation, this may be required when the pace must be maintained in a field still bunched together with about 200 m remaining to the finish. Thus, in some practice runs, it is wise to include an occasional maximal effort actually maintained to the end.

For out-of-bend practice, acceleration to near-maximal running pace need not be achieved until the runner is about 150 m from the finish. Then the pace can be maintained or even increased slightly through the bend until the runner reaches the finishing straight. From a point between 80 m and 100 m from the finish, the final do-or-die kick is launched. As can be imagined, it is not the quantity of these bend-run repeats as much as the preservation of excellent running form and learning the technique of sudden pace change that improves racing effectiveness. A few such repetitions can provide an effective learning stimulus.

Therapeutic Runs

At times all runners begin to develop thoughts that they may not or cannot run well in an upcoming competition. Their attitude seems more negative than positive, and they often complain of tiredness or fatigue. The coach should not dismiss these feelings, because as we shall learn in chapter 8, some of these emotions may indeed signal overtraining. Loss of vigor and the will to win often go hand in hand with excessive fatigue. The coach, in a supportive role, should on one hand offer positive words of comfort directed toward reviewing the good aspects of the athlete's recent development, but on the other attempt to elicit objective reasons as to why the feelings of doubt exist. (Is it fear of a particular competitor, real symptoms of overtraining, or rumors of what a competitor has been doing during training?) At such moments the runner can benefit from a brief respite from hard work and also by some positive physical evidence that running can indeed be enjoyable and done quickly and easily.

One approach to this problem is to find a suitable training course, preferably one that is very slightly downhill, the distance of which is compatible with training for the forthcoming race, and even better, with a slight prevailing wind in the running direction. The athlete's task is to run the course, not hard but quickly. It will be easy to do and not exhausting. The athlete should preferably run it alone, moving at a pace that feels satisfying. At the end the athlete's feeling of strength and well-being and ability to have good turnover should put to rest any doubts about being competent to perform. Of course, if the athlete attempts such a run and barely finishes it, this may indeed be good evidence of the development of overtraining, a bout of the flu, or a head cold. This objective evidence may then allow a better-informed decision about perhaps canceling the upcoming race.

Seb Coe found himself in just such an unhappy situation on one particular occasion, wondering whether he was really ready for a scheduled competition. A run that met the criteria just described was selected; it was just outside and high above the city of Sheffield in a spot called Moscar Top. From this point the road gently descends toward the city, with exhilarating views. With a brisk swinging stride, Seb covered those 5 mi quickly and easily, feeling very fresh at the finish. He slept that evening with his doubts and fears far up on the moors where they belonged. Long after having figured out the reasoning behind this rather sly coaching tactic, Seb still found that such a run had almost a magic "battery-recharging" effect. And far more than once since, when the moment has been ripe, either Seb or his coach would ask the other, "How about going out for a therapeutic?"

Anthony Sandoval had such runs in Los Alamos, New Mexico, often in the middle of hard training weeks during his X_1 and X_2 mesocycles when he was preparing for the U.S. Olympic Marathon Trials of 1980 and 1984. (He won the Trials in 1980, was sixth in 1984, and was fourth in 1976, and his personal best for a loop marathon course stands at 2:10:20.) It was a 10-mi jaunt down Bandelier Canyon. After a short jog into the forest outside the city and onto a narrow trail, a sharp switchback descent of several hundred feet down into the bottom of the canyon put Anthony into a world of his own. Paralleling a rushing stream that flows through the canyon, a scarcely used hiking trail of packed dirt provided a steady downhill run. The noise of the bubbling water as well as its cool spray, the green ferns and other lush vegetation along the way, and the incredible ease of dashing along miles of trail at a 6:00 min/mi pace with scarcely elevated breathing allowed Anthony's love of running to return undiminished. Of course, a breakfast of fresh, warm, blueberry muffins and juice brought by his wife and a few hugs from his children, who drove to the mouth of the canyon to pick him up, completed the picture of a runner in tune with his environment. That's a therapeutic!

Using Altitude Training as a Fitness-Enhancing Stimulus

Any endurance runner who has journeyed from the altitude at which he or she resides to an altitude higher by a few thousand feet and then tried to train or race knows very clearly that it feels more difficult than at sea level. The effort required to maintain a familiar submaximal pace seems increased. And it is especially difficult to perform at a high intensity.

Comparison is often made of performance times in the endurance running events at the 1968 Mexico City Summer Olympic Games (at 2,300-m altitude) with the sea-level best times of those same athletes achieved earlier that year. Their altitude paces were consistently slower, even though there's no doubt these athletes were supremely fit at the Games. Virtually every medalist from 1,500 m through the marathon was either a higher-than-sea-level altitude native or had trained extensively at altitude before competing in Mexico City. Thus, for the longer distance races, altitude is definitely a physiological stressor that slows the maximally sustainable pace. Those adapted to it perform better at altitude than those who are not.

Is training at higher altitude effective for improving sea-level performance? This is a complex topic, about which much has been written. We know the basic mechanism by which altitude training ought to enhance performance. But a real problem exists in going to altitude to obtain the physiological benefits without disrupting all the other facets of lifestyle that contribute to the well-being of a healthy athlete. Let us examine this in greater detail.

Altitude Effects on Performance

By how much does altitude slow a distance runner's performance? We can provide both specific examples and general indications. One specific example is a comparison of the performance of two altitude-dwelling Mexican marathon runners racing at sea level and altitude. Dionicio Ceron won the Mexico City marathon on 29 August 1993 with 2:14:47; Maurilio Castillo was fifth with 2:18:12. Seven months prior to the Mexico race, Castillo ran 2:13:04 to win a marathon at Beppu, Japan. Four months following the Mexico City race, Ceron ran 2:08:51 to win the Fukuoka, Japan, Marathon. All of these races were run in cool, good weather conditions, and over flat courses. The race in Mexico City was at 2,300 m; Beppu and Fukuoka are at sea-level. The difference between Ceron's two performances was 4.4%, for Castillo, 3.7%.

A general indication of the effect of altitude is seen by the present policy of the governing body for athletics in the United States regarding the acceptance of competition results for athlete entry into its national outdoor championships. A 3% "altitude allowance" is permitted for track performances at distances of 1,500 m or longer achieved above 4,000 ft (1,219 m).

The Hypoxic Stimulus of Altitude

What causes the slowing of performance with increasing altitude? The fundamental cause is hypoxia—decreased available O_2 for the working tissues, notably cardiac and skeletal muscle. The reason should be obvious. Distance running is primarily an aerobic (O_2-requiring) event. Breathing environmental air provides this O_2, and it moves from the lungs into the blood. As we ascend to altitude, the inspired O_2 concentration decreases. In the blood, 98.5% of the O_2 chemically binds to hemoglobin, found in the red blood cells. The cardiovascular system distributes this blood everywhere, particularly to the working tissues. The higher the altitude, the greater is the challenge to ensure adequate O_2 transport.

The extent to which altitude, with its decreasing available inspired O_2, first begins to impair endurance performance was initially identified as roughly a 1% decrease in maximal aerobic power for every 100 m above 1,500 m (Buskirk and Kollas 1967). Refinement of measuring techniques (Squires and Buskirk 1982) later lowered this threshold altitude of apparent physiological change to about 1,200 m and suggested a linear reduction in $\dot{V}O_2$max of 8% for each 1,000-m rise in altitude above 700 m. The most recent thinking (Terrados 1992) suggests that a measurable decrease in maximal aerobic power among elite athletes is detectable even at 900 m. This corroborates reports of sea-level endurance athletes who perceive performance impairment when they race at altitudes as low as 700 to 800 m and compare their sea-level performance times during the same competitive season under conditions of similar temperature, humidity, and terrain.

Adaptation to Altitude Hypoxia

Can one adapt to altitude hypoxia by simply living at altitude, or is training at altitude required? Both bring about an adaptation. When sedentary people travel to altitude and remain there for an extended period (a month or more), their tolerance to the hypoxic stress of occasional exercise improves even though they do not train (Grover, Weil, and Reeves 1986). Beneficial physiological adaptations have obviously occurred. Training at altitude provides an additional hypoxic stress, to which additional adaptation also occurs. The response is similar to the changes seen with hard training at sea level, which also is a hypoxic stress due to the high level of effort that requires more O_2 than can be provided by complete fuel metabolism.

How does the body adapt to the hypoxia caused by training at altitude? Several physiological changes occur. More enzymes are produced by the working muscles for oxidative metabolism. These are found particularly in the skeletal muscle mitochondria, which increase both in size and number. Also in the working skeletal muscles there is greater reliance on fatty acids as a primary fuel than on glycogen. As a result, blood lactic acid production is reduced during submaximal work. The heart rate response varies. In some athletes an initial elevation of resting heart rate occurs and persists. In others it returns to the sea-level value. Maximal achievable heart rate is unchanged, but it now occurs at a smaller work rate than at sea level. The stroke volume typically decreases. Thus, even with optimal altitude adaptation, maximal cardiac output never reaches that seen at sea level. This helps to explain why an athlete's VO_2max at altitude is less than at sea level. Blood plasma volume decreases immediately upon arrival at altitude. With adaptation over many weeks this is often restored close to sea-level values.

Hypoxia also stimulates the kidneys to increase their output of the hormone *erythropoietin*. In turn, this stimulates the bone marrow to produce more red blood cells, which contain hemoglobin. This adaptation occurs a little more slowly than the plasma volume response. Eventually, if the increases in plasma volume and red blood cell volume are equivalent, the total blood volume will rise with no change in either the hemoglobin level or the hematocrit. If red blood cell mass increases slightly more than plasma volume, both hemoglobin and hematocrit will be higher than at sea level. In either case, the blood's O_2-carrying capacity is increased.

Benefits and Liabilities of Altitude Training

If altitude residence improves an athlete's ability to compete at altitude, does altitude residence improve the ability to compete at or near sea level, where virtually all of the world's major competitions are held? Here the evidence is far from clear (Dick 1992; Smith and Sharkey 1984; Wolski, McKenzie, and Wenger 1996). If athletes train at altitude, return to sea level, and race successfully, it is impossible to know whether they would have raced just as well without the altitude training block; they cannot return to their prior fitness level, redo the training block at sea level, and then race the same competitions under the same conditions, with the only difference being the altitude stimulus.

When athletes successfully complete an altitude training block, that is, they return to sea level and have successful competitions, several factors in addition to simply training at altitude have played a contributory role, making it difficult to assess specifically the role of their increased O_2-carrying ability. For example, greater attention may have been devoted to creating and carrying out an optimally effective training plan. If they moved temporarily to a high-altitude location, they may have had more free time for ensuring adequate sleep and nutrition, because of being away from the pressures of a job or family. Additional attention may have been given to regenerative modalities such as massage. The hillier terrain typically found at altitude may have provided an additional stimulus if their former residence was virtually flat.

Not all athletes complete an altitude training block successfully. Because of either injury or prolonged fatigue, some have poor competitive success and disappear from the athletic scene. Because of this disappearance, one tends to hear only the success stories of athletes who trained at altitude, returned to sea level, and competed well. No one knows the real washout rate of those who attempted altitude training and failed to achieve later competitive benefits.

There are many reasons why altitude training can be unsuccessful. Traveling to higher altitudes in remote mountainous parts of foreign lands without thoroughly considering the consequences can bring boredom, excessive fatigue, inadequate nutrition, chronic dehydration, and inadequate facilities for enhancing regeneration, not to mention homesickness. Thus, while expected physiological adaptations to altitude hypoxia do indeed suggest improved aerobic endurance, this is only one facet of an individual's multidimensional adaptability to environment and training.

Why don't all athletes adapt to altitude to the same extent? There are primarily two reasons: the interaction of altitude with other aspects of lifestyle, as just described, and individual physiological differences. The primary physiological factors involve differences in the quantity of hemoglobin and in lung function. These factors, along with such other factors as running efficiency, cause variability in maximal aerobic power among athletes.

Athletes with hemoglobin levels on the higher end of the normal range will manage hypoxia more easily and be less susceptible to overtraining at altitude than those with values on the low end. They simply have greater O_2-carrying ability. Also, for any particular height, age, and sex, considerable normal variation exists in (1) the size of the lungs, (2) the rate at which air can rush into and out of the lungs without the airways reflexively constricting, and (3) the ease with which O_2 diffuses from lungs into blood. Those with better lung function will adapt to altitude more easily. Typically, cooler, drier weather prevails at altitude, which might feel refreshing to those coming from subtropical heat and humidity. However, some athletes have airways that are hyperreactive and likely to reflexively constrict when exposed to cold, dry, rapidly moving air. These athletes are bothered with what has been termed exercise-induced asthma (EIA) or exercise-induced bronchospasm (EIB). For those athletes altitude training may prove difficult and, in some instances, not beneficial.

Additional Variables With Altitude Training

Other factors add to the variability in altitude responsiveness. First, depending on place of normal residence, one particular altitude may or may not seem stressful. As an example, athletes native to Mexico City do not consider their 2,300 m as altitude. Instead, they find it appropriate to go to 3,500 m in the mountainous hills around Toluca for an altitude stimulus. Athletes living along the seacoast, however, find the altitude of Mexico City quite challenging. Almost all sea-level-dwelling elite athletes find that living or prolonged training above 2,750 m is too stressful for predictably consistent benefits. The combination of skeletal muscle wasting, slowness of tolerable training pace, and ongoing tendency toward dehydration more than negate any benefits of additional oxygen transport capability caused by the adaptive increase in red cell mass. Occasional day trips to such altitudes, and higher, however, are often included as part of a training mesocycle by those living routinely at moderate altitude. Again, it has not been possible to quantify whether those specific sessions by themselves have a measurable physiological benefit in competitive performance.

Second, depending on event specialty, altitude training may fit differently in the overall plan of a training macrocycle. Middle-distance runners, for example, find it difficult to maintain or improve their turnover (leg speed, quickness) at altitude. Hence, their altitude stimulus may best be reserved for their aerobic base period early in the training macrocycle. Appropriately for long-distance runners, periods of altitude training could be included through a sizable portion of the macrocycle, alternating with sea-level blocks of faster training to maintain leg speed. For either group of athletes there is a useful strategy for maintaining leg speed at altitude. That is to maintain sea-level pace during interval training, but reduce the interval distance considerably (e.g., 400-m intervals become 200 m or 300 m), and lengthen the recovery. Thus, neuromuscular quickness is maintained.

Realizing that higher-altitude training is indeed stressful, although the red blood cell stimulus is desirable, raises an interesting question. Why not reside at the higher altitude to provide the chronic hypoxic stimulus (both by residence and by longer-distance runs), and then travel briefly to a lower altitude two or three times each week for the quickness-oriented aspects of training? Experiments are currently underway in an attempt to quantify the differing benefits among the several possibilities of living high or low, and training only high, only low, or doing longer-but-slower sessions high and shorter-but-quicker sessions low (Levine and Stray-Gundersen 1992). Recent conclusions (Levine, Friedmann, and Stray-Gundersen 1996) seem to confirm that four weeks of living at altitude and training near sea level provides a combination of acclimatization and increased fitness that benefits sea-level performance. A few such training sites—with sizable altitude differences close to each other, which have both trails for pleasant distance running and synthetic tracks for faster sessions—exist in the United States. The combination has been used for many years with considerable success. In California, South Lake Tahoe (1,909 m) and Orangevale (120 m) are separated by only 132-km driving distance. In Arizona, Flagstaff (2,107 m) and Phoenix (332 m) are separated by 222 km of driving.

How does one effectively time the return to sea level for optimal performance? This is the key to whether the efforts devoted to an altitude training experience were really beneficial. Primarily, the optimal time to return and compete well is determined by a combination of (1) maintaining increased blood volume (red cell mass and plasma volume), (2) restoring neuromuscular quickness and leg turnover, (3) optimal tapering and regeneration, and (4) return to normal breathing dynamics. The average life span of red blood cells in hand-training distance runners is 80 days, so the increased aerobic power caused by the additional hemoglobin within these cells remains for a few months after return to sea level. Neuromuscular quickness can be regained quickly—within a few weeks of faster-paced sessions. The ventilatory dynamics can be explained briefly by outlining what occurs with both ascent and descent.

Ventilatory and Metabolic Dynamics With Changing Altitude

Normal ventilation is controlled peripherally in the body by the level of O_2 and CO_2 in the blood and centrally by the acidity of the cerebrospinal fluid. Carbon dioxide from fuel metabolism diffuses into the cerebrospinal fluid and thus contributes to its acidity. Increased metabolism raises acidity and thereby stimulates breathing centrally. Ascent to altitude reduces the amount of O_2 inspired with each breath, thereby lowering blood O_2 and providing a peripheral stimulus to increase ventilation. Also, the hypoxia starts to increase red blood cell production within a week, raising the O_2-carrying capacity of the blood and eventually decreasing the peripheral stimulus to increase breathing. However, since CO_2 is a major component of the expired air, increased breathing lowers the CO_2 concentration in the blood and cerebrospinal fluid.

This has two effects. First, the decrease in blood acidity permits a slightly increased work output, and the first week of training at altitude often appears rather easy. Also, since the brain's nervous stimulus to breathe comes from increased cerebrospinal fluid acidity, which has now been reduced, the central breathing stimulus falls. As full altitude adaptation is achieved, ventilation returns back to normal, balanced by an increased O_2-carrying capacity and a normal cerebrospinal fluid acidity.

Upon return to sea level following altitude adaptation, the reverse situation occurs. Athletes now enter an O_2-rich environment. Thus, the peripheral stimulus to breathe is reduced. A small accumulation of CO_2 in the blood and cerebrospinal fluid occurs, which continues for several days. The slight blood and tissue acidosis brings symptoms of sluggishness, drowsiness, and decreased ability to tolerate intense anaerobic work. The gradually increasing cerebrospinal fluid acidity eventually increases ventilation to rid the body of accumulating metabolic acid. Also, after a few weeks, the decreased erythropoietin-producing stimulus lowers red blood cell production rates to those normally seen at sea level. As the O_2-carrying ability of the blood starts to fall, the peripheral breathing stimulus increases slightly.

Eventually, normal sea-level ventilation returns as blood and cerebrospinal fluid regulation of O_2 and CO_2 levels also normalize. Although these ventilatory changes are typically completed within a week, from the standpoint of athletes performing competitively, another several days are often required for adaptation to both the fatigue-related consequences of the altitude sojourn and the fatigue resulting from return to faster sessions for refining racing skills on return to lower altitude.

Hints for Using Altitude Training Successfully

Our experience is that the optimal period of altitude residence is approximately four weeks: This increases red blood cell concentration in the bloodstream, thereby increasing O_2-carrying ability, and also permits an unhurried training block. The optimal time for return to lower altitudes and racing appears to be roughly two to three weeks: sufficient time to return breathing dynamics and acid-base levels to normality and to permit recovery from the fatigue of hard training at altitude. Another conclusion that we have found useful, particularly for middle-distance runners, is to use the period from roughly 12 to 18 days after return from altitude as a period for very intense speed work, which can take advantage of the aerobic boost to increase the combination of blood volume, neuromuscular quickness, and mental confidence. Then, following several days of rest, the high-level competition period can begin, about three-and-a-half weeks post–altitude stimulus.

Realizing that athletes who have acquired the aerobic boost from altitude training will likely have an increased $\dot{V}O_2$max and thus an increased ability to compete at a higher level, serious athletes who have not considered altitude training ought to do so. Those who have done so but who have experienced poor results ought to rethink the details of their experience and try it again. Their bad experience may simply have resulted from poor planning and not knowing what questions to ask in preparation. As with any new aspect of training, however, remember that altitude training is only one facet of a total lifestyle, and it must not cause lifestyle disruption. The key points to remember for adding altitude training to a training macrocycle are the following:

- Don't wait until it's time to prepare for an important championship to try altitude training for the first time.
- Use laboratory physiological testing before going and after returning to quantify the extent of change in such variables as VO_2max, anaerobic threshold, and hemoglobin.
- Don't go so high or train so hard that the altitude stress is excessive.
- Ensure that the terrain used for training permits the option for flat as well as hilly running.
- Stay long enough to acquire sufficient adaptation to make the effort worthwhile: at least three to four weeks.
- Create a homelike lifestyle and an entirely hospitable training environment by thorough advance planning (including a prior "tourist trip" to the locale for initial arrangements and to develop useful personal contacts).
- If the important competitions following altitude training are planned for sea level, return home early enough (roughly two weeks) to permit appropriate sea-level ventilatory and neuromuscular adaptation before racing begins.

Keep a Training Diary

This chapter has greatly emphasized the necessity of planning and managing an athlete's career. It is impossible to do this effectively without the proper records needed to assess the long-term results of training. Very often yesterday's comments point to the answers for today's and tomorrow's questions. A good training log forms a unique educational base from which it often becomes delightfully obvious what needs yet to be done or how what is being done is affecting performance (whether positively or negatively). Winston Churchill once remarked that people "occasionally stumble over the truth, but most of them pick themselves up and hurry off as if nothing had happened." A good log makes it more difficult to stumble without realizing what caused it and easier to identify how the truth can be achieved without falling at all.

We have seen many printed examples of training logs and diaries; they are for sale seemingly everywhere. And we have devoted countless hours to poring over the training logs of the runners with whom we have worked closely. It is interesting how the two seem to differ. Relatively few elite runners with whom we have worked use these fine-looking but ever-so-regimented formats. There is so much diversity in training details that no real regimented format is possible. Specifics of track sessions, unique and novel names given to specific running routes, mental notes about the effort sense of a session, details of weather or daily activities that may have added frustration or spirit to the training, and much more, all have varying importance on different days. The staunchly independent and free-spirited mental framework of most runners demands that the simplest, most adaptable system be the basis for noting the appropriate details that make each training day unique and noteworthy.

We have urged our athletes to document some details precisely on a consistent basis. Table 5.16 suggests a format for such a training log. Notice that the space provided for each section is purposely small, to emphasize thoughtful, succinct, specific comments that stimulate all the recall necessary to put that day's training into conversational form for discussion. For interval sessions, include the sets, the repetitions, the recovery times, the distances run, the feelings of perceived exertion, and the nuances that gave bother or pleasure at the moment. For aerobic conditioning (longer runs), include the time and distance and an indicator of effort sense (with an established communicated agreement that such terms as "easy," "steady," and "hard" have rough physiological equivalents, e.g., a heart rate of roughly 135, 145, and more than 160 beats/min). Physiological observations such as morning heart rate, hours of sleep, weight measured at a meaningful time (for repeatability), and aches and pains ought to be recorded, but not in such detailed fashion that it becomes a drudge. Finally, comments after the day's training to give a perspective on ease of recovery, lasting fatigue, findings after massage, and so on can be very useful to gauge developing fatigue or malaise that ought to be corrected by a few days of rest. Essays need not be written; shorter, almost cryptic, but still understandable comments make it much more likely that the athlete will maintain a daily record-keeping routine.

Table 5.16 also gives a suggested race summary format, again with space devoted to room for short, cryptic, but pithy commentary that lays bare the essentials of that important moment. Several kinds of information need to be recorded. First, record the specific details, including split times if possible. Second, was preparation okay? What could have been done to prepare better? Or did everything go well according to plan? Third, what were the immediate primary impressions about the competition and the entire experience? Often athletes write very little if they performed well; their thoughts are on celebrating. Similarly, if they raced poorly, they would prefer to forget the whole thing. Such emotional responses may be understandable, but still an objective postmortem assessment of the event is of inestimable value. First thoughts and impressions, honestly written, can be very useful later on in helping to recall the entire event in a more reasoned light.

Other types of logs and journals can also be quite useful, depending on one's penchant for documentation. One is a week-by-week graph of total running distance, roughly proportioned by aerobic and anaerobic aspects, with a note of races and time trials. This provides a global view of training breaks and helps athletes and coaches visualize the periodization aspect of training.

SUMMARY

Building Better Fitness by Running

1. Hard work over a long period of time is the primary route to developing athletic performance potential. The art of coaching is to identify the smallest amount of the most specific work needed to ensure continual progress in performance ability. All other training is overtraining and increases the risk of injury, excessive fatigue, or the problems of staleness. There is also a science to coaching—how the body responds to the stress of training in specific ways, with either physiological adaptation that brings performance improvement or pathological deterioration that precipitates illness or injury, is well known.

2. Both coaches and athletes must have short-term and long-term goals. With goals, training plans can be easily designed. Without goals, no plans make sense. Any training program must reflect an athlete's beginning fitness level. The ath-

TABLE 5.16

A Sample Training Summary

Date _____ Total distance run _____

Morning pulse _____ Sleep _____ Weight _____

Morning session:

Description _____

_____

_____

_____

_____

Afternoon session:

Description _____

_____

_____

_____

_____

Items:

Course

sets

reps

Tempo

Recovery

Conditions

Perceived exertion

Nuances

Comments:

_____

_____

_____

_____

Competitions/Time Trials

Date _____ Event _____

Distance _____ Time _____

Splits _____

Notes on final preparation: _____

_____

_____

_____

_____

Notes on the race: _____

_____

_____

_____

_____

Notes for the future: _____

_____

_____

_____

_____

lete must take the time to recover completely from the previous training and competition season—both physically and mentally—and then begin again reasonably, realizing that all good things take time. Athletic excellence requires months of steady and proper preparation during which the body's homeostatic processes adapt at their own rate. For this reason, it is preferable to train around individual excellence and needs.

3. Athletes should perform all training sessions with a desire for perfection, pride in achievement, variety, and purpose. Every training session should end with the athlete still capable of doing more. If there is ever a question of whether to do more, do less. Keep good records, realizing that although no training program can be used more than once, the knowledge gained from progress and development during one season can be used to fine-tune a subsequent season for more effective improvement.

4. The training process has a stimulus and a response. The response is physiological breakdown caused by the work done, along with the body's adaptation during the rest period following recovery. Unless there is recovery, there is no chance for even performance restitution, let alone performance improvement. Thus, regenerative rest is absolutely essential to the training process. Good nutrition, fluid replacement, adequate sleep, use of recuperative modalities such as warm and cold baths and massage, and enjoyment of activities that contribute to the wholeness of life beyond running are all important.

5. Periodization is the term given to the reasoned division of a training season (macrocycle) into intermediate-length time blocks (mesocycles), which have a broad focus of improvement, and into shorter time blocks (microcycles), which contain daily training assignments for specific development.

6. The primary goals of training are to improve strength (muscular force capacity), speed or power (quick mobilization of strength), stamina (management of speed for sizable periods of time), and endurance (long-term resistance to submaximal effort fatigue). Training sessions involving running consist of a given distance traversed (the volume, or interval) a specific number of times (the frequency, or repetitions) at a specific pace (the intensity, or tempo). If there is more than one repetition, there is a specific recovery period (the density, or rest).

7. Important physiological adaptations occur with effective training: increased blood volume, larger ventricular chambers, more stored fuels in muscle cells, increased enzyme capability in muscle cells for metabolizing fuel, increased effectiveness of the nervous system in recruiting more muscle fibers, stronger muscles, and increased tolerance of supporting connective tissues to the chronic impact stress of thousands of miles or kilometers of running each year.

8. The most successful training plan is one that provides the greatest gains in $\dot{V}O_2$max and elicits the fastest pace at which one can race the selected distance. The higher the $\dot{V}O_2$max, regardless of race distance, the less the lactate production at any given work load, and the faster one can race before lactate begins to accumulate. The more efficient the athlete, the faster this pace can be. Although the greatest gains in $\dot{V}O_2$max initially will be gained through higher-volume, lesser-intensity training, such training has limitations for two reasons. First, because runners adapt to the stimulus, ever-greater training volumes are required for greater gains, increasing the risk for connective tissue injury. Second, the fast-twitch (FT) muscle cells are stimulated to develop only by medium- to higher-intensity effort, and they too have an important aerobic component as well as an anaerobic component. Thus, a variety of training paces—changing over the training year—provide the best stimulus for complete devel-

opment. Since training at altitude provides an additional hypoxic stimulus, it also can be helpful in improving $\dot{V}O_2$max.

9. The running portion of training can be divided into four performance intensity zones, named for the predominant physiological benefit resulting from a manageable training session in each. The running pace in each zone is based on a percentage of the pace at which one reaches maximal O_2 consumption ($\dot{V}O_2$max pace). This pace can be determined easily using results obtained from treadmill testing or from a track time trial (assuming that 100% $\dot{V}O_2$max pace can be maintained for 10 to 12 min).

10. *Aerobic conditioning* involves conversational-pace, longer-distance runs and forms the bulk of the volume of most distance runners' training. *Anaerobic conditioning* consists of comfortably harder distance runs from 15 to 25 min at approximately lactate/ventilatory threshold pace. *Aerobic capacity training* consists of longer-distance intervals of running at essentially 5,000-m to 10,000-m race pace. *Anaerobic capacity training* involves shorter-distance intervals at faster-than-5,000-m race pace. As the intensity of running increases, so does the amount of recovery rest required between intervals, although improving fitness can tend to reduce the time needed.

11. Particularly with more challenging training sessions, work load tolerance is specific to each individual. Thus, over time the effect of differences in genetics, starting fitness, and rate of adaptation will cause a variable rate of improving fitness. This variability will be most evident with the most difficult sessions. Sensitivity to this variability will effectively prevent slower-responding athletes from overtraining, incurring injury, or becoming frustrated. Switching to more individualized sessions in the latter stages of a macrocycle very often provides the best approach to hone the talents of each athlete optimally.

12. The best method for identifying these specific details of training responsiveness and for improving on the plan for improving fitness is to keep reasonably detailed records in the form of a training log or journal. No two training years will ever be identical, but conclusions from one year can be applied to improve strategies for the next.

13. A carefully designed plan of development, in which the training load is regulated to ensure steady improvement, will provide satisfying rewards in the form of a healthy, happy athlete with a much-improved ability to perform. Both athlete and coach will be delighted.

References

Bompa, T. 1988. Physiological intensity values employed to plan endurance training. *New Studies in Athletics* 3(4):37-52.

———. 1993. *Periodization of strength: The new wave in strength training.* Toronto: Veritas.

Bondarchuk, A. 1988. Constructing a training system. *Track Technique* 102:3254-3268.

Bunc, V.; Hofmann, P.; Leitner, H.; and Gaisl, G. 1995. Verification of the heart rate threshold. *European Journal of Applied Physiology* 70:263-269.

Buskirk, E.R., and Kollas, J. 1967. Physiology and performance of track athletes at various altitudes in the United States and Peru. In *The effects of altitude on physical performance*, ed. R.F. Goddard, 65-71. Chicago: Athletic Institute.

Charniga, A., Jr.; Gambetta, V.; Kraemer, W.; Newton, H.; O'Bryant, H.S.; Palmieri, G.; Pedemonte, J.; Pfaff, D.; and Stone, M.H. 1986-87. Periodization. *National Strength and Conditioning Association Journal* 8(5):12-22; 8(6): 17-24; 9(1):16-26.

Conconi, F.; Ferrari, M.; Ziglio, P.G.; Droghetti, P.; and Codeca, L. 1982. Determination of the anaerobic threshold by a noninvasive field test in runners. *Journal of Applied Physiology* 52:869-873.

Costill, D.L. 1986. *Inside running.* Indianapolis: Benchmark Press.

Coyle, E.F. 1990. Detraining and retention of training-induced adaptations. *Sports Science Exchange* 2(23):1-4.

Cullinane, E.M.; Sady, S.P.; Vadeboncoeur, L.; Burke, M.; and Thompson, P.D. 1986. Cardiac size and $\dot{V}O_2$max do not decrease after short-term exercise cessation. *Medicine and Science in Sports and Exercise* 18:420-421.

Daniels, J. 1989. Training distance runners—A primer. *Sports Science Exchange* 1(11):1-4.

Daniels, J.T., and Gilbert, J. 1979. *Oxygen power: Performance tables for distance runners.* Tempe, AZ: Oxygen Power.

Daniels, J., and Scardina, N. 1984. Interval training and performance. *Sports Medicine* 1:327-334.

Dellinger, B., and Freeman, B. 1984. *The competitive runner's training book.* New York: Macmillan.

Dick, F.W. 1975. Periodization: An approach to the training year. *Track Technique* 62:1968-1970.

―――. 1992. Training at altitude in practice. *International Journal of Sports Medicine* 13:S203-S205.

Edwards, S. 1992. *The heart rate monitor book.* Sacramento, CA: Fleet Feet Press.

Fox, E.L.; Bartels, R.L.; Billings, C.E.; Matthews, D.K.; Bason, R.; and Webb, W.M. 1973. Intensity and distance of interval training programs and changes in aerobic power. *Medicine and Science in Sports* 5:18-22.

Freeman, W.H. 1989. *Peak when it counts.* Los Altos, CA: Tafnews Press.

Galloway, J. 1984. *Galloway's book on running.* Bolinas, CA: Shelter.

Grover, R.F.; Weil, J.V.; and Reeves, J.T. 1986. Cardiovascular adaptation to exercise at high altitude. *Exercise and Sport Sciences Reviews* 14:269-302.

Guralnick, M. 1996. The PR promise. *Running Times* 19(1):23-25.

Humphreys, J., and Holman, R. 1985. *Focus on middle distance running.* London: Adam and Charles Black.

International Amateur Athletic Federation. 1977. *Scoring table for men's track and field events.* London: International Amateur Athletic Federation.

Karvonen, M.J.; Kentala, E.; and Mustala, O. 1957. The effects of training on heart rate. *Annales Medicinae Experimentalis Biologica Fennicae* 35:307-315.

Knuttgen, H.G.; Nordesjo, L.-O.; Ollander, B.; and Saltin, B. 1973. Physical conditioning through interval training with young male adults. *Medicine and Science in Sports* 5:220-226.

Lacour, J.R.; Padilla, S.; and Denis, S. 1987. L'inflexion de la courbe fréquence cardiaque-pussiance n'est pas un témoin du seuil anaerobic (The inflection on the graph of heart rate versus work is not a proof of the anaerobic threshold). *Science et Motricite* 1:3-6.

Larsen, H., and Bentzen, H. 1983. The effect of distance training and interval training on aerobic and anaerobic capacity, muscle fiber characteristics and performance in endurance trained runners. *Twelfth European Track Coaches Congress,* Acoteias, Portugal, January, 1983.

Léger, L.; Mercier, D.; and Gauvin, L. 1986. The relationship between %$\dot{V}O_2$max and running performance time. In *The 1984 Olympic Scientific Congress proceedings.* Vol. 3, *Sport and elite performers,* ed. D.M. Landers, 113-120. Champaign, IL: Human Kinetics.

Lenzi, G. 1987. The marathon race: Modern training methodology. *New Studies in Athletics* 2:41-50.

Levine, B.D.; Friedmann, B.; and Stray-Gundersen, J. 1996. Confirmation of the "high-low" hypothesis: Living at altitude—training near sea level improves sea level performance. *Medicine and Science in Sports and Exercise* 28:S124.

Levine, B.D., and Stray-Gundersen, J. 1992. A practical approach to altitude training: Where to live and train for optimal performance enhancement. *International Journal of Sports Medicine* 13:S209-S212.

Matthews. P. 1996. *Athletics 1996. The International Track and Field Annual* (pp. 247-258). Surbiton, England: SportsBooks Ltd.

Matveyev, L. 1981. *Fundamentals of sports training.* Moscow: Progress.

McInnis, A. 1981. Systematized approaches to peaking. In *Track technique annual,* ed. V. Gambetta, 25-30. Los Altos, CA: Tafnews Press.

Miller, D. 1992. *Sebastian Coe: Born to run.* London: Pavilion Books.

Nett, T. 1965. Die Lehre der Leichtathletik (The teaching of athletics). *Leichtathletik* 16:1023.

Okkels, T. 1983. The effect of interval- and tempo-training on performance and skeletal muscle in well-trained runners. *Twelfth European Track Coaches Congress,* Acoteias, Portugal, January, 1983.

Péronnet, F., and Thibault, G. 1989. Mathematical analysis of running performance and world running records. *Journal of Applied Physiology* 67: 453-465.

Renström, P., and Johnson, R.J. 1985. Overuse injuries in sports. *Sports Medicine* 2:316-333.

Robinson, S.; Edwards, H.T.; and Dill, D.B. 1937. New records in human power. *Science* 85:409-410.

Saltin, B.; Kim, C.K.; Terrados, N.; Larsen, H.; Svedenhag, J.; and Rolf, C.J. 1995. Morphology, enzyme activities and buffer capacity in leg muscles of Kenyan and Scandinavian runners. *Scandinavian Journal of Medicine, Science, and Sports* 5:222-230.

Smith, M.H., and Sharkey, B.J. 1984. Altitude training: Who benefits? *Physician and Sportsmedicine* 12(4):48-62.

Spiriev, B.; Spiriev, A.; and Kovacs, G. 1992. *Scoring tables of athletics.* Budapest: Elite.

Squires, R.W., and Buskirk, E.R. 1982. Aerobic capacity during acute exposure to simulated altitude, 914-2286 meters. *Medicine and Science in Sports and Exercise* 14:36-40.

Terrados, N. 1992. Altitude training and muscular metabolism. *International Journal of Sports Medicine* 13:S206-S208.

Tokmakidis, S.P., and Léger, L.A. 1988. External validity of the Conconi's heart rate anaerobic threshold as compared to the lactate threshold. In *Exercise physiology: Current selected research.* Vol. 3, eds. C.O. Dotson and J.H. Humphrey, 43-58. New York: AMS Press.

———. 1992. Comparison of mathematically determined blood lactate and heart rate "threshold" points and relationship with performance. *European Journal of Applied Physiology* 64:309-317.

Vigil, J. 1987. Distance training. *Track Technique* 100:3189-3192.

———. 1995. *Road to the top.* Albuquerque, NM: Creative Designs.

Wilt, F. 1968. Training for competitive running. In *Exercise physiology,* ed. H.B. Falls, 395-414. New York: Academic Press.

Wolski, L.A.; McKenzie, D.C.; and Wenger, H.A. 1996. Altitude training for improvements in sea level performance: Is there scientific evidence of benefit? *Sports Medicine* 22:251-263.

Yakovlev, N.N. 1967. *Sports biochemistry.* Leipzig: Deutsche Hochschule für Korperkultur (German Institute for Physical Culture).

DEVELOPING TOTAL FITNESS: STRENGTH, FLEXIBILITY, AND HEALTH

The act of running is a fundamentally simple form of exercise, but it is also highly specific in that certain skeletal muscle groups are stimulated out of proportion to others. Accomplished distance runners train anywhere from 70 mi/wk (110 km/wk) to 150 mi/wk (240 km/wk) for many weeks in sequence. The greater the magnitude of this running stimulus, the greater is the relative difference among the stimulated and unstimulated muscles. The posterior lower-limb muscles (hamstrings, gastrocnemius, soleus) and lower-back muscles develop enormous strength and endurance. Other muscle groups, however, such as the anterior lower-limb muscles (quadriceps) and abdominal muscles, are relatively less stimulated. Still other muscles, notably in the upper limbs and trunk, receive even less development. Athletes with such large imbalances in strength and endurance among major muscle groups have an increased risk for injury. If there is a "secret" to improving performance excellence over time, it is training around inherent excellence and not around periodic injuries.

Runners who have been able to incorporate what we have termed a *comprehensive conditioning program* into their training scheme—which increases general strength and balance of *all* their various major muscle groups—tend to have a sizable competitive advantage over those who have not done so. There are at least three reasons for this:

- Submaximal work loads of greater intensity can be managed more easily.
- Greater muscular strength decreases the risk of joint injury or overuse strain by minimizing stress on the connective tissues of the musculoskeletal

253

system (ligaments, tendons, and cartilage) that share in maintaining joint integrity.

- A conditioning program also strengthens these connective tissues, making the entire support system more durable.

As previously mentioned, in a sport in which musculoskeletal injuries from overuse and overtraining are the dominant cause of lost time, giving attention to an effective conditioning program is a wise investment for improving an athlete's longevity.

An important aspect of comprehensive conditioning is the maintenance of adequate flexibility. This is ensured by consistently stretching muscles before and after vigorous use in training. It is essential to have a joint range of motion greater than that required during the exercise; otherwise there is a real risk of muscle tears. Studies of hamstring muscle pulls suggest that muscles that are weak, inflexible, or both are the most susceptible to strain and injury (Christensen 1972; Nicholas 1970). A well-developed balance in strength between the extensors and flexors of the hips and legs, as well as adequate joint range of motion (greater than that required during the exercise), optimizes tolerance to the repetitious nature of thousands of footstrikes logged during each day or week of training. It also permits safe execution of the powerful strides essential for end-of-race sprints to the finish or for quick interval training sessions.

Total-body fitness thus has three components:

- Efficient cardiovascular and fuel-metabolizing systems developed by running, which provide aerobic and anaerobic fitness specific to the act of running
- Adequate joint flexibility as well as strength, power, and endurance in all the major muscle groups, which improve structural balance and reduce the risk of musculoskeletal injury, developed by a comprehensive conditioning program
- An acceptable body composition, which consists of an optimal lean body mass (providing the highest possible power-to-weight ratio) and minimal body fat to ensure good health

Table 6.1 presents a useful self-test of physiological performance and assessment that will give runners an overview of where they fit in terms of high-level comprehensive conditioning for their sport. Distance runners find it relatively easy to hone the cardiovascular endurance component of fitness to a high standard, for that is their specialty area. On the other hand, runners who have not emphasized comprehensive conditioning in their training programs often perform poorly in this self-test. A low score should not be thought of negatively but rather as a stimulus for future development, with accompanying rewards in improved performance.

Athletes seeking to develop and maintain a high standard of comprehensive fitness often find themselves confronted with a bewildering array of fundamental questions regarding the details of training plans and the best equipment to use for such training. Even worse, the answers they receive from alleged experts in various types of conditioning programs can range from appropriate to inappropriate to contradictory. In part, this confusion occurs because of considerable sales pitching regarding the potentially greater benefits of one particular

TABLE 6.1

A Physiological Performance Evaluation of Total-Body Fitness for Talented Distance Runners

Athlete's name _____ Height _____ Weight _____

I. Basic running ability

Stamina test: Run for 15 min around the track, covering as much distance as possible in that time.

> 4,000 m = 52.8 ml $\cdot$ kg^{-1} $\cdot$ min^{-1} $\dot{V}O_2$max= poor for elite men; fair for women
> 4,500 m = 61.1 ml $\cdot$ kg^{-1} $\cdot$ min^{-1} $\dot{V}O_2$ = fair for elite men; good for women
> 5,000 m = 69.5 ml $\cdot$ kg^{-1} $\cdot$ min^{-1} $\dot{V}O_2$ = good for elite men; world-class for women

Speed test: Sprint 40 yd (36.6 m) from a standing start. 6 s = poor, 5.5 s = fair, 5 s = good, 4.5 s = very good

II. Muscle performance ability—strength, power, stamina, agility

Muscular endurance test:

a. Maximum number of press-ups in 1 min. 30 = poor, 40 = fair, 50 = good.
b. Maximum squat thrusts in 1 min. Knees must reach level of arms. 30 = poor, 40 = fair, 50 = good.
c. Maximum sit-ups in 1 min. Lying supine, legs outstretched, hands resting on thighs, head raised with chin pressed to chest, reach forward and touch hands to knees. 40 = poor, 50 = fair, 60 = good.
d. Maximum pull-ups in 1 min, holding bar with palms forward, no leg assistance. Men: 3 = poor, 6 = fair, 9 = good. Women: 2 = poor, 3 = fair, 4 = good.

Muscular power tests for legs:

a. Hop test: Hop 25 m on each leg and count the hops required. 14 hops = poor, 12 = fair, 10 = good.
b. Standing broad jump: Distance equal to own height = poor; distance equal to own height + 10% = fair; distance equal to own height + 25% = good.
c. Sargent jump: Face the wall, make the highest mark possible with chalk-dusted fingertips of an upstretched arm; now turn sideways, leap up, and again touch fingertips to the wall, making a mark with chalk dust; measure the distance between the 2 marks. 12 in. = poor, 18 in. = fair, 24 in. = good
d. Do a full squat with barbell weights. Half body weight = poor, 3/4 body weight = fair, body weight = good.

Strength/weight ratio:

a. Standing medium grip barbell curl. 1/4 body weight = poor, 1/2 body weight = fair, 6/10 body weight = good.
b. Standing barbell press, starting with the barbell placed either on the chest (military press) or on the upper back. 1/4 body weight = poor, 1/2 body weight = fair, 3/4 body weight = good.

III. Range of motion

Flexibility test:

a. Attempt to touch toes with fingertips, keeping legs straight.
b. Lying prone (on stomach), raise the chest off the ground and hold 10 s.
c. Lying supine (on back), legs raised and straight at a 45° angle with the ground, hold for 10 s.
d. Lying prone, raise the chest and legs off the ground for 10 s.
e. Lying supine, knees well bent, hands behind the neck, rise to a sitting position.
f. Lying prone, arms outstretched to the sides, bring right foot over to touch left hand, and vice versa, with minimal chest movement.

IV. Body composition

Percent body fat:

If % body fat is > 8% for men and > 14% for women, fat weight is in excess for quality performance in running.

Height/weight ratio:

Men	Women
71.5 in. (182 cm)/138 lb (62.7 kg)	68.5 in. (174 cm)/116 lb (52.7 kg)
70.0 in. (178 cm)/135 lb (61.3 kg)	66.6 in. (169 cm)/113 lb (51.3 kg)
68.5 in. (174 cm)/132 lb (60.0 kg)[a]	64.9 in. (165 cm)/110 lb (50.0 kg)[a]
66.9 in. (170 cm)/129 lb (58.6 kg)	63.1 in. (160 cm)/107 lb (48.6 kg)
65.4 in. (166 cm)/126 lb (57.3 kg)	61.5 in. (156 cm)/104 lb (47.3 kg)

[a]Middle values represent means of top ten world-ranked athletes in 1996 for 800 m through the marathon; values above and below are calculated based on a metric height/weight ratio of 2.9 cm/kg for men and 3.3 cm/kg for women, or an Imperial ratio of 1.9 lb/in. for men and 1.7 lb/in. for women. For men, variations ± a few kilograms are common, with marathon runners tending to be lighter than runners from 800 m through 10,000 m. For women, variations are larger, with a more noticeable increase in weight from 10,000 m toward 800 m. Longer-distance runners of both sexes tend to be shorter on the average than shorter-distance runners.

kind of conditioning equipment or regimen over another. It also results from our modern-day dilemma of overspecialization: A marathon runner querying a strength coach in the football program at a major American university may get advice more appropriate for a quarter-miler, whose needs are more like those of a quarterback. However, the conditioning requirements of a 400-m or 800-m runner are considerably different from those of a marathoner.

Serious distance runners who will achieve consistent success typically are an intelligent bunch. They want bottom-line answers to many specific questions that will help them with their long-term goals—which typically center around steady improvement year after year. How do strength, power, flexibility, and endurance interact to improve performance? Are increases in muscle mass really necessary for distance runners to become stronger? Are there suggestions for general conditioning (and injury prevention) that would be helpful for middle- as well as long-distance runners, and if so, how can these be implemented using the many available kinds of modalities (free weights, machines, etc.)? How do circuit training and stage training contribute to conditioning? Of the three primary methods for strengthening muscles (identified by whether tension, length, or velocity is held constant during training), which is best for runners attempting to improve their athletic performance? How do eccentric, concentric, and plyometric loading of muscles relate to these three strengthening methods? Similarly, how do flexibility and stretching exercises fit into the training process? What is optimal leanness (or fatness) for distance runners? How do men and women differ in this regard? Does amenorrhea predispose a runner to increased skeletal injury risk, and if so, how does this relate to fatness and bone mineral mass?

With all these complex questions, it is understandable why distance runners often neglect to develop a comprehensive conditioning program and concentrate simply on running. But such a decision is a real error. This chapter should provide a better understanding of and solution to the challenge of developing a comprehensive conditioning plan. This in turn should help prevent injuries and provide the kind of balanced fitness a runner requires to move toward the goals of extended competitive excellence.

Adapting Muscles to Stress Loading

In chapter 2 we outlined some of the important anatomical and physiological principles that explain skeletal muscle function. Now let us apply some of this knowledge practically to improvement through specialized training of the various components of muscular performance.

The terminology for each of these components is quite specific, but often the terms are used incorrectly. Just as we defined clearly in chapter 5 all the various terms related to training sessions, let's first explain the concepts; this will make their practical application much easier as we discuss fitness development.

Definitions: The Terminology of Conditioning

Strength is often defined as the maximal force that can be developed during muscle activation (tension generation). If we think of strength as equivalent to force, its units of measurement would be the *newton* (N) in the metric system or the *pound* (lb) in the Imperial system, where 1 N = 0.225 lb and 1 lb = 4.4 N.

Commonly the term *contraction* is used as an alternative to *activation* or *tension generation*, implying that the muscle shortens. But we shall soon see that, depending on circumstances, the muscle could also either lengthen or remain unchanged in length and still produce tension and exert force. Thus, contraction (i.e., shortening) does not always describe accurately what is happening. Tension generation is indeed occurring when force is being exerted, regardless of whether the muscle is changing in length, so it is a more accurate phrase. By using appropriate descriptors such as *lengthening* or *shortening*, we can characterize more clearly the kind of tension generation occurring.

Strength is often said to be determined by a *muscular component* and a *neural component*, but there is a third, mechanical component as well, which shall be discussed later. The muscular component of strength has three contributing variables: cross-sectional area, muscle fiber length, and muscle architecture (McDonagh and Davies 1984). *The greater the cross-sectional area*, as seen when muscles incorporate more protein and become larger, *the greater the muscle force production capability. The longer the muscle*, as seen when muscle cells add sarcomeres on either end, *the greater its potential shortening or lengthening capability.* Force output will be greatest when the overlap among tension-generating proteins (actin and myosin) is maximal. In chapter 2 we illustrated the variety of possible architectural arrangements in muscle—fusiform, multipennate, and so on. These variations change the force development pattern during muscle shortening or lengthening as movement occurs.

The neural aspect has two variables: stimulus frequency and recruitment. Recall that skeletal muscle cells are each influenced by their connecting motor neurons. *As stimulus frequency increases, force production rises* (Person and Kudina 1972) because more and more motor units are activated. The relationship is sigmoidal (S-shaped) rather than linear (Rack and Westbury 1969). *Recruitment* refers to a predictable and sequential activation of motor units as work intensity increases (Denny-Brown 1949). Low-threshold stimuli activate slow-twitch (ST) motor units preferentially. *The higher the stimulus strength, the greater is the recruitment of motor units*, as those with a higher threshold of response are gradually brought into action. Interestingly, however, the sequence of motor unit activation with a *natural* (neural) increase in the intensity of muscle stimulation is the opposite of that seen when *artificial* (electrical) stimulation occurs. Neural stimulation recruits motor units in the following sequence (Burke 1981): ST with fatigue-resistant (slow oxidative) muscle cells, FT with intermediate fatigability (fast oxidative-glycolytic muscle cells), and FT with rapidly fatigable (fast glycolytic) muscle cells. Because of considerable overlap, however, even at low work intensities some FT motor units will be activated.

Electromyostimulation, however, produced simply by sending electrical current through a stimulating electrode placed on the skin over the surface of a muscle, brings the opposite response in the motor units. This is related to the response characteristics of the motor neurons to electrical stimulation. The largest nerve axons have the lowest threshold of stimulation, and thus the rapidly fatigable FT muscle cells are stimulated first (Eccles, Eccles, and Lundberg 1958; Henneman 1957). Only with higher-intensity stimulation will the smaller neurons, which innervate the ST fatigue-resistant muscle cells, be activated. These different responses have important implications in the rehabilitation of injured muscles as well as in their normal function.

Various skeletal muscles differ in their relative combinations of stimulus frequency and motor unit recruitment that permit force production. Even at relatively low force outputs, some muscles will have nearly all their motor units active but stimulated at a rather low frequency. Other muscles will produce an equivalent force but rely initially on only a few fibers being stimulated at a higher frequency. Both stimulus frequency and recruitment are related to the level of outflow from the central nervous system. This is often termed the *central drive* and is determined in large measure by such ill-defined but powerful factors as motivation.

It becomes technically more correct to add a few additional constraints to our earlier definition of strength. John Atha (1981) defined strength as "the ability to develop force against an unyielding resistance in a single contraction of unrestricted duration." Time, however, is a critical factor in distance running performance. The quicker athletes run, the faster they reach the finish line. The concepts of velocity and speed thus become crucial. *Velocity* is simply *the rate of change in position over time.* It can be expressed in a variety of units. For example, at the 1996 Brussels Memorial Ivo Van Damme track meet, when Morocco's Salah Hissou set a world record in the men's 10,000-m run, we could say that this performance of 26:38.08 represented an average running velocity around the track of 6.3 m/s, or 14.0 mi/hr (or a pace of 63.9 s/400 m). *Speed,* however, is a more general term relating to *quickness;* a runner with inherent speed can run quickly.

When force is applied to move a particular resistance through a given distance, work is done. Thus, *work* can be defined as the product of the force used for displacement times the distance the resistance is moved. It represents the energy output of activated muscles. The appropriate units for work measurement are *newton-meters* ($N \cdot m$) or *joules* (J) in the metric system and *foot-pounds* ($ft \cdot lb$) in the Imperial system: $1 N \cdot m = 1 J = 0.738 ft \cdot lb$, and $1 ft \cdot lb = 1.356 J$. If no movement occurs, regardless of the force exerted on a given resistance, no work is done.

Torque is defined as the force required to move an object around an axis of rotation (Laird and Rozier 1979). Some find it useful to think of torque as angular work. It is calculated as the product of the rotary component of the exerted force and the length of the involved lever arm. In turn, *lever arm* is a line drawn perpendicular to the direction of muscle force (the muscle force vector), from the axis of rotation of a movable joint to the point where muscle force is applied (figure 6.1). Thus, the units of torque are the same as those for work—$N \cdot m$ or $ft \cdot lb$. As the muscle shortens or lengthens, producing limb rotation around the joint, the resulting changes in lever arm length can produce changes in torque without changing the muscular force applied. Thus, in addition to the neural and muscular components of strength identified earlier, inclusion of this *mechanical component* is essential. However, although a strength training program may improve the body's ability to neurally recruit more muscle fibers or increase the total available muscle protein, it has very little effect on changing lever arm relationships. These are anatomically determined.

Power is the rate at which work is done. The metric unit for power is the *watt* ($1 N \cdot m/s$ or $0.7376 ft \cdot lb/s$). Thus, power can be calculated as force times velocity, or as torque times angular velocity. A powerful athlete can produce force rapidly. An increase in power can occur either by increasing the rate at which a given work output occurs or by increasing the amount of work accomplished in a given time period. Thus, strength as well as the velocity of shortening or lengthening of muscle cells are important aspects of power output. Training in a manner that improves power output through modest gains in both strength and velocity may be less injurious and fundamentally more useful than attempting impressive gains in either strength or velocity alone.

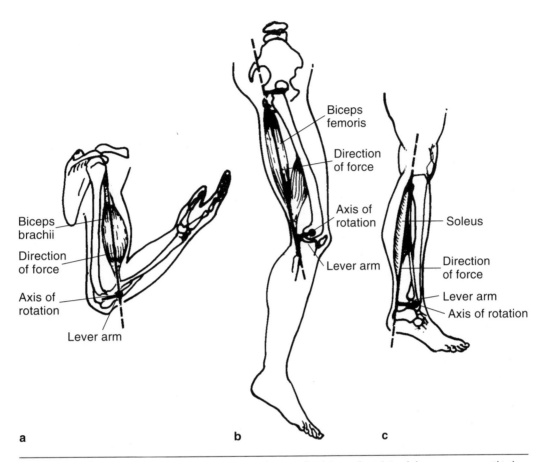

Figure 6.1 Lever arms for three common muscles: (*a*) the biceps brachii of the upper arm, (*b*) the biceps femoris of the upper leg (one of the hamstrings), and (*c*) the soleus of the lower leg. In each instance the lever arm extends from the axis of rotation of the distal (movable) joint attachment to the muscle force vector, indicating the muscle's direction of force output.

Methods for Building Muscle Strength and Power

Over the years a great many different approaches have been developed for improving strength and power. Some have used free weights, often called barbells. Others have used any of several sophisticated mechanical devices called weight machines. It is important to understand the concepts that explain how these approaches achieve their goal. Only then can serious athletes decide which approach is best for helping them achieve their specific goals for improving athletic performance.

Static Resistance Training: Isometrics

When we attempt to push or lift a fixed or otherwise immovable object (referred to as an external force), our skeletal muscle fibers generate tension but cannot exert sufficient internal force to produce movement. Some fibrillar shortening within the muscle occurs, but the elastic components stretch, and the external length of the whole muscle remains unaltered. Because of this relatively unchanging length, the muscles are said to be under *isometric* or *static tension.* They can produce maximal tension or any amount of varying submaximal tension at essentially any joint angle.

Isometric training was brought to the forefront of the fitness world in 1953 when Hettinger and Muller announced their surprising finding that essentially a single isometric effort of only 6-s duration at as little as two thirds of maximal intensity could be effective in improving muscular strength. Thus, hours of barbell lifting and other kinds of hard work might be unnecessary for strengthening muscles. Quite logically, as athletes have used other forms of strength training for centuries to build muscle size and strength, this report of the benefits of isometric training was scrutinized carefully, and a large number of subsequent studies followed in the ensuing two decades. The current status of these studies has suggested that the initially reported 5% increase per week in strength was not very repeatable, but a smaller increase, approaching 2%, could be expected. Thus, isometric training does increase strength, and the initial gains are sizable, but they fall off rapidly after about five weeks. These gains typically are localized to within about 20° of the training angle (Knapik, Mawdsley, and Ramos 1983). Thus, several joint angles must be selected over a broad range to ensure reasonably uniform strength development over a joint's entire range of motion.

One of the most familiar examples of isometric tension generation in runners is seen when they lean toward and push against a wall or tree as a warm-up exercise before a training run or a race (look ahead to figure 6.19). Although the intent of the exercise may be to stretch the posterior lower-limb muscles, the upper-torso and upper-limb muscles come under isometric tension. A second example of isometric stimulation involves training at specific joint angles where increased strength is required—for example, in the knee joint at takeoff in the high jump. In the weight room, athletes may use a power rack to produce isometric tension in their quadriceps muscles at this takeoff knee joint angle by pushing a bar upward against appropriately positioned restraining pins. Isometric activity is also used during rehabilitation of limbs that have been injured and immobilized as a result of recent surgery. Exercises that produce isometric tension can slow or prevent muscle cell atrophy.

A few problems can occur with performance of isometric exercises. The most important is a sizable increase in both systolic and diastolic blood pressures. This occurs even if the active muscles form a rather small fraction of the total muscle bulk. Another difficulty involves joint discomfort and stress from excessive bone and joint compression. Some of the exercises used in isometric conditioning are ill advised for beginners until the vertebral column becomes well protected by associated musculotendinous development. For example, using a standard isometric squat rack can direct excessive force to the vertebral column, increasing the risk of lower-back pain and possible injury.

A third difficulty involves the absence of natural ballistic action in body segments. Most sport activities require far more than simply isometric strength capabilities. They involve a high degree of automatic control of skilled ballistic movements. Neuromuscular coordination, effective utilization of multiple joints, and a broad range of movement of those joints are crucial for success. These movements have large initial accelerations that require considerable strength followed by fine-tuned control that requires split-second timing and optimal movement economy. As described in chapter 1, fast motion and multiple joint actions are the mainstay of distance running, integrated in a repetitive, ballistic sequence of footstrike, midsupport, takeoff, follow-through, forward swing, foot descent, and then another footstrike. Although joint stability may be improved by static resistance training, the resulting increased muscle strength does not translate well to improved sport performance. Hence, if a runner can choose between static and dynamic strength-training exercises, the latter would be preferred because they transfer more directly to running.

Dynamic Resistance Training

If an unchanging resistance such as a barbell or some other weighted object can be moved, either directly by lifting it or indirectly through action on cables and pulleys, then tension generation, force production, and length changes will all occur in the muscles utilized. This is called *dynamic resistance exercise,* and it refers to the training of skeletal muscles by application of loads of such magnitude that the muscles can lengthen or shorten within their normal movement limits. The tension generated will vary in magnitude depending on leverage relationships, gravitational influences on inertial and velocity changes, and number of actomyosin cross-bridge connections. The term *dynamic tension* is often used to describe this continually changing tension. There are three different types of dynamic resistance training: *isotonic, isokinetic,* and *plyometric.*

If the resistance is unchanging, as with lifting a barbell, the term *isotonic training* is used, suggesting constant tension or tone but actually referring to a constant load. Some familiar examples of working against a constant resistance include the use of one's own body weight to perform exercises such as push-ups (press-ups), chin-ups (pull-ups), or sit-ups. Another form of constant resistance exercise can be achieved through the use of free weights such as barbells. Plates of varying weights are placed at either end of a metal bar. As the athlete assumes various positions of standing, sitting, or lying, these weights are lifted, pushed, or maintained in position while some other part of the body is moved (see figures 6.5, 6.8, 6.9, 6.10, 6.15, and 6.17 later in this chapter).

Isokinetic training requires the use of certain specialized equipment to be described shortly. The equipment permits athletes to train their muscles by moving them at a constant velocity, that is, isokinetically, through their entire range of motion. Tension generation can be maximal or submaximal, and the equipment provides an accommodating resistance to permit constant velocity.

With either the isotonic or isokinetic forms of dynamic exercise training, the muscle fibers may either lengthen (called *eccentric loading*) or shorten (called *concentric loading*). For example, when we do sit-ups, the abdominal muscles, particularly the rectus abdominis, shorten as we sit up and then lengthen as we return to the supine position. During concentric tension generation, work is done *by the muscles on the load,* which here is overcoming the force of gravity in raising the head, upper limbs, and upper torso. This is termed *positive work.* During eccentric tension generation, work is done *by the load on the muscles;* this is called *negative work.* The energy cost of negative work is less than for positive work, and the muscles involved are under higher tension than during either positive work or isometric tension generation (Olson, Schmidt, and Johnson 1972). Presumably, during eccentric work fewer motor units and thus fewer muscle cells are involved, but they are involved more intensely. This may explain the relatively greater postexercise soreness that accompanies eccentric work (e.g., long downhill runs) than other types of muscle activation. Finishers of the Boston Marathon comment frequently that their muscle soreness and recovery are greater for that event than for other marathons. The Boston Marathon course is net downhill for the first 16 mi and for the final 5 mi, resulting in extensive eccentric muscle loading. Thus, the probable best strategy for a good finish at the Boston Marathon is not to race the downhills so vigorously (which can be debilitating), but rather, be gentle on the downhills and race the uphill portion ("Heartbreak

Hill") aggressively. This proved to be the winning strategy for Kenya's Cosmas Ndeti in the 1993, 1994, and 1995 editions of that famous race.

Using the biceps brachii in the upper arm to lift the body in performing a chin-up is an example of isotonic *concentric* tension generation. The corresponding antagonist muscles (triceps) are relaxed during this activity. Returning to the starting position would involve isotonic *eccentric* tension generation in the biceps. The antagonists also remain relaxed. Similarly, the act of sitting or squatting involves negative work by the leg extensors; moving to the supine position from a sitting position requires negative work by the hip flexors. Standing from the squatting position, or sitting up from the recumbent position, involves positive work by the same respective muscles. Their antagonist muscles (leg flexors for sitting, hip extensors for lying) are inactive during this period of activation.

Plyometric training involves a specialized coupling of eccentric and concentric loading, with the aim of increasing the muscle power output. This type of training includes the so-called bounding exercises that are especially popular for jumpers, but which can also be beneficial for runners. This will also be described in greater detail shortly.

How can the force generated by dynamic resistance training be quantified? Using Newton's *second law of motion*, the force (F) developed by such dynamic exercise is determined by the sum of the weight (W; the downward pull of gravity acting on the mass of the involved object—the weight of a barbell, for example) and the product of the mass (m) of the object and its acceleration (a). Thus,

$$F = W + ma \tag{6.1}$$

Initially, considerable force is required to start the muscle movement, whether it be pushing, pulling, or lifting, because inertia must be overcome. Once movement begins, the same applied force can now maintain acceleration as the pace quickens. As a constant pace is achieved, this rate of acceleration slows to zero. Fatigue will decrease the extent to which such initial accelerations are easily achieved.

Isotonic Training: Unchanging Resistance. The phenomenon of skeletal muscles getting bigger and stronger through a program of gradually more challenging isotonic loading is probably one of the oldest observations in physiology and is certainly as old as sport itself. Hardly a lecture or article describing the principles of strength training fails to mention the legendary feats of Milo of Crotona. Milo was a wrestler with a very long and successful career during the sixth century B.C. who allegedly earned a victory wreath at the ancient Olympic Games (Young 1984). The story is often recited of how, as a shepherd, he would hoist a small lamb across his back and shoulders, then squat down and return to his standing position several times in succession. As the lamb grew and gained weight, this provided a greater resistance to which Milo could gradually adapt. The legend becomes misty in suggesting that he could steadily increase his own strength development until the animal reached adulthood. Nevertheless, he eventually became so strong that no one could match him, and his enormous strength put him almost in a class by himself when he entered the wrestling arena.

It was the Romans, however, rather than the Greeks who developed and refined the techniques that form the basis of what we do today for systematically improving strength. The three fundamental principles of strength training date back so far that their originators have long been lost. One of these is the *principle of progressive resistance*, which states that if skeletal muscles are overloaded, they will gradually adapt in such a manner that this new load will become better tolerated. Then if the resistive load is again increased progressively and over time as a new level of overload, an eventual new level of adaptation will occur; this is why the example of Milo is so often used in teaching the principles of strength training. Adaptation occurs in the skeletal and nervous systems as well as in the muscles. We may define *overload* as a substantially larger training load than the muscle normally experiences, consisting of either a larger resistance or an increased number of repetitions (reps) that the resistance is managed, or both.

The *principle of increasing intensity* states that it is the intensity of muscle stimulation rather than the frequency that is important in strengthening muscle. An interesting study by MacDougall, Wenger, and Green (1982) confirmed this rather nicely. Both body builders and power lifters were studied in an attempt to learn more about the mechanism by which muscle training produces hypertrophy. These two types of athletes train quite differently: Body builders typically do many repetitions at submaximal loads, and power lifters generally do only a few reps using very heavy loads. A common denominator of these two groups, however, is that both train to failure, that is, to the point of virtually complete fatigue. Thus, they both provide a maximally intense stimulus to their muscles. Both types achieve a similar end result in terms of hypertrophy (increased muscle mass). The cellular mechanisms that trigger the hypertrophy have not yet been identified.

Two pioneering studies set the stage for the enormous interest in strength training that began shortly following World War II. Benedetto Morpurgo (1897) at the University of Siena verified that as muscles get bigger with training, it isn't the *number* of fibers that increases, but rather an increase in individual fiber *size*. John Eyster (1927) later showed that the *intensity* of work performance rather than simply the *work load managed* is the stimulus for increasing muscle size and increasing its strength.

Thomas DeLorme in 1945 published one of the first scientific reports on the effects of isotonic resistance training on skeletal muscle development. If anyone can be identified as the originator of the phrase *progressive resistance exercise*, it is he. Strength is improved best through high-resistance and low-rep exercise. Endurance, on the other hand, is developed through low-resistance and high-rep exercise without training to failure. Strength increases in muscle accrue largely through an increase in intracellular muscle protein, whereas endurance is improved by increased capillarization and intracellular mitochondrial dynamics. Strength training will not build the performance qualities that are developed by endurance training, and vice versa. This is the important *principle of specificity:* The adaptation to training is determined by the nature of the training stimulus. Thus, weeks and weeks of slow distance running do not improve the ability to run quickly as much as they provide an endurance base on which fast running can then be added to effectively improve racing capabilities.

A few years later DeLorme and Arthur Watkins (1948) provided a systematized format for using progressive resistance exercise to increase gross muscle strength and endurance. They used an arrangement of cables and pulleys combined with the weight of the extremity to be trained (arms or legs) and counterbalancing weights. Their strength-building regimen required three sets of lifting, each set based on an amount of weight that could be lifted no more than 10 times (called a 10-rep maximum, or 10 RM). The first two sets of 10 lifts were at

50% and 75% of maximum, thereby serving as a warm-up for the maximal effort that followed. This final third set contributed most as the actual strength-building stimulus. As strength gains occur, athletes can eventually manage easily more than 10 reps at the original 10 RM. Arbitrarily, DeLorme and Watkins suggested that when 15 reps can be managed at the 10-RM load, an increase in loading should then occur to permit a new strength-building challenge.

Subjects who used such a format often reported considerable fatigue, muscular pain, and inability to maintain full range of motion from doing so much work before the primary strength-building stimulus. Zinovieff suggested that instead of decreasing the volume of the two warm-up sets, the stimulus format be reversed. In 1951 he outlined a program of 10 sets of 10 reps, the very first to be done at the 10-RM intensity when the muscles were fresh. Each set thereafter was done with decreasing resistance; the ideal situation would be one in which increasing fatigue would be matched exactly by decreasing load so that all 100 reps would be at a functional maximum.

As one might imagine, these studies were followed over the next few decades by literally hundreds more, each suggesting a different variation on the same goal, namely, how to arrive at the best combination of sets, reps, interval of rest, and size of load that would bring the greatest gains in performance. At about this same time the pioneering ultrastructural studies of muscle function began to reveal how muscle tension generation occurred. As we described in chapter 2, the sliding filament theory (A.F. Huxley and Niedergerke 1954; H.E. Huxley and Hanson 1954) postulated an enzyme-mediated movement of actin and myosin molecules past one another to permit shortening or lengthening. It provided a fascinating breakthrough in knowledge on the molecular level to accompany that occurring at the gross level regarding the mechanisms for improving muscular performance.

Depending on the athlete, performance aspirations will differ. Muscle hypertrophy is very important for a body builder. A middle-distance runner desires considerable strength and power but with a minimal increase in muscle size. For a long-distance runner, adequate overall joint strength and reasonable increases in both strength and power in the major muscle groups connecting to those joints is desirable, again with no need to increase muscle mass. No generic program is suitable for all athletes; based on present fitness level, genetic predisposition regarding FT/ST fiber types, event specificity, past experience at comprehensive conditioning programs, and individual strengths and weaknesses, a workable plan can be designed for each individual.

During the early 1960s Richard Berger (1962) published a prodigious amount of work aimed at identifying the optimal mix of sets and reps to permit gains in muscular strength. His criterion for a strength gain was improvement in a 1-RM lift. His conclusion was that, for most people, three sets of four to eight reps done three times per week produced optimal strength gains. Unlike the DeLorme/Watkins system, however, where only the final set was at maximum, all three sets are done at maximal intensity. Thus, using a 6-RM load as an example, it may not be possible during the first training session to complete the assigned load. Instead of three sets of 6 RM, the first may be six reps, the second five reps, the third only four or five reps. Gradually, however, increasing strength permits six reps at the 6 RM, showing nicely the adaptive improvement over time. When this work load can be tolerated routinely, Berger recommends increasing the load by 5%.

In 1979 Wayne Westcott proposed a system of lifting that requires less total effort yet provides gains in strength similar to those of other systems in use.

Using an individual's 1 RM as the basis for identifying the training load, Westcott suggested three sets with decreasing reps (for example, 10 to 5 to 1) along with increasing resistance (55%, 75%, and 95% of maximum). The obvious conclusions when programs such as those of DeLorme, Berger, and Westcott are compared is that it isn't the total number of reps or the total weight lifted that is crucial for initiating a strength-building stimulus. Instead, as indicated earlier, it is the exercise intensity. The various combinations of submaximal efforts, either preceding or following the most intense (improvement-stimulating) part of the lifting session, merely vary the pattern of warm-up or cool-down as well as neural recruitment and total work output.

Because of individual differences in the FT/ST composition of skeletal muscles, the number of reps that can be managed at any work intensity will vary considerably. In chapter 2 we described the greater fatigue resistance in ST fibers. Although both FT and ST fibers will be recruited at high-intensity work loads (Lesmes et al. 1983), as is done during weight training or very fast running, athletes with a majority of FT fibers will fatigue more quickly. Thus, whereas one set of 8 to 12 reps may be commonly advocated, the ultimate decision regarding fewer or greater numbers of reps should be based on each individual athlete's predisposition toward endurance or strength excellence.

A typical result observed after several months of a strength-building program is a plateau in performance gains. The initial improvements are due largely to improved neurological recruitment abilities and gains in efficiency of performing each exercise. Skeletal muscle fiber adaptations, however, contribute as well. Once recruitment and efficiency begin to plateau, however, continued gains in strength occur but are more specifically a result of intrinsic muscle cell adaptation (Häkkinen and Komi 1983). For a runner relatively uninterested in producing muscle hypertrophy, this slowdown in improvement is not as important as the continued maintenance training effect that aids in injury prevention in the muscles and their associated connective tissues.

With isotonic training, although the load may remain constant, the mechanical advantage of lever systems changes through the range of joint motion, particularly as the load is distributed among different muscle groups. Lifters are then limited to the weight they can manage at the weakest point in their range of motion—this is the *sticking point*. During the 1960s and 1970s a wide variety of so-called *variable resistance machines* appeared on the market as a preferable alternative to free weights. One type (Universal Gym), developed by Harold Zimkin, had multiple stations, arranged around a central axis, using pulley and lever systems. An entirely different concept, pioneered by Arthur Jones (Nautilus Industries, Inc.), consists of many separate machines utilizing eccentrically placed cams. In this way the equipment's resistive load can be effectively lightened when the body's lever arms are working at their least mechanical advantage and maximized when the muscles are working most advantageously. A variety of investigative reports which not only assessed the performance capabilities of Nautilus equipment but also compared it to other types of equipment then available were later published by one of Nautilus's technical specialists, Ellington Darden (1977).

The net effect of variable resistance provides a velocity profile through the range of motion that differs greatly from that seen commonly in normal sport movements, however. In particular, the achievement of high acceleration is dampened. But the relatively slow training movements provide a high level of muscle fiber tension throughout the entire range of motion, and this is the preferred mode of training using this equipment. The consensus based on individual experience with such equipment seems to indicate that one set of 8 to 12 reps using a sizable load is most successful for strength gains. Fast training movements are possible but often impractical because the ballistic movements cause problems with bouncing stacks of weights.

Plyometrics: Coupling Eccentric and Concentric Loading. Bounding and jumping exercises involve isotonic tension generation but do so in a unique manner. As a jumper strikes the ground after having been in midair, an initial brief period of eccentric tension generation occurs as the landing legs absorb the impact effects of body weight and gravity by momentarily flexing at the knee. Forward momentum as well as body weight contribute to this eccentric tension. A split second later, this is followed by concentric tension generation. During concentric tension, forward and upward movement then occurs. Every impact of feet striking the ground is accompanied by this eccentric-concentric tension-generation pattern: Bounding and jumping simply exaggerate it.

According to Matveyev (1981) the body's ability to improve the operational qualities of eccentric-concentric coupling with specialized training provides an enormous opportunity for improving power, particularly in jumping. Yuriy Verkhoshanskiy (1973) referred to exercises that improve tolerance to this kind of stress (typically jumping off boxes, landing, and then explosively leaping upward) as *shockloading*. Atha (1981) termed them *bounce-loading* exercises. The term currently used is *plyometrics,* which refers to training exercises that augment or increase concentric power output by means of a closely linked preceding eccentric (stretch) loading.

When eccentric-concentric coupling occurs, several phenomena interact to enhance power output. One of these is a *muscle stretch reflex*. As an example, let us consider a simple bounding exercise in which a lower limb is about to absorb landing shock and at the same time provide the push-off that begins the next bound in the sequence. Lengthening tension in the quadriceps muscle cells stretches small receptor endings called muscle spindles. Activation of the sensory neurons connecting to these spindles produces a reflex stimulation of the motor neurons innervating the quadriceps muscle cells. An active generation of concentric tension occurs, producing a tendency for knee extension. If this reflex stimulation is timed perfectly with the nearly simultaneous volley of information from the cerebral cortex to voluntarily initiate takeoff, both will summate, enhancing total neuromuscular output at the knee joint and providing a powerful knee extensor response.

A second phenomenon resulting from eccentric tension is the storage of energy in elastic components within the muscle cells (Thomas 1988). These are arranged both in series with and parallel to the muscle cell proteins that slide past each other during tension generation. This elastic energy can be recovered during the subsequent shortening. The magnitude of recovery will be greatest when

- there is minimum time delay between lengthening and shortening tension (Komi and Bosco 1978),
- the lengthening tension is not too great (Cavagna 1977), and
- the velocity of lengthening tension is greatest (Burke 1981).

Specific plyometric exercises are used actively by athletes in such disciplines as high jumping and triple jumping, where a major emphasis is developing the greatest possible vertical or horizontal trajectories in flight (D.E. Martin et al. 1987). On first consideration it might not seem appropriate for distance runners to be interested in improving their jumping ability. Efficient running is characterized by, among other things, minimal vertical oscillation, thereby ensuring optimal conversion of energy into forward motion. A modest amount of plyometric training, however, particularly for middle-distance runners (800 m, 1,500 m, steeplechase), will add a beneficial power component that would not be acquired through the more traditional isotonic training techniques. Such power can be beneficial in racing situations for sudden pace changes through effective use of the large hip and leg extensors. Additionally, any increase in joint strength resulting from such training will benefit the athlete in terms of injury prevention.

Plyometric exercises for leg muscles typically include various types of depth-jumping exercises using boxes or other gymnastic equipment. Receiving and immediately pushing back a medicine ball is an example of plyometric exercise challenging the upper body. The kinds of equipment needed for plyometric exercises can be quite simple: sturdy boxes 10, 15, 20, 25, and 30 in. (25, 40, 50, 65, and 75 cm) in height, weighted vests (10, 15, 20, and 25 lb; 5, 7, 9, and 11 kg), a few adjustable hurdles, and a smooth grassy surface. Using these, an individualized program can be devised to provide a variety of challenging plyometric stimuli for developing muscle and joint strength and power. Exact numbers of reps and sets (and heights of hurdles or boxes) depend on the athlete's prior experience, position in a training macrocycle, and event specialty. We have found that for hurdle hops (jumping over five hurdles closely spaced to permit one two-footed landing between them) or box jumping (jumping onto and off of four boxes closely spaced to permit one two-footed landing between them), more than 20 to 25 bounds is excessive. If the athlete can easily manage sequences such as five sets of five bounds using low boxes or low hurdles, then the intensity can be increased gradually by increasing the athlete's body weight (using a weighted vest) or the height to which the center of gravity must be lifted. The athlete can also do bounding exercises on a soft grassy surface, performing three sets of 10 elongated strides with the exaggerated knee lift used in the step phase of the triple jump.

Plyometrics should be considered highly specific exercises to be scheduled judiciously and are potentially dangerous when done improperly or in a fatigued state. These guidelines are therefore appropriate:

- Because of their intensity and ballistic nature, plyometrics should be preceded by thorough warm-up and stretching exercises.
- Plyometrics should not be done after serious weight training or fast running sessions, but rather should be scheduled as a first item on a training agenda, when muscles and joints are fresh.
- Because these exercises have a large anaerobic component and require good technique and considerable concentration, nearly complete recovery should occur between sets.
- Use of a weighted vest is recommended as an add-on only after considerable proficiency has been developed using normal body weight that can be very easily managed.
- Anaerobic running sessions should not be scheduled for the day following a quality plyometric session; one day of easy running is needed to ensure recovery.
- Athletes should always use soft, resilient landing surfaces, such as grass or suitable mats, along with shoes that provide plenty of support (it is best not to use a track surface).

- Plyometrics should be introduced only after a substantial base of strengthening and conditioning; not all distance runners ought to consider plyometrics to be crucial or essential.

In summary, plyometrics are an advanced form of specific training intended to provide primarily middle-distance runners with an explosive component in their leg and hip extensors that can be beneficial for specific aspects of racing.

Isokinetic Training: Accommodating Resistance. The commercial availability of machines in the 1970s that could essentially remove ballistic movement and permit overload training with maximal muscle tension generation at a *constant velocity throughout the full range of motion* provided an entirely new dimension to fitness training. This was termed *isokinetic training.* Probably the first isokinetic device was built in the 1920s (Levin and Wyman 1927), using a needle valve to regulate oil flow between two connecting chambers. In 1968, 41 years later, Los Angeles bioengineer James J. Perrine published his research with a more sophisticated device eventually marketed commercially under the trade name of Cybex (Lumex Industries, Inc.). Since then an expanding technology using everything from hydraulics to pneumatics and clutch plates in tandem with flywheels has given us a wide variety of devices to provide resistance that is essentially a mirror image of the active force provided by the muscles. Thistle and colleagues (1967), in their first published study using the Cybex isokinetic dynamometer, pointed out that an *accommodating resistance* is provided to the tension-generating muscles, and it matches almost exactly their force output. Because the velocity of muscle shortening is virtually unchanged throughout the movement range, the muscle cells are being isokinetically trained. Thus, the activated muscle cells are generating maximal tension at every point in their associated joint's range of motion.

Figure 6.2*a* illustrates knee joint extension and flexion evaluation using the Cybex II isokinetic dynamometer. Our athlete test subject is Laurie Henes (whose runner-up 10,000-m finish [32:05.02] at the 1995 U.S. track championships earned her a berth on the traveling team to the Göteborg World Championships). Before starting her test, the torque-measuring arm of the device is first aligned with her knee joint axis (figure 6.2*b*). We then use a broad range of nine angular velocities, starting at 300°/s and decreasing by 30°/s increments down to 60°/s, to evaluate the dynamic properties of her lower-limb musculature. Any additional force greater than that required to achieve these velocities is resisted (passively) by an equal and opposite force. This force can be quantified in various ways (Laird and Rozier 1979; Moffroid and Kusiak 1975). For example, peak torque, torque at specific joint angles, peak torque per body weight, work, and power can all be measured.

The isokinetic effort depicted in figure 6.2*a* is considerably different from a knee extension and flexion maneuver with a weighted leg extension machine (similar to that shown in figure 6.14, *a* and *b*). On a leg extension machine, movement from 90° of knee joint flexion to 0° requires concentric quadriceps tension, and movement back to 90° requires eccentric quadriceps tension. Isokinetic movement from 90° of knee joint flexion toward 0° requires concentric quadriceps tension, but in contrast, movement from 0° of flexion back to 90° requires concentric tension in the hamstrings and gastrosoleus muscles. Thus, the instructions given to our athletes are first to kick out as hard as possible (i.e., reduce knee flexion from 90° toward 0° using quadriceps tension) and then to pull back as hard as possible (i.e., increase knee flexion back toward 90° using gastrosoleus and hamstrings tension). Thus, eccentric tension generation is not

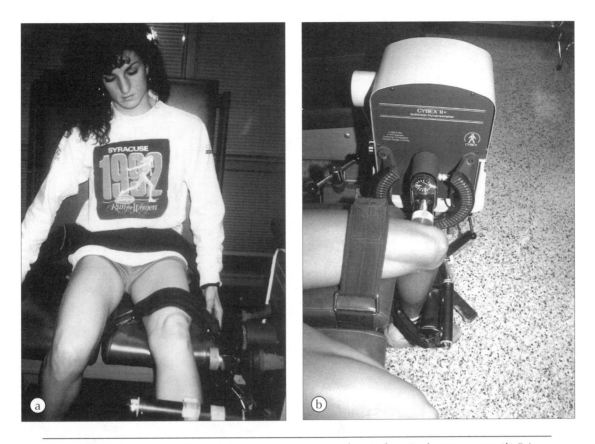

Figure 6.2 (*a*) Evaluation of knee joint function using a Cybex isokinetic dynamometer. (*b*) Prior to testing, the torque-measuring arm must be aligned with the subject's knee joint axis. In (*b*) the subject's left knee is in 90° of joint flexion (and extension). Extending the knee, beginning in (*a*), brings the knee toward 0° of flexion.

involved and would need other types of equipment, such as the isotonic leg extensor machine and the hamstring curl machine (see figure 6.16 later in this chapter).

Figure 6.3, *a* through *c*, depicts graphically the maximal torque produced by knee extension as it proceeds from 90° to 0° and returns by knee flexion to 90°. Tracings are illustrated for three different movement velocities: 60°/s, 180°/s, and 300°/s. Each muscle or muscle group has its own unique force production curve in causing joint rotation; the difference between knee extensors and flexors in figure 6.3 can readily be seen. Notice also that maximal torque production varies not only with joint angle but with velocity of tension generation as well. This torque variation with different movement velocities relates to the number of cross-bridge linkages in place at any given moment in time. The faster the movement velocity, the fewer the number of cross bridges linked at any moment, resulting in less tension. Mary Moffroid and her colleagues (Moffroid and Whipple 1970; Moffroid et al. 1969) expanded on these early studies to provide a wealth of practical information concerning the value and utilization of isokinetic evaluation and training in clinical practice.

In nature, accommodating resistance can be imitated somewhat by exercising in water. Water surrounding a limb provides considerably more resistance than air does, which tends to dampen or reduce the velocity of movement achievable. Thus, the limb will move at a more constant velocity throughout its range of motion.

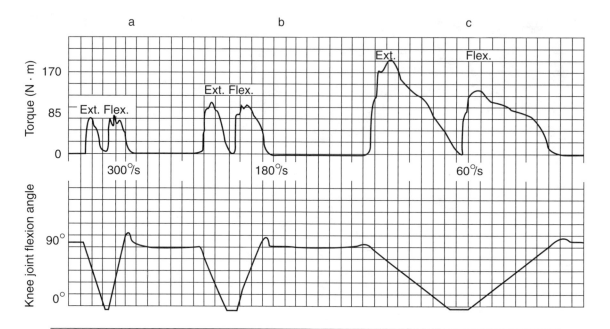

Figure 6.3 Tracings depicting the pattern of maximal torque output for isokinetic knee joint extension and flexion at three different movement velocities: (a) 300°/s, (b) 180°/s, and (c) 60°/s. Torque output varies with both specific joint angle and movement velocity.

ISOTONICS VERSUS ISOKINETICS: WHICH IS BEST?

There are some identifiable advantages and disadvantages regarding free-weight systems and the several variable and accommodating resistance devices available for use in a comprehensive conditioning program. Appreciating some of these differences may help athletes and coaches make the best decisions for their own needs.

Free weights and the use of one's own body weight are particularly effective at improving strength and power while at the same time integrating balance and coordination of many major muscle groups in a manner that closely matches the neuromuscular patterns utilized in sport skills, particularly the ability to accelerate. Examples include squats and power cleans using free weights, and sit-ups and dips using one's body weight. Both eccentric and concentric tension can be developed, which seems to be better than developing either one alone. Muscle group isolation can be achieved through isotonic strength training, as well as strengthening those muscles playing a stabilizing and assisting (synergizing) role in ensuring stable joint function.

With free weights, only the very sophisticated lifter needs more than relatively little specialized equipment. A bench and rack on which to position the weights can be purchased (or built) for relatively little expense and permits training in the privacy of one's basement or garage. An almost infinite combination of hand spacings on the bar, foot positions, and format of movements is possible, providing both variety and subtle stimulus variability from session to session. Identification of progress comes objectively by such measurements as the maximum manageable weight for one rep, the numbers of reps and sets that can be managed, and subjective assessment of the effort required. Free weights are relatively inexpensive and can be stored compactly. The use of one's body weight coupled with a chair, an overhead bar, and a box provides even greater simplicity.

Free weights have relatively few liabilities. One relates to the risk of injury unless the athlete learns proper technique before starting serious lifting. A spotter may be needed to provide assistance in order to minimize injury risk. If the free-weight area of a training room is busy with many athletes of various abilities attempting the same lifts, effective alternation between athletes may require the continual addition or removal of weight plates from the lifting bar to meet individual requirements. This can detract from athletes' concentration and can keep the activity level too high during the rest period. The best alternative may be to arrange a different time for training.

It is probably inappropriate to suggest assets and liabilities for fitness machines in general, because of their enormous variety in mode of operation. Essentially all of the variable resistance machines, however, have the user move a weight or resistance along some specific unchanging path. This permits greater isolation of individual muscles or specific muscle groups, providing localized overload. Both concentric and eccentric tension can be produced. Progress can be monitored by identifying how many plates or how much resistance is moved and by counting reps to reach fatigue. Machines with stacks of weights are typically safer than free weights because the weights slide up and down on metal bars, supported indirectly by the lifter (via cables or chains). The design of each piece of equipment provides for easy setup in minimal time. With some equipment the athlete can perform a variety of exercises simply by moving from one station (position) to another around it.

Variable resistance equipment has some liabilities as well, however. Much of the equipment is so expensive that it is beyond the price appropriate for home purchase. Some brands are designed so that developing each major group requires a separate machine. Caution is then necessary to ensure that for any agonist muscle group being trained, the appropriate machine is available for training the antagonist group. Very tall or very short individuals often cannot use these machines because most are constructed to fit people whose height is relatively close to the mean height for men and women. Finally, because many of these machines dampen acceleration to ensure a slower speed for optimal strength development, the movement patterns have little direct transfer to sport skills. These machines therefore are tools to help develop comprehensive fitness rather than tools for specific sport skill development.

Isokinetic resistance equipment, marketed under such brand names as Cybex, Orthotron, Biodex, Kin-Com, and Lido, has provided an alternative to variable resistance equipment and free weights (Malone 1988; Perrin 1993). Perhaps these machines' greatest asset is that they provide the opportunity to develop maximal tension across the entire range of joint motion at a wide variety of velocities. In turn, this optimizes the development of strength, power, and work output. Injuries are minimal because the machines provide mainly passive resistance matching that is initiated by the user. There are no free weights or stacks of plates that must be controlled. Newer versions often are equipped with video screens that graphically depict muscle responses. This biofeedback, which gives the user instantaneous visual display of force output or developing fatigue, can have considerable value. On some models, computerized data storage and retrieval can provide comparative and statistical analysis of responses from repeated sessions.

A variety of factors cause these machines to be less user-friendly, however, than free weights and variable resistance machines. First, they too are quite expensive, making home use almost out of the question. Second, many joint-testing functions are carried out on the same unit, requiring considerable machine readjustment for each joint tested. Professional assistance may be necessary to ensure proper joint alignment and calibration. Thus, these machines' primary use seems to be either for diagnostic evaluation and rehabilitation or for specialized training for patients or athletes. In our work with elite-level distance runners we find that isokinetic evaluation, particularly of lower-limb muscles, can be very useful for identifying similarities or differences in right side versus left, extension versus flexion, and so on. The rate of recovery from an injury can be tracked in this manner, and the possibility of a developing imbalance that might predispose to an athletic injury can also be identified, along with the usual measurement of performance changes brought about by training.

Another point to consider is that, of the accommodating resistance machines on the market, only Cybex (which also produced Orthotron) has been thoroughly validated as the result of a few decades of use by clinicians worldwide. The others are less established and validated. Another disadvantage is that eccentric tension generation is not always possible with accommodating resistance equipment. Also, the newer machines are computer-controlled or computer-driven with already-programmed software packages. Individualized muscle testing or training sequences are not always easy to implement unless the existing software is modified or additional software is created. Finally, testing and training are intended for relatively specific, isolated muscle groups; multiple muscle group testing or training is difficult to accomplish. Thus, there is little of the integrative neuromuscular coordination that is so important in transfer to sport skills.

Circuit and Stage Training

During the 1950s the pursuit of an active, health-oriented lifestyle became popular, and many people began to seek programs for building a high level of comprehensive fitness in its own right without pursuing the competitive aspects of body building, weight lifting, or other formally organized sports. The idea seemed plausible that a series of exercises could be designed and sequenced in such a manner that, when they were performed one after the other, a combination of strength, power, stamina, agility, flexibility, and cardiovascular conditioning could be stimulated. If such an exercise regimen were followed for a period of weeks, this would serve as an overload stimulus that would bring adaptive improvements in the performance variables challenged. At the University of Leeds in England, Morgan and Adamson (1957) developed just such a routine and called it *circuit training*. Specific tasks were assigned for completion at a series of exercise stations, some with simple pieces of equipment to assist with the exercise. These stations were arranged to fit available space. In this manner as many people as there were stations could train at the same time, each person moving from one station to another at a similar pace. The muscle groups stimulated at each adjacent station were quite different so as to minimize the chance for inappropriate localized fatigue.

Circuit work is now recognized as a useful means of both developing general conditioning as well as stimulating specific muscle groups. The number and intensity of reps can vary, and so can the rest interval between individual reps or sets of reps; the number of exercise stations; the emphasis on strength, power, or flexibility; and the extent of anaerobic and aerobic involvement. A large variety of circuit-training regimens have been devised (Sorani 1966), revealing considerable ingenuity and creativity to meet the needs of various athletic populations and workout environments.

Some circuits consist solely of calisthenic exercises done against body weight that require no special equipment. These can be done either all in one place or at various sites, for example, around each of the four corners of a track with the athlete jogging or running from point to point to begin each new exercise. Other circuits can be done indoors, using the selection of wall bars, benches, and adjustable vaulting boxes commonly found in a gymnasium. Seb Coe's physical education instructor at Loughborough University, George Gandy, devised a plan during the mid-1970s that involved such varied exercises as a rope climb, depth jumps onto and off of a box, dips, burpees (sometimes called squat-jumps), leg raises, inclined push-ups (sometimes called press-ups), and step-ups onto a bench. This circuit merged plyometrics, strength training, flexibility, and cardiovascular development into a single program (Gandy 1983). This is comprehensive conditioning at its finest.

Improvement in conditioning from such a program, done two to three times per week, can be measured in various ways (Wilmore et al. 1978). Subjectively, people sense that it becomes gradually less stressful to proceed through the circuit at a given volume and intensity of work. Careful observation by a coach or by other athletes can reveal better or worse performance of particular exercises. Objectively, measurements can be made of the number of reps, amount of weight managed, or total time required for completion of specific exercises. Motivation typically is high even from the beginning of such a program. Initially there is the satisfaction of learning new exercises. Later there is improvement of skill competency. Once this plateaus, further improvements occur with performance gains in strength or total work output.

Several simple guidelines can be outlined to assist athletes in constructing appropriate circuit-training programs:

1. Schedule no more than about 8 to 12 exercises (5 to 9 for beginners), and ensure through variety that all major muscle groups are exercised. Next, assign an acceptable number of reps to permit completion of the circuit in about 12 to 15 min. This restricts each exercise to about 1/2 min in duration. The number of reps assigned can be determined through a prior test session. For more difficult exercises, count the maximum number of reps achievable in 45 s; for easier exercises count the reps attainable in a 60-s test period. Then, take half the total number of reps completed in each of these test sessions and assign that for the circuit-training assignment. The intent is for athletes to remain continuously active, be at each station for about the same period of time, and not become excessively fatigued.

2. Plan to do from two to five reps of the circuit, depending on fitness level, which provides a training period lasting approximately from 30 min to 1 hr. Take no more than 2 to 3 min of rest between the completion of one circuit and the start of the next circuit repetition.

3. Challenge different muscle groups at each adjacent station.

4. Emphasize quality of performance output (good technique); do not rush through each exercise.

5. Give special attention to the development of those muscles that are not emphasized during specialized event-related training.

6. Incorporate all aspects of fitness into the circuit program: flexibility, agility, strength, and endurance, with additional emphasis on components of total fitness that are rather poorly developed in relation to others.

Two important variants to circuit training have developed that are quite different from simply changing the combination of basic exercises indicated previously. One involves the use of specific strength-training equipment such as free weights and machines (Allen, Byrd, and Smith 1976). This approach is appropriately termed *circuit weight training*. In a prescribed short time limit (such as 30 s), as many reps as can be managed are completed at a given station at about 50% of the 1 RM. Immediately the athlete moves to the next station, challenging different muscle groups in an equivalent manner. Stations that require push-ups, chin-ups, or sit-ups can also be inserted easily into such a routine.

The second variant is *stage training*. Here, a variety of exercises are arranged in circuit fashion, but the athlete proceeds through the circuit only once. At each stage, the athlete completes either several sets of reps—for example, one third of the maximum number that can be done in 45 or 60 s, with an appropriate rest period between each set—or one very long set. This permits specific and intense localized muscle loading as a stimulus to improve strength and endurance. Seb Coe devised a stage-training routine that he could do almost anywhere because it required only a chair and a box or low table. Particularly during extended periods of travel away from his home training environment, when workout facilities were not conveniently located, he preserved a high level of overall conditioning that otherwise would have tended to be neglected. Here is a brief summary of the stage-training routine that he used:

Half-squats: Ranging from two sets of 5 × 200 reps to two sets of 500 each; recovery equal to the duration of one set.

Bent-knee sit-ups: Alternating straight trunk curls with oblique trunk curls (alternate elbows touching the opposite knee); one set of 200 to 250 reps.

Push-ups (press-ups): With feet elevated to incline the lower limbs; five sets of 20 reps.

Back extensions: Using a chair and either a friend or some immovable object to stabilize both legs; three to four sets of 20 to 30 reps; no more than 100 reps per session.

Step-ups: Done onto a box or a low sturdy table as one continuous set; 2×10 reps each with alternate legs, then 2×20 reps each with alternate legs.

Guidelines for Comprehensive Conditioning

One of the questions most commonly asked by athletes interested in designing an effective set of exercises to meet their particular conditioning requirements is simply, "What works? What equipment should I use, and what is the best plan for me?" An indirect answer is that the kind of equipment isn't necessarily as important as doing the training without getting injured. There is no doubt that the various strength training routines that we have thus far described—free weights, plyometrics, circuit work, machines—have the capability of increasing strength (with or without gains in muscle mass), power, and endurance (as does swimming, although this has not been discussed). Just as circuit training with weights became popular in the 1950s, in the 1980s the use of cycling and swimming became popular, nonspecific, supplemental training activities for runners, heralding the triathlon and duathlon boom.

All these additional comprehensive conditioning activities have what has been termed a *crossover effect*; that is, they do provide an increase in overall general fitness among many muscle groups, as well as increased joint strength, which can help improve performance through reducing injury risk and providing an increased general fitness base (Foster et al. 1995). For this reason, the term *cross-training* has often been applied to these kinds of activities. An additional advantage of cross-training is that it tends to prevent injuries because it offers multi-plane joint stimulus rather than the high-volume single-plane joint loading characteristic of participation in only one sport. While no single method has been shown to be unequivocally superior, for athletes engaged in movement-oriented sports such as running, isometric training would definitely receive lower priority than isotonic and isokinetic training. The six keys to successful conditioning with cross-training as it relates to improving fitness for running are these:

1. Train regularly.
2. Train the muscle groups most in need of conditioning and that are of greatest benefit to running.
3. Ensure muscle balance by training antagonists as well as agonists (e.g., hamstrings as well as quadriceps, triceps as well as biceps).
4. Provide a progressive overload stimulus.
5. Work the muscles through their full range of movement.
6. Allow adequate time between training sessions for recovery and physiological adaptation to occur.

For several reasons it has been difficult to effectively compare the various types of strength- and power-training equipment available (Clarke 1973; Kraemer, Deschenes, and Fleck 1988; Pipes and Wilmore 1975; Weltman and Stamford

1982). First, untrained individuals will initially accrue sizable strength gains using any of several types of resistance work for training because of neurological adaptation and recruitment. The rate of neurological gains diminishes considerably as fitness increases, leaving a slower rate of improvement from variable increases in muscle protein. Thus, to assess the relative benefits of one system or machine over another, groups of subjects that are all at the same level of initial training must first be identified. Then they must be assigned similarly stressful work loads. Both of these constraints are difficult to manage in scientific studies but are crucial if the conclusions are to have practical value for athletic training.

The second reason for difficulty in equipment comparisons is the quite variable credibility of the vast sales-oriented literature available from manufacturers of the more specialized machines for improving fitness. Manufacturers have an intense desire to acquire even a small percentage of a very lucrative market, which encourages aggressive marketing. The more aggressive this promotion, the more slick the sales pitches suggesting that one or another piece of equipment is so revolutionary, so effective, so research-tested, and so ideal for the purpose that one would be a fool not to purchase it for spa or home. These companies may also hire scientists to produce studies that characterize the performance capabilities of the particular equipment being marketed. This vested-interest relationship increases the need for particular caution in interpreting the published reports that result.

Third is the problem of transferring fitness gains and performance improvement on various machines to increased racing effectiveness as a distance runner. Machines that isolate individual muscle groups for development may not provide strength transfer as useful as that obtained from training modalities that stimulate multiple muscle groups, thereby improving agility and coordination, and mimicking the individual sport activity. Comprehensive fitness training will indeed very likely improve general fitness, but it will be the total synergistic effect of this improved general fitness along with other specific training superimposed on it that provides sport-related performance gains. A psychological component also accompanies the performance gains that might accrue from such a comprehensive training program: The knowledge that nothing is being overlooked and that a winning edge may result from being just a little more completely prepared than a competitor is difficult to quantify.

Fourth is the phenomenon of specificity of adaptation to training. It is difficult to compare objectively the strength gains in groups of athletes who have trained using different types of equipment, because each type challenges the musculoskeletal system differently as a result of individual biomechanical variations. An exercise at a particular intensity for intended muscle groups using one piece of equipment may result in quite a different total work output compared to another piece of equipment, simply because either the same muscles are challenged using a different anatomic arrangement or additional muscles are involved. Though these differences may give each of the many kinds of variable resistance equipment its marketability (being touted as "better than the rest" or "unique"), they also prevent comparison of their functional effectiveness. Although these differences may be of great importance to a body builder, they may make little difference to a runner who is using this equipment for the more general purpose of overall conditioning for musculoskeletal balance and injury protection.

Some examples of training specificity may serve to stimulate readers to think of additional examples germane to their own training programs. One example relates to the effect of the direction of a joint's movement on the training of muscles attached to that joint. Let us consider the act of pushing a barbell over-head. This requires activity in the pectoralis muscles, perhaps the most impor-tant chest muscles. When we stand and push the barbell overhead, primarily the portion of this muscle nearest the collarbone (clavicle) is activated. When we lie supine on a bench with trunk parallel to the floor, the middle portion of the muscle is most utilized. When we lie on an inclined bench with hips higher than the shoulders, mainly the lower portion of the pectoralis major is challenged.

Another example of specificity involves the consideration of linear versus rotary motion. Typically, muscles exert force in a straight line, but the effect of this shortening or lengthening is to produce rotary movement of a bone around a joint axis. Only if two joints are involved can linear motion be produced. In a squat, for example, the trunk moves up and down (linearly), due to rotary mo-tion produced simultaneously at the ankles, knees, and hips. A leg extension involving only the knee joint, however, produces rotary movement.

A third example of specificity concerns the intricate interrelationships between skeletal muscles in permitting body movement to occur. We have been concerned primarily with those muscles directly involved in producing movement—the *agonists* or *prime movers*. Other muscles influence the function of these prime movers. There are at least four groups of these. We have already mentioned the *antagonists,* which typically act in the opposite direction to the agonists, but which, when the agonists are active, remain relaxed or else help stabilize the joints on which the agonists are acting. *Synergistic muscles* help the prime movers and may partially compensate for movement loss if paralysis or extreme fatigue oc-curs in the prime movers. *Stabilizer muscles* fix a relevant body part in such a way that motion can occur in the proper direction. *Neutralizer muscles* eliminate one of the two possible directions of movements by a prime mover.

A few examples that identify the various muscles involved in what we would consider as fairly simple joint actions provide an impression of the real com-plexity that is involved. Refer back to figures 1.6, 2.2, and 2.3 to help locate the position of these various muscles. For *knee joint flexion* the prime movers are the biceps femoris, semitendinosus, and semimembranosus, collectively termed the hamstrings group. Synergists include the gracilis, sartorius, popliteus, and gas-trocnemius. Neutralizers include the biceps femoris on one side and flexors on the other side. Stabilizers include flexors of the hip joint. For *hip flexion* the prime movers are the iliopsoas group. Synergists include the adductors longus and brevis, sartorius, rectus femoris, tensor fasciae latae, parts of the gluteus medius and minimus, and pectineus. Neutralizers include the tensor fasciae latae and pectineus. Stabilizers include the extensors of the lumbar spine and the abdomi-nal muscles. As a final example, for *hip extension* the prime movers are the glu-teus maximus, biceps femoris, semitendinosus, and semimembranosus. Syner-gists include parts of the gluteus medius and minimus and the entire adductor magnus. Neutralizers include the gluteus medius and adductors. Stabilizers in-clude the abdominal muscles and extensors of the lumbar spine.

From these considerations, it should be evident that during running much more is occurring than simply the activation of a few prime movers. Many other muscles are utilized, with different attachment points on several involved joints. These all must be adequately strengthened if they are to do their job of permit-ting distance runners to meet their competitive needs. These needs can vary from great strength or enormous quickness in short, fast races to prolonged per-formance at submaximal work loads in long-distance races. Though running itself provides the most specific development stimulus to the prime movers, conditioning programs should include exercises that effectively improve the performance abilities of these accessory muscles in assisting the prime movers.

In summary, combining hard work with a well-developed plan and specific monitoring will go far in providing an optimal level of comprehensive as well as specialized fitness. For comprehensive conditioning, the bulk of experience over the past few decades suggests the following:

- Exercises that develop balance and coordination of *many* major muscle groups provide a better practical and total conditioning effect for runners than those that isolate just one or a few muscle groups.

- Examples of such exercises typically include the use of free weights, one's own body weight, or arrangement of cams or pulleys connected to stacks of weights.

- The best plan is to identify the major muscle groups that need development and then create a training plan that best takes advantage of all the various kinds of equipment in a particular training facility.

- By keeping detailed records of amount of work done (reps and sets) using isotonic training or by using electronically-produced records of torque, power, and work using isokinetic resistance equipment, both progress over time and symmetry between right and left sides and between agonist and antagonist muscle groups permit long-term awareness of improvements or deficits in performance. This information is helpful for identifying strength and power gains that one hopes will translate into improved performance in running. The information can also be useful for injury prevention or for following the progress of rehabilitation from an injury.

Designing Your Strength- and Power-Training Program

Figure 6.4 provides an overview of the interrelationships between comprehensive conditioning and the various aspects of running as they contribute not only to strength and speed but also to endurance and stamina. For distance running, total-body conditioning does not directly contribute as much to competitive success or failure as it does toward achieving the goals of injury prevention and provision of a comprehensive fitness base for more event-specific training (i.e., running). This injury freedom and excellent general fitness forms a useful pedestal upon which other more specific aspects of fitness can be structured with the aim of producing an athlete with competence in a specific area (middle-distance, long-distance, steeplechase, etc.)

Table 6.2 provides some suggestions for distance runners interested in devising circuit-, stage-, and free-weight-training sessions. These exercises or lifts should be quite familiar to all readers, and a few are illustrated on the following pages (figures 6.5 to 6.18) by three elite-level runners who have benefited substantially from such training: Seb Coe, Pat Porter, and Wendy Sly, Olympians all. An almost infinite variety of such exercises can be developed to fit the kinds of equipment available, whether in a gymnastics hall, a health spa, or a living room. Once a general outline of numbers of sets, reps, and rest breaks has been established, fine-tuning should provide the necessary alterations to optimize development and minimize unnecessary fatigue. Then this program can become an effective and integral part of the overall training plan.

The exercises shown in figures 6.5 through 6.18 can improve strength, power, and endurance in the major muscle groups that are important to distance

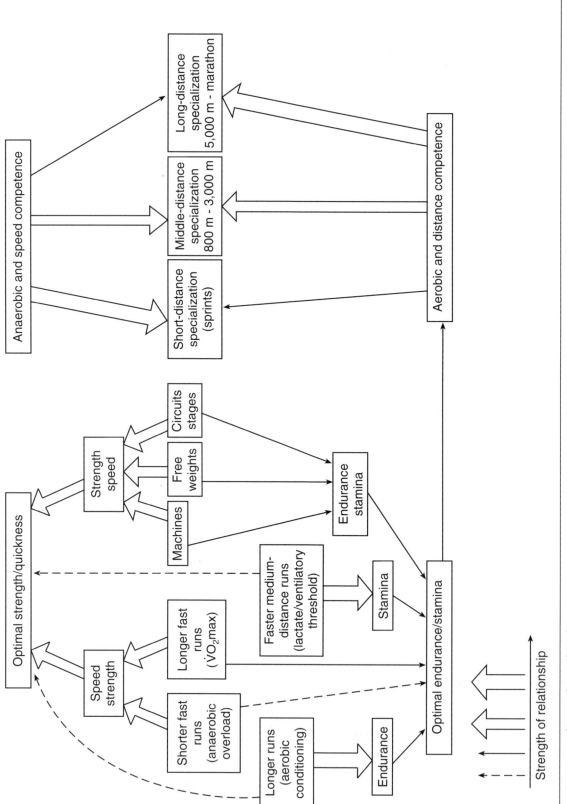

Figure 6.4 Summary of interrelationships between comprehensive conditioning and running in the development of strength/quickness and endurance/stamina in the three groups of runners (sprinters, middle-distance, and long-distance).

TABLE 6.2

Suggestions for Comparing Light, Medium, and Hard Training Sessions Using Circuit, Stage, and Weight Training

The exercises to be performed in each set or circuit are marked with an X	Circuits[a] Number of circuits			Stage training[b] Number of stages		
	2-3 Easy	3-4 Medium	4-5 Hard	5-6 Easy	7-8 Medium	8-10 Hard
Dips		X	X			
Back extensions	X	X		X		
Back extensions over chair[c]			X[c]		X[c]	X[c]
Bent-knee sit-ups, straight raise	X			X		
Bent-knee sit-ups, twisting raise		X			X	
Bent-knee sit-ups, inclined			X			X
Press-ups (push-ups)	X	X		X		
Press-ups, feet elevated			X		X	X
Squat thrusts (frog jumps)	X		X	X		
Burpees		X	X		X	X
Leg raise			X			
Rope climb		X	X			
Chin-ups (pull-ups)	X	X				
Barbell step-ups			X	X	X	X

Strength + endurance weight training	Repetitions/set			Sets		
	Easy	Medium	Hard	Easy	Medium	Hard
Barbell curls	3	6	10	3	4	6
Bent-arm pullovers	2	5	8	3	3	2
Barbell bench press	2	4	6	4	4	4
Barbell half-squats	2	4	6	6	6	6
Barbell-alternated front lunge	2	4	6	3	3	6
Vertical rowing	2	3	5	4	5	6
Barbell steps-ups (moderate load)	10	15	20	2	4	5-6

[a]Each circuit should consist of between about 8 and 12 exercises when athlete is fully accustomed to this kind of training.
[b]Each stage is a single exercise done a given number of repetitions.
[c]Use caution with this exercise if there is known low-back weakness; as with other exercises, initially always use care.

runners. This sequence proceeds from upper to lower body. Athletes will want to consider carefully the design of a training sequence that is best for them in terms of specific needs and well-rounded balance. Typically, an appropriate combination of exercises is selected to train those muscle groups that most need additional development. A training sequence is designed to prevent excessive fatigue by challenging different muscle groups at each station. Depending on an athlete's access to various kinds of equipment, for developing certain muscle groups it may be entirely appropriate to substitute another training modality for those illustrated here. Emphasis ought to be on good technique and an appropriate training stimulus for improving the strength, endurance, flexibility, and agility components of fitness.

Whereas strength is increased by emphasizing *higher-intensity work with fewer reps*, and endurance is best improved by emphasizing *many reps of a submaximal stimulus*, stamina bridges the gap between the two. *Stamina* represents a high level of strength sustainable for a considerable number of reps. Experience will

Figure 6.5 *Standing medium grip barbell curl* for developing the biceps brachii. (*a*) Using a palms-up grip, hold the barbell at arm's length against the upper thighs, with feet and arms spaced about 15 in. (38 cm) apart. (*b*) Inhale as the bar is curled up toward the top of the shoulders. Keep the back straight with legs and hips locked. Return to the starting position in a smooth, controlled manner using eccentric tension generation accompanied by exhalation.

dictate exactly how (which exercises) and when (during the training year) the athlete's focus needs directing toward strength, stamina, or endurance to match personal needs. Although strength and stamina are typically stimulated in separate sessions, it is possible to incorporate both into single training sessions. Such patterns form the basis for sessions in which the number of reps per set decreases but the amount of weight lifted per rep increases and will provide an equivalent stimulus to those muscle cells being recruited. As an example, for Seb Coe (130-lb [59-kg] body weight) doing six sets of half-squats, the number of reps per set will be 15, 15, 15, 10, 10, and 5, with the weight increasing by 10 lb (4.5 kg) per set from 140 to 190 lb (63.5 to 86 kg). Admittedly, this is a challenging session—more than 11,000 lb (5,000 kg) moved in 70 lifts—but over the years Seb became an accomplished weight lifter, and while this training session was not a "killer," nevertheless it would have been accompanied by only an easy run that day and also the day following. The recovery permitted the payoff, which was increasing development of enormous muscle stamina: better tolerance to very intense work and greater resistance to injury.

Stronger muscles can respond more effectively to the impact stress that occurs at footstrike during running. This is particularly valuable for stabilizing joints and for reducing fatigue during repetitive stress. Muscle injuries typically occur at the muscle end of musculotendinous junctions (Garrett et al. 1987). The muscle tissue attaching to the tendons has more connective tissue and fewer sar-

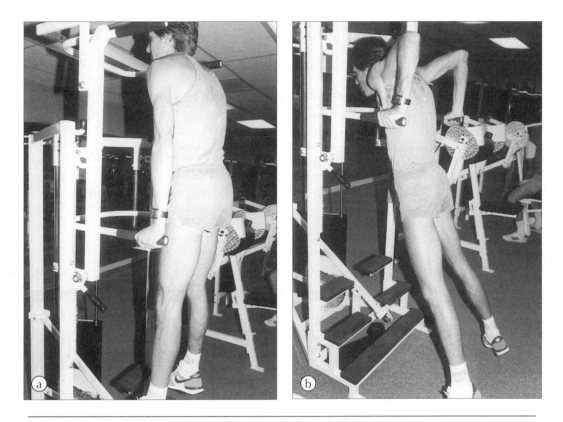

Figure 6.6 *Dips* to develop pectoralis and triceps. Find a set of parallel bars or a dip stand built specifically for this purpose. The bars should be high enough to prevent the feet from touching the floor at the lowest point of the exercise. In the starting position (*a*), the athlete is supported in an erect position by the arms. (*b*) With elbows at the sides as much as possible, the body is lowered by bending the arms until the biceps and the forearms come close together. An inhalation occurs during this descent. After a very brief pause, triceps shortening tension will permit the athlete to press back up to full arm's length, thereby allowing maximal activity in the triceps and pectoralis muscles. Exhalation occurs during this return phase. The body will tend to swing to and fro during the exercise, but the athlete must develop control to minimize this movement.

comeres, and this difference apparently renders it weaker than the muscle tissue adjacent to it. Larger muscle mass at these junctions makes tears less likely to occur.

The fitness an athlete develops from such training can contribute to making the difference between winning and simply performing well, and between being injury-prone and injury-resistant. In a sense, this kind of work forms the real "secret training system" of a championship-caliber athlete—few people besides the coach know that the athlete is doing this work. It provides the strength, suppleness, stamina, and potential for speed that other athletes will not develop unless they work equally hard. Once such complete conditioning begins to reward the athlete in terms of total fitness, the added mental confidence that develops from having done the extra measure of effort makes this athlete just that much tougher to defeat in competition.

Some comments are in order concerning training safety. Just as conditioning exercises are intended to reduce the injury risk from running by producing comprehensive musculoskeletal development, an injury risk occurs with a conditioning program unless appropriate safety precautions are taken. First, sturdy shoes that give lift and support to the heels and arches are a must. Well-constructed training shoes for running are appropriate; never use racing flats. Second, when the vertebral column is stressed, as with squat exercises, a

BREATHING PROPERLY WHILE LIFTING

A proper breathing pattern is an important part of effective weight training, and some comments are appropriate to help in this regard (Austin et al. 1987). The traditional view is to exhale on the way out, down, or up (during the action phase) and inhale on return (during recovery phase). Essentially, this strategy is correct. However, from a physiological and structural point of view, during the most difficult part of the pushing or pulling movement—out, down, or up—it is entirely appropriate to hold the breath *briefly*. This permits a temporary increase in intrathoracic pressure, creating a rigid rib cage and thereby providing additional support for the thoracic spine. Breath holding also produces tension in the abdominal muscles, contributing additional support for the lower spine.

The act of breath holding when accompanied by tension generation in the abdominal muscles and an attempt to exhale against a closed glottis is termed a *Valsalva maneuver* (after its original descriptor, the Italian anatomist Antonio Valsalva). If this maneuver is sustained for too long, the increase in intrathoracic pressure may reduce venous return to the heart, decreasing cardiac output. This could predispose the athlete to fainting. Thus, to have the best of both worlds—minimal reduction in venous return to the heart yet adequate support to the spine—it is suggested that athletes strive to develop an effective breathing pattern to accompany their own lifting patterns that takes advantage of the information provided here. As mentioned, a brief holding of breath at the moment of maximal tension seems ideal.

Figure 6.7 *Push-ups (press-ups)* to develop pectoralis and triceps. These exercises are very familiar to almost everyone, and there are many possible varieties. The simplest version is the medium-grip push-up with feet on the floor. When the hands are closer together, the inner pectoralis receives more emphasis; hands spaced farther apart put emphasis on the outer pectoralis. This exercise is made even more difficult through increasing the resistance, as shown here by raising the position of the feet. Begin the exercise in the position shown, with the body rigid and the triceps and pectoralis under tension but locked. From this position the body is lowered as far as possible. Following a very brief pause, the body is pushed upward again to return to the starting position. Inhalation with breath holding occurs on the descent, with exhalation during ascent.

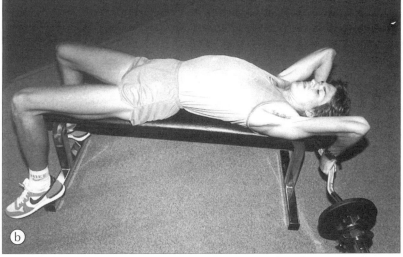

Figure 6.8 *Bent-arm barbell pullover* to develop upper pectoralis and muscles of the rib cage. This exercise is begun lying supine on a bench, shoulders near one end, head resting at the end, a barbell supported by the arms just above the chest and over the nipples using a palms-down handgrip a little wider than the width of the chest (*a*). Inhale as the weight is moved closely along and over the chest and face and finally lowered until it nearly touches the floor (*b*). The return motion is essentially the reverse; exhalation as the bar is pulled upward, then past the face, and back to the chest.

well-fitting leather waist belt is recommended. This belt teams up with the abdominal muscles that are developing tension at the same time. It helps to reduce some of the interarticular shearing force that is particularly stressful on the vertebrae of the lumbar spine.

How much time during any portion of a training macrocycle should be devoted to comprehensive conditioning? Remember that conditioning is merely an aid to running; it is not a substitute for it and must not be overdone. Thus, during any week of training, running will always occupy the majority of the total training effort.

Figure 6.9 *Seated barbell press in front of and behind the neck* to develop the front and outer deltoid muscles. This exercise begins from a sitting position, with a barbell cleaned either to the front or the back of the shoulders, using a palms-down handgrip, as shown in (*a*). The barbell is then pressed upward to arm's length overhead (*b*) and returned; if the starting position was behind the neck, return is in front of the neck. Inhalation is during the press; exhalation is during the eccentric return.

An effective conditioning plan will very likely be different for each individual athlete. Middle-distance runners will need more strength, power, and flexibility than long-distance runners. The athlete's individual strengths and weaknesses should be identified, with emphasis on developing those muscle groups that require greater conditioning and on doing maintenance work for those groups already well conditioned.

During the higher-volume training portions of a macrocycle (e.g., during mesocycles X_2 and X_3, as illustrated in figure 5.3), comprehensive conditioning should receive more emphasis than during other periods. Table 6.3 provides an overview of the varied intensity and pattern of circuit, stage, and weight training that Seb Coe found useful during his yearly training macrocycle. The accompanying hourglass-shaped figure alongside the table is an attempt to provide a dimensional image of the total conditioning work load. Its width dimension represents volume, and its vertical dimension represents time. Notice that circuit and stage training form an initial conditioning base and account for a sizable volume of weekly work. During period A, as introductory training progresses, the volume of circuit and stage training increases. Then this kind of training is gradually replaced by more intense weight training (periods B and C) as the midpoint of the training macrocycle is reached. Up to this point, as we described more fully in chapter 5, the running aspects of training have been

TABLE 6.3

Suggested Format to Incorporate Total Body Conditioning Into a Distance-Running Program

Month	Wk		
Oct.		Complete rest, no running, only easy calisthenics and flexibility exercises	A
	4		
Nov.		One circuit training or easy stage training session each week	
	8		
Dec.		Two stage sessions, one easy, one hard, each week	
	12		
Jan.		Two stage training sessions, both hard, each week	B
	16		
Feb.		One moderate stage session, one easy weight session using light weights for endurance each week	
	20		
Mar.		One moderate stage session and one endurance weight session using heavier weights each week	
	24		
Apr.		One week with one hard endurance weight session alternating with one week with a pyramid lifting session @ 90%-95%	C
	28		
May		One easy endurance weight session, one easy stage session, each week	D
	32		
June		Alternating weeks of one easy endurance weight session with one easy stage or circuit session	
	36		
July		One easy circuit or stage session each week	
	40		
		Mobility work only; competition period	E
	44		
Aug.		Mobility work only; competition period	
	48		
Sept.		Mobility work only; competition period	
	52		

Note. As illustrated, this pattern is for a year-long macrocycle; appropriate rearrangement (but not increase in work load) would be required for shorter macrocycles.

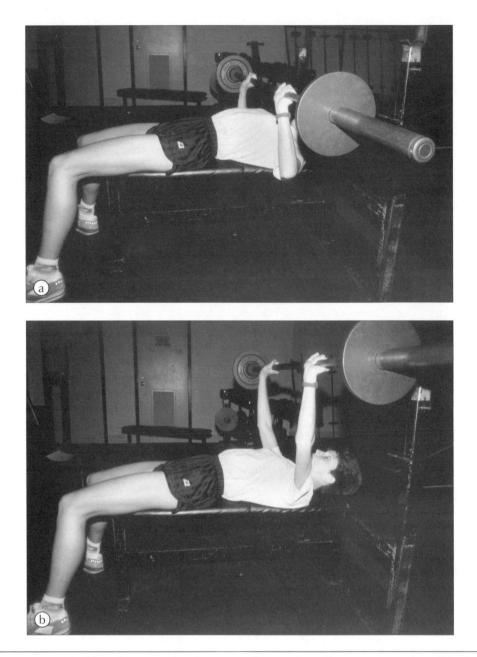

Figure 6.10 *Barbell bench press* to develop pectoralis muscles. The outer pectoralis will be best developed if the palms-out bar grip is wide; the inner pectoralis best activated with a close grip. As the athlete lies supine on a flat bench with legs positioned on the sides of the bench and feet on the floor, the barbell is lifted off its rack, with inhalation occurring as the bar is being lowered to the chest (*a*). Following a brief but definite pause, exhalation occurs as the bar is pressed upward to arm's length (*b*). The back may arch a little, but the hips (and the head) must remain on the bench.

directed more toward increased volume to improve aerobic fitness. As running now includes more anaerobic components and the athlete enters the precompetitive sharpening phase, the intensity of total-body conditioning will continue to decrease (periods D and E), with one additional brief period of increased volume (D) prior to a decrease (E) to permit recovery, regeneration, and freshness before the actual competitive phase begins.

Figure 6.11 *Lat pull-down* to develop the latissimus dorsi. This exercise is best done using a machine with a bar attached to a cable, which in turn winds around a pulley arrangement and connects to a weight stack. With hands grasping the bar (either a wide palms-down handgrip as shown in photo *a* or a close handgrip) and supporting the weight stack, arms extended in front to head level, inhale and pull the bar straight down until the bar touches the top of the thighs (*b*). The more the arms are locked at the elbows, the greater the stimulus applied to the latissimi. Exhalation occurs with a return to the starting position. Variations of this exercise can be done in the kneeling position, beginning with the arms extended overhead, with pull-down either in front to the top of the chest or in back to the neck.

Flexibility: The Essence of Joint Motion

Our joints are limited in their ability to provide movement because of the arrangement of muscles and ligaments that connect to them. With typical day-to-day activities sedentary people typically do not move their joints through what is termed their maximal *range of motion*. Only by more vigorous activities—calisthenics, sports, or a sudden burst of motion, for example, to bound up a flight of stairs—do people greatly challenge the range of movement around specific joints. Muscular lengthening or shortening plays a large role in allowing this to occur. However, if connective tissues attaching to joints are not periodically stretched to their normal limits, they tend to become more dense and less stretchable over time, increasing the difficulty of achieving what earlier was considered the full range of motion for that joint. We say we are now less flexible. The word *flexibility* defines a condition of suppleness characterized by the ability to move joints through their intended normal range of motion. The dictionary definition of flexibility is a capability of being bent without breaking. In the body, breaking corresponds to a tearing of connective or muscle tissue.

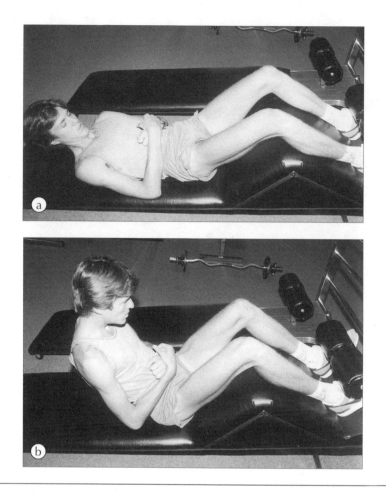

Figure 6.12 *Bent-knee simple and compound sit-up* to develop the four pairs of abdominal muscles. This exercise can be done using either a level sit-up board, as illustrated, or an inclined board. Some kind of strap or pad needs to be in place around which to restrain the feet. (*a*) Thighs should make a 45° angle with floor. Hands may be placed behind the head, cradling it, or behind the head and extended, or held at chest or stomach level. For quite accomplished athletes, a weight may be held behind the neck. Upon inhalation, the torso is raised. The extent and direction of the raise is also variable; trunk flexion may be straight up to the midrange of movement (*b*), at which point flexion can continue straight upward or be twisted right or left to promote oblique abdominal development. Trunk flexion can continue far enough so that the shoulders nearly touch the knees. When maximal flexion is reached, exhale and return to the original position. As abdominal muscle fatigue develops, hip flexors such as the iliopsoas become increasingly active, and lower back stress increases. Thus, high reps are neither necessary nor recommended (sets of 25 to 30 are adequate).

The topic of joint flexibility receives discussion on almost an annual basis in popular running magazines (Anderson 1989; Festa 1988; Robertson 1991; Waldron 1994) and has been discussed frequently in the coaching and scientific literature (Alter 1996; Anderson et al. 1984; Beaulieu 1981; Cornelius 1985). The benefits of adequate joint mobility (or flexibility) for athletes should already be evident. When an athlete is strong as well as flexible, more force is required to produce muscle or connective tissue tearing, and more stretch is required before tearing occurs. The greater these limits of strength or stretch, the greater the performance capacities of these tissues and the less liable the athlete is to injury (Beaulieu 1981; Corbin and Noble 1960). When athletes remain uninjured for

Figure 6.13 *Leg raise* to develop hip flexors. This exercise can be done using either dip bars or some other arrangement of parallel bars, or a single bar as shown here. The starting position can have the athlete hanging (*a*), or in the position to begin dips (see figure 6.6*a*); in either situation, elbows are locked out. Inhale and bend at the waist, raising the legs until they are parallel to the floor (*b*). Try not to bend the knees. Exhale as the return to the starting position occurs. Primary hip flexors developed here are the psoas major and iliacus, but the rectus femoris, sartorius, and tensor fasciae latae are strengthened as well. Abdominal muscles are active as stabilizers.

long periods, they can continue to make progress in their training, which permits them to more closely approach their performance potential. Losing such valuable development time from injury slows this process.

Individual differences make it inappropriate to compare one person's flexibility with another's, and it may very well be unwise to attempt to achieve or surpass the flexibility level of someone else who is better endowed. One difference involves genetic variability in the positioning of muscle attachments to tendons and bones. Another involves the extent of recovery of muscles from intense anaerobic work. Inflow of H_2O into muscles to maintain osmotic equilibrium changes their shape, making them shorter and thus decreasing flexibility of the joints to which they attach. A third difference involves the effect of diurnal postural changes, particularly as we transition from sleeping to waking. The movement of water out of intervertebral disks as a person changes from the horizontal posture (during sleep) to the vertical posture (while moving about during the day) slowly decreases body length, thereby increasing back flexibility. This is one reason why we are more flexible in the evening than in the

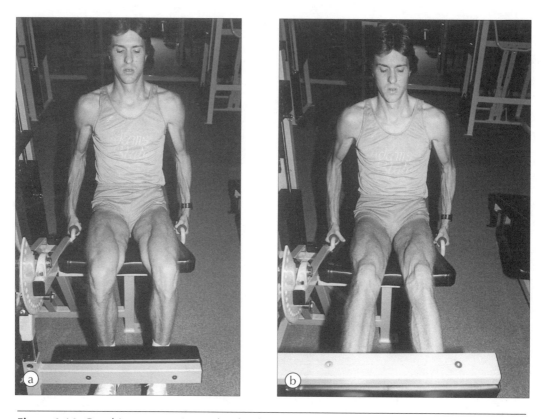

Figure 6.14 *Quadriceps extension* to develop lower anterior thigh muscles (quadriceps group). Any of various leg extension machines may be used. The best sitting position is where the end of the seat is against the rear or the knees. The seat should be grasped with hands just behind the buttocks; usually handgrips are provided (*a*). Toes are pointed slightly downward. With inhalation, the weight stack is raised until legs are essentially parallel with the floor (*b*). The upper body should remain fixed during this activation of the thigh muscles. Return to the starting position is accomplished by exhalation.

morning: As the day goes on we become shorter people (D.E. Martin et al. 1986). A fourth difference involves the attention given to maintaining flexibility. People who routinely put their joints through a full range of motion on a daily basis will be blessed with considerably greater joint suppleness than those who do not. It is suggested that athletes be aware of and assess their own present state of flexibility and attempt in a reasonable manner to develop and maintain sufficient flexibility so that a margin of safety exists between their sport-specific needs and their limits of joint range of motion.

There is less correlation between flexibility and such variables as body build (somatotype), age, and sport skill level than there is between the performance of exercises intended to develop flexibility and an actual improvement in joint range of motion. Adequate flexibility is almost guaranteed in those athletes who, by performing comprehensive conditioning exercises properly, emphasize activity through what for them is their full range of motion (Anderson et al. 1984). As an example, pull-ups should be started from an arms-overhead hanging position (the same position as when doing leg raises, illustrated in figure 6.13*a*) to ensure full stretch as well as strength development through the movement range from 0° of elbow flexion upward past 90° as the exercise is completed. However, because it is quite difficult to complete this exercise through the initial phase, athletes often begin with the elbows closer to 90°. One means of permitting a complete stretch of the biceps brachii until this strength deficit is overcome is to

Figure 6.15 *Barbell alternated front lunge* to develop anterior thigh muscles and biceps femoris of the posterior thigh (hamstrings group). A barbell is placed either on the rear shoulders as if in preparation for a barbell squat, using a palms-up grip (*a*), or held in position at the level of the upper chest as if in preparation for a barbell push press (again using a palms-up grip). The back is kept straight, the head up, and the feet planted firmly on the floor next to each other. The exercise is begun by inhaling and taking a step forward as far as possible until the thigh of the stepping leg is almost parallel with the floor (*b, c,*). The rear leg should be as straight as possible; do not bend the knee any more than necessary. From here, two possibilities exist. The athlete can step back to the starting position (exhaling in the process) and either repeat the same movement with the other leg or repeat the movement with the same leg. A more intense training stimulus occurs if the set is completed using just one leg stepping forward.

include a few reps beginning at 90° of elbow flexion and to proceed back toward 0° using eccentric tension generation. In training jargon, this is often referred to as *doing negatives* (the concentric form of the exercise is termed a *positive*). In this manner, stretch is ensured, and strength is gradually developed to permit full-range concentric movement.

Categories of Stretching Exercises

Stretching exercises are intended to help a joint achieve and maintain its normal range of motion. Various terms have developed to describe such exercises, depending on the nature of the activity. *Static stretching* exercises involve slow and gentle tissue lengthening as the athlete assumes certain specific postures, some of which are illustrated in figures 6.19 to 6.28. These exercises can be active—that is, done by the athlete—or passive, with the athlete being assisted by a partner. *Dynamic* (or *ballistic*) *stretching* exercises involve bouncy or swinging movements that are beyond the joint range of motion typically seen in sedentary living, and which may equal or exceed the range of movement found in typical athletic endeavors. Such movements are not so excessive that the joint's maximal range of motion is exceeded, because joint injury would occur. Finally, *proprioceptive neuromuscular facilitation* (PNF) exercises permit further lengthening of an agonist muscle beyond its normal maximal length by stimulating isometric tension in its antagonist counterpart. By appropriate inhibitory interneuronal connections involving both agonist and antagonist muscles via the spinal cord, increased relaxation of tone will occur in the agonist. These PNF exercises can be done either alone or with a partner's assistance (Hatfield 1982).

Stretching exercises to enhance range of motion should be an integral part of routine training sessions that involve running. Some training sessions involve easy to moderate or steady running and do not vigorously challenge the maximal range of motion of the joints to which the major muscle groups attach. These sessions usually begin with easy jogging, gradually increase in intensity as the body warms up and metabolic reaction rates speed up, and culminate in completion of the training assignment for a particular distance over a specific pace range. An example might be an easy morning run. Stretching is best left as the final activity *after* the session of running, as part of the cool-down process. The still-elevated body temperature as well as the prior physical activity will have increased muscle stretchability, making it easier to do the exercises. In a reasonably short time—no more than 15 to 20 min—all of the exercises that will be described shortly in figures 6.19 to 6.28 can be completed. This permits a systematic physical assessment of right and left agonist-antagonist similarities and differences and provides a stimulus to achieve the usual maximal range of motion appropriate to that athlete.

For those running sessions that are considerably more challenging—either interval training, tempo runs, time trials, or actual races—an athlete's maximal joint range of motion may be more fully challenged. Stretching exercises then become an important part of preparation and must be integrated into the warm-up routine. One appropriate sequence is an initial easy warm-up period of jogging or easy running, followed by a short-duration stretching session that includes the full range of motion required during the running session, and then a series of strides that take the athlete up to the pace anticipated during the racing or fast running portion of the day's activity. Following the training session, it is best to again include a period of easy running (cool-down) followed by a second stretching session that statically stretches the lower-limb joints through the same range of motion as before the session. This will help restore body symmetry.

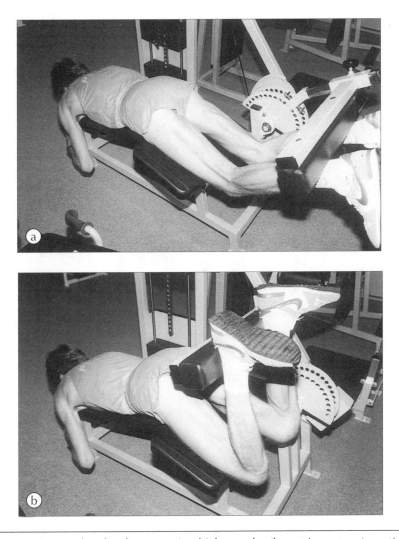

Figure 6.16 *Hamstrings curl* to develop posterior thigh muscles (hamstrings group), particularly the biceps femoris. Either a specific hamstrings curl machine or a leg extension machine can be used. Lie face down on the bench, straighten the legs, and place the heels under the appropriate foot pads (*a*). Grasp the front of the machine for support. On inhalation, curl the legs upward until the lower and upper legs nearly come together, lifting an appropriate stack of weight (*b*). Along with exhalation, return to the starting position.

Creating an Effective Stretching Routine

The best stretching routine is one that is easy to complete, is so repeatable that it becomes almost automatic, and includes the major joints and muscle groups used in running. The routine should not be hurried; it should provide mental relaxation as well as the needed stretching and opportunity for physical assessment. The series of exercises shown in figures 6.19 through 6.28 are certainly not unique; they have probably appeared in print dozens of times before, most likely because they are useful. Our model for these exercises is Bo Reed, an established U.S. 10,000-m track runner. He's not the most flexible athlete in the world, but he works consistently at maintaining an acceptable level of flexibility. He thus is a more preferable model than an aerobics instructor whose suppleness most runners can only dream of imitating (and which is probably not needed for running excellence).

Figure 6.17 *Barbell squat* for developing the entire body. The athlete begins this exercise in an erect standing position, with a barbell held on the shoulders using a palms-down handgrip (the photo in *a* was taken a split second after the squat portion began). The feet may be flat on the floor, or heels may be slightly raised. The chest is kept high, a deep inhalation occurs, and the athlete moves in a steady, controlled fashion down to the squat position illustrated in *b* and *c*. There is a definite momentary pause with exhalation, followed by a second inhalation during return to the standing position and then exhalation. A fairly light weight can be used, because for distance runners it isn't muscle bulk that is important, but rather strength together with stamina. Five reps constitute a typical set. For the second or third set, three or four breaths may be appropriate instead of the initial two.

Figure 6.18 *Total-body conditioning* exercises need not be restricted to a formal setting in which specific muscle group development is emphasized. As illustrated here with (*a*) leapfrogging and (*b*) partner-carries done outside on a grassy but hilly surface, the combined principles of circuit work, stage training, and weight training can be carried out in an exhilarating and challenging atmosphere. Seb Coe emphasized such training for many of his developmental months, including one session each week that lasted as long as a few hours and gained the understandable nickname "Sunday slogs."

A few cardinal rules apply for performing stretching exercises:

- Stretch the muscles on both sides of the body.
- Do not exceed the threshold for discomfort or pain.
- Do not bounce or jerk, but rather gradually induce the stretch.
- Maintain each stretch stimulus at or near maximum for between 20 and 40 s to ensure optimal lengthening.
- Be aware of whether one side of the body is more or less flexible than the other—is this a result of structural differences, recovery from injury, or possible indication of developing injury?

One of the most common hamstrings and calf stretching exercises is illustrated in figure 6.19. As shown here, with the left leg forward and the right leg supporting most of the body's weight, lean forward and balance with the hands against a sturdy object. Keep the head up and slowly bend the arms, thereby leaning farther forward and increasing the stretch on the right hamstrings and calf. Try to keep the heel of the back leg on the ground. Reverse leg positions and repeat the exercise to stretch the left hamstrings and calf muscles.

Figure 6.20 adds two muscle groups to the posterior limb stretch maneuver just described. With hands on the hips for balance, raise the right leg upward and forward, and step up to an adjacent raised object as shown. This stretches

Figure 6.19 Hamstrings and calf stretching exercise.

Figure 6.20 Adding a stretch of the groin muscle and hip flexors (iliopsoas) to the hamstrings/calf exercise.

the adductor muscles in the right groin region as well as the hip flexor (iliopsoas group) on the left side. Again, keeping the head as well as the right rear foot pointed straight ahead, increase the angle of flexion of the bent right knee, thereby moving the hips forward and slowly increasing the stretch. Return to the original position, and switch leg positions to complete the stretching exercise.

Another stretching exercise for the hamstrings is depicted in figure 6.21. Lying in the supine position as shown, with the right leg partially bent at the knee, grab the left leg below the calf and pull it toward the shoulders, stopping and maintaining that position at the first detection of discomfort. After 10 to 15 s additional stretch can probably be applied. Switch leg positions and repeat the exercise.

An exercise similar in nature to figure 6.20 done in the supine position adds a component of stretch to the iliopsoas group along with the hamstrings. As depicted in figure 6.22, with the left leg (and left iliopsoas) outstretched, grasp the

Figure 6.21 Stretching the hamstrings from the supine position.

Figure 6.22 Adding a hip flexor (iliopsoas) stretch (keeping the left leg straight) to the supine hamstrings stretching exercise (pulling the right knee toward the chest).

right knee and pull it slowly toward the chest. The left leg should remain out-stretched if the iliopsoas on that side is adequately stretched, but if not, it will begin to rise up as the right leg is pulled farther. Maintain this stretch for 30 to 40 s without forcing a stretch of any of these important muscles. Then switch sides.

In figure 6.23 the quadriceps muscles are being stretched. Standing on the right foot, grab the left foot and pull it upward and toward the left hip. After a 10- to 20-s stretch, repeat the exercise, standing on the left foot and pulling the right foot toward the right hip to stretch the quadriceps group on that side.

Figure 6.24 illustrates a useful stretching exercise for the neck, chest, abdominal, iliopsoas, and quadriceps muscles. From the recumbent position, use the arms to lift the upper torso, helping to increase the stretch by lifting the head back as far as possible. The sternocleidomastoid muscles are also stretched. These muscles originate on the sternum and collarbone and insert on the mastoid process of the temporal bone around the ear. They protect the carotid artery, jugular vein, and vagus nerve along either side of the neck, permitting chin elevation, head movement toward the shoulder, and flexion of the vertebral column.

Two exercises are useful for the back muscles and spine. Simply by rocking back and forth several times in the supine position with knees pulled gently toward the chest (figure 6.25), a stretch of the back muscles can be produced. Figure 6.26 depicts what sometimes is called the Oriental squat position. By gently pulling forward with the arms and resisting this with the quadriceps group, using the body weight to keep from sliding forward, a gentle stretch will be applied to the lower back muscles, hips, and knees.

Figure 6.23 Quadriceps muscles stretch.

Figure 6.24 Stretching exercise for the neck, chest, abdominal, iliopsoas, and quadriceps muscles.

Figure 6.25 Stretching the lower back and spine.

Figure 6.27, *a* and *b*, illustrates two methods for stretching adductor muscles. In figure 6.27*a* the hands are applying gentle downward pressure on the knees. In figure 6.27*b* the hands are being used to move the feet a little closer to the torso, with additional stretch applied to the legs by elbow pressure.

In figure 6.28, *a* and *b*, several muscle groups on both sides of the body are stretched. From a sitting position with the left hand on the ground and right arm clasped around the distal portion of the left upper leg, the left hip rotators, left abdominal obliques, and right-side back muscles can be stretched as depicted in figure 6.28*a*. Also, turning the head to the left provides a stretch to the right trapezius and sternocleidomastoid muscles. When these positions are reversed, the corresponding muscles on the opposite side of the body will be stretched. In figure 6.28*b* this exercise is repeated in the supine rather than sitting position. The left leg has been brought over toward the right side, and gentle pressure by the right arm brings the left leg toward (but not touching) the floor.

Figure 6.26 Using the Oriental squat position to stretch the low back, hips, and knees.

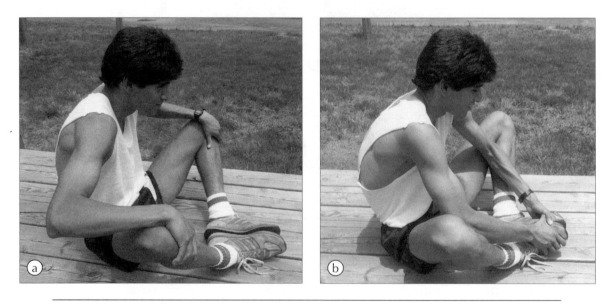

Figure 6.27 Stretching the major adductor (groin) muscles.

The head is turned toward the left to enhance the stretch of the hip rotators and abdominal obliques. Again, remember to reverse this body position to complete the stretching routine.

We have deliberately omitted some stretching exercises from this routine because they present for some people, particularly those who have had specific muscle or joint injuries, a sizable element of reinjury risk. For those athletes who have not been injured and who can indeed complete these exercises successfully, they are both beneficial and acceptable. One exercise is the familiar reach-

Figure 6.28 Stretching multiple muscle groups, including hip rotators and abdominal obliques.

ing down to touch the toes while keeping the legs straight. This can be excessively stressful to the lower back, particularly if done by overweight beginners or if accompanied by any bouncing. Another involves the so-called *hurdler's stretch*, which is done in a sitting position. For athletes who have suffered rotational problems with the knee joints, hamstring pulls, or low back injuries, this exercise can be more injurious than beneficial. A third exercise is sometimes called the *plow*, named because the position of the head, torso, and lower limbs resembles an old-style agricultural plow blade. The individual first lies supine, then raises the legs and brings them over the head and back far enough so that the toes touch the ground. The combination of body weight plus momentum can place excessive stress on the spine, even when the hands are used to provide partial back support. The exercises illustrated in figure 6.19 to 6.28 are a more-than-adequate substitute for these three exercises to provide adequate flexibility for running at any intensity.

Body Composition: Importance and Measurement

One of the more popular topics of interest to athletes and coaches as they query sport scientists about technical aspects of training and health maintenance is body composition. Runners in particular desire a high power-to-weight ratio; that is, they desire optimal *leanness*, or muscularity, in relation to their total weight. Although just their highly active training lifestyles typically cause them to have very little fat accumulation, the element of *fatness* as it relates to body composition is of concern as well. This is excess baggage that can potentially slow running performance if it is excessive. How much is optimal? How can lean body mass and body fat be quantified? Does low body fat in women due to excessive leanness predispose them to amenorrhea? What is the relationship between the estrogen-related loss of bone calcium from amenorrhea and the potential risk for skeletal injury? Along with the concept of lactate/ventilatory threshold, few topics in exercise physiology have generated more interest and controversy among coaches and athletes than the question of ideal body composition for health and performance.

Fatness Versus Leanness

It seems a simple conclusion that our total body weight has two components: fat (or adipose tissue) and lean body mass. But beyond the fact that fat is less dense than H_2O and therefore floats, while the rest of our tissue mass sinks because it is more dense than H_2O, not much else regarding body composition is unequivocal. There are indeed sex-related differences in fat storage, and racial/ethnic differences as well—not only in sites of preferential fat storage but also in the density of various tissues.

The balance between training intensity (energy outgo) and nutritional status (energy intake) determines how much stored fat is present. In technologically advanced societies, where food is abundant and physical requirements of the working population are reduced, obesity becomes a chronic and important problem affecting that society's health. Thus, the desire among many nonathletes to begin an exercise program is often motivated by their realizing that it is a more satisfying alternative than simply eating less. Because protein turnover can increase during very intense training states, lean body mass can also change, increasing or decreasing depending on whether the training stimulus was appropriate or excessive. Thus, total body weight, lean body mass, and body fat are all useful variables in assessing an individual's changing body composition over time.

Athletic performance can be affected in diverse ways by the presence of body fat. Swimmers, for example, find that a certain amount of fat beyond the minimum required for health maintenance is advantageous because it contributes to buoyancy. Competitive swimmers are still relatively lean people, however. Athletes in contact sports such as American football and English rugby find a certain amount of fat useful as a cushion against impact injury. Runners, though, discover that excess body fat is simply excess baggage. It increases inertia and mass and thus requires additional energy for its transport.

A certain amount of fat is absolutely essential in everyone for life, however, so runners need reminding that an obsession for trying to become excessively thin can be as unhealthy as gaining too much weight. Many hormones (particularly the steroid hormones such as cortisone, estrogen, progesterone, and testosterone), as well as vitamins A, D, E, and K, for example, are fat soluble rather than water soluble. Thus, fat is required for these hormones to be transported through the blood and into the tissues where they play their important role in life processes.

The presence of a certain amount of fat is hormonally determined. Estrogen hormone levels are higher in women's circulating blood than in men's. These have a hypolipemic (fat-storing) effect, with fat typically deposited in subcutaneous areas such as the buttocks and lower limbs. Fat storage also occurs in such places as bone marrow and around the internal organs. Men have lower circulating blood levels of estrogen than women and thus less stored fat, but men exhibit higher levels of protein-building hormones such as testosterone.

Muscle tissue is more dense than adipose tissue, containing about 75% water as compared with only 10% for adipose tissue. Because of its greater density than fat, it occupies less space per unit mass. Thus, a 60-kg man at 8% fat will *appear* smaller than a 60-kg woman at 15% body fat. Table 6.4 provides some basic information concerning percent fat in various groups of men and women. There is a certain amount of non-sex-specific essential fat in the body, which refers to lipids that are intimately associated with the life of our tissues: most cell membranes, the coverings of nerve cells, and in the brain. This is small in quantity, roughly between 2% and 3% of body weight. Usually, the term *lean body mass* includes this essential lipid (Buskirk and Mendez 1984), with estrogen-related *storage fat* referring to the remainder. The term *fat weight* actually refers to all fat tissue, leaving the rest as fat-free body weight. Equations (6.2) and (6.3) summarize these relationships (BW = body weight):

$$\text{Total BW} = \text{fat-free BW} + \text{fat weight} \tag{6.2}$$

and

$$\text{Total BW} = \text{lean body mass with essential fat} + \text{storage fat} \tag{6.3}$$

Highly trained distance runners, as shown in table 6.4, are at the very bottom of the range of values for fat content among healthy people, because of their large training loads (which are energy consuming) and their generally careful selec-

TABLE 6.4

Selected Anthropometric Data for Men and Women

Category	% body fat	
	Men	**Women**
Non-sex-specific essential body fat	2-3	2-3
Fat in healthy, trained distance runners	5-8	10-14
Fat in active, healthy, young adults	12-20	16-25
Clinical obesity	> 25	> 30

Category	Body mass index[a]	
	Men	**Women**
Active, healthy, young adults	25	25
Trained distance runners	18-22	18-20
Clinical obesity	> 30	> 30

[a]Body mass index = weight in kilograms/square of height in meters.

tion of nutritious but lower-fat-content foods. Thus, their percent fat ranges from about 5% to 8% for men and 10% to 14% for women, because of the estrogenic effect. Unfortunately, some runners develop the erroneous belief that all fat can be dispensed with if they simply eat less and train harder. This is simply untrue and, as will be described shortly, can cause health problems. Our elite-level marathon runners tend toward the low end of these ranges (5% to 7% for men, 10% to 12% for women), probably because their consistently high training volume makes their energy intake similar to their energy outgo with very little extra fat available to store. In contrast, our healthy middle-distance runners, with total training loads not quite so high in terms of energy requirement, tend toward the high end of these body fat ranges (6% to 8% for men, 11% to 14% for women).

We do not know precisely the extent to which variation in the density of various tissues occurs with racial/ethnic differences. By racial we refer to a group of individuals with certain common biological features and by ethnic we refer to a group distinguished by cultural differences such as language or religion. Often there is considerable overlap, but great diversity can occur as well. If such differences exist, then the equations of Siri (equation 6.6; 1961) and Brozek et al. (equation 6.7; 1963), validated for the healthy American white (European stock) young adult population, may not apply to other groups. Data of Robert Malina (1973), for example, suggest that black American athletes when compared with white American athletes tend to display a more linear physique, smaller skinfolds, higher body density, and greater skeletal muscle mass and density. A more recent study by James Schutte et al. (1984) has extended some of these observations, comparing young, healthy, black and white American males. Certainly because of a greater bone mineral content in blacks, and perhaps also because of greater muscle density, the body density for blacks has been estimated as 1.113 gm/cc, compared with 1.100 gm/cc for whites (Behnke, Osserman, and Welham 1953). Schutte et al. (1984) thus suggest the following formula for converting density to body fat in blacks instead of those used for whites:

$$\% \text{ fat} = [(4.374/\text{BD}) - 3.928] \times 100 \tag{6.4}$$

Depending on how fat content is expressed, it can appear to change when in fact it is remaining stable. As an example, if a 60-kg (132-lb) male runner gains 2 kg (4.4 lb) of lean body mass through a serious strength-building program, although his *total* fat content may not change (we'll say he has 3.6 kg [7.9 lb] of body fat), his *percent* body fat will decrease from 6.0% to 5.8%.

Methods of Measurement

People with even a cursory interest in body composition have probably heard mention of (or have been measured by) such procedures as underwater weighing (densitometry), skinfold assessment using calipers (anthropometry), or any of several newer techniques. Densitometry determines body density directly, and anthropometry estimates it indirectly. Density measurement typically is the first step in quantifying leanness/fatness. Once density is determined, estimates can be made of percent fat and nonfat mass or lean body mass by use of regression equations developed by measurements made on large numbers of individuals. Either technique can provide useful information, depending on the accuracy of data collection and whether the equations used are appropriate for the individual being measured. This topic is being actively researched, with several timely reviews of new developments occurring regularly (Barr, McCargar, and Crawford 1994; Brodie 1988; Heyward 1996; A.D. Martin and Drinkwater 1991).

Densitometry

During the 1940s and 1950s several groups of scientists did the primary investigative work that led to the wide use of densitometry as a primary method for evaluating human body composition. Brozek and Keys (1951) suggested that density differences in healthy people could be explained simply by differences in their relative amounts of lean and fat tissue. Detailed investigations of healthy, young, white, adult subjects gave values for the density of body fat as 0.9007 gm/cc (Fidanza, Keys, and Anderson 1953), with lean tissue mass averaging 1.100 gm/cc (Behnke, Osserman, and Welham 1953). However, the human body's irregular shape makes it impossible to quantify its exact volume. Because only fat tissue is less dense than H_2O, the ingenious notion developed that one ought to be able to use Archimedes' principle and determine body density (D_B) by weighing people underwater (called hydrostatic weighing) and then using this D_B value to estimate percent fat using a regression equation developed from data representing a large subject population (Buskirk 1961). *Archimedes' principle* states that a body immersed in water is buoyed up with a force equal to the weight of the water displaced. Two measurements of body weight are made, one out of water and the other when immersed, and a correction is made for residual lung volume. D_B can then be calculated using the following equation, where D_B = body density, OWBW = out-of-water body weight, UWW = underwater weight, RV = residual volume, and WD = water density:

$$D_B = \frac{OWBW}{\dfrac{OWBW - UWW}{WD} - RV} \tag{6.5}$$

Two different equations have resulted for converting D_B values to percent body fat. The equation of Siri (1961), developed from cadaver examination, in which

$$\% \text{ fat} = [(4.95/D_B) - 4.50] \times 100 \tag{6.6}$$

assumes fat density as 0.9 gm/cc and fat-free tissue density as 1.1 gm/cc. The equation of Brozek et al. (1963), in which

$$\% \text{ fat} = [(4.57/D_B) - 4.142] \times 100 \tag{6.7}$$

is based on idealized values for the so-called reference man of 70 kg and 14% body fat.

Hydrostatic weighing is reasonably accurate but requires specialized equipment, several time-consuming repetitive measurements, and the subject's willingness to be dunked into a tank of water. But the importance of obesity as a problem in clinical medicine as well as the interest of physical educators in the effect of body fat on physical performance has brought the procedure into widespread use.

At least five technological sources of error contribute to an inability to measure body density precisely using underwater weighing. Most of these can be controlled reasonably well. One is the *dry-land weight* obtained using a measuring scale. Another is measurement of *body volume*. A third is the weighing chamber *water temperature;* only at 39.2° F (4° C) does water have a density of 1 gm/cc. (This method would be even more unpopular with subjects if that were the water temperature used during submersion! The preferred water temperature of 85° F [29.4° C] has a density of 1.004 gm/cc.) A fourth error comes from the presence of *intestinal gas,* which is more difficult to estimate than to reduce by using dietary guidelines the day before testing to minimize intestinal gas production. Finally, there is *lung volume,* which can be minimized (i.e., reduced to residual lung volume) by having the subject exhale maximally prior to submersion (Weltman and Katch 1981). Using predicted nomographic values for residual volume based on age, sex, and height instead of measured values, however, can also add considerable error (Morrow et al. 1986) and should be avoided.

In addition to these five sources of technological error, other constraints can cause problems in interpreting densitometric data accurately. We do not yet know precisely how an intense training program maintained over a period of months may change subtle aspects of body composition. MacDougall, Sale, Elder, and Sutton (1982) suggest that athletes may have denser bones and muscles than nonathletes. If true, this would cause an overestimation of percent fat using the equations that assume lesser body density.

Even when these technological sources of error are minimized, there is still a roughly 3% margin of error that represents the biological limitation of using only two components—fat weight and fat-free body weight—in the measurement model. There are individual variations in body H_2O content and in lean tissue density, yet the assumption is made that body density is a fixed value. Thus, a male runner measured as having 6% body fat might actually have anywhere between 3% and 9% body fat depending on how closely his or her body density approaches the idealized value used in the equation. Such limitations might seem so large that coaches and athletes, who are accustomed to timing race performances in 100ths of a second, might consider measurements of percent fat a waste of time, especially if it means dunking an athlete in a tank of water each time the measurements are made. They shouldn't worry, however, because usually they are not interested in identifying the so-called *absolute value* for percent fat as much as they are in quantifying *changes in the measured value over time* as fatness and fitness vary. Sequential measurements made on a given individual over a period of time, particularly if the same instrument and measurer are used, will have much less error associated with them because of minimal technological variability and density changes in that individual between measurements. Still, the relative inaccessibility of underwater weighing tanks has resulted in coaches and athletes seeking other means for quantifying leanness and fatness.

Anthropometry

Given the logistical and other constraints of densitometry, it is not surprising that alternative simpler methods would be sought to provide similar information regarding leanness and fatness. Particularly when a coach desires to measure such variables as height, weight, lean body mass, and percent fat in an entire sport team, it has been desirable to have available methodology that can be implemented simply, conveniently, quickly, and inexpensively using techniques with good reliability. A number of anthropometric variables (those which measure body structural features) have been evaluated over the past few decades for their possible predictive value in estimating body density. Among these are bone diameters, height and weight indices such as the body mass index (table 6.5), circumference of selected body parts, and skinfold thicknesses.

TABLE 6.5

Body Mass Index, Body Density, and Percent Body Fat

Athlete _____ Test date _____

Birth date _____ Exact age _____

Weight (kg) _____ (lb) _____ Height (cm) _____ (in.) _____

Body mass index = weight (kg)/square of height (m^2) = _____

Skinfold thicknesses (mm):

Triceps	_____	Thigh	_____
Pectoralis	_____	Midaxillary	_____
Subscapular	_____	Suprailiac	_____
Abdominal	_____		

Sum of skinfolds = E = _____ (mm)   Sum squared = E^2 = _____

Calculated estimate of body density:

Women (Reference: Jackson, Pollock, and Ward 1980):

D_B = [1.097 − 0.00046971 × E] + [0.00000056 × E^2] − [0.00012828 × age]

= 1.097 − _____ + _____ − _____

= _____

Men (Reference: Jackson and Pollock 1978):

D_B = [1.112 − 0.00043499 × E] + [0.00000055 × E^2] − [0.00028826 × age]

= 1.112 − _____ + _____ − _____

= _____

Calculated estimates:

% body fat = [4.57/D_B − 4.142] × 100 = _____

Nonessential fat mass = weight × %BF = _____ (kg) _____ (lb)

Fat-free body mass = weight − fat mass = _____ (kg) _____ (lb)

An effective interaction between the disciplines of physiology and biostatistics has produced a large variety of prediction equations for estimating body density from the kinds of variables mentioned previously. Evidence has gradually favored the use of several skinfold measurements alone rather than in combination with other anthropometric variables such as bone diameters and various circumferences. As a result, the seven-site skinfold equations developed by Andrew Jackson and Michael Pollock for men (1978) and women (Jackson, Pollock, and Ward 1980) have achieved considerable popularity. In a subsequent review of literature, Timothy Lohman (1981) agreed with this notion of using a variety of skinfold measures.

Jackson and Pollock (1978) and Jackson, Pollock, and Ward (1980) detailed the nature of some of the important problems that must be considered when using anthropometry to estimate body density. First, the relationship between body density and skinfold fat is nonlinear. Thus, quadratic rather than linear regression equations are needed for greater accuracy. Second, skinfold fat is not distributed uniformly between the sexes; it is thicker at some sites than at others. The larger quantity of sex-specific essential fat in women means that a given skinfold thickness in women represents a greater quantity of fat. Third, body composition is age related; that is, beyond age 35, adults tend to increase their stored fat, and this relates in part to activity level. Fourth, sizable prediction errors can occur if equations are used that were created for one specific population (e.g., middle-aged, white, sedentary men) and are then applied to data representing a different population (e.g., trained, college-age, male distance runners). It is preferable to develop prediction equations that generalize from large populations rather than equations based on specific populations. The equations of Jackson and Pollock for men and women are just that—they best fit the data from a heterogeneous sample.

Racial/ethnic differences in skinfolds thickness also occur, meaning that a prediction equation for one group may not apply to another (Robson, Bazin, and Soderstrom 1971). Blacks and Mexican-Americans, when compared with whites, tend to have less subcutaneous fat on their extremities than on their trunk (Malina 1973; Mueller, Shoup, and Malina 1982). This has been observed by measuring thinner triceps and thicker subscapular skinfolds. Further work is needed to determine whether the skinfolds sites chosen for anthropometry in whites are equally diagnostic for body density within other ethnic groups.

Because of such variations in skinfolds thickness and density as well as possible differences in tissue density caused by the training stimulus, some investigators prefer simply to assess changes in the numerical sum of skinfold thicknesses over a given time period. Though this does reduce the confounding influence of some of the possible errors identified here, it does not permit the evaluation of changes in leanness that may also occur with fluctuating body weight. Loss of storage fat from intense training and net energy outgo with no net change in leanness is an entirely different energy picture than the reverse. Typically, both fatness and leanness changes occur in varying degrees. Thus, measuring the sum of skinfolds along with total body weight to permit calculation of percent fat as well as lean body mass is needed to give an adequate picture of ongoing metabolic dynamics.

Obtaining Accurate Skinfold Measurements

As in many forms of data analysis, proper acquisition of the data is crucial; a good analysis of poor-quality information is worse than a poor analysis of good-quality information. When using skinfold assessment for estimation of percent body fat, keep four primary considerations for valid data collection in mind:

- Use reliable measuring calipers, and use the same calipers from one measurement session to another.
- Make repeatable measurements at the proper site using the correct technique.
- Have a trained (preferably the same) individual make the measurements.
- Once reliable data are obtained, use a regression equation that has been validated for the population group being studied.

The equations published by Jackson and Pollock (1978) for men and by Jackson, Pollock, and Ward (1980) for women, shown in table 6.5, have been validated for trained white distance runners whose percent fat tends to be below the 12% and 16% values that might suggest the lower end of the normal range for healthy young men and women, respectively.

Guidelines for identifying and measuring the various skinfolds are best provided by a combination of illustrations (figures 6.29 through 6.37) and written descriptions (Lohman, Roche, and Martorell 1988). The following suggestions should help ensure reliability and repeatability:

- Use the right side of the body for all measurements.
- Use the thumb and index finger of one hand to grasp the skin, and use the calipers, held in the other hand, to measure the skinfold thickness.
- Have the calipers perpendicular to the skinfolds when making the measurement; use the full caliper grip pressure (typically this is about 10 gm/mm^2).
- Make repeated measurements at each site until repeatability is ensured.
- Practice measuring the entire series of skinfolds with at least 50 different subjects before considering that technical competency is minimally acceptable.
- Make the measurements when the athlete is in a normal hydrated state, typically as part of preliminary data acquisition before a treadmill stress test to measure fitness or before a training session. Dehydration will decrease skinfold thickness, thus decreasing the value calculated for percent fat.

Dual-Energy X-Ray Absorptiometry (DEXA)

Underwater weighing and the use of skinfold measurements to estimate percent body fat are based on the notion that the body is divisible into two distinct compartments: fat mass and fat-free mass. These so-called two-compartment models rely for their accuracy on the mean values obtained for the density of these two tissue types from a relatively small number of cadavers, and thus their validity has often been questioned. How can results from such a small subject population be applicable to people of different ethnic groups, ages, and fitness? Quite simply, it cannot, as has been mentioned on several occasions in the foregoing text. Recent new technology has provided a method for getting around this dilemma (Kohrt 1995; Mazess et al. 1990; Nichols et al. 1995).

The technique uses a total-body scanner with two X-ray beams at different energy levels. These two X-ray energy beams are attenuated differently by body tissues, giving rise to the name of the procedure (dual-energy X-ray absorptiometry, or DEXA). Using technology that is irrelevant to describe here, body mass can be divided into three components: bone mineral content and soft tissue mass, with the latter subdivided into lean tissue mass and fat mass. As shown in figure 6.38a, using U.S. elite-level middle-distance star Kristen Seabury as our subject, the X-ray beam makes consecutive transverse scans at 1-cm inter-

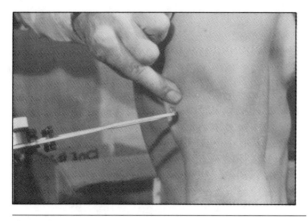

Figure 6.29 *Triceps:* A vertical fold is taken over the muscle belly, midway between the olecranon and the tip of the acromion processes of the humerus; the elbow is extended and the entire limb is relaxed.

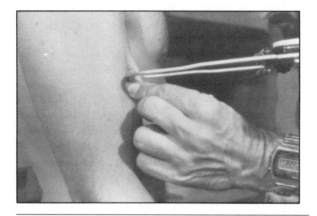

Figure 6.30 *Biceps:* A vertical fold is taken over the midpoint of the muscle belly, midway between the anterior axillary fold (above) and the antecubital space (below); the elbow is extended and the entire limb is relaxed.

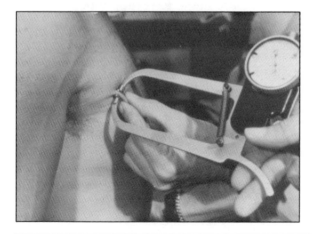

Figure 6.31 *Pectoralis:* A diagonal fold is taken halfway between the nipple and anterior axillary line for men, and two thirds of the distance toward this anterior axillary line for women.

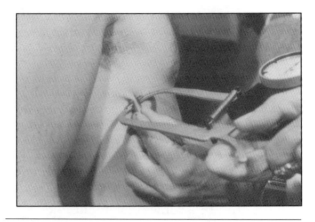

Figure 6.32 *Midaxillary:* A vertical fold is taken at the level of the xiphoid process of the sternum, on the midaxillary line.

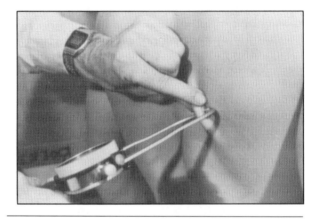

Figure 6.33 *Subscapular:* A diagonal fold is taken no more than 2 cm below the inferior angle of the scapula.

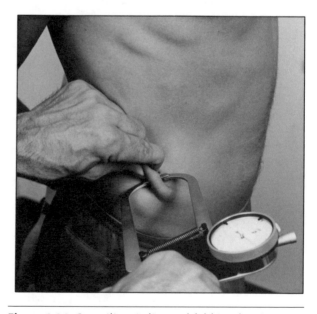

Figure 6.34 *Suprailiac:* A diagonal fold is taken just above the iliac crest at the midaxillary line.

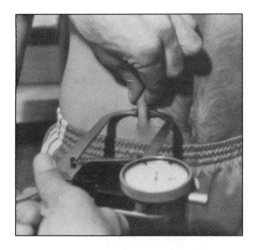

Figure 6.35 *Abdominal:* A vertical fold is taken about 2 cm to the right of the umbilicus.

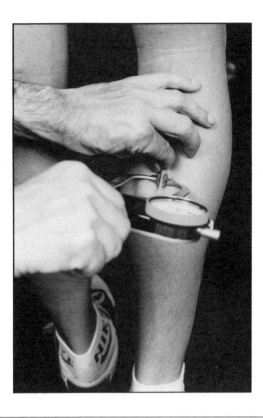

Figure 6.37 *Calf:* A vertical fold is taken at the largest portion of the posterior non-weight-bearing lower limb, over the belly of the gastrocnemius.

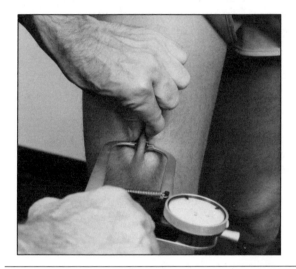

Figure 6.36 *Thigh:* A vertical fold is taken at the anterior midline of the non-weight-bearing lowering limb, halfway between the hip and knee joints.

vals, moving from head to toe at a rate of about 8 cm/s. Kristen is 66 in. tall (168 cm), and thus, after about 21 min a completed image of her bone mineral content—which looks like a mini-X-ray—appears on the machine's video screen, as illustrated in figure 6.38*b*. The level of X-ray exposure is so small as to be unimportant: Each total-body scan provides approximately 0.02 to 0.05 millirem (mrem) of radiation exposure, compared with 40 to 50 mrem from a standard chest X-ray or 0.45 mrem per day that we all receive from background radiation. Thus, the procedure is eminently safe, in addition to providing accurate, detailed information in a short time span. Accompanying the image is a detailed report that quantifies both total bone mineral density and percent fat as well as providing such information for specific body regions.

We have been using this technology since 1992 as athletes visit our laboratory for physiological profiling. By combining the information gained from

• a 3-day dietary profile to estimate food intake, including calcium,

- a computerized time-line energy analysis based on an interview to outline the 24-hr time dynamics of when this food is eaten (Benardot 1996),
- assessment of menstrual status of female athletes,
- DEXA technology to evaluate both bone mineral status as well as percent fat,
- skinfold estimation of percent fat, and
- evaluation of injury status since the previous visit,

we have been able to provide practical guidance to our runners regarding what to eat and how to eat it to stay "lean and mean" and how to minimize the risks of musculoskeletal injury.

As one practical example, the dietary assessment provides an indication of daily calcium intake, and the DEXA scan provides information regarding bone mineral density at various sites. Among our runners, ordinarily the mineral density in their legs is considerably higher than that normally seen in healthy, sedentary people. For these runners this is an expected consequence of their increased impact stress from training. We hope that this additional calcification is of dietary origin rather than having been "stolen" from other skeletal areas of the body. If in fact we observe that the mineral density of other skeletal sites is below normally expected values, perhaps additional dietary calcium would be beneficial. By suggesting such dietary supplementation (for example, an extra 8-oz glass of calcium-fortified orange juice every day) and by then reevaluating the athlete at 6-month intervals using DEXA, the changing calcium dynamics can be monitored.

The Dangers of Being Too Thin

Particularly for female athletes, the combination of information about diet, leanness, and bone mineral density just described has been long needed and helpful for better understanding and managing a particularly devastating condition that has only recently even been given a name (American College of Sports Medicine 1992). The so-called *female athlete triad* involves a combination of *amenorrhea* (reduced menstrual cyclicity), *osteoporosis* (bone demineralization), and *disordered eating* (sufficient to cause excessive weight loss) that can be the end result of what starts out as a perfectly logical sequence of thought oriented toward athletic success, but that gets out of hand.

Female athletes striving for excellence in sport are under enormous pressure to succeed. While such pressure is an inextricable facet of sport competition and considered desirable, it can get out of hand. The triad just mentioned has been commonly seen among gymnasts as well as endurance runners and swimmers. To the uninformed these may seem entirely unrelated problems, but they are not. They result from a behavioral mind-set that carries to excess an ongoing perception that "being thin is in," and that, among athletes especially, one must "be thin to win." The consequences can be tragic—injurious at best, career-ending at worst—and are only now starting to be fairly well explained.

In part because the clinical identification of this triad is both difficult and delayed, diagnosis too often is too late to save the athlete from disabling injury or emotional scarring. Male coaches outnumber female coaches, particularly in running and gymnastics circles, and this peculiarly female syndrome is often not even known to men, much less understood. Let's try to outline what's oc-

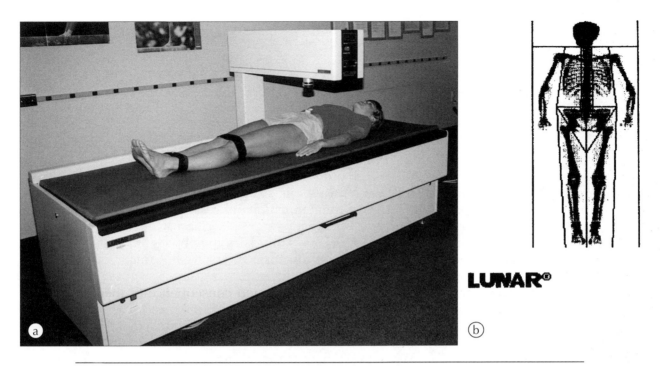

Figure 6.38 The use of dual-energy X-ray absorptiometry provides accurate quantification of bone mineral content, lean tissue mass, and fat mass. A total-body scan (*a*) requires about 20 min and produces a video screen image (*b*) along with a detailed data summary.

curring with this complex and frustrating phenomenon and how it might be addressed, with the hope of saving some athletic careers and optimizing the performance potential of talented female distance runners.

Current Western societal values suggest that a lean body is associated with fitness, competitiveness, self-discipline, and attractiveness. Generally, a body composition of not less than about 10% to 14% fat using skinfold assessment is common among elite-level, highly fit, female distance runners. At least this level of fatness is required to transport the steroid hormones and the fat-soluble vitamins (A, D, E, and K), to provide foot cushioning by the plantar fat pad on impact in running, and to promote normal menstrual cyclicity (Bale 1994).

Being too lean, however, particularly for athletes participating in impact stress sports, predisposes them to skeletal injury. This increased injury risk is often not fully realized by athletes until too late, for several reasons. First, although amenorrhea, osteoporosis, and disordered eating can all occur by themselves, only recently has the relationship between these three factors in association with excessive leanness been explored. Second, the onset of injury varies among athletes due to training loads, structural integrity, and body type. Third, there is no uniformity among people. We are all different. Leanness in one person is not equivalent to leanness in another because differences in hormone levels vary the extent to which fat is used and distributed. Some women may stop having their menstrual cycle when body fat gets down to 12%; for others this may be 10%. What is sufficiently lean but still healthy in one may predispose another to injury (Oppliger and Cassady 1994).

Development of the Problem

How do we distinguish between those athletes who are susceptible to development of the triad of amenorrhea, osteoporosis, and disordered eating and those who do not have such problems? Let's first review the healthy situation as unaffected female runners train successfully for a major championship. And let's use the fall U.S. cross-country season; this is a period when both collegiate and postcollegiate athletes from a variety of track specialties all come together to build a strong aerobic competitive base for a late-November peak. We'll assume these women all start their fall training season fairly fresh, in good health, with normal menstrual cyclicity.

Particularly for the college and club athletes, a spirited eagerness in coming together for this new training block begins. These athletes are hungry to train, work together in a group, push each other in training, and dream of excellence come November. They also know full well that to be successful, in addition to optimal training, they will require optimal nutrition, injury freedom, a positive mental attitude, no illness, and an ideal taper before the big race. Concentration is on beating the best, and clear in everyone's mind are the photos in the latest running magazines showing the stars at top form in last year's major races. Seeing them decked out in their competitive finery, looking super-sleek, super-confident, and super-cool with their fresh flowing stride, the goal is to emulate their success. Periodic races of varying intensity provide practice for the upcoming championships. Quality performances result, which in turn make it rewarding to take some well-deserved down time, permitting "the body to heal, and the fires to rekindle." When everything clicks, it's so easy!

For certain other athletes susceptible to the female athlete triad, however, this is not the scenario. The unprecedented pressure placed upon all female athletes to excel has already been mentioned. They may experience pressures from academic work, living needs, financial constraints, family, the need for good sport performances that start the path to success to bring financial and personal satisfaction, and wanting to perform well for themselves, their coach, and others. Because their peers also are doing this, there is competition. However, perhaps due to a slightly smaller genetic endowment with talent, or a slightly less developed level of maturity, or a reduced level of starting fitness as the hard training season begins, or some difficulties in managing the academic course load, they are not quite as well prepared as others to cope with their environment.

The real problems for these vulnerable athletes typically begin several weeks into their season, when they not only begin to experience chronic fatigue from lifestyle overload, but also have a bad race. What's going wrong, they wonder? Their coach wrote the plan and is allegedly a competent coach, and other athletes are managing the same load, so the athlete must be at fault.

A two-pronged focus of attention now occurs. First, there is the attentional focus toward those athletes at the front of the competition—they seem so thin, and they run so fast—they must be running fast because they are thin. Second, there is an attentional focus toward whatever can be done to emulate these thin athletes at the front. The disciplines of competitiveness, perfectionism, and self-control now are centered toward weight loss, food deprivation, and more intense training to burn more energy.

Thus, all focus is now channeled toward the twin goals of losing weight and training harder. This will be stressed even more if the athlete has a naturally stockier body type or if the coach dwells upon the topic of getting thin or losing weight as a means of performing better. Becoming thin can occur quickly and relatively easily, at least initially, simply by not eating, and this will surely please the coach. It is, however, a recipe with the potential for disaster. The extreme hunger leads to an enormous desire for food, which is now accompanied by a fear of its energy content. This may now stimulate the coping behavior of eating and immediately getting rid of the food (via vomiting or laxatives) before its nutritional benefits can be gained (bulimia). In the worst instances this leads to a panic situation about possible greater weight gain, which is compensated for by more training. Not only are fat stores depleted, but there is also an ongoing inadequate absorption of fat-soluble vitamin D to ensure calcium intake. Dieting continues, the training load increases, frustration increases, sleeping decreases, performance worsens, and all this in turn stimulates more of the same rigid behavior.

Interestingly, quite often in the early stages as stored body fat is lost and body weight decreases, training and racing performance increase for awhile. This is because the athletes are still fairly healthy, and in addition, their power-to-weight ratio has increased. Their still-fairly-fit lean body mass is powering a lighter frame faster than before. In turn, this performance improvement fuels their desire to continue what they have been doing: denying themselves food to remain thin. Similarly, the first poor performance as energy storage levels become performance-inhibiting fuels an even stronger denial of energy so as to become even more lean.

Now the risk of injury or illness skyrockets. Both of these are also feared like the plague, because they will require forced rest, which increases the risk of weight gain or not being able to compete. If illness or injury do occur, athletes steadfastly try to hide them. The sum of these emotional challenges brings moodiness, a feeling of inadequacy, and isolation. An accompanying factor to this elevated stress load, along with the greatly decreased body fat, is loss of menstrual cyclicity. Athletes in this situation often are delighted with this, for two reasons. First, they've heard that their very thin competitors at the front also tend not to have menstrual cyclicity. And even better, now they need not worry about premenstrual cramping as an inhibitor to successful competition. By this time, however, any thoughts of a successful competition are typically dashed from either developing stress fractures, profound fatigue from overtraining, or illness.

Medical Aspects

Earlier we alluded to the three features of the female triad, and we've mentioned them in the foregoing description of the problem-athlete scenario. Let's briefly provide some medical notes regarding these three problems, so that we can use this information to offer suggestions for improving the situation. First, *disordered eating* manifests itself in several ways that all emphasize excessive weight loss: depriving oneself of food; use of laxatives, diuretics, and diet pills; and even vomiting of food just eaten. If continued long enough, it can lead to eating disorders, such as bulimia nervosa and anorexia nervosa. Both of these disorders are associated with a distorted body image (not only a fear of fatness, but also thinking that one looks fatter than one really is) and with behaviors focused on minimal food intake. *Bulimia* includes secretive binge eating episodes with subsequent purging to prevent any caloric benefit.

There are a few warning signs of disordered eating, but they are often difficult to observe: not eating with others, disappearing after meals, and increasingly noticeable weight loss or weight cycling. Clinically, the presence of fine body hair (lanugo) is also a telltale sign. Additional aerobic training well beyond that normally assigned (health-spa stair climbing, treadmill running, cycling, swimming, etc. after hours simply to burn calories) is another indication.

Disordered eating can dramatically increase the incidence of amenorrhea and osteoporosis, both of which increase greatly the risk for skeletal degeneration and injury.

Osteoporosis implies bone demineralization, such that bone calcium loss may be similar to that in an early menopausal woman. It has at least two distinguishing features: (1) decreased bone mass and (2) microarchitectural changes in bone that increase bone fragility and risk of fractures. Bone health depends upon an interplay between available calcium, exercise, and estrogen levels. Both exercise and estrogen stimulate bone mineralization. Within the first four years after menopause, bone demineralization is greatest, caused by dramatically decreased estrogen levels. In postmenopausal women, if estrogen supplements are begun promptly, along with emphasis on continued dietary calcium intake and exercise, much of this loss can be minimized. But if such supplements are not begun promptly, the mineral loss will not be fully replaced.

Amenorrhea may be the most easily recognizable aspect of this triad. The eating behaviors are hidden, and changes in bone density require specialized equipment not readily available. Amenorrhea is defined as the absence of 3 to 12 consecutive menstrual periods per year. Its incidence is 2% to 5% in the general population, 3.4% to 66% among all athletes in general (figure skaters, gymnasts, and distance runners are at the high end of this range). Amenorrhea in young female athletes is not simply a result of hard training, but rather indicative of something going wrong. Its development is not completely understood but is probably multifactorial and in particular involves a reduction in the hormonal output from the hypothalamus, pituitary gland, and ovaries. Coupled with this is an energy drain: decreased food intake, increased emotional and physical stress from high training loads, and decreased body fat below a critical limit, which is different for each person.

For those who are less than 27 years of age and who have never been pregnant, the incidence of amenorrhea is greatest. Their near-zero blood estrogen levels promote bone demineralization (and thus an increased skeletal injury risk) even if they exercise and maintain normal dietary calcium. Provided that they can regain normal cyclicity, bone mineral density can be improved by about 6% after one year, but only about an additional 3% will occur after the second year. Then there is a plateau with little change thereafter. This suggests that complete bone remineralization may never occur. Thus, the longer the period of amenorrhea and the greater the extent of bone mineral loss, the greater is the risk of a young athlete being left with "old bones."

Psychological Aspects

What we are witnessing in the female athlete triad seems to be a crossing beyond the fine line between the effective interaction of mind and body into a situation where mind and body are at odds with each other. Three aspects of a naturally occurring and essential cognitive style characterize how highly competitive athletes get out of control. One aspect is *competitiveness*. The healthy behavior is hard training and keeping an adequate diet of carbohydrates and fats that provides all or very nearly all of the needed energy required, with only a slight reduction in weight during the more intense final phases. When out of control, the focus becomes one of "How hard can I train, how much fat can I lose, and how low can my weight get?"

A second aspect is *perfectionism*. The healthy behavior is a normal self-criticism, which realizes that occasional days of dismal performance are a natural occurrence in hard training and indicative of the essential need for recovery.

When out of control, an all-or-nothing mentality dictates that no workout is hard enough, rest is inappropriate, and even the good performances should have been better. And achieving the so-called "perfect weight" becomes first and foremost.

A third aspect is *self-control*. The healthy behavior is mentally coping with the fatigue of hard training and pushing onward, within reason. When out of control, this is replaced by a denial of feelings of tiredness or need for rest and a dominating obsession to put such thoughts away as unacceptable. As the overriding determination to perform better and better develops, losing becomes ever more severely threatening. A rigidity sets in that removes the possibility of reason—lack of discipline cannot be tolerated.

Managing and Preventing the Problem

The challenge to ensure that female athletes do not fall victim to the female athlete triad is to emphasize a performance-based stereotype rather than one that is appearance-based. The *appearance stereotype* focuses on the logic that "if you're thin you'll win" and "if you win, it's because you're thin." Or, to state it slightly differently, "the less I eat, the thinner I'll get, and the greater are my chances of getting thin enough to win." Clearly, this is faulty logic. One cannot drive from New York to Los Angeles on 10 gallons of fuel. The tank needs to be filled periodically. Quality fuel gives better mileage. No fuel gives no mileage. Think nutritious food, not denial of food. Life is not solely a bagel, a piece of fruit, and a bowl of plain spaghetti. This is a tragic mind-set, a blueprint for athletic failure and premature aging.

The *performance-based stereotype* focuses on the logic that if you train hard and eat right, you'll get lean and mean and that it isn't fatness but fitness that's crucial. Or, to state it slightly differently, "The secret is eating to win, so if I eat healthy food and train within my limits, I'll get thin automatically. But this is a healthy thinness, and however thin that is, it's irrelevant, because I'll have the fitness to be awesome." The flaw with the appearance-based stereotype should be obvious—it isn't thinness that wins races, rather, it's fitness and desire, along with marvelous health and an optimal combination of diet and training. The high training load is optimal for improving fitness without producing injury but mandates a high caloric intake. A high-carbohydrate diet with adequate fat and protein provides plenty of minerals, vitamins, and electrolytes without weight gain. Temporary periods of slight caloric deficit will produce more leanness from the use of stored calories, but this is a "healthy leanness."

The performance-based stereotype is presently the mind-set that identifies most of today's truly elite female distance runners who are enjoying long-term success. The advice for athletes is simple: Train hard, be very sensitive to the need for recovery, look forward to food, and focus on the healthy food that you know you need instead of on food that you think you shouldn't eat. Once emphasis on *quality* nutrition dominates over *no* nutrition, the entire energy environment works to the betterment of the athlete. Weight gain during downtime is reduced. The chance of nutrient deficiencies (minerals, electrolytes, vitamins) is reduced. The risks of anemia, overtraining, and injury decrease. And percent fat does not go so low as to cause amenorrhea, thereby preserving estrogen balance for maintaining bone integrity.

Clearly, we have entered a new age of sport. Sport is big business that thrives on performance. A college scholarship or apparel contract demands performance. Always there is pressure for performance improvement. Better is not good enough. Best never occurs because one can always do better, which is never good enough. An athlete is barely as good as her last race, because very likely someone else ran even better more recently somewhere else. One might hope that coaches, administrators, and all the others in control of this new age of sport will assume a leadership role and develop a new age of knowledge for their athletes. Until this occurs, however, athletes themselves must take on this responsibility, and many are simply not aware of the fundamental nature of the problem.

It is to be hoped that athletes can become informed adequately about the female athlete triad problem, either through an informed support group or through self-realization. Chances are that informed athletes will cope successfully. The uninformed athlete without outside assistance is the victim—she takes what seems a logical course of action, because short-term success can be perceived, but does not realize the tragedy she will eventually suffer (amenorrhea, osteoporosis, injury) because it is months or years in the future. She can't see the eventual tragedy by reminding herself of those athletes who now are injured—they are out of the picture: disappeared, depressed, and in despair. Educational guidance and awareness regarding identification and management of the problem, among coaches as well as athletes, are the keys (Yeager et al. 1993). We hope the few nuggets contained herein will serve as a jumping-off point for additional reading and awareness.

SUMMARY

Running Improvement Through Total-Body Conditioning

1. After training, probably the single most important contributor to improved performance is remaining injury free for long periods. This permits steady, long-term progress over time. Distance runners who simply run tend to have more injuries than do distance runners who engage in a comprehensive total-body fitness program intended to improve the output capabilities of those muscle groups that are not specifically challenged by running but that assist running and that also contribute to overall joint strength for injury prevention.

2. Complete body fitness also includes an adequate program of stretching exercises to maintain effective joint range of motion. Athletes must take care, however, not to overdo either conditioning or stretching. Runners should not experience such ongoing residual fatigue from conditioning that their ability to manage the running aspects of their training plan is compromised. Similarly, they should not strive so diligently for improved flexibility that stretching injuries result.

3. Strength (force-generating capability) is determined by muscular factors (cross-sectional area of working muscle, fiber length, and muscle architecture) as well as neural factors (stimulus frequency and recruitment). A strengthening program will improve the functional capabilities of ligaments, tendons, and bones as well as the working muscles. Bones move as a result of muscle-directed rotation around the axis of the joint to which they connect. The torque generated by a limb as it moves around its axis of rotation is given by the product of force and the distance between axis of movement and point of contact.

4. When muscles generate tension, they can either lengthen (eccentric movement), shorten (concentric movement), or not change length at all. Muscles can

be strengthened using principles that maintain relatively constant tension (isotonic training), length (isometric training), or velocity (isokinetic training). The principle of specific training for sport suggests that dynamic (i.e., movement) training is preferable to static (isometric) training, with isotonic training having more direct transfer to running than isokinetic training.

5. Athletes can improve their muscle strength through a program of gradually increasing the intensity of the load applied. A stimulus requiring at least 80% maximal effort and involving about three sets of six to eight reps is required to stimulate muscle growth. As adaptation occurs, the size of the stimulus is appropriately increased. A wide variety of training equipment and techniques is available for implementing such a program. When possible, muscle groups that play a synergistic, stabilizing, and neutralizing role in running should be developed in addition to the prime movers. The equipment used can include one's own body weight, free weights (such as barbells), and specialized machines that provide variable or accommodating resistance. The techniques can include several types of muscle activation (isokinetic, isotonic, and isometric) as well as variable sequencing of multiple activities to provide a comprehensive conditioning stimulus (circuit and stage training).

6. Skeletal muscles respond to the intensity of their training overload rather than to the actual method of the overload. Thus, relatively nonchallenging activities will provide generalized conditioning, whereas more intense exercises that simulate movement patterns, velocities, and forces characteristic of the chosen event will contribute to specialized performance enhancement. By progressively increasing the resistance provided via an overloading stimulus, continued performance improvement should occur. A wide variety of training equipment and techniques is available for implementing such a program. In this chapter we have provided a brief introduction to some of them.

7. Performance of exercise in any form requires adequate joint range of motion. The longer the stride, as with faster running, or the more uneven the terrain, as with cross-country running or the steeplechase, the more important becomes maintenance of adequate flexibility. Athletes who do not achieve this functional range for the needs of their event risk injury or impaired performance in training and competition. Thus, stretching exercises should be an essential part of any athletic training regimen, not only to ensure adequate movement potential in all joints, but also to provide the margin of safety required for excellence in a given event specialty.

8. In sport activities such as running, where the body weight is transported, it is important not to be burdened with excessive nonfunctional weight. Thus, body composition analysis for determining body fat and nonfat body mass has become popular. Densitometry (underwater weighing) provides a measure of density, from which percent fat can be estimated. Anthropometry (skinfold measurements) attempts to predict the percent body fat that would exist if hydrostatic weighing were done. Percent fat measured by the two techniques often yields similar results, and it is not uncommon for both to be used at least once for comparison. For practical reasons, skinfold assessment seems to be done more frequently with athletes, as it is less time-consuming and uses more easily accessible equipment. Also, athletes are more interested in knowing whether changes in fatness or leanness have occurred over time in relation to diet and training than in knowing absolute values.

9. Particularly for female athletes, ensuring that percent body fat does not get too low is crucial to help maintain their general health. Recent techniques

(such as dual-energy X-ray absorptiometry) have permitted a more accurate assessment of percent fat than skinfold and densitometry techniques. With it, a simultaneous estimate of bone mineral density can also be made. Current concern about the increased risk for bone injuries among women whose fatness gets so low that the incidence of amenorrhea increases (with its accompanying decrease in calcium-storing estrogen hormones) has urged further study of, and dissemination of information about, what has been called the female athlete triad. It is but another facet of the important realization that comprehensive general health and fitness synergize with the adaptive effects of specific training to produce a competent athlete.

References

Allen, T.E.; Byrd, R.J.; and Smith, D.P. 1976. Hemodynamic consequences of circuit weight training. *Research Quarterly* 47:299-306.

Alter, M.J. 1996. *Science of flexibility.* 2nd ed. Champaign, IL: Human Kinetics.

American College of Sports Medicine. 1992. The female athlete triad: Disordered eating, amenorrhea, osteoporosis: Call to action. *Sports Medicine Bulletin* 27:4.

Anderson, B. 1989. The flex factor. *Runner's World* 24(2):38-43.

Anderson, B.; Beaulieu, J.E.; Cornelius, W.L.; Dominguez, R.H.; Prentice, W.E.; and Wallace, L. 1984. Coaches roundtable: Flexibility. *National Strength and Conditioning Association Journal* 6(4):10-22.

Atha, J. 1981. Strengthening muscle. *Exercise and Sport Sciences Reviews* 9:1-73.

Austin, D.; Roll, F.; Kreis, E.J.; Palmieri, J.; and Lander, J. 1987. Roundtable: Breathing during weight training. *National Strength and Conditioning Association Journal* 9(5):17-25.

Bale, P. 1994. Body composition and menstrual irregularities of female athletes. *Sports Medicine* 17:347-352.

Barr, S.I.; McCargar, L.J.; and Crawford, S.M. 1994. Practical use of body composition analysis in sport. *Sports Medicine* 17:277-282.

Beaulieu, J.E. 1981. Developing a stretching program. *Physician and Sportsmedicine* 9(11):59-69.

Behnke, A.R.; Osserman, E.F.; and Welham, W.L. 1953. Lean body mass. *Archives of Internal Medicine* 91:585-601.

Benardot, D. 1996. Working with young athletes: Views of a nutritionist on the sports medicine team. *International Journal of Sports Nutrition* 6:110-120.

Berger, R.A. 1962. Effects of varied weight training programs on strength. *Research Quarterly* 33:168-181.

Brodie, D.A. 1988. Techniques of measurement of body composition. *Sports Medicine* 5:11-40, 74-98.

Brozek, J.; Grande, F.; Anderson, J.T.; and Keys, A. 1963. Densitometric analysis of body composition: Revision of some quantitative assumptions. *Annals of the New York Academy of Sciences* 110:113-140.

Brozek, J., and Keys, A. 1951. The evaluation of leanness-fatness in man: Norms and intercorrelations. *British Journal of Nutrition* 5:194-205.

Burke, R.E. 1981. Motor units: Anatomy, physiology, and functional organization. In *Handbook of physiology.* Sec. 1, *The nervous system.* Vol. 2, *Motor control, Part I,* ed. V.B. Brooks, 345-422. Bethesda, MD: American Physiological Society.

Buskirk, E.R. 1961. Underwater weighing and body density, a review of procedures. In

Techniques for measuring body composition, eds. J. Brozek and A. Henschel, 90-106. Washington, DC: National Academy of Sciences, National Research Council.

Buskirk, E.R., and Mendez, J. 1984. Sport science and body composition analysis: Emphasis on cell and muscle mass. *Medicine and Science in Sports and Exercise* 16:584-593.

Cavagna, G.A. 1977. Storage and utilization of energy in skeletal muscle. *Exercise and Sport Sciences Reviews* 5:89-129.

Christensen, C.S. 1972. Strength, the common variable in hamstring strain. *Medicine and Science in Sports* 2:39-42.

Clarke, D.H. 1973. Adaptations in strength and muscular endurance resulting from exercise. *Exercise and Sports Sciences Reviews* 1:73-102.

Corbin, C.B., and Noble, L. 1960. Flexibility: A major component of physical fitness. *Journal of Physical Education and Recreation* 51:23-60.

Cornelius, W.L. 1985. Flexibility. The effective way. *National Strength and Conditioning Association Journal* 7(3):62-64.

Darden, E. 1977. *Strength training principles: How to get the most out of your workouts.* Winter Park, FL: Anna.

DeLorme, T.L. 1945. Restoration of muscle power by heavy resistance exercises. *Journal of Bone and Joint Surgery* 27:645-667.

DeLorme, T.L., and Watkins, A.L. 1948. Technics of progressive resistance exercise. *Archives of Physical Medicine* 29:263-273.

Denny-Brown, D. 1949. Interpretation of the electromyogram. *Archives of Neurology and Psychiatry* 61:99-128.

Eccles, J.C.; Eccles, R.M.; and Lundberg, A. 1958. The action potentials of the alpha motoneurons supplying fast and slow muscles. *Journal of Physiology* 142:275-291.

Eyster, J.A.E. 1927. Cardiac dilation and hypertrophy. *Transactions of the Association of American Physicians* 25:15-21.

Festa, S. 1988. Stretching: The truth. *Runner's World* 23(2):39-42.

Fidanza, F.; Keys, A.; and Anderson, J.T. 1953. Density of body fat in man and other animals. *Journal of Applied Physiology* 6:252-256.

Foster, C.; Hector, L.L.; Welsh, R.; Schrager, M.; Green, M.A.; and Snyder, A.C. 1995. Effects of specific versus cross-training on running performance. *European Journal of Applied Physiology* 70:367-372.

Gandy, G. 1983. Overview of Coe's non-track training. In *Track technique annual,* ed. V. Gambetta, 89-91. Los Altos, CA: Tafnews Press.

Garrett, W.E., Jr.; Safran, M.R.; Seaber, A.V.; Glisson, R.R.; and Ribbeck, B.M. 1987. Biomechanical comparison of stimulated and non-stimulated skeletal muscle pulled to failure. *American Journal of Sports Medicine* 15:448-454.

Häkkinen, K., and Komi, P. 1983. Electromyographic changes during strength training and detraining. *Medicine and Science in Sports and Exercise* 15:455-460.

Hatfield, F.C. 1982. *Flexibility training for sports: PNF techniques.* New Orleans: Fitness Systems USA.

Henneman, E. 1957. Relation between size of neurons and their susceptibility to discharge. *Science* 126:1345-1347.

Hettinger, T., and Muller, E.A. 1953. Muskelleistung und Muskeltraining (Muscle performance and muscle training). *Arbeitsphysiologie* 15:111-116.

Heyward, V.H. 1996. Evaluation of body composition. *Sports Medicine* 22:146-156.

Huxley, A.F., and Niedergerke, R. 1954. Structural changes in muscle during contraction. *Nature* 173:971-973.

Huxley, H.E., and Hanson, J. 1954. Changes in the cross-striations of muscle during contraction and stretch and their structural interpretation. *Nature* 173:973-976.

Jackson, A.S., and Pollock, M.L. 1978. Generalized equations for predicting body density of men. *British Journal of Nutrition* 40:497-504.

Jackson, A.S.; Pollock, M.L.; and Ward, A. 1980. Generalized equations for predicting body density of women. *Medicine and Science in Sports and Exercise* 12:175-182.

Knapik, J.J.; Mawdsley, R.H.; and Ramos, M.V. 1983. Angular specificity and test mode specificity of isometric and isokinetic strength training. *Journal of Orthopaedic Sports Physical Therapy* 5:58-65.

Kohrt, W.M. 1995. Body composition by DXA: Tried and true? *Medicine and Science in Sports and Exercise* 27:1349-1353.

Komi, P., and Bosco, C. 1978. Utilization of stored elastic energy in leg extensor muscles by men and women. *Medicine and Science in Sports* 10:261-265.

Kraemer, W.J.; Deschenes, M.R.; and Fleck, S.J. 1988. Physiological adaptations to resistance exercise: Implications for athletic conditioning. *Sports Medicine* 6:246-256.

Laird, C.E., Jr., and Rozier, C.K. 1979. Toward understanding the terminology of exercise mechanics. *Physical Therapy* 59:287-292.

Lesmes, G.R.; Benhain, D.W.; Costill, D.L.; and Fink, W.J. 1983. Glycogen utilization in fast and slow twitch muscle fibers during maximal isokinetic exercise. *Annals of Sports Medicine* 1:105-108.

Levin, A., and Wyman, J. 1927. The viscous elastic properties of muscle. *Proceedings of the Royal Society* (London) B101:218-243.

Lohman, T.G. 1981. Skinfolds and body density and their relation to body fitness: A review. *Human Biology* 53:181-225.

Lohman, T.G.; Roche, A.F.; and Martorell, R. 1988. *Anthropometric standardization reference manual*. Champaign, IL: Human Kinetics.

MacDougall, J.D.; Sale, D.G.; Elder, G.C.B.; and Sutton, J.R. 1982. Muscle ultrastructural characteristics of elite powerlifters and bodybuilders. *European Journal of Applied Physiology* 48:117-126.

MacDougall, J.D.; Wenger, H.A.; and Green, H.J. 1982. *Physiological testing of the elite athlete*. Toronto: Canadian Association of Sports Sciences.

Malina, R.M. 1973. Biological substrata. In *Comparative studies of blacks and whites in the U.S.*, eds. K.S. Miller and R.W. Dreger, 53-123. New York: Seminar Press.

Malone, T.R. 1988. Evaluation of isokinetic equipment. *Sports Injury Management* 1:1-92.

Martin, A.D., and Drinkwater, D.T. 1991. Variability in measures of body fat. *Sports Medicine* 11:277-288.

Martin, D.E.; Stones, D.; Joy, G.; and Wszola, J. 1987. *The high jump book*. Los Altos, CA: Tafnews Press.

Martin, D.E.; Vroon, D.H.; May, D.F.; and Pilbeam, S.P. 1986. Physiological changes in elite male distance runners training for Olympic competition. *Physician and Sportsmedicine* 14(1):152-171.

Matveyev, L. 1981. *Fundamentals of sports training*. Moscow: Progress.

Mazess, R.B.; Barden, H.S.; Bisek, J.P.; and Hanson, J. 1990. Dual-energy x-ray absorptiometry for total-body and regional bone-mineral and soft-tissue composition. *American Journal of Clinical Nutrition* 51:1106-1112.

McDonagh, M.J., and Davies, C.T. 1984. Adaptive response of mammalian skeletal muscles to exercise with high loads. *European Journal of Applied Physiology* 52:139-155.

Moffroid, M.T., and Kusiak, E.T. 1975. The power struggle: Definition and evaluation of power of muscular performance. *Physical Therapy* 55:1098-1104.

Moffroid, M.T., and Whipple, R.H. 1970. Specificity of speed and exercise. *Journal of the American Physical Therapy Association* 50:692-699.

Moffroid, M.T.; Whipple, R.H.; Hofkosh, J.; Lowman, E.; and Thistle, H. 1969. A study of isokinetic exercise. *Physical Therapy* 49:735-746.

Morgan, R.E., and Adamson, G.T. 1957. *Circuit training.* London: G. Bell and Sons.

Morpurgo, B. 1897. Über aktivitäts-hypertrophie der willkürlichen Muskeln (Concerning the hypertrophy of voluntary muscle). *Virchow's Archiv für Pathologie und Physiologie* 150:522-554.

Morrow, J.R.; Jackson, A.S.; Bradley, P.W.; and Hartung, G.H. 1986. Accuracy of measured and predicted residual lung volume on body density measurement. *Medicine and Science in Sports and Exercise* 18:647-652.

Mueller, W.H.; Shoup, R.F.; and Malina, R.M. 1982. Fat patterning in athletes in relation to ethnic origin and sport. *Annals of Human Biology* 9:371-376.

Nicholas, J.A. 1970. Injuries to knee ligaments: Relationship to looseness and tightness in football players. *Journal of the American Medical Association* 212:2236-2239.

Nichols, D.L.; Sanborn, C.F.; Bonnick, S.L.; Gench, B.; and DiMarco, N. 1995. Relationship of regional body composition to bone mineral density in college females. *Medicine and Science in Sports and Exercise* 27:178-182.

Olson, V.L.; Schmidt, G.L.; and Johnson, R.C. 1972. The maximum torque generated by eccentric, isometric, and concentric contractions of the hip abduction muscles. *Physical Therapy* 52:148-149.

Oppliger, R.A., and Cassady, S.L. 1994. Body composition assessment in women. *Sports Medicine* 17:353.

Perrin, D.H. 1993. *Isokinetic exercise and assessment.* Champaign, IL: Human Kinetics.

Perrine, J.J. 1968. Isokinetic exercise and the mechanical energy potentials of muscle. *Journal of Health, Physical Education, and Recreation* 39(5):40-44.

Person, R.S., and Kudina, L.P. 1972. Discharge frequency and discharge pattern of human motor units during voluntary contraction of muscle. *Electroencephalography and Clinical Neurophysiology* 32:471-483.

Pipes, T.V., and Wilmore, J.H. 1975. Isokinetic versus isotonic strength training in adult men. *Medicine and Science in Sports* 7:262-274.

Rack, P.M.H., and Westbury, D.R. 1969. The effects of length and stimulus rate on tension in the isometric cat soleus muscle. *Journal of Physiology* 204:443-460.

Robertson, J.W. 1991. An ounce of prevention. *Runner's World* 26(2):40-46.

Robson, J.R.K.; Bazin, M.; and Soderstrom, R. 1971. Ethnic differences in skinfold thickness. *American Journal of Clinical Nutrition* 29:864-868.

Schutte, J.E.; Townsend, E.J.; Hugg, J.; Shoup, R.F.; Malina, R.M.; and Blomqvist, C.G. 1984. Density of lean body mass is greater in blacks than in whites. *Journal of Applied Physiology* 56:1647-1649.

Siri, W.E. 1961. Body composition from fluid spaces and density: Analysis of methods. In *Techniques for measuring body composition,* eds. J. Brozek and A. Hensheld, 223-244. Washington, DC: National Academy of Sciences.

Sorani, R. 1966. *Circuit training.* Dubuque, IA: Brown.

Thistle, H.G.; Hislop, H.J.; Moffroid, M.; and Lohman, E.W. 1967. Isokinetic contraction: A new concept of resistive exercise. *Archives of Physical Medicine and Rehabilitation* 48:279-282.

Thomas, D.W. 1988. Plyometrics—More than the stretch reflex. *National Strength and Conditioning Association Journal* 10(5):49-51.

Verkhoshanskiy, Y. 1973. Depth jumping in the training of jumpers. *Track Technique* 51:1618-1619.

Waldron, M. 1994. Stretching: The next generation. *Runner's World* 29(2):76-81.

Weltman, A., and Katch, V. 1981. Comparison of hydrostatic weighing at residual volume and total lung capacity. *Medicine and Science in Sports and Exercise* 13:210-213.

Weltman, A., and Stamford, B. 1982. Strength training: Free weights versus machines. *Physician and Sportsmedicine* 10(11):197.

Westcott, W.L. 1979. Female response to weight lifting. *Journal of Physical Education* 77:31-33.

Wilmore, J.H.; Parr, R.B.; Girandola, R.N.; Ward, P.; Vodak, P.A.; Barstow, T.J.; Pipes, T.V.; Romero, G.T.; and Leslie, P. 1978. Physiological alterations consequent to circuit weight training. *Medicine and Science in Sports* 10:79-84.

Yeager, K.K.; Agostini, R.; Nattiv, A.; and Drinkwater, B. 1993. The female athlete triad: Disordered eating, amenorrhea, osteoporosis. *Medicine and Science in Sports and Exercise* 25:775-777.

Young, D.C. 1984. *The Olympic myth of Greek amateur athletics.* Chicago: Aires.

Zinovieff, A.N. 1951. Heavy resistance exercises: The Oxford technique. *British Journal of Physical Medicine* 14:129-132.

PREPARING TO RACE: STRATEGIES FOR EXCELLENCE

This chapter is written as a discussion with those reading this book who are athletes. Quite obviously, however, coaches can obtain much benefit in "listening in" on our perspectives for showing athletes how to use the knowledge we have put forth in the preceding chapters to achieve good racing outcomes. And scientists can begin to get a useful appreciation for not only the challenges facing athletes when they race, but also how science plays an interactive role with the art of putting together an effective race plan. However, athletes are the ones who are doing the work. They have done the training, using suggestions and guidelines based on what has been presented thus far, and now they are going to the starting line. They will be the ones who execute race strategies as they compete, and to that end we desire to give them some special, direct attention.

We have considered Olympic distance events from the 800 m through the marathon, and we hope to stimulate you to develop successful strategies for the following aspects of competition:

- Race assessment and preparation
- Getting a good start, and establishing and maintaining optimal race position
- Running a race that best balances efficient use of energy resources with the sometimes energy-inefficient realities of racing
- Considering tactics for varying race circumstances that will provide the best opportunity for a successful finish

It must be emphasized that this chapter is by no means a complete guide to the "secrets" of winning races. Every competition, along with the preparation leading up to it, is unique. No one can identify all potential scenarios and suggested outcomes. Even if we could do this, it would remove the element of the unknown that adds so much enjoyment to racing. We can, however, identify patterns of thought that are useful for considering each event. These in turn might provide a more informed basis for discovering the tools you can use for creating your own best performance.

General Concepts for Race Preparation

You'll find five underlying principles mentioned again and again as we discuss what it takes to compete successfully in each of these events. While the events themselves change some of the details of how the principles are implemented, these common points still hold true:

- Be well prepared, realistic, and thoughtful before any race, but don't overdo it.
- Have an accurate sense of pace: estimating it, keeping it as even as possible for economy of effort, and knowing when and how to quicken it.
- Stay physically and mentally apace with your competitors.
- Know *racing tactics*—a structuring of the race pattern so as to be more advantageous to you than to your opponents—but use these only if you can manage them and can gain a meaningful edge over opponents.
- Realize that it is not always necessary or appropriate to derive satisfaction only from winning— placing well in a very deep field of top-class athletes can be perfectly acceptable. So can running a personal best, or a technically excellent race.

This final point deserves some additional discussion, as there are at least two examples where focusing on winning may be entirely irrelevant to the intended goal. In the heats of a championship series, for example, conserving as much energy as possible while placing high enough to move you up to the next race in the series is what is really crucial. As another example, in a race where you may find yourself in the company of several athletes with much more skill and experience than you have at that moment, running your best race is the key to placing well. Of course, that's also the surest way to score an upset victory! To glorify the adage that winning is everything makes defeat all the more devastating. Not winning is not losing if the quality of effort was excellent or appropriate for the situation. As athletes, you train hard so that you can be fit enough to race successfully, and that can mean many things entirely apart from winning: using tactics well, maintaining concentration throughout, running a personal best, racing well the first time out after an injury, picking up the pace as desired near the end; success has many facets. Having a successful race is the single best indicator of being able to race better. Over a career, victories come most often from consistently successful racing. Successful racing requires knowledge and application of racing principles. That is what this chapter is all about.

The 800-Meter Run

The 800-m run is probably the most unforgiving of all track events. It requires a combination of strength, raw speed, and anaerobic endurance, but on top of all this, split-second judgment to decide when tactics can be invoked to help achieve a victory or, at the very least, the best possible performance. The shorter events (100 m through 400 m) are run in lanes throughout, limiting many tactical options. The 100 m is a straight, forward explosion of running, and starting technique is of utmost importance. The 200 m demands good judgment of bend running. The 400 m is now so fast that any attempt to float at 200 m to snatch a brief respite before the remainder of the race is no longer possible. Only the first bend of the 800 m, however, is run in lanes. During the space of time between the break from lane assignments and when the bell announces the final lap, which is only 300 m, athletes need a very sharp tactical sense in addition to superb fitness to set up the best environment for the final lap. Victory then goes most likely to the runner with a combination of the greatest drive to win and the most accomplished ability to endure the remaining physiological race demands.

Not long ago the 800-m distance was considered the shortest middle-distance event. But in 1981 on a warm and steamy sea-level June evening in Florence, Italy, Seb Coe lowered his own men's 800-m world record to 1:41.73. He achieved this by running laps of 49.7 and 52.1 s. Two years later in 1983 Jarmila Kratochvilova lowered the women's 800-m record to 1:53.28 by running laps of 56.1 and 57.2 s. The thought of men coping with an under-50-s opening lap or women with an under-56-s opener makes it functionally more sensible (both in terms of training and racing) to consider the 800-m distance as a kind of extended sprint. Such fast racing requirements place ever greater emphasis on the speed (anaerobic) aspects of speed-endurance. Similar changes are occurring now in the longer distances as well, notably in the 5,000-m and 10,000-m events, as athletes become willing to challenge themselves to race ever faster, at paces that would have been thought impossible only a few years ago.

Running nearly all out for a large part of the 800-m distance, trying to remain afloat in a sea of hydrogen ions, is difficult enough without the added requirements of staying alert and thinking clearly. In a fast 800-m race with a field of your peers, there is never time to recover from mistakes. Thus, mistakes must never be made. Yet to err is human. Therein lies the dilemma—minimizing your chance for error and coping where possible. One wrongly placed and inappropriately excessive burst of speed can be the undoing of a good race; thus pace management throughout the race must always be considered carefully, with the strongest effort left for the finish.

Anaerobic and Aerobic Expertise Are Essential

The requirement for both anaerobic and aerobic expertise for success at 800 m puts unique demands on your abilities. In effect, you must be expert at utilizing both energy systems. Think about what is required. An international-class male 800-m runner needs the ability to run 400 m in roughly 45.5 to 47 s, plus sufficient speed-endurance to run a world-class mile. Similar effort output holds true for less accomplished runners performing to their limit, although the times will be appropriately slower.

Reconsideration of table 5.4 , which summarizes the relative balance between the aerobic and anaerobic energy contributions for various racing distances, not only adds some perspective to the logistics of running 800 m but also raises some interesting practical questions. The relative percentages of aerobic-to-anaerobic energy needs for 800 m are 57% to 43%. For a 400-m race, the ratio is 30% to 70%. Let us create a race scenario and attempt to better understand its energy dynamics. We'll use in this example the split times for a top-level man and woman (the woman's times in parentheses), and let you create split times that fit your own abilities. The concept is more important at this point than specific times.

Let's assume that you plan to run an 800-m race in 1:43 (1:56), with 400-m split times of 50 s (56.5 s) and 53 s (59.5 s). Your personal best for 400-m is 48 s (54 s), and as you run your 800-m race, you cover the first lap at 96% of your best 400-m pace. What is the ratio of aerobic to anaerobic energy needs for this first 400 m? Certainly not 30% to 70%, because it is not an all-out 400-m race effort. Let us suggest that it is at 65% to 35% or 60% to 40% and that a sizable O_2 debt has now accumulated as you begin the second lap. You run the second 400-m lap in 53 s (59.5 s) at 90% of your maximal 400-m velocity. Your effort is virtually all-out, and you work very hard to maintain good form. Now, what is the aerobic percentage of your almost all-out second 400 m of this 800-m race? We suspect the aerobic-to-anaerobic ratio is more on the order of 35% to 65% or 40% to 60%. Thus the two laps are quite different in physiological terms. Particularly for the 800-m event, this kind of analysis is useful because it helps to clarify the need for specialized intensive training to manage what in fact are quite different metabolic loads for each lap. This will give you an important edge over your competitors.

Your training for 800-m racing must permit the development of both strength and endurance in your skeletal muscles, especially your legs. They must be able to tolerate an intense sustained work load. It is our belief that only a combination of running plus weight-room and circuit training will provide adequate preparation for 800-m excellence. Your body must increase its ability to cope with acidosis so well that not only can you maintain pace, but you can also run steadily faster even when tissue discomfort is making your body plead with you to stop running altogether—and maintain a smooth running style as well. Maintaining adequate flexibility, nutrition, and hydration for your working muscles are of course also important complementary pieces of the picture of total preparation.

Be Alert at the Start

In contrast to the other middle- and long-distance events, nearly all 800-m races have the first bend run-in lanes. This requires a staggered start to ensure that all the runners cover the same distance. In major races and championships, the staggered start is always used. With this method, runners start in lanes and stay with them through the first turn. Then they may break away from this ordered sequence and use any lane suitable. This system delays the jockeying for optimal position until the back straightaway portion of the track.

Several strategic complications affect a staggered start. The outside runners are up front and cannot see those behind. (One coaching tip often given to the outside runners, however, is that if you can sense a runner on your left, you're behind.) The inside runners have a marked advantage in this regard, as they can see most of their opposition. In a somewhat slow start, those who go out fast can opt to run hard from the gun. If inside runners do this, outside runners then have the double problem of closing the gap and also achieving their desired position early on into the race. In a fast start, however, the runners farthest back who start a bit slowly may not see the outside runners up front until the break from lanes is almost reached and may not realize until then the deficit they need to remove. Bearing in mind the *rule of speed—it's easier to ease up than it is to speed up*—and realizing the frustration of finding yourself behind nearly from the beginning, it's clear that no matter which way the race begins, your strategies and attitudes should be geared toward a fast, safe start with the greatest odds of achieving an optimal position as early as possible.

In a race employing the seldom-used simple-curved start, this method often creates a situation that, as with much of life itself, has no small amount of unfairness. The jostlng that occurs can cause bumps and bruises at best, spiking and falls at worst. Some of the larger competitors are not the most agile and often figure prominently in this initial melee, being least affected because of their size. Thus, it is not necessarily a disadvantage to be at the outside edge of the pack. This may provide the safest vantage point for choosing the proper moment to slip into the best position within the pack.

Run the Shortest Distance

We mentioned earlier the rule of speed. Now we remind you of the equally obvious *rule of distance:* the shortest distance between two points is a straight line. Failing to use this principle can get you into many difficulties in 800-m races. If your starting position in the staggered start is in the outer lanes, when the breakpoint from lanes is reached, you should move to the outside of the inner lane gradually. Ideally you would reach it by the far back turn as illustrated in figure 7.1, which shows the path you would take if you ran tangentially from lane 8 after the first 100 m to the outside edge of lane 1 by the start of the approaching bend. Remember that a tangent to a circle is the straight line that just touches the circle but does not cut into it. We have drawn a tangent line from the edge of lane 1 on the far back turn in a manner such that it extends to lane 8 at the 100 m mark. Following this path, or a similar one, should minimize participation in the associated collisions and elbowing that result from joining the immediate dash for the inside lane. If you overestimated the pace of your

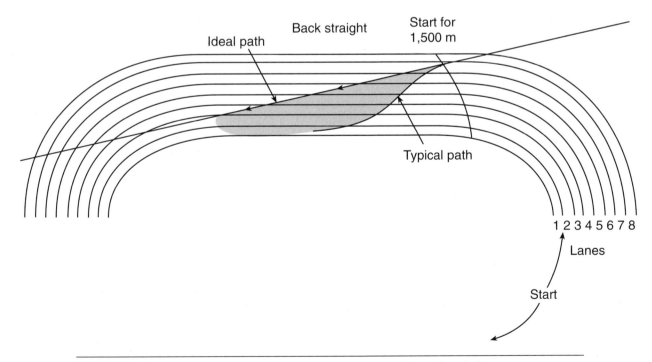

Figure 7.1 Diagram of an idealized (compared with the typically used) path for an 800-m (or 1,500-m) runner from the 100-m breakpoint to reach the start of the back turn.

first 200 m, it is easier to avoid taking the lead prematurely. Simply move over gradually and adjust your pace accordingly.

Even this tactic may have its problems, particularly if you are a runner caught in a middle lane and are being pushed by those outside bullying their way toward the inside. The 800-m event is indeed a race with physical contact, and you must defend very firmly space fairly won. It is, however, entirely unacceptable to struggle with another competitor for space simply because it is desired (it is also a waste of energy). A fall or blow in the wrong place could bring needless and premature loss of the race.

An enduring myth about track running holds that an enormous cost in distance results when running wide, that is, in the outer lanes. This is limited to bend running, and even then the added distance per bend is not much: roughly 2.8 m in lane 2 compared to lane 1. But because it is very easy to run side by side in one lane, the added distance will be as little as 1.6 m. At a 52 s/400 m pace, this costs only 0.21 s—a small price in time to pay for staying out of tactical trouble and also remaining free to take the lead. For top-level women running at a 58-s pace, the time loss is still only 0.23 s. Much more time—and perhaps victory in the race—could be lost by being trapped behind the front-runner while the pack makes its move around.

Because of the extended-sprint nature of the 800-m event, it is essential to distribute your race energy as economically as possible. There are good reasons for this, whatever the specific race strategy. If you are aiming for a personal best, a more even pace instead of a fast-slow or slow-fast lap combination will minimize anaerobic energy production (although it still is high, as the intensity will be as high as 135% of your $\dot{V}O_2$max pace). If victory is your goal and if you fall a little behind early on, it may not be possible for you to muster the physical strength needed to catch up by increasing your stride length or stride frequency, even if you can endure the anaerobic stress. Thus, you must maintain contact with the leaders throughout.

Strong front-runners typically avail themselves of a fast start. In part this is because they are still fresh during the first 14 to 16 s, although an O_2 debt is developing rapidly as a result of blood perfusion to skeletal muscles initially falling short of metabolic demands. Such runners hope that they will get far enough in front that they can slow their pace slightly during midrace, thereby having just enough recovery to permit a strong final-lap effort.

Establish Optimal Position During the First Lap

The best position for your first lap is probably in the wind-shadow of the front-runners. You conserve energy by drafting and apply psychological pressure to the leaders, who realize that they are now the hunted, not the hunters. You have no catching up to do. Instead, as the hunter, you are poised and ready, assessing the optimal moment to launch an assault that will overcome your prey and bring victory. An example using the real world of racing illustrates the point. In a 50-s lap for the first 400 m, the average running velocity is 8 m/s. As the bell lap begins, an athlete 6 m in back of the lead will need to race at a nearly 49-s pace just to catch the leader. Any decision to wait until later suffers from the problem of accumulating acidosis, which tends to slow cadence as well as shorten stride length. Even if the leader is caught, victory isn't at hand, because now this potential winner must take the lead.

Probably the best position to occupy as the race develops is on the outside portion of the inside lane. This permits running wider if necessary and reduces the chances of being blocked by a runner in front. Picture the following scenario: You are running along the back straight, approaching the final bend just behind and slightly wide of the leader's shoulders. Someone from behind launches a sudden powerful surge to the front, darting past you and the leader and taking a position alongside the curb. This leaves the earlier leader trapped behind the new replacement, and to the inside of the smartest athlete in the race—you! By maintaining pace and position at the outer edge of the inside lane, you are still unimpeded, virtually at the front, ready to cope with other would-be front attackers, and poised to initiate your own assault at the proper moment.

Achieve an Excellent Finish

If you are clearly the best athlete in the field, you may attempt the fastest possible time in addition to a victory. An all-out effort to leave the pack far behind always requires courage but is a dramatically powerful psychological tactic in its own right. Often such an opportunity isn't provided. The presence of other talented athletes in the competition having a quality race will put individual finish times much closer, making tactical decisions ever more important.

In these situations you must not only study both the field of competitors and the developing race while under increasing anaerobic stress, but also determine the best kind of decisive maneuvering for the final stages. If the field has one or two well-known fast finishers, one of your options is to lead the entire field through the first lap at a rather fast pace, accepting the energy drain from breaking the wind but realizing that the edge must be removed from their fast-finish abilities. If you do this carefully so as not to inhibit your finishing kick, the final lap then becomes a test of strength-endurance more than speed-endurance. Here is where the benefits of a long-term, total-body strength and endurance training program involving weight-room and circuit work has its delightful payoff.

After a manageable first lap a variant of this theme is for you to provide the pressure of a steadily increasing acceleration during the second lap. This application of gradually increasing speed calls for courage as much as gun-to-tape front-running, but it can shatter the will of your would-be pursuers, who must accelerate even more just to remain in contention with you. One of the more well-known proponents of this gradual acceleration tactic was Jurgen Straub of the German Democratic Republic, who was actually a 1,500-m specialist and steeplechaser. In the 1980 Moscow Olympic Games 1,500-m final race, at the 700-m point he initiated a powerful dash for the finish at an 800-m pace of 1:46. Beginning with the final 300 m, each succeeding 100 m was faster than the previous. After Straub had broken a fine field of runners, Seb Coe, who had stuck to him like glue, was able to beat him at the finish line using an even faster 12.1-s final 100-m effort. Again, such an achievement is your prerogative only if you have a profound background of complete conditioning.

In a race in which many of the top competitors have similar abilities, your primary strategy becomes one of making the crucial attack first. This must be a shrewd blow, delivered as late as possible to avoid a counterattack, but early enough that it is the first strike. It needs to be a decisive breakaway in a few quick strides. Maintaining that gap or even only a part of it is much easier than trying to catch up, which all the rest must do.

In summary, total awareness of the ongoing race plus a willingness to commit completely and attack hard when the fleeting opportunity to strike presents itself are probably the two most crucial attributes for success in 800-m racing.

Sufficient talent, preparation, and authority to create opportunities are excellent, but the ability to assess and seize appropriate opportunities as well rounds out the creation of a grand master. Just as the race is multifaceted, so also must be the totality of your preparation. Superb fitness comes from a complete training plan: strength, quickness, stamina, and endurance for all your major muscle groups. The gift of race confidence comes from practice in continuing to work when it hurts, that is, building the ability to tolerate anaerobic stress. This is not the fatigue of the long-distance runner. Rather, it's the raw pain of fast, prolonged speed. It makes little difference whether you race among the fastest athletes in the world, or in your local club or school. Whether it is a 50 s/400 m lap (8 m/s) or a 57.1 s lap (7 m/s), if it's a highly competitive 800-m race, the principles are the same. Even the strategies of running wide remain the same: The time lost running wide will be longer for a slower race, but the distance covered by everyone each second is also less.

The 1,500-Meter Run

A 1,500-m race unfolds in roughly twice the time of an 800-m event. This can be a double-edged sword. There is added time to recover from errors incurred, but there is more time to encounter difficult circumstances. Often the field of start-

IMPROVING THE 800-M WORLD RECORD

Seb Coe's fastest 800-m time and his best time at the companion distance of 1,000 m are presently the oldest sea-level world records in men's track, dating all the way back to 1981. This is despite the 800-m event still being one of the more popularly contested distances around the world. Coe's last track race was in 1990 at the Auckland Commonwealth Games. For nostalgia, and also to document a little-known bit of history, figure 7.2 shows Seb in his last victory—an invitational 800-m race won in 1:47.66 in Sydney on 14 January 1990. It was a tune-up for the Commonwealth Games; Seb was 33 years of age.

Meet promoters love world records, and with the Grand Prix circuit in Europe over the past several years little has been left to chance in meticulously setting up pace-making for arrival at 400-m and 600-m points perfectly on course to break the 800-m record. It is remarkable that so few performances since 1981 have put Seb's records dangerously close to being broken. Often, from 600 m onward, things seem to go wrong, and it's very plain that those in the hunt do not have what it takes to conquer the problem of maintaining the required pace for the final 200 m.

The summer of 1995, particularly after the World Championships in Göteborg, saw some excellent examples of this. At Zürich's famed Weltklasse meeting, for example, there were so many top-class 800-m runners that two separate races were staged. And with a reported $3 million budget with which to both entice and reward performance excellence, the stage was certainly set for records to fall. Indeed, world records did get broken in both the men's 10,000 m and in the 3,000-m steeplechase—but not in the 800 m.

In one of the 800-m races, five athletes were inside 1:44.00; in the other, five were inside 1:45.00. That was the good news. The disappointing news was that only one of the performances even qualified for the all-time top-30 list! That was a 1:42.87, good for 12th on the all-time list, and the first time someone had even broken the 1:43.00 barrier since 1990. The result was achieved by 25-year-old Wilson Kipketer, a Kenyan citizen who competed for Denmark at Göteborg (winning the 800-m world title the previous week). Unfortunately his application for Danish citizenship was not approved in time for him to compete at the 1996 Atlanta Olympic Games.

Figure 7.2 Sebastian Coe in his last winning race, in Sydney on 14 January 1990, staged as an invitational 800-m tune-up for athletes preparing for the Auckland Commonwealth Games; his time was 1:47.66.
Photo courtesy of Mark Shearman.

Two weeks after the Atlanta Games, again in Zürich, two 800-m races were staged for men, and again Wilson Kipketer scored the fastest time. His 1:42.61 was even faster than that achieved in 1995—again, the only sub-1:43.00 performance of the evening, although six performances were inside 1:44.00. He is mentored by a Polish coach, Slawomir Nowak, who also lives in Denmark. These notes are presented because they may help in our answering the question of what is required to topple Seb's record.

In our opinion a combination of several factors explain why it hasn't been broken. The record breaker must master the essence of performing a long and continuous sprint after having first developed a sound endurance base. The endurance base is not created by long slow distance running, but rather by high-end near-$\dot{V}O_2$max stamina training. Once $\dot{V}O_2$max has gotten about as high as possible, the remaining task is very simply a quest in mastering tolerance of the attendant abundant and intense pain that accompanies a few sessions per week (for many weeks) of longer-distance intervals at very near to even greater than 800-m race pace.

The only athletes with any hope of conquering such a humbling challenge will have been blessed with several circumstances and characteristics. First, they will have developed an extraordinarily strong will and matching discipline over several years of very focused training. This most likely will require the direction of a very knowledgeable coach who can impassively design the punishing work required while still remaining very sensitive to the athlete's human frailties (Nowak's sophisticated Eastern European training is important in this regard). Second, this development will have been carefully laid out to ensure that (1) the work required was achieved without undue injury or burnout and (2) an effective tapering plan was matched with well-choreographed racing opportunities. Third, athlete and coach will have realized that extended sprinting is a strength game, manageable only through a long-term plan of progressive-overload, total-body strength development using weight training. These weight-training sessions will have been added to the ongoing plan of running-related training (again, Nowak's sophistication in giving Kipketer the kind of development that most Kenyans remaining at home will find difficult to obtain just may make the difference).

Disciplined hard work is the key. Over time it leads to improvement, which brings excellence and is rewarding, but this satisfaction must then in turn stimulate further discipline for additional training. This ever-increasing work requirement can be achieved only by an almost cold-blooded, hard-driving hunger for excellence. It must be remembered about Seb's world record in 1981 that he already *was* the world-record holder, with 1:42.33 dating back to 1979. It took two additional years of hard work before the time was ripe to challenge that mark again.

A long-lasting career can only be fruitful with relative freedom from injury. At the top level, injuries are far more of a nemesis than are illnesses, because there is the risk for injuries to become chronic. In a sense, the head colds and viruses that athletes get when they are in the thick of training and competing can be a blessing in disguise. If they in reality are suggesting training or lifestyle overload, better it be managed by a week off to stop sneezing and then moving on, than by a month off while an Achilles tendon repairs and then continually remains a weak point. One great result of correct strength training, particularly for middle-distance runners, is the protection that it confers from injury.

Finally, given that metabolic efficiency is the key and that the inevitable pace-slowing effects of metabolic acidosis during the second 400 m will occur, the first 400-m pace must be selected precisely to match the athlete's ability. Racing *effort* may be similar during both laps, but the manageable pace will slow as efficiency decreases. It is our conclusion that the first lap will need to be run faster than 50 s. The best way of running the required second lap is to be muscularly so strong that this pace will still be submaximal in terms of effort, and thus the slowing of pace will be minimal. At Zürich in 1995 and 1996, seeing those four incredibly talented fields of 800-m men faltering with 200 m remaining told the story clearly—if there is any secret, it is *sustaining power over the distance*. That explains why the losers so often are more exhausted than the winner! Such sustaining power is developed by long-term strength training and speed training on a very high level of endurance base fitness.

Of all the present-day 800-m runners, we see Wilson Kipketer as the closest candidate for a chance to reign for a while over the men's 800-m event. In addition to his two sub-1:43.00 performances in 1995, during his superb summer of racing in 1996 he delivered seven more—while not another soul managed it even once! In two short years at the top, his nine sub-1:43.00 races surpass the entire career total (six) of Brazil's prolific Joaquim Cruz. (Seb himself only managed two.) Kipketer seems focused on maintaining excellence as a middle-distance athlete. Just as important, he has joined forces with a coach who is accustomed to designing difficult training plans that emphasize both periodization and technical competence. His racing strategy during the summer of 1996 was similarly methodical, not excessive, and brought consistency: 1:42.76 at Oslo, 1:42.51 at Nice, 1:42.59 at Monte Carlo, 1:42.61 at Zürich, 1:42.77 at Brussels, 1:43.34 at Berlin, 1:41.83 at Rieti, and 1:42.17 at Tokyo. Just as with Coe, for Kipketer, racing in the world-record time frame is now essentially routine. We wish him the best of patience and success in his conquest! But a parting note to those who may not quite be at the level where they can attempt such a record—the preceding discussion can be just as informative if you substitute "new personal best" for "world record"; the concepts are the same regardless of the actual race time achieved.

ers may number as many as 12 to 15. Thus, positioning yourself optimally early on and as the race proceeds takes on considerable importance.

Establish Good Position and Maintain Contact

An outside draw in the selection of track position in a 1,500-m or mile race should not be a source of worry. It is a safe place. When you reach the start of the back straight, the logical move is to run the same path that gradually puts you at the inside lane as described for the 800-m staggered start (figure 7.1). If your selection is on the inside, run the first 100 m briskly, regardless of the presence of a known pacemaker, to permit a gradual easing up with a position in the second lane at or near the front. If your initial pace was overestimated, it is safer to ease up in lane 2 than in lane 1, where you may be boxed in easily by surrounding athletes. If a pacemaker has been assigned to the race, this runner may not be the fastest of starters, and a place for that person needs to be "reserved" in lane 1, at the front, as he or she directs the initial stages of the race.

While it is certainly nice if you maintain close contact with the early leaders, this is not absolutely essential to achieve an eventual victory. Several circumstances can cause you to fall behind the lead pace. A slow start can bring some bumping and stumbling during the first lap and perhaps during the second as well. A spike wound or a sharp elbow to your ribs can be so frightening that you tend to fall back simply from frustration or fear. Even if you are aggressive by nature, your rhythm can be disrupted, which can also slow your pace. A tactical acceleration by the leaders has an effect on runners farther back in the pack similar to what occurs with a string of automobiles in highway traffic. Precious time is lost until space provided by the acceleration of the leaders permits those in the back of the pack to respond as well. By then, the leaders may have opened up a difference of 15 m or more.

One possible strategy for gaining lost distance, particularly when the deficit occurs early, is to steadily and economically reduce the gap by gradual acceleration. An excellent example of this occurred in the 1995 USA Mobil Outdoor Championships at Sacramento. In heat 2 of the women's 1,500 m, 1984 Olympian Ruth Wysocki took a hard fall at 650 m, and by the time she recovered, she was 20 m behind the pack. She used her 15-plus years of track savvy correctly—she needed to qualify for the final in the most efficient manner possible. She used the next lap to make up the lost ground, and by 1,200 m led the group in 3:26.83. She placed fourth (4:15.36), and the top four places advanced to the final.

While all of this sounds quite logical, such suggestions must fit the exigencies of the real world, and the real world has a habit of adding unexpected complexities. If the aforementioned race had been the 1,500-m final and if the front-runners had a good sense of tactics, just as Wysocki reached them, their best strategy for diminishing her effectiveness would be to collectively increase their pace. From both a psychological and physiological perspective, Wysocki would then be at a disadvantage.

If this race had been the final, however, in today's level of competition, it's doubtful that she would have used this same strategy. Most likely, she would then have taken the same best option as for any runner stuck early in the middle or back of the pack simply because of poor position. She would have inserted a prompt submaximal short sprint to get back up near the outside shoulder of the lead runner. Delivery of this kind of anaerobic burst is best developed by repeatable 400-m sprint practice, which we discussed in chapter 5. This improves particularly well your nervous system's ability to recruit additional FT muscle cells. Distributing this anaerobic metabolism to larger numbers of muscle fibers optimizes energy production while minimizing excessive buildup of acidosis in each. Athletes often refer to this ability as *surging power*, or the ability to quickly *shift gears.*

A steady pace is, of course, most economical. The faster you attempt to run—for example, when a personal best is desired—the more sensible is an even pace. But many more races will be tactical battles, where victories often go to those who have imposed (and better managed) great demands of pace variation on their adversaries. Again, you must remain in a position close to the early leaders, ready to respond, whether it be to maintain pace or to initiate a tactical move.

Decide When to Strike

Three well-known racing tactics have been used with awesome effectiveness to win 1,500-m and mile races. Each was used distinctively by Britain's superb trio of male middle-distance runners during the 1980s. Steve Ovett was an accomplished fierce kicker during the later stages of a race, especially in his sprints down the final straight. One racing response to this was the Steve Cram style of beginning a powerful acceleration from 300 m out, removing the sting from any accompanying sprinter experts. Two responses that Seb Coe perfected were either to sense when to begin the final drive for home just before a long-surging competitor did or to stay with that athlete's surge, saving energy by running in his wind-shadow until it was appropriate to shift gears once again, quickening the pace even further in the closing meters. The need for the comprehensive fitness required to permit such a fierce kick, long acceleration, or quick pace change has already been described for 800-m racing, and in this regard the 1,500-m run is similar.

Being up with the leader is crucial for each of these tactics to succeed. Not only do you gain the advantage of surprise, but virtually everyone else must accelerate more to remain abreast of you. An experienced athlete can sense when others around are laboring, which helps to determine the most opportune moment to strike. Also, if a competitor in the lead is attempting to maintain an optimal pace for his or her finish style, you may be well advised to insert a midrace pace increase. This will help to neutralize, both psychologically and physiologically, that runner's notion of a race going according to an optimal plan. Front-running an entire 1,500-m race is energy costly and mentally stressful, but occasional front-running can have a useful purpose, particularly if it permits you to keep the race pace within your manageable limits.

Some races are directed for a considerable period by a prearranged, assigned pacemaker. Interestingly, not always do such paced races produce fast finish times. The psychological realization that much work is being done for these athletes by someone who intentionally takes them around at a preestablished pace can lessen their competitive resolve. Some runners will not break away from the field early on as they might in a less-orchestrated race. These psychological negatives may not be compensated for completely by the physiological energy-saving benefit of drafting behind the pacemaker.

A real risk exists in such a race of the pacemaker stealing the show with an unexpected victory, especially if the pacemaker is also a gifted athlete. Hardly a track fan during the early 1980s will forget the drama of the United States' star miler, Tom Byers, setting the pace for an excellent field in the Oslo Bislett Games 1,500-m run in June 1981. Tom took the field through 400 m in 57.6 s and 800 m in 1:54.9, developing an enormous 30-m lead. The trailing pack unknowingly was given Byers' split times instead of their own, thus clouding their usually unerring pace sense. Only too late did they realize the discrepancy. Tom was too far ahead for them to successfully close. They tried, but Tom earned his victory (over Steve Ovett) by 0.52 s with 3:39.01.

The cover photo of this Second Edition illustrates some practical wisdom that we have described for both 800-m and 1,500-m racing. The photo shows athletes entering the final straightaway from the back of the turn of the New York Games mile on 14 May 1992. Notice how Said Aouita (1) has moved out into lane 3, clear to launch his final surge that gave him the victory (3:58.20).

John Trautmann (15) placed second (3:58.23). Not quite able to match their sustainable speed, Marcus O'Sullivan (12) was third in 3:58.95. Jim Spivey was struck in the "sled dog" positioin behind O'Sullivan in lane one and couldn't get out and around; hence, he was relegated to fifth (4:00.54) behind Kevin McKay (3:59.92), seen just behind Trautmann. Remember the key points: To win means to run faster than the rest, but to do so requires optimum position when it counts.

The Steeplechase

The steeplechase is an intriguingly different running event, complicated by both Imperial and metric aspects of course measurement and design, and requiring multiple athletic talents. The speed-strength of a quality middle-distance runner and the endurance of a quality long-distance runner need to be combined with well-developed hurdling abilities. If you remember these three attributes for success and train for them, you can race the steeplechase successfully. In fact, there is probably a much better name for this event than the steeplechase. It is known as the *distance hurdle event* in the vocabulary of the most successful steeplechase coach in the United States, Chick Hislop. Coach Hislop loves the steeplechase to the extent that it is the main focus of his distance-running program at Weber State University in Utah. In too many other schools it seems to be the event left for those athletes who haven't been selected to represent the team in other distance events. It is thus no secret that most of the recent top-level U.S. steeplechase athletes have either been part of Hislop's program or have profited by hours of mentoring at his special clinics.

A quick glance at the steeplechase medal list for the 1988, 1992, and 1996 Olympic Games, and for the 1991, 1993, and 1995 World Championships, shows that 13 out of 18 medals have been won by eight athletes from Kenya. They'll tell you confidently that they "own" the event. And Kenya's Moses Kiptanui in 1995 became the first athlete to run under 8 min in the event. Many suggest that the Kenyan training lifestyle sets them up to perform well in the steeplechase, because so much of their over-distance training as children is off roads: in pastures and through forests—where it becomes second nature to develop hurdling skills—over tree logs, ditches, fences, large boulders, small bushes, while running at varying paces uphill and downhill. This may be a primary reason why Coach Hislop suggests that his athletes, in order to consider themselves as developing adequately over a year's time, ought to aim for roughly 14,000 hurdle clearances using a variety of drills.

Although the steeplechase for years has been primarily a men's event, involving a 3,000-m run over a series of obstacles of very specific height and placement on the track, this is changing. A strong international interest is developing to encourage women to participate. Whether they will end up with a race over a similar or different distance, or use obstacles of similar or different dimensions, will become clear over the next decade.

Unique Aspects of the Event

There are indeed obstacles, and some call them hurdles, but they are not all the same, and they aren't hurdles in the typical sense—they might best be termed barriers. True, they are the same height as those used for the 400-m intermediate hurdle race—established in the Imperial system as 3 ft (91.4 cm). But they are not regulation hurdles used for the sprint hurdle events. Particularly for the beginning athlete, these are gigantic barriers, measured Imperially as 13 ft wide (3.96 m), and there are three of them placed evenly around the track. They are very heavy, with the weight established metrically as between 80 and 100 kg (from 176 to 220 lb). A barrier of this size is so heavy that a runner hitting it will not change its position, as with a standard hurdle. Depending on the track design, barriers are spaced roughly 80 m apart. Thus, for the 3,000-m distance there will be 28 track barrier clearances.

An additional barrier, a little narrower than the others (12 ft or 3.66 m), is fixed at one end of the track, either just within the track oval or just outside it. It is placed at the near end of a water-filled depression as you approach it, 0.7 m deep just below the barrier. This depression slopes upward and reaches the track surface by 12 ft (3.66 m).

Because tracks can have this water jump inside or outside the contour of the track, each lap covered will be either longer or shorter than 400 m, respectively.

In turn, this makes the start of the race different for almost every track, due to additional variations in radius of curvature and length of straightaway portions. There are seven laps in the 3,000-m event, measured from the sprint finish line, with any additional distance then measured back appropriately. This extra distance could range anywhere from 130 m to 270 m. Never are there any barriers in this initial prelap segment. The first barrier always occurs 10 m into the first full lap. If all this sounds complicated, think about the civil engineer who has to make the correct track measurements to get it right!

There are no special rules for clearing these barriers, except that your entire body must cross each completely. As shown in figure 7.3, being demonstrated by the grand master Moses Kiptanui, quality athletes clear the track barriers without touching them using a modified hurdler's style. Notice how far away he is—both his angle of ascent and clearance over the barrier are as low as possible, with his trail leg off to the side. This sets him up to land on the midfoot of his lead leg, with his trail-leg knee never higher than his hip. Figure 7.4, however, shows clearly that barrier clearance—even at the highest levels of competition—is an individual matter. Kenya's barefoot Christopher Koskei ran a fantastic race and cleared each barrier with a style that for him was optimally energy efficient. The water jump, in contrast, is typically cleared by placing the lead-leg foot on the cross-beam and then pushing off to almost clear the water-filled pit.

The presence of these barriers adds several practical challenges. First, it is nearly impossible to develop a consistent stride pattern. Second, as the barriers are cleared, especially if the runners are still bunched together, the opportunity for entangled legs and misjudged beam position sets the stage for falls. Third, a well-developed sense of pace is essential, particularly awareness of the effect of fatigue caused by the presence of 35 barriers. Fourth, the much slower pace of this event, in comparison to the sprint hurdle events, requires a brief acceleration toward each barrier in order to ensure enough momentum for economical clearance. Fifth, the water jump is sufficiently different from the track barriers, and crossed enough times, that it needs a considerably different clearance strategy.

Now, given all of these complexities, how do you become an excellent competitor at the steeplechase? First and foremost, develop a good base of distance-running fitness—that's described in the rest of this book, so that's a problem solved! However, because the 3,000-m event is mathematically closer to the 1,500-m distance than to the 5,000-m, and because 35 barriers to cross give an interruption of rhythm that causes a potent buildup of anaerobic metabolites, anaerobic expertise is absolutely essential.

Second, develop *accelerative ambidexterity* in barrier clearance: Accelerate toward each barrier and clear it without even thinking of which leg is leading. This is the secret to gaining time over the barriers. The alternative is slowing down and stutter-stepping as each barrier is approached, using one favorite leg as your lead leg. That is not world class—purge that style from your repertoire! Third, improve your hurdle skills; unless you are a Kenyan, aim for 14,000 annual hurdle clearances!

Developing Hurdle Expertise

We have learned much from Coach Hislop and with his permission would like to share with you some of his exercises, so those 14,000 hurdlings will have some variety. One point agreed upon by almost everyone regarding the teaching of ambidexterity over the barriers is that athletes ought to practice this con-

Figure 7.3 Clearing the barriers in the steeplechase requires a harmonious coordination of running and hurdling which, if mastered, permit acceleration toward the barrier and use of either leg for takeoff. Shown here is the 1995 Göteborg gold medalist, Moses Kiptanui (7), in action, running 8:04.16; he bettered his own world record five days later.

Figure 7.4 No specific rules define how the steeplechase barrier must be cleared. While one could suggest that Kenyan Christopher Koskei's technique might be unorthodox, as shown here at Göteborg in 1995, for him it was very effective: He earned the silver medal with 8:09.30.

stantly. Do not spend a month doing right lead-leg hurdling, then a month leading with the left. Each day you do hurdle drills, do half with one leg leading, half with the other. Teach your brain to think either way all the time.

One hurdle drill is termed by Hislop the *hurdle ritual,* because it teaches hurdling fundamentals. These are important because the other drills are applications of this basic technique. Set up two hurdles on the track side by side at the 400-m hurdle/steeplechase height of 3 ft (0.91 m), facing in opposite directions. Now, run for 10 m toward one hurdle, clearing it on its side using a given lead leg. Continue for 10 m, turn around, and return to clear the other hurdle with the same lead leg. Do 10 round trips for each lead leg, and then do 10 more round trips with each leg going over the hurdle as the trail leg. Now do 10 additional round trips going over the *center* of the hurdle to develop a more complete hurdling technique. Each time you turn around, do it at a slightly different point, so you will never know which leg will end up being the lead leg until you are two steps from the approaching hurdle. With only a small adjustment you will now find yourself quickly developing confidence with either leg as lead leg.

The second drill emphasizes the trail leg, and is called the *10-ft hurdle drill* or *3-m hurdle drill* because 10 hurdles (again at the standard 400-m hurdle/steeplechase height of 3 ft [0.91 m]) are placed 10 ft (3 m) apart. This distance should be adequate for beginners to clear 5 hurdles, and eventually 10 for more experienced athletes. Clear the first hurdle with your trail leg, take one step, then clear the next hurdle again with the same trail leg, and so on through the series. Returning to the starting point, now proceed along the opposite side of the hurdles, using your other leg as the trail leg. Practice moving that trail leg quickly, keeping it parallel to the ground as it clears. Do this drill three times with each leg.

A third drill can be called the *alternate leg drill* because it involves alternate legs clearing a series of hurdles. Set up a flight of 10 hurdles on a track straightaway at the standard 3-ft height, but this time spaced for the men's 100-m hurdle competition (established as 10 yd, which converts to 9.14 m). Approach these hurdles at your estimated steeplechase racing pace. Clear the first hurdle with one leg as lead leg, and run four steps to the next hurdle. Now your other leg will be the lead leg. Continue alternating lead legs through the entire flight of hurdles. Depending on experience, do this drill two to four times. It is challenging, and it will go far to help you eventually eliminate any remaining tendency for stutter-stepping or chopping your stride, because it demands the use of both legs.

A final drill can be called the *finish form drill* because it is a running drill that gives you practice in getting up on your toes. This will help you develop additional muscles that you'll enjoy bringing into action in the finishing stages of the race when fatigue is setting in. It uses a full flight of hurdles set at the standard 3-ft height, but which are now positioned over the women's 100-m hurdle marks. This hurdle spacing, in contrast to the men's, is measured metrically as 8.5 m (27.9 ft). Now, running at your anticipated finishing-lap steeplechase pace, you will only be able to fit three steps between each hurdle. Thus, you will have to rise up on your toes as you race in between these hurdles. Run this using one lead leg, and then go back and lead with the other leg. Train both legs at least twice.

When should such hurdle drills be incorporated into training? We can discuss this from two aspects: the period during a yearly macrocycle and the period within any microcycle. Assuming a yearly macrocycle starting with cross-country training in the fall and ending with a peak in late summer of the following year, start hurdle exercises after cross-country season, that is, beginning with mesocycle X_2 as described in chapter 5. Then, within any given training week, use the following hints: (1) Do hurdle drills three times a week during mesocycles X_2, X_3, and X_4, or until the period when some track racing begins; and (2) during event fine-tuning in mesocycle X_5, continue drills three times a week if not racing a steeplechase, otherwise do drills twice in the week that a steeplechase is contested.

How should such drills be incorporated into a training day? They should not be part of a standard training session, but done separately, for example, in place of an easy morning run or before weight training. Never do more than two of the drills previously described during any given training session. Remember that these drills are not intended to provide a cardiovascular workout but are intended to develop hurdling technique; enjoy taking the time to do them properly, focus on developing technical competence, and leave the session fresh, so that the rest of the training day can be completed without undue fatigue.

Hurdle practice can also be incorporated into regular training sessions, in addition to the specific drills previously mentioned. They can be cleared during long-interval track sessions. For example, during a session of repeated 1,000-m runs, a hurdle can be set up in a track lane and cleared every other lap. If a covered water jump is available, that also could be cleared on the same lap, providing the extra small measure of fatigue that will be quite familiar on race day.

Delivering Your Best Race

Racing a steeplechase now becomes a matter of bringing all these various instruments of the orchestra into a symphonic performance. First, realize clearly the major differences between the steeplechase and other distance running events:

- Each stadium has its starting point positioned differently, depending on its radius of curvature and length of straight sections.
- Lap split times are meaningless, as the laps are not a familiar distance such as 400 m.
- There are often many competitors in the race, crossing barriers bunched together.
- The distances between barriers vary, depending on layout.

Perfected hurdle technique will ensure economical barrier clearance, giving energy savings. Excellent aerobic fitness, and middle-distance-oriented strength work developed through anaerobic conditioning and aerobic capacity training, will provide a powerful engine to drive the machine. Special attention toward clearance of each water jump, together with acceleration into the track barriers, will ensure that split-second quickening of race pace that others not so focused (and well-trained) will lack. More so than the other distance running events, this is also a technique event. Think of yourself as a performer on stage. Focus on form and execution throughout the race, and you'll have the greatest chance of racing well.

The 5,000-Meter Run

We are now considering a race 6.25 times longer than the 800 m and 3.3 times longer than the 1,500 m. This event is contested at a pace approaching 100% of aerobic capacity. Thus, as with the 800 m and 1,500 m, we hope that your $\dot{V}O_2$max has been raised as high as possible during training. Carbohydrates will by far be the predominant energy source for this race. Even with a steady pace, the energy demands are such that you will be racing faster than your lactic/ventilatory threshold pace. Thus, lactic acid accumulation will occur and must be managed effectively. In fact, very likely your per-lap pace throughout will be fast enough that you'll not be able to manage much more than a one-lap final surge to the finish. The most economical strategy, therefore, is to run an evenly paced race to keep skeletal muscle and blood acidosis as low as possible until near the end. In chapter 5 we stressed the importance of developing effective pace sense in training. For the longer distance races, this facet of race savvy is crucial. A trait of particular value is accurate pace assessment during varying states of fatigue.

We can learn from the grand masters of the event. Consider Haile Gebrselassie, whose 12:44.39 at Zürich on 16 July 1995 was nearly an 11-s improvement on Moses Kiptanui's existing world mark of 12:55.30 set 10 weeks previously in Rome. The details of his epic race have been well documented (Watman and Matthews 1995). Frank O'Mara was the early pacemaker, going through 1,000 m in 2:34.04. He was replaced at 4 min into the race by Worku Bikila, who brought Gebrselassie through 3,000 m in 7:42.92—the planned pace was 7:45. However, given that this world record attempt was a carefully choreographed affair, what is particularly relevant for our discussion of high-quality 5,000-m racing is a look at Gebrselassie's remarkably even 400-m split times: 60.4, 62.4, 62.4, 63.2, 60.3, 60.6, 62.3, 61.7, 60.4, 60.2, 60.1, and 60.2 got him to 4,800 m. His final two 200-m split times were 29.9 and 29.8 s. Thus, the faster you race over the entire distance, the less anaerobic reserve you'll have at the finish, making it imperative that you select your pace and manage it carefully.

Gebrselassie's method for racing fast is very often not available to you. Realize that he had the luxury of pacemakers to assist him in his world record attempt. For most distance running events, it would appear that the world record is out of reach of someone running without such assistance. Because the athlete runs behind the pacemaker, there is a reduction in effort from being in the pacemaker's wind-shadow. This conservation of energy can be substantial, thereby delaying the point in the race where accumulating lactic acidosis starts to slow the pace. Debate rages about whether these track world records are little more than the equivalent of downhill road-race courses. Obviously, the athlete scoring the world record had to have a high degree of fitness, but there's little doubt that the performance was aided by the energy-conserving influence of the initial pacemakers.

Often, however, there is no such pacemaking available, and neither is the 5,000-m race run in the most economical manner. It is more likely that the competitor lineup will have a mixture of runners who are famous for their fast, strong finish, runners who may insert very fast midrace laps, runners who insert shorter but even quicker and more sudden bursts of speed, and runners who prefer a strong pace throughout to remove the sting from any would-be final kickers. Among the top men in recent history, some well-known examples of each of these styles include, respectively, Marty Liquori (United States), Brendan Foster (Great Britain), Dave Bedford (Great Britain), and Antonio Leitão (Portugal). Now that this distance is an Olympic event for women, similar distinct racing styles are showing up among them as well: Ireland's Sonia O'Sullivan has a punishingly blazing finish, and Portugal's Fernanda Ribeiro grinds her competitors into the turf with her strong pace throughout. These racing styles are good examples of individually different tactics: Each style allows the athlete to take advantage of a particular talent, with the hope that its use by that athlete will be less costly than for all the others. This points to the importance of knowing your competition in an event, and even more important, knowing yourself and devising your own individual strategy to utilize your strengths optimally.

Establish an Early Race-Pace Rhythm

Running too fast too early has several consequences, all bad. The agonies of accumulating metabolic acidosis inhibit muscle operational efficiency prematurely. Added to this is the important psychological contribution ("I'm hurting this badly and it's so early in the race!?"), which reveals the importance of the mind-body interaction. A slowing finish pace is the likely unfortunate result, with other runners passing you instead of you passing them. Try as you might to bring additional accessory muscles of the limbs and trunk into use in a valiant but vain struggle to keep pace, this simply decreases running economy and increases even further the O_2 consumption required. Even multi-tier training cannot rectify the mistakes of premature and unnecessarily excessive speed. However, it can provide the capability for enduring and initiating the sizable kinds of pace changes that may be required to either respond to or create conditions in which victory comes to the most-prepared athlete.

For most people the 5,000-m race pace is too quick to permit widely varying pace changes. After those first few laps done smartly because you feel fresh, you must resist the trend to begin pushing the pace or to take the lead because the pace seems slow unless you are in substantially better form than the rest and truly believe you can manage a faster pace. The reality is that after the first two laps, 10 laps and a little more yet remain. Reserve the fastest of these 10-plus laps for the end, not the beginning. Short bursts that are not sustained will quickly be closed by smarter runners not far behind who are keeping a more even pace. At this same time, those in the lead will have an increased energy requirement when compared with those behind because they are breaking the wind.

The easiest of all race options is simply to calculate a fixed per-lap pace that best estimates your potential performance, given the existing weather conditions and your level of physical fitness. If the early stages are run on the slow side of this pace, a feeling of freshness in the later stages permits a delightful increase in tempo. Feed off the positive psych that derives from passing those who were less accurate (or less sensible) in their pace judgment. Maintain good form throughout, and you'll have the best chance for your fastest possible race.

Such a strategy is wonderful in a race where you face relatively little opposition. Take the lead and go for it. It works at all levels of racing. Dave Moorcroft's world-record 13:00.42 at Oslo in 1982, where he found repeat 62-s and 63-s laps relatively easy, is an almost legendary example. Just as with Haile Gebrselassie in 1995, we can only presume that on that day 13 years earlier, Dave's lactate/ventilatory threshold pace was very close to an already high $\dot{V}O_2max$ pace, thereby keeping his tissue and blood lactic acid accumulation minimal at his race pace. In both races, for whatever reason, the winners had a remarkably greater fitness level than the excellent competitive fields behind them; Moorcroft won by 20 s, whereas Gebrselassie did so by 17 s.

Could these athletes have run faster? How often have we heard spectators remark after witnessing such a front-running effort, "What a splendid race! That runner was clear all the way. I wonder how much faster his finish time would have been had other runners been good enough to push him harder?" The athlete clearly ran a smart race—optimally pace efficient. But had the winner been challenged by being forced to alternately quicken and slow the pace in responding to surges, such changes, with their increase in blood acidity for the faster-paced running, would have been costly.

In many races the challenging athletes aren't so gentle as to simply encourage the leader onward. We prefer to call these runners the *spoilers* because they delight in applying pressure in a most effective and unnerving way, using their own special tactics to ruin another runner's intended race plan. A well-known victim of such tactics was Britain's Dave Bedford, who had his very effective fast-pace running destroyed on several occasions by competitors who moved repeatedly to the front, then slowed ever so slightly and reduced the pace. He wasn't actually impeded, though he had the spike marks on his shins to show what had occurred. Such antics shattered his concentration.

The spoilers, of course, also run the risk of tiring, for it is physiological folly to insert short bursts to open gaps in a vain attempt to split the field. However, if several runners do this to slow the fast pace of a front-runner, they all can benefit, thereby neutralizing the would-be pacesetter and permitting the next phase of the battle to unfold. If you are a spoiler, however, be aware of the energy cost for such moves. If you are a front-runner in the process of being spoiled, you have an option, if it is in your repertoire. Use your repeatable, fast 400-m capability to make a serious and relatively long surge and hope it will drive you free of all attackers. This tactic is energy costly as well, but if it brings home a victory, it is an effective use of proper training.

Strategies for a Successful Finish

If a decisive push to set the stage for victory is to be attempted during the final five or six laps, it must indeed be a sustained drive: at the very least, one full lap, preferably two, and it may require a third to get clear. It should begin early enough to keep the would-be fast-finish sprinters from tagging along, remain modest enough to prevent you from slowing down toward the finish, and be sufficiently prolonged to let anyone in pursuit realize you are very serious. Once you have established your temporary supremacy, slow down to the overall pace that you believe you can manage and that you believe will win, because you most likely cannot maintain that excessive pace throughout the race. For example, if you believe the race will be won in 13:20 or 13:45 (for men), or 15:00 or 15:25 (for women), resume running at the average pace per lap for each of those finish times: 64 or 66 s, and 72 or 74 s, respectively. Running any faster may require a pace faster than you can manage. If you run any slower you will not reap the benefit of that sudden injection of speed, because those behind will catch up too quickly. Ideally, they need to catch you only by about 5,001 m!

Not everyone can manage this strategy, however, and many have failed in the attempt. This tactic requires good anaerobic tolerance, an ability to cope with the pressure of knowing that you are "the hunted," an excellent sense of pace judgment, and a feel for how others are handling the pace before you make your move. There is, however, the mental satisfaction of knowing that you have forced the others into running faster and (for them) less economically. If you have overestimated your competitors, you may be able to slow down slightly, thereby gaining a small measure of recovery as you prepare for your final acceleration to give your best effort. Of course, there is always the risk of one star in the field who is having a magnificent race remaining right beside you after your perfectly executed surge. Such is the nature of good competition, and of course the crowd loves it. What to do about it? Do the best you can, and hope that you can get more out of yourself than you believed possible.

Seb Coe remembers very well a two-lap, 5-mi road race in Italy in which a very good Italian distance runner simply was not intimidated by Seb's three long, fast surges. It required a fourth, very close to the finish, before the race was decided. This points out an interesting similarity between successful racing in athletics and successful negotiations in the rest of life: To win, you must be committed willingly, without any doubt, to endure at least one moment longer than your adversary! And that requires the twofold combination of both physical and mental toughness and freshness.

It used to be fairly common that, even in top-level 5,000-m races, an athlete with a strong finish kick could stay back in the pack throughout the race, catch up fairly quickly over the penultimate lap, and utilize a strong finish kick to emerge victorious. Fast mile and 1,500-m athletes can manage this best and often try such a strategy when moving up to the 5,000 m. One notable example is Ireland's Sonia O'Sullivan, who in 1995 was the World Champion at 5,000 m but who also was fastest in the world over 1,500 m (3:58.63) and the mile (4:23.83). But that seems now to be more an exception than the rule. Only one of the other two World Championship 5,000-m medalists among the women made the top-25 lists in the mile or 1,500 m, and none of the three men's medalists were among the top 50 in those events.

Final-kick sprinting ability is not necessarily all genetic endowment. You can develop it in various ways to fit your own strengths and limitations using multi-tier training. It is merely one facet of overall speed development. To race fast you must have had fast training sessions, and that brings development of both speed-strength and speed-endurance. Today's 5,000-m runners, both men and women, need to realize that both speed and strength must be incorporated into an extensive endurance base if they desire consistent success. Excellence in all areas provides the greatest number of options and thus the best chance for quality performances. Practice at racing distances on either side of 5,000 m can provide such expertise by challenging your ability to manage speed with endurance (as in 3,000-m track racing) as well as the reverse (as in 10-km road racing).

The 10,000-Meter Run

From both physiological and tactical viewpoints, the 10,000-m event has some similarity to the 5,000 m. The former is raced at roughly 92% of $\dot{V}O_2$max pace, the latter nearer to 100%. With optimal development, your lactate/ventilatory threshold will probably not much exceed 88% to 90% of $\dot{V}O_2$max. Unless you can raise your $\dot{V}O_2$max or lactate/ventilatory threshold so high that a winning race pace would be within aerobic limits, a gradually accumulating metabolic acidosis will occur during both events. This accumulation is less intense at 10,000-m race pace than for the 5,000-m run, however, which makes more viable the option of inserting occasional supra-race-pace surges as a tactic to increase the chances of victory. These observations give some clues about the parameters of development that must be emphasized during training:

- Refining an accurate sense of pace
- Raising lactate/ventilatory threshold
- Raising $\dot{V}O_2$max
- Honing an excellent speed capability for midrace surging and a strong finish

As with the other events, periodic performance monitoring using treadmill testing as well as time trials in repeatable conditions can be useful to identify the extent to which training has in fact brought improvement over time. These principles were discussed earlier in chapters 4 and 5.

A typical pace for 10,000-m races is typically about 3 s per 400 m slower than for a 5,000 m of equivalent difficulty. This is shown in Table 7.1. Compare the 63.9 s/400 m pace of Salah Hissou's 10,000-m world record with the 61.2 s/400 m pace of Haile Gebrselassie's 5,000-m world record. (On the women's side, the 70.9 s/400 m pace for Wang Junxia's 10,000-m world record is so similar to the 70.1 s/400 m pace of Fernanda Ribeiro's 5,000-m world record that it points out the extraordinary quality of Wang's performance.) However, while this approximately 3-s slower pace may sound comfortable, it must be maintained twice as long. The pace difference also explains the greater requirement for stamina-endurance training in 10,000-m development, as compared to speed-stamina for the 5,000 m. Table 7.2 provides a detailed pace chart for use in determining the average 400-m lap time for a wide range of 10,000-m performances, as well as intermediate times at varying stages of such races.

You are probably fully aware of the accumulating stress of attempting to sustain for 25 laps a race pace that is even 1 s/400 m beyond your manageable optimum. Being the leader means that, because you are breaking the wind, physiologically you are racing at a slightly faster pace than those in your wind-shadow.

TABLE 7.1

Selected Noteworthy Running Paces for the 5,000 m and 10,000 m

Athlete	Time	Date	Venue	Pace (s/400 m)
5,000 m				
Haile Gebrselassie[WR]	12:44.39	16 August 1995	Zürich	61.2
	13:00			62.4
	13:30			64.8
	14:00			67.2
	14:30			69.6
Fernanda Ribeiro[WR]	14:36.45	22 July 1995	Hechtel	70.1
	15:00			72.0
	15:30			74.4
	16:00			76.8
	16:30			79.2
	17:00			81.6
	17:30			84.0
10,000 m				
Salah Hissou[WR]	26:38.08	23 August 1996	Brussels	63.9
	27:00			64.8
	27:30			66.0
	28:00			67.2
	28:30			68.4
	29:00			69.6
	29:30			70.8
Wang Junxia[WR]	29:31.78	08 September 1993	Beijing	70.9
	30:00			72.0
	30:30			73.2
	31:00			74.4
	31:30			75.6
	32:00			76.8
	32:30			78.0
	33:00			79.2
	33:30			80.4
	34:00			81.6
	34:30			82.8
	35:00			84.0

[WR] = world record

TABLE 7.2

200-M and 400-M Intermediate Split Times for Selected Race Distances Between 600 M and 10,000 M

Average per 200/400 m (s)	600	800	1,000	1,500	2,000	3,000	4,000	5,000	6,000	8,000	10,000
25.0/50.0	1:15.0	1:40.0	—	—	—	—	—	—	—	—	—
25.5/51.0	1:16.5	1:42.0	—	—	—	—	—	—	—	—	—
26.0/52.0	1:18.0	1:44.0	2:10.0	—	—	—	—	—	—	—	—
26.5/53.0	1:19.5	1:46.0	2:12.5	—	—	—	—	—	—	—	—
27.0/54.0	1:21.0	1:48.0	2:15.0	—	—	—	—	—	—	—	—
27.5/55.0	1:22.5	1:50.0	2:17.5	—	—	—	—	—	—	—	—
28.0/56.0	1:24.0	1:52.0	2:20.0	3:30.0	—	—	—	—	—	—	—
28.5/57.0	1:25.5	1:54.0	2:22.5	3:33.8	—	—	—	—	—	—	—
29.0/58.0	1:27.0	1:56.0	2:25.0	3:37.5	4:50.0	—	—	—	—	—	—
29.5/59.0	1:28.5	1:58.0	2:27.5	3:41.3	4:55.0	—	—	—	—	—	—
30.0/60.0	1:30.0	2:00.0	2:30.0	3:45.0	5:00.0	7:30.0	—	—	—	—	—
30.5/61.0	1:31.5	2:02.0	2:32.5	3:48.8	5:05.0	7:37.5	10:10.0	—	—	—	—
31.0/62.0	1:33.0	2:04.0	2:35.0	3:52.5	5:10.0	7:45.0	10:20.0	12:55.0	—	—	—
31.5/63.0	1:34.5	2:06.0	2:37.5	3:56.3	5:15.0	7:52.5	10:30.0	13:07.5	15:45.0	—	—
32.0/64.0	1:36.0	2:08.0	2:40.0	4:00.0	5:20.0	8:00.0	10:40.0	13:20.0	16:00.0	21:20.0	—
32.5/65.0	1:37.5	2:10.0	2:42.5	4:03.8	5:25.0	8:07.5	10:50.0	13:32.5	16:15.0	21:40.0	27:05.0
33.0/66.0	1:39.0	2:12.0	2:45.0	4:07.5	5:30.0	8:15.0	11:00.0	13:45.0	16:30.0	22:00.0	27:30.0
33.5/67.0	1:40.5	2:14.0	2:47.5	4:11.3	5:35.0	8:22.5	11:10.0	13:57.5	16:45.0	22:20.0	27:55.0
34.0/68.0	1:42.0	2:16.0	2:50.0	4:15.0	5:40.0	8:30.0	11:20.0	14:10.0	17:00.0	22:40.0	28:20.0
34.5/69.0	1:43.5	2:18.0	2:52.5	4:18.8	5:45.0	8:37.5	11:30.0	14:22.5	17:15.0	23:00.0	28:45.0
35.0/70.0	1:45.0	2:20.0	2:55.0	4:22.5	5:50.0	8:45.0	11:40.0	14:35.0	17:30.0	23:20.0	29:10.0
35.5/71.0	1:46.5	2:22.0	2:57.5	4:26.3	5:55.0	8:52.5	11:50.0	14:47.5	17:45.0	23:40.0	29:35.0
36.0/72.0	1:48.0	2:24.0	3:00.0	4:30.0	6:00.0	9:00.0	12:00.0	15:00.0	18:00.0	24:00.0	30:00.0
36.5/73.0	1:49.5	2:26.0	3:02.5	4:33.8	6:05.0	9:07.5	12:10.0	15:12.5	18:15.0	24:20.0	30:25.0
37.0/74.0	1:51.0	2:28.0	3:05.0	4:37.5	6:10.0	9:15.0	12:20.0	15:25.0	18:30.0	24:40.0	30:50.0
37.5/75.0	1:52.5	2:30.0	3:07.5	4:41.3	6:15.0	9:22.5	12:30.0	15:37.5	18:45.0	25:00.0	31:15.0
38.0/76.0	1:54.0	2:32.0	3:10.0	4:45.0	6:20.0	9:30.0	12:40.0	15:50.0	19:00.0	25:20.0	31:40.0
38.5/77.0	1:55.5	2:34.0	3:12.5	4:48.8	6:25.0	9:37.5	12:50.0	16:02.5	19:15.0	25:40.0	32:05.0
39.0/78.0	1:57.0	2:36.0	3:15.0	4:52.5	6:30.0	9:45.0	13:00.0	16:15.0	19:30.0	26:00.0	32:30.0
39.5/79.0	1:58.5	2:38.0	3:17.5	4:56.3	6:35.0	9:52.5	13:10.0	16:27.5	19:45.0	26:20.0	32:55.0
40.0/80.0	2:00.0	2:40.0	3:20.0	5:00.0	6:40.0	10:00.0	13:20.0	16:40.0	20:00.0	26:40.0	33:20.0
40.5/81.0	2:01.5	2:42.0	3:22.5	5:03.8	6:45.0	10:07.5	13:30.0	16:52.5	20:15.0	27:00.0	33:45.0
41.0/82.0	2:03.0	2:44.0	3:25.0	5:07.5	6:50.0	10:15.0	13:40.0	17:05.0	20:30.0	27:20.0	34:10.0
41.5/83.0	2:04.5	2:46.0	3:27.5	5:11.3	6:55.0	10:22.5	13:50.0	17:17.5	20:45.0	27:40.0	34:35.0
42.0/84.0	2:06.0	2:48.0	3:30.0	5:15.0	7:00.0	10:30.0	14:00.0	17:30.0	21:00.0	28:00.0	35:00.0
42.5/85.0	2:07.5	2:50.0	3:32.5	5:18.8	7:05.0	10:37.5	14:10.0	17:42.5	21:15.0	28:20.0	35:25.0
43.0/86.0	2:09.0	2:52.0	3:35.0	5:22.5	7:10.0	10:45.0	14:20.0	17:55.0	21:30.0	28:40.0	35:50.0
43.5/87.0	2:10.5	2:54.0	3:37.5	5:26.3	7:15.0	10:52.5	14:30.0	18:07.5	21:45.0	29:00.0	36:15.0
44.0/88.0	2:12.0	2:56.0	3:40.0	5:30.0	7:20.0	11:00.0	14:40.0	18:20.0	22:00.0	29:20.0	36:40.0
44.5/89.0	2:13.5	2:58.0	3:42.5	5:33.8	7:25.0	11:07.5	14:50.0	18:32.5	22:15.0	29:40.0	37:05.0
45.0/90.0	2:15.0	3:00.0	3:45.0	5:37.5	7:30.0	11:15.0	15:00.0	18:45.0	22:30.0	30:00.0	37:30.0

This contributes to the dilemma of whether to lead during a sizable portion of the race, as illustrated in figure 7.5. If you are racing for time, such as to achieve a qualifying mark or a personal best, you need to ensure that some predetermined pace is maintained. If no one else is capable of, or interested in, doing the work, the race becomes yours. Or, if your stride is particularly long and free-flowing and if the pace is quite manageable relative to your fitness, you might feel more comfortable to be away from the body contact when other runners are bunched together. However, if the race is a qualifier for a final to be staged a few days later, the ideal is to remain in another athlete's wind-shadow until the final stages, thereby conserving energy.

The ability to sustain concentration during extended periods of track running—for pace identification and maintenance, and as well for staying alert—is mandatory for 10,000-m runners. This focus of attention can only be ensured by being mentally and physically rested before an important competition. Still, the length of this event provides considerably more options for responding to changing conditions than do the shorter events previously described. Unless the race is in the final stages when a sudden pace change brings a competitor surging forth, you have adequate time to judge its significance, that is, its potential effect on the race outcome and the extent to which you can fit it into the context of your own intended strategy for competitive effectiveness.

Figure 7.5 When to lead during the long 10,000-m race and when to remain tucked away in the pack is always a debated question, even at the highest level of racing, as shown here during the first qualifying round at Göteborg in 1995 by four world-class female runners known for their aggressive racing excellence. From front to back, Laurie Henes (USA), Yvonne Murray (GBR), Jill Hunter (GBR), and Kathrin Wessel (GER).

The Influence of Weather and Pacemaking

The elements of weather influence the outcome of 10,000-m racing more profoundly than the shorter events, if for no other reason than the increased time of exposure. Higher ambient temperatures mandate a shunting of blood flow to the skin for cooling. Coupled with sweat losses, this can reduce the amount of blood volume available for skeletal muscle perfusion. If the humidity is high as well, the evaporation rate decreases, even though perspiration may continue at a high rate. A 10,000-m race in such difficult weather conditions becomes a 24-lap exercise in energy conservation through optimal pace management with a final one-lap test of who has the greatest sprinting ability. It was under such conditions at the 1985 University Games in Kobe, Japan, that Keith Brantly achieved thus far the United States' only 10,000-m University Games gold medal. He carefully combined excellence in managed pace control with a slightly quicker last lap that involved an all-out sprint down the final straightaway. On an early-evening track still warm from the day's sun (temperature 29.5° C [85° F]; relative humidity 68%) his 29:11.24 victory was 0.47 s ahead of Mexico's Jesus Herrera and 0.49 s in front of Japan's Shuiji Yoneshige.

Wind can also affect performance. A headwind along one straightaway and a tailwind along the other typically produce an accordion-like effect as the space occupied by a pack of runners alternately shortens (into the wind) and lengthens (with the wind). For the leaders the increased energy cost when running into the headwind is not regained as they proceed downwind. For those midpack during the upwind portion the increased chances of being spiked by a runner in front, coupled with the need to shorten stride as the pack comes together, can be unnerving and debilitating even to the freshest and most seasoned competitors. Both mental and physical toughness are crucial in combating the negative effects of these race conditions on performance.

When weather conditions are more favorable and when the races are more tactical, the abilities of today's top-level racers to deliver fast final laps, even after quality racing for 23 or 24 laps, attest to their well-rounded athletic abilities: not only a well-developed speed component in their training, but also a tolerance to high-level acidosis for a brief period. Many coaches will recall the en masse finish of the men's 10,000-m final in the 1983 Helsinki World Championships. At 9,600 m, 13 runners remained in a tight pack. As they passed the ringing bell, announcing the last lap, Werner Schildhauer (German Democratic Republic) launched a ferocious change of pace, eventually delivering a 54.8-s final 400 m. But Hans-Jörg Kunze (German Democratic Republic) ran exactly as fast. Martti Vainio (Finland) ran even faster (54.5 s), and Gidamis Shahanga (Tanzania) ran very nearly as fast (54.9 s). Yet none of these athletes won the race! Alberto Cova (Italy) delivered a 53.9-s 400 m to beat Schildhauer by 0.14 s in 28:01.04. The other three were so close that only 0.89 s separated first place from fifth.

When the racing is extremely fast, however, such final-lap surges are not possible because there is already too little additional anaerobic reserve. Ten weeks before Haile Gebrselassie's 1995 world record at 5,000 m, described previously, he used a similar strategy to break the 10,000-m record at Hengelo on 5 June 1995. Again, because the present world record was already so fast, having itself been set using pacemakers to break the wind in front of the athlete, the best way to break it was to repeat the process with as many similarly paced laps as possible, running in someone else's wind shadow. Ireland's Paul Donovan led the first six laps, and then Ethiopia's Worku Bikila brought Gebrselassie through 5,000 m in 13:21.4. His 400-m splits were predictably very similar: 64.9, 65.3,

64.5, 65.1, 62.5, 63.4, 64.0, 63.1, 62.9, 63.7, 64.6, 64.8, and a 200 m in 32.6 s to complete the first 5,000 m. Shortly thereafter Haile was on his own to do the work. Around 8,000 m he slowed for two laps, allowing some lactic acid to clear, and then steadily increased his pace to the finish. Starting with 5,000 m, his 400-m splits were 65.5, 64.7, 63.2, 64.2, 64.6, 65.2, 66.0, 65.7, 64.1, 63.1, and 61.5, with the final three 200-m segments in 31.2, 30.3, and 30.2 s.

Road Racing

Racing on roads is very different from racing on a track for a variety of reasons, both physical and mental. Thus, simply being a fit athlete from preparation to excel on the track does not guarantee success in road racing. Knowing the four major differences between track and road allows you to plan strategies for excellence in each environment.

One difference is in course layout. Tracks may differ in the length of their straightaway portion, radius or curvature, texture of surface, and visual appearance from stadium to stadium, but this is minuscule compared to the diversity of racing on public streets. Road race courses may be out and back, point to point, loops within loops, or anything else imaginable. Course distances may be either similar to track distances (5 km, 10 km, etc.) or various similar distances (12 km, 14 km, half-marathon), or distances that seem entirely illogical until one realizes that they resulted either from geographic convenience or the local historical significance of having the start and finish at specific points. Bridge gratings, railroad tracks, irregular pavement, and more all need to be negotiated. Some races may be entirely into the wind or entirely with a tailwind.

A second difference relates to the "people dynamics" of racing. At the start, you may be surrounded by hundreds or thousands of other runners, with a start line spanning six wide street lanes, instead of 20 to 30 runners spaced across eight narrow track lanes. Many of these athletes may not belong there, being less-talented athletes who slipped into your time-group area on a whim. The finish line will be unique to each race: single versus multiple chutes, overhead photographic platforms under which you may be directed, a finish line variably visible because of the mass of humanity crowding around.

A third difference is the presence of hills varying in placement and difficulty: large versus small, steep versus gradual, at the beginning versus later in the race. Training must be specially devised to develop useful hill-running skills. Here is where track athletes who develop an initial base fitness using cross-country training have an advantage over those who train essentially only on flat surfaces.

A fourth difference relates to event logistics, which often are greatly different from track races. Road races tend to be morning events, whereas track races are scheduled more often in the afternoon or evening. The question of how to help time pass during the day becomes one of managing very early morning arousal: when, where, and what to eat; ensuring normal bowel function; and finding the start line, which may very simply be a line drawn in a street instead of a standard start point in a stadium. The larger the event, the more complicated are the dynamics of caring for athletes prerace—as anyone will attest who has entered races with 25,000 or more participants.

Some suggestions for building racing simulations into preparations for a competitive road-racing season might be useful at this point. Thoughtful discussions over many years with one of the world's consummate road racers—Jon Sinclair, whose two or three visits to our testing lab each year for 13 years have helped keep him healthy and racing well in addition to providing a most fascinating and informative data base—has provided a one-word answer: *strength*—both mental and physical. Jon has now retired from the highest level of racing, to the delight of many competitors, because for more than a decade he was a terror on the world road circuit, the only athlete to be ranked among the world's top 100 by *Runner's World* for 14 years, from 1979 through 1992 (Wischnia 1993).

Think about what occurs in top-level road racing, and you'll see why physical strength is so important. Frequent surging is routine, and those who do surge seem fearless about trying it anywhere: on the uphills, on the downhills, around sharp turns. Pace changing is common, which results in more frequent transitions into and out of anaerobic metabolic states. Given that these changing dynamics can occur anywhere during the race, it is understandable that mental tenacity also is well developed.

Taking advantage of the mountainous terrain around Fort Collins, Colorado, Sinclair's repertoire for his pre-road-race development phase included periodic, very serious sessions (in mesocycles X_4 and X_5 as outlined in chapter 5) devoted to hill-related strength development. After initial development of an endurance base of aerobic fitness, three types of hill-training sessions were carefully introduced using a variety of courses and intensities. A few examples can serve as a guide to stimulate you to take advantage of your own local running terrain and to design equivalent sessions. Compare these with the concepts of hill-training that we developed in chapter 5 and you'll see how one athlete has adapted the training concept very well to his local terrain.

One type of prerace-season hill training focuses on over-distance hill running. Initially Jon did his Poudre River Canyon workout: 8 to 12 mi (12.8 to 19.3 km) steadily uphill at an aerobic pace. This prepared him later for his Rist Canyon workout: a challenging 8-mi uphill with three components. First came 3 1/2 mi of moderately tough running with a final, steep 1/2 mi. Then after a brief level stretch at a jogging pace, he began a 2 1/2-mi uphill run steeper than the first but ending with a brutal 600-m finale. Finally, after another brief, level stretch of jogging this canyon road provided another mile of even steeper running with an annihilating 200-m climax. In addition to the ever-steeper ascent was an altitude increase from 6,000 ft (1,828 m) to 8,000 ft (2,438 m). Jon did not do this workout very often; instead, it was arranged carefully to provide a useful indication of whether strong racing skills were developing successfully. Of course, it goes without saying that considerable attention is also given to recovery from such hard sessions.

The second type of prerace hill training is best described as up- and downhill racing practice. Out in the countryside around a large reservoir Jon had an 8-mi (12.8-km) course with four fairly evenly spaced, challenging hills, each roughly 1,400 m long. The idea was to run both uphill and downhill at what could best be termed a hard aerobic effort. This meant being aggressive on the uphills, but then honing specifically the best technical skills for arm and leg coordination over the fairly fast-paced downhill.

A third pre-race-season hill conditioner is best conceptualized as a bounding and striding session. Midway through a roughly 5-mi run, Jon included 8 to 10 reps of a loop that climbed up a fairly steep slope (about 75 m) and glided down a more tapered slope (about 120 m). The uphill run was done in bounding fashion, using vigorous arm and leg running mechanics. After cresting the top, the downhill portion required a dramatic change of form to long, loose, relaxed, free-flowing strides.

Training is not the only solution to preparing you for good road racing. There are plenty of specific prerace activities that can help set you up to be a winner. First, drive over the course the day before (better yet, run over parts of it) to identify places in the course where surges can be made effectively—by you or another runner. Second, identify structural landmarks leading up to the finish line. Since the course is typically measured as the shortest straight-line distance on the road surface, note when you'll be drifting from one side of the road to the other. It may sound strange, but if you are in the lead, you cannot always depend on proper course guidance: On many occasions the lead vehicle or police err in directing you over the officially measured course. Obviously, this is unintentional, but it's the athlete who races the correct distance and reaches the finish line first who wins!

Third, use the hills or turns to your advantage. If there is a downhill finish, think about a hard surge a few hundred meters *before* this, especially if downhill running is not your forte. You'll have an extra edge. Similarly, surge hard 50 m *before* a 90° turn at an intersection, thereby ensuring that you cut the corner as sharply as legally permissible, and well out of the tangle of legs and arms as the pack bunches up.

Fourth, develop a mental checklist of important "items of business" that you attend to almost reflexively during the 24 hr prerace. This will permit you to focus more specifically on the race itself. One item relates to clothing: what to do with your warm-ups prerace and how to reclaim them after the race. Another relates to the finish line: Check it out either the day before or the morning of the race; you should have no doubts about how to cross that line if you're involved in a sprint finish. At the start, do not position yourself directly behind the press truck; if it fails to start properly, so do you. If the first turn comes fairly early in the race, position yourself at the start so that you aren't caught among the masses at the turn; it's better to run wide. Big races—and big money—can be won or lost by split-second control, or lack thereof, over your own destiny. Although road racing is vastly different from track racing, it is without doubt just as enjoyable to those who know its nuances.

The Marathon

The marathon is a vastly different event from the races just described in several respects. Racing for a much longer time is only one of the challenges. Consider first the pace dynamics of this race; table 7.3 will help in this regard. Had Ethiopia's Belayneh Dinsamo run his world-best marathon performance on a track, he would have averaged the equivalent of 105 continuous laps of 400 m plus an additional 195 m at an average pace of 72.1 s per lap. Similarly, Ingrid Kristiansen's marathon world record represents an average pace of 80.3 s per lap. The marathon thus demands well more than two hours of concentrated pace running while managing dehydration and fuel exhaustion and avoiding physical debilitation.

The athlete may also need the reserve to insert a decisive increase in pace at a moment precisely timed to break a competitive field both mentally and physically. This most often occurs during the final 7 km of the race, but increasingly, marathons at the highest level are becoming sprints to the finish. Picture the three top Japanese female athletes in the 1994 edition of the Osaka International Ladies Marathon all entering the stadium track together just after 41.5 km and literally racing as fast as their legs could carry them before tens of thousands of

TABLE 7.3

Approximate Pace Equivalents for Selected Marathon Performance Times

Athlete	Time	Venue	Date	Min/mi	Min/km
Belayneh Dinsamo[WR]	2:06:50	Rotterdam	17 April 1988	4:50	3:00
	2:07:00			4:51	3:01
	2:08:00			4:53	3:02
	2:09:00			4:55	3:03
	2:10:00			4:57	3:05
	2:11:00			5:00	3:06
	2:12:00			5:02	3:08
	2:13:00			5:04	3:09
	2:14:00			5:07	3:11
	2:15:00			5:09	3:12
	2:20:00			5:20	3:19
Ingrid Kristiansen[WR]	2:21:06	London	21 April 1985	5:23	3:21
	2:25:00			5:32	3:26
	2:26:00			5:34	3:28
	2:27:00			5:36	3:29
	2:28:00			5:39	3:30
	2:29:00			5:41	3:32
	2:30:00			5:43	3:33
	2:31:00			5:45	3:35
	2:32:00			5:48	3:36
	2:33:00			5:50	3:38
	2:34:00			5:52	3:39
	2:35:00			5:55	3:40
	2:40:00			6:06	3:48

[WR] = world record

screaming spectators who had waited more than two hours on a bitterly cold day. The end result? Tomoe Abe won with a photo finish over Nobuko Fujimura, both timed in 2:26:09, with Stuttgart World Champion Junko Asari 1 s behind—all bettered their national record. Anyone who believes that a marathon is a simple event for which to prepare is terribly misinformed!

Unique Aspects of Marathon Preparation

These long, grueling races often give the impression that success is as much genetically determined as in the 100-m dash. Instead of possessing the reflexes of a squirrel with a genetic predominance of FT skeletal muscle fibers, marathoners will probably be generously ST-endowed with a well-honed running efficiency and a relatively low lactate production even at high work loads. But performance is still determined by the interaction of genetic gifts with proper training, coupled with incredible mental tenacity and a gift of pace sense. Training to build strength and improve technique is of as great a value for marathoners as it is for sprinters. Your training will need to emphasize an ability to store plenty of energy supplies for 2- and 3-hr runs. You'll need to train in such a way to increase both your aerobic power ($\dot{V}O_2max$), using higher-intensity volume-overload training, and your lactate/ventilatory threshold pace, using near-marathon-pace training sessions.

However, racing successfully over this distance requires even more than genetics and training. At least three other considerations take on importance with this longer distance, which is more than four times longer than even the 10,000-m event. First, environmental conditions have an enormous impact on performance. Regardless of whether the field of athletes is highly competitive, many environmental variables must all come together to optimize chances for a fast time: A flat course that is correctly measured (to minimize the added stress of hills), cloudy skies (to minimize radiant heat gain), cool weather (to minimize sweat losses), and minimal wind (to reduce energy cost) will bring out the best in everyone. Admittedly, these may seem almost like laboratory conditions, but statistical records show that the vast majority of the world's best performances for both men and women have been achieved under such conditions (Buoncristiani and Martin 1993). The most dependable circumstances for achieving these performances occur in Japan during their marathon season (December to March) and in Europe. Cities such as Rotterdam, London, Berlin, Fukuoka, Tokyo, Nagoya, and Osaka are meccas for those athletes who race the clock in an attempt for a personal record. Such performances are rarely achieved in the United States, where athletes all too commonly have the fruits of several months of hard training sadly spoiled by a hot day, subfreezing temperatures, or blustery winds—conditions that may leave a marathoner mentally destroyed and physically debilitated.

In addition to course conditions, a second challenge not encountered in racing shorter distances is the real risk of exhausting available energy supplies for maintaining a competitive race pace and for maintaining adequate hydration. Thus, tapering prior to a marathon race must involve nutritional considerations as well as physical rest. Fuel and water intake during the race must both be adequate. Additional factors, often considered trivial, such as clothing and shoes that do not cause problems with chafing or blisters, also assume greater importance during marathon racing.

A third dilemma that you'll face in moving up to the marathon from shorter events comes in designing training plans. An important loss is the ability to include training runs considerably longer than your race distance. Top-level 800-m and 1,500-m men may run distances as long as 10 to 15 mi in training; women typically a little less. Enormous confidence can come from training at distances from 15 to 30 times longer than your primary racing event. If you have decided to become a marathoner, you've just lost this option. Top-level middle-distance runners have a much more favorable ratio of weekly training to race distance than do marathon runners. For a male 1,500-m runner, this ratio may average 112,500:1,500 m = 69.9:0.93 mi = 75:1 over a training macrocycle. For a female 1,500-m runner, the ratio is less—perhaps 50:1. A marathoner's weekly training-to-racing ratio is from 3.5:1 to 5.5:1 at best. This may explain why the more consistently successful marathon runners can race effectively in no more than two to three marathons per year.

A fourth difference between marathon runners and shorter-distance specialists is the marathoner's need for what we will term very long runs, ranging between 30 km (18.6 mi) and 40 km (24.8 mi) and done about once every 12 to 20 days during the two- to three-month period before a marathon race. These are aerobic runs, typically at between 55% to 70% of $\dot{V}O_2$max pace (70% to 80% of maximum heart rate). The wearing effect of these very long runs is of such magnitude that they need to be considered almost as race equivalents. They will condition you mentally to tolerate sustained periods of running at a constant pace and introduce you to the sensation of profound fatigue that begins as muscle carbohydrate supplies begin to deplete.

When added to the remainder of a training week, the stress of these very long runs means that for marathon runners a much greater chance exists than for runners in the other distance events for the results of training to initiate the sequence whereby fatigue leads to exhaustion which in turn cause breakdown.

In chapter 8 we will outline the various kinds of injury that occur, primarily tendon injuries as muscles fatigue and fail to do their share of load bearing during training. If one warning can be issued for the prevention of injury, it is the *rule of specific quantity:* Do the least amount of the most sensible training to bring about improvement in performance. Do very long runs but not too frequently, and ensure proper recovery. Do shorter runs and longer-distance interval runs, but again, ensure recovery. If the choice is yours, it is better to err on the side of undertraining rather than overtraining.

Another warning invokes the *rule of individuality:* Every athlete is an experiment of one, and the more elite the athlete, the more unique the experiment. Each athlete has a slightly different genetic endowment of FT and ST skeletal muscle fibers as well as a different training base, fitness level, and level of personal commitment. The previous training load on the day before your very long runs and the ideal pace for these runs will be quite different, depending on the period in your training cycle, your recovery, and your genetics. This is one of the problems with training too frequently as part of a group. For some in the group the pace will be too quick, producing excessive fatigue; for others it will be a perfect training stimulus. If your optimal training pace is 6:00 min/mi (3:44 min/km) for 20 mi, then running at a 5:50 min/mi (3:38 min/km) pace is dangerously too quick. It isn't worth the risk of excessive fatigue or injury simply to have companionship on a long run. A winner crossing the finish line is all alone; here's your chance to practice just that (unless your training partners are your clones!).

Excellent marathoners quite often possess admirable shorter-distance (i.e., 10,000-m) racing abilities. This demonstrates once again the importance of strength, speed, and stamina in improving the ability of working muscles to endure a given submaximal work load for a long period. Within limits, the faster you can run, the easier any particular submaximal pace becomes. Dinsamo's 2:06:50 represents a 15:04/5,000-m pace, while Kristiansen's 2:21:06 is at a 16:43/5,000-m pace. The ability to race back-to-back 5,000-m repeats at 15:50 for men (running at a 2:13:35 pace) or 18:00 for women (running at a 2:31:54 pace) can be developed nicely by training designed to raise as much as possible both your $\dot{V}O_2$max and your anaerobic threshold. We aren't necessarily suggesting here that men who are under-4-min milers make fast under-2:20:00 marathoners (scarcely 60 runners have achieved this double in the history of running). We are indeed suggesting, however, that good shorter-distance racing ability, in both men and women, can contribute to competent marathon racing, provided that the required marathon training component of periodic very long runs is included to create connective tissue adaptation; increased skeletal muscle fuel reserves, mitochondria, and capillarization; and mental readiness for extended pace maintenance.

Marathons are raced seriously by most everyone at about 95% to 97% of their lactate/ventilatory threshold pace. This means typically about 80% to 84% of $\dot{V}O_2$max pace for elite-level athletes, slower for those with less genetically endowed running efficiency. Relying on adequate stored supplies of carbohydrates on board, your respiratory exchange ratio (R) will be around 0.93 to 0.95 during the race. This suggests a fat-to-carbohydrate energy utilization ratio between 24% to 76% and 17% to 83%. If you possess a generous ST muscle fiber endowment, have a $\dot{V}O_2$max on the high side of that found among elite endurance athletes (e.g., 75 ml · kg^{-1} · min^{-1} or higher for men, 65 ml · kg^{-1} · min^{-1} or higher for women), and are economical (i.e., consume less O_2 at submaximal paces than most other runners of similar expertise), then you have the best tools for fast performance. The key to achieving these fast performances is initiating a pace slow enough in the beginning to ensure an optimal ratio of fuel utilization, thereby maintaining adequate carbohydrate stores to carry you through the entire race. This topic of energy provision will be discussed further later in this chapter.

Strategies for Racing Marathons

For those competing in their first marathon who have never (or very seldom) traversed the actual race distance, the experience will be unique and unforgettable. Indeed, the varying terrain, weather, and past training history will make very nearly every marathon race quite different from any other. You very much want your first experience to be favorable, and so we'll assume you have prepared quite diligently. One useful approach is to utilize both the metric and Imperial measurement systems in your race plan.

Breaking the Race Into Familiar Pieces

In a marathon, the "running" usually occurs during the first 20 mi, and the "racing" during the final 10 km. Thus, if there is still a pack of competitors remaining at 20 mi, aggressive surges that with luck will split the group aren't generally made until somewhere in the vicinity of 32 to 35 km. The 20-mi point is at 32.2 km. Ideally, your training should have been such that you have developed the strength in your legs to get to 20 mi as if you were simply on a long run. Now, focus on racing as well as possible for the remaining 10 km.

Particularly if you are from the United States or Britain, where miles and kilometers are quite often used interchangeably (10-km races, for example have 1-mi splits, and marathons have both mile and kilometer points marked), mentally divide your marathon race into an initial 20-mi fairly hard run followed by a 10-km race. Psychologically you are always in familiar territory. Thus, the 21-mi mark is sensed as the first mile of the 6.21 mi remaining, and so on to the end of the race. Since these high-mileage indicators are not often encountered in training, emphasis always centers about familiar indicators of progress. Mentally picture your last successful 10-km road race, and as each mile mark ticks by, imagine yourself in a similar racing effort. Your focus is thus not that you should be starting to feel the agony of having covered so many miles in your marathon, but that this is a competitive race with only a few "friendly" miles yet to cover.

Practice Taking in Fluids

It is crucial to stay cool if the weather is warm, and it is also crucial to keep hydrated as much as possible. This topic will be described in greater detail later in this chapter. Practice during training will be required to master the art of drinking adequate fluids at water stations, splashing fluid on your skin if the sun is shining and the humidity is low, and at the same time remaining relaxed. Gaining experience on your long training runs is the only way to develop the skill of continuing to carry your bottle until it is empty and swallowing the fluid while still staying close to race pace. During races, if on-course feeding stations are provided for elite runners to pick up bottles containing special fluids, care must be given to labeling (good visibility), shape (for easy capture), and content.

Figure 7.6 shows the top two finishers of the women's marathon at the 1995 Göteborg World Championships in Athletics in action at a refreshment station. Both athletes were drinking, and both were splashing additional water onto

Figure 7.6 During marathon racing, especially in warm weather, drinking is crucial to minimize the risk of dehydration as well as to ensure intake of energy. Use of water-soaked sponges, especially in low humidity, can enhance evaporative cooling.

their skin on that sunny, dry day by use of water-soaked sponges to enhance evaporative cooling. Romania's star marathoner Anuta Catuna, shown here behind eventual winner Maria Manuela Machado (713) of Portugal, also decided to reduce the sun's glare through the use of sunglasses. Their poise while performing this mix of racing and drinking at a race pace of 85 to 86 s/400 m is impressive and is a reflection of their racing competence.

Minimizing Fatigue Through Pace Management

One theoretical strategy for minimizing the slowing of pace is to deviate as little as possible from the mean pace of your intended finish time. This is difficult to achieve, however, because you will not know how fast you'll run until the race is finished, making it difficult to decide on an acceptable mean 5-km split pace. Given the typical scenario that more races are lost by mistakes in the first 20 mi and that more are won by excellent performance in the final 10 km, one safe suggestion is simply to begin every marathon race with some degree of conservatism. This can be difficult because of the combination of prerace excitement and a wonderful sense of freshness in the working muscles from the few days of tapering.

As a method for assessing the dynamics of pace management during marathon racing, we have analyzed the intermediate 5-km split times for a fairly large population of top-level marathon runners who race in the wintertime Japanese marathon circuit (Buoncristiani and Martin 1993). These races are conducted under almost laboratory conditions: ideal weather conditions and fairly flat courses, with great attention to detail in collecting accurate intermediate split times for all participants. One useful conclusion is that deviating from the mean race pace by more than ± 2% is metabolically more costly than remaining within this pace window. Athletes with early-race fast splits all too often pay a price later on in the form of a dramatic slowdown, with proportionately slower late-race splits.

This important psychophysiological consideration needs to be appreciated. It is in distinct contrast to the other distance races we have thus far discussed, which typically require a sizable pace increase near the end. What sets the stage for causing this tendency to slow, and can it be minimized? We may have a partial answer. Another interesting conclusion from our studies of 5-km marathon splits is that for both men and women, even for those whose 5-km split times suggest a very sensible pace management, beyond 30 km there is a statistically measurable slowing of maintainable race pace. The likely explanation is that metabolic changes in the active tissues combine to increase the energy cost to run the distance. The contributory factors are no doubt several: energy fuel depletion, increased viscosity of connective tissues and working muscles, hemoconcentration from fluid losses through sweating, gradual decrease in O_2 delivery to the working tissues, and cooling of these tissues if the ambient temperatures are sufficiently low. Thus, the anaerobic threshold pace may decrease slightly as the race proceeds. The best method for minimizing the combined adverse effects of these changes is to ensure fluid, energy, and electrolyte replenishment by ensuring that your body is well-fueled and hydrated before the race begins and by taking effective advantage of the available refreshment stations.

Another psychological consideration relates to the increased effort sense and elongated perception of time that occurs with developing fatigue. Thus, a given time-distance relationship—for example, running 1 mi in 6 min (or 1 km in 3:44)—is distorted so that it seems to take longer. For those of us who have run marathons, there is little worse than not only realizing that a slowing of pace is occurring from real fatigue, but also perceiving that slowing as even greater than it really is! The psychological explanation for the lengthened time perception is still being studied. Is it a reduction in neurotransmitter chemicals that link nerve cells with muscle cells, or a decreased sensory input, or neurological manifestations of the metabolic effects of prolonged fatigue? Perhaps the best way to deal with it is to prevent its occurrence by maintaining an early pace commensurate with the eventual mean pace for the race.

Planning Ahead for Comfort

More than for the shorter-distance events, small often seemingly insignificant elements of preparation can affect the outcome of a marathon. Shoes must fit perfectly to prevent blisters and allow for foot swelling during the late stages. Clothing should not chafe or bind. Shoes and clothing that will be used in a race should all have been worn before the race to verify their suitability. For marathoners selected as part of traveling teams, early issue of team clothing should be a high priority.

Using Split Times in a Practical Way

Tables 7.4 and 7.5 provide a ready reference for intermediate times, using both the metric and Imperial systems, for you to chart appropriate splits during marathon racing. Ideally, you should run the first portion of the race a little slower

TABLE 7.4

Metric Marathon Pace Chart With Selected Intermediate-Distance (Split) Times

1 km	5 km	10 km	15 km	20 km	Half	25 km	30 km	35 km	40 km	Marathon
3:00	15:00	30:00	45:00	1:00:00	1:03:18	1:15:00	1:30:00	1:45:00	2:00:00	2:06:35
3:05	15:25	30:50	46:15	1:01:40	1:05:03	1:17:05	1:32:30	1:47:55	2:03:20	2:10:06
3:10	15:50	31:40	47:30	1:03:20	1:06:49	1:19:10	1:35:00	1:50:50	2:06:40	2:13:37
3:15	16:15	32:30	48:45	1:05:00	1:08:34	1:21:15	1:37:30	1:53:45	2:10:00	2:17:08
3:20	16:40	33:20	50:00	1:06:40	1:10:20	1:23:20	1:40:00	1:56:40	2:13:20	2:20:39
3:25	17:05	34:10	51:15	1:08:20	1:12:05	1:25:25	1:42:30	1:59:35	2:16:40	2:24:09
3:30	17:30	35:00	52:30	1:10:00	1:13:50	1:27:30	1:45:00	2:02:30	2:20:00	2:27:40
3:35	17:55	35:50	53:45	1:11:40	1:15:35	1:29:35	1:47:30	2:05:25	2:23:20	2:31:11
3:40	18:20	36:40	55:00	1:13:20	1:17:21	1:31:40	1:50:00	2:08:20	2:26:40	2:34:42
3:45	18:45	37:30	56:15	1:15:00	1:19:07	1:33:45	1:52:30	2:11:15	2:30:00	2:38:13
3:50	19:10	38:20	57:30	1:16:40	1:20:52	1:35:50	1:55:00	2:14:10	2:33:20	2:41:44
3:55	19:35	39:10	58:45	1:18:20	1:22:38	1:37:55	1:57:30	2:17:05	2:36:40	2:45:16
4:00	20:00	40:00	60:00	1:20:00	1:24:24	1:40:00	2:00:00	2:20:00	2:40:00	2:48:48
4:05	20:25	40:50	61:15	1:21:40	1:26:09	1:42:05	2:02:30	2:22:55	2:43:20	2:52:18
4:10	20:50	41:40	62:30	1:23:20	1:27:54	1:44:10	2:05:00	2:25:50	2:46:40	2:55:49
4:15	21:15	42:30	63:45	1:25:00	1:29:40	1:46:15	2:07:30	2:28:45	2:50:00	2:59:20
4:20	21:40	43:20	65:00	1:26:40	1:31:25	1:48:20	2:10:00	2:31:40	2:53:20	3:02:51
4:25	22:05	44:10	66:15	1:28:20	1:33:11	1:50:25	2:12:30	2:34:35	2:56:40	3:06:21
4:30	22:30	45:00	67:30	1:30:00	1:34:56	1:52:30	2:15:00	2:37:30	3:00:00	3:10:57
4:35	22:55	45:50	68:45	1:31:40	1:36:42	1:54:35	2:17:30	2:40:25	3:03:20	3:13:14
4:40	23:20	46:40	70:00	1:33:20	1:38:47	1:56:40	2:20:00	2:43:20	3:06:40	3:16:55
4:45	23:45	47:30	71:15	1:35:00	1:40:13	1:58:45	2:22:30	2:46:15	3:10:00	3:20:26
4:50	24:10	48:20	72:30	1:36:40	1:41:58	2:00:50	2:25:00	2:49:10	3:13:20	3:23:57
4:55	24:35	49:10	73:45	1:38:20	1:43:44	2:02:55	2:27:30	2:52:05	3:16:40	3:27:28
5:00	25:00	50:00	75:00	1:40:00	1:45:30	2:05:00	2:30:00	2:55:00	3:20:00	3:31:00

than your expected mean pace, thereby conserving carbohydrate supplies. Later on, as conditions become more tactical as you initiate or respond to pace increases intended to break apart the lead pack, adequate carbohydrate supplies will be available to provide energy for these pace increases as well as for a strong finish.

This is the concept of *negative-splitting* a marathon: covering the second half in a shorter time than the first half. This seldom occurs, however, for three reasons, some of which we have already suggested. First, very few marathon competitions occur in what we refer to as laboratory conditions, that is, on a flat course out and back with minimal wind and ideal weather (cool and cloudy), and where accurate split times are recorded every 5 km to permit ongoing (and postrace) analysis. Second, typically athletes do not have the patience initially to maintain a pace that seems well within their comfort zone; the temptation is to race faster. The agony of the second half of a previous marathon raced has been all but forgotten, and the same mistake is about to be made again. Third, lactate/ventilatory threshold pace most likely slows during the final stages of the race. The trend toward dehydration reduces blood volume, which reduces the extent of skeletal muscle perfusion. This decreases $\dot{V}O_2$max and also causes

TABLE 7.5

Marathon Pace Chart With Selected Metric and Imperial Intermediate-Distance (Split) Times

Mile pace	5 km (3.1 mi)	5 mi	10 km (6.2 mi)	15 km (9.3 mi)	10 mi	20 km (12.4 mi)	Half-marathon	15 mi	25 km (15.5 mi)	30 km (18.6 mi)	20 mi	35 km (21.7 mi)	40 km (24.8 mi)	Marathon
4:40	14:30	23:20	29:00	43:30	46:40	58:00	1:01:11	1:10:00	1:12:30	1:27:00	1:33:20	1:41:30	1:56:00	2:02:22
4:45	14:46	23:45	29:31	44:17	47:30	59:02	1:02:17	1:11:15	1:13:48	1:28:33	1:35:00	1:43:19	1:58:04	2:04:33
4:50	15:01	24:10	30:02	45:03	48:20	1:00:04	1:03:22	1:12:30	1:15:05	1:30:06	1:36:40	1:45:07	2:00:08	2:06:44
4:55	15:17	24:35	30:33	45:50	49:10	1:01:06	1:04:28	1:13:45	1:16:23	1:31:39	1:38:20	1:46:56	2:02:12	2:08:55
5:00	15:32	25:00	31:04	46:36	50:00	1:02:08	1:05:33	1:15:00	1:17:40	1:33:12	1:40:00	1:48:44	2:04:16	2:11:06
5:05	15:48	25:25	31:35	47:23	50:50	1:03:10	1:06:39	1:16:15	1:18:58	1:34:45	1:41:40	1:50:33	2:06:20	2:13:17
5:10	16:03	25:50	32:06	48:09	51:40	1:04:12	1:07:44	1:17:30	1:20:15	1:36:18	1:43:20	1:52:21	2:08:24	2:15:28
5:15	16:19	26:15	32:37	48:56	52:30	1:05:14	1:08:50	1:18:45	1:21:33	1:37:51	1:45:00	1:54:10	2:10:28	2:17:39
5:20	16:34	26:40	33:08	49:42	53:20	1:06:16	1:09:55	1:20:00	1:22:50	1:39:24	1:46:40	1:55:58	2:12:32	2:19:50
5:25	16:50	27:05	33:39	50:29	54:10	1:07:18	1:11:01	1:21:15	1:24:08	1:40:57	1:48:20	1:57:47	2:14:36	2:22:01
5:30	17:05	27:30	34:10	51:15	55:00	1:08:20	1:12:06	1:22:30	1:25:25	1:42:30	1:50:00	1:59:35	2:16:40	2:24:12
5:35	17:21	27:55	34:41	52:02	55:50	1:09:22	1:13:12	1:23:45	1:26:43	1:44:03	1:51:40	2:01:24	2:18:44	2:26:23
5:40	17:36	28:20	35:12	52:48	56:40	1:10:24	1:14:17	1:25:00	1:28:00	1:45:36	1:53:20	2:03:12	2:20:48	2:28:34
5:45	17:52	28:45	35:43	53:35	57:30	1:11:26	1:15:23	1:26:15	1:29:18	1:47:09	1:55:00	2:05:01	2:22:52	2:30:45
5:50	18:07	29:10	36:14	54:21	58:20	1:12:28	1:16:28	1:27:30	1:30:35	1:48:42	1:56:40	2:06:49	2:24:56	2:32:56
5:55	18:23	29:35	36:45	55:08	59:10	1:13:30	1:17:34	1:28:45	1:31:53	1:50:15	1:58:20	2:08:38	2:27:00	2:35:07
6:00	18:38	30:00	37:16	55:54	1:00:00	1:14:32	1:18:39	1:30:00	1:33:10	1:51:48	2:00:00	2:10:26	2:29:04	2:37:18
6:05	18:54	30:25	37:47	56:41	1:00:50	1:15:34	1:19:45	1:31:15	1:34:28	1:53:21	2:01:40	2:12:15	2:31:08	2:39:29
6:10	19:09	30:50	38:18	57:27	1:01:40	1:16:36	1:20:50	1:32:30	1:35:45	1:54:54	2:03:20	2:14:03	2:33:12	2:41:40
6:15	19:25	31:15	38:49	58:14	1:02:30	1:17:38	1:21:56	1:33:45	1:37:03	1:56:27	2:05:00	2:15:52	2:35:16	2:43:51
6:20	19:40	31:40	39:20	59:00	1:03:20	1:18:40	1:23:01	1:35:00	1:38:20	1:58:00	2:06:40	2:17:40	2:37:20	2:46:02
6:25	19:56	32:05	39:51	59:47	1:04:10	1:19:42	1:24:07	1:36:15	1:39:38	1:59:33	2:08:20	2:19:29	2:39:24	2:48:13
6:30	20:11	32:30	40:22	1:00:33	1:05:00	1:20:44	1:25:12	1:37:30	1:40:55	2:01:06	2:10:00	2:21:17	2:41:28	2:50:24
6:35	20:27	32:55	40:53	1:01:20	1:05:50	1:21:46	1:26:18	1:38:45	1:42:13	2:02:39	2:11:40	2:23:06	2:43:32	2:52:35
6:40	20:42	33:20	41:24	1:02:06	1:06:40	1:22:48	1:27:23	1:40:00	1:43:30	2:04:12	2:13:20	2:24:54	2:45:36	2:54:46
6:45	20:58	33:45	41:55	1:02:53	1:07:30	1:23:50	1:28:29	1:41:15	1:44:48	2:05:45	2:15:00	2:26:43	2:47:40	2:56:57
6:50	21:13	34:10	42:26	1:03:39	1:08:20	1:24:52	1:29:34	1:42:30	1:46:05	2:07:18	2:16:40	2:28:31	2:49:44	2:59:08
6:55	21:29	34:35	42:57	1:04:26	1:09:10	1:25:54	1:30:40	1:43:45	1:47:23	2:08:51	2:18:20	2:30:20	2:51:48	3:01:19
7:00	21:44	35:00	43:28	1:05:12	1:10:00	1:26:56	1:31:45	1:45:00	1:48:40	2:10:24	2:20:00	2:32:08	2:53:52	3:03:30
7:05	30:00	35:25	43:59	1:05:59	1:10:50	1:27:58	1:32:51	1:46:15	1:49:58	2:11:57	2:21:40	2:33:57	2:55:56	3:05:41
7:10	22:15	35:50	44:30	1:06:45	1:11:40	1:29:00	1:33:56	1:47:30	1:51:15	2:13:30	2:23:20	2:35:45	2:58:00	3:07:52
7:15	22:31	36:15	45:01	1:07:32	1:12:30	1:30:02	1:35:02	1:48:45	1:52:33	2:15:03	2:25:00	2:37:34	3:00:04	3:10:03
7:20	22:46	36:40	45:32	1:08:18	1:13:20	1:31:04	1:36:07	1:50:00	1:53:50	2:16:36	2:26:40	2:39:22	3:02:08	3:12:14
7:25	23:02	37:05	46:03	1:09:05	1:14:10	1:32:06	1:37:13	1:51:15	1:55:08	2:18:09	2:28:20	2:41:11	3:04:12	3:14:25
7:30	23:17	35:30	46:34	1:09:51	1:15:00	1:32:06	1:38:18	1:52:30	1:56:25	2:19:42	2:30:00	2:42:59	3:06:16	3:16:36
7:35	23:33	37:55	47:05	1:10:38	1:15:50	1:33:08	1:39:24	1:53:45	1:57:43	2:21:15	2:31:40	2:44:48	3:08:20	3:18:47
7:40	23:48	38:20	47:36	1:11:24	1:16:40	1:34:10	1:40:29	1:55:00	1:59:00	2:22:48	2:33:20	2:46:36	3:10:24	3:20:58
7:45	24:04	38:45	48:07	1:12:11	1:17:30	1:35:12	1:41:35	1:56:15	2:00:18	2:24:21	2:35:00	2:48:25	3:12:28	3:23:09
7:50	24:19	39:10	48:38	1:12:57	1:18:20	1:36:14	1:42:40	1:57:30	2:01:35	2:25:54	2:36:40	2:50:13	3:14:32	3:25:20
7:55	24:35	39:35	49:09	1:13:44	1:19:10	1:37:16	1:43:46	1:58:45	2:02:53	2:27:27	2:38:20	2:52:02	3:16:36	3:27:31

hemoconcentration, effectively increasing the blood acidity. To keep this acidity from increasing further, running pace may have to be slowed. Thus, run the first portion of the race only minimally faster than your expected mean pace to allow for late-race slowing.

To illustrate the dynamics of pace management more specifically, in figure 7.7 we show the 5-km splits of Japan's Takeyuki Nakayama for three races in his outstanding career. This talented athlete made a breakthrough in 1984 with a 2:10:00 victory at Fukuoka. In figure 7.7a we see how sensibly he started that race, well within the ±2% window. He increased his pace between 25 and 30 km to break free of accompanying athletes, and only Michael Heilmann (German Democratic Republic) stayed with him. Although Nakayama moved outside the ±2% window during this surge, this increased pace was more within his limitations than it was for Heilmann, who slowed after 35 km, giving Nakayama a 36-s margin of victory.

Figure 7.7b shows Nakayama's next marathon, a brilliant personal best (by 1:45) at Hiroshima in April 1985. It was also a new national record. He delivered

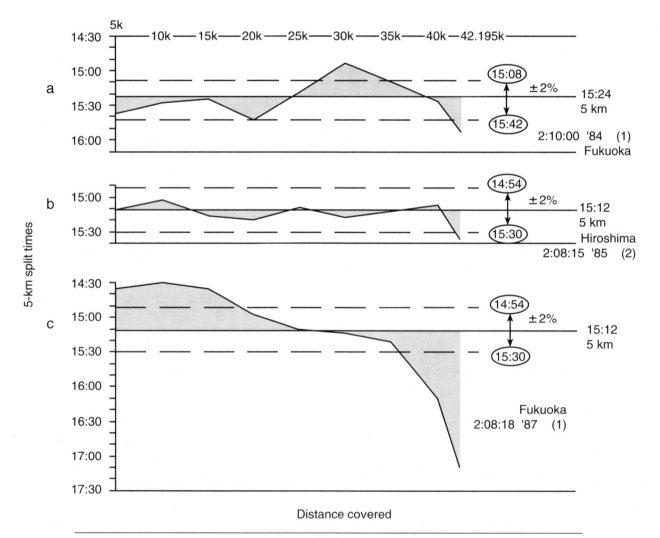

Figure 7.7 Racing in the marathon. Examples, using 5-km split times for three marathons of Takeyuki Nakayama, illustrate how even-paced running throughout can reduce pace slowing at the end. Numbers in parentheses represent finish places.

virtually identical 5-km splits throughout, going head to head with Djibouti's Ahmed Salah through 40 km. Only then, as Ahmed gradually moved ahead and broke contact, did the cumulative physiological (and now psychological) effects of the competition begin to slow Nakayama's average pace. Finally, figure 7.7c shows the debilitating effects of an excessively fast early pace. At the Japanese Olympic Trials in Fukuoka in December 1987 Nakayama felt obliged to deliver a performance of sufficient quality to ensure team selection. He led the pack through amazingly quick 5-km splits of 14:30, 14:35, and 14:30 (on target for an under-2:03:00 performance) before slowing to a pace (between 20 and 35 km) closer to his mean race pace. The effects of increasing metabolic acidosis, perhaps combined with decreasing carbohydrate availability, then took their toll, and he began to slow. His decreased heat production from the slower pace, coupled with the added hypothermic effects of a chilling rain, gave him a finish time of 2:08:18, a scant 3 s short of a personal best. We wonder just how much faster he would have run had his pace been as sensibly controlled as at Hiroshima, particularly because he had successfully improved his 10,000-m racing speed from 28:07:0 to 27:35:33 during the preceding summer on the European track circuit.

Breaking Records in the Marathon

One of the questions most asked by the sports media when writing about the marathon is, "When will a woman break the 2:20:00 barrier in a marathon race?" Obviously, there's no way anyone can predict this. Most likely, what they are probably asking is, "Do you believe it is possible for a woman to run faster than 2:20:00?" Having worked with elite athletes so long, we certainly wouldn't suggest that it is impossible; athletes have a habit of embarrassing people who suggest that they have performance limits.

Our typical answer to this question is, "A woman will indeed break 2:20:00 someday, and when she does, the men's record will probably have been lowered as well, down to about 2:05:51." This time for men is based simply on extrapolating the existing difference between the present women's (2:21:06) and men's (2:06:50) marathon record of 10.1%. Table 7.6 provides some additional perspective by summarizing the present-day differences between the men's and women's world records in the running events from 100 m through the marathon. It is remarkable that, over such a wide range of distances, contested with such varied combinations of aerobic and anaerobic energy dynamics, the male-female differential is fairly similar. At the shorter distances the difference is primarily due to the greater strength of male distance runners. At the longer distances where strength is less important, men still have an advantage in their greater blood O_2 content. Some of the events (e.g., the track 20 km, 25 km, and 30 km) have been raced only infrequently by men, but much less by women. The larger differences between the sexes for these latter events thus result primarily from the much smaller contributing pool of female athletes. Nevertheless, taking all 15 events together, the average difference between all of the men's and women's times is 9.8%, which is surprisingly similar to the difference between just the two marathon performances.

It is anyone's guess as to exactly when women will actually break the 2:20:00 barrier, but we have no doubt that it will occur sooner or later. We leave it to the athletes to tell us where and when! As should be clear from the preceding discussion, a vast number of variables related to fitness, pace, course layout, and weather will have to come together in an optimal manner if either record is to fall.

TABLE 7.6

Performance Differences Between Male and Female Sea-Level World Track Records in Running (as of 01 September 1996)

Distance	Record	Velocity m/s	mi/hr	Male athlete	Year	Performance equivalent (ml · kg⁻¹ · min⁻¹)
100 m	9.84	10.16	22.7	Donovan Bailey	1996	
200 m	19.32	10.35	23.2	Michael Johnson	1996	
400 m	43.29	9.24	20.7	Harry Reynolds	1988	
800 m	1:41.73	7.86	17.6	Sebastian Coe	1981	82.6
1,000 m	2:12.18	7.57	16.9	Sebastian Coe	1981	82.0
1,500 m	3:27.37	7.23	16.2	Noureddine Morceli	1995	83.1
1 mi	3:44.39	7.24	16.2	Noureddine Morceli	1993	82.9
2,000 m	4:47.88	6.95	15.5	Noureddine Morceli	1995	81.7
3,000 m	7:20.67	6.80	15.3	Daniel Komen	1996	83.5
5,000 m	12:44.39	6.54	14.6	Haile Gebrselassie	1995	84.1
10,000 m	26:38.08	6.26	14.0	Salah Hissou	1996	83.8
20,000 m	56:55.60	5.85	13.1	Arturo Barrios	1991	81.0
25,000 m	1:13:55.80	5.64	12.6	Toshihiko Seko	1981	78.9
30,000 m	1:29:18.80	5.60	12.5	Toshihiko Seko	1981	79.4
Marathon	2:06:50	5.54	12.4	Belayneh Dinsamo	1988	80.6

Record	Velocity m/s	mi/hr	Female athlete	Year	Performance equivalent (ml · kg⁻¹ · min⁻¹)	% difference
10.49	9.53	21.3	F. Griffith-Joyner	1988		6.2
21.34	9.37	21.0	F. Griffith-Joyner	1988		9.5
47.60	8.40	18.8	Marita Koch	1985		9.1
1:53.28	7.06	15.8	J. Kratochvilova	1983	72.9	10.2
2:28.98	6.70	15.0	Svetlana Masterkova	1996	71.5	11.3
3:50.46	6.51	14.6	Qu Yunxia	1993	73.5	10.0
4:12.56	6.37	14.3	Svetlana Masterkova	1996	72.2	12.0
5:25.36	6.14	13.7	Sonia O'Sullivan	1994	71.0	11.5
8:06.11	6.17	13.8	Wang Junxia	1993	74.7	9.4
14:36.45	5.70	12.8	Fernanda Ribeiro	1995	71.8	12.8
29:31.78	5.64	12.6	Wang Junxia	1993	74.2	9.8
1:06:48.80	5.55	12.4	Izumi Maki	1993	67.3	14.8
1:29:29.20	4.66	10.4	Karolina Szabo	1988	63.3	17.4
1:47:05.60	4.67	10.4	Karolina Szabo	1988	64.4	16.6
2:21:06	4.98	11.1	Ingrid Kristiansen	1985	71.2	10.1

Fuel and Fluid Replenishment for Marathon Training and Racing

In chapter 3 we discussed the essentials of both fuel metabolism and fuel replenishment for athletes racing over the standard track distances and strategies for ensuring an adequate diet to promote optimal nutrition. Whether for training or racing, the guidelines are similar. For marathon training and racing, however, while the basic principles are similar, there are many additional details that need discussion. Recall that fatty acid energy stores are plentiful, whereas carbohydrate stores (in the form of muscle, blood, and liver glucose and glycogen) are not. For race distances shorter than the marathon carbohydrates contribute the largest energy source, and sufficient stored carbohydrate exists to satisfy these needs. Although fatty acid utilization increases its role as an energy source during long races, even for the marathon distance the role of carbohydrates is so great that carbohydrate exhaustion in the working muscles, with subsequent slowing of race pace, is a real possibility. This can occur during the very long training runs of marathon runners as well. The details of this interaction among fuels are interesting.

Consider the metabolic dilemma that exists. Fats are the logical energy source for a long race such as the marathon, because they are available in large quantity. But recall that fatty acid molecules contain very little O_2 and thus must rely on a plentiful circulating O_2 supply through the bloodstream. By comparison, glucose contains much more O_2 in its molecular structure and thus needs less additional O_2 for its metabolism. Thus, for every mole of O_2 provided by the blood, 5.05 kcal (21.1 kJ) of energy are derived from glucose, compared to 4.69 kcal (19.6 kJ) from fatty acids (Dwyer and Dyer 1984). How is this important?

If you begin your marathon race at a sensible pace (slightly less than lactate/ventilatory threshold pace), your fuel consumption ratio will be about 25% fatty acids to 75% carbohydrates. During the race, if your muscle carbohydrate supplies begin to dwindle, this ratio will have to change as fatty acid utilization increases. This shift in fuel preference requires an increased blood flow to the working muscles to provide the increased O_2 for fatty acid metabolism. However, since cardiac output equals stroke volume times heart rate and since developing dehydration from sweating, especially on a warm day, is already decreasing the maintainable stroke volume, it isn't likely that this increased blood flow can occur. Especially if you are already racing close to your lactate/ventilatory threshold pace, such an increase in pace will not be sustainable because of accumulating acidosis. If carbohydrate supplies dwindle substantially, shifting the fuel consumption to an even greater reliance on fatty acid metabolism may slow your race pace by an additional increment. The combination of all these factors is often the cause for the profound slowing of race pace that occurs in marathon racing somewhere after 20 mi (32.2 km). In runner's jargon, you have *hit the wall.*

What can you do to ensure an adequate blood volume, as well as adequate carbohydrate supplies, throughout your long-distance race (marathon distance and beyond)? Clearly, the answer is multifaceted:

- Have as much glycogen in your skeletal muscles as possible *before* the race.
- Be well hydrated *before* the race.
- Drink water periodically *during* the race.
- Have carbohydrate energy mixed with the water drunk *during* the race, to provide a continuing bloodborne carbohydrate reserve to supplement diminishing muscle glycogen stores.
- Practice drinking fluids on many long training runs months *before* the race, thereby learning all the tricks of the trade: the size and shape of bottle that best fits your hand, the best fluid/energy mixture that tastes good and absorbs well, and the patience to continue carrying the bottle until all the contents are ingested.

It should be clear from the preceding advice that good race management of energy supplies begins well before the actual race. It begins before every training session on a day-to-day basis and becomes more specialized in the few days prior to a race, and the energy intake pattern is modified still more during the actual race period. These topics deserve some additional attention.

Posttraining Energy Replenishment

Knowledge about the relationship of high-volume training and carbohydrate repletion dates back to the studies of Hultman and Bergstrom (1967). These workers (and others since) showed that if skeletal muscle glycogen stores are largely depleted by prolonged exercise (e.g., a 20-mi [32.2-km] run), the depleted muscles will respond during postexercise nutritional replenishment by storing even more glycogen than had been present before the depletion. This phenomenon is called *muscle glycogen supercompensation*. If your muscle cells had a personality, we could picture them not at all enjoying the loss of so much of their stored energy sources and deciding to stuff some extra fuel into their cytoplasm after such a depletion, under the assumption that you might attempt a similarly crazy antic again sometime in the future. Supercompensation will occur during the day or so following the long run if adequate nutritional replacement is provided. This increased glycogen-storing stimulus in the working muscles, which can best be triggered by the very long distance runs, is thus an essential part of competitive marathon preparation.

During aerobic running you will consume about 1.04 kcal · kg^{-1} body weight · km^{-1} of distance (or 4.34 kJ · kg^{-1} · km^{-1}). Thus, a 20-mi (32.2-km) run for a 60-kg man or a 50-kg woman has an energy requirement of 2,009 kcal (8,739 kJ) for the man and 1,674 kcal (7,281 kJ) for the woman (Anonymous 1989; Margaria et al. 1963). This requirement is related more to distance than to pace (the faster the aerobic pace, the greater the rate of energy production, but the training distance will be covered in less time). This puts you as much as two meals behind in your daily nutritional requirements. Following this long run, energy intake needs to replace the energy lost. Muscle glycogen will deplete quickly with daily high-volume distance running unless it is replenished completely (Costill and Miller 1980).

It is recommended that athletes doing high-volume aerobic training maintain a diet composed of a mixture of 60% carbohydrate, 25% fat, and 15% protein to ensure adequate energy replacement (Hecker 1987). One problem for athletes doing such high-volume training—even those who do two training sessions each day instead of one long run, which still may total 18 or more miles per day (29 km/day)—is that they find it difficult to schedule several feedings of such high-carbohydrate items as baked potatoes, rice, sweet potatoes, and pasta. It thus becomes easy to enter a state of negative energy balance in which outgo exceeds intake. Athletes in hard training need at least 5 gm (though optimally 6 to 7 gm) of carbohydrate per kilogram of body weight per day. This problem of not being able to take in enough carbohydrates after a high-volume workout underscores the importance of periodic recovery days.

An interesting recent finding is that carbohydrate replacement immediately following training—within the first 90 min—will permit as much as 300% more carbohydrate assimilation (glycogen synthesis) than if it is delayed until a few hours postexercise (Ivy et al. 1988). Athletes typically do not eat much during this period immediately after training, as they are either traveling to or from their training site or ending their training session with a shower or massage. Carbohydrate replacement can be managed nicely by bringing liquid carbohydrate sources to the training site, readily available for immediate ingestion when the training session is finished. Dozens of commercially available energy/electrolyte beverages are now available, most of which contain carbohydrate polymers as well as simple sugars with an appropriate amount of commercial hype touting the excellence of one over the other as "the one to buy." There isn't any real advantage of one over another except individual taste preference or ease of purchase. They are easily digested and absorbed, refreshing, and acceptable in flavor. Such rapid posttraining intake of high-energy fluids provides a beneficial alternative to the solid forms of complex carbohydrates mentioned previously and ensures a high-energy intake when the body is most receptive to it.

Most of the research studies of fluid and energy intake dynamics have involved cyclists rather than runners, in part because of the interest in the nutritional needs of athletes engaged in multiday cycling competitions such as the Tour de France. There is no reason to believe that runners would have different metabolic dynamics than cyclists in terms of their daily energy needs, because they often have similar energy requirements during heavy training and competition. However, running is very different from cycling in terms of jostling of the viscera. If this adversely affects the absorptive characteristics of the intestinal tract, then runners as a group may be more diverse in their responses to fluid ingestion during training and competition.

Prerace Energy Loading

Most marathoners have experimented with various regimens suggested in the literature for topping up fuel reserves (especially carbohydrates) in the final few days preceding a marathon. This is popularly known as *carbohydrate loading*, and the strategies used by runners have been based on the concept of glycogen supercompensation described earlier. An earlier preference was to do a long depletion run several days before the race, include a day of noncarbohydrate intake (only protein), and then steadily taper the training and shift the dietary emphasis to complex carbohydrates, hoping to optimize glycogen supercompensation. The more recent preference is to eliminate the noncarbohydrate day. Really, what's best is what works for you. As always, the best advice is practice, practice, practice. Set up multiday regimens during your training that integrate both dietary and training patterns: a long depletion run followed by recovery and dietary loading and then either a hard, longer race (such as a 25- or 30-km event) or a long, hard training run. Keep accurate notes about your energy intake pattern and its apparent efficacy in terms of how you performed during the final race or long run.

Our experience with elite-level marathon runners suggests an increasing tendency not to tamper very much with established dietary habits before races. Instead, they (1) integrate a moderate-intensity longer run several days prerace into a framework that permits several days preceding the race of steady tapering and a slightly higher intake of complex carbohydrates, (2) eliminate the sometimes too stressful protein-only day, and (3) realize that increased fuel storage will occur automatically because of tapering the daily training load. Thus, energy intake exceeds energy outgo, and if the intake has a substantial carbohydrate emphasis (60% or more), the excess will be stored, providing the desired energy loading.

Another important strategy occurs during the several hours before the race. The idea is to top off fuel stores that were lost simply from the overnight fast and to ensure optimal fluid on board for the race. It does no good to drink excessive amounts of water hours before a race, as it will simply be excreted as urine for reasons that we shall discuss shortly. However, fluids ingested during the final hour prerace will still be in the process of being absorbed when the race begins. Then, as kidney blood flow diminishes because of the shunting of blood from the viscera to the skeletal muscles, this absorbed fluid will remain available for use by the body. A light carbohydrate meal 4 to 5 hr prerace, including such items as oatmeal, low-fat milk, unbuttered toast, and orange juice is easily absorbed and can top off fuel reserves quite nicely.

Contrasting this rather common practice of fuel intake several hours prerace, Oxford University biochemist Eric Newsholme (1986) suggests that carbohydrate-containing drinks and snacks be omitted from the near-race period and that just water be ingested. Costill and his co-workers (1977) pointed out some theoretical justification for refraining from carbohydrate ingestion from about 2 hr to 30 min prerace. Such ingestion typically increases insulin release into the blood, promoting glucose absorption throughout the body. The combination of insulin and an elevated blood sugar reduces the liver's usual glucose output into the bloodstream. Then, as the race begins, a gradually lowering blood sugar level deprives the working muscles of a steady glucose infusion until such time as insulin levels fall and liver output of glucose is restored. It would be preferable to maintain that steady infusion throughout the race.

What explains the difference between these theoretical views of eminent scientists and the real world of competitive sport? The answer might reside in the additional effects of increasing blood adrenaline levels as the starting time of the race approaches. Adrenaline mobilizes blood sugar from the liver and thus counteracts the insulin-induced energy storage.

Energy Intake During Marathon Racing

During the race many runners prefer to ingest only water, as it leaves no stickiness if spilled, has minimal chance for spoilage, and will be absorbed at least as quickly as most nutrient solutions. However, we have already emphasized the need for supplemental and continual glucose diffusion into the working muscles to provide a carbohydrate source to supplement falling muscle glycogen supplies. Current research suggests that you can ingest carbohydrate solutions of up to 7% to 8% with acceptable absorption and no reduction in total water intake. This provides a ready source of blood glucose for working muscles (Coyle et al. 1986; Tsintzas et al. 1995). Thus, the threefold combination of energy replacement during the race with energy-rich drinks, training-related fuel increases as a result of very long runs followed by adequate energy replenishment, and prerace carbohydrate loading is an important strategy to help optimize marathon race performance.

Variation among athletes makes none of these regimens uniformly tolerable by everyone's gastrointestinal system. Your own experimentation done as a part of very long training runs will provide the best practical information to develop a workable strategy for you. The gastrointestinal system typically functions best by habitual periodic activity as typified by eating three meals a day. Altering the system's functional pattern by introducing sizable changes in mealtimes and type of food ingested tends to increase the likelihood of dysfunction. Even mild diarrhea or constipation can be unpleasant and debilitating, particularly during a race. It would be sad to lose the rewards of months of preparation by experiencing stomach distress caused by inability to manage nutrient intake.

Ensuring Optimal Hydration

Although few popular world marathons are intentionally scheduled during hot-weather periods (exceptions being Honolulu and Bangkok), the chances are fairly good that some spring and early fall marathons may take place during unseasonably warm weather. The major summertime international world competitions, such as the Olympics and World Championships, however, are rather often awarded to cities with weather that ends up being warm to hot and often humid. Even if you are not training to race a warm-weather marathon, training in warm to hot weather must continue during the summer if competitive summertime fitness is to remain high, especially for the shorter-distance road-racing circuit. The body has a powerfully effective cooling mechanism in the form of evaporation of sweat from the body surface. This process is only effective when there are plenty of available body fluids. These can be obtained only by drinking.

For runners in hard training during almost all kinds of weather, drinking adequate quantities of fluids to ensure optimal muscle hydration is essential—remember that muscles are 75% water. How can training and racing be managed to cope with this problem of potentially dangerous fluid loss? Is simply drinking lots of fluids during and after such runs adequate for maintaining normal hydration? Or is it essential to drink plenty of fluids before such runs or races, especially during warm weather? Are there any alternative strategies that might be helpful?

The process of losing body fluids is termed *dehydration,* and it occurs typically because of a combination of excessive fluid loss (by sweating) and inadequate fluid intake (through drinking). Once body fluids have gotten excessively low, then one is said to be in a state of *hypohydration.* Fluid losses through sweat from fairly vigorous running on a warm day can easily reach 1 to 1 1/2 L/hr. For some who sweat profusely this loss can exceed 2 L/hr during the first few hours of a hot-weather race. Even under the best of conditions, however, fluid intake from absorption of ingested fluids will reach barely 1 L/hr. Thus, while fluid intake both during and after training and racing over long distances is important, having plenty of fluids on board *before* exercise begins is crucial.

During shorter training runs (less than an hour) and road races up to 10,000 m in length, elite-level runners typically do not drink fluids. Unless it is extraordinarily warm, the distance covered and the time of heat exposure are short enough that neither fluid nor energy losses are sufficient to impair performance. Also, fluids may not be conveniently available. In addition, during racing the high work intensity (90% or more of $\dot{V}O_2$max pace for a 10-km race) greatly reduces blood flow to the gastrointestinal system, because blood is shunted to the working skeletal muscles (for O_2 delivery) and skin (for heat dissipation). Thus, absorption is reduced, and runners may be left with a bloated feeling and possible gastrointestinal distress if they attempt to drink. Despite this situation for elite runners, it is common to provide fluids during large road races conducted in hot weather. Many of the slower runners who are not working so intensely may be out on the course for a much longer period. Indeed, their fluid losses may be great enough that fluid replenishment is essential.

Long training runs, however, and longer races (marathons and ultradistance events) occur at a slower pace. Not only does this slower pace make it easier for everyone to ingest fluids easily, but the possibility of large fluid loss makes drinking essential. During warm weather any run or race of a half-marathon distance or greater can produce a combination of hypohydration and energy depletion sufficient to impair performance in the majority of athletes: Their pace may slow, and some athletes may not even be able to finish the planned distance. The explanation for this impairment is simple. As hypohydration sets in, the body diminishes its skin blood flow and sweat rate to conserve remaining body fluid supplies. This reduction is necessary to ensure sufficient blood pressure to continue perfusion to the working muscles. But this can have severe consequences, because now the body's evaporative heat loss mechanism no longer functions adequately. Unless the pace is slowed drastically, continuing loss of evaporative potential from decreased skin blood flow very likely will cause the body to overheat, in turn causing potentially sizable performance decrements and even endangering health. During a long training run or a long competitive race, it would be preferable that neither pace slowing nor debilitation occur. Hyperhydration can help prevent them.

Glycerin-Induced Hyperhydration for Increasing Fluid Volume

One possible strategy for overcoming hypohydration during prolonged exercise in the heat—whether a long race or simply a very long training run—is to induce hyperhydration before the exercise. *Hyperhydration* means storing greater than normal amounts of water in the body. One might logically think that the simplest method for achieving this would be to drink a large volume of water or electrolyte drink. This would be absorbed directly into the bloodstream and increase the total circulating blood volume. For an interesting reason, this rapidly ingested fluid will quickly be urinated away. Within the cardiovascular system very sensitive receptors detect changes in blood volume, acting both rapidly and powerfully to keep it constant. This helps to explain the very long lines at the Port-a-Johns set up near the start line of road races! The kidneys have increased their urine output to compensate for the increased prerace drinking, and this will restore the blood volume to normal levels.

What is needed is a modified strategy that will permit the distribution of an increased fluid intake into *all* of the body's major fluid compartments—not just the intravascular compartment (the blood plasma), but also the two extravascular compartments, namely, the interstitial fluid between cells and the intracellular fluid within cells. This will minimize loss through urination. There is such a method for total-body hyperhydration, which involves the ingestion of a mixture of glycerin with water. Glycerin (or glycerol) is a naturally produced substance, is well tolerated by the body, and can be taken orally. By osmotic action, water absorbs along with the glycerin, and the combination distributes itself rapidly and evenly within all of the body's major fluid compartments.

The larger the fluid compartment, the more it will expand with glycerin infusion. All three aforementioned compartments contribute fluid to sweat, especially the two extravascular compartments. This results in little water loss via the kidneys because of minimal stimulation of the receptors that control the constancy of plasma volume. The plasma volume is the smallest of these compartments, but its percentage contribution to sweat is the largest. Thus, *glycerin-induced hyperhydration* through expansion of the two extravascular compartments provides a reservoir for maintaining plasma volume as fluid losses from sweating continue. In turn, this keeps the skin surface of the body cooler, maintains cardiac output, and delays the onset of fatigue. As the glycerin is metabolized during the period that includes the race or long training session, its osmotically bound water then becomes available to maintain the steadily decreasing blood volume. Glycerin is metabolized to dihydroxyacetone phosphate as part of the anaerobic portion of the pathway for glucose breakdown (recall figure 3.12) and thus is converted into usable energy.

Research studies involving the use of glycerin for runners in long-distance training or competition are not extensive, but some experimental results suggest a potential benefit. One well-known study (Lyons et al. 1990) was conducted at the University of New Mexico during the late 1980s. A half dozen recreational runners recruited from the Albuquerque area each agreed to do three 90-min treadmill runs in a hot, humid room over a several-week test period using three different fluid-replacement regimens. During one of these runs subjects were permitted to drink only a small amount of water, with a similarly small portion of water provided before the run. During another of the runs the subjects drank plenty of a water-and-orange-juice mixture and were permitted to drink a sizable amount of this before their run as well. During the remaining run glycerin was added to the water–orange-juice mixture to promote fluid retention and redistribution of fluid through the body fluid compartments.

Physiological responses were sought that might indicate whether the runners who hyperhydrated with glycerin and then drank adequate glycerin-containing fluid during the run were in fact more protected against heat injury than under the other two circumstances. When little fluid was ingested, not only was there minimal urination (the kidneys were retaining what little fluid was available), but also the body temperature rose considerably. When plenty of fluid without glycerin was ingested, urination was considerable, and the body temperature also rose. When fluids as well as glycerin were ingested, urination was less, and body temperature was not as high, suggesting that glycerin served to redistribute the water throughout the body and that plenty of fluid was available for use in evaporative cooling.

Since that study we have assisted several of our elite-level marathon runners, who were selected to national teams competing in hot weather, in the effective use of glycerin (Martin 1992). Our experience with marathoners at the 1991 Tokyo World Championships, the 1992 and 1996 Olympics, and the 1995 Mar del Plata Pan American Games suggests that prerace hyperhydration with glycerin-water can be very beneficial as an accompaniment to drinking during the race for helping to maintain adequate fluid volume.

An optimal amount of glycerin and water ingestion, which seems well tolerated in terms of no gastrointestinal discomfort and a practical level of hyperhydration, is 1 gm glycerin per kilogram of body weight mixed with 21 ml water per kilogram of body weight. Glycerin is easily obtainable from a local grocery or drug store; no prescription is needed. However, it is absolutely essential to realize that *glycerin cannot be ingested in its pure form* directly from the bottle. It must be greatly diluted with water—approximately 26-fold—before consumption. Because glycerin is heavier than water (with a density of 1.26 gm/ml compared with water at 1.00 gm/ml), 60 gm of glycerin, for example, occupies 47.6 ml of volume, whereas 60 gm of water occupies 60 ml of volume. This must be factored into any recipe for preparing a glycerin solution. Let's take some examples. A 60-kg (132-lb) male distance runner should add 48 ml of glycerin to $60 \times 21 = 1,260$ ml water, mix it, and then ingest it over a period of 1 to 2 hr before a marathon or long training run. (About 300 ml of water can be replaced by electrolyte drinks to add some flavor.) A female distance runner weighing 50 kg (110 lb) would prepare a solution containing $50 \times 21 = 1,050$ ml of water mixed with 40 ml of glycerin. The ratio of water to glycerin described here is about 26.2:1.

An equivalent Imperial conversion would be about 3 tablespoons of glycerin into 36 ounces (oz) of water (1 tablespoon = 14.8 ml, for a total of 44.4 ml of glycerin). In the U.S. fluid measurement system, 1 oz = 29.6 ml, whereas in the British system, 1 oz = 28.4 ml. Thus, 36 oz of water = 1,066 ml in the U.S. system or 1,022 ml in the British system. These ratios for water to glycerin (23:1 for the British system, 24:1 for the U.S.) are slightly more concentrated than in the aforementioned metric system. Both have been tolerated quite well by our runners with no side effects.

What is the best strategy for using glycerin? First, this is primarily intended for substantially long training runs or races (two hours or more) done in warm weather. For short training runs or races done during cool weather, fluid losses are not large, and glycerin loading is entirely unnecessary. Second, as with the techniques of energy intake previously described, practice the use of glycerin hyperhydration during long warm-weather runs *before* attempting its use in a race. Get clear answers to the relevant questions that will make this a workable technique for you. How long will it take to drink the glycerin-water mixture comfortably? How long before the run or race will be required before the fluid has cleared your gastrointestinal tract? Is it more palatable when mixed with an electrolyte beverage? Will you have a bloated feeling, and if so, when will it disappear? These important questions need thoughtful answers that can be obtained only through experience. It is essential to ensure that not only the required volume of fluid can be consumed, but also that gastrointestinal comfort with this prerace procedure is optimal.

Some final caveats about fluid intake during training and racing in the heat can also be offered (Gisolfi and Copping 1974). First, while fluids at a cooler temperature do help to cool the body, this is not as important as ensuring that fluids are indeed taken in, whether warm or cool, because it is their evaporation that provides the larger cooling potential. Second, prehydration with water or water-glycerin does not mean that it is unnecessary to drink *during* the long run or race. It is indeed important to drink during the activity as well, because of the potentially greater loss than gain of fluids during the same time period. Third, if there is a choice between drinking and splashing water over the head, although the latter probably feels better, the former will provide ultimately more cooling.

Preparing for and Delivering Successful Competitions

It was probably John Landy who first went on record as stating that he would rather lose in a very fast race than win in a very slow one. That's the mentality of a pacer—a runner who is essentially challenging the clock. In contrast, Seb Coe stated in a televised interview, "I have to give up so many things, make so many personal sacrifices to perform at my level, that I cannot even contemplate losing." If Landy was the classic pacer, then Coe was the consummate racer. As an athlete you will probably find yourself in both sets of shoes on one occasion or another—perhaps during the same race! You may even use pace as a tactic in its own right, although your inner predilection may be solely striving to win. Seb Coe's medals in two consecutive Olympic Games and then at the European Championships in Stuttgart were won in come-from-behind tactical battles. Many of his other top-level victories have come from shrewdly assessing the pace that the rest of the field could not manage and then proceeding to run away from them. Morocco's incredible Noureddine Morceli fits this mold in present-day major championship racing. Ideally, the best prepared athlete may be both racer and pacer: the complete athlete, developed optimally through multi-tier training, who needs only to select the correct ploy for the race at hand. An utterly simple desire, but so challenging to achieve!

Philosophical Considerations: Racer Versus Pacer

Each athlete has his or her own basic philosophy about winning and losing, about racing and pacing, determined partly by genes and partly by training.

Very few athletes are so gifted that their training eventually brings them to a level at which they have only themselves for competition. For these athletes the clock is the challenge. Younger athletes who are progressing faster than their peers may find themselves in this position. At the highest levels are athletes like Said Aouita, Ingrid Kristiansen, Seb Coe, Noureddine Morceli, and Haile Gebrselassie, who at various moments of their careers have been out in front of everyone else in performance capability. Typically, this is short lived, however, and eventually they all find that the competition dictates whether they will be racers or pacers.

The racer and the pacer form two ends of the spectrum of competitive mentalities. The pacer mentality is synonymous with the classic Olympic ideal, in which participation and doing one's best (running fastest) is what matters, not simply winning. The racer mentality takes the view that failing to win, regardless of the pace, is unacceptable. Every nation's sport journalism archive probably has its notable quote that drives home this desire to win. In Britain the 1,500-m and 5,000-m star Ian Stewart remarked, "First is first and second is nowhere." In the United States the late Green Bay Packer football coach Vince Lombardi tempered this thinking somewhat with a phrase that went something like "Winning isn't everything, but *wanting* to win is the only thing."

The desire to win is laudable for any athlete—it's the ultimate purpose that justifies training to compete. But athletes can run wonderfully and not win. Consider the field of athletes behind Haile Gebrselassie in that incredible Zürich Weltklasse world-record 5,000-m race on the evening of 16 August 1995. Tenth place was 13:10.20. Of those nine behind Gebrselassie, six achieved personal bests, and another athlete equaled his personal best. It was the best-ever marks for place for those who finished fifth and seventh through tenth. Should these runners have been disappointed at not winning? It depends on the extent to which they are more racer or pacer in their approach to sport. For the real racer, defeat is a very bitter pill to swallow, and rationalizing isn't easy.

In today's highly competitive world the choice of which camp to be in is not so simple. Very often three or four runners with similar ability find themselves racing each other, and all are very fit. Whatever the strategy, there is little room for error in planning exactly how best to utilize experience and aptitudes. If everyone holds back, it's a race of who has the fastest kick. If the pace is very fast from the start, then it's a race between those who have a combination of the greatest depth of fitness and natural talent. In both track and road races it is becoming ever more difficult to win with slower times unless conditions of heat or humidity are influential, and even then the work load is enormous. Thus, though an athlete may be interested primarily in winning (racing), the need to run the fastest possible time to win (pacing) may also be required. Here is where the confidence of knowing that you're fit as a result of having trained properly and optimally is of greatest ultimate benefit.

The decision of whether to be racer or pacer typically becomes blurred during actual competition, because in addition to those you are trying to defeat, you are also competing against yourself by attempting to do your best. On occasion you may find it appropriate to select specific races or set up special race conditions in which racing or pacing can be emphasized. In his initial athletic years Seb Coe had a burning desire to win every race. But as time passed and he approached the world's best in capabilities, he became desirous of challenging a standing record with a definitive performance, hoping to get the most out of himself and to push the record just a little farther from the hands of anyone else. This attitude inevitably led him to several of his world records in races that he selected as fitting optimally with his preparation and that had some form of prearranged pacesetting for the early stages.

Coaches have similar dilemmas in working with athletes: Do they desire racers or pacers? They would prefer to develop the optimally well-rounded athlete—the so-called Renaissance man or woman—and thus they are probably directed more toward producing winners. Athletes who are winners see themselves as successful, both as athletes and as people. The confidence they project as a result of their high self-esteem is perceived as desirable by others, and provides a source of admiration. The pursuit of excellence carries with it the idea of being number one, the very best. To challenge the best and win leaves no doubt. Coaches want their athletes to challenge the top spot, whether at the club, school, or world level. No one can win all the time, but a person's real character can develop and shine forth while he or she learns how to cope with both victory and defeat. That's also what keeps coaches interested in working with athletes: their interest in helping them be the very best athletes (and yes, the best people as well) that they can be.

Mental Preparation

It is unlikely that a maximal training effect is ever achieved if it is not carried out with a strict mental discipline and with full concentration on the task at hand. An important part of your training, therefore, ought to be devoted to developing the willpower and mental discipline required to endure arduous physical training and competitive preparation. We can define at least five especially important mental characteristics that ought to be developed in this regard. These are confidence, motivation, controlled aggressiveness, anxiety management, and relaxation. Let's describe each of these briefly.

Confidence

Regardless of the level of competition, success is most likely to come consistently when you are not only physically prepared but also rid of doubts about your readiness: You *know* you are as ready as you can be under the circumstances. There are two facets to this mental confidence. One relates to training. The sessions you completed had variety, and they were achievable. Although some training days were more successful than others—that's life—still, you have seen yourself improving in several areas. You have a clear awareness of your strong points and areas still needing improvement. You are prepared to design an effective race plan that takes advantage of your strengths. You and your coach have designed your training together, and he or she has assumed as much responsibility as you in ensuring that it is correct. The two of you have developed alternative training plans if you got sick or were injured. Each step along the way, the two of you have agreed that your revised plan is both acceptable and achievable. Confidence thus comes from being in control, being proactive, and being organized in your actions.

The other facet relates to competing. Wanting to win and even needing to win can be motivational in themselves, but at the starting line you must have everything together mentally and physically. To have made the decision genuinely in your own mind that "I am ready to race really well," or "I am ready to go after a victory" can be a very settling thought. It provides a frame of reference geared toward both a plan and control. The plan will require that you are prepared to endure some hardship as you try your best, and control will focus your mind toward racing with a specific purpose.

When you travel to competitions, especially as part of a team, small interferences can create large difficulties in maintaining a winning confidence. Changes that you had not predicted can add uncertainty or frustration. A roommate who snores, cafeteria food that is cold or greasy, transportation delays, a practice stadium that's locked instead of open—these complications and more can sap your energy and drain your confidence. Such problems can be minimized if you plan ahead, think clearly, and communicate well with the coaching staff or other appropriate authorities. It is better to expend energy in a positive way to create viable options than to expend the same amount complaining and achieving no solution to the problem. For your own individual trips, develop a checklist of important items to bring along (clothing, toiletries, snacks, competition schedule, telephone contacts, spikes or other unique competitive items, etc.) that give you your independence. Double-check predeparture details in advance to ensure that mistakes haven't been made and that you have set yourself up to be well looked after. As just one example, always check airline tickets when received to be sure your planned dates of departure and return are really on the ticket. Then call the airlines, make your seat assignments, and order special meals if available. Having better control over your own destiny enhances your confidence and reduces the effects of negative influences that are counterproductive to proper preparation.

An example of how mental attitudes are important in providing the environment for physical success, even over many months, can be found by briefly examining Seb Coe's preparation before the 1984 Los Angeles Olympic Games. During the first several months of 1984 Seb's physical preparation had progressed well, although it was delayed by illness. However, Seb was unsettled and unresolved in his attitude about being prepared adequately. Two years of setbacks had left him unsure of himself. He needed to get back into the proper mental state that befitted his level of training. Both Seb and coach decided that this was best done by Seb himself. The logic for that decision was quite simple: Even in a crowded competition, a track can be a lonely place. The larger the meeting, the lonelier it can become. When the big test comes, the athlete is out there on his or her own and had better have mind and body together. In Seb's case it was something he would have to do by himself, and it was crucial that he begin to do it well in advance of the Games. Thus, it was decided that his coach would not go with him for his several-week pre-Olympic training camp (summarized in table 7.7).

Shortly before making this decision, Seb had been defeated in a selection meeting, giving a poor performance in a slow time. His next race was in Oslo, where he won a top-class 800-m race in a very fast time. The change for the better had already commenced. Knowing when and how to intervene is the key to coaching, but the athlete must also have the self-discipline to accept that there are times when the coach can do little more. This is not coaching defeatism; it is simply being wise enough to know when a rich and heady brew is best left to its own fermentation. Seb traveled to the Chicago area and proceeded through his pre-Olympic preparation at his own pace. When coach and athlete next met for a visit at the Olympic Village, Seb was radiantly confident as never before, and no further verbal confirmation was required to his coach that all was well.

If nothing else, what is important here is that the athlete was permitted the freedom to get himself together. The stresses of travel, training, and acclimatizing to Olympic Village life were all very real, but they were Seb's to deal with. He knew it, and he set himself about doing it. This aggressive decision making, more than anything else, gave him the impetus he needed to begin the next phase, the competition. Even after winning his silver medal in the 800 m, Seb was happy and confident that a gold in the 1,500 m could be his. He was buoyant throughout the qualifying rounds—so much so after the semifinal that his coach was rash enough to tempt the gods by saying publicly that his athlete

TABLE 7.7

Training and Tapering for Competitive Excellence: Sebastian Coe's Five Weeks Before His 1984 Los Angeles 1,500-M Gold Medal

Week 1—38 mi

—Tue. 10 Jul: Fly 18 hours from England to Chicago; easy, yet steady P.M. run @ 6:00 to 6:30 per mile pace to get refreshed.

—Wed. 11 Jul: A.M. tempo session to ease into a faster pace and couple this with some speed endurance—3 × 1,600 m @ 4:40 per mile pace, 3-min recovery; cool-down of two laps @ 90-sec pace followed by easy jogging.

—Thu. 12 Jul: A.M. easy recovery run of 6 mi; P.M. a tempo session to turn Wednesday's A.M. tempo session into a continuous run—3 mi in 14:30.

—Fri. 13 Jul: Introduction to race pace, but not deeply anaerobic—after warm-up, 30 × 200 m @ 27/28 s; cool-down of 2 laps @ 90-s pace followed by easy jogging.

—Sat. 14 Jul: Lengthening the short-distance intervals and speed, but keeping good recovery—after warm-up, 2 x (3 x 300 m) @ 39 s, with 3-min recovery, 9 min between sets; cool-down of 2 laps @ 90-s pace followed by easy jogging.

—Sun. 15 Jul: Easy run of 6 mi for recovery, rest, rehabilitation, and "charging the battery."

Week 2—36 mi

—Mon. 16 Jul: The first of the harder tempo runs—A.M. after warm-up, 6 × 800 m @ 2:00 with 3-min recovery; cool-down of 2 laps @ 90-s pace followed by easy jogging; P.M. 4 mi easy.

—Tue. 17 Jul: The first cadence session—A.M. 5 mi easy; P.M. after warm-up, 10 × 100 m steady acceleration to 60 m, maximum speed to 80 m, then float to 100 m, walk back to start position and repeat.

—Wed. 18 Jul: Progressing from the Saturday 300-m session but run 2 s slower and as a single set—A.M. after warm-up, 6 × 300 m @ 41 s, with 3-min recovery; cool-down of 2 laps @ 90-s pace followed by easy jogging; P.M. 4 mi easy.

—Thu. 19 Jul: Short intervals to sharpen speed and still maintain a good heart/lung stimulus but keeping mileage low— A.M. after warm-up, 20 × 200 m @ 27/28 s; cool-down of 2 laps @ 90-s pace followed by easy jogging; P.M. 5 mi easy.

—Fri. 20 Jul: Adjusting to increasing speed with increasing distance—11 sprints, progressing in distance from 100 m to 200 m in 10-m increments, @ 14, 15, 16, 17, 18, 19, 20, 21, 22, 23, 24, 25 s, with jog-back recovery to the start position.

—Sat. 21 Jul: Maintained endurance run, but without locking into a set pace—6-7 mi including mixed accelerations (mini-fartlek).

—Sun. 22 Jul: Complete rest from running—traveled to Los Angeles and processed into Olympic Village.

Week 3—31 mi

—Mon. 23 Jul: Start of alternating hard and easy sessions, taking particular care not to carry over fatigue from the previous day; A.M. after warm-up, 6 × 800 m hard (@ 2:00 pace) with 2-min recovery; cool-down of 2 laps @ 90-s pace followed by easy jogging; P.M. 4 mi easy.

—Tue. 24 Jul: 30 min easy running over grassy slopes.

—Wed. 25 Jul: A 400-m session as part of progression from 200 m and 300 m; A.M. after warm-up, 6 × 400 m @ 51/52 s with 5-min recovery; cool-down of 2 laps @ 90-s pace followed by easy jogging; P.M. 5 mi easy.

—Thu. 26 Jul: 30 min easy running over grassy slopes.

—Fri. 27 Jul: Similar to 300-m intervals of 18 July but 2 s faster; A.M. after warm-up, 6 × 300 m @ 38/39 s with 3-min recovery; cool-down of 2 laps @ 90-s pace followed by easy jogging; P.M. 5 mi easy.

—Sat. 28 Jul: Complete rest from running.

—Sun. 29 Jul: Not as fast as Wednesday, but shorter recoveries—after warm-up, 400 m/600 m/400 m/300 m/200 m in 55/ 82/53/36/25 s; cool-down of 2 laps @ 90-s pace followed by easy jogging.

Week 4—24 mi

—Mon. 30 Jul: Interval pace maintained, but recovery reduced; A.M. 4 mi easy; P.M. after warm-up, 6 × 300 m @ 38/39 s with 2-min recovery; cool-down of 2 laps @ 90-s pace followed by easy jogging.

—Tue. 01 Aug: A.M. 4 mi easy; P.M. a first session to maintain the feeling of 800-m race pace—after warm-up, 10 × 200 m @ 27 s with 2-min recovery; cool-down of 2 laps @ 90-s pace followed by easy jogging.

—Wed. 02 Aug: A second session to maintain the feeling of 800-m race pace—after warm-up, 3 × 400 m @ 52/51/51 s; cool-down of 2 laps @ 90-s pace followed by easy jogging.

—Thu. 03 Aug: Rest, but some easy jogging to stay loose.

—Fri. 04 Aug: A.M. easy 3 mi, including some strides during the run; P.M. race 800-m heat #1; late evening easy jogging to stretch the legs.

—Sat. 05 Aug: Exactly identical to Friday; race 800-m heat #2.

—Sun. 06 Aug: A.M. easy jogging to stretch the legs and stay loose; P.M. race 800-m semifinal; late evening easy jogging to stretch the legs.

Week 5—17 mi

—Mon. 07 Aug: A.M. easy jogging if desired; P.M. 800-m final.

—Tue. 08 Aug: 8 mi easy running; no fast-paced racing-style efforts.

—Wed. 09 Aug: No fast-paced racing-style efforts; 10 × 100 m easy strides and accelerations.

—Thu. 10 Aug: A.M. 3 mi easy plus a few faster paced strides than those of Wednesday; P.M. race 1,500-m heat #1; late evening easy jogging to stretch the legs.

—Fri. 11 Aug: A.M. easy jogging as desired; P.M. race 1,500-m semifinal; late evening easy jogging to stretch the legs.

—Sat. 12 Aug: A.M. easy jogging as desired; race 1,500-m final.

Note. In the preceding summary, note carefully the pattern of progression of interval running. The principle is simple: First, establish the speed, then begin decreasing the recovery time to bring speed endurance into focus. This is done by eliminating the added rest time between sets. The intermediate step is a slight reduction of speed in going from sets to a continuous series of runs, with gradual return to the faster speed. This can best be done by simultaneous reduction in quantity of training. Speed and freshness become foremost in the athlete's mind, both of which are crucial for racing.

would win. Once again, coach and athlete were together; the coach's confidence now added to Seb's increasing knowledge that indeed everything was coming together. At the final race Seb went to the line with a determined "This medal is mine" attitude, and it was going to be very difficult to defeat him. No one did.

Motivation

Motivation is defined simply as the urge to succeed, and figure 7.8 identifies two basic types of motivation. One is an urge to succeed that originates from outside your own psyche: That's *extrinsic*. Recognition and praise from others, monetary rewards, a love of trophies all have little to do with any inner desire to succeed, but they can strongly influence your desire to perform well. We believe it is preferable to have motivation that is *intrinsic*, that is, to have the urge to do well because it gives you great personal pleasure and a sense of inner achievement. Malcolm Firth, a national coach to the British Cycling Federation, once remarked that "in the last analysis the athlete who aspires to the very top must have a high degree of self-motivation [that's intrinsic] and enthusiasm for the task. Athletes who get to the top and *remain there* [our emphasis] are capable of pulling themselves out of the depths of despair that overtake all athletes at some stage of their career."

No one enjoys the challenge of returning to quality fitness after an illness, injury, or other serious setback. But once such problems occur, athletes who are motivated intrinsically have a better chance of returning to their former greatness. What attributes characterize intrinsically motivated athletes, and can these be developed? There are two features that seem innate within us all, but to varying degrees: our perception of competence and our perception of control over the situation. It's anyone's guess as to whether these traits can be developed by coaching, but we can list five additional factors that we believe could be incorporated into a training lifestyle to benefit the athlete:

- Be involved in the design of your own training plan.
- Take pride in your performances.
- Work toward attainable goals.

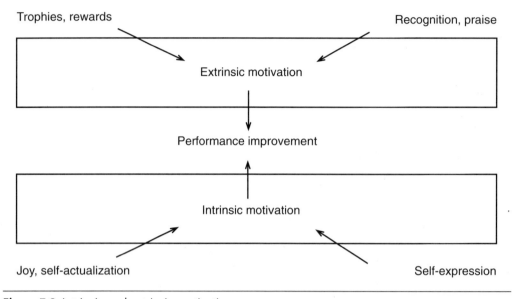

Figure 7.8 Intrinsic and extrinsic motivation.

- Evaluate your progress periodically; take the time to review these factors as a form of conscious self-assessment with a view toward self-improvement.

- Above all, enjoy what you are doing; take a genuine self-interest in training and competing, for this is what motivation is all about.

It was such contemplation and such attitudes that kept Seb Coe in the proper frame of mind after his withdrawal (due to illness) from the 800-m final in the 1986 Commonwealth Games. He needed to recover, regroup, take positive action, and continue on his course toward good performances at the European Championships just over a month later (where he earned his coveted first and only major championship 800-m gold medal).

Controlled Aggressiveness

In running, *aggressiveness* is best identified as a single-minded determination to prevail over the opposition at all costs, within the rules. In a race it can be demonstrated by unleashing an irresistible tactical maneuver at precisely the proper moment. Concentration and aggressiveness are interwoven inextricably in a successful athlete. Single-minded pursuit of any goal requires concentration to shut out the trivial. Aggressive behavior added to this concentration can make the athlete flourish. There is a lot of possessiveness—almost a greediness—in this behavior. Those who heard Keith Brantly's prerace assertion, "When I'm gone, I'm gone," as his planned strategy to break away from the pack at 5 mi into the 1989 Gasparilla 15-km Distance Classic in Tampa have a perfect example. His two months of prerace preparation had been flawless, and his confidence and motivation were both very high. The competitive field, however, was so good that only a powerfully decisive burst of aggressive action—in the form of a sudden, maintained, and powerful surge in race pace—could be effective. It was, and his 42:50 victory was the third-fastest time in the race's 12-year history.

It should be clear, then, that aggressiveness in sport is beneficial only if it is controlled, that is, used at the proper moment and directed within reason toward a successful performance. All too often stories surface about athletes completing an absolutely awesome track session several nights before a weekend competition, ostensibly as a confidence-builder, only to be metabolically flat as a pancake on race day, delivering a dismal performance. Here, their aggressiveness was prematurely directed. Their previous overall development should have given them the required confidence, with no need for a race-quality effort before the actual race to provide last-minute assurance. That final track session should serve more to keep the engine fine-tuned than to damage the cylinders. Focus your aggressiveness toward your competition rather than toward your own self-destruction!

Anxiety Management

Anxiety is a form of nervous tension that typically arises out of fear. Fear can rear its ugly face in many ways:

- We fear the unknown, not knowing how we will perform.
- We fear failing, or looking bad during a competition.
- We fear letting down those we hold in esteem.
- We fear danger.
- We may be intimidated by our opponents.

Still another source of anxiety for athletes is that the greater the importance assigned to a race, the greater the fear of not performing well. A national championship or the Olympic Games are very different from a small local sports meeting. As an athlete, you are well aware of the concept of being *psyched*—too much, not enough, or just enough—for a competition or for training. The term relates to the interaction between arousal and attentiveness. In figure 7.9 performance quality is plotted as a function of the extent of arousal. An inverted-U relationship results. Simply stated, *best performances come from being aroused optimally* (at the top of the curve) in terms of mobilizing nervous energy. Under- or overarousal often results in poor performance. Attentional focus is also important: Attention directed too broadly, too intensely, or too negatively detracts from performance.

The fear of losing can be lessened in a way that reduces total anxiety. This may improve the outcome of an upcoming performance. Again, think positively. Don't fear the worst or consider how disappointed you will be with a poor effort. Instead, use this attitude: "I'm going to see just how fit I am, and if I don't win I'm going to assess what still needs to be done for improvement; then I'll have the means for a better race next time." An understanding coach can suggest these subtle differences in attitudes about appraising performance and in so doing can reduce considerably an athlete's level of anxiety. Fear of the opposition is, of course, normal to some extent, unless everyone else in the competition is indeed considerably inferior to you in abilities, and then perhaps you shouldn't be in that race. Fear, along with other emotions, contributes to the required elevated state of arousal. It merely needs to be reduced and placed in its proper perspective as a useful motivating factor.

Thus, reducing anxiety is all about developing confidence, which in turn is best achieved by having knowledge. It's trite but true: Knowledge is power. Incorporate into your lifestyle those attitudes and behaviors that center around being knowledgeable: assess yourself, listing positive attributes and things to work on. Compliment yourself regarding your positive traits, and work on being better. You then become in better control of your own destiny, which reduces anxiety because you are doing the best you can.

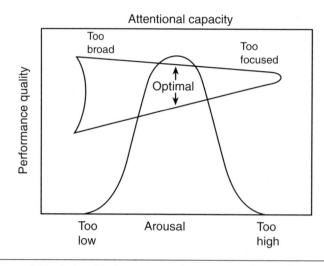

Figure 7.9 The inverted-U relationship between performance quality and arousal level and its relationship to attentional capacity.

Relaxation

Relaxation is a governor of excessive anxiety: It reduces nervous tension that can detract from optimal performance. The purpose of relaxation when an athlete is already motivated for competition may already be obvious. How can you prepare to stay on top of the inverted U when it's time for competition? Balance anxiety with relaxation. Figure 7.10 illustrates a wide variety of tasks and activities that you may find useful to incorporate as part of your precompetition game plan. Note again that the emphasis is on objective and positive goal-oriented tasks. When completed, these tasks contribute to the confidence that you are doing the best possible things for preparation.

Each successive level of activity in figure 7.10, indicated by roman numerals, is more specific and occurs closer to the time of competition. Thus, well before any important race you will have evaluated your training success, included adequate racing simulations, and considered possible applicable racing strategies. You will have done this days or weeks before the competition. Such objective assessment reduces the anxiety that comes with panicked judgment of fitness that might arise when embellished stories circulate about almost unbelievable training accomplishments of competitors.

Consistency of readying procedures should also reduce the incidence of anxiety. A master checklist of what's required when you travel to a competition will minimize the need for sudden, frenzied activity during last-minute packing. Do not try dramatically new preparation techniques without having practiced them at home. Identify what has worked best previously, and at the same time keep an open mind toward including improvements.

The finishing touches to optimal competitive readiness are often found in your prerace warm-up. Ensure that this is not so ritualized and specialized that it cannot be adapted to different conditions, which may cause you irritability. At this moment you as well as your competitors will be reaching your highest levels of pre-event focusing. You are now a different person from who you are during periods of noncompetitive social interaction. Statements made to you by friends or coaches may be interpreted quite differently or unknowingly ignored. These changes from the norm can be sources of frustration and misunderstanding to both parties. It is here that being alone can be an advantage. Coaches

I. Expectations in performance
   A. Know what you can do: Assess your training.
   B. Practice possible racing scenarios using simulation.

II. Consistency in readying procedures
   A. Before a competition get a good night's sleep.
   B. Ensure suitable meals and adequate fluid replacement evening before a competition.
   C. During training practice any new racing innovations to be tried.
   D. Maintain familiar, previously effective routines.

III. Optimal competitive readiness
   A. Prepare as you did before previous best performances.
   B. Arrive early enough to ensure a proper warm-up.
   C. Strive for an optimal attentional (mental, emotional) state.

IV. Use autogenic relaxation, imaging, and focusing
   A. Relax
      1. Develop mental images (words, experiences, colors, etc.) that evoke a relaxation response when brought to mind.
      2. Reduce excessive muscular tension to levels similar to those at the top of the inverted U.
   B. Image
      1. Imagine performing the event as desired for best results.
      2. If you imagine that you can do well, then the psychological environment for doing well is optimal.
   C. Focus
      1. Concentrate on one or two relevant elements of the competition.
      2. Do not be overattentive to irrelevant cues.

Figure 7.10 Task/activity sequence, with minimal anxiety risk, to permit an orderly approach to competition.

must also realize that you are a different person; they should minimize the detailed instructions or last-minute advice. Only relevant cues for that race are needed or appropriate.

The use of *autogenic* (self-induced) *relaxation* can be effective in reducing excessive muscular tension. Powerful emotions are often accompanied by muscular tension in various parts of the body. Such tension is needlessly energy wasteful, much like when an automobile engine idles too fast. Thought processes directed toward returning to more manageable levels of neuromuscular tone will thus reduce the overall level of arousal. For some, a single word or phrase or recalling a particular experience elicits memories of activity sufficiently low-key to bring about relaxation of excessively tense musculature.

Two other techniques, *imaging* and *focusing*, can assist in relaxation. Mentally picturing the race as you would ideally like it to proceed or imagining yourself delivering the correct racing response to specific attacks by competitors is effective in removing anxieties about fear of failure. You are taking positive action and acting with control, which are less fearful by nature. This kind of behavior serves as a prelude for the final prerace (and even during-race) task of focusing. Identify and prioritize the primary focal points on which you will base your race assessment as it develops. Is it not losing contact with the leaders? Is it remembering to use strong arm action and lift with hip flexors to better attack hills in cross-country or road races? Is it not being boxed in behind the leader in a track race, unable to change position? Focusing squarely on key items permits quicker response when most appropriate.

A number of quite good books have emerged in recent years on sport psychology. Though some of these deal with sport in general (Bell 1983; Elliott 1984; Loehr 1994; Orlick 1990; Vernacchia, McGuire, and Cook 1992), some include considerable useful emphasis on running events (Lynch 1987; Nideffer 1976). As an athlete, you would do well to read as many of these as possible; the psychological aspect of sport preparation is as integral a part of total development as the physiological aspect. When the two work as one, the synergism is incredibly powerful.

Tactical Preparation

It has often been said that tactics are only the icing on the cake, and the basis of racing is fitness and preparation. Back in the 1960s when a few New Zealand runners were seemingly on top of the distance-running world, their coach, Arthur Lydiard, suggested that the days of utilizing tactics were numbered. When well-trained athletes were running at their limit, tactics wouldn't be used because everyone would be maintaining a fairly similar pace to optimize efficiency, each hoping he or she had more left at the end than anyone else. Indeed, in many close, fast races this often is true. But just as often tactics can add a sparkle of decisiveness that clearly sets the stage for the supremely fit athlete to run away with a victory.

The use of tactics, however, need not be left until the race itself. In training, tactics can be practiced as you prepare for specific race requirements. Identify any aspect about the manner in which a race may need to be run to achieve victory, and then plan for it during your period of training. One anecdote from Seb Coe's experience involves his contending with Steve Ovett's enormous talent for suddenly surging very quickly over the final few hundred meters of mile and 1,500-m races. In response to this, some very specific sessions in Seb's training were directed at giving him practice in starting a finishing kick from a variety of paces with the goal of then maintaining the fastest speed possible for as long as possible. This gradually improved Seb's mental and physical ability to cope with such race problems. When Steve Ovett then unleashed a furious sprint, though it may have been debilitating to most competitors, it wasn't for Seb, who confidently countered with equal fury.

Remember that the tactics available to any athlete will depend in part on genes and in part on race preparation. If your attributes don't allow you to "perform like a sprinter," then don't plan to rely on a fast finish as the key to success. Perhaps you are a better front-runner, more able to maintain a steady fast pace throughout that is just a little too fast for all the rest. Select your best option and go with it. An excellent example of this was seen when Ingrid Kristiansen established a lead of as much as 15 s, beginning with lap 2 in her 10,000-m final at the 1987 Rome World Championships. Returning from a period of injury without having had opportunities to hone her speed, she was concerned that a sprint down the final straightaway would more likely play into the hands of runners who had excellent speed training, such as the Soviet Union's Elena Zhupieva. Ingrid opted valiantly to maintain a very lonely position well out in front of the greatest field of women's 10,000-m runners that had ever been assembled. She eked out a victory by a scant 3.55 s as Elena's brilliant 61.1-s final 400 m came not quite close enough to surpass Ingrid's sense of lonely but sustainable pace in front.

Being Prepared for Important Races

Whatever the basic tactic that you have opted to employ, you simply must be on par with your finest competitive abilities at your top-level meetings, wherever they might be. Thus, a mix of intelligent training, tapering, and handling of prerace details becomes a very important consideration for both athlete and coach. After every race a debriefing of sorts should be done, with written notes made of what could have been improved—from all viewpoints. Later as these notes are re-read, further consideration will add more accuracy. Eventually a pattern will emerge of the overall strategy that is most effective for you when racing season arrives.

At major competitions it is sometimes incredible how penalizing even the slightest deviation from peak form can be, and it hurts here the most, particularly if it prevents you from advancing through heats or semifinal rounds. A few illustrations will make the situation painfully clear. As a theoretical example, let's consider a 1,500-m final race for a male athlete that will be won in 3:35, a time that is also his personal record. To be only 1/2 of 1% below this ability is to concede 7 m, roughly 1.08 s—enough to leave him unplaced in a tight finish. As a historical example, let's again consider that amazing 1983 Helsinki World Championships men's 10,000-m final. It was won in 28:01.04, a time slower than the personal best times of most of the finalists. If you had been in the race, and ran 1/2 of 1% slower than Alberto Cova's winning time, you would have been 8.4 s back, relegated to 9th place! In each of the two heats, the same closeness prevailed: 1/2 of 1% back of the winning time would have been 9th place for the faster heat (won in 27:45.54), 11th place for the slower (won in 28:04.69).

Top-level finals in the longer distances usually tend not to be quite so close and so deep at the same time. But great care must be reserved for the qualifying rounds. Very close races may occur when a large group of runners, who have not run a completely exhausting race because they are keeping as much in reserve as possible for the upcoming final, make a final dash to the finish tape. As a specific example, consider the two semifinal races of the 1988 Seoul Olympic Games men's 5,000 m. The first race was won in 13:22.44, the second in 13:24.20. In either race, finishing 1 s behind the winner would have meant eighth place. In each race the top six finishers qualified for the final by place, and the seventh qualified by time. In the second semifinal, only 0.61 s separated first place from seventh! The lessons to be learned are the following:

- Be sure your sense of pace is excellent for proper acceleration during the final stages.
- Develop a readily mobilizable speed component during training to permit such acceleration.
- Aim always for qualification on the basis of place rather than time.

The tapering period for a major race is as important as the training and actual competition. When we recall that the *training process* consists of the *breakdown phase* (the training) and the *building-back phase* (the recovery), *tapering* becomes the final aspect of the recovery process. Several guiding principles might assist in final preparation. First, when a racing phase is about to begin, particularly for middle-distance runners, the more endurance-oriented aspects of training (such as long runs) are replaced by rest, recovery runs, or some form of interval training (recall our discussion of periodization in chapter 6). Marathoners fit into a special category here, as their racing phase may be only one event, requiring little final preparation in the way of quicker-paced, shorter-distance intervals. For all events the mental state of an athlete prepared for racing is not conducive to coping with continued serious training.

Second, to permit the supercompensation phase of recovery to have full effect, rest during the period of tapering should be considerable. Give the body time to heal itself. Third, the quickness aspect of the training process, rather than the endurance aspect, begins to deteriorate first when training ceases or dramatically decreases. Thus, faster sessions ought to be the mainstay of maintenance training during a tapering phase. The athlete begins to "think speed" in the context of feeling fresh and desirous of racing; both feelings are essential in producing a mentality geared toward racing to win. Shorter, faster training sessions can maintain cardiovascular and neuromuscular systems in a high state of readiness between races scheduled over a period of a few weeks. And the developing freshness should make it possible to manage these sessions more quickly, which in turn gives a psychological boost.

More careful analysis of table 7.7, which summarizes Seb Coe's pre-Los Angeles Olympic Games pattern of final preparation, shows how these concepts were utilized effectively. Our old friends—volume, intensity, density, and frequency—were adjusted to permit reduction in total work but maintenance of quickness. Seb commenced with 200-m interval runs, initially with full recoveries. These intervals were then gradually reduced in number, with recovery maintained and then discontinued as faster work was introduced. Similarly, the 300-m repetitions began during week 1 as two separate sets of three, run fairly quickly but with adequate recovery between repetitions and added recovery between sets. The running time was steadily decreased (the pace was increased) and the recovery time shortened (but each week only one variable was altered). This same logic was continued with the 800-m runs. Always the emphasis was on staying sharp (fresh and quick), ensuring good form, not getting tired, and feeling good about the results. Although some might call these "buildup" weeks to the Olympic Games, the difficult, exhausting work had been built up many weeks before—this was tapering! By use of short-distance, faster-paced work (200 m, 300 m, 400 m) as well as longer-distance, slower-paced work (1,600-m runs and a pyramid-style combination of 200-m, 300-m, 400-m, and 600-m runs), the multitier training philosophy was maintained in a context of work reduction to ensure freshness when required.

SUMMARY

Running Your Best Race

1. Running quickly and intelligently during races provides the best opportunity for victory. To run quickly, an athlete must develop fatigue resistance, strength, and speed. Running intelligently demands proper management of pace and tactics. The longer the race distance, the greater the influence on racing effectiveness of such factors as heat, humidity, wind, and the dynamics of energy replacement.

2. In any race, it is crucial to (a) be prepared physically and mentally, (b) run efficiently but effectively, (c) be poised to act and react as necessary to remain in the best possible position to win, and (d) use tactics as appropriate to gain additional advantage. Every race will be unique but will have striking similarities to other races. Learning from every race you run should be an important goal.

3. If you are successful, you have geared your preparation to match all possible needs of the distance being raced. These include (a) scheduling appropriate proportions of aerobic and anaerobic work, (b) completing race-scenario simulations, (c) assessing personal strengths and weaknesses as well as those of competitors, and (d) improving your intuitive sense of manageable pace.

4. The best competitor is one who is completely fresh: physically tapered, well hydrated and well fueled, and mentally confident. When training load is reduced, speed is lost more quickly than endurance. Thus, during tapering, reduce the volume of endurance training and maintain speed. The accompanying volume reduction permits physical recovery and builds increasing hunger for competition. With motivation and confidence high and aggressiveness and anxiety under control, good racing is the logical sequel.

5. Although a mind-set focused on an excellent race effort is essential, winning is not always of sole importance. A personal best may be satisfaction enough. In the heats of semifinals, however, the primary goal is to advance to the next round of competition; racing for place here is the foremost priority.

6. When you race against peers, there are no guaranteed formulas for winning any race, let alone every race, because the possible strategies are limitless. Being fit and well trained are essential. But being alert, sharp-witted, and ready to respond are all virtues that increase the chances for achieving your best performance. Excessive mental rehearsal can leave you perplexed and beaten before the race, particularly if it has produced a plan that cannot be amended or dropped in an instant for a better alternative that fits changing circumstances.

7. Remember to put competitive sport into the perspective of your overall life. Success in sport is not final, and failure is not fatal. What is important is to work hard to be better than you were yesterday and the best that you can be today. Competitive sport is and must be only a wonderful game whose rules set an exciting stage for helping you achieve the best years of your life. So do the very best you can, and put the results into a healthy perspective.

References

Anonymous. 1989. *Walking and running.* Alexandria, VA: Time-Life Books.

Bell, K.F. 1983. *Championship thinking.* Englewood Cliffs, NJ: Prentice-Hall.

Buoncristiani, J., and Martin, D.E. 1993. Factors affecting runners' marathon performance. *Chance* 6(4):24-30.

Costill, D.L.; Coyle, E.; Dalsky, G.; Evans, E.; Fink, W.; and Hoopes, D. 1977. Effects of elevated plasma FFA and insulin on muscle glycogen usage during exercise. *Journal of Applied Physiology* 43:695-699.

Costill, D.L., and Miller, J.M. 1980. Nutrition for endurance sport: Carbohydrate and fluid balance. *International Journal of Sports Medicine* 1:2-14.

Coyle, E.F.; Coggan, A.R.; Hemmert, M.K.; and Ivy, J.L. 1986. Muscle glycogen utilization during prolonged strenuous exercise when fed carbohydrate. *Journal of Applied Physiology* 61:165-172.

Dwyer, T., and Dyer, K.F. 1984. *Running out of time.* Kensington: New South Wales University Press.

Elliott, R. 1984. *The competitive edge.* Englewood Cliffs, NJ: Prentice-Hall.

Gisolfi, C.V., and Copping, J.R. 1974. Thermal effects of prolonged treadmill exercise in the heat. *Medicine and Science in Sports and Exercise* 6:108-113.

Hecker, A.L. 1987. Nutrition and physical performance. In *Drugs and performance in sports,* ed. R.H. Strauss, 82-151. Philadelphia: Saunders.

Hultman, E., and Bergstrom, J. 1967. Muscle glycogen synthesis in relation to diet studied in normal subjects. *Acta Medica Scandinavica* 182:109-117.

Ivy, J.L.; Katz, A.L.; Cutler, C.L.; Sherman, W.M.; and Coyle, E.F. 1988. Muscle glycogen synthesis after exercise: Effect of time of carbohydrate ingestion. *Journal of Applied Physiology* 64:1480-1485.

Loehr, J.E. 1994. *The new mental toughness training for sports.* New York: Penguin Books.

Lynch, J. 1987. *The total runner.* Englewood Cliffs, NJ: Prentice-Hall.

Lyons, T.P.; Riedesel, M.L.; Meuli, L.E.; and Chick, T.W. 1990. Effects of glycerol-induced hyperhydration prior to exercise in the heat on sweating and core temperature. *Medicine and Science in Sports and Exercise* 22:477-483.

Margaria, R.; Cerretelli, P.; Aghemo, P.; and Sassi, J. 1963. Energy cost of running. *Journal of Physiology* 18:367-370.

Martin, D.E. 1992. Glyzerin als Marathon-Wundermittel? *Der Läufer* 9(5):46-48.

Newsholme, E.A. 1986. Application of principles of metabolic control to the problem of metabolic limitations in sprinting, middle-distance, and marathon running. *International Journal of Sports Medicine* 7(suppl. 1):66-70.

Nideffer, R.M. 1976. *The inner athlete.* New York: T.Y. Crowell.

Orlick, T. 1990. *In pursuit of excellence: How to win in sport and life through mental training.* 2nd ed. Champaign, IL: Human Kinetics.

Tsintzas, O.K.; Williams, C.; Singh, R.; Wilson, W.; and Burrin, J. 1995. Influence of carbohydrate-electrolyte drinks on marathon running performance. *European Journal of Applied Physiology* 70:154-160.

Vernacchia, R.A.; McGuire, R.T.; and Cook, D.C. 1992. *Coaching mental excellence.* Dubuque, IA: Brown and Benchmark.

Watman, M., and Matthews, P. 1995. Epic world records at Zürich. *Athletics International* 3(21):1.

Wischnia, B. 1993. The road warrior. *Runner's World* 28(9):76-83.

8

MANAGING BALANCED TRAINING

Training in any form—intervals, long runs, a weight-lifting session—is stressful. The good news about stress is that the body can adapt well to a variety of fairly enormous loads—both in quality and quantity. But the bad news is that there is a limit: If one "goes over the edge," the consequences very often can be disastrous. Be it injury, illness, or, even worse, a state of chronic fatigue known variously as burnout, overreaching, overtraining, and staleness—the end result is that a distance runner's days as a fit, competitively successful athlete are stopped, temporarily or forever. The purpose of this concluding chapter is to have a look at the continuum between adequate training, which brings improvement, and excessive training, which is counterproductive to improvement from any of several consequences: injury, physical burnout, and mental staleness.

Fatigue: A Natural Consequence of Training

It is useful to view the *training process* as a two-step *stimulus-response* pattern. The *stimulus* is provided by the work done, be it a long run, an interval session, or a session in the weight room. The stimulus causes many alterations in normal body and mental functioning. The *response* by the athlete over time, one hopes, is full physiological and mental recovery from these alterations and ideally some adaptation such that eventually an even stronger work load can be tolerated. This stimulus can be short lived, as with a given day's assignment. Or, it can be longer lasting, as with the work load over an entire few-week microcycle. Similarly, the response can be short term, as with an overnight recovery, or long term, as with the improvement in fitness during a training microcycle. Many of these adaptive processes were described in chapters 2, 4, 5, and 6. Harvard University physiologist Walter Cannon described the physiological alterations in

387

1929, coining the term *homeostasis* to refer to those dynamic, self-regulating processes by which the body's internal cellular environment is maintained at a constant level of function.

Let's take a simple example. During a long weekend aerobic run on a warm day, evaporative cooling will cause a sizable depletion of body fluids. Partial depletion of energy reserves will also occur, causing hunger. Mild accumulation of metabolites such as lactic acid in working muscles may cause muscle cell swelling as water moves in to restore the osmotic balance. Stiffness and a sense of fatigue may result. During the body's recovery process in the hours after the run, increased thirst and hunger promote ingestion of sufficient fluids and fuels to promote restoration of nutrient, electrolyte, fluid, and fuel supplies. Massage, a relaxing bath, and a good night's sleep also promote restoration of normal cell function. Ideally, the next day finds the athlete feeling fresh, rested, and able to train effectively.

During the training process the work load stimulus of hard work causes a partial breakdown, or *catabolism*, of tissue integrity in both skeletal muscle cells and their associated connective tissues. Sensations of fatigue and soreness, as well as energy and electrolyte imbalances in the working muscles, are common. Psychological changes, such as tiredness and decreased motivation, that parallel the physiological changes also occur. During the subsequent recovery phase, intracellular metabolic function is restored back to the prestimulated state or even beyond (this is called *anabolism*), thereby providing recovery and, one hopes, enhancement of performance ability. Psychologically, increased vigor and the urge to compete return as well. This is really homeostasis in action.

Thus, the rewards from the physical aspects of training come *after* recovery, when a sense of freshness replaces the dullness of fatigue, and performance abilities are improved. A key ingredient to achieving a successful race effort, therefore, is performing under the influence of an optimal combination of the beneficial effects of physical training and recovery. Ideally, when it is time for an athlete's major competitions, the adaptive effects of training should by far dominate over any residual detrimental debilitating effects of fatigue. The art of achieving optimal athletic preparation is therefore in designing a breakdown stimulus as challenging as can be managed, followed by an appropriate recovery period that is timed to bring the athlete into the competition period in perfect condition for an excellent performance. Unfortunately, a very small difference exists between training just enough for optimal preparation and good health and training too much, which can bring injury, illness, staleness, or a combination of these. Both science and artistry are involved on the part of athletes, coaches, and their technical support people to ensure that this threshold of excessive total stress load is not reached.

We've mentioned previously a variety of strategies for incorporating specific kinds of training stimuli into a successful developmental program. If it hasn't been clearly enough emphasized thus far, let us mention again that the essence of optimal training is in getting the mix correct. Along with doing the proper kinds of training, there are three simple points:

- Don't do too much.
- Ensure plenty of time for recovery.
- Remember that being mentally hungry and physically fresh will win far more races than being mentally and physically flat.

Thus, the proper response to the oft-heard phrase "You can never do enough training" ought to be "But is it really necessary?" What differentiates the fatigue sensed after a hard day of training—but which goes away after a day or two—from the far-worse, seemingly chronic condition of poor performance that has often been given names such as burnout and overtraining? What causes limb soreness? Is it a problem with the muscles, with their associated connective tissues, or with both? Does excessive fatigue or soreness in muscle tissues represent injury? If so, what is the causal mechanism of such injury? Is there truth to the oft-heard comment that the incidence of illness and injury increases when an athlete is in an overtrained or stale state? If so, what causes this susceptibility? When athletes get so overtrained that staleness results, what explains the very long time required for recovery? How can overtraining be avoided? How does an athlete strike a balance between quantity of training and adequate recovery to permit optimal adaptive benefits for beginning the ensuing training or competitive phase? It is far easier to ask these questions than to provide answers.

In this chapter we will attempt to identify how the transition from acceptable, challenging training, to which physiological adaptation can occur, can progress to unacceptable training, in which excessively difficult work loads maintained for too long, especially in the face of other lifestyle constraints, bring pathological debilitation. Once these concepts are understood, guidelines for preventing this transition from occurring may be more logically identifiable.

The Dynamics of Adaptation

It is appropriate to view overuse injuries, overtraining, and staleness as pathological elements of the training process. Ideally, none of these should occur, but if they do occur, careful athlete management is required to bring prompt recovery. Fatigue and muscle soreness are quite different from overtraining or staleness, although they may exist during such states. They are normal physiological elements of what may be termed the *training process,* which is defined as a set of interactions between a stimulus and a response intended to initiate adaptive (beneficial) physiological changes. This process has both somatic and psychological aspects (body and mind) that are linked inseparably. When the training process is overdone, then overtraining, staleness, and overuse injuries are very likely to occur.

Figure 8.1 depicts the relationship between training, recovery, and performance over time for three different training loads. In the context of a training athlete, these loads could quite nicely represent the two- to three-week requirement to complete a particular microcycle of training. In figure 8.1*a* notice that a given training stimulus (indicated by T in the shaded area) decreases immediate performance abilities during its time of application. Following adequate recovery, shown by the shaded area labeled R, the original performance level is restored or perhaps even enhanced to a small extent. Highly talented athletes interested in ever-greater performance excellence would not enjoy the adaptive effects of such a training stimulus: They desire significant performance improvements. For thousands of serious fitness devotees, however, this is exactly what they seek: excellent health through vigorous activity, a minimal injury risk, and maintenance of enjoyable and consistent athletic activities. Fatigue and some mild muscle soreness may likely occur, but these are transient, expected, and tolerable.

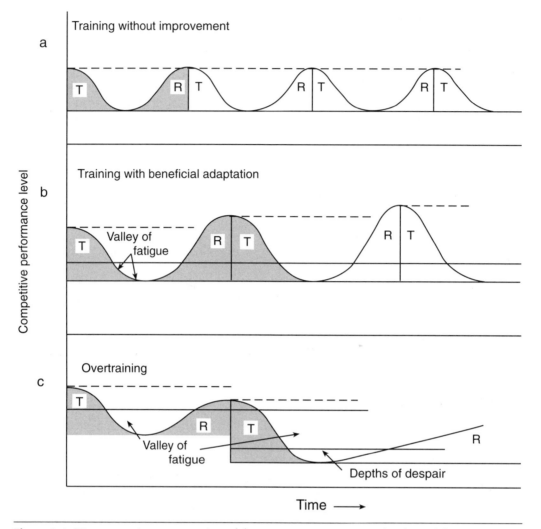

Figure 8.1 Diagrammatic representation of the response to training under three different conditions. In (a) insufficient training occurred to elicit performance improvement upon recovery. In (b) such a performance improvement did occur, caused by a beneficial training effect. In (c) a performance decrement occurred as a result of not only an excessive training stimulus but also its beginning before recovery had fully occurred; overtraining was the result.

In figure 8.1b the training stimulus is quantitatively more profound, intended for the competitive athlete. The stimulus either is applied longer or is more intense. Thus, the energy cost is higher, the adaptive challenge is larger, and muscle fatigue and soreness will be greater. The initial performance decrements are more sizable than those in figure 8.1a, and additional recovery time is required after removal of the training stimulus. But the performance ability following full recovery is now increased considerably. The greater training load has initiated homeostatic changes designed to permit greater tolerance to such a challenge. The athlete has improved; that is, performance abilities are now greater than they were previously. If the training load was not too severe and if the recovery was adequate, the risk for injury or illness should also be minimal.

One of the coaching grand masters in the art of varying the quantity and quality of such work loads—providing an adequate stimulus just long enough to yield excellent results without putting athletes over the edge—was Indiana University swimming coach James Counsilman. His excellent book *The Science of Swimming,* published in 1968, served as a stimulus for others to consider carefully the strategies for training and peaking for top-level performance when it was most important. Since then, although much jargon has sometimes confused the picture, his general concepts for administering and removing training stimuli have become widely used and modified.

In figure 8.1*a* our athlete has been within what we could term a *zone of normalized homeostatic adaptation.* By this we mean that when recovery was permitted (note the R in the shaded area) through reduction in the training load (indicated by T), there was not necessarily an actual improvement in performance ability. The athlete simply returned to normal performance capabilities. In figure 8.1*b,* however, our training athlete progressed into a *zone of improved homeostatic adaptation.* The extra training load, characterized by athletes' psychological awareness that they are working very hard, puts them into a so-called "valley of fatigue." Physiologically, this manifests itself in extensive skeletal muscle fuel depletion and possibly also muscle protein breakdown. The enlarged training load must then be followed by an increased recovery period. The reward is an improved performance level caused by the various physiological adaptive changes that have taken place: increased $\dot{V}O_2$max, restored (perhaps increased) fuel supplies to the working muscles, greater size and numbers of mitochondria, and so on. Slower training paces will initiate this adaptive response primarily in the ST fibers, providing little if any stimulus to the FT fibers. Faster-paced work would provide a continuing adaptive stimulus to both ST and FT muscle fibers (explaining the need for never venturing very far away from speed all through the training year). To climb out of this valley of fatigue and reap the training benefits in the form of improved work tolerance, proportionately more recovery time to regain optimal organ function is required than for the earlier example given in figure 8.1*a.*

Thus, improved athletic performance has a *psychological component* (the athlete knows that hard training has been managed well and has a proper attitude about the use of the performance improvements) and a *physiological component,* which in turn has two aspects. There is a neuromuscular improvement (more muscle fiber recruitment, more tension generation with less fatigue) and a metabolic improvement (increased fuel storage and utilization). Few scientists studying human performance have emphasized enough the intricate interaction of these two components—physiological and psychological (Morgan 1985)—in raising performance potential. Even fewer physiologists have emphasized the interaction of the two physiological aspects involved (Noakes 1988).

Appreciation of this latter interaction, for example, helps to explain observations from both animal experiments and human training experience. Sprint training in rats (Davies, Packer, and Brooks 1982) as well as strength training in young men (Weltman et al. 1986) can increase $\dot{V}O_2$max without increasing mitochondrial numbers or mitochondrial enzyme content in individual muscle cells, suggesting that it is tension-generating ability that is improved (through recruitment of more muscle cells and therefore more muscle protein) rather than increasing O_2 usage in individual muscle cells. When performance capacity falls, we ought to look at any or all of these three components as possible causes.

Fatigue: Friend or Foe?

When we defined fatigue in chapter 5 as a sensation of increased difficulty to maintain a previous level of working effectiveness, we were implying that specific physiological processes such as muscle tension generation were challenged, thereby decreasing our ability to sustain submaximal or maximal work. An understanding for how physiological changes bring about such limitation in function is quite important for athletes and coaches alike. Fatigue can be a friend or foe depending on how it is used or abused in the training process. Recall from chapter 2 that skeletal muscle cells exist in several varieties. Some emphasize glycolytic (anaerobic) work (FT Type IIb), others oxidative (aerobic) work (ST), and some do both quite well (FT Type IIa). ST fibers are used predominantly to maintain posture and allow walking, jogging, and lesser-intensity running, whereas FT fibers are not recruited in appreciable numbers except during higher-intensity running (faster speeds or uphill).

Fatigue decreases the maximal tension-generating velocity attainable by all types of skeletal muscle fibers. This is a biochemical process: Increasing numbers of H^+ ions from anaerobic metabolism at higher work rates decrease the effectiveness of myosin ATPase as an enzyme in permitting interaction with adjacent actin myofilaments. The slower the rate of cross-bridge linking between the actin and myosin myofilaments (see figures 2.6 and 2.7), the slower these myofilaments can slide past each other, and the slower the rate of tension generation in the muscle. Because power is the rate of performing work, this decreased power output manifests itself as a slowing of performance. Free H^+ ions also decrease the rapidity with which actin-myosin complexes are broken. In turn, relaxation of skeletal muscle tension is slowed; this is noticeable as a shortened running stride.

Runners are keenly aware in very practical terms of the limitations brought about by fatigue. There is the fatigue caused purely by acidosis, seen as competitive middle-distance runners find that they simply cannot maintain pace in the final few hundred meters. But there is the fatigue caused partly by acidosis and partly by depleted energy supplies. Here is an example: At the end of an exhausting and intensive weight-room session, particularly one in which three or four sets have already been completed in addition to other exercises, an athlete attempts eight repetitions of the bench press or quarter-squat with a sizable amount of resistance. The desire to work is there, but the fuel metabolism operates at a diminished rate.

Fatigue can be an even more complex phenomenon. For a first-time marathon runner who has attempted (and failed) to maintain an excessively fast pace relative to performance abilities, or for an experienced marathoner who has not taken in adequate quantities of energy-containing drinks to maintain stored muscle glycogen, fatigue has a different feeling. For them, there is an indescribably overwhelming urge late in the race to sit down at the edge of the road, quit the race altogether, and have a cold drink. The desire to endure has been lost almost completely. The definition of *endurance*—the ability to continue at a given work intensity over increasingly long periods—might thus be considered the opposite of fatigue.

What caused these marathon runners to develop the overwhelming urge to stop? Unlike the examples of the track runner and the weight lifter who still had continuing motivation but had to slow their work rate (the mind said "Go" but the body said "No"), for these marathon runners it was an eventual central nervous system decision to stop (the mind said "Stop" and the body said, "I'm glad you agree; I've been suggesting this for some time!"). Fatigue is thus a psychophysiological phenomenon, explainable completely only by the interactive result of many cellular functions that are no longer in a stable equilibrium. Depleted fuel supplies, dehydration, and accumulating acidosis in the working muscles are only parts of the picture. There are other less-understood central nervous system signals from overworked tissues that all contribute to work intensity. An increase in these central nervous system signals—for example, by cheering from friends to continue competing—can recruit additional less-fatigued motor units. Such stimulation, of course, is temporary, eventually bringing even greater fatigue. This same emotional contribution, however, from a full stadium of screaming track fans can provide the additional stimulation for an athlete to push on despite the overwhelming fatigue.

No single physiological or psychological measurement can quantify fatigue, and its complete explanation remains a dilemma. In 1905, an Italian worker, Angelo Mosso, described its most important features. Research since then has not added much more to our understanding. As outlined in a 1915 translation of Mosso's work, with fatigue two sets of phenomena demand attention. The first is *diminution of the muscular force*. The second is fatigue as a *sensation*. Thus, muscle cells seem to weaken, and the central drive to work is reduced. The sensation can occur long into the resting state after the physical activity has ceased.

Possible Explanations of Fatigue

Over the years, various alterations in cellular physiology have been proposed as contributing to fatigue in working muscles. Some workers have suggested that ATP supplies become exhausted. Studies of biopsied muscle tissue, however, as well as newer reports using magnetic resonance imaging, show that ATP levels aren't changed very much during intense or prolonged work. ATP is never in very large supply, and it is quickly regenerated from ADP (using the CP reservoir) as it is broken down (recall chapter 3).

Other workers have suggested reduced intracellular O_2 availability, and thus the increasing inhibitory effects of acidosis from anaerobic metabolism, as the cause of fatigue. Though this may play a role in high-intensity exercise, it doesn't explain the reason why marathon runners working within their aerobic limits achieve such a state of fatigue that they simply run out of reasons for running. Inhibition of performance by the accumulation of acidosis should be minimal in less-competitive runners, including those thousands of serious fitness athletes who run primarily at an aerobic pace as they enjoy participating in popular marathons and other long-distance road races. But they fatigue as well.

Probably the best single physiological indicator that correlates well with the sensation of fatigue is a fall in muscle glycogen levels. Major credit goes to the work emanating out of the laboratory of David Costill for pioneering nutritional and fuel metabolism studies in working muscles of athletes (Costill 1988). This glycogen depletion probably accounted for a large part of the eventual decision of the marathon runners described earlier to quit their race efforts.

Many practical suggestions for dealing appropriately with fatigue have resulted from the work of Costill and his many graduate students. A few of these suggestions are listed below:

- Include adequate recovery time following intense training periods to permit proper nutrient, electrolyte, and fuel replenishment.
- Use multiple muscle groups during exercise (for example, when running up hills, use a vigorous arm swing to accompany leg motion), thereby diminishing the fall in muscle cell glycogen for any particular muscle group.
- Increase stored fuel supplies in the working muscles before a major competition (such as through carbohydrate loading for marathon racing, which was outlined in chapter 7).

- Ensure adequate hydration by drinking water or energy-containing sport drinks; the best coaching advice is that, while athletes ought to drink whenever they are thirsty, a much better philosophy would be to drink *before* they become thirsty. Because muscles are 75% water, athletes cannot afford to have these working tissues dehydrated.

Returning to Mosso's conceptualization of fatigue, we see that this phenomenon derives only in part from actual weakness and that it also involves several other variables about which we know very little. There is a decrease in the central nervous system drive to motor units: A fatigued runner has less desire to compete than one who is fresh. There are the decreased intracellular energy reserves we referred to earlier. Fatigued endurance runners may have decreased plasma volume from prolonged perspiration, which in turn decreases optimal perfusion of their working muscles. There are most likely several other aspects contributing to fatigue, which can occur well after the termination of exercise. Fatigued muscles can be sensed even when they are not in use. Witness the continuing fatigue in our muscles when we arise the next day after a hard training session—even before we do any additional exercise! The complexity of this picture hints that, as will be discussed later in this chapter, it may be unlikely that we will find any single blood chemistry variable or other criterion more reliable than our own sensual perception as an indicator of either the onset or the cessation of fatigue.

Muscle Soreness and Connective Tissue Injury

Athletes in hard training often report considerable soreness in their lower limbs, usually a day after intense, fast-paced running sessions or following back-to-back, very hard training days or after a hard race. The longer and more intense the effort, the greater the chance for such discomfort. However, the same soreness can occur if athletes suddenly begin a hard training cycle without adequate transition from moderately intense training. This so-called *delayed-onset muscular soreness* (DOMS) was defined by Robert Armstrong (1984) as a sensation of discomfort or pain in the skeletal muscles that occurs following unaccustomed muscular exertion. The key word here is "unaccustomed," because such soreness does not typically occur following routine submaximal-intensity training.

Such lower-limb muscle soreness is particularly noticeable after a marathon, but it can occur after challenging shorter-distance races or training sessions as well. For both marathoners and shorter-distance runners, the soreness can require a several-day recovery process. About a day following their race they discover that their quadriceps and gluteal muscles are especially tender to palpation and sore as they descend stairs. For marathoners the soreness peaks between two and four days postrace, varies in intensity depending on the marathoner's fitness and the stress of the race, and often disappears completely within a week. It manifests as a combination of tenderness and stiffness.

Is this pain indicative of actual tissue injury? If so, are the muscles or the connective tissues (or both) affected? Is inflammation present? Because such soreness may be nearly unavoidable after racing efforts, should training that produces such soreness be avoided at all costs? These and other questions have characterized quite active recent investigation of the problem, although scientists have studied the phenomenon for a long time.

Muscle Response to Excessive Loading

More than 90 years ago, the notion was advanced (Hough 1902) that hard work in muscle unadapted to such loads caused a microscopic tearing or rupturing of the cells. This could, of course, involve damage to the muscle cells, to their associated connective tissues, or to both. The soreness may occur all along the involved muscles and is often greatest near the muscle-tendon junctions. Newham et al. (1982) have suggested that at these junctions the long axes of muscle fibers are least parallel to the long axis of the entire muscle. Also, pain receptors are very common in the tendons and connective tissue. In several of the long lower-limb muscles, the tendons, instead of being restricted to the ends of the muscle (e.g., near the hip, knee, or ankle), extend a considerable distance along the muscle to which they connect (recall the diagram of penniform hamstring muscles in figure 2.3). During soreness the tension-generating abilities of the muscle cells are reduced (Francis and Hoobler 1988). According to Newham et al. (1983) more muscle cells than previously (i.e., before the onset of the soreness) will need recruiting to achieve a given level of force output. This may explain why racing effectiveness (or continued fast-paced work) is so difficult during such a period. Clearly, tissue breakdown has been extensive, involving both skeletal muscle cells and connective tissue.

Armstrong (1984) has surmised that this debilitation of muscular force occurs because of an increased Ca^{2+} ion level in the muscle cells. Cell membrane damage from intense activity permits more Ca^{2+} ions to diffuse inward (because their concentration outside these cells is greater than that inside). An elevated cell Ca^{2+} level inhibits the rate at which Krebs cycle enzymes permit fuel breakdown. The ionic disruption is entirely transitory, thanks to homeostatic processes that permit complete regeneration of membrane integrity during the recovery period. Calcium entry is restored to an acceptable rate, and fuel metabolism proceeds normally.

During the days when delayed-onset muscular soreness is manifested, the best means for enhancing recovery seems to be very mild exercise. There are several plausible explanations for this. First, breaking up the connective tissue adhesions between muscle cells may decrease the stretch that stimulates pain-mediating neurons in the region. Second, the brain and spinal cord produce opiumlike substances called *endorphins* that, when released into the bloodstream and allowed to circulate, have potent analgesic properties; they are released with even mild exercise. Third, elevated activity of sensory neurons from working muscles and tendons may inhibit the activity of smaller pain-mediating neurons. Fourth, increased circulation of blood through these tissues increases the influx of nutrients and helps the efflux of cellular breakdown products from tissue catabolism. Such mild exercise will not magically bring about a recovered state after its completion. The muscular soreness will return and will continue until recovery processes restore the cells to normal health. But this kind of gentle restorative exercise can help speed the overall recovery process.

In contrast to the limited tissue breakdown, soreness, and rapid recovery of a middle-distance athlete, for a marathoner the cellular destruction is sufficient to cause the dissolution of tension-generating proteins and the complete destruction of sizable numbers of sarcomeres. Recent studies of athletes following completion of marathon races (Evans 1987; Hagerman et al. 1984; Siegel, Silverman, and Lopez 1980; Warhol et al. 1985) and multiday ultra-endurance races (Dressendorfer and Wade 1983) have documented clearly the extensive pathological disruption that can occur in skeletal muscle cells from such prolonged physical work. Intracellular enzymes leak into the bloodstream as a result of increased muscle membrane permeability, the most well known of these enzymes being creatine kinase (CK). This is also observed in the milder forms of delayed-onset muscular soreness caused by intense short-term training. Studies often report peak serum CK levels correlating positively with the subjective sensation of muscle soreness (Dressendorfer and Wade 1983; Schwane et al. 1983). White blood cells eventually move into these damaged muscle cells and metabolize the intracellular debris, permitting recovery so that renewed protein synthesis will restore cellular integrity (tension-generating ability and membrane stability). While the muscular soreness may subside within a week in marathon runners, as long as a month may be required for effective repair of the muscle cell destruction (Warhol et al. 1985). This rebuilding of muscle cells is one good reason why training and racing should be minimal for several weeks after a marathon race.

Lengthening (eccentric) tension generation seems more prone to causing soreness than shortening (concentric) tension generation, although both can do it (Ebbeling and Clarkson 1989; Schwane et al. 1983). Examples of eccentric tension include running downhill, stepping down, or reverse bicycle pedaling. Eccentric tension is an integral part of running even on level ground, occurring with every stride as the gastrosoleus, anterior and posterior tibialis, and quadriceps absorb much of the impact forces placed on the knee joint and foot at footstrike. This explains the soreness an athlete often experiences in these muscle groups after a particularly grueling training or racing effort. Perhaps this provides a partial explanation for the general consensus among road racers that considerably more recovery time is required before resuming normal training patterns following a downhill marathon (such as at Boston) or other shorter-distance hilly road race. Training patterns do not provide sufficient adaptation to the tissue loading to make such an experience routine.

At least three mechanisms may explain this debilitation. First, electromyographic evidence suggests that fewer muscle fibers are recruited during lengthening tension generation. Thus, fewer involved muscle fibers must generate relatively more force at any given work rate than if they were active during shortening tension. Second, the muscle force production requirements are greater during downhill running because the body's center of mass is lowered (Margaria 1972). Because braking against gravity is required when running downhill, the additional momentum of limb movements must be counteracted by antagonistic muscles. This requires greater involvement of connective tissue elements such as tendons. It is not surprising, therefore, that delayed muscle soreness and elevated CK levels are both greater when running is predominantly downhill rather than uphill or on level terrain (Schwane et al. 1983). Third, during prolonged exercise, FT muscle cells that may have been used and subsequently fatigued enter a state of rigor. Passive lengthening from eccentric exercise can mechanically damage or destroy them (Lieber and Friden 1988).

The renowned British exercise physiologist Archibald Hill suggested as far back as 1951 the novel theoretical viewpoint that the best way to prevent delayed-onset muscular soreness may in fact be to train harder. Assuming that adaptation occurs, this would make the routine tolerable work load more similar to the work load producing the soreness (remember that it is the unaccustomed load that causes the soreness). As one might expect, the training stimulus must be very specific. That is, hard eccentric training will protect against muscular soreness from a very difficult eccentric session much better than it will from a sudden concentric session, and vice versa. More recent work (Schwane, Williams, and Sloan 1987) has confirmed this notion.

Thus, an important strategy for the U.S. male and female marathoners training for their 1996 Olympic trials in hilly Charlotte, North Carolina, and Columbia, South Carolina, was to include plenty of training specifically directed toward building their tolerance to performing effectively for long distances over tough, hilly terrain. Two of the three men who earned Olympic berths, Mark Coogan and Bob Kempainen, included training blocks in the Colorado mountains (where Mark lived), while Keith Brantly, living in the flatlands of south Florida, did most of his initial hard training in the mountains of North Carolina. Anne Marie Lauck earned a berth on the women's team thanks to her hard training in the very hilly northside Atlanta metropolitan area. Of course, training under such challenging conditions brings with it an increased injury risk, unless care is taken to provide the increased accompanying rest between hard work loads.

Overuse Injuries in Connective Tissue

To become the best, an athlete must challenge the body to its *reasonable* limits, and the crucial element of the art of athletic development is always to stop short of *excessively* intense or prolonged hard work. A manageable challenge followed by beneficial adaptation ought to provide enhanced tolerance to intense work and improve performance potential. Athletes and coaches are always aspiring toward better performance and thus are quite willing to assign or to endure the most difficult of sessions. But the work must not be overdone. What occurs when insufficient recovery or rest time is provided, when too many back-to-back sessions are assigned, or when the athlete does this increasing training in the face of notable biomechanical imperfections (such as excessive genu valgum [knock-knees], ligamentous laxity, or wearing overworn shoes)? Aren't we suggesting that athletes push themselves very close to the point of doing too much (overuse) and developing injury? Yes, we are. The essence of optimal athletic development is to achieve as close to tolerable load limits as possible, no more.

The dilemma for coach and athlete should be strikingly obvious: How much is too much? It is easy enough to be idealistic and accept that there is obviously a limit to hard training and that it isn't wise ever to exceed this limit. But how does one sense this limit? It is not easy, but these suggestions may help:

- Keep accurate records of training work loads and recoveries.
- Learn from experience the kinds of loads that can be tolerated (this is one of the rewards of working with athletes over a period of many years).
- Do not wait until fatigue is excessive, but rather plan fairly frequent recovery periods in advance.
- Proceed to the next hard session only when a feeling of freshness of both body and spirit returns, which suggests that recovery is complete.

The key to comprehending an inappropriate overuse injury risk is to realize that this implies *excessive tissue stress over time without adequate recovery.* It is important to remember that our limbs are interconnected bone-tendon-muscle links in a kinetic chain responsible for absorbing impact stress and providing push-off forces. It should be obvious that the weakest link in this chain will deteriorate first. Thus, once again it is important to have a feel for the physiology of these three major tissue types to gain an appreciation for how they work and how overuse occurs.

When athletes have overuse lower-limb injuries, what typically is their presenting problem? A myositis (problem with the muscles)? No. An osteitis (problem with the bones)? No. Rather, it's a connective tissue problem—plantar fasciitis, Achilles tendinitis, patellar tendinitis, or iliotibial band syndrome. What's the mechanism? Bones are structurally very stable. And muscles, when fatigued either by excessive acidosis or loss of energy, simply fail to generate tension. The connective tissues are caught in between.

Tendons and ligaments adapt less readily than muscle and bone to long-term, repeated stimulation (Archambault, Wiley, and Bray 1995). Understanding the physiology of connective tissue provides an understanding of its recovery dynamics. Ligaments are composed largely of a connective tissue molecule called *elastin,* a stretchable fibrous protein, whereas tendons are essentially nonstretchable and composed of *collagen* molecules. Collagen is the most common protein in the body. In tendons, collagen fibrils are arranged in parallel bundles and have enormous tensile strength—even more than steel wire. Unfortunately, tendons have poor blood circulation. The repetitive mechanical stresses of running increase collagen metabolism. There is a limit to the dynamics of this tissue maintenance (breakdown and buildup) in its healthy state. When tendons are stressed beyond this limit, tendon disruption occurs in the form of microtears. These tears heal, by the formation of either good-quality new collagen or lesser-quality fibrotic scar tissue. The poorer a tendon's vascularity, the greater the incidence of inadequate recovery from excessive use. The more incomplete the healing process, caused most frequently by depriving the tissue of adequate rest, the greater the risk of scar tissue formation resulting from continuing chronic inflammatory processes.

There is thus a fine line between a healthy training challenge (with physiological adaptation) and an unhealthy excessive training challenge that brings chronic overuse (with pathological consequences). The essence of successfully applying proper training loads is to realize in advance how much will be excessive and then to provide periodic rest to ensure that training serves as a temporary rather than continual overload. The rest period must be long enough to permit recovery. If only a bell could ring when that exact amount of loading occurred—life would be simple! We know only *after* the repetitive stress by the pathological consequences that it has been excessive. Thus, keeping adequate records of training loads and recovery periods, as well as notes concerning the response to the loading, is essential.

All overuse injuries to muscle and connective tissues are the result of excessive repetitive microtraumas, which result in *inflammation* as the pathological response. The action of prostaglandins within circulating blood brings vasodilation, which increases capillary permeability and thereby causes fluid to pass into tissues with accompanying swelling and pain. Anti-inflammatory agents such as aspirin work by blocking prostaglandin synthesis and thus mildly reducing the intensity of the body's repair processes. Incoming white blood cells, especially lymphocytes, neutrophils, and monocytes, digest cellular debris and clear the area for repair to begin. Recapillarization and growth of new collagen then begin, but this takes time. Only limited motion can occur during this period, which varies depending on the tissue and the extent of injury. Some inflammation is thus an ongoing and essential component of the postinjury healing process, but chronic inflammation indicates a lack of progress in repair. Thus, injured athletes who are experiencing inflammation as part of their normal healing process must be advised strongly to make the rest period sufficiently profound that tissue recovery in fact occurs.

Collagen and elastin contain sizable quantities of a unique amino acid called *4-hydroxyproline*. When connective tissues containing these molecules break down, their metabolites appear in the blood and are eventually excreted in the urine. Thus, urinary excretion of 4-hydroxyproline can serve as a marker for increased tendon and ligament metabolism (Abraham 1977). It is therefore not surprising that studies of delayed muscle soreness that included urinary measurements of 4-hydroxyproline in the days following very hard muscular exercise showed increases in this metabolite. Increased plasma hydroxyproline levels are also seen (Hodgdon et al. 1988). To ensure that what is being measured actually reflects extracellular structural collagen breakdown from tissue such as tendons, it might be preferable to measure plasma levels of metabolites (such as hydroxypyridinoline) that are restricted to this type of collagen (Riedy et al. 1988).

Depending on the intensity of exercise or the challenge to the metabolic integrity of the tendons involved, these connective tissue metabolites and skeletal muscle enzyme elevations in the blood may parallel nicely the occurrence of delayed muscle soreness. Such elevations are not always observed, however (Dressendorfer and Wade 1983), showing that a particular threshold of volume and intensity overload is required. In turn, this will be determined individually by the athlete's fitness, the environmental conditions, and the athlete's genetic constitution (muscle fiber type and biomechanical efficiency). Another variable that may require consideration in such studies is dietary vitamin C intake. Vitamin C is *ascorbic acid*, which is required for the enzymatic hydroxylation of proline to form 4-hydroxyproline for collagen biosynthesis. Distance runners frequently include oral vitamin C supplementation of as much as 500 mg to 1 gm per day as part of their diets. The interrelationships among high weekly training volumes, measured connective tissue turnover, and possible benefits of increased vitamin C intake have not yet been determined precisely.

Achilles Tendinitis

The *calcaneal tendon* (or Achilles tendon) is often a victim of the strain of overuse from running. This tendon originates about halfway down the lower leg and is formed when the superficial and deep fasciae of the triceps surae (the soleus plus the two heads of the gastrocnemius) merge. It inserts on the posterior portion of the calcaneus, or heel bone. Chronic stress can bring inflammation, thickening, and fibrosis to the tendon sheath (called the *mesotendon*). When such changes occur in the calcaneal tendon, the resulting condition is termed *Achilles tendinitis*. Overpronation is a common cause of Achilles tendinitis. Excessive internal tibial rotation causes pronation (as outlined in chapter 1) and draws the Achilles tendon medially, producing a whipping action of the tendon that can cause microtears.

The blood supply to tendons is usually via their surrounding mesotendon. Thus, reduction in mesotendon vascularity can even further inhibit the tendon's ability to cope with chronic loading. If the accompanying pain from tendinitis does not cripple the runner, partial tendon rupture may. Excessive strain on an inflamed tendon (particularly sudden overload) can initiate partial rupture.

Interval training and hill sessions are particularly stressful on lower-limb muscles and tendons. It is therefore especially useful for such exercises to be introduced very early into the training plan and begun very gently at first to ensure the kind of intermediate adaptive limb strengthening that permits tolerance to meaningful (and intense) sessions later on. Even then, adaptation may never be sufficient to permit strong *daily* challenges to the lower-limb tendons with such training. This explains why either a sudden initiation of high-intensity hill or track sessions or an assignment of several in one week often results in a painful flare-up of Achilles tendinitis. If this occurs, runners find themselves severely compromised. There is absolutely no other choice but rest for the needed tendon repair: Microhealing can only occur if there is no stress on the tendon. This is why even easy running on an inflamed Achilles tendon is ill advised; to an individual tendon cell, easy running is a megastress. Alternative activities (such as deep-water pool swimming using a flotation vest) can be considered to maintain cardiorespiratory fitness, although even then considerable caution is needed to ensure that the tendon isn't stressed by vigorous movement in the water.

Bursitis

Another problem related to overuse involves inflammation in the bursa that is often associated with tendons or muscles that need to glide over bony prominences. A *bursa* is a closed sac lined with a synovial membrane that produces a thick, viscous fluid with a texture similar to that of an egg white. One example is the retrocalcaneal bursa, which lies between the calcaneus and the Achilles tendon. Only a small amount of fluid, sufficient to serve as a marvelously effective lubricant, is produced. Repetitive trauma caused by excessive pressure of the tendon on this bursa can lead to inflammation, increasing synovial fluid production and causing even greater tissue pressure in this region. Eventually, debilitating pain and decreased mobility result. A typical diagnostic feature in *retrocalcaneal bursitis* is a decreased passive dorsiflexion of the foot. An effective ongoing health maintenance program designed to stretch and strengthen the gastrocnemius-soleus muscle complex is ideal for minimizing not only the pressure of the Achilles tendon on its bursa, but also the risk of bursitis (and tendinitis) from high-volume training.

Iliotibial Band Friction Syndrome

It is not solely the effects of overload training that can predispose an athlete to overuse pathology. Biomechanical imbalances, particularly when coupled with improper footwear, can hasten the development of overuse problems. In chapter 1 we mentioned the need for a certain amount of pronation to occur as each foot lands on its running surface. Wearing shoes that excessively limit subtalar joint pronation reduces the foot's ability to absorb landing shock. Running on crowned roads also tends to limit pronation in the downhill foot. Frequently the iliotibial band (see figure 2.2) is affected, with pain manifested on the lateral surface of the knee as this band of connective tissue moves over a bony protuberance on the femur called the *lateral femoral epicondyle* (Jones and James 1987). The pain arises predictably after a certain distance is covered, is especially noticeable with downhill running, and subsides when the athlete stops running and switches to walking (because the band no longer moves over the epicondyle). Fairly sudden increases in training distance covered and an excessive emphasis on faster running (especially over distance runs) seem to hasten its onset.

Ironically, this *iliotibial band friction syndrome* may result after a runner has been told to wear shoes and special inserts (orthotics) intended to limit the excessive pronation that had produced a pain syndrome called runner's knee. The twisting of the lower limb resulting from excess pronation causes excessive asymmetric tension on the ligaments supporting the patella (kneecap). The stress at the ligament-bone junction produces an inflammation response. Pain around the patella has an onset after a predictable running distance, is noticeable when ascending or descending stairs, and increases while sitting for prolonged periods with the knees bent. The proper amount of correction will alleviate the symptoms of runner's knee. But it must not be overcorrected.

There is perhaps only one thing worse than the correction of one overuse problem by creating another. And that is when an athlete displays some symptoms of two problems but doesn't know how the injured tissues are responding (resolution or exacerbation) to the treatment being applied. Because of travel to different locales or frustration over being told that they should briefly curtail their running, runners often visit several health care professionals and are given different diagnoses or suggested therapeutic regimens. The presenting problem is indeed different at various times because of the changing nature of the injury. For good reason, both athletes and professionals are dismayed. The athletes do not enjoy hearing different diagnoses or requests for rest, and the professionals are often insufficiently aware of the athletes' preceding medical history to integrate it with the presenting problems. Clearly, prevention is by far the best way to manage this situation. Given that this ideal may not always be achieved, it is probably most useful for athletes to maintain close contact with the same support team of competent, medically knowledgeable experts. This ensures consistency in health care.

Preventing Overuse Injuries

What is the best way to prevent assigned training loads from being so excessive that pathology replaces physiology, that is, maladaptation replaces adaptation? Ensure that periodic rest is programmed into all training regimens. This implies taking a day off here and there voluntarily, rather than being forced to take off the same amount of time or more when it may not be at all desirable. It also implies keeping careful records to compare assigned with achieved training loads and developing the attitude in both athlete and coach that *because rest is part of training, it should be given the same importance as the work load.*

Some useful thoughts from the profession of psychological counseling are useful here to help ensure that this combination of assigned work and rest is implemented. Any type of lasting behavioral change must be coupled with an attitude change, which in turn requires a change in thought patterns. Here, athletes and coaches must not think of the need for rest as a sign of an inability to tolerate arduous training, but rather as a mechanism for increasing the chances of adaptation without injury. If there is ever a doubt about whether an athlete should insert additional rest or press onward relentlessly, by all means rest is the preferred choice. The physiological recovery will certainly be beneficial because the risk for injury will have been reduced. Also, the mental respite will bring renewed enthusiasm for the ensuing training session. Freshness is far more functional than fatigue in achieving overall quality in training.

Overtraining and Staleness: Beyond Fatigue

Let us now return to figure 8.1c and examine a third possible scenario of training and recovery. In figure 8.1c our athlete did not allow adequate homeostatic recovery from the first sizable work load before resuming intense training. This next training load was even more intense than the previous one. Often such an increased load/decreased recovery sequence results when the previous training mesocycle went very successfully. Both athlete and coach decide (in this instance, erroneously), "We're ahead of schedule, so let's pick up the pace." In the ensuing enthusiasm a training excess occurs. During the second training period the athlete not only reaches the bottom of the valley of fatigue, but enters the *depths of despair,* or *fatigue plus.*

This athlete is experiencing *short-term overtraining,* which we will refer to as *overtraining* and define as a condition characterized by a temporary imbalance between training and recovery. It is sensed as fatigue that doesn't disappear with normal rest and that is accompanied by a wide variety of additional signs and symptoms. The essence is that an athlete cannot perform optimally after what would normally be considered an acceptable period of recovery (Fry et al. 1992). Just as with the two training intensities depicted in figure 8.1, *a* and *b,* initially catabolism is greater than anabolism, and there is a metabolic tearing down of tissues. However, the breakdown has affected the body much more profoundly, and much more than the usual amount of time will be required for recovery. Figure 8.2 outlines some of the adaptive mechanisms that will occur if recovery from high training loads is adequate, and the degenerative processes that may occur if recovery is inadequate or if the training load was inappropriately excessive.

When athletes enter this state of overtraining, they typically sense that they are not quite as recovered as would normally be expected and often wisely opt to ease up on their training for a few days. Unfortunately, anywhere from three

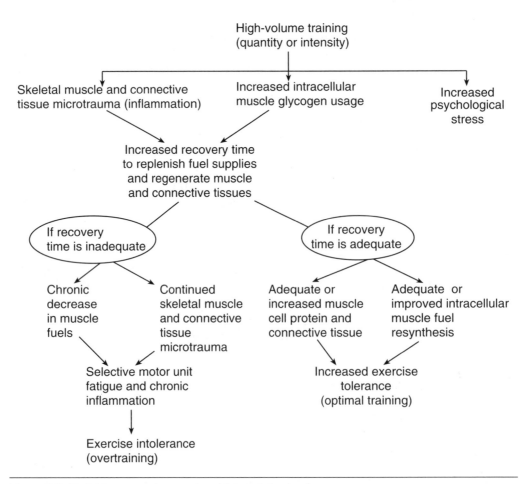

Figure 8.2 Variable responsiveness to a high training load.

to five days or more may be required. Thus, the likelihood that athletes will resume training prematurely is very high. If they now step up the intensity of their training even more, either to "make up for lost time" or because of the sense that "the more I train, the fitter I'll become," they may set themselves up for disaster.

If our athlete in figure 8.1c continues to push onward with training despite continuing symptoms of overtraining—which we shall describe shortly—eventually (typically within a few weeks) a kind of physiological and psychological breakdown can occur. This marks the onset of what is called *long-term overtraining*, or simply *staleness* (Kuipers and Keizer 1988). It can be defined as a combination of (1) inability to train or race at an acceptable level, (2) an extended period of fatigue, and (3) often an increased occurrence of sickness (Budgett 1990). This represents a complex combination of psychophysiological signs and symptoms of a more far-reaching nature than simple fatigue. It suggests a trend toward actual cellular injury, profound fuel exhaustion, breakdown of the body's defense mechanisms, neurological and endocrine disturbances, or perhaps all of these together. Decrements in performance that before were occasional are now chronic and large. Along with increased risk of injury, illness occurs with increasing frequency. Altered mood states, altered hormonal patterns, and other metabolic changes can occur, and these can vary enormously among individuals. A very long time will be required for recovery to restore performance abilities: weeks, months, maybe even a year!

Using the psychological approach of Morgan, Brown, Raglin, O'Connor, and Ellickson (1987), it is convenient to view excessive training and overtraining as stimuli in the context of the classic stimulus-response paradigm. *If excessive training is the stimulus, then overtraining is the response.* Similarly, *if overtraining is the stimulus, then staleness, however it is manifested, is the response.* The development of long-term overtraining (staleness) should be avoided by athletes like the plague, because it could spell the end of a competitive season or even a career. Optimal training ought to be the goal of all athletes, but overdoing it becomes almost a fact of life for those who are highly motivated, particularly those just at the edge of moving up to a higher level of performance. Being sensitive to the early identification of overtraining and having the good sense and strategy to take the proper corrective steps to return to optimal training is of crucial importance for proper development.

The difference between hard training and overtraining is not so much in the kinds of work done as in the manner by which the body responds to the work assigned. Overtraining results when either the load is too great for the tissues or insufficient recovery is provided after the load is applied. Figure 8.3 depicts some of the interrelationships and differences between hard training and overtraining as they potentially contribute to or affect adaptation, fatigue, muscular soreness, overuse injury, and staleness. Hard training is essential for eventual improvement in performance. Although it causes a temporary diminution of performance abilities through catabolic changes in the working muscles and other energy-storage tissues, it is done for relatively short periods, and the anabolic recovery phase then permits the kind of adaptation that yields even greater performance potential.

Overtraining can be thought of as the result of overdoing hard training, such that the ongoing very high level of activity can no longer be managed effectively. There is a fine line between hard training, to which the body can adapt if the stimulus is not too great and if the recovery is adequate, and excessive hard

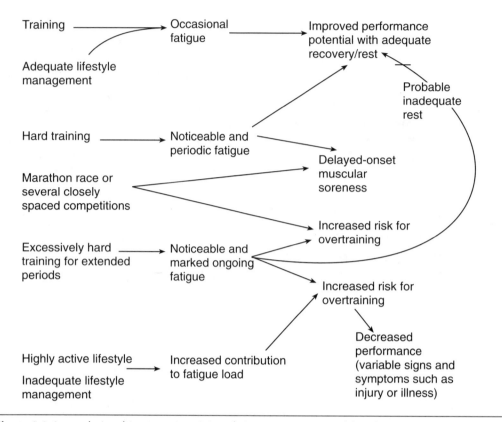

Figure 8.3 Interrelationships among training, fatigue, overtraining, lifestyle, overuse injury, staleness, and athletic performance.

training, which is simply too much to manage. As soon as that line is crossed, a major reduction in work load must be initiated until regenerative processes restore homeostatic equilibrium.

Lifestyle Overload and Overtraining

From a holistic or total-body viewpoint, the performance abilities of athletes for training and competition are a function of coping adequately with their lifestyles. If their adaptation to training is excellent, performance will likely improve, showing that other lifestyle activities are not excessive. If adaptation is inadequate, then substandard or diminishing performance may occur, suggesting the onset of overtraining unless athletes redesign their lifestyle. Mechanical engineers define *stress* as load per unit area. We might analogize here and write the following relationship:

$$\text{stress} = \text{lifestyle load} / \text{athletic performance} \tag{8.1}$$

Lifestyle load refers to enhancing factors (adequate nutrition, rest, and relaxation; emotional stability; positive family and other support group assistance; and proper training) as well as inhibitory factors (imbalances in any of the aforementioned enhancers as well as other competing pressures caused by ongoing problems of life in the real world).

Athletes differ in important ways in their likelihood of developing overtraining or staleness when presented with a given high-volume training work load. An excessive load for one athlete may not necessarily be excessive for another, even if the athletes are of similar age, weight, and $\dot{V}O_2$max and have similar previous personal bests. The many aspects of total lifestyle, including the other activities that compete for the athlete's available energy supplies—a full-time job, frequent promotional or other travel related to sport, demands imposed by media, raising children, responsibilities of maintaining a complete household, and so on—must also be considered, along with differing states of fitness at the time the work load is assigned.

One of the difficulties that coaches often experience in attempting to work effectively with elite athletes is that they do not understand some of the unique personality traits of these gifted performers. The work of psychologist Frank Farley (1986) has been quite illuminating in this regard. Highly talented and motivated athletes exhibit what Farley classifies as a *type T personality:* T for thrill-seeker, which implies having a high predilection for taking risks. These individuals become bored quickly, have a large need for ongoing stimulating activities, are very adventuresome, have an enormous capacity for energy-consuming activity, and have no difficulty rationalizing putting all their abilities on the line in risky (competitive) environments. They may lose everything, but they have the resiliency (and the temperament) to recover, regroup, and do it all over again.

It may now be easier to comprehend why the most-motivated athletes may have the greatest risk for overtraining and staleness. The type of personality just described is a prerequisite for the mind-set with which the athlete is able to achieve goals that have a relatively small chance of success. To optimize the chance for success, no amount of energy output in preparation is considered excessive. This high-level enthusiasm carries over into the athlete's daily affairs, which can also be energy draining. If an active lifestyle coupled with intense training eventually becomes too demanding, manifestations can be evident in the form of poor competitive performance, overuse injury, or profound fatigue. Figure 8.4 illustrates this cycle of events that sets the scene for the development of staleness from too much training. This is a sad irony that needs attentive intervention to prevent. The best coach is very often not one who emphasizes solely the motivation to work harder. The best coach instead may be someone who realizes when motivation is indeed appropriate but who also is

Figure 8.4 Psychophysiological event sequence causing overtraining.

ever alert to the need for moderation, reassessment, and redirection of the total work output. This is in keeping with our previously stated view that the least amount of specific work required to achieve the best results is a powerfully effective training strategy.

It should be obvious from the preceding discussion that it is not just excessive training loads that can culminate in overtraining. Training itself may be within reasonable limits, but the sum of all the other facets of the athlete's lifestyle may compete inappropriately with the total energy available. We may think of an athlete's "energy pie" as the total energy level at which the athlete can maintain daily activities over extended periods. It can have many or few pieces, but the total energy available—the size of the pie—doesn't change. Increasing the size of those pieces unrelated to running or increasing the number of pieces (the number of lifestyle activities) mandates that the training, racing, and recovery pieces must be appropriately reduced. Athletic performance then diminishes accordingly. The intelligent athlete with a passion for excellence must choose wisely in lifestyle management.

A short practical anecdote can exemplify this interrelationship of training and lifestyle as well as the need to monitor total lifestyle demands. It concerns the buildup to Seb Coe's first world record in the 800 m, run in Oslo on 5 July 1979. During the previous winter and on into the early spring of 1979 Seb had been studying diligently for his honors degree in economics and social history. At the same time, of course, he was training very hard for the coming Olympic season. As a means of deriving a sense of whether he was developing optimally in preparation for the Moscow Olympic Games, on 31 May he ran an 800-m race for his university against a representative team from the British Amateur Athletic Association. His time was 1:47.8, and he felt slightly ill at the time. In the eyes of his coach, Seb looked a bit drawn from the effort. Nothing at all would have suggested that Seb had anything in him to permit running much faster. He ended up with subsequent sniffles and the aches and pains all over that characterize a typical viral cold.

The obvious response was to accept the fact that an overload was occurring and to back off training, because it was impossible to dismiss the difficult academic regimen that was coming to a peak. In addition to his head cold, a few psychological symptoms of overtraining were also noticeable. With the training stimulus greatly reduced, Seb finished his final exams with excellent results. Then it was as if a huge element of strain that had been consuming his energy reserves was lifted. His academic load was removed, and his volume of physical training had already been reduced. In the transition back to high-level athletic work, his spirits brightened, and his physical freshness returned just as quickly. His subsequent achievement was extraordinary. Two races later and a Bislett Games 1:42.33 world record was his.

The decision not to push on in view of the warning signals, which required interpreting them properly, was by far more proper than to have pushed on despite the warning signs. Excellent grades were crucial, as was a quality athletic performance. Attempting both simultaneously was too much. The writing was on the wall, and the message, fortunately, was both read and heeded. Seb had rearranged his priorities correctly. Doing less ultimately meant gaining more.

Physiological Dimensions of Overtraining

In 1976 the noted Canadian biochemist Hans Selye identified in somewhat general terms what might be occurring as the initial challenge of overtraining merges with the more prolonged response of staleness. Hans Selye and Walter Cannon were contemporaries, and both attempted to quantify a concept introduced by W.A. Engelhardt (1932), which defines the *training process* as a physiological breakdown that serves as a specific stimulus for subsequent adaptive recovery processes. Selye was particularly interested in the difference between short-term physiological breakdown (e.g., hard training, from which normal recovery occurs without problems) and pathological breakdown (e.g., overtraining and then staleness, from which recovery requires much additional time and from which it is likely that complete functional restoration of homeostatic processes may not occur). His most well-known experiments did not involve athletes in physical training but instead used laboratory animals injected with noxious agents. He found in his animals a predictable series of events, initiated through increases in pituitary and adrenal gland hormonal activity essentially directed at mobilizing increased amounts of circulating fuels—carbohydrates, fats, and proteins—to provide energy for the body to fight off the effects of the injected agents.

An initial alarm reaction (figure 8.5), as the body fails to keep up with the sudden increased metabolic demands, is characterized also by a lowered resistance, perhaps caused by a depletion of lymphatic tissue. Following this is a period whose duration varies, depending on the assault, during which the animals maintain a heightened state of resistance and tolerance to the noxious agents. Presumably, during this period adequate energy reserves are available to cope with the body's needs to combat the effects of the injected agents. Eventually, however, unless recovery occurs as a result of the elevated metabolism being sufficient to combat the tissue assault, a state of progressive exhaustion will develop, with death or illness resulting shortly thereafter. The staleness seen with prolonged overtraining in athletes may be analogous to Selye's stage of exhaustion.

Galbo (1983), Berdanier (1987), and Urhausen, Gabriel, and Kindermann (1995) have reviewed the endocrine and metabolic responses that are mobilized to help athletes cope with the long-term overloading of prolonged overtraining, which may be similar to the stress placed upon Hans Selye's laboratory animals. The response is multidimensional, involving several organ systems.

The adrenal glands increase their output of adrenaline and noradrenaline, the former more than the latter. Both increase liver blood flow and increase the metabolism of glycogen, fats, and proteins in an attempt to provide the additional fuel required. The pituitary gland is also stimulated, increasing its output of adrenocorticotropic hormone. This substance in turn stimulates the adrenal

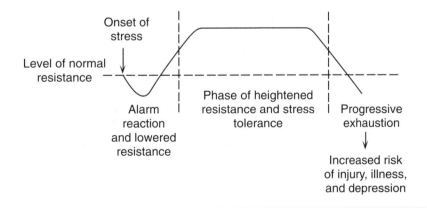

Figure 8.5 The three phases of Hans Selye's general adaptation syndrome. *Note.* From *The Lore of Running* by T.D. Noakes, 1991, Champaign, IL: Leisure Press. Copyright by Timothy D. Noakes. Adapted by permission.

cortex to increase its release of steroid hormones, notably aldosterone and a group of hormones best known as glucocorticoids (a good example is cortisone). Aldosterone assists with maintaining electrolyte balance; glucocorticoids have anti-inflammatory properties and also help mobilize fats and proteins for energy purposes. Testosterone levels in both men and women may be reduced or unaltered for reasons not clearly understood. Pituitary growth hormone levels are also elevated, increasing the potential for protein synthesis. Because many of the immune system substances (such as immunoglobulins) are proteins, this increased protein synthesis may be of benefit for improving the body's immunocompetence. Intense physical exercise stimulates protein breakdown in the working muscles.

All of the previously mentioned hormones inhibit both the release of insulin and its action on glucose uptake by muscle and fat cells. In turn, the liver responds by increasing its own glucose production. Along with an increased fatty acid secretion into the bloodstream, this provides an additional fuel source. An increased level of heat production with this fuel metabolism decreases the amount of chemical energy that can be harvested (as ATP) for any given quantity of fuel consumed. During severe stress this energy inefficiency can be increased as much as 10-fold, which mandates a considerably increased nutritional requirement.

An unscientific analogy to the body's reaction to stress could bring to mind a "reservoir of antistress" in the body that can be used to counteract the effects of applied stress. This reservoir could represent stored energy fuels, the immune system, and all the hormones and enzymes related to fuel metabolism and maintenance of immunological integrity. Overtaxing the performance limits of these systems may disrupt their synergistic interactions and deplete energy supplies, thereby decreasing the effectiveness of homeostatic mechanisms that previously were effective in handling the body's response to hard work. When this reservoir is depleted, continued resistance to the stress is not possible, and breakdown occurs.

Selye's work did not include the psychological and illness manifestations of stress because he worked with laboratory animals, but these aspects are no less important. In particular, the studies of Rahe (1972) provide useful insight. It was Rahe's contention that life experiences relate to disease prevalence. He developed a *life stress and illness model* whereby the ability of an individual's psychological defenses to cope with life problems determines the likelihood of acquiring illness. Excessive and prolonged anxiety, depression, and emotional distress, representing the inability to manage life problems effectively, carry with them a sizably increased risk for physical symptoms of illness. In part this is developmental. The studies of Weiner (1972) suggest that early behavioral experiences when growing up influence the nature of our responses to changing environmental situations. We'll describe additional psychological aspects of overtraining and staleness shortly.

The possibility of immunological suppression and thus an increased risk of infection accompanying hard training and excessively hard training (which can produce overtraining or staleness) has been difficult for epidemiologists to quantify. Three major difficulties have hindered forward progress:

- The great variability among individuals in response to exercise
- Difficulty in assigning equivalent long-term work loads to experimental study subjects
- The still incompletely understood nature of the immune system

There is both anecdotal (Jokl 1974) and epidemiological (J.G. Cannon 1993; Pedersen and Bruunsgaard 1995; Peters and Bateman 1983; Weidner 1994;) evidence that athletes seem to exhibit less resistance to minor infections than untrained people, suggesting a decreased effectiveness of the acquired (or specific) immune system. Through the abilities of specialized cells to recognize foreign macromolecules of infectious agents, this system results in the production of antigen-specific antibodies and certain other chemicals (called *interleukins*) that can increase the potency of the overall immunological response. The cells involved are lymphocytes, which become very specialized and metabolically highly active to carry out their task.

Work by Ardawi and Newsholme (1985) has suggested an almost certain interdependence between skeletal muscle cells and lymphocytes. Lymphocytes derive their energy from two fuel sources: glucose and glutamine. A major site for glutamine biosynthesis in the body is skeletal muscle, and its ability to produce adequate glutamine seems to be compromised when it is in a state of extensive repair following long-term intense exercise. If a glutamine debt should occur, the extent to which lymphocyte function is compromised may determine the prevalence of viral invasions or the rate of recovery from the effects of viral illnesses or fever.

A variety of recent studies have described the extent to which specific subtypes of lymphocytes are either increased or decreased in numbers as a result of long-term intense exercise. Current evidence points toward ratios of these subtypes that are altered in such a manner as to produce temporary immunological suppression (Mackinnon and Tomasi 1983; Nieman et al. 1989). Whether this is hormonally induced has not yet been clearly established. Corticosteroid hormones, elevated during exercise, are typically immunosuppressive, but hormones such as adrenaline and noradrenaline can increase lymphocyte populations (Galbo 1983). It also isn't clear yet how specific cell subtype ratios are changed in favor of immunosuppression or activation during chronic hard training.

Decreased resistance to infection is not limited to human athletes. Veterinarians working with race horses have also characterized a poor performance syndrome (Mumford and Rossdale 1980) that involves a positive relationship between upper respiratory tract infections and lackluster race efforts.

The interaction of psychological aspects of stress with immunological competency is also only beginning to be explored. The discovery of decreased immunoglobulin A levels in the saliva of students under the duress of major university examinations (Jemmott et al. 1983) suggests that immunosuppression to some extent can occur during periods of psychological stress. In this instance, immunosuppression is probably related to elevated adrenaline levels. The interaction of psychological with physiological mechanisms in permitting proper adaptation to a training load is well known. It appears as though physiological maladaptation can also be negatively affected by the interaction of psychological factors.

Psychological Dimensions of Overtraining

How do the psychological dimensions of overtraining and staleness interact with physiological changes? A common subjective report of an athlete who has entered an overtrained state is, "I'm training as hard as I ever have, but my gains are getting smaller and smaller. I just feel like giving up, but I know I shouldn't." The increased frustration, accompanied by decreased enthusiasm and dedication, can be so profound as to bring clinical signs of depression. Table 8.1 lists the wide variety of symptoms that may be observed to a limited extent during overtraining but that become more prevalent in both number and severity during staleness. A perusal of this list suggests that we are seeing a psychophysiological deterioration of stability: Both mind and body are affected. Eventually, this deterioration can have pathological consequences as well. This is to be expected because of the complex neuroendocrine interactions that direct the subtleties of human performance. A review of recent studies in this area (Kuipers and Keizer 1988) suggests that two types of staleness may be identifiable, depending on whether the sympathetic or parasympathetic portions of the autonomic nervous system are increased in their activity.

Staleness thus may be an athlete's manifestation of a combination of the pathophysiological exhaustion identified by Selye with additional psychological components. The kinds of detailed metabolic investigations that might identify the extent to which Selye's stress syndrome is similar to staleness are just beginning to be carried out in athletes. There are indeed some similarities (Kuipers and Keizer 1988), but the picture is far from clear. Medical diagnosticians have reported a condition seen in the general population known variously as *post-viral fatigue syndrome* (David, Wessly, and Pelosi 1988), *chronic fatigue syndrome* (Eichner 1989b), or *inadequate recovery syndrome* (Hendrickson and Verde 1994). It is characterized by a similarly wide variety of psychological and physiological symptoms, persistent malaise, and even a positive titer to Epstein-Barr virus. Distance runners who have entered what we would term staleness, characterized by a sizable number of the signs and symptoms listed in table 8.1, frequently also have a positive test result for Epstein-Barr virus (Roberts 1986).

The multifaceted nature of staleness frustrates those who would like to more precisely define it. Perhaps staleness and the syndrome (or syndromes) just discussed are variants of the same entity; we do not know at present. Eichner (1989a) brushes the syndrome aside for distance runners, considering it purely psycho-

---

TABLE 8.1

The Major Warning Signs of Overtraining and Staleness

Training-related

Unusual muscle soreness the day after a training session

Progressive increases in soreness with continued training

Performance plateau or decrement despite increased training

Inability to complete previously manageable training load

Elevated effort sense; delay in recovery from training

Thoughts of quitting training, skipping training

Lifestyle-related

Increased tension, depression, anger, fatigue, confusion; inability to relax

Decreased vigor in completing daily activities; things once pleasurable now are not

Poor-quality sleep

Health-related

Swelling of lymph nodes

Constipation, diarrhea

Increased incidence of illness (fever, head colds, etc.)

Increased blood pressure; increased morning pulse

Loss of weight; loss of appetite

logical, suggesting that positive thinking is the solution for affected runners who desire to restore their presyndrome excellence. We would suggest the alternative view: that the head does indeed have a body and that the two work together. When the body is not functioning properly, it lets the head know that indeed an imbalance is occurring that ought to be addressed.

Given the enormous mental drive that powers a runner to train and compete at a high level, an overtrained runner who continues to overwork may likely find it necessary to recruit more than the usual additional muscle cells from accessory muscles to complete a workout at a prescribed pace. These muscle cells may not be as fatigued as those that ordinarily serve as the prime movers. Their tension-generation velocities may be relatively normal, and their recruitment may permit attainment of the desired running paces. However, these muscles are not designed for the task at hand as specifically as the (now fatiguing) prime movers. We could hypothesize that there is a greater O_2 cost for this submaximal work output and that this runner's economy (movement efficiency) has decreased. If true, and if the decrease is large enough, this decreased economy could be detected by comparing O_2 consumption at various submaximal paces with previous values. Subjectively, the increased fatigue can be detected as an increased effort sense, but thus far no evidence exists to show that a runner who feels fatigued does in fact run less economically.

Athletes experiencing overtraining are more likely to perform worse in competition than if they were undertrained or optimally trained. This may not relate as much to physiological performance decrements as to the interaction of performance decrements with psychological attitudinal deficits, as indicated in table 8.1. The two summate, and during a competitive phase, when an optimal mental attitude directed toward successful performance assumes enormous importance, the interaction is seen clearly. A useful testing instrument for profiling psychological tension (McNair, Lorr, and Droppelman 1971) known as the *profile of mood states* (POMS) describes these attitudinal changes predictably. The pioneering studies of University of Wisconsin sport psychologist William Morgan characterized the onset of performance decrements in elite runners using this evaluation instrument. He found similar attitudinal changes in both men (Morgan and Pollock 1977) and women (Morgan, O'Connor, Sparling, and Pate 1987) as manageable training changed to overtraining and, just as important, as marginal overtraining changed back to recovery when tapering preceded a competitive period. Figure 8.6 illustrates two profiles, one from an athlete training normally in a properly prepared state for top-level competition and one from the same athlete showing symptoms of overtraining. During optimal preparation, attitudes such as depression, fatigue, confusion, anger, and tension are minimal in comparison to vigor. The overtrained athlete's profile shows an essential inversion of these measures of affective behavior.

In the jargon of sport psychologists, if the profile of the optimally prepared athlete is likened to a floating iceberg (figure 8.6a) and called an *iceberg profile,* then the overtrained athlete (figure 8.6b) will likely exhibit a *flipped iceberg profile* (Morgan 1985). This is where long-term monitoring of athletic performance and behavior can be useful for optimizing preparation. As training intensities are manipulated, appropriate changes in mood states may likely occur. Though fatigue and vigor may, respectively, increase and decrease during a period of intense training, these mood states should reverse during recovery or tapering. The continuum of performance abilities with training thus has undertraining at one end and staleness at the other, with optimal training and overtraining fitting somewhere in between. Both physiological and psychological variables can

a

b

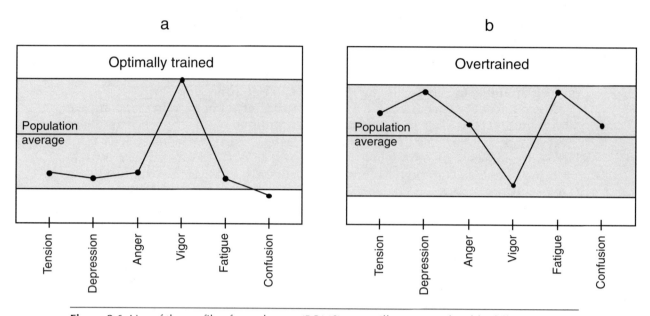

Figure 8.6 Use of the profile of mood states (POMS) test to illustrate predictably different mood states in overtrained and optimally prepared athletes. During optimal preparation, athletes score quite low in such measures of affective behavior as tension, depression, anger, fatigue, and confusion but very high in vigor, giving the so-called "iceberg profile" as shown in *a*. The overtrained state is characterized by a reversal of these mood states, causing a so-called "flipped iceberg profile," indicated in *b*. *Note.* From "The Facts and Fallacies of Overtraining and Staleness" by J. Kimiecik, 1988, *American Coach*, March/April, p.12. Copyright 1988 by Human Kinetics. Reprinted by permission.

be monitored to assess the possible shift from an optimally productive state to one suggestive of overtraining or staleness.

Preventing Overtraining

The earlier the symptoms of overtraining can be identified and managed, the more rapid and successful will be a return to effective progress and the less likely will be the development of staleness. This often is not easy to do. It is unfortunate but evident that a peculiar tunnel vision frequently impairs the perception of outstanding athletes and their coaches (perhaps because of their T personalities) regarding total work load management. They cannot imagine that doing too much will happen to them. Too often an individualized training plan has not provided periodic rest. Training is pushed into the realm of excess, either unknowingly (because coach and athlete do not jointly assess the results of work assigned) or simply because of a work ethic that continually promotes the attitude that more is better, that there is no gain without pain, and that the need for rest is a sign of weakness.

An athlete's body cannot become a bottomless sink-hole for physical training, and an athlete's mind cannot become obsessed with the fear that time allotted for recovery will diminish the fitness gains acquired from the physical work. Such a preparation regimen is an almost guaranteed prescription to initiate overtraining, overuse injury, or eventual staleness. Just as an effective doctor-patient relationship requires a correct diagnosis, a correct prescription, and faithful adherence to taking the medication, so it is with an athlete and coach in developing an effective training plan. When coach and athlete ask whether it is appropriate to train harder or increase volume, the more important question really is, "Is more really necessary?" Athletes who are products of such an environment have long and productive careers with few setbacks.

Unfortunately, a percentage of coaches go overboard, either because of their aggressive personality, or because they unknowingly are a kind of cult leader. In unbending fashion these coaches write generic training plans for the athlete group and expect that all will tolerate the assigned training loads without discussion or debate (Newton and Durkin 1988). Often such coaches are frustrated ex-athletes, whose careers may have been terminated by injury or simply not being quite talented enough to make the grade, and who now see their charges as the athletes they wished they could be. Because of these coaches' dictatorial natures, for the athletes, thinking is out of the question and obeying is the only alternative; they will simply push on and not admit that they are unduly fatigued, depressed, or even marginally injured. If the coach's record in previous years has been successful, the athletes may even convince themselves that this state of profound fatigue, depression, or injury is necessary or appropriate for victory. Even if conversations between coach and athletes occur, the athletes may be afraid to admit any deficiencies that could be construed as signs of weakness. The coach may rationalize any orneriness from the athletes as simply a little irritability from a certain amount of expected fatigue caused by hard training. The emotional environment simply does not permit athletes and coach to appreciate that, by continuing high-level work output without compensatory rest, a high risk of developing overtraining or overuse injury is inevitable.

Attempting to resolve such a situation reminds us of trying to pick up an irritated porcupine. There is no good direction from which to begin making progress! Individual athletes eventually become incapable of excellent performance or get injured and are eliminated from further competition. The coach doesn't learn the reasons for the various athletes' overstress partly because the environment for two-way exchange hasn't developed. And if the team does well, thanks to a sufficiently large group of athletes still running well who can amass scoring points in the championship meet, the injured athletes are simply viewed as people who didn't respond properly to the training program.

Hopefully, the kind of coaching mentality portrayed here is on its way out of the profession, thanks to expanding programs of coaching education. We can only hope that athletes seeking to develop an effective coaching relationship will be sensitive at the outset to the genuine need for a harmonious two-way relationship based on a mutual desire for forward progress rather than a one-sided game of imposed dominance and control by one over the other. Athletes should, as well, keep good records of progress, thereby permitting easy identification of steady rises, plateaus, or declines in performance. In this way, if it becomes appropriate to change coaching relationships over time, they will have a reliable record of their development, which can be used functionally in the next stage of their development.

Can Overtraining Be Identified Before It Occurs?

Three primary circumstances in the training environment most frequently set the stage for the kind of fatigue that elicits either overtraining or overuse injury. One is the conclusion that performance in either training or racing has started to deteriorate because the athlete simply has not been training enough in quantity, quality, or both. The logic behind this conclusion seems simple, but is incorrect:

Because training should bring improvement of performance, and no training should result in no improvement, then a falling-off in performance can be caused only by inadequate training. This logic is incorrect because at the point of performance deterioration, the athlete is no longer capable of responding in the usual manner to a training stress. No longer does more beget more; here, more will beget less and less will beget more. The third variable in the developmental equation—recovery/rest in addition to quantity and quality—needs to be greater.

The second circumstance occurs following a successful series of races or a few quality mesocycles of training. A feeling of invincibility or a feeling that better results would accrue through more training, particularly because the athlete achieved good results without feeling overtaxed from a previous difficult training load, helps ingrain the belief that more work can be tolerated. In fact, as stated, the situation may be quite the opposite. The excellent results probably resulted from just the correct balance of quantity, quality, and recovery. Very slight increases in work load may continue to raise the athlete to a new plateau. Substantial increases may very likely be excessive.

The third circumstance occurs when an athlete has recovered from a setback such as an injury or illness, particularly when relatively little time remains for proper preparation for an upcoming important competitive period. Instead of not competing and adjusting goals for a later competitive period, the athlete rapidly increases the quantity and quality of training without incorporating adequate rest. Initially, the athlete is fresh, both physically and mentally, from the layoff. But the body is inadequately prepared to manage the training load. Enormous improvements occur initially, but benefits do not accrue because of either inadequate rest or excessive loads.

Athletes and coaches thus find themselves in a dilemma when they devise a training plan. Three crucial questions need answers:

1. How much training can be done so that improved performance will occur but overtraining will not?
2. What kinds of training or other lifestyle patterns pose increased risks of overtraining?
3. Are there any telltale early-warning signs that may mark the onset of overtraining and staleness?

The first question is the most difficult to answer, because for each athlete it is different. The three major groups of variables that contribute to stress as training volume begins to increase are lifestyle, genetic factors, and initial fitness level. One suggestion for identifying optimal manageable training loads resides in careful examination of training logs from similar training periods to identify the combination of lifestyle and training loads previously manageable for favorable progress. A rule of thumb (with only the evidence of experience to back it up) suggests that no more than a 5% increase in training load each week can be managed effectively over a period such as a microcycle with healthy and progressive homeostatic adaptation. Also, volume and intensity of training should not be increased simultaneously.

Such deliberations, however, demand well-documented training records and a healthy athlete at the start of the training period. Tabulations should include data such as the weekly and monthly distance run; the total weekly distance that represents aerobic, long-interval (marginally anaerobic), and short-interval (considerably anaerobic) work; the number of rest days per week or month;

quantification of running paces and interval rests for faster sessions; and a summary of interruptions in the continuity of routine (family or job difficulties, long distance travel, illness, small injuries, etc.). Often when such data are viewed in tabular fashion and are not hidden among pages of daily training details, trends of shifts away from an optimal pattern of work and rest can be discerned clearly.

An important unsolved problem for coaches that scientists ought to help resolve is the development of a method for assigning a numerical indicator of intensity to all training sessions, permitting a more specific comparison of such sessions, and also a cumulative indicator of training load. The body does this very nicely as it accommodates to each day's training assignment. Weather, terrain, psychological factors, muscle cell O_2 and fuel availability, range of motion, and many other factors all contribute to the totality of the body's response to a training session. As soon as we can quantify this net effect as well as the body itself does, we can better distinguish between training load and overload. With the computer age upon us, this should be simple. Canadian physiologist Eric Banister is making substantial progress in this direction, and his published work should be available soon (Anderson 1995). A major breakthrough in better estimating when hard training turns into overtraining could occur when such analyses are possible.

The second question about training and lifestyle patterns is a little easier to answer, again provided that adequate documentation of training records and responses is available for perusal. Several kinds of activity patterns should be red-flagged because of their high risk of causing the kind of overwork that brings on overtraining. These include the following:

- Too many competitions closely spaced without adequate recovery between them or without a well-defined rest break after the series
- A sudden rather than gradual increase in quantity or intensity of training
- Increased emphasis on one training format, so that certain muscle groups are challenged excessively
- Increased non-training-related, extraneous stress factors (travel, irregular daily schedule, inadequate sleep, emotional confrontations, negative energy or water balance, etc.)

Athletes often fail to realize the magnitude of both the inhibitory and summating effect of these extraneous factors on optimal recovery from hard training. They very definitely increase the total lifestyle load. Conversely, however, the enhancement of recovery and thereby a possibility for absorbing even more difficult training as a result of having these extraneous stressors removed underlies the desire of many athletes to adjourn periodically to training camp environments. Some nations maintain such camps on a year-round basis for their developing athletes. Nutritious food at regular intervals, excellent training facilities, massage and other recuperative therapeutic modalities, recreational diversions, and minimal outside influences form an ideal environment for a motivated athlete. However, the risk of excessive training in such a sport haven is very great. Therefore, these training camp sessions are usually restricted to no more than two weeks, and recovery, tapering, and some form of small competition or time trial are typically scheduled in the following week.

Keith Brantly has made use of such a training camp situation very successfully. In his fall preparations for a successful U.S. men's marathon championship performance in January 1995 at Charlotte, North Carolina, he alternated two to three weeks of easy training at home in flat, sea-level, warm and humid Florida (emphasizing volume training and practicing fluid intake during long runs) with two to three weeks of hard training in the mild-altitude mountains of North Carolina (emphasizing quality training to build strength on challenging, hilly terrain). The modest altitude stimulus provided a small increase in red blood cell production for increased blood O_2-carrying ability. The minimal time required to travel between the two locations was not stressful, and the two quite different training formats ensured that a variety of muscle groups were stimulated in the training process. Freedom from extraneous stressors also ensured the freshness required to best accommodate to the work loads assigned. The strategy worked so well that he utilized it in his preparations for the 1996 Olympic marathon in Atlanta. During the late spring and early summer, the heat, humidity, and hills simulated perfectly the Atlanta marathon racing environment.

Subjective Indicators

Although a quest among the scientific and medical community has been intense in its efforts to discover blood chemistry markers that might suggest the onset of overtraining, the evidence at the moment suggests that "self-reported ratings of well-being" may be actually more useful (Hooper and Mackinnon 1995). Put simply, fine-tuned athletes know themselves very well; if they only believe what they are sensing, they probably can clearly recognize all the telltale signs of impending overtraining in their perception of training effectiveness.

The essence of how to sense that one has "gone over the edge" and is failing to adapt to the ongoing combination of training load and lifestyle is fairly simple to explain, as shown in table 8.1. Any of the warning signs summarized in table 8.1 may occur on occasion in isolated fashion and simply suggest a temporary setback in training continuity. But when hard training becomes overtraining, these symptoms begin to summate, and performance shows consistent deterioration. Our collective experience in the close management of several dozen elite-level distance runners over nearly 10 years suggests that four primary behavioral indicators—when they can be observed *in combination*—are signs of developing overtraining and possibly staleness unless prompt and aggressive recovery measures are begun. These indicators are as follows:

- A clearly greater effort sense required to finish a speed session, time trial, or race effort at a pace that previously was entirely manageable under similar environmental conditions. Running intervals cannot be done at previously manageable paces unless considerably longer recovery is provided.

- A clearly recognizable inadequacy of the usual day-to-day recovery time for completion of a training assignment, often seen as an increased morning heart rate or poor-quality sleep and an ongoing feeling of dehydration.

- Problems of attitude (moodiness, being argument-prone and complaining, etc.). This might be likened to the burnout that workers in high-stress jobs in the business world experience.

- A decreased drive to train. Athletes no longer look forward to the challenge of a hard training session and have almost a dread of achieving expected poor results.

Heeding the signs immediately and taking aggressive recovery measures can very often provide the recovery turnaround that prevents further performance degeneration. These recovery measures are indeed aggressive: Examples include reducing the training volume by 50% to 60%, foregoing an upcoming competition, improving regularity and quality of sleep and nutritional intake, and removing the effects of other extraneous stressors by rearranging priorities. Even then, however, a few weeks of tempered training are needed, and the previously intense training regimen should be resumed only slowly, thereby preventing a return to the earlier total stress load. The signal to resume full training is a renewed interest in and ability to train hard in a normal, adaptive fashion.

Overtraining and staleness should be considered as very real and important setbacks in forward development. Their effects must be removed by decreasing the stress load. There is typically no other choice. Cross-training or other forms of active rest are often appropriate to maintain at least some level of fitness, but the question will always remain of how much is too much. And doing too much does not promote recovery.

In our discussions over the years with elite-level runners who have experienced overuse injuries or staleness, it has become evident that they indeed experienced the previously described early-warning signs, but they ignored them. Their training goals had been identified in terms of an upcoming competitive phase, and the thought that overtraining or overuse injury could ever occur was simply not in those plans. When these symptoms occurred, it was simply assumed that somehow they would go away, and the athletes' tolerance to their developing effects was seen as another indicator of overall toughness. Just as often these athletes were under the direction of coaches who would not tolerate injury or the suggestion of inserting recovery time to permit restoration of normal adaptive mechanisms. Only when it was too late, when injury, illness, or profound staleness developed, did the athletes realize that their training plan design was inappropriate to their adaptive abilities. They felt inferior and tended to blame themselves for their deterioration rather than even considering as a contributory element the unbending coach who permitted no deviation or discussion and who concluded that the reason the athletes failed was that they simply didn't respond adequately to the training regimen.

Objective Indicators

Just as a physician makes use of the clinical laboratory to monitor the patient's health status, so also it is appropriate and useful for athletes and coaches to develop a collaborative relationship with knowledgeable sport science or sports medicine personnel who have a sincere interest in the performance success of the athletes being monitored. Increasing study of overtraining and staleness has provided a better diagnostic awareness for early detection through the use of psychological evaluation (such as the POMS test for mood changes described earlier) and blood chemistry profiling (quantifying variations in blood chemistry variables that suggest metabolic imbalance).

The serious setback resulting from staleness has stimulated great interest in a search for either one or a small number of easily measurable physiological variables that would be highly suggestive of overtraining and its consequences. Because the overstress phenomenon is multifaceted, such a simple solution seems unlikely. But the search goes on, though it has not been easy (Rowbottom et al. 1995). Ideally, to identify overtraining before it occurs is best. But this in itself may be difficult. If specific variables unique to overtraining are identifiable, these wouldn't occur until after overtraining had begun.

A primary difficulty in identifying such variables is that arduous training by itself causes measurable changes in cellular physiology that can be seen by profiling various blood chemistry and physiological values. The difference between serious but manageable training and the onset of overtraining is essentially one of degree. There is a gray area where adaptive physiological responses are not quite keeping up with demand. The problem of inter- and intraindividual variability in blood chemistry makes it difficult to suggest specific overtraining threshold values applicable to everyone. However, deviations from normal limits in a group of selected variables measured somewhat frequently (e.g., monthly or quarterly) and compared with the particular athlete's baseline blood chemistry profile may be enough to suggest that the body is not maintaining homeostatic equilibrium, with overtraining a likely result. Some of the more commonly measured blood chemistry variables, which we have already discussed in this chapter and in chapter 4, include hemoglobin (an indicator of anemia), ferritin (an indicator of latent anemia), creatine kinase (an indicator of muscle cell membrane permeability increases), hydroxyproline (an indicator of tendon breakdown), reticulocytes (an indicator of adequate red blood cell production), and haptoglobin (an indicator of increased hemolysis).

Our experience in interpreting blood chemistry profiles for elite distance runners suggests a substantial reduction in training, along with reevaluation of training loads and nutritional status, when the four behavioral markers previously listed are substantially altered and when additional physiological changes, to be mentioned shortly, occur. These athletes typically have not developed symptoms of overtraining, so it's tempting to suggest that this is one acceptable regimen for preventing overtraining. Scientifically, of course, we could only prove this by continuing the training load and finding that overtraining symptoms and eventual staleness resulted. We are interested in this occurring, and so we play it safe.

Some have suggested the value of monitoring generalized human performance data, such as hours of sleep each night or morning heart rate (Ryan et al. 1983; Dressendorfer, Wade, and Scaff 1985). Similar difficulties occur in acquiring and interpreting these data as well. As an example, recording *hours of sleep* each night may provide a useful estimate of needed rest. But going to bed late and sleeping late the next morning do not typically provide as restful a night's sleep as the usual sleeping pattern. Thus, quality of sleep and also sleep patterns should be documented. The measurement of *morning pulse* may be useful as an index of generalized recovery. But different conditions of measurement can increase variability considerably: awaking naturally versus with an alarm, measuring before or after arising from bed, and so on.

A third potentially useful variable is *body weight*. Again, when and how to measure is critical. The same weighing device ought to be used for each measurement. Following a training session might be the best time to measure this so-called training weight. But not all sessions are similar, because of weather conditions and the nature of the training load. And depending on circumstances, athletes may or may not drink fluids during the session, further modifying the weight loss picture. Morning weight is also sometimes used, following bladder and bowel activities and before breakfast. Notable elevations in heart rate, decreases in body weight, or either decreased sleep or insomnia, particularly when they occur together, should raise suspicion that an overtrained state is imminent. The lesson to be learned from this is that poorly collected data can be an excellent source of noninformation. Useful conclusions can be derived only from well-collected data obtained through meaningful planning.

SUMMARY

Extending a Running Career

1. Optimal training loads should bring optimal improvement in performance capability. A crucial question is how to ensure an optimal training load. The nature of competitive sport, that is, a contest requiring athletes to perform at their very best, mandates a high level of motivation for doing all the work required to achieve the greatest possible fitness. This intense motivation, a personality trait in gifted athletes, often clouds athletes' ability to discern the difference between optimal and excessive work.

2. Fatigue and delayed-onset muscle soreness are accompanying components of the training process of athletes who desire substantial improvements in their performance capabilities. This is because they are manifestations of the metabolic effects of hard training on organ systems. Unusually challenging exercise of a temporary nature typically induces delayed-onset muscular soreness, recovery from which occurs in a few days. Overuse injuries are more likely to result from extended periods of inappropriately high training volume or intensity (overtraining). Rapid turnover rates for tissues such as muscles and tendons occur as a result of sizable periods of anaerobic metabolism and thus of near-maximal or maximal work rates. If optimal physiological adaptation occurs, recovery should find the trained individual more capable of enduring similar work loads.

3. Short-term overtraining (or simply overtraining) results when inadequate recovery is permitted from a challenging training load. Both psychological and physiological signs and symptoms announce its presence, and a considerably greater period of recovery is required than usually is provided for homeostatic restitution to occur. Performance in races is typically poor.

4. Long-term overtraining (or staleness) results when overtraining continues unabated. Again, psychological and physiological indicators signal its existence, but these now are more numerous and obvious, accompanied by increased incidence of illness and a predilection to overuse injuries. Recovery may require anywhere from weeks to a month or more.

5. The risks of inhibiting good performance because of fatigue or the risks of preventing continued progress because of overuse injury or staleness are so great that all athletes and coaches desirous of achieving sport excellence must make it a top priority to take appropriate steps to minimize their occurrence. Hard training does not become overtraining at any precise moment, because the latter occurs as a result of the sum of hard training occurring too long without adequate compensatory recovery or rest. Although it is difficult to back away, even temporarily, from continued hard training when one feels confident that development is proceeding well, somehow the mind-set of an athlete must be geared toward the reality that planned adequate rest is a part of training and essential for continuing this excellent development. When rest is indeed adequate, athletes consistently feel good about themselves and their training and have a positive attitude and sense of confidence.

6. The single best method for minimizing the risk of overtraining includes careful monitoring of the past and present training history and present lifestyle

status and using this knowledge in the training plan design with appropriate reassessment. Combinations of unusual increases in training volume or quality, adverse changes in training environment (warmer weather or the addition of hilly terrain), or the addition of other lifestyle stress factors when unaccompanied by a corresponding increase in rest, nutrition, or use of recuperative and restorative therapeutic modalities is unwise and can best be avoided by careful consideration of written training records. Accurate record keeping with periodic objective review and analysis should form the first line of defense against overtraining. The conclusions from such analyses can also predict the possibility of risk.

7. Subjective indicators of the accumulating effects of very hard training can be effective early warning signs that overtraining is occurring. The best subjective indicators include (a) increased effort sense for a given pace, (b) decreased performance abilities despite the typically allocated rest, (c) increased irritability and moodiness, and (d) decreased drive to train.

8. Individualized training plans, updated continually to reflect an athlete's ongoing adaptations to training, have far less risk of inducing overtraining than generic training plans intended for a group. Too often such group plans stimulate overtraining in the less fit or less talented athletes and understimulate the more gifted ones, causing the latter to include additional work that may also bring overtraining if not controlled appropriately. Athletes need to be constantly aware of whether their developmental environment—an effective two-way communication relationship with their coach and appropriate interaction with other athletes in their training environment—is appropriate for their optimum improvement.

9. Metabolic indicators, as measured by changes in the values reported for blood chemistry variables, are at present imprecise indicators for the actual onset of overtraining, because no consistently identifiable threshold level exists for this condition. Individual differences are sizable. Periodic blood chemistry profiling as part of routine health evaluation of athletes in training will be valuable in providing an ongoing accurate picture of what is typical for each athlete. For those athletes who have the luxury of periodic, long-term (i.e., several years) health care monitoring, changes in such variables are useful indicators that overtraining may be likely. When alterations from this normally stable blood chemistry picture occur in a direction that logically suggests possible metabolic imbalance, prompt consideration of these changes in the context of that athlete's training and lifestyle can be useful for restoring equilibrium. A few such blood chemistry variables have been described. Other important physiological alterations that can be monitored include an increase in morning heart rate, progressive weight loss, decreased sleep effectiveness, and a loss of appetite. Caution must be taken, however, to obtain information that has consistency and validity for useful interpretation.

References

Abraham, W.M. 1977. Factors in delayed muscle soreness. *Medicine and Science in Sports* 9:11-20.

Anderson, O. 1995. Precision training. *Runner's World* 30(4):36.

Archambault, J.M.; Wiley, J.P.; and Bray, R.C. 1995. Exercise loading of tendons and the development of overuse injuries. *Sports Medicine* 20:77-89.

Ardawi, M.S., and Newsholme, E.A. 1985. Metabolism in lymphocytes and its importance in the immune response. *Essays in Biochemistry* 21:1-43.

Armstrong, R.B. 1984. Mechanisms of exercise-induced delayed onset muscular soreness: A brief review. *Medicine and Science in Sports and Exercise* 16:529-538.

Berdanier, C.D. 1987. The many faces of stress. *Nutrition Today* 22(2):12-17.

Budgett, R. 1990. Overtraining syndrome. *British Journal of Sports Medicine* 24:231-236.

Cannon, J.G. 1993. Exercise and resistance to infection. *Journal of Applied Physiology* 74:973-981.

Cannon, W.B. 1929. Organization for physiological homeostasis. *Physiological Reviews* 9:399-431.

Costill, D.L. 1988. Carbohydrates for exercise: Dietary demands for optimum performance. *International Journal of Sports Medicine* 9:1-18.

Counsilman, J.E. 1968. *The science of swimming.* London: Pelham.

David, A.S.; Wessly, S.; and Pelosi, A.J. 1988. Post-viral fatigue syndrome: Time for a new approach. *British Medical Journal* 296:696-699.

Davies, K.J.A.; Packer, A.; and Brooks, G.A. 1982. Exercise bioenergetics following sprint training. *Archives of Biochemistry and Biophysics* 215:260-265.

Dressendorfer, R.H., and Wade, C.E. 1983. The muscular overuse syndrome in long-distance runners. *Physician and Sportsmedicine* 11(11):116-130.

Dressendorfer, R.H.; Wade, C.E.; and Scaff, J.H. 1985. Increased morning heart rate in runners: A valid sign of overtraining? *Physician and Sportsmedicine* 13(8):77-86.

Ebbeling, C.B., and Clarkson, P.M. 1989. Exercise-induced muscle damage and adaptation. *Sports Medicine* 7:207-234.

Eichner, E. 1989a. Chronic fatigue syndrome: How vulnerable are athletes? *Physician and Sportsmedicine* 17(6):157-160.

———. 1989b. Chronic fatigue syndrome: Searching for the cause and treatment. *Physician and Sportsmedicine* 17(6):142-152.

Engelhardt, W.A. 1932. Die Beziehungen zwischen Atmung und Pyrophatumsatz in Vögelerythrocyten (The relationships between respiration and phosphate turnover in bird erythrocytes). *Biochemische Zeitschrift* 251:343-368.

Evans, W.J. 1987. Exercise-induced skeletal muscle damage. *Physician and Sportsmedicine* 15(1):89-100.

Farley, F. 1986. The big T in personality. *Anthropology and Education Quarterly* 20(5):44-52.

Francis, K., and Hoobler, T. 1988. Delayed onset muscle soreness and decreased isokinetic strength. *Journal of Applied Sports Science Research* 2:20-23.

Fry, R.W.; Morton, A.R.; Garcia-Webb, P.; Crawford, G.P.M.; and Keast, D. 1992. Biological responses to overload training in endurance sports. *European Journal of Applied Physiology* 64:335-344.

Galbo, H. 1983. *Hormonal and metabolic adaptation to exercise.* Stuttgart: Thieme Verlag.

Hagerman, F.C.; Hikida, R.S.; Staron, R.S.; Sherman, W.M.; and Costill, D.L. 1984. Muscle damage in marathon runners. *Physician and Sportsmedicine* 12(11):39-46.

Hendrickson, C.D., and Verde, T.J. 1994. Inadequate recovery from vigorous exercise. *Physician and Sportsmedicine* 22(5):56-64.

Hill, A.V. 1951. The mechanics of voluntary muscle. *Lancet* 261:947-954.

Hodgdon, J.; Riedy, M.; Goforth, H.; Norton, J.; Murguia, M.; Mandelbaum, B.; and Vailas, A.C. 1988. Plasma hydroxyproline and its association to overuse training. *Medicine and Science in Sports and Exercise* 20:S10.

Hooper, S.L., and Mackinnon, L.T. 1995. Monitoring overtraining in athletes. *Sports Medicine* 20:321-327.

Hough, T. 1902. Ergographic studies in muscle soreness. *American Journal of Physiology* 7:76-92.

Jemmott, J.B.; Borysenko, J.Z.; Borysenko, M.; McClelland, D.C.; Chapman, R.; Meyer, D.; and Benson, H. 1983. Academic stress, power motivation, and decrease in secretion rate of salivary secretory immunoglobin A. *Lancet* 1:1400-1402.

Jokl, E. 1974. The immunological status of athletes. *Journal of Sports Medicine* 14:165-167.

Jones, D.C., and James, S.L. 1987. Overuse injuries of the lower extremity. *Clinics in Sports Medicine* 6:273-290.

Kimiecik, J. 1988. The facts and fallacies of overtraining and staleness. *American Coach* (March/April):12.

Kuipers, H., and Keizer, H.A. 1988. Overtraining in elite athletes. *Sports Medicine* 6:79-92.

Lieber, R.L., and Friden, J. 1988. Selective damage of fast glycolytic muscle fibers with eccentric contraction of the rabbit tibialis anterior. *Acta Physiologica Scandinavica* 133:587-588.

Mackinnon, L.T., and Tomasi, T.B. 1983. Immunology of exercise. *Annals of Sports Medicine* 3:1-4.

Margaria, R. 1972. Positive and negative work performances and their efficiencies in human locomotion. In *Environmental effects on work performance,* eds. G.R. Cummings, D. Snidal, and A.W. Taylor, 215-228. Toronto: Canadian Association of Sports Sciences.

McNair, D.M.; Lorr, M.; and Droppelman, L.F. 1971. *Profile of mood states manual.* San Diego: Educational and Industrial Testing Service.

Morgan, W.P. 1985. Selected psychological factors limiting performance: A mental health model. In *Limits of human performance,* eds. D.H. Clarke and H.M. Eckert, 70-80. Champaign, IL: Human Kinetics.

Morgan, W.P.; Brown, D.R.; Raglin, J.S.; O'Connor, P.J.; and Ellickson, K.A. 1987. Psychological monitoring of overtraining and staleness. *British Journal of Sports Medicine* 21:107-114.

Morgan, W.P.; O'Connor, P.J.; Sparling, P.B.; and Pate, R.R. 1987. Psychological characterization of the elite female distance runner. *International Journal of Sports Medicine* 8:S124-S131.

Morgan, W.P., and Pollock, M.L. 1977. Psychologic characterization of the elite distance runner. *Annals of the New York Academy of Sciences* 301:383-403.

Mosso, A. [1905] 1915. *Fatigue.* 3rd ed. Trans. M. Drummond and W.G. Drummond. London: Allen and Unwin.

Mumford, J.A., and Rossdale, P.D. 1980. Virus and its relationship to the "poor performance syndrome." *Equine Veterinary Journal* 12:3-9.

Newham, D.J.; Mills, K.R.; Quigley, R.; and Edwards, R.H.T. 1982. Muscle pain and tenderness after exercise. *Australian Journal of Sports Medicine and Exercise Science* 14:129-131.

———. 1983. Pain and fatigue after concentric and eccentric muscle contractions. *Clinical Science* 64:55-62.

Newton, J., and Durkin, J.D. 1988. *Running to the top of the mountain.* Roselle, IL: J and J Winning Edge.

Nieman, D.C.; Berk, L.S.; Simpson-Westerberg, M.; Arabatzis, K.; Youngberg, S.; Tan, S.A.; Lee, J.W.; and Eby, W.C. 1989. Effects of long-endurance running on immune system parameters and lymphocyte function in experienced marathoners. *International Journal of Sports Medicine* 5:317-323.

Noakes, T.D. 1988. Implications of exercise testing for prediction of athletic performance:

A contemporary perspective. *Medicine and Science in Sports and Exercise* 20:319-330.

———. 1991. *The lore of running*. Champaign, IL: Leisure Press.

Pedersen, B.K., and Bruunsgaard, H. 1995. How physical exercise influences the establishment of infections. *Sports Medicine* 19:393-400.

Peters, E.M., and Bateman, E.P. 1983. Ultra-marathon running and upper respiratory tract infections: An epidemiological survey. *South African Medical Journal* 64:582-584.

Rahe, R.H. 1972. Subjects' recent life changes and their near-future illness susceptibility. *Advances in Psychosomatic Medicine* 8:2-19.

Riedy, M.; Hodgdon, J.; Goforth, H.; Norton, J.; Murguia, M.; Mandelbaum, B.; and Vailas, A.C. 1988. A serum marker for monitoring the exercise-induced degradation of connective tissues. *Medicine and Science in Sports and Exercise* 20:S10.

Roberts, J.A. 1986. Virus illness and sports performance. *Sports Medicine* 3:298-303.

Rowbottom, D.G.; Keast, D.; Goodman, C.; and Morton, R.A. 1995. The haematological, biochemical and immunological profile of athletes suffering from the overtraining syndrome. *European Journal of Applied Physiology* 70:502-509.

Ryan, A.J.; Brown, R.L.; Frederick, E.C.; Falsetti, H.L.; and Burke, E.L. 1983. Overtraining of athletes: Round table. *Physician and Sportsmedicine* 11(6):93-110.

Schwane, J.A.; Johnson, S.R.; Vandenakker, C.B.; and Armstrong, R.B. 1983. Delayed-onset muscular soreness and plasma CPK and LDH activities after downhill running. *Medicine and Science in Sports and Exercise* 15:51-56.

Schwane, J.A.; Williams, J.S.; and Sloan, J.H. 1987. Effects of training on delayed muscle soreness and serum creatine kinase activity after running. *Medicine and Science in Sports and Exercise* 19:584-590.

Selye, H. 1976. *The stress of life*. New York: McGraw-Hill.

Siegel, A.J.; Silverman, L.M.; and Lopez, R.E. 1980. Creatine kinase elevations in marathon runners: Relationship to training and competition. *Yale Journal of Biology and Medicine* 53:275-279.

Urhausen, A.; Gabriel, H.; and Kindermann, W. 1995. Blood hormones as markers of training stress and overtraining. *Sports Medicine* 20:251-276.

Warhol, M.J.; Siegel, A.J.; Evans, W.J.; and Silverman, L.M. 1985. Skeletal muscle injury and repair in marathon runners after competition. *American Journal of Pathology* 118:331-339.

Weidner, T.G. 1994. Literature review: Upper respiratory illness and sport and exercise. *International Journal of Sports Medicine* 15:1-9.

Weiner, H. 1972. The transduction of experience by the brain. *Psychosomatic Medicine* 34:335-380.

Weltman, A.; Janney, C.; Rians, C.B.; Strand, K.; Berg, B.; Tippitt, S.; Wise, J.; Cahill, B.R.; and Catch, F.I. 1986. The effects of hydraulic resistance strength training in pre-pubertal males. *Medicine and Science in Sports and Exercise* 18:629-638.

INDEX

ABOUT THE AUTHORS

David Martin

Sebastian Coe & Peter Coe

No two authors are better qualified than David Martin and Peter Coe to address both the physiology and coaching of distance running.

Martin has served as marathon chair of USA Track & Field's (USATF) Men's Development Committee since 1979 and as chair of the national governing body's Sport Science Subcommittee since 1984. These positions have allowed him to coach, advise, and scientifically evaluate many of America's best men and women distance runners. They have also provided him the opportunity to work with and learn from other top coaches and sports scientists around the world.

A fellow of the American College of Sports Medicine, Martin is the author of four books, including *The High Jump Book, The Marathon Footrace,* and *Training Distance Runners.* He also is a contributor *to New Studies in Athletics,* the technical journal of the International Amateur Athletic Federation.

Dr. Martin is a regents professor of health sciences at Georgia State University, which has three times honored him as a distinguished professor. He is also a results statistician for the Association of International Marathons and the Association for Track & Field Statisticians.

Peter Coe has successfully coached domestic and foreign runners at all levels, but he is probably best known for guiding his son Sebastian to one of the greatest middle-distance running careers of all time. Under Peter's tutelage, Sebastian won two Olympic gold medals in the 1500-meter run and two Olympic silver medals in the 800-meter run; a bronze, a silver, and a gold at the European championships; and 12 world records.

A retired engineer, Coe is a recognized international lecturer and a writer. He is author of *Training Distance Runners* and *Winning Running.* Coe was presented the Senior Coaching Award by the British Athletics Association and was named Coach of the Year by the British Milers' Club—an organization for which he served as chairman for several years.

More Resources for Runners

Marathon & Beyond

Journal
Richard Benyo, Editor

Frequency: Bimonthly (January, March, May, July, September, November)
ISSN: 1088-6672 • **Item:** JMAB
Call for subscription rates.

Each issue of *Marathon & Beyond* focuses on the specific needs of marathoners and ultrarunners. The journal features up-to-the-minute news on training techniques, race strategies, nutrition, and health concerns; profiles of important races; stories from the race travels of women's marathoning pioneer Kathrine Switzer; well-known runners' recollections of their most memorable races; and answers to your running questions from our panel of experts.

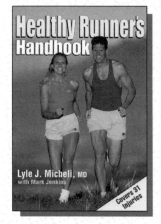

Healthy Runner's Handbook

Lyle J. Micheli, MD, with Mark Jenkins

1996 • Paper • 264 pp • Item PMIC0524
ISBN 0-88011-524-6 • $16.95 ($24.95 Canadian)

> **"If you want to train injury free, *Healthy Runner's Handbook* is a book you cannot live without."**
> **Arturo Barrios**
> Professional runner, Reebok Racing Club
> Two-time Pan-American Games gold medalist
> Two-time Olympian

Healthy Runner's Handbook will help you continue running safely and successfully. The book shows runners how to diagnose, care for, and rehabilitate 31 common overuse injuries, plus it provides useful advice on how to prevent such injuries.

Better Runs

25 Years' Worth of Lessons for Running Faster and Farther
Joe Henderson
Foreword by Jeff Galloway

1996 • Paper • 264 pp • Item PHEN0866
ISBN 0-87322-866-9 • $14.95 ($19.95 Canadian)

> **"A treasure trove of helpful hints, with amusing anecdotes, stories, and personalities from running's rich history. Definitely a book that will enlighten and inspire."**
> **Joan Ullyot, MD**
> Top Master's Runner, sports physician, and author of *Women's Running*

Drawing on 25 years of editorial work for *Runner's World*, more than 700 races, and his experience as author of more than a dozen books and countless articles, Joe Henderson shares what he and others have learned about running. *Better Runs* will boost your motivation, performance, and enjoyment as a runner.

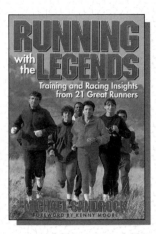

Running With the Legends
Michael Sandrock
Foreword by Kenny Moore
1996 • Paper • 592 pp • Item PSAN0493
ISBN 0-87322-493-0 • $19.95 ($29.95 Canadian)

> **"I feel I have 21 new friends in the running community. When I have a question about my own running career, I can just open *Running With the Legends*, read a chapter, and my question will be answered."**
> **Gwyn Coogan**
> 10,000-meter Olympian, 1992
> Twin Cities Marathon winner, 1995

From special tips you can use to incredible feats that will motivate you, *Running with the Legends* is full of material to enhance your own running and appreciation of those who have set the standard for excellence.

Boston Marathon
The First Century of the World's Premier Running Event
Centennial Race Edition
Tom Derderian
Forewords by Joan Benoit Samuelson and Bill Rodgers
1996 • Paper • 664 pp • Item PDER0479
ISBN 0-88011-479-7 • $21.95 ($32.95 Canadian)

> **"I heard about the Boston Marathon as I was growing up in Kenya, and Tom's book gave me a better understanding of all those who have run before me. It makes my victories here even more special."**
> **Cosmas Ndeti**
> Three-time Boston Marathon Champion
> Boston Marathon Men's Record Holder, 2:07:15

Take a fascinating look at the personalities and passions of the runners as well as the history and evolution of the Boston Marathon.

Lore of Running
(Third Edition)
Timothy D. Noakes, MD
Foreword by George Sheehan, MD
1991 • Cloth • 832 pp • Item PNOA0437 • ISBN 0-88011-437-1 • $30.00 ($44.95 Canadian)
1991 • Paper • 832 pp • Item PNOA0438 • ISBN 0-88011-438-X • $22.95 ($32.95 Canadian)

> **"Noakes has a training, an intelligence, a sensitivity, and experience that few writers on the athletic life can equal."**
> **George Sheehan, MD**
> Author of *Doctor George Sheehan's Medical Advice for Runners* and
> *Personal Best*

Lore of Running combines the expertise of Tim Noakes—a runner, physician, and exercise physiology researcher—with important new findings about running. In a down-to-earth way that every reader can understand, Noakes explains physiology, training, history, and health and medical considerations.

To place your order, U.S. customers call
TOLL FREE 1-800-747-4457. Customers outside the U.S. place your order using the appropriate telephone/address shown in the front of this book.

Human Kinetics
The Premier Publisher for Sports & Fitness
http://www.humankinetics.com/

Prices subject to change.